Paris

timeout.com/paris

Penguin Books

PENGUIN BOOKS

Published by the Penguin Group
Penguin Books Ltd, 80 Strand, London WC2R ORL, England
Penguin Books USA Inc., 375 Hudson Street, New York, New York 10014, USA
Penguin Books Australia Ltd, 250 Camberwell Road, Camberwell, Victoria 3124, Australia
Penguin Books Canada Ltd, 10 Alcorn Avenue, Toronto, Ontario, Canada M4V 3B2
Penguin Books (NZ) Ltd, cnr Rosedale and Airborne Rds, Albany, Auckland, New Zealand

Penguin Books Ltd, Registered Offices: Harmondsworth, Middlesex, England

First published 1989
Second edition 1990
Third edition 1992
Fourth edition 1995
Fifth edition 1997
Sixth edition 1998
Seventh edition 1999
Eighth edition 2000
Ninth edition 2001
Tenth Edition 2002
10 9 8 7 6 5 4 3 2 1

Reprographics by Quebecor Numeric, 56 bd Davout, 75020 Paris
Cover reprographics by Precise Litho, 34-35 Great Sutton Street, London EC1
Printed and bound by Cayfosa-Quebecor, Ctra. de Caldes, Km 3 08 130 Sta Perpètua de Mogoda, Barcelona, Spain

Edited and designed by
Time Out Paris
100 rue du Fbg-St-Antoine
75012 Paris
Tel: +33 (0)1.44.87.00.45
Fax:+33 (0)1.44.73.90.60
Email: editors@timeout.fr
www.timeout.com/paris

For
Time Out Guides Ltd
Universal House
251 Tottenham Court Road
London W1T 7AB.
Tel: +44 (0)20 7813 3000
Fax:+44 (0)20 7813 6001
Email: guides@timeout.com
www.timeout.com

Editorial

Editor Paul Hines
Consultant Editor Natasha Edwards
Production Editor Alison Culliford
Researchers Frances Dougherty, Natalie Whittle, Cara Young
Proofreader Rosalind Sykes

Editorial Director Peter Fiennes
Series Editor Ruth Jarvis
Deputy Series Editor Jonathan Cox
Guides Co-ordinator Jenny Noden

Design

Art Director Paris Richard Joy
Ad Design Philippe Thareaut

Group Art Director John Oakey
Art Director Mandy Martin
Picture Editor Kerri Miles

Advertising

Sales & Administration Manager Philippe Thareaut
Advertising Co-ordinator David Jordan
Advertising Executives Olivier Baenninger, Clothilde Redfern

Group Commercial Director Lesley Gill
Sales Director Mark Phillips
International Sales Co-ordinator Ross Canadé

Administration

Managing Director Paris Karen Albrecht

Publisher Tony Elliott
Managing Director Mike Hardwick
Group Financial Director Kevin Ellis
Marketing Director Christine Cort
Marketing Manager Mandy Martinez
Group General Manager Nichola Coulthard
Production Manager Mark Lamond
Production Controller Samantha Furniss
Accountant Sarah Bostock

Features for the tenth edition were written or updated by: History Alison Culliford (A brief history of harlotry), Michael Fitzpatrick, Gildas Launay (This man is a revolutionary). **Never mind the Balzacs** Lisa Guérard (Existentialism), Hélène Hines, Paul Hines (Weller-weller-weller ooh!). **Architecture** Natasha Edwards. **Paris Today** Jon Henley, Michael Fitzpatrick (Paris stats), Rosa Jackson (Is French food finished?). **Islands, Right Bank, Left Bank, Beyond the Périphérique**, Richard Bermingham (Right Bank Refresher), Alison Culliford, Natasha Edwards, Paul Hines (Paris, city of lights out, The mob wars: killing in style, Wass up? Chuck, May 68 & all that, Mind your language, The writing's on the wall, Subterranean bone-pit views, Drancy, A *banlieusard* rain's a-gonna fall), Gildas Launay (Bertrand Burgalat), Kevin Titman (Meaty culture at La Villette), Natalie Whittle (Glorious galleries). **Museums** Natasha Edwards, Paul Hines (Happy birthday, dear Victor), Nicola Mitchell (A passion for fashion). **Restaurants** adapted from *Time Out Eating & Drinking in Paris Guide*. Lulu Gédouin (Michelin Man), Rosa Jackson (Mince and the revolution). **Bars, Cafés & Tearooms** Adapted from *Time Out Eating & Drinking in Paris Guide*, Paul Hines (Coolest shaker), Katherine Spenley (Red-eye refuges), Rosa Jackson. **Shops & services** Alison Culliford, Maja David (The nose how), Rosa Jackson (All crescent and accounted for), Gildas Launay, Nicola Mitchell, Kate Thirwall (How to be a boho goddess, RIP Marks & Spencer), Lauren Trisk, Natalie Whittle. **By Season** Cara Young. **Cabaret, Circus & Comedy** Cara Young. **Children** Kate Horne (From cheeseboard to clapperboard), Dinah Nuttall (Marvelling at the sheer Gaul of it). **Clubs** Gildas Launay, Lucia Scazzocchio. **Dance** Thierry Amouzou, Rosa Jackson (Stepping Out). **Film** Simon Cropper. **Galleries** Natasha Edwards. **Gay & Lesbian** Gildas Launay. **Music: Classical & Opera** Stephen Mudge, Nick Petter (Liberty, equality and do-re-mi). **Music: Rock, Roots & Jazz** Gildas Launay, Nick Petter (Heeeeere's Johnny!), Lucia Scazzocchio (Chansons for a new generation), Kevin Titman (Stop press). **Sport** Thierry Amouzou (PSG: Please score goals), Kate Horne (Friday night fever). **Theatre** Thierry Amouzou, Kate Thirlwall (Holy Moses, it's all gone showbiz!). **Trips out of Town** Hélène Hines, Louise Rogers. **Directory** Alison Culliford, Kate Horne, Cara Young.

Maps p398-409 by Mapworld, p410-412 courtesy RATP.

Photography by Karl Blackwell, Tom Craig, Adam Eastland, Jon Perugia, Colm Pierce. **Additional photography** Daniel Agneli, Jean-Louis Faverole, Nathalie Jacqualt, Oliver Knight, Crescenzo Mazza, PMVP: Habouzit, Joffre, Pierrain, Ladet **Additional photos courtesy** Collections Photographiques du Musée Carnavalet, Opéra National de Paris, Théâtre de la Ville, Photothèque des Musées de la Ville de Paris, Mairie de Paris, Parc Astérix.

Contents

Introduction

Paris is a tantalising city. One of its lesser-spotted (but most deadly) temptations is the one it presents to the travel guide editor; namely, that of writing a toe-curler of an introduction. How many of us have had to make a lunge for the smelling salts after reading cliché-drenched phrases larded with references to *l'art de vivre* and that quote from *Casablanca*? You and I know that Paris – the most visited city in the world – is a pudding that doesn't need or deserve to be over-egged. To business, then.

This guide has three aims. The first is to give you an accurate picture of what Paris is like in 2002. The second is to tempt you to visit, and the third is to provide you with all the information you'll need when you do.

Paris is in good shape in 2002. Last year the Parisians elected a new mayor, Bertrand Delanoë, the first socialist to hold that office for well over a hundred years. If he carries out the promises he made in his manifesto (a massive 'if' with any politician, of course), Paris is going to become a cleaner, greener and even more visitor-friendly city. (And, just to bust a superannuated cliché, Parisians *are* welcoming. As city-dwellers, they're busy and they're probably often stressed, but they are most definitely not unfriendly.)

As far as tempting you to visit without ladling on the purple prose, well, just imagine what the world would be like without Paris: no Louvre; no ooh-la-la; no gummy drunks slurring oratory on the Métro; no views from bridges across the Seine; no gorgeous women in shades who exist on a diet of lettuce leaves, Gitanes and attitude; no Napoleonic monuments; no blue-chin tough guys shamelessly carrying rheumy-eyed miniature poodles as they bowl down the *rue* looking forward to their 8am grenadine. If Paris didn't exist, we'd only have to invent it. Thankfully, a bunch of French people have already done it, and it really would be rude not to come and have a look.

And as for giving you all the information you'll need, here comes a book full of it. So uncurl your toes and enjoy.

ABOUT THE TIME OUT CITY GUIDES

The *Time Out Paris Guide* is one of an expanding series of *Time Out* City Guides produced by the people behind London's and New York's successful listings magazines. This tenth edition has been thoroughly revised and updated by writers resident in Paris who have striven to provide you with all the most up-to-date information you'll need to explore the city, whether you're a local or a first-time visitor.

For events each week, see the *Time Out Paris* section (in English) inside French listings magazine *Pariscope*, available at all Paris-area newsstands. The quarterly *Time Out Paris Free Guide* is available in selected hotels, bars and visitor centres. For detailed reviews of 850 Paris restaurants, cafés and bars, buy the *Time Out Paris Eating & Drinking Guide*. Penguin's *Time Out Book of Paris Walks* features 23 themed itineraries by eminent writers and journalists.

THE LOWDOWN ON THE LISTINGS

Above all, we've tried to make this book as useful as possible. Addresses, telephone numbers, transport details, opening times, admission prices, credit card details and, where possible, websites, are all included in our listings. And, as far as possible, we've given details of facilities, services and events, all checked and correct at the time we went to press. However, owners and managers can change their arrangements at any time. Before you go out of your way, we'd strongly advise you to telephone and check opening times, dates of exhibitions and other particulars. While every effort has been made to ensure the accuracy of the information contained in this guide, the publishers cannot accept responsiblity for any errors it may contain.

PRICES AND PAYMENT

The prices we've supplied should be treated as guidelines, not gospel, especially in the light of the changeover to the euro. Inflation and fluctuations in exchange rates can cause prices to change. If you encounter prices that vary wildly from those we've quoted, ask whether there's a good reason. If not, go elsewhere. We have noted whether venues such as shops, hotels, restaurants, bars and clubs accept credit cards or not but have listed only the major cards – American Express (**AmEx**), Diners Club (**DC**),

There is an online version of this guide, as well as monthly events listings for more than 30 international cities, at www.timeout.com.

SFMOMA
MUSEUM STORE

→ with the sfmoma
   artists gallery

   four embarcadero center
   lobby level
   san francisco
   california 94111

→ new international
   terminal

   san francisco
   international airport

→ 151 third street
   san francisco
   california 94103

   tel 415 357 4035
   fax 415 357 4043

e-mail: museumstore@sfmoma.org

www.sfmoma.org

become a member

receive a 10% discount
on your
museumStore purchases

SFMOMA

call membership
at
415 357 4135

visit SFMOMA and
shop the museumStore
at

The euro

MasterCard (**MC**) and Visa (**V**). Note that shops, restaurants, cafés and museums often will not accept credit cards for sums of less than €15.

CROSS-REFERENCING

Where we mention important places or events also listed elsewhere in the guide, or in detail later in the chapter, they are highlighted in **bold**.

THE LIE OF THE LAND

Paris is divided into 20 *arrondissements,* which form a snail-shell spiral beginning at Notre-Dame and finishing at the Porte de Montreuil on the eastern edge of the city. Paris addresses include the *arrondissement* at the end of the postcode, following the prefix 750 (*see p373,* **Addresses**). In this guide we have referred to the *arrondissements* as 1st, 2nd, 3rd, 4th and so on. Chapters on **Accommodation**, **Sightseeing** and **Eating & Drinking** have been divided into area categories that roughly follow *arrondissement* guidelines. In each of the other listings categories (**Rock, Roots & Jazz**, for instance), entries are placed in order of *arrondissement.* Addresses within the area covered on the **colour street maps** have also been given map references. An **arrondissement map** is on page 398.

TELEPHONE NUMBERS

All French phone numbers, including mobile (*portable*) numbers have ten digits. The area code for Paris is (01). All telephone numbers printed in this guide start with this code, unless otherwise stated. From outside France, dial the country code (33) and leave off the zero at the beginning of the number.

ESSENTIAL INFORMATION

For all the practical information you might need for visiting the city – including getting yourself in the Paris mood, visa and customs information, disabled access, health and emergency telephone numbers, tips for doing business and dealing with French bureaucracy, a list of useful websites, a compendium of essential vocabulary, more information on the euro and the lowdown on the local transport network – turn to the **Directory** chapter at the back of this guide. It starts on *p365.*

MAPS

We've included a series of fully indexed colour maps to the city, including a map of the Paris area and transport maps, at the back of the guide – they start on *p397* – and, where possible, we've printed a grid reference against all venues that appear on the maps.

LET US KNOW

We hope you enjoy the *Time Out Paris Guide* and we'd like to know what you think of it. We welcome tips for places that you consider we should include in future editons and we value and take notice of your criticisms of our choices. There's a reader's reply card at the back of this book – or you can simply email us on editors@timeout.fr.

Advertisers

Teamsys.

A WORLD OF SERVICES

 Teamsys is always with you, ready to assure you all the tranquillity and serenity that you desire for your journeys, 365 days a year.

Roadside assistance always and everywhere, infomobility so not to have surprises, insurance... and lots more.

To get to know us better contact us at the toll-free number **00-800-55555555**.

...and to discover Connect's exclusive and innovative integrated infotelematic services onboard system visit us at:

www.targaconnect.com

In Context

History

From bog-trotters to *beau monde* in 2000 years – how did the Parisians do it? Well, a lot of people lost their heads...

IN THE BEGINNING

Traces of habitation in the Paris basin have been found from both the fourth and second millennia BC in Montmorency and Villejuif. Within Paris, Neolithic canoes, clear evidence of early river traffic, were discovered at Bercy in the early 1990s. Bronze Age tombs and artefacts have also been discovered here. In about 250BC a Celtic tribe called the Parisii established a fishing settlement on the Ile de la Cité. The Celts grew prosperous – witness the hoard of gold coins from the first century BC in the **Musée des Antiquités Nationales**.

ROMAN HOLIDAY

Its strategic position also made the city a prime target. By the first century BC the Romans had arrived in northern Gaul. Julius Caesar mentions the city of the Parisii, on an isle in the Seine, known as Lutétia, in his *Gallic Wars*. In 53BC when the Celtic tribes, the Senones and the Carnutes, refused to send delegates to the Assembly of Gaul at Amiens, he ordered the assembly to keep watch over the rebellious tribes. In 52BC, the Celt Vercingétorix spearheaded a revolt, joined by Camulogenus, who took control of Lutétia, while his army camped on Mons Lutetius, now site of the Panthéon. Caesar's lieutenant Labienus crushed the rebels at Melun, marched downstream and camped in an area now occupied by the Louvre. The Parisii and Gaul were under Roman rule.

Lutétia thrived. The Roman town centred on what is now the Montagne Ste-Geneviève on the Left Bank. Many of its villas were of masonry, brick and mortar, some embellished with frescoes and mosaics. Around AD50-200 Lutetia acquired its grandest public buildings. The remains of a forum have been uncovered on rue Soufflot, a trio of bathing establishments, parts of the city wall and a heating system at the **Crypte Archéologique de Notre-Dame**. There was also a temple to Jupiter, where the cathedral now stands. Christianity appeared in the third century AD, when Athenian St-Denis, first bishop of Lutétia, was sent to evangelise its people. Legend has it that in 260, he and two companions began to knock pagan statues off their pedestals. Not a good idea: they were arrested and decapitated on Mount Mercury, thereafter known as Mons Martis (Mount of Martyrs), later Montmartre.

As Roman power weakened, Lutétia (renamed Paris in 212) was under increasing attack from barbarians from the east. Many inhabitants retreated to their ancestral island and a wall was built around the Cité. In 313 Emperor Constantine made Christianity the new religion of the Empire.

357-363: JULIAN'S APOSTATE HELL

In 357, a new governor, Constantine's nephew Julian, arrived. He improved the city's defences, and sought to return to Platonic ideals in opposition to what he saw as the brutality of Constantine and subsequent Christian emperors. In 361, after victories over the barbarians, his army declared him Roman Emperor in Paris. Condemned by Christian historians as 'Julian the Apostate', he could do little to turn back the new faith or the decline of Rome; he was killed in battle in 363. By the early fifth century, Roman rule had effectively collapsed in northern Gaul. In the ensuing chaos, the exemplary life of Ste-Geneviève – and the threat of war – helped confirm many converts in the new faith. As the legend goes, in 451 Attila the Hun and his army were approaching Paris. Its people prepared to flee, but Geneviève told them to stay, saying the Hun would spare their city so long as they repented of their sins and prayed with her. Miraculously, Attila moved off to the south. Geneviève was acclaimed saviour of Paris.

FRANK EXCHANGES

The reprieve was temporary. In 464 Childéric the Frank attacked Paris, and in 508 his son Clovis made it his capital, seated at the old Roman governor's palace on the Ile de la Cité. The now-aged Geneviève converted the new king to Christianity; he was baptised by St Rémi in **Reims** in 496. Clovis (ruled 481-511) began the Merovingian dynasty of 'long-haired kings'. On the Left Bank he founded the abbey of St-Pierre et St-Paul (later Ste-Geneviève), where he, queen Clotilde and Geneviève could be buried side by side. The Tour de Clovis, within the Lycée Henri IV, is a last relic of the basilica. Ste-Geneviève, who died about 512, remains the patron saint of Paris; a shrine to her and relics are in the church of **St-Etienne-du-Mont**. Clovis' son and successor Childéric II founded the equally renowned abbey of **St-Germain-des-Prés**. Not that the Merovingians went very far out of their way to be pious: under their law an inheritance had to be divided equally among heirs, which led to regular bloodletting and infanticide and the eventual snuffing-out of the line in 751.

CHARLEMAGNE

Next came the Carolingians, named after Charles Martel ('the Hammer'), credited with halting the spread of Islam after defeating the Moors at Poitiers in 732. In 751 his son Pepin 'the Short' was proclaimed king of all the Franks. His heir Charlemagne extended the Frankish kingdom and was made Holy Roman Emperor by the Pope in 800. He chose Aix-La-Chapelle (Aachen) as his capital.

After Charlemagne, the Carolingian empire gradually fell apart, helped by famine, flood and marauding Vikings (the Norsemen or Normans), who sacked the city repeatedly between 845 and 885. When Emperor Charles II the Bald showed little interest in defending the city, Parisians sought help from Robert the Strong, Count of Anjou. His son Eudes (Odo), succeeded him as Count of Paris, and led the defence of the city in a ten-month-long Viking seige in 885, sharing the throne (893-898) with Charles III the Simple. The feudal lords thus came to outpower their masters. In 987, the Count of Paris, Hugues Capet, great-grandson of Robert the Strong, was elected king of France and made Paris his capital. A new era had begun.

THE MAGIC CAPET

The ascension of Hugues Capet, founder of the Capetian dynasty, is the point from which 'France' can be said to exist. For a long time, however, the kingdom consisted of little more than the Ile-de-France. Powerful local lords would defy royal authority for centuries.

'France' would largely be created through the gradual extension of Parisian power.

Paris continued to grow in importance, thanks to its powerful abbeys and the fairs of St-Germain and St-Denis. By the twelfth century, three distinct areas were in place: religion and government on Ile de la Cité, intellectual life around the Left Bank schools, and commerce and finance on the Right Bank.

A major figure in this renaissance was Suger, Abbot of St-Denis and minister to a series of weak monarchs, Louis VI (the Fat) and Louis VII (the Younger). The latter rather unwisely divorced the first of his three wives, Eleanor of Aquitaine, who then married Henry II of England, bringing a vast portion of southwest France under English control. Suger did much to hold the state together and give it an administration; as priest, he commissioned the new **Basilique St-Denis** to house pilgrims flocking to the shrine. Considered to be the first true Gothic building, St-Denis set the style across France and northern Europe for four centuries. In 1163, Bishop Sully of Paris began building **Notre-Dame**.

LOVE ON THE ROCKS

Paris was developing a reputation as a centre of learning. The abbeys kept scholastic traditions alive and, by the 11th century, the Canon school of Notre-Dame was widely admired. By 1100, scholars began to move out from the cathedral school and teach independently in the Latin Quarter. One such scholar was Pierre Abélard, a brilliant logician and dialetician who had rooms in the rue Chanoinesse behind Notre-Dame. He would be forever remembered for his part in one of the world's great love stories.

In 1118, at 39, Abélard was taken on by Canon Fulbert of Notre-Dame as tutor to his 17-year-old niece Héloïse. The pair began a passionate affair, but were found out by the Canon. Following an illegitimate pregnancy and a secret marriage, the enraged father had Abélard castrated and his daughter consigned to a monastery. Abélard went on to write refined works of medieval philosophy, while Héloïse continued to send tormented, poetic missives to her lost lover. The two were reunited in death at the Paraclete, the oratory-cum-convent which Abélard had himself established and given to Héloïse, who became a famous abbess. In 1817 their remains came to rest in a fanciful neo-Gothic tomb in **Père Lachaise** cemetery.

In 1215 the Paris schools combined in a more formally organised 'university' under papal protection. Most famous was the **Sorbonne**, founded in 1253 by Robert de Sorbon, Louis IX's chaplain. The greatest medieval thinkers attended this 'New Athens': German theologian Albert the Great, Italians Thomas Aquinas and Bonaventure, Scot Duns Scotus, Englishman William of Ockham.

AN AUGUSTE MONARCH

The first great Capetian monarch Philippe II (Philippe-Auguste 1165-1223) became king in 1180. He won Normandy from King John of England and added Auvergne and Champagne. The first great royal builder to leave a mark on Paris, he built a new, larger fortified city wall, chunks of which can still be seen in rue des Jardins-St-Paul in the Marais and rue Clovis in the Latin Quarter. He began a new fortress on the Right Bank, the **Louvre**, but his main residence was still on Ile de la Cité *(see p74-75* **Conciergerie***)*. In 1181, he established the first covered markets, **Les Halles**, on the site they occupied until 1969. He also ordered the paving of streets and closed the most pestilential cemeteries.

A SAINTLY MONARCH

Philippe's grandson Louis IX (1226-70) was famed for his extreme piety. When not out and about on crusade, he put his stamp on Paris, commissioning the **Sainte-Chapelle**, convents, hospices and student hostels. But it was his grandson, Philippe IV (Le Bel, 1285-1314) who transformed the fortress on the Cité into a palace fit for a king, with the monumental Salle des Gens d'Armes in the Conciergerie. The end of his reign, however, was marred by insurrection and riotous debauchery. In suspiciously quick succession, his three sons ascended the throne. The last, Charles IV, died in 1328, leaving no male heir.

WAR, PLAGUE AND PESTILENCE

All this proved irresistible to the English, who claimed the French crown for young Edward III, son of Philippe IV's daughter. The French

The best Roman Paris

Crypte Archéologique
Great Roman left-overs under the front square of Notre-Dame *(see p76)*.

Arènes de Lutèce
10,000 paying customers used to show up for a touch of the gladiatorials *(see p123)*.

Musée de Cluny
Hot-and-cold wash-house, with bidets and some great mosaics (and a medieval museum to boot). Salve! *(see p117)*.

The Gauls: hemlines may come and go, but a good glass of wine is a drink.

refused to recognise his claim, as Salic law barred inheritance via the female line. Philippe de Valois, the late king's cousin Philippe VI, claimed the crown for himself (1328-50), and thus began the Hundred Years' War.

The Black Death arrived in Europe in the 1340s and, in Paris, outbreaks of the plague alternated with battles, bourgeois revolts, popular insurrections and bloody aristocratic vendettas. In 1355, Etienne Marcel, a rich draper, *prévôt* of the Paris merchants (a kind of mayoral precursor) whose house was on the site of the future Hôtel de Ville and member of the *Etats-généraux* (it had met for the first time in Paris in 1347), seized Paris. His aim was to limit the power of the throne and gain a constitution for the city from Dauphin Charles (then regent – his father Jean II had been captured by the English). In January 1357 Marcel declared a general strike, armed his merchants and demanded the release of Charles 'the Bad', King of Navarre, direct descendant of the Capetians, ally of the English – and prisoner of the French king. The Dauphin accepted the *Etats'* extended powers but, after Charles of Navarre escaped prison and received a glorious welcome in Paris, offered to defend the city only if the *Etats* footed the bill. Treachery and murder ensued until, in 1358, the Dauphin's supporters retook

the city and Marcel and his followers were executed. France's first popular revolution died with its leader.

The former Dauphin distanced himself from the mob by transferring his residence to the Louvre. He extended the city walls and had a new stronghold built, the Bastille. Despite political turmoil, the arts flourished.

After the battle of Agincourt in 1415 the English, in alliance with Jean, Duc de Bourgogne, seemed to prevail. From 1420-36 Paris (and most of the rest of France) was under English rule, with the Duke of Bedford as governor. In 1431, Henry VI of England was crowned in Notre-Dame. But the city was almost constantly besieged by the French, at one time helped by Joan of Arc. Eventually, Charles VII (1422-61) retook his capital.

RENAISSANCE AND HERESY

Booksellers Fust and Schöffer brought print to the city in 1463, supported by wily Louis XI (1461-81) against the scribes' and booksellers' guilds. In 1470, Swiss printers set up a press at the Sorbonne. By the 17th century Parisian printers had published 25,000 titles.

In the last decades of the 15th century the restored Valois monarchs sought to reassert their position. Masons erected flamboyant

Gothic churches (*see chapter* **Architecture**), as well as posh mansions commissioned by nobles, prelates and wealthy bourgeois, such as **Hôtel de Cluny** and **Hôtel de Sens**. The city's population tripled in the 16th century.

FRANK AND CHARLES

The most spectacular Valois was François 1er (1515-47), epitome of a Renaissance monarch. He engaged in endless wars with great rival Emperor Charles V, but also built sumptuous châteaux at **Fontainebleau**, **Blois** and **Chambord**, and gathered a glittering court of knights, poets and Italian artists, such as Leonardo da Vinci and Benvenuto Cellini. He also set about the process of transforming the Louvre into the palace we see today.

François 1er, however, was unable to prevent the advance of Protestantism, even if ever more heretics were sent to the stake. Huguenot (French Protestant) strongholds were mostly in the west; Paris, by contrast, was a citadel of virulent, often bloodthirsty Catholic orthodoxy, complicated by complex interwoven aristocratic squabbles between the factions of the Huguenot Prince de Condé and the Catholic Duc de Guise, supported by Henri II (1547-60).

HACK UP A HUGUENOT

By the 1560s, the situation had degenerated into open warfare. Henri II's scheming widow Catherine de Médicis, regent for the young Charles IX (1560-74), was the power behind the throne. Paranoia was rife. In 1572, a rumour ran round that Protestant Huguenots were plotting to murder the royal family; in anticipation, on St-Bartholomew's Day (23 August), Catholic mobs slaughtered over 3,000 people suspected of Protestant sympathies. Henri III (1574-89) attempted to forge a peace, but Paris turned on its sovereign and he fled. His assassination by a fanatical monk ended the Valois line.

MAKE MINE A BOURBON

Henri III had recognised his ally Henri of Navarre, a Huguenot, as heir. The latter proclaimed himself King Henri IV, founding the Bourbon dynasty. Fervently Catholic Paris continued to resist in a siege that dragged on for nearly four years. Its inhabitants ate cats, rats, donkeys and even grass. Henri IV agreed to become a Catholic in 1593, and was received into the church at St-Denis, declaring that '*Paris vaut bien une messe*' (Paris is well worth a mass). On 22 March 1594, he entered the city.

Aided by minister Sully, Henri IV worked to unify the country and re-establish the monarchy. He also set about changing the face of his ravaged capital. He commissioned place Dauphine and Paris' first enclosed, geometrical square – the place Royale, now **place des**

Vosges. In 1610, after at least 23 assassination attempts, the king was stabbed to death by a Catholic fanatic while caught in a bottleneck on the rue de la Ferronnerie. The *ancien régime* began as it would end: with regicide.

RICHELIEU TAKES CARE OF BUSINESS

On Henri's death, son Louis XIII (1610-43) was only eight years old, and Henri's widow, Marie de Médicis, became regent. She commissioned the **Palais du Luxembourg** and a series of 24 panels glorifying her role painted by Rubens (now in the Louvre). In 1617 Louis took over. But Cardinal Richelieu, chief minister from 1624, held the real power.

Richelieu won the confidence of tormented Louis, who stuck by his minister through numerous plots hatched by his mother, wife Anne of Austria, assorted princes and various disgruntled grandees. A brilliant administrator, Richelieu created a strong, centralised monarchy, paving the way for the absolutism of Louis XIV and grinding down what he perceived as the two major enemies of the monarchy: Spain, and the independence of the aristocracy (especially the Huguenots). A great architectural patron, he commissioned Jacques Lemercier to build him what was to become the **Palais-Royal**, and rebuilt the **Sorbonne**. This was the height of the Catholic Counter-Reformation, and the very best architects were commissioned to create such lavish Baroque churches as the **Val-de-Grâce**.

The literary lights of the *Grand Siècle* often found their patrons in the elegant Marais *hôtels particuliers*, where salons hosted by lettered ladies like Mlle de Scudéry, Mme de la Fayette, Mme de Sévigné and the erudite courtesan Ninon de l'Enclos rang with witty asides and political intrigue. By comparison, Richelieu's Académie Française (founded 1634) was a fusty, pedantic reflection of the establishment.

MAZARIN'S MACHINATIONS

Richelieu died in 1642. The next year Louis XIII died, leaving five-year-old Louis XIV as heir. Anne of Austria became regent, with Cardinal Mazarin (a Richelieu protégé whose palace is now part of the **Bibliothèque Nationale Richelieu**) as chief minister.

In 1648 the royal family was made to flee Paris by the Fronde, a rebellion of peasants and aristocrats led by the Prince de Condé against taxes and growing royal power. Parisians soon tired of anarchy. When Mazarin's army entered Paris in 1653 with the boy-king, they were warmly received. Mazarin died in 1661, shortly after Spain had been decisively defeated, leaving France stronger than ever, with military capacity to spare.

Louis XVI: a 'golden age' that ended in ruin and bloodshed.

LOUIS XIV, THE SUN ALSO RISES

This was the springboard for Louis XIV's move towards absolute rule, with the classically megalomaniac statement '*L'Etat, c'est moi*' (I am the state). Louis XIV's greatness demanded military expansion and France waged continual wars against the Dutch, Austria and England.

An essential figure in Louis' years of triumph was minister of finance Jean-Baptiste Colbert. He amassed most of the other important ministries over the 1660s and determined to transform Paris into a 'new Rome', with grand, symmetrical vistas – a sort of expression of absolute monarchy in stone. In the 1680s, he commissioned the finely proportioned **place des Victoires** and **place Vendôme** and opened up the first boulevards along the line of Charles V's wall, with triumphal arches at **Porte St-Denis** and **Porte St-Martin**.

Louis XIV took little interest in the schemes. Such was his aversion to Paris that from the 1670s he transferred his court to **Versailles**.

The arts flourished. In 1659 Molière's troupe of actors settled in Paris under the protection of the king, presenting plays for court and public. Favoured composer at Versailles was the Italian Lully, granted sole right to compose operas (in which the king often appeared). Rameau and Charpentier also composed, while the tragedies of Racine were encouraged.

Despite Colbert's efforts, endless wars left the royal finances in permanent disorder, reflected in growing poverty, vagrancy and a great many crippled war veterans. The **Invalides** was built to house them on one side of town, the **Salpêtrière** to shelter fallen women on the other. Colbert died in 1683, and the military triumphs gave way to the grim struggles of the War of the Spanish Succession. Life at Versailles soured under dour Mme de Maintenon, Louis' last mistress, whom he secretly married in 1684. Nobles began to sneak away to the modish Faubourg-St-Germain.

PHILIPPE D'ORLEANS

Louis XIV had several children, but both his son and grandson died before he did, leaving five-year-old great-grandson Louis XV (1715-74) as heir. The Regent, Philippe d'Orléans, an able general and diplomat, returned the Court to Paris. Installed in the Palais-Royal, his lavish dinners regularly degenerated into orgies. This degeneracy filtered down through society; Paris was the *nouvelle Babylone*, the modern Sodom. The state remained chronically in debt. Taxation came mainly in duties on commodities such as salt. Collection was farmed out to a private corporation, the *Fermiers généraux*, who passed an amount to the state and kept a proportion for themselves. This system bore down on the poor, was riddled with corruption and never produced the required funds. The Regent thought he had a remedy with Scottish banker John Law's investment scheme in the French colonies, which inspired a frenzy of wheeler-dealing. But in 1720, a run on the bank revealed there was very little gold and silver on hand to back up the paper bills. Panic ensued. Law was expelled from France; the Regent, and to some extent royal government, were deeply discredited. The South Sea Bubble had burst.

PARIS SEES THE LIGHT

As soon as he was his own man, Louis XV left Paris for Versailles, which again saw sumptuous festivities. But in the Age of Enlightenment, Paris was the real capital of Europe. 'One lives in Paris; elsewhere, one simply vegetates,' wrote Casanova. Paris salons became the forum for intellectual debate under renowned hostesses such as the Marquise du Deffand and Mme Geoffrin. The king's mistress, the Marquise de Pompadour (1721-64), was a friend and protectress of Diderot and the *encyclopédistes*, of Marivaux and Montesquieu, and corresponded with Voltaire. She urged Louis XV to embellish his capital with striking monuments, such as Jacques Ange Gabriel's **Ecole Militaire** and place Louis XV **(place de la Concorde)**. Intellectual activity was matched by a flourishing of fine arts with painters such as Boucher, Van Loo and Fragonard coming to the fore.

Dr Marat condemned Louis XVI, only to be murdered in the bath.

THE ROAD TO RUIN

The great failure of Louis XV's reign was the defeat in the Seven Years' War (1756-63), in which France lost most of its colonies in India and Canada to Britain. As his grandson Louis XVI (ruled 1774-91) began his reign, France was expanding economically and culturally. Across Europe, people craved Parisian luxuries. In the capital, roads were widened, lamps erected, gardens and promenades created. Parisians were obsessed with the new, from ballooning (begun by the Montgolfier brothers in 1783) to the works of Rousseau.

French intervention in the American War of Independence drove finances towards bankruptcy. In 1785, at the behest of the *Fermiers généraux*, a tax wall was built around Paris, which only increased popular discontent (*see chapter* **Architecture**). Louis XVI's only option was to appeal to the nation; first through the regional assemblies of lawyers and, if all else failed, the *Etats-généraux*, the representation of the nobility, clergy and commoners, which had not met since 1614, and which would inevitably alter the relationship between society and an absolute monarchy. In early 1789 Louis XVI continued to prevaricate.

RIGHT IN THE NECKER

The spring of 1789 found Louis XVI increasingly isolated as unrest swept through France. In Paris, the people were suffering the results of a disastrous harvest, and there were riots in the Faubourg-St-Antoine. The king finally agreed to convene the *Etats-généraux* at Versailles in May. The members of the Third Estate, the commoners, aware that they represented a far larger proportion of the population than nobility and clergy, demanded a system of one vote per member. Discussions broke down, and a rumour went round that the king was sending troops to arrest them. On 20 June 1789, at the Jeu de Paume at Versailles, the Third Estate took an oath not to separate until 'the constitution of the kingdom was established'. Louis backed down, and the *Etats-généraux*, newly renamed the Assemblée Nationale, set about discussing a constitution.

Debate also raged in the streets among the poor *sans-culottes* (literally, 'without breeches'; only the poor wore long trousers). It was assumed that any concession by the king was intended to deceive. Louis had posted foreign troops around Paris and, on 11 July, dismissed his minister, Jacques Necker, considered the commoners' sole ally. On 13 July an obscure lawyer named Camille Desmoulins leapt on a café table in the Palais-Royal. Likening Necker's dismissal to St-Bartholomew's Day, he called to the excited crowd: '*Aux armes!*' ('To arms!').

BASTILLE DAY

On 14 July, the crowd marched on **Les Invalides**, carrying off thousands of guns, then moved on to the hitherto invincible **Bastille**, symbol of royal repression. Its governor, the Marquis de Launay, refused to surrender, but the huge crowd outside grew more aggressive. It seems that one nervous Bastille sentry fired a shot, and within minutes there was general firing on the crowd. The mob brought up cannon to storm the fortress. After a brief battle, and the deaths of 87 revolutionaries, Launay surrendered. He was immediately killed, and his head paraded throughout Paris on a pike. Inside were only seven prisoners. Nevertheless, the Revolution now had the symbolic act of violence that marked a real break with the past.

Political debate proliferated on every side, above all in the rapidly multiplying political clubs, such as the Cordeliers, who met in a Franciscan monastery in St-Germain, or the radical Jacobins, who had taken over a Dominican convent on rue St-Honoré. Thousands of pamphlets were produced, read avidly by a remarkably literate public.

But there was also real hardship among the poor. As disruption spread through the country, wheat deliveries were interrupted, raising bread prices still further. In October, an angry crowd of women marched to Versailles to protest – the incident when Marie-Antoinette supposedly said, 'let them eat cake'. The women ransacked part of the palace, killing guards, and were only placated when Louis XVI appeared with a revolutionary red-white-and-blue cockade and agreed to be taken to Paris. The royal family were now virtual prisoners in the Tuileries.

In the Assembly, the Girondins, who favoured an agreement with the monarchy, prevailed, but came under intense attack from the openly Republican Jacobins. On 20 June 1791, Louis and his family tried to escape by night, hoping to organise resistance from abroad. They got as far as the town of Varennes, where they were recognised and returned to Paris as captives.

In 1792, the monarchies of Europe formed a coalition to save Louis and his family. A Prussian army marched into France; the Duke of Brunswick threatened to raze Paris if the king came to harm. Paranoia reigned and anyone who showed sympathy for Louis could be accused of conspiring with foreign powers. On 10 August, an army of *sans-culottes* demanded the Assembly officially depose Louis. When they refused, the crowd attacked the Tuileries. The royal family were imprisoned in the **Temple** by the radical Commune de Paris, led by Danton, Marat and Robespierre.

1792-94: A TIME OF TERROR

The next month, as the Prussians approached Paris, the September Massacres took place. Revolutionary mobs invaded prisons to eliminate anyone who could possibly be a 'traitor' – around 2,000 people. The monarchy was formally abolished on 22 September 1792, proclaimed Day I of 'Year I of the French Republic'. Soon after, the French citizen army defeated the Prussians at Valmy.

The Apotheosis of Napoléon: something funny happened on the way to the forum.

The most radical phase of the Revolution had begun. The Jacobins proclaimed the need to purge 'the enemies within', and Dr Guillotin's invention was installed in the place de la Révolution (formerly Louis XV, now **Concorde**). Louis XVI was executed on 21 January 1793; Marie-Antoinette in October.

In September 1793 the Revolutionary Convention, replacing the Assemblée Nationale, took decisive action against foreign spies and put 'terror on the agenda'. Most of the leading Girondins, and even Danton and Camille Desmoulins, would meet the scaffold. In the *Grande Terreur* of 1794, 1,300 heads fell in six weeks at place du Trône Renversé ('Overturned Throne', now **place de la Nation**), the bodies dumped in communal graves.

THE AGE OF REASON

Cultural transformation now proceeded apace; churches were confiscated in November 1789, made into 'temples of reason' or put to practical uses – the Sainte-Chapelle was used to store flour. All titles were abolished – *monsieur* and *madame* became *citoyen* and *citoyenne*. Artists participated in the cause: as well as painting portraits of revolutionary figures and the *Death of Marat*, David organised the Fête de la Régénération in August 1793 at the Bastille. The Terror could not endure. In July 1794 a group of moderate Republicans led by Paul Barras succeeded in arresting Robespierre, St-Just and the last Jacobins. The former heroes were then immediately guillotined.

The wealthy, among them some Revolutionary *nouveaux riches*, emerged blinking into the city's fashionable corners. Barras and his colleagues set themselves up as a five-man Directoire to rule the Republic. In 1795, they were saved from a royalist revolt by an ambitious young Corsican general Napoléon Bonaparte, in a shootout at the **Eglise St-Roch**. France was still at war with most European monarchies. Bonaparte was sent to command the army in Italy, where he covered himself with glory. In 1798, he took his army to Egypt, which he almost conquered.

THE NAPSTER PLAYS HIS ACE

When he returned, he found a Republic in which few had any great faith, and where many were prepared to accept a dictator who had emerged from the Revolution. There had always been two potentially contradictory impulses behind the Revolution: a desire for a democratic state, but also for an effective, powerful defender of the nation. Under Napoléon, democracy was put on hold, but France was given the most powerful centralised, militaristic state ever.

In November 1799 Bonaparte staged a coup; in 1800 he was declared first consul. Between continuing military campaigns, he set about transforming France – the education system (the *Grandes Ecoles*), civil law (the *Code Napoléon*) and administration all bear his stamp. In 1804, he crowned himself emperor in an ostentatious ceremony in Notre-Dame. Napoléon's first additions to the city were the **Canal St-Martin**, *quais* and bridges, notably the **Pont des Arts**. He desired to be master of the 'most beautiful city in the world', with temples and monuments to evoke Augustan Rome – as in the **Madeleine** and the **Bourse**. The Emperor's official architects, Percier and Fontaine, also designed the **rue de Rivoli**.

Parisian society regained its brio. After Bonaparte's campaign, Egyptomania swept town, seen in Empire-style furniture and in architectural details in the area around rue and passage du Caire; fashionable ladies mixed Greek draperies and *couture à l'égyptienne*.

France seemed unstoppable. In 1805, Napoléon crushed Austria and Russia at Austerlitz. But disaster followed with his Russian invasion in 1812; Paris was occupied, for the first time since the Hundred Years' War, by the Tzar's armies in 1814. Napoléon escaped confinement in Elba to be finally defeated by Wellington at Waterloo in 1815.

ANOTHER ROUND OF BOURBONS

In 1814, and then again in 1815, the Bourbons were restored to the throne of France, in the shape of Louis XVI's elderly brother, who had spent the Revolution in exile, as Louis XVIII. Although his 1814 Charter of Liberties recognised that the pretensions of the *ancien régime* were lost forever, he and his ministers still sought to establish a repressive, Catholic regime and turn back the clock.

The capital, however, still nurtured rebellion. Paris, especially the working-class east, was far more radical than the rest of the country. Its disproportionate weight in French affairs meant it was often seen as imposing its radicalism on the nation at large. At the same time, this radicalism was fed by a progressive press, liberal intellectuals – among them artists and authors Hugo, Daumier, Delacroix and Lamartine – radical students and a growing underclass. This coalition proved explosive.

THE 1830 REVOLUTION

Another brother of Louis XVI, Charles X, became king in 1824. On 25 July 1830 his minister Prince Polignac, in violation of the Charter of Liberties, abolished freedom of the press, dissolved the Chamber of Deputies and altered election laws. Next day, 5,000 printers and press workers were in the street. Three newspapers defiantly published. When police tried to seize copies, artisans and shopkeepers joined the riot. On 28 July, the disbanded National Guard came out rearmed, Republicans organised insurrection committees, and whole regiments of the Paris garrison defected. Three days of fighting followed, known as *Les Trois Glorieuses*. Charles was forced to abdicate.

THE UMBRELLA KING

Another leftover of the *ancien régime* was winched on to the throne: Louis-Philippe, Duc d'Orléans, son of Philippe-Egalité. A father of eight who never went out without his umbrella, he was eminently acceptable to the bourgeoisie. But the workers, who had spilled blood in 1830 only to see quality of life worsen, simmered throughout the 'July Monarchy'.

In the first half of the century, the population of Paris doubled to over a million, as a building boom – in part on land seized from the nobility and clergy – brought floods of provincial workers. After 1837, when France's first railway line was laid between Paris and St-Germain-en-Laye, there were stations to build too. The overflow emptied into the poorest quarters. Balzac, Hugo and Eugène Sue were endlessly fascinated by the city's underside, penning hair-raising accounts of dank, tomb-like hovels and of dismal, dangerous streets.

The well-fed, complacent bourgeoisie regarded this populace with fear. For while the Bourse, property speculation and industry

Yet another revolution: a defecting national guard wounded in **1848**.

Massacre of the Swiss guards by bayonet in the **1830 Revolution.**

flourished, workers were still forbidden from forming unions or striking. Gaslight cheered up the city streets but enabled the working day to be extended to 15 hours-plus. Factory owners pruned salaries to the limit and exploited children, unfettered by legislation. The unemployed or disabled were left to beg, steal or starve. An 1831 cholera epidemic claimed 19,000 victims, and aggravated already bitter class divisions. Louis-Philippe's *préfet* Rambuteau made a pitch to win Bonapartist support, finishing the **Arc de Triomphe** and the **Madeleine**, and also initiated some projects, notably the **Pont Louis-Philippe** and **Pont du Carrousel**.

1848: REVOLUTION AGAIN

On 23 February 1848 nervous troops fired on a crowd on boulevard des Capucines. Again, demonstrators demanded blood for blood and barricades covered the city. The Garde Nationale defected. Louis-Philippe abdicated.

The workers' revolution of 1848 brought in the Second Republic, led by a progressive provisional government. Slavery in the colonies and the death penalty for political crimes were abolished and most French men (but only men) got the vote; National Workshops were set up to guarantee jobs for all. But the capital had not counted on the provinces. In May 1848 a conservative commission won the general

election. It disbanded the 'make work' scheme as too costly and allied with socialism.

Desperate workers took to the streets in the 'June Days'. This time the insurgents got the worst of it: thousands fell under the fire of the troops of General Cavaignac, and others were massacred in later reprisals.

A HERO IN THE DOGHAUSS

At the end of 1848, to widespread surprise, Louis-Napoléon Bonaparte, nephew of the great Emperor, won a landslide election victory. An ambitious man, he decided he didn't merely want to preside but to reign, seizing power in a *coup d'état* on 2 December 1851. In 1852, he moved into the Tuileries Palace as emperor of France: *Vive Napoléon III.*

At home, Napoléon III combined authoritarianism with crowd-pleasing social welfare in true Bonapartist style. Abroad, his policies included absurd adventures such as the attempt to make Austrian Archduke Maximilian emperor of Mexico. He had plans for Paris too: to complete the **Louvre**, landscape the **Bois de Boulogne**, construct new iron market halls at **Les Halles**, and open up a series of new boulevards and train stations. To carry out these tasks he appointed Baron Haussmann *Préfet de la Seine* from 1853. Haussmann set about his programme with unprecedented energy, transforming the aged, malodorous city (*see chapter* **Architecture**).

The new Paris was a showcase city, with the first department stores and the International Exhibition of 1867. With so much building work, there was plenty of opportunity for speculation. The world capital of sensual pleasure was again decried as a 'New Babylon'. The combination of sensuality and indulgent opulence of the Second Empire can be seen in the regime's most distinctive building, Charles Garnier's **Palais Garnier** opera house. Haussmann was forced to resign in 1869 after some of his projects were found to be based on highly questionable accounts.

1870-71: PULVERISED BY PRUSSIA

In 1870, the Emperor was maneouvred into war with the German states, led by Bismarck's Prussia. The French were crushed at Sedan, on 4 September 1870; Napoléon III abdicated.

Days later, a new Republic was proclaimed to much cheering at the Hôtel de Ville. Yet within weeks Paris was under Prussian siege. Beleaguered Parisians starved. The French government negotiated a temporary armistice, then hastily arranged elections for a National Assembly mandated to make peace. Paris voted republican, but the majority went to conservative monarchists. The peace agreed at Versailles on 28 January 1871 – a five billion-franc indemnity, occupation by 30,000 German troops and ceding of Alsace-Lorraine – was seen as a betrayal. Worse, the new Assembly under Adolphe Thiers spurned the mutinous capital for Versailles.

1871: A COMMUNE MISTAKE

Paris was rife with revolutionary activity throughout the 19th century. The period of the Commune (March to May 1871) was to prove a savage and bloody turning point, memorably documented in the collection of the **Musée d'Art et d'Histoire de St-Denis**.

On 18 March 1871, Adolphe Thiers sent a detachment of soldiers to Montmartre to collect 200 cannons from the Garde Nationale, paid for through public subscription to defend the city during the German siege. The mission ended badly; insurrectionists led by schoolteacher Louise Michels fended off the troops.

Thiers immediately ordered all government officials and the army to head for Versailles, leaving the city in the hands of the poor and a wide-ranging spectrum of radicals. On 26 March, the Commune of Paris was proclaimed at the Hôtel de Ville. The Commune's Assembly comprised workers, clerks, accountants,

Napoléon's statue in place Vendôme is toppled during the **1871 Commune**.

journalists, lawyers, teachers, artists, doctors and a handful of small business owners, who decreed the separation of Church and State, the secularisation of schools, abolition of night work in bakeries, creation of workers' co-operatives, and a moratorium on debts and rents. There was no question of abolishing private property, since the worker's fundamental aim was to own an *atelier*.

Artists got swept up in Commune fever. A federation established in April 1871 attracted such talents as Corot, Daumier, Manet and Millet. Its mission: to suppress the Academy and the Ecole des Beaux-Arts, in favour of art freed of governmental sanctions. Courbet reopened the Louvre and the **Muséum d'Histoire Naturelle**. On 12 April, the column on place Vendôme celebrating Napoléon's victories was knocked down.

While support for the Commune was strong among workers and intellectuals, their lack of organisation and political experience proved fatal, and they were also outnumbered. In a matter of days Thiers and his Versaillais troops began their assault on the city. On 4 April, the Commune's two principal military strategists, Flourens and Duval, were taken prisoner and immediately executed. By 11 April, Thiers' troops had retaken the suburbs.

ANOTHER BLOODY WEEK!

Soon barrages of artillery encircled the city, while inside Paris barricades of sandbags and barbed wire sprung up. On 21 May, in the week dubbed the *Semaine sanglante* (Bloody Week), Thiers' Versaillais entered the city through the Porte de St-Cloud, and captured Auteuil, Passy and the 15th *arrondissement*. Within three days more than half the city was retaken. On 28 May, among the tombs of the **Cimetière du Père Lachaise**, 147 Communards were cornered and executed, against the 'Mur des Fédérés', today a memorial to the insurrection.

An estimated 3,000-4,000 Communards were killed in combat, compared with 877 Versaillais. The Commune retaliated by kidnapping and killing the Archbishop of Paris and other clergy, setting fire to a third of the city. 'Paris will be ours or Paris will no longer exist!' vowed 'the red virgin' Louise Michels. The Hôtel de Ville and Tuileries palace were set ablaze. Although the Hôtel de Ville was rebuilt, the Tuileries was ultimately torn down in 1880.

At least 10,000 Communards were shot, many buried under public squares and pavements. Some 40,000 were arrested and over 5,000 deported, including Louise Michels to New Caledonia for seven years.

Bon appétit! Dish of the day during the **siege of 1871.**

THE THIRD REPUBLIC

The Third Republic, established in 1871, was an unloved compromise, although it survived for 70 years. The right yearned for the restoration of the monarchy; to the left, the Republic was tainted by its suppression of the Commune.

Paris' busy boulevards, railway stations and cafés provided inspiration for the Impressionists, led by Monet, Renoir, Manet, Degas and Pissarro. Rejected by the official Salon, their first exhibition took place in 1874 in photographer Félix Nadar's *atelier*, on boulevard des Capucines.

The city celebrated its faith in science and progress with two World Exhibitions. The 1889 exhibition was designed to mark the centenary of the Revolution and confirm the respectability of the Third Republic. The centrepiece was a giant iron structure, the **Eiffel Tower**.

On 1 April 1900 another World Exhibition greeted the new century. A futuristic city sprang up along the Seine, of which the **Grand** and **Petit Palais**, ornate **Pont Alexandre III** and Gare d'Orsay (now **Musée d'Orsay**) remain. In July, the first Paris Métro shuttled passengers from Porte Maillot to Vincennes in the unheard-of time of 25 minutes. The 1900 Exhibition drew over 50 million visitors.

AN AFFAIR TO REMEMBER

After the defeat of 1870, many were obsessed with the need for 'revenge' and the recovery of Alsace-Lorraine; a frustration also expressed in xenophobia and anti-Semitism. These strands came together in the Dreyfus case, which polarised French society. In 1894, a Jewish army officer, Captain Alfred Dreyfus, was accused of spying for Germany, quickly condemned and sent off to Devil's Island. As the facts emerged, suspicion pointed clearly at another officer. Leftists and liberals took up Dreyfus' case, such as Emile Zola, who published his defence of Dreyfus, *J'Accuse*, in *L'Aurore* in January 1898. Rightists were bitterly opposed, sometimes taking the view that the honour of the army should not be questioned, although divisions were not always clear: radical future prime minister Clemenceau supported Zola, but so also did the prince of Monaco. Such were the passions mobilised that fights broke out in the street. Dreyfus was eventually released in 1900.

THE NAUGHTY 90S

Paris of the flamboyant 1890s was synonymous with illicit pleasures. In 1889, impresario Maurice Zidler opened the **Moulin Rouge**, which successfully repackaged a half-forgotten dance called the *chahut* as the can-can. In 1894, what is believed to have been the world's first strip joint opened nearby on rue des Martyrs, the Divan Fayouac, with a routine titled *Le Coucher d'Yvette* (*Yvette Goes to Bed*). The *belle époque* ('beautiful era', a phrase coined in the 1920s in a wave of nostalgia after World War I) was a time of prestigious artistic activity. The city was an immovable feast of oysters and champagne – until August 1914.

THE GREAT WAR

On 2 August 1914, France learned that war with Germany was imminent. Many Parisians rejoiced. It seemed that the long-awaited opportunity for 'revenge' had come. However, the Allied armies were steadily pushed back. Paris filled with refugees, and by 2 September the Germans were just 15 miles from the city. The government took refuge in Bordeaux, entrusting Paris' defence to General Galliéni. What then occurred was later glorified as the 'Miracle on the Marne'. Troops were ferried to

the front in Paris taxis. By 13 September, the Germans were pushed back to the Oise; Paris was safe. In the trenches battles raged on.

Defeatism emerged after the catastrophic battle of Verdun in 1916 inflicted appalling damage on the French army. Parisian spirits were further sapped by a flu epidemic and the shells of 'Big Bertha' – a gigantic German cannon levelled at the city from 75 miles away. The veteran Clemenceau was made prime minister in 1917 to restore morale. On 11 November, the Armistice was finally signed in the forest of Compiègne. Celebrations lasted for days, but the war had cut a swathe through France's population, killing over a million men.

INTERWAR UNEASE

Paris emerged from the War with a restless energy. Artistic life centred on Montparnasse, a bohemian whirl of colourful *émigrés* and daring cabarets. The Depression did not hit France until after 1930, but when it arrived, it unleashed a wave of political violence. On 6 February 1934, Fascist and extreme right-wing groups tried to invade the Assemblée Nationale. Fire hoses and bullets beat them back. Fifteen were killed, 1,500 wounded. Faced with Fascism and the economic situation, Socialists and Communists united to create the Popular Front. In 1936, Socialist Léon Blum was elected to head a Popular Front government. In the euphoric 'workers' spring' of 1936, workers were given the right to form unions, a 40-hour week and, for the first time, paid holidays.

By the autumn, debates about the Spanish Civil War had split the coalition, and the economic situation had deteriorated. Blum's government fell in June 1937. The working class was disenchanted, and fear of Communism strengthened right-wing parties. Tragically, each camp feared the enemy within far more than what was waiting on its doorstep.

THE SECOND WORLD WAR

Britain and France declared war on Germany in September 1939, but for months this meant only the *drôle de guerre* (phoney war), characterised by rumour and inactivity. On 10 May 1940, Germany invaded France, Belgium and Holland. By 6 June, the French army had been crushed and the Germans were near Paris. A shell-shocked government left for Bordeaux; archives and works of art were bundled off to safety. Overnight the city emptied. The population of Greater Paris was 4.96 million in 1936, by the end of May 1940 it was 3.5 million. By 27 June about 1.9 million remained.

Paris fell on 14 June 1940 with virtually no resistance. The German army marched along the Champs-Elysées. At the Hôtel de Ville, the

A brief history of harlotry

Prostitution has always done wonders for Parisian tourism. For centuries, the city, with its reputation for sensuality and libertinism, was the Bangkok of Europe. And let us not forget harlotry's cultural contribution – without the Parisian tart French literature would be a desert, its art a series of drab landscapes.

It was in the Middle Ages that prostitution boomed, and it did so right under the nose of the church. Religious fanaticism brought festivals such as the annual jamboree at St-Denis, where tarts offered their wares alongside candyfloss and Papal indulgences.

Les Halles was an area steeped in the sex trade. The fact that the clergy were among their best clients made it tricky to legislate against the prostitutes, who were now organised and dangerous, having formed their own proto-guilds. King Louis IX tried to restrict whores to certain areas, bolstering this move with the criminalisation of the wearing of bourgeois dress (shoe buckles, embroidered belts, furs – fair sets the loins aflame, eh?)

The history of Parisian whoredom brings heart-warming tales. Take Margot Roquier, a country lass who came to Paris to learn embroidery. Finding the needlecraft market fallow, Margot was forced to whore for a royal chamberlain and hand over all her earnings to her sister-in-law. When the authorities found out what was afoot, the in-law was burnt at the stake. The sullied but fundamentally pure Margot was released back to her sewing kit, and one can but hope that her experiences now invested her tapestries with an earthy quality they had hitherto lacked.

During François 1er's reign prostitutes were freely soliciting in the choir of Notre-Dame. But then this was in an age when the king openly had a mistress. The liberal approach continued in the reign of Henri IV, whose toytown around the place des Vosges made bed-hopping easy. Of course, the trollops were by no means all thick-eared, cellulite-ridden floozies with droopy drawers and surly demeanours: courtesans such as Ninon de Lenclos were cultured women who surrounded themselves with poets and held literary soirées from their beds. One can only imagine the limericks they inspired.

In the nineteenth century, the focus moved to the 9th *arrondissement*, where a colony of prostitutes sprang up when developers rented out rooms to give the impression the area was well-populated. The Grands Boulevards

also provided a stage for the prostitutes to flaunt their charms. Flaubert wrote of his first experience of Paris, feeling 'a shock from the asphalt pavement on which every evening so many whores drag their feet and trail their rustling skirts'. Throbbing quills gave rise to literary courtesans such as Zola's Nana, scarlet women who used their sexual power to hob – and knob – with the beau monde.

It was somehow a natural progression from the cafés of the Grands Boulevards to cabarets such as the Moulin Rouge and the Elysées Montmartre. At the same time, the celebrated *maisons closes* opened their velvet curtains to such guests as the Prince of Wales. The richest Parisian prostitute in history was a certain Thérèse Lachmann, who invested her filthy lucre wisely and controlled blocks of shares in South American railways and nickel mines in New Caledonia.

Tragically, prostitution has taken a stylistic downturn in this day and age. A quick bang in a van in the Bois de Vincennes is about as classy as it gets. The scene is truly international: most of the girls working the streets around Porte de Bagnolet and rue St-Denis are from eastern Europe and Africa. As for the tariff, the going rate is €45 for a blow-job, and a bit more for sex. Some girls charge as little as €12. Perhaps some modern-day Flaubert would like to give us a few rhapsodic lines on the reality of that.

Bal du Moulin Rouge: naughty but nice in the **1890s.**

tricolore was lowered and the swastika raised. The French cabinet voted to request an armistice, and Maréchal Pétain, an elderly World War I hero, dissolved the Third Republic and took over. The Germans occupied two-thirds of France, while the French government moved south to Vichy. A young, autocratic general, Charles de Gaulle, went to London to organise a Free French opposition movement.

The Nazi insignia soon hung from every public building, including the Eiffel Tower. Hitler visited Paris only once, on 23 June 1940, taking in the Palais Garnier, Eiffel Tower and Napoléon's tomb at the Invalides. Leaving the city, he observed: 'Wasn't Paris beautiful?… In the past, I often considered whether we would not have to destroy Paris. But when we are finished in Berlin, Paris will only be a shadow. So why should we destroy it?'

THE OCCUPATION

Paris was the Germans' western headquarters and a very attractive assignment compared to, for example, Russia. They lapped up luxury goods and swamped Paris' best night spots, restaurants and hotels. There was no shortage of Parisians who accepted them and warmed to an enemy who offered a champagne lifestyle. Maurice Chevalier and the actress Arletty were later condemned for having performed for, or

having still closer contacts with the Germans, as was Coco Chanel.

Private cars were banned and replaced with horse-drawn carriages and *vélo*-taxis, carts towed behind a bicycle. Bread, sugar, butter, cheese, meat, coffee and eggs were rationed. City parks and rooftops were made into vegetable gardens and a substitute for coffee, dubbed *café national*, was made with ground acorns and chickpeas.

Occupied Paris had its share of pro-Vichy bureaucrats who preferred to work with the Germans than embrace a seemingly futile opposition. There were also *attentistes* (wait and see-ers) and opportunist black marketeers. Even so, many were prepared to risk the Gestapo torture chambers at rue des Saussaies, avenue Foch or rue Lauriston. By summer 1941, in response to the activities of the patriots organised from Britain, the executions of French underground fighters had begun.

THE JEWISH QUESTION

There was also the rounding-up and deportation of Jews, in which the role of the Vichy authorities remains a sensitive issue. On 29 June 1940, Jews were ordered to register with the police; on 11 November, all Jewish businesses were required to post a yellow sign. The wearing of the yellow star was introduced in May 1942, soon followed by regulations prohibiting Jews from restaurants, cinemas, theatres, beaches and most jobs.

The first deportations of Jews (most foreign-born) took place on 14 May 1941. In July 1942, 12,000 Jews were summoned to the Vélodrome d'Hiver (the winter cycling stadium) in Paris. The Vichy Chief of Police ensured that not only Jews aged over 18, but also thousands of young children not on the original orders, were deported in what is known as the *Vél d'Hiv*. A monument commemorating the event was installed on the quai de Grenelle in July 1994.

Not everyone went along with the persecution of the Jews. Many were hidden, and a number of government officials tacitly assisted them with ration cards and false papers. While one-third of French Jews were killed in concentration camps during the war, the remaining two-thirds were saved, largely through the efforts of French citizens.

THE LIBERATION

In June 1944, the Allies invaded Normandy. German troops began to retreat east and Parisians saw a real opportunity to retake their city. On 10 to 18 August there were strikes on the Métro and in public services; people began to sense that liberation was at hand.

On 19 August, a *tricolore* was hoisted at the Hôtel de Ville, and the Free French forces launched an insurrection, occupying several buildings. On 23 August, Hitler ordered his commander,Von Choltitz, to destroy the capital. Von Choltitz stalled, an inaction for which he would later be honoured by the French government. On 25 August, General Leclerc's French 2nd Armoured Division, put at the head of the US forces so that it would be French troops who first entered Paris, arrived by the Porte d'Orléans. The city went wild. There were still snipers hidden on rooftops, but in the euphoria no one seemed to care. Late in the afternoon, de Gaulle made his way down the Champs-Elysées to the Hôtel de Ville. 'We are living minutes that go far beyond our paltry lives,' he cried out to an ecstatic crowd.

THE POST-WAR YEARS

Those who had led the fight against Vichy and the Germans felt that now was the time to build a new society and a new republic. The National Resistance Council's postwar reform programme was generally approved and de Gaulle was proclaimed provisional President. At first vigilante justice prevailed and severe punishments were doled out. However, many former Vichy officials escaped trial and rose within the administration.

As the economy began to revive, thousands flocked to the capital. In 1946, there were 6.6 million inhabitants in greater Paris, by 1950 that number had increased by 700,000. In response, the state built *villes nouvelles* (new towns) and low-income housing.

THE ALGERIAN WAR

De Gaulle relinquished office in 1946, and the Fourth Republic was established. Thereafter, French troops were constantly engaged in a battle to save France's disintegrating Empire. Vietnam was lost in 1954, but after revolt broke out in Algeria in 1956 socialist prime minister Guy Mollet sent in almost half a million troops. Mutinous army officers, opposed to any 'sell-out' of the French settlers in Algeria, took over government headquarters in Algiers. The Fourth Republic admitted defeat. In May 1958 de Gaulle came back.

DE GAULLE AND THE FIFTH REPUBLIC

De Gaulle appeared to promise one thing to French settlers while negotiating with rebel leaders for Algeria's independence. On 17 October 1961, the pro-independence FLN demonstrated in Paris, and police shot at the crowd. Officially only three were killed, but recently released archives show that over 300 bodies were fished out of the Seine alone. On 17 October 2001, a plaque commemorating the tragedy was unveiled at Pont St-Michel. Algeria became independent in 1962, and some 700,000 embittered colonists returned to France.

The state was again under pressure to provide housing and radical urbanisation plans were hastily drawn up. Historic areas were considered sacrosanct, but large areas succumbed to the ball and chain: the 'Manhattanisation' of Paris had begun. André Malraux, Minister of Culture, however, did ensure the preservation of the historic Marais.

The post-war mood of crisis was over, and into the breach thundered a sharp, fresh 'new wave' of cinema directors, novelists, critics and filmmakers who gained international status, including Truffaut, Melville and Godard.

MAY 1968

Meanwhile trouble was brewing in the student quarter. Their numbers swelled the over-stretched French educational system and dissatisfaction with the authoritarian nature of the state was widespread. In May 1968 the students took to the streets. On 3 May, paving stones were torn up, perhaps inspired by the Situationist slogan *'sous les pavés, la plage'* ('beneath the paving stones, the beach'). By mid-May, workers and trade unions at Renault and Sud-Aviation had joined in; six million people went on strike across France.

De Gaulle's proposed referendum was rejected with the worst night of violence. An anti-strike demonstration was held on the Champs-Elysées; workers went back to their factories.

If not a political revolution, May 1968 forced an attitude of open debate and consolidated a new generation, many of whom now constitute the French establishment. De Gaulle lost a referendum in early 1969, and retired to his provincial retreat, where he died in 1970.

1970: GEORGES POMPIDOU

Georges Pompidou or Pom-Pom – as de Gaulle's successor was often called – didn't preside over any earth-shattering political developments. What the conservative leader did do was to give the go-ahead to a building that radically changed the architectural face of Paris, the uncompromisingly avant-garde

Centre **Pompidou** (he died before the building was completed). He also built the expressways along the Seine and gave the go-ahead to the redevelopment of Les Halles.

VALERY GISCARD D'ESTAING

After Pompidou's sudden death, Valéry Giscard d'Estaing became president in 1974. He made clear his desire to transform France into 'an advanced liberal society'. Notable among his decisions were those to transform Gare d'Orsay into a museum and to create a science museum at the old abattoirs at **La Villette**.

FRANÇOIS MITTERRAND

In an abrupt political turnaround, the Socialists, led by François Mitterrand, swept into power in 1981. The mood in Paris was initially electric, although after nationalising some banks and

This man is a revolutionary

His name is Bertrand Delanoë, he is 52 years old, he is a Socialist and, since March 2001, he has been the mayor of Paris. His election was a revolution in local politics: Mr Delanoë is the leader of the first left-wing administration to run Paris since 1871.

There are other ways in which Delanoë is far from your average Paris mayor. First – and, of course it shouldn't be important, but it is – he's openly gay. Not that that bothers Parisians. Then there's the way his political career seems to have been conducted in an astonishingly un-Machiavellian way. His election as a councillor at the age of 27 in 1977 was the start of a long career in the Town Hall, the hallmarks of which were diligence and industriousness. In 1993, he became head of the Paris Socialists and was elected to the Senate two years later. Not for Delanoë the naked careerism, flashy publicity stunts and keen eye for the photo opportunity that we expect from our public servants; the man is low-key. He only really made his mark on *l'homme dans la rue* in 1995, when he masterminded the Socialists' civic election campaign, and managed to dent the right wing's stranglehold on Paris politics. Despite that success, Delanoë was not seen as the natural candidate for the Paris 2001 mayoral elections, as his perceived lack of charisma was considered a drawback to holding a position that had come to be seen as a showbiz pitstop on the way to the presidency. Even though Delanoë found himself having to convince his own party of his suitability right

up until just before polling day, the voters had no qualms. The quiet man of Parisian politics found himself in power on 18 March 2001.

By voting for Delanoë, Parisians have clearly signalled a desire for change (*see chapter* **Paris Today**), and the new mayor has no small task in front of him; a big challenge will be to change public perception of the town hall, which has become the focus of suspicions of top-level corruption. To combat this, he is insisting on glasnost and perestroika in local administration and, ironically, he also wants to decentralise, by giving Paris' 20 local mayors more power, more resources and more responsibility. The mayor must concern himself with improving the quality of life in Paris. Crime has risen disturbingly in the city over the last five years, and Delanoë aims to start tackling this (and appease the vociferous police lobby) by creating 1,000 new police jobs, while setting up what might be described as a junior police force to look after traffic circulation and school security. He also intends to provide 2,000 pre-school places for young children and 2,500 slots in community playgroups.

In order to enact policies effectively, the mayor will also have to alter the mindset of his civil servants after 20 years of dancing to the conservatives' tune. He must also satisfy his main allies, the Greens, whose support he needs for policy implementation. Delanoë will impress us all if he manages to juggle his finances in such a way that the voters do not feel ripped off: before he was elected, he industries, Socialist France of the prosperous 1980s turned out to be not wildly different from Gaullist France. In Paris, the period was defined by the feuding between Mitterrand and Jacques Chirac, Paris' right-wing mayor since 1977.

Mitterrand cherished ambitions to transform Paris. His *Grands Projets* began with the **Louvre** and the Louvre pyramid and included the **Grande Arche de la Defénse**. He transferred the Ministry of Finance to a new complex at **Bercy** as one part of a major programme for the renewal of eastern Paris along with **Opéra Bastille**. The controversial **Bibliothèque Nationale de France François Mitterrand** was completed after Mitterrand's death in January 1996.

The last years of the Mitterrand era were marked by the President's ill health and a seeping away of his prestige. Despite policies of decentralisation, Paris remained the intellectual and artistic hub of France. Competition between government and mayor actually helped the capital's artistic growth: large-scale Paris-funded exhibitions at the **Petit Palais** and **Musée d'Art Moderne de la Ville de Paris** rivaled those held at the national **Grand Palais** and **Centre Pompidou**.

CHIRAC AND A NEW REVOLUTION

The start of Jacques Chirac's presidency, which began in May 1995, was marred by strikes, terrorist attacks, corruption scandals and a prime minister, Alain Juppé, whose unpopularity exceeded even that of previous record-holder – France's only woman PM, Edith Cresson. In May 1997, in a strategic miscalculation, Chirac called a general election a year early. A socialist coalition under Lionel Jospin won by a landslide. Chirac was sidelined into a largely ceremonial role. The socialist coalition (which includes Greens and Communists) started its reign with a record number of leading female ministers and unprecedented popularity.

In March 2001, Paris witnessed a local government revolution, when the left took control of Paris for the first time in 130 years with the election of a new mayor, Bertrand Delanoë (*see left*). The election of Mr Delanoë has a meaning that extends beyond his political orientation. He is the first openly gay man to hold such high political office in France. One of the most persuasive aspects of his manifesto was a promise to purge Parisian local government of the corruption with which it has latterly become synonymous.

As the 2002 general and presidential elections approach, several broad political tendencies are worth noting. The political right seems too badly organised to capitalise on the biggest ace in its pack, Jacques Chirac's enormous personal popularity. The socialist coalition may well survive the economic impact of whatever happens as a result of the destruction of the World Trade Center. It does seem that socio-political concerns for the next year will centre on recession, redundancy, security concerns and a growing awareness that France is losing its status as a great power.

The distraction of the very public bickering between Chirac and Jospin towards the close of the outgoing administration has damaged the country's reputation and even led some commentators to suggest that a system of cohabitation whereby the president and prime minister come from opposite ends of the political spectrum is unworkable (if, perhaps, democratically worthy) and should be abandoned. Time for the Sixth Republic?

claimed that he would keep taxation stable, yet his reforms will come at a conservatively estimated price of nearly 2 billion euros. Now there's a challenge.

So far, there are grounds for hoping that Bertrand Delanoë is not just another careerist bullshitter. The fact that he is uncomfortable with political glitz is a heartening sign, as is the fact that he eschews as much pomp as possible (the mayoral penthouse in the Hôtel de Ville is being turned into a nursery on his orders). If he carries out his promises, Paris will be a better place for everyone. So come on, Bertrand, make our day.

Defining moments

EARLY HISTORY
250 BC Lutétia founded on the Ile de la Cité by a Celtic tribe, the Parisii.
52 BC Paris conquered by the Romans.
260 AD St Denis executed on Mount Mercury.
360 Julian, Governor of Lutetia, is proclaimed Roman Emperor by his troops.
451 Attila the Hun nearly attacks Paris.
496 Frankish king Clovis baptised at Reims.
508 Clovis makes Paris his capital.
543 Monastery of St-Germain-des-Prés founded.
635 King Dagobert establishes Fair of St-Denis.
800 Charlemagne becomes first Holy Roman Emperor. Moves capital from Paris to Aix-la-Chapelle (Aachen).
845-880 Paris sacked by the Vikings.
987 Hugues Capet, Count of Paris becomes king of France.

THE CITY TAKES SHAPE
1136 Abbot Suger begins Basilica of St-Denis.
1163 Building of Notre-Dame begins.
1181 Philippe-Auguste establishes market at Les Halles.
1190-1202 Philippe-Auguste constructs new city wall.
1215 University of Paris recognised with Papal Charter.
1246-48 Louis IX (St-Louis) builds the Sainte-Chapelle.
1253 Sorbonne founded.
c1300 Philippe IV Le Bel rebuilds Conciergerie.
1340 Hundred Years' War with England begins.
1357 Revolt by Etienne Marcel.
1364 Charles V moves royal court to the Louvre and builds Bastille and Vincennes fortresses.
1420-36 Paris under English rule; 1422 Henry V of England dies at Château de Vincennes.
1463 First printing press in Paris.

THE WARS OF RELIGION AND AFTER
1528 François 1er begins rebuilding the Louvre.
1572 23 Aug: St Bartholemew's Day massacre of Protestants.
1589 Henri III assassinated.

1593 Henri IV converts to Catholicism, ending Wars of Religion.
1605 Building of place des Vosges and Pont Neuf, the first bridge without houses atop it.
1610 Henri IV assassinated.
1635 Académie Française founded by Richelieu.
1643 Cardinal Mazarin becomes regent.
1648-53 Paris occupied by the *Fronde* rebellion.
1661 Louis XIV begins personal rule – and to transform Versailles; fall of Fouquet.
1667 Paris given its first street lighting.
1671 Building of Les Invalides.
1672 Creation of the Grands Boulevards on line of Charles V's city wall. Portes St-Denis and St-Martin built.
1680 Comédie Française founded.
1682 Louis XIV transfers court to Versailles.
1685 Colbert commissions place des Victoires.

ROYALTY TO REPUBLICANISM
1700 Beginning of War of the Spanish Succession.
1715 Death of Louis XIV; Philippe d'Orléans becomes regent.
1751 First volume of Diderot's *Encyclopédie.*
1753 Place Louis XV (later Concorde) begun.
1785 Fermiers Généraux Tax Wall built.
1789 First meeting of Etats-Généraux since 1614.
1789 14 July: Paris mob takes the Bastille. Oct: Louis XVI forced to leave Versailles for Paris.
1791 20 June: Louis XVI attempts to escape Paris.
1792 September Massacres. 22 Sept: Republic declared. Royal statues removed.
1793 Execution of Louis XVI and Marie-Antoinette. Louvre museum opens to the public.
1794 The Terror – 1,300 heads fall in six weeks. July: Jacobins overthrown; Directoire takes over.
1799 Napoléon stages coup, becomes First Consul.
1804 Napoléon crowns himself emperor in Notre-Dame.
1806 Napoléon commissions the Arc de Triomphe.

1814 Napoléon defeated; Russian army occupies Paris; Louis XVIII grants Charter of Liberties.
1815 Napoléon regains power (the 'Hundred Days'), before defeat at Waterloo. Bourbon monarchy restored, with Louis XVII.
1830 July: Charles X overthrown; Louis-Philippe of Orléans becomes king.
1836 Completion of Arc de Triomphe.
1838 Daguerre creates first daguerreotype photos.
1848 Louis-Philippe overthrown, replaced by Second Republic. Most men get the vote. Louis-Napoléon Bonaparte elected President.

CULTURAL EVOLUTION
1852 Louis-Napoléon declares himself Emperor Napoléon III: Second Empire. Bon Marché, first department store, opens.
1853 Haussmann appointed Préfet de Paris.
1862 Construction of Palais Garnier begins. Hugo's *Les Misérables* published.
1863 Manet's *Déjeuner sur l'Herbe* exhibited.
1866 *Le Figaro* daily newspaper founded.
1870 Prussian victory at Sedan; siege of Paris. Napoléon III abdicates.
1871 Commune takes over Paris; May: *semaine sanglante*.
1874 First Impressionist exhibition in Nadar's *atelier* on bd des Capucines.
1875 Bizet's *Carmen* at Opéra Comique.
1889 Paris Exhibition on centenary of Revolution: Eiffel Tower built. Moulin Rouge opens.
1894-1900 Dreyfus case polarises opinion.
1895 Dec: world's first public film screening by the Lumière brothers at the Jockey Club (Hôtel Scribe).
1900 Paris' *Exposition Universelle*: Grand Palais, Petit Palais, Pont Alexandre III built. First Métro line.
1904 Pablo Picasso moves to Paris.
1910 Floods in Paris.

THE WORLD WAR YEARS
1914 As World War I begins, Germans beaten back from Paris at the Marne.
1918 11 Nov: Armistice signed in the forest of Compiègne.
1919 Peace conference held at Versailles.
1927 La Coupole opens in Montparnasse.

1934 Fascist demonstrations.
1936-37 France elects Popular Front under Léon Blum; first paid holidays.
1940 Germans occupy Paris. 18 May: de Gaulle's call to arms from London.
1941-42 Mass deportations of Paris Jews.
1943 Nativity of Jean-Philippe Smet (aka Johnny Hallyday).
1944 25 Aug: Paris liberated.
1946 Fourth Republic established. Women given the vote.
1947 Christian Dior's New Look. The Marshall Plan gives post-war aid to France.
1949 Simone de Beauvoir's *The Second Sex* published.
1955-56 Revolt begins in Algeria; demonstrations on the streets in Paris.
1957 Opening of CNIT in new La Défense business district.
1958 De Gaulle President: Fifth Republic.

EUROPEAN UNION AND NEW WORLD ORDER
1959 France founder member of the EEC.
1962 Algerian War ends.
1968 May: student riots and workers' strikes in Paris and across France.
1969 De Gaulle resigns, Pompidou becomes President; Les Halles market closes.
1973 Boulevard Périphérique inaugurated.
1977 Centre Pompidou opens. Jacques Chirac wins first mayoral elections. Marie Myriam wins the Eurovision Song Contest with *L'Oiseau et L'Enfant*.
1981 François Mitterrand elected President; abolition of the death penalty.
1986 Musée d'Orsay opens.
1989 Bicentenary of the Revolution: Louvre Pyramid and Opéra Bastille completed.
1995 May: Jacques Chirac elected President.
1996 Dec: Opening of Bibliothèque Nationale de France François Mitterrand.
1997 General election: Socialist government elected under Lionel Jospin.
1998 July: France wins football World Cup at Stade de France.
2001 Socialist Bertrand Delanoë elected Mayor. *Le Monde* declares 'We Are All Americans' following the destruction of the World Trade Center. France officially admits that Paris police murdered 200 Algerian demonstrators in 1961.

Paris Today

The recent revolution in local government might just make Paris the city it really ought to be, says Jon Henley.

Historic, we all wrote. A break with the past, a turning of the page. The collapse of the house that Jacques built. And, journalistic hyperbole aside, it was: on 18 March 2001, for the first time (we dutifully recalled) since the days of the Commune, the left took control of Paris. For a day, every socialist in the capital became a champagne socialist. Jean-Paul in his kiosk near Opéra even served up a glass of the bubbly stuff to his early customers. The victory may have been foretold, but it still brought to an end 130 years of conservative rule.

For, despite their well-deserved reputation for taking to the streets at every available opportunity (and, if necessary, devising entire new systems of execution to dispose of more than usually unpopular leaders), Parisians have always tended to the right in local elections. So dominant were the conservatives that twice during the 1980s, all 20 *arrondissements* were captured by President Jacques Chirac's RPR party. But the second round vote gave the Socialist-Green alliance led by Bertrand Delanoë, a modest if peculiarly charisma-free

52-year-old, control of 12 *arrondissements* and 92 of the 163 seats on the city council.

The jury is still out on what that will mean for the capital. Paris mayors wield enormous power and preside over an unimaginable €5.36bn budget. But most previous incumbents, as is often the way in France, have had their eyes on bigger things. Chirac was mayor of Paris for 18 years from 1977 to 1995, and turned the town hall into a formidable party-political fighting machine that launched him into the highest ranks of French politics. He handed the reins to a loyal lieutenant, Jean Tiberi, on his election to the Elysée Palace. Under Chirac, and later Tiberi, the city became undeniably a cleaner, smarter, wealthier, more bourgeois and ultimately a more boring place. But under them, too, the wildly ornate town hall fell prey to practices that could charitably be described as dodgy. Truckloads of evidence collected by three investigating magistrates now suggests that luxury city apartments were given to friends and relatives for little or no rent; electoral rolls were stuffed with non-existent (sometimes non-living) voters; RPR activists were given well-paid but fictitious city jobs; and building companies lined various parties' pockets with multimillion-franc commissions in exchange for valuable public contracts.

Chirac has so far waded free of the rising tide of scandal lapping at the Elysée doors by pleading presidential immunity (although if he loses May's presidential elections, he may not stay that way for long). Tiberi, however, who refused to be made the RPR's scapegoat and fought a renegade campaign for re-election, is under police investigation. Delanoë fought a determinedly local campaign that emphasised the novel values of openness and honesty, and stressed the clean break represented by his Socialist ticket. It appealed to Parisians fed up with their town hall being exploited as a political springboard to the national stage.

'Delanoë promises to rescue Paris from museumification.'

Under its new mayor, the first openly gay politician to hold such an elevated position in France, the capital can certainly hope for more transparency. He has also promised to do his best to roll back the Chirac years; to make the world's most visited city a younger, more open and more adventurous place, restoring the mood of cultural innovation and vitality it has lost over the past two decades and rescuing it from what he calls 'conformism, self-satisfaction and museumification'. The rest of his projects are about quality of life: creating more green spaces in Europe's most densely-packed capital by taking over unused land from the army and the railways; cutting car use by 20%; making rental bikes available at Métro stations; turning the polluted Grands Boulevards into a haven for pedestrians, cyclists and roller-bladers; multiplying the number of places in crèches and pre-school classes.

On the whole, he has not made a bad start, although he may have committed a strategic error by taking aim first at that most sacred of Gallic cows, the automobile. It was many years ago now, in the early 1970s, that the late President Georges Pompidou declared that it was time for Paris to enter the age of the automobile. In little more time than it takes a Parisian motorist to lean on his horn and accuse the driver of the car in front of being born in a brothel, the Right Bank of the Seine between the Tuileries and the Place de la Bastille became the *voie* Georges-Pompidou, otherwise known as the shortest stretch of motorway in France.

Delanoë, for his part, has decided that it is now time for Paris to do something drastic

Paris stats

10,000,000 tourists visited the city in 2000. You are not alone

100 lions, tigers and panthers are estimated to be kept as pets in the city's apartments

5g of uranium 235 (the isotope in nuclear weapons) was seized by police in 2001

1932 was the year in which the world's first printed horoscope appeared, in evening newspaper *Paris-Soir*

20 cats used to be burned alive on the eve of St John's Day

1,000 dogs made up the personal canine collection of Henri III – and you thought the pavements were in a state today!

317 traffic cameras observe drivers going through countless emotions

2,500,000 rivets hold the Eiffel Tower together

4.5 million people use the Métro each day

1,200 end the journey without their purse or wallet

30,000 handbags were snatched in 2000

20,000 mobile phones were stolen in that year

1,705 passports were stolen between July 1999 and June 2000

0.0000075ha is the average size of a Parisian window box

2,000,000 people live inside the Périphérique

1653 was the year in which the post box was invented in Paris

23 species of fish live in the Seine

1310 was the year of the first public execution. The last one was in 1830

260,000,000 oysters were consumed by Parisians in 1866

500 Parisians per day were carried off during the plague of 1348

34,000 works of art reside in the Louvre

194 litres of rain per square metre fell in the first two weeks of July 2001 (the heaviest fall ever)

65% of residents were reckoned to be evading tax in 1848. Today it's 5%. Yeah, right

25 litres of carbonic gases are anally expelled by visitors to Notre-Dame every hour. How could you?

Is French food finished?

Has the unthinkable happened? Has French cuisine become a joke? Even the country's best chefs are daring to ask. A recent issue of culinary bible *GaultMillau* had star chef Alain Ducasse on the cover next to the quote, 'French cuisine no longer has any influence'.

The problem doesn't derive from one single factor, such as pompous service in certain haute cuisine restaurants, unimaginative cooking in too many bistros (think of the poor, abused *tarte Tatin*, so often sapped of all its juices in the microwave) or inflexible serving hours. As the Paris restaurant scene grows ever more international, French cooking seems to be gripped by a general malaise.

'Are we not having fun when we go out to eat? That's not just something I feel, it's something I'm sure of,' says Jacques Pourcel of the celebrated Le Jardin des Sens in Montpellier, who recently opened the funky Maison Blanche. 'If you can't put your fingers in your plate or laugh out loud, it's a bore.'

Pourcel defends French food – but only up to a point. 'I don't think we're naff; we're no worse than anybody else. But we have trouble making the leap into modernity – the problem is that we're still too timid with complex flavours and foreign cuisines.'

Bernard Pacaud, chef of the luxury restaurant L'Ambroisie, is far less charitable. 'If in many brasseries and bistros we eat disgusting things, it's because technically or financially some of them can't do any better. Customers have really started to like foreign cuisines because the image of French gastronomy is a bit square. A *tartare-frites*, a *magret*, a *steak au poivre* or a *crème brûlée* doesn't interest many people these days.'

Daniel Boulud, who runs New York's most renowned French restaurant, Daniel, is frustrated by the slow pace of change in Paris. 'You can't blame three-star restaurants for being attached to tradition. But I eat in a lot of these restaurants and I feel that, for the money they charge, many of them could be doing much more. In the younger generation of bistro chefs, there is wonderful talent but limited knowledge of technique. I worry that the French techniques will gradually be lost.'

Boulud also complains of surly service. 'Three Michelin stars often means pretention, and that's totally unnecessary. Last time I ate at Taillevent I was surprised at how nice the waiter was. He made the guests feel very good and relaxed, that's how it should be.'

The most talked-about new restaurant of the past year, L'Astrance, seems to point the way forward. The chef, Pascal Barbot, trained with Alain Passard – one of Boulud's favourite chefs. His reasonably priced cooking offers surprises such as a soup made with nearly burnt breadcrumbs and Asian-inspired red mullet cooked in a banana leaf, served with tamarind sauce. Service from a young team is relaxed and unintimidating.

Another chef who is forging his own identity is Gilles Choukroun of Le Café des Délices. Choukroun made his name in Chartres before opening his own restaurant, where he has ditched the bells and whistles that feature on every Michelin inspector's checklist. Rather than calling on some big-name designer, Choukroun decorated his own dining room, and the resulting space feels warm and stylish. His menu proves that he is having fun, with dishes such as a *pièce de boeuf* with a risotto-like mix of wheat and mimolette cheese (not unlike a sophisticated cheeseburger; would that Elvis had lived to see it) and sliced dates with fresh orange, crunchy pistachios, mint leaves and lemon sorbet.

It's fairly easy, unless you're wary, to eat horrid food in France – we ordered an Alsatian *flammeküche* in a Vincennes café and, a full hour later, the waiter slammed down a flabby white crust topped with rubbery cheese and chunks of frankfurt sausage. But, as an adventurous new breed of chefs is proving, French cuisine isn't in its death throes just yet – when the food and service are good, they are still very, very good. But, of course, you're only as good as your last *côq au vin*.

about the unhealthy domination of the motor-car. In August 2001 he ordered the *voie* Georges-Pompidou closed to all traffic between the hours of 6am and 11pm, with a view to a possible permanent ban at some future date. The move was popular with tourists, lovers and small but dangerous children learning how to ride bicycles. But the traffic jams in central Paris had to be seen to be believed. Some 70,000 cars a day had to find another route, and the tailbacks stretched across to the Left Bank and even out to the Périphérique. At one point police measured a total of 108 miles of gridlock.

Similar cries of outrage greeted the Mayor's second major initiative, the reinforcement of some 80km of city bus lanes with specially-constructed mini-pavements impossible for cars to cross. One result of this was that the habitual honking, snarling, three-lane, three-mile traffic jam that is (for example) the rue de Rivoli turned, overnight, into a honking, snarling, two-lane, five-mile traffic jam. Delanoë's opponents claimed he risked actually increasing city-centre pollution by blocking the traffic.

The Mayor says he expects 'a bit of initial fuss'. He should be careful, though, on two counts. First, it is a brave politician who comes between a French motorist and his machine. Second, the broad boulevards the Mayor is busily narrowing were designed that way precisely to prevent revolting Parisians from manning the barricades.

The new administration is, however, introducing Parisians to political correctness. At the time of writing, a fine Parisian row was raging over a 110-yard long street on the border between the 1st and 8th *arrondissements*. It centred on the fact that the street concerned is named after one General Antoine Richepance, a famed Napoleonic commander who walloped the Austrians at Hohenlinden and put down an unseemly rebellion on the French island of Guadeloupe. In commemoration of the former, the general's name is engraved on the Arc de Triomphe, a monument to the diminutive Corsican emperor. Richepance's second memorable feat, however, entailed the slaughter of some 10,000 former slaves and is seen by many more enlightened Parisians (Delanoë included) as a rather more dubious achievement.

'Rescuing Paris' cutting-edge vitality will take more than renaming a few streets.'

The Mayor has no intention of allowing ambiguous traces of France's history to persist on the walls of Paris; the rue Richepance must be 'debaptised' as soon as administratively possible. Ideally, he would like it renamed the rue du 27 avril 1848, the day that France outlawed slavery. François Lebel, the right-wing Mayor of the snooty 8th, disagrees and has accused Delanoë of 'revisionism of the most worrying kind, worthy of a totalitarian regime'.

Rescuing Paris' vitality will take more than renaming a few streets. Every year, another landmark falls prey to the capital's creeping gentrification, every month another horse-meat butcher's closes and is reopened as an estate agency, a web bar or a Tex-Mex joint. Recently it was the turn of the Café de l'Hôtel de Ville, the scene of Robert Doisneau's *Kiss*, the best-known of all Paris photographs. It turned into a patisserie and tearoom. Doisneau shot *le Baiser de l'Hôtel de Ville*, the archetypal picture of Paris' archetypal open-air activity, from the café terrace in 1950. The photo of a young man planting a kiss on the lips of a girl became a symbol of Gallic romance. That terrace is gone. There, at least, a bit of museumification might have been welcome. Paris gleams, Paris sparkles, Paris (inside the Périphérique) is smart and smug and one of the world's greatest and most infuriating cities. Local politics will not do much to change that. Fewer cars, holier-than-thou street names, even better public transport, wonderful. But *The Kiss*? Please Mr Delanoë, Paris isn't Paris without *The Kiss*.

Jon Henley is Paris correspondent for The Guardian.

LE CAFÉ DU COMMERCE

Quality and tradition since 1921

51, rue du Commerce (15th)
Open every day - 01 45 75 03 27
M° La-Motte-Picquet-Grenelle / www.lecafeducommerce.com

Never mind the Balzacs

Parisian literature's not all Quasimodos and quasi-intellectualism. It's as feisty and vivacious as the city itself.

Paris is not some stately, strait-laced grande dame of a city. Never has been. It's a sexy, provocative town that has inspired some of the most vigorous literature ever to emerge from quills, typewriters and laptops. The following is an entirely subjective whistle-stop selection of some authors who have brought this enthralling city to life in ways you don't always get in the guide books.

The mysterious life story of **François Villon** (1431-some time after 1463), author of some of the most beautiful lyric verse in the French language, is as arresting as his portrayal of the city. This street punk and priest killer transports us to a working-class, late-middle-ages Paris that heaves with life, much of it of the low variety. His work is populated by cops and robbers, tarts and

pimps, bent magistrates and depraved monks. But it's not all grime; Villon nails the balance between sleaze and exquisiteness that remains a hallmark of the city today and, in *The Women of Yesteryear*, creates a poetic homage to an aspect of Paris that has never changed – the sensuality of its women.

Perhaps surprisingly for a man whose name is a byword for bawdiness (but then what can you expect when he wrote an entire chapter about a giant's quest to find the perfect object with which to wipe his bum?), **François Rabelais** (1494-1553) was a monk, lawyer and doctor. The author of the irrepressible burlesque epics *Pantagruel* and *Gargantua* possessed one of the keenest minds of the Renaissance, and never has there been a more acute satirist of Paris pretensions: Rabelais mocked the Sorbonne, an institution he judged reactionary. (As if to prove his point, the university tried to have his works censored.) Rabelais' *Animal House*-style Paris makes no attempt at realism, but it shows us a city of immense intellectual activity and ribald vitality. In fact, Rabelais' work can even reach down the centuries and provide succour today. If you're ever feeling the pinch on a crowded Métro train, reeling from the stunning indifference of a waiter or stuck in a traffic jam, just close your eyes and think of the moment where the giant Gargantua sits on the tower of Notre-Dame and gleefully pees over the population below.

Existentialism

Even though popular consciousness tends to bracket existentialism in with the Left Bank black-polo-neck brigade, it didn't actually start with the French. It was Kierkegaard who kicked things off by insisting that the highest good for an individual is to find his unique path in life, regardless of objective standards (in plain terms – do your own thing).

But the works of Camus and Sartre are usually associated with existentialism because of their insistence on the apparent absurdity of life and the terrifying indifference of the universe (one gets the feeling that neither guy would have enjoyed a sparkling career in the Samaritans). The notions of freedom and responsibility to make sense of life in a universe without a God inspired feelings that Sartre dramatically termed 'nausea' and 'anguish', but he offered an antidote to these malaises, namely the necessity of engagement in a just cause (in plain terms – get a life).

Existentialism could be termed the philosophy of convenient excuses. Think of it: if you turn a delicate shade of green during a choppy trip along the Seine, you can always claim to be suffering from existential nausea; or, if you're exposed as a secret bingo fiend, just tell your posse that it's simply a way of engaging in a just cause to keep anguish at bay. But, before you do, why not check out *Nausea* by Jean-Paul Sartre and *The Rebel* and *The Plague* by Albert Camus.

For a selection of Paris' best book shops and places to buy black polo-neck sweaters, see **Shops & Services**.

Honoré de Balzac (1799-1850) gave the world much more than a dodgy rhyme for Prozac. In *La Comédie humaine*, he presents a vivid tableau of Parisian society in the early 19th century; for Balzac, the individual existed only in relation to society, and he presents each area of Paris as representing a different element of contemporary society. For example, Rastignac, hero of *Le Père Goriot* (which was based on *King Lear*), a young and penniless noble driven by ambition moves from Montagne Sainte-Geneviève, quarter of students and the poor, to the Faubourg Saint-Germain, which represented *ancien régime* aristocracy. The area around Saint-Lazare and the Chaussée d'Antin symbolised the new aristocracy of money, and bourgeois society was incarnated by the Faubourg Saint-Honoré. The Palais-Royal was the hub of pleasure and debauchery and the Tuileries the home of the elegant. Balzac also tended to anthropomorphose Paris in much the same way as Peter Ackroyd does London. For Balzac, Paris had the power to intimidate: at the end of *Goriot*, Rastignac lays down a gloves-off challenge to the city itself: '*A nous deux maintenant!*', something of an '*OK, Paris, make my day*' moment.

'Every time I've been here, I have gradually felt slipping away from me the desire to go elsewhere.' Breton

Paris will, of course, provide a landscape for anybody's imagination, and it is no surprise that many Surrealist texts are set in the city. Notable Surrealist works are *Nadja* and *Les Vases communicants* by **André Breton** (1896-1966), *le Paysan de Paris* by **Louis Aragon** (1897-1982) and *Les dernières Nuits de Paris* by **Philippe Soupault** (1897-1990). In *Nadja*, the author meets a strange, beautiful woman and walks with her through the city streets, a trip that could derail the most stable of minds (the person who inspired this tale and who set out to live without distinguishing between reality and dreams – the point where the two fuse being a definition of Surrealism – eventually went mad). The modernity of the city allowed the Surrealists to discover new analogies between Paris and human desires, particularly sexual ones: for Breton, the square du Vert-Galant is the vagina of Paris, showing that one person's uber-perv is another's Surrealist visionary. In contrast to Surrealism, **Louis-Ferdinand Céline** (1894-1961) gives a gritty portrayal of early 20th-century Paris (although Gide said, intriguingly, that Céline did not portray reality

Weller-weller-weller ooh!

He may be 44, he may have a degree in agricultural engineering, he may try to hide his baldness with an upper-cranial sweepover and he may look like the sort of chap whose idea of a good time is looking after the class gerbil for the weekend, but Michel Houellebecq (it's pronounced 'wellerbeck') is a veritable literary punk rocker. Houellebecq's method is to use outrage and insult to bring what he sees as the hypocrisy and *petit bourgeois* values of French society into question. Regardless of his abilities as a social commentator and satirist, he certainly knows how to use sex and controversy to shift books. His autumn 2001offering *Plateforme*, whose subject is sexual tourism and whose target is Islamic fundamentalism (it is, of course, coincidental that the book, which features a multi-fatality Islamic attack on a Thai sex hotel, was published two weeks before the destruction of the World Trade Center), sold 240,000 copies in the first three weeks after its publication and has whipped up enough publicity to keep it in the bestseller lists for many a month to come. Not surprisingly, opinions on Houellebecq tend to polarise, but at least he gives the Parisian chattering classes, whose values he obviously despises, plenty to chatter about as he launches his offensives from his home in Cork. Two of his novels (*Atomised* and *The Elementary*

Michel Houellebecq, punk penman.

Particles) have now been published in English. Those thinking of dipping into his work should be warned that meticulously described scenes of kinky sex (sometimes featuring only one participant, some five or six) are a staple of the Houellebecquian oeuvre. Cue the stampede...

but 'the hallucinations that reality provokes'). Céline spent his childhood in the passage Choiseul, which he describes in *Le Voyage au bout de la nuit* and *Mort à crédit*; the alley where his parents had a shop is described as a place of suffocation and stagnation, 'more squalid than the inside of a prison', and Paris is seen as a city of hopelessness. Montmartre, where the writer lived in adulthood, is also examined in his work. *Féeries pour une autre fois*, the tale in which he describes the lives of bohemian artists, is set there.

Léo Malet (1909-96) gives us 'Paris noir' fiction. In 1954 he started writing the *Nouveaux mystères de Paris*, the idea of which was to situate a crime story in each *arrondissement* (only 15 tales were complete at the time of the author's death). True to the genre in which he operated, Malet invented the ace detective, Nestor Burma, a *filles*-and-fisticuffs 'tec. Malet takes you into unfamiliar parts of Paris that evoke lipstick, booze and Gauloises and groan with crime and fear.

This noir underbelly is mixed with surrealism by **Daniel Pennac** (born 1944). Pennac is the author of a series of thrillers set in Belleville, in which he presents a harsh view of this currently fashionable area. Pennac shows a locale whose multi-ethnic tensions, drug culture and lunatic inhabitants (a male detective who goes undercover in the guise of an old lady in *La Fée carabine*, for example) are the back-drop for wild whodunnits.

Paris has caused some great minds to reach literary heights and, of course, you don't have to be French to be inspired. So, when you visit, why not pack your notebook or charge up your laptop? The person who catches your eye in a café one day could turn out to be your very own Rastignac, Nadja or – God forbid – Gargantua.

▶ 2002 is the 200th anniversary of the birth of Victor Hugo. For more information on this author, see **Sightseeing: Museums** p147.

Architecture

Architecture spells prestige; from the perfectly planned royal city to the recent pranks of the city's restaurateurs.

Whether by way of walls, squares and boulevards or *grands projets*, Paris has developed through periods of conscious planning: its apparent homogeneity stems from use of the same materials over the centuries: local yellow limestone and slate – later zinc – roofs. It was only early in the 20th century that brick became widely used and, with a few exceptions, only since World War II that large-scale use of glass, concrete and steel have created more obtrusive landmarks.

THE ROMANESQUE
The medieval city was centred on the Ile de la Cité and the Latin Quarter. The main thoroughfares of the medieval – and even the modern – street plan of the area, in the rue St-Jacques and rue Mouffetard, followed those of Roman Paris. Paris had several powerful Romanesque abbeys outside the city walls, but remains of this simple style are few. The tower of **St-Germain-des-Prés**, topped by a later spire, still has its rounded arches, while some decorated capitals survive in the nave.

GOTHIC PARIS
It was in the **Basilique St-Denis**, begun in 1136, under the patronage of the powerful Abbot Suger, that the Gothic trademarks of pointed arches, ogival vaulting and flying buttresses were combined for the first time. Gothic vaulting allowed buildings to span large spaces and let light in, bringing with it an aesthetic of brightness and verticality. A spate of building followed with cathedrals at Chartres, Sens and Laon, as well as **Notre-Dame**, which incorporated all the features of the style: twin-towered west front, soaring nave, intricate rose windows and buttressed east end.

Shortly after work on Notre-Dame had begun, in the 1190s, King Philippe-Auguste began the building of the first **Louvre**, with a solid defensive keep, part of which can be seen within the museum complex today. In the following century, ribbed vaulting become ever more refined and columns more slender, in the Rayonnant or High Gothic style. Master mason/architect Pierre de Montreuil continued work on St-Denis with the rose windows. His masterpiece, the 1246-48 **Sainte-Chapelle**, takes the Gothic ideal to its height.

The later Flamboyant-Gothic style saw a wealth of decoration. **Eglise St-Séverin**, with its twisting spiral column, is particularly original. The pinnacles and gargoyles of the early 16th-century **Tour St-Jacques** and the porch of **St-Germain-l'Auxerrois** are typical. The **Tour Jean Sans Peur** is a rare fragment of an early 15th-century mansion, while Paris' two finest medieval mansions are the Hôtel de Cluny (now **Musée National du Moyen-Age**) and **Hôtel de Sens**.

THE RENAISSANCE

The influence of the Italian Renaissance came late to Paris, and was largely due to the personal impetus of François 1er. He installed Leonardo da Vinci at **Amboise** and brought over Primaticcio and Rosso to work on his palace at **Fontainebleau**. The pretty, hybrid church of **St-Etienne-du-Mont** shows that Renaissance style remained a largely superficial effect: the structure is Flamboyant Gothic, the balustrade of the nave and the elaborate roodscreen are Renaissance. A heavier hybrid is the massive **St-Eustache**. The **Hôtel Carnavalet**, altered by Mansart, and the **Hôtel Lamoignon**, both in the Marais, are Paris' best examples of Renaissance mansions.

THE ANCIEN REGIME

France's first Bourbon king, Henri IV, built the **Pont Neuf** and **place Dauphine** on the Ile de la Cité and **place des Vosges** in the Marais. Both followed a symmetrical plan, with red brick vaulted galleries and very pitched roofs.

The 17th century was a high point in French power; the monarchy desired buildings that reflected its grandeur, a need satisfied by the Baroque style. Great architects emerged under court patronage: Salomon de Brosse, François Mansart, Jules Hardouin-Mansart (his nephew), Libéral Bruand and Louis Le Vau, decorator Charles Lebrun and landscape architect André Le Nôtre. But even at **Versailles** Baroque never reached the excesses of Italy or Austria. French architects followed Cartesian principles of harmony and balance.

The **Palais du Luxembourg**, built by de Brosse in Italianate style for Marie de Médicis, combines classic French château design with elements of the Pitti Palace in Marie's native Florence. Counter-Reformation churches such as the **Chapelle de la Sorbonne** followed the Gésu in Rome. The **Eglise du Val-de-Grâce**, designed by Mansart, and later Jacques Lemercier, is one of the grandest examples of Baroque architecture in Paris.

Nouveaux-riches flocked to build mansions in the Marais and the Ile-St-Louis. Those in the Marais follow a symmetrical U-shaped plan, with a secluded courtyard: look through the archways to the *cour d'honneur* of the **Hôtel de Sully**, Hôtel Libéral Bruand or Hôtel Salé (now **Musée Picasso**), where facades are richly decorated, in contrast with their street faces. In contrast, along rue du Faubourg-St-Antoine, a working district, the buildings where the furniture-makers lived and worked were tall, with arches leading from the street to cobbled courtyards lined with workshops.

Under Colbert, Louis XIV's chief minister, the creation of stage sets to magnify the Sun King's power proceeded apace. The Louvre grew as Claude Perrault created the sweeping west facade, while Hardouin-Mansart's circular **place des Victoires** and **place Vendôme**, an elegant octagon, were both designed to show off equestrian statues of the king.

ROCOCO & NEO-CLASSICISM

In the early 18th century, the Faubourg-St-Germain overtook the Marais in fashion. Most of the mansions there are now ministries or embassies; today you can visit the Hôtel Bouchardon (now **Musée Maillol**), which has some original carved panelling.

Under Louis XV, the severe lines of the previous century were softened by rounded corners and decorative detailing, such as satyr masks over doorways, at the Hôtel Chenizot (51 rue St-Louis-en-l'Ile) and **Hôtel d'Albret** (31 rue des Francs-Bourgeois). The main developments came in interior decoration, with the frivolous French rococo style. The finest example is the **Hôtel de Soubise**, with

The best **of medieval**

Notre-Dame
Gruesome gargoyles and flying buttresses. *See p34.*

Sainte-Chapelle
A holy relic in itself. *See p35.*

Tour Jean Sans Peur
For those with a good head for heights *See p35.*

Philippe-Auguste's city wall
One of the first *grands projets*. *See p34.*

Hôtel de Cluny
The building, the baths and medieval-inspired garden. *See p34.*

panelling, plasterwork and paintings by decorators of the day including Boucher, Restout and Van Loo.

From the 1750s geometry was back as Ancient Rome inspired another monument to royal majesty, Jacques Ange Gabriel's neo-classical **place de la Concorde**; and Soufflot's domed **Panthéon** on a Greek cross plan was inspired by the one in Rome.

One late addition by the *ancien régime* was the tax wall, the *Mur des Fermiers Généraux*, built around the city in 1785. Utopian Claude-Nicolas Ledoux's **toll gates** played games with pure geometrical forms; circular at Parc Monceau and La Rotonde de la Villette, and rectangular pairs at place Denfert-Rochereau and place de la Nation.

THE NINETEENTH CENTURY

The Revolution largely confined itself to pulling buildings down. Royal statues bit the dust along with the Bastille prison, and churches became 'temples of reason' or grain stores. Napoléon, however, soon brought Paris back to a proper sense of its grand self. Land confiscated from aristocracy and church was built up. A stern classicism was preferred for the **Arc de Triomphe**, the Greek-temple-inspired **Madeleine** and Brongniart's **Bourse**.

By the 1840s classical style was under challenge from a Gothic revival led by Eugène Viollet-le-Duc. Critics accused him of creating a romanticised notion of the medieval; his use of colour was felt to pollute these monuments. Judge for yourself in the choir of Notre-Dame and the Sainte-Chapelle or visit the castle he (re)built largely from scratch at **Pierrefonds**. Historical eclecticism ruled, though, with the neo-renaissance **Hôtel de Ville** (rebuilt after the Paris Commune), **Hôtel de la Païva** and **Eglise de la Trinité**. Hittorrf chose Antique polychromy in the **Cirque d'Hiver**, while Byzantium and the Romanesque made a comeback from the 1870s.

Engineering innovations made the use of iron frames in buildings increasingly common. Henri Labrouste's reading room at the **Bibliothèque Ste-Geneviève** (1844-50), in the place du Panthéon, was one of the first to use iron for the entire structure. Stations like Hittorff's **Gare du Nord** (1861-65) and such apparently massive stone structures as the Grande Galerie de l'Evolution (**Muséum d'Histoire Naturelle**) and **Musée d'Orsay** are but shells around an iron frame, allowing spacious, light-filled interiors. The most daring iron structure of them all was the **Eiffel Tower**, built in 1889, then the tallest structure in the world.

BARON HAUSSMANN

Appointed Napoléon III's *Préfet de la Seine* in 1853, Haussmann was not an architect but an administrator. Aided by architects and engineers including Baltard, Hittorff, Alphand and Belgrand, he set about making Paris the most modern city of its day. Broad boulevards

Palais de Chaillot: monumental classical modernism as a model of state prestige.

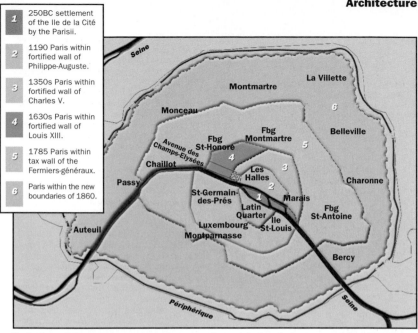

1	250BC settlement of the Ile de la Cité by the Parisii.
2	1190 Paris within fortified wall of Philippe-Auguste.
3	1350s Paris within fortified wall of Charles V.
4	1630s Paris within fortified wall of Louis XIII.
5	1785 Paris within tax wall of the Fermiers-généraux.
6	Paris within the new boundaries of 1860.

Paris through the ages, as successive ramparts and ring roads have spread from the centre.

were cut through the old city. Ile de la Cité was decimated, but some old districts were left unaltered. An estimated 27,000 houses were demolished and some 100,000 built. The boulevards answered real communication and health problems in a city that had grown from 500,000 in 1789 to 1 million in 1850.

Haussmann constructed asylums (Hôpital Ste-Anne, 14th), prisons (Prison de la Santé, 14th), new schools, churches (**Eglise St-Vincent de Paul**), hospitals, and the water and sewage systems. He landscaped the Bois de Boulogne and other parks, and gave Paris its new market pavilions at Les Halles.

Amid the upheaval, one building epitomised Second Empire style: Charles Garnier's sumptuous **Palais Garnier** opera of 1862-75 perfectly expresses the ambition of mid-century Paris. The city also acquired the Haussmannian apartment block, which has lasted until well into the 20th century and beyond.

THE TWENTIETH CENTURY

The 20th century began with an outburst of extravagance for the 1900 Exposition Universelle. Laloux's Gare d'Orsay (now **Musée d'Orsay**) and the **Train Bleu** brasserie were ornate examples of the heavy beaux arts floral style and eclectic classical motifs of the period.

Art nouveau looked to nature and fluid forms. It is seen at its most flamboyant in Guimard's Métro stations and his 1901 **Castel Béranger**, the entrance to the luxury apartment block by Jules Lavirotte at 29 avenue Rapp, or in shop 2 of La Samaritaine, built 1905-10 by Frantz Jourdain, with its whiplash-style staircase, *verrière* and frescoes, as well as in a wave of restaurants and brasseries, notably Julien and Maxim's.

It was all a long way from the roughly contemporary work of Henri Sauvage, innovative but too eclectic to be identified with any movement. After the geometrical Cité Commerciale Argentine flats (1904), his tiled apartment block at 6 rue Vavin (1911-12) was the first to use stepped-back terraces as a way of getting light into the different storeys. He went to a bigger social housing project in rue des Amiraux, tiled artists' studios-cum-flats in rue La Fontaine, and the more overtly art deco 1920s extension of **La Samaritaine**. Social housing began to be put up citywide, funded by philanthropists, such as the Rothschilds' estate in rue de Prague, 12th.

THE MODERN MOVEMENT

After World War I, two names stand out for their innovation and influence – Auguste Perret and Le Corbusier. Perret stayed largely within a classical aesthetic, but his use of reinforced

Paper palaces

The history of a city is also a history of what might have been. Long before the Louvre Pyramid was a twinkle in architect I M Pei's eye, Louis-Ernest Lheureux had plans in 1889 for a pyramidal-shaped Monument to the Glory of the French Revolution, resembling some elaborate Hindu temple, on the site of the burned-down Palais des Tuileries (instead Paris got the arguably equally daft Eiffel Tower). The other side of the Louvre might have looked a bit different, too, had Louis XIV stuck to his original idea of bringing in Rome's flamboyant Baroque maestro Bernini rather than Claude Perrault along rue du Louvre. Under the Enlightenment, the 18th-century rationalists naturally found an ideal of beauty in pure geometry.

Of course, paper architecture has existed since the Renaissance and some Utopian schemes were always set to rest on paper, like Etienne-Louis Boullée's radical Cenotaph for Isaac Newton – his built works were far more modest. Ledoux built the ring of geometrical toll gates but not his spherical house. In the 1860s, Haussmann's broad vistas merely paved the way for future grandiloquent visions of urban order. Had Le Corbusier wreaked his way in his Plan Voisin, the 12th would have been covered by a zigzag swathe of housing blocks. In the 1920s, his one-time master and fellow modernist Auguste Perret hoped to replace the Champs-Elysées with an avenue of Maisons-Tours, while a belt of 20-storey towers, each housing 3,000 people, was intended to ring the city. Nearer to the present, Jean Nouvel was just one of the architects who participated in a competition for *la Tour sans fin*, a theoretical never-ending skyscraper, at La Défense. Most far-fetched of all were plans for an Exposition Universelle in 1989, where the search for space led Renzo Piano to envisage a vast manmade Ile Flottante in the Seine.

concrete (which he had used less visibly for the **Théâtre des Champs-Elysées**) gave scope for more varied facades than traditional, supporting walls, as in his flats and own office in rue Raynouard (16th) and the circular Conseil Economique et Social at place d'Iéna. Le Corbusier tried out his ideas in private houses, such as the Villa La Roche (**Fondation le Corbusier**) and Villa Savoy. His Pavillon Suisse at the **Cité Universitaire** and **Armée du Salut** hostel in the 13th can be seen as an intermediary point between these villas and the mass housing schemes of his Villes Radieuses, which became so influential and so debased in projects across Europe after 1945.

A third architect, Robert Mallet-Stevens, stands unrivalled for his elegance, best seen in the mix of Cubist forms and decorative metalwork on **rue Mallet-Stevens**. Paris is one of the best cities in the world for Modern Movement houses and studios. Other examples include Adophe Loos' house for Dadaist poet Tristan Tzara in avenue Junot, 18th, supposedly the epitome of his maxim 'ornament is crime', Chareau's influential Maison de Verre (31 rue St-Guillaume, 7th, not visible from the street), houses by Lurçat and Perret near parc Montsouris, Pierre Patout's steamboat-style apartments (3 bd Victor, 15th) and Studio Raspail at 215 bd Raspail by Elkouken.

In a diluted form, the Modern Movement showed its influence in town halls, low-cost public housing and in numerous schools built in the socially minded 1930s, while the love of chrome, steel and glass found its way into art deco brasseries including **La Coupole**, and the **Grand Rex** cinema. For the 1937 Exposition Universelle, modernism met classicism as the **Palais de Chaillot** and **Palais de Tokyo** embodied official state culture.

POST-WAR PARIS

The aerodynamic aesthetic of the 1950s saw the 1958 **UNESCO** building, by Bernard Zehrfuss, Pier Luigi Nervi and Marcel Breuer, and their **CNIT** building that marked the birth of La Défense. The *bidonvilles* or shanty-towns that had emerged around the city, many occupied by immigrant workers, cried out for a solution. In the '60s and '70s, tower blocks sprouted in the suburbs and new towns were created at Sarcelles, Mantes la Jolie, Cergy-Pontoise, Evry, Melun-Sénart and Créteil. Redevelopment inside the city was limited, although new regulations allowed taller buildings, noticeably the Tour Montparnasse and in the 13th. Renzo Piano's and Richard Rogers' high-tech **Centre Pompidou**, opened in 1977, was the first of the daring prestige projects that have become a trademark of modern Paris.

Palais-Royal: originally a modest pied-à-terre for Cardinal Richelieu.

THE 1980S & BEYOND

Mitterrand's *grands projets* dominated the 1980s and early '90s as he sought to leave his stamp on the city with Nouvel's **Institut du Monde Arabe**, Sprecklesen's **Grande Arche de la Défense**, as well as Ott's more dubious **Opéra Bastille**, Perrault's **Bibliothèque Nationale** (a curious throwback to the 60s) and Chemetov's Bercy finance ministry. Urban renewal has transformed previously industrial areas to return the balance of Paris eastwards. Stylistically, the buzz word has been 'transparency' – from I M Pei's **Louvre Pyramid**, and Nouvel's **Fondation Cartier** with its clever slices of glass, to Armstrong Associates' Maison de la Culture du Japon – while also allowing styles as diverse as Portzamparc's **Cité de la Musique**, with geometrical blocks round a colourful internal street, or Richard Meier's neo-Modernist Canal+ headquarters. The city also invested in public housing: of note are the human-scale housing round parc de la Villette and parc André-Citroën, Piano's red-tile-and-glass ensemble in rue de Meaux (19th), La Poste's apartments for young postal workers designed by young architects such as Frédéric Borel, also responsible for the vertiginous clashing angles at 131 rue Pelleport.

Curiously, some of the most impressive buildings of the late 1990s have been either sacred or sporting. It's not easy to develop a new religious vernacular; Architecture Studio at Notre-Dame de l'Espérance in the 15th and Botta at the cylindrical **Evry Cathedral** have responded with more or less successful

solutions. Sports facilities have been boosted by Henri and Bruno Gaudin's streamlined Stade Charléty, Zublena and Macary's flying-saucer-like **Stade de France** and Architecture Studio's new copper-roofed Institut National du Judo. The Métro has also made a return to style not seen since Guimard's station entrances, with Antoine Grumbach's and Bernard Khon's stations for the new Météor line.

At the dawn of the 21st century, the age of the *grands projets* is over, although Chirac's Musée des Arts Premiers designed by Jean Nouvel is under construction by the Seine. Paris has gained two footbridges: the **passerelle de Solférino** by French architect-engineer Marc Mimram and the future passerelle de Bercy by young Austrian architect Dietmar Feichtinger. Although construction continues apace in the ZAC Rive Gauche around the new Bibliothèque Nationale and ZAC Alésia-Montsouris, issues of conservation and conversion of the existing urban fabric and the city's industrial heritage are at long last on the agenda: Valode et Pistre have rehabilitated the row of wine warehouses in the **Cour St-Emilion**, and the Compressed Air Building and Grands Moulins de Paris will be preserved within the ZAC Rive Gauche.

Moving indoors, the look of the new is back in favour, alongside the eternal neo-Louis and faux-Napoléons, as architect/designers like Christian Biecher (**Korova**, **Sentou**, Joseph), Jakob and MacFarlane (**Georges**), Imad Rahouni (La Maison Blanche) or Paillard and Jumeau (**Nouveau Casino**) put their stamp on restaurant, shop and club interiors.

ShortBreaks Ltd

NEED A FEW DAYS AWAY?

Short Break packages
quality hotels
central locations
unbeatable prices

020 8402 0007   www.short-breaks.com

Accommodation

Accommodation

For crisp, white-sheet romance, nothing beats waking up in Paris. From Rococo excess to total zen cool, there's a hotel to suit any taste.

With over 1,500 hotels in central Paris you can take your pick from beams-r-us hideaways to temples to minimalist chic. Paris' palace hotels are a hedonist's idea of heaven, crammed full of everything you could possibly need for extremely sweet dreams – although the cost might give you nightmares.

A more down-to-earth approach can usually be found at one of the many small, family-run hotels that are dotted round the city. For those on a limited budget it is still possible to find a perfectly clean, basic room with *en suite* bathroom for around €40, which is more than can be said for many cities.

Official star ratings are not listed here because the French classification system is based on standard factors such as room size, the presence (or lack) of a lift, services and so on but doesn't reflect decor, staff or atmosphere. Our advice: unless you're after a major *luxe* blow-out, forget star snobbery as a two-star might well be better (but not necessarily cheaper) than a three-star.

Hotels are often booked solid during peak months and it's practically impossible to find a stylish sleep during fashion weeks (January and early July for couture, March and October for *prêt-a-porter*). However, in quieter times, including August, hotels do offer relatively reasonable deals; it's worth phoning to find out if there are any discounts to be had. Same-day reservations can be made in person (for a small fee) at the Office de Tourisme de Paris (*see chapter* **Directory**). Prices quoted are for rooms including bath or shower (unless otherwise stated), and we have divided the hotels into five categories roughly representing the following price ranges for a double room: Palace (€600+); Deluxe €200-€600; Expensive €140-€200; Moderate €80-€140; Budget up to €80. All hotels are obliged to charge an additional room tax (*taxe de séjour*) of €0.15-€1.07 per person. In all categories you can expect a good level of creature comfort; thus amenities such as lifts and mini-bars are not listed in the Budget to Expensive categories; nor is porter service listed in Palace and Deluxe.

The Best Hotels

Royal Monceau
Luxuriate in the best spa in town. See p53.

Pershing Hall
The newest, chicest address. See p60.

Hôtel François 1er
Glamour off the Champs-Elysées. See p53.

Hôtel Brighton
Great value, great views. See p47.

Pavillon de la Reine
Sensual seclusion. See p49.

La Manufacture
The 13th is lucky for some. See p59.

Hôtel des Grandes Ecoles
Country living on the Left Bank. See p59.

Hôtel Eldorado
Half-price hip. See p56.

The Islands

Deluxe

Hôtel du Jeu de Paume
54 rue St-Louis-en-l'Île, 4th (01.43.26.14.18/ fax 01.40.46.02.76/www.hoteldujeudepaume.com). Mº Pont Marie. **Rates** single €151-€201; double €213-€263; suite €412-€435; breakfast €14. **Credit** AmEx, DC, MC, V. **Map** p406 K7.
Louis XIII ordered a tennis court to be built here in 1634 when the Ile St-Louis was at the height of fashion. Subsequently a warehouse and then a crafts-men's workshop, in 1988 the timber-framed court was converted into a dramatic, airy breakfast room, centrepiece of this romantic 32-room hotel.
Hotel services *Baby-sitting. Bar. Conference services. Laundry. Sauna.* **Room services** *Hairdryer. Radio. TV. Whirlpool bath.*

Expensive

Hôtel des Deux-Iles
59 rue St-Louis-en-l'Île, 4th (01.43.26.13.35/fax 01.43.29.60.25). Mº Pont Marie. **Rates** single €125; double €145; breakfast €10. **Credit** AmEx, MC, V. **Map** p406 K7.

Silk and swags at the **Hotel Meurice**. *See p45.*

This refined, peaceful hotel in a 17th-century townhouse on Ile St-Louis has 17 rooms done up in faintly colonial style with cane furniture, print curtains and a lovely fireplace in the lobby. The Hôtel de Lutèce up the road at No 65 (01.43.26.23.52), under the same management, features a similar sense of period style.
Hotel services *Air con. Baby-sitting. Laundry. Lift.* **Room services** *Double glazing. Hairdryer. Modem link. Radio. Safe. TV.*

Budget

Hôtel Henri IV

25 pl Dauphine, 1st (01.43.54.44.53). M° Pont Neuf. **Rates** single or double €25.92-€68.60; breakfast included. **Credit** MC, V. **Map** p406 J6.
This legendary dosshouse has been a hotel for 250 years and can't have been redecorated for at least a hundred. If you can ignore the smells and damp patches on the walls, you can enjoy the large rooms and beautiful views on to the square. It has a loyal following, so book a month in advance.

The Louvre, Palais-Royal & Les Halles

Palace

Hôtel Meurice

228 rue de Rivoli, 1st (01.44.58.10.10/fax 01.44.58.10.15/www.meuricehotel.com). M° Tuileries. **Rates** single €470-€550; double €600-€740; suites from €1200-€2,520; breakfast €30-€40. **Credit** AmEx, DC, MC, V. **Map** p401 G5.
Known as the hotel of kings – Queen Victoria and George VI were regulars and the Duke and Duchess of Windsor took refuge here after the abdication – this former English bastion has been painstakingly restored to its full glory. Revel in silk-laden Louis XVI rooms, acres of Italian marble and gold leaf paint galore; Kofi Annan and Robert De Niro do.
Hotel services *Baby-sitting. Bar. Fitness centre. Garden. Laundry. Restaurant.* **Room services** *CD-player. Fax. Hairdryer. Modem link. Room service (24hr). Wheelchair access.*

Hôtel Ritz

15 pl Vendôme, 1st (01.43.16.30.30/fax 01.43.16.31.78/www.ritz.com). M° Concorde or Opéra. **Rates** single €580-€730; double €680-€690; suite €800-€7,700; breakfast €32.5-€56.5. **Credit** AmEx, DC, MC, V. **Map** p401 G4.
Coco Chanel, the Duke of Windsor and Proust stayed here; Hemingway hoped heaven would be as good. Now owned by Mohamed Al Fayed, the Ritz was the setting for Dodi and Di's infamous last supper. The Oriental-carpeted corridors go on forever and the windows on place Vendôme are bullet-proof. There are 142 bedrooms and 45 suites, from the romantic 'Frédéric Chopin' to the glitzy 'Impérial'.

Hotel services *Baby-sitting. Fitness centre. Nightclub. Pool.* **Room services** *CD-player. Fax. Modem link. Radio. Room service (24hr). Wheelchair access.*

Deluxe

Hôtel Costes

239 rue St-Honoré, 1st (01.42.44.50.00/ fax 01.42.44.50.25/www.hotelcostes.com). M° Tuileries. **Rates** single €304.90-€458.11; double €609.80-€686.02; suite €990.92-€2,286.74; breakfast €28.97, parking €18.29, **Credit** AmEx, DC, MC, V. **Map** p401 G5.
The Costes continues to pull in just as many film, fashion and fluff A-listers as it did at its opening in 1995 – probably due to the Second Empire bordello decor, courtyard and good-looking (but often staggeringly rude) staff. It also boasts possibly the best pool in Paris, a sybaritic Eastern-inspired affair with Sade playing underwater.
Hotel Services *Air con. Baby-sitting. Bar. Bureau de change. Laundry. Fitness centre. Pool. Restaurant. Sauna. Nightclub.* **Room services** *CD-player. Fax. Radio. Room service. Safe. TV. Wheelchair access.*

Hôtel de Vendôme

1 place Vendôme, 1st (01.55.04.55.00; fax 01.49.27.97.89; www.hoteldevendome.com). M° Concorde. **Rates** single €427; double €488-€549; suite €732-€2,287; breakfast €28. **Credit** AmEx, DC, MC, V. **Map** p401 G4.

No-frills, but legendary – **Henri IV**. *See p45.*

In complete character with place Vendôme itself is this small but very *luxe* hotel located in the 1723 mansion of Pierre Perrin, secretary of the Sun King. During the 1998 refurbishment acres of marble were imported for the jewel-box foyer, bathrooms and the hotel's Lebanese restaurant. Each of the 29 rooms and suites is individually decorated with passementerie, antiques and original art in styles ranging from Louis XIV to art deco. There is also a clubby piano bar and an elegant café on the ground floor. **Hotel services** *Air con. Bar. Laundry. Restaurants.* **Room services** *Triple glazing. Fax. Hairdryer. Modem link. Radio. Room service (24-hr). Safe. TV.*

Expensive

Hotel Brighton

218 rue de Rivoli, 1st (01.47.03.61.61/fax 01.42.60.41.78/www.esprit-de-france.com). M° Tuileries. **Rates** single €104; double €142; suite €183; breakfast €6.90. Credit AmEx, DC, MC, V. **Map** p401 G5.

Excellent value for its location, the marble and mosaic Hotel Brighton dates back to the end of the 19th century when, for once in their history, France and England shared a friendship. Book early and reserve one of the 11 beautifully refurbished rooms overlooking the Tuileries gardens then perch on the balconette and ooooooh! at the view. The rest of the rooms, though more modest, are reasonably priced and unusually spacious. **Hotel services** *Bureau de change. Tea salon. Laundry.* **Room services** *Double glazing. Hairdryer (some rooms). TV. Room service (breakfast only). Safe.*

Hôtel des Tuileries

10 rue St-Hyacinthe, 1st (01.42.61.04.17/ fax 01.49.27.91.56/www.hotel-des-tuileries.com). M° Tuileries. **Rates** single €135.68-€182.94; double €176.17-€213.43; breakfast €11.43. **Credit** AmEx, DC, MC, V. **Map** p401 G5

A delightful small hotel on a quiet street near the Tuileries gardens. Ethnic rugs, antique furniture and original pictures decorate the lobby and 26 rooms. The centrepiece is a latest spiral staircase. The cellar breakfast room gets natural light from an interior greenhouse. It's not swish and newly decorated by any means, but it is cosy and truly individual. The fashion world has snapped it up as a hip address, so book ahead. **Hotel services** *Air con. Baby-sitting. Bureau de change. Laundry.* **Room services** *Double glazing. Hairdryer. Radio. Room-service (24hr). Safe. TV. Wheelchair access.*

Moderate

Hôtel du Cygne

3 rue du Cygne, 1st (01.42.60.14.16/ fax 01.42.21.37.02). M° Etienne Marcel or Châtelet. **Rates** single €72; double €84-€90; triple €99; breakfast €6.10. **Credit** MC, V. **Map** p402 J5.

The Cygne occupies a renovated 17th-century building in pedestrianised Les Halles. Exposed beams abound, while assorted antique furniture collected by the two sister-owners adds interest. Rooms are on the small side, but 'La Grande' under the eaves is particularly delightful. **Hotel services** *Bar.* **Room services** *Hairdryer. Safe. TV.*

Budget

Hôtel de Lille

8 rue du Pélican, 1st (01.42.33.33.42). M° Palais Royal or Louvre-Rivoli. **Rates** single €33.50 (without bathroom); double €43 (without bathroom)-€50; triple €60 (without toilet)-€65; no breakfast. **No credit cards. Map** p401 H5.

None of the glamour of the Palais-Royal, just a few steps away, has rubbed off on this 13-room hotel. Still, at these prices, who cares? The fake flowers and Toulouse-Lautrec prints hung here and there are unimpressive, but all rooms are clean and the doubles are a reasonable size.

Hôtel Tiquetonne

6 rue Tiquetonne, 2nd (01.42.36.94.58/fax 01.42.36.02.94). M° Etienne Marcel. Closed August and over Christmas. **Rates** single €23.32-€35.52; double €40.55; shower €4.57; breakfast €4.58. **Credit** AmEx, MC, V. **Map** p403 J5.

On a cobbled street near Les Halles, this superb-value hotel has 47 basic but clean rooms. Some are very large for the price, and high ceilings on the lower floors give even more of a sense of space. All doubles have bathrooms; some singles are without. **Hotel services** *Lift.*

Opéra & the Grands Boulevards

Deluxe

Hôtel Scribe

1 rue Scribe, 9th (01.44.71.24.24/fax 01.42.65.39.97/www.accorhotels.com). M° Opéra. **Rates** single or double €111.61-€457.35, suite €533.57-€670.78; breakfast €19-€24. **Credit** AmEx, V, MC. **Map** p401 G4.

A few steps from the Opéra Garnier, the Scribe is a study in discreet, intimate comfort: its hallmarks are Haussmannian architecture, Empire furniture, Baccarat chandeliers and luxuriant fabrics. It has a rich artistic history: the Lumière brothers held the world's first public film projection here in 1895 and Hemingway and Proust were *habitués*. In 1999, artists were invited to set up installations in the rooms, continuing the hotel's artistic tradition. **Hotel services** *Air con. Baby-sitting. Bar. Bureau de change. Laundry. Restaurant.* **Room services** *CD-player. Double glazing. Fax. Hairdryer. Modem link. Radio. Room-service (24hr). Safe. TV. Wheelchair access.*

Hotel Victoires Opéra

56 rue Montorgueil, 2nd (01.42.36.41.08/
fax 01.45.08.08.79/www.victoiresopera.com).
M° Sentier. **Rates** single or double €213-€274;
suites €335; breakfast €12. **Credit** AmEx, DC,
MC, V. **Map** p402 J5.

Smart and spotless with spic, span and smiling
staff, the Victoires Opéra, re-opened in 2000,
attracts a mixture of business and holiday makers.
The tasteful brown/cream decor, smoothly lit and
dotted with unobtrusive artworks, is immaculate,
if unimaginative. However, if what's on the outside
counts you'll find all the pleasures of Paris on
colourful and authentic rue Montorgueil.
Hotel services *Air con.* **Room services**
Double glazing. Hairdryer. Modem link. Radio. Safe.
TV. Wheelchair access.

Moderate

Hôtel Baudelaire Opéra

61 rue Ste-Anne, 2nd (01.42.97.50.62/
fax 01.42.86.85.85). M° Quatre-Septembre or
Pyramides. **Rates** single €99; double €120; duplex
€160; breakfast €7.50. **Credit** AmEx, DC, MC, V.
Map p401 H4.

Although it wouldn't win prizes for highbrow style,
you'll certainly feel at home at the colourful
Baudelaire Opera. Some rooms have a slightly
shabby edge but the staff are delightful and the
rooms are great value for this part of town, particularly the 'mezzanines' which sleep up to three.
British proprieter Linda has plenty of touring tips.
Hotel services *Lift. Safe.* **Room services** *Double*
glazing. Hairdryer. Modem link. Radio. Room service
(24-hr). Safe. TV.

Résidence Hôtel des Trois Poussins

15 rue Clauzel, 9th (01.53.32.81.81/
fax 01.53.32.81.82/www.les3poussins.com).
M° St-Georges. **Rates** single €75; double €99;
triple €124; with kitchenette €15 extra; breakfast
included. **Credit** AmEx, MC, V. **Map** p401 H2.

The Résidence has been done up and gone upmarket. Between Opéra and Montmartre, it offers a rare
opportunity for self-catering. Of the 40 beamed, floral rooms, 24 are studios equipped with kitchens.
For the special prices quoted above please mention
Time Out when booking.
Hotel services. *Air con. Garden. Laundry.*
Room services *Double glazing. Hairdryer. Modem*
link. Room service. Safe. TV. Wheelchair access (two
rooms).

Budget

Hôtel des Arts

7 cité Bergère, 9th (01.42.46.73.30/
fax 01.48.00.94.42). M° Grands Boulevards.
Rates single €62; double €65.50-€68.50; triple
€86; breakfast €5.50. **Credit** AmEx, DC, MC, V.
Map p402 J4.

In a tiny, tranquil alley of hotels, this is the best, if
most unconventional, of the cheapies. Run by the
friendly Bernard family, the reception area is
bohemian, with Babar the parrot, a bubbling fish
tank, and a gaudy grandfather clock. The stairwells
are pasted over with theatre and museum posters.
The 26 rooms vary in size and species of flowery
wallpaper, but all are fresh and clean.
Hotel services *Safe.* **Room services** *Double*
glazing. Radio. TV.

Hôtel Chopin

46 passage Jouffroy or 10 bd Montmartre, 9th
(01.47.70.58.10/fax 01.42.47.00.70).
M° Richelieu-Drouot or Grands Boulevards. **Rates**
single €62-€70; double €69-€80 triple €91;
breakfast €6.10. **Credit** AmEx, MC, V. **Map** p402 J4.
The Chopin was built with the passage Jouffroy in
1846 and forms part of its magical appeal. Behind
the entrance hall with its Chesterfield and piano is
a warren of salmon-coloured corridors and 36 rooms;
all (except one single) have *en suite* bathrooms.
It's popular with visiting Japanese musicians so
book ahead.
Hotel services *Hairdryer. Lift. Safe.* **Room
services** *TV.*

Hôtel Vivienne

40 rue Vivienne, 2nd (01.42.33.13.26/
fax 01.40.41.98.19). M° Bourse or Grands
Boulevards. **Rates** single €48; double €78-€84;
breakfast €6. **Credit** MC, V. **Map** p405 H7.
Soft yellows and oranges in the reception, wood
floors, chandeliers and wicker add to the charm of
this hotel that looks as if it's straight out of a
Van Gogh painting. There's a noisy bar below, but
the hotel is close to the Palais Garnier, the *grands
magasins* and pretty Galerie Vivienne.
Hotel services *Lift. Safe.* **Room services** *Double
glazing. Hairdryer. TV.*

Hôtel Chopin hits the right notes. *See left.*

Beaubourg & the Marais

Deluxe

Pavillon de la Reine

28 pl des Vosges, 3rd (01.40.29.19.19/
fax 01.40.29.19.20/www.pavillon-de-la-reine.com).
M° Bastille or St-Paul. **Rates** single €330; double
€355-€495; suite €495-€700; breakfast €20-€25;
extra bed €50. **Credit** AmEx, DC, MC, V.
Map p406 L6.
Entered from the arcades of the place des Vosges,
Pavillon de la Reine is set back behind an enchanting formal garden. The 55 rooms and suites are all
tastefully decorated, but if you are booking in with
your lover ask for one of the duplexes, decked out in
purple velvet and taffeta, and hope to emulate the
'petite nuit tellement intense' described by one satisfied customer in the guest book.
*Hotel services Air con. Baby-sitting. Bar. Bureau de
change. Garden. Laundry. Parking. Restaurant.
Room services Double glazing. Hairdryer. Modem
link. Room service (24-hr). Safe. TV/VCR.*

Expensive

Hôtel St-Merry

78 rue de la Verrerie, 4th (01.42.78.14.15/
fax 01.40.29.06.82). M° Hôtel de Ville.
Rates double €146-€210; triple €250; suite €305;
breakfast €10. **Credit** AmEx, MC, V. **Map** p406 K6.

Chic but not *cher*, the contemporary
comforts of the **Axial Beaubourg.**

Nestled against the Gothic church of the same name,
the 11 room, 17th-century St-Merry basks in
eccentricity. A confessional box serves as a phone
cubicle and iron candelabras, stone walls and
beams add to the charm. The biggest surprise is
the flying buttress straddling the bed in No 9.
Book in advance. Because it's a historic building
there isn't a lift.
Hotel services *Baby-sitting.* **Room services**
Double glazing. Hairdryer. Safe. TV in suite only.

Moderate

Hôtel Axial Beaubourg

11 rue du Temple, 4th (01.42.72.72.22/fax
01.42.72.03.53/www.axialbeaubourg.com).
M° Hôtel de Ville. **Rates** single €89.95-€105.19;
double €120.44-€144.83; breakfast €6.87. **Credit**
AmEx, DC, MC, V. **Map** p406 K6.
The new-look Axial Beaubourg has been stunning
passers-by with its red velvet armchairs and bell-
shaped lights seen through the windows. Véronique
Turmel took over the running of the hotel from her
mother and has put a contemporary stamp on it
while retaining features such as the beams in the
reception and first-floor bedrooms. The warm decor
is based around aubergine and ginger and there
are sparkling modern bathrooms, but the personal
touch of a family-run hotel is still much in evidence.
Hotel services *Air con. Lift.* **Room services**
Double glazing. Hairdryer. Modem point. Safe. TV.

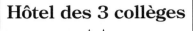
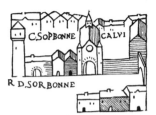

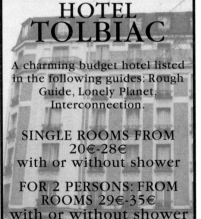

fully
(booked)
7/17 11:30 pm

Accommodation

53 € single w/toilet
CITI/ MasterCard.

Hôtel Caron de Beaumarchais

12 rue Vieille-du-Temple, 4th (01.42.72.34.12/
fax 01.42.72.34.63/ www.carondebeaumarchais.com).
M° Hôtel de Ville. **Rates** double €128-€142;
breakfast €9. **Credit** AmEx, DC, MC, V.
Map p406 K6.

Named after the 18th-century playwright who lived
just up the street, this charming hotel in the heart
of the Marais re-creates the refined tastes of
Beaumarchais' era, from gilded mirrors to Chinese-
style bathroom tiling. The 22 rooms are comfortable
if not always spacious.
Hotel services *Air con. Baby-sitting. Garden.*
Laundry. Safe. **Room services** *Double glazing.*
Hairdryer. Minibar. TV.

Hôtel St-Louis Marais

1 rue Charles V, 4th (01.48.87.87.04/
fax 01.48.87.33.26/www.saintlouismarais.com).
M° Sully Morland or Bastille. **Rates** single €90;
double €105-€120; breakfast €8. **Credit** MC, V.
Map p406 L7.

Built as part of a 17th-century Célestin convent, the
Hôtel St-Louis' thick walls offer a cosy welcome. 16
rooms are decorated in dark green or deep rose; terracotta floor tiles in half of them (the others have
plush carpets), tapestries on the walls and beams
add to its charm. Spacious single rooms are especially good value. There's a sister hotel on the Ile St-
Louis itself.
Hotel services *Baby-sitting. Meeting room.* **Room**
services *Double glazing. Fax. Hairdryer. Modem*
link. Safe. TV. Wheelchair access.

Hôtel du Septième Art

20 rue St-Paul, 4th (01.44.54.85.00/
fax 01.42.77.69.10). M° St-Paul. **Rates** single €50-
€90; double €105-€120; extra bed €20; breakfast
€7. **Credit** AmEx, DC, MC, V. **Map** p406 L7.

Though it's looking a bit scruffy, the Septième Art
has a loyal following of movie buffs and media
types. The lobby has black and white checked floors,
while the rooms are dominated by posters depicting
such torrid classics as *Niagara* and *Gone with the*
Wind. If the sedentary life of the cinephile is getting
you down, don't worry – there is now a room with
fitness apparatus to work off the flab.
Hotel services *Bar. Fitness room. Laundry.*
Room services *Double glazing. Hairdryer. Safe. TV.*

Budget

Grand Hôtel Jeanne d'Arc

3 rue de Jarente, 4th (01.48.87.62.11/
fax 01.48.87.37.31). M° St-Paul. **Rates** single €53-
€64; double €67-€78; triple €107; quad €122;
breakfast €5.80. **Credit** MC, V. **Map** p406 L6.

The attractive stone-built Jeanne d'Arc is on the corner of a pretty Marais street. Inside are interesting
touches, from 3D door numbers and murals to the
heraldic mosaic mirror in the reception area. The
cheapest of the 36 rooms are small but still good value.
Hotel services *Lift. Safe. Hairdryer.* **Room**
services *TV.*

Hôtel Castex

5 rue Castex, 4th (01.42.72.31.52/
fax 01.42.72.57.91/www.castexhotel.com).
M° Bastille. **Rates** single €39-€51; double €51-€57;
triple €65-€73; extra bed €10; breakfast €5.
Credit MC, V. **Map** p406 L7.

The Perdigãos have recently taken over this good-
value Marais hotel and added a small salon. Neon-lit
drinks and snacks machines are incongruous but no
doubt handy. The 29 rooms are plain but pleasant.
A couple of rooms don't have a loo *en suite*, but all
have a shower or bath.
Room services *TV.*

Hôtel de la Herse d'Or

20 rue St-Antoine, 4th (01.48.87.84.09/
fax 01.48.87.94.01). M° Bastille. **Rates** single
€30.30 (without bathroom); double €36 (without
bathroom)-€48; breakfast €4. **Credit** V.
Map p406 L7.

Enter this 17th-century building down a stone-
walled corridor, and you'll find a cheap and cheer-
ful hotel offering good-sized basic rooms in an
excellent location. The 35 rooms (many without
bathroom) look on to small dark courtyards or the
noisy rue St-Antoine. There isn't a lift so if you have
heavy luggage book a lower floor.
Hotel services *Safe.* **Room services** *Double glazing.*
TV (€4).

Hôtel du Séjour

36 rue du Grenier-St-Lazare, 3rd (01.48.87.40.36).
M° Etienne Marcel or Rambuteau. **Rates** single €30
(without bathroom); double €42 (without bathroom)-
€54; shower €3; no breakfast. **No credit cards.**
Map p402 K5.

No frills, flounces or phones here, but this 20-room
hotel is a welcoming haven for budget travellers.
Run by a friendly Portuguese couple for 25 years,
most rooms and bathrooms have been smartened up
and the courtyard is freshly painted.
Room services *Double glazing.*

The Bastille, eastern & north-eastern Paris

Deluxe

Libertel Terminus Est

5 rue du 8 mai 1945, 10th (01.55.26.05.05/fax
01.55.26.05.00/www.libertel-hotels.com). M° Gare de
l'Est. **Rates** single €143-€168 ; double €151-€245;
suite €307-€449 ; breakfast €12.50. **Credit** AmEx,
DC, MC, V. **Map** p402 K3.

One of the great railway hotels, the Terminus Est
has been imaginatively restored by Libertel, combining sleek, modern interior design with elements
that evoke the age of steam: leather luggage handles
on wardrobes, nostalgic photos, Edwardian-style
bathroom fittings and a library in the lobby. Red-
jacketed porters and polite receptionists give an
impression of quiet efficiency. An added boon is the

Personal training reaches new heights at the **Hotel Royal Monceau**. *See p53.*

health club and sauna. Don't miss the 1912 stained glass in the bar and breakfast room lobby.
Hotel services *Air-con. Baby-sitting. Bar. Laundry. Health club.* **Room services** *Double glazing. Hairdryer. Room service. Safe. TV.*

Moderate

Hôtel Beaumarchais

3 rue Oberkampf, 11th (01.53.36.86.86/ fax 01.43.38.32.86/www.hotelbeaumarchais.com). Mº Filles du Calvaire or Oberkampf **Rates** single €69-€85; double €99-€130; breakfast €7. **Credit** AmEx, MC, V. **Map** p402 L5.
This stylish hotel in the hip Oberkampf area was modernised by its architect owner, with brightly coloured walls, mosaics in the bathrooms, wavy headboards and Milan glass bedlamps. 33 rooms range from small singles to a good-sized suite; some overlook a pretty courtyard.
Hotel services. *Air con. Lift.* **Room services** *Double glazing. Hairdryer. Room service (24hr). Safe. TV.*

Le Pavillon Bastille

65 rue de Lyon, 12th (01.43.43.65.65/fax 01.43.43.96.52/www.pavillon-bastille.com). Mº Bastille. **Rates** single/double €130; suite €213; breakfast €12. **Credit** AmEx, DC, MC, V. **Map** p407 M7.
Directly opposite the Opéra Bastille, the Pavillon Bastille is a stylish choice in an area of unexceptional hotels. The hotel is set back behind an attractive courtyard and rooms feature bright, contemporary yellow and blue decor and exceptionally crisp-looking bedlinen. Breakfasts include freshly squeezed orange juice and fresh fruit salad and there is a limited room service menu. If you ask for a Forfait VIP, an extra €24 gets you a bathrobe, slippers, bowl of fruit, umbrella and more flexible

checking out hours, in addition to the complementary half-bottle of white wine that greets all guests. Non-smoking rooms available.
Hotel services *Air con. Bar. Laundry. Lift. Patio.* **Room services** *Hairdryer. Room service (24-hr). Safe. TV. Wheelchair access.*

Budget

Hôtel Apollo

11 rue de Dunkerque, 10th (01.48.78.04.98/ fax 01.42.85.08.78). Mº Gare du Nord. **Rates** single €37-€55; double €41-€76; extra bed €9; breakfast €5.30. **Credit** MC, V. **Map** p402 K2.
Opposite the Gare du Nord, the Apollo is a great find in an area full of doubtful budget joints. The 45 rooms have the rustic charm of a traditional railway hotel; rooms are decorated with large wardrobes and florid wallpaper and are thankfully not invaded by the roar of the *TGV*.
Hotel services *Lift.* **Room services** *Double glazing. Hairdryer. Safe. TV.*

Hôtel de Nevers

53 rue de Malte, 11th (01.47.00.56.18/ fax 01.43.57.77.39/www.hoteldenevers.com). Mº République. **Rates** single or double €30 (no bathroom)-€46; triple €56; quad €70; shower €3.05; breakfast €5. **Credit** MC, V. **Map** p402 L4.
A good-value base ten minutes from the Marais and within striking distance of Oberkampf, this hotel is ideally placed for those wanting to make the most of the capital's nightlife. Three languid cats welcome you as one of the family. The vintage lift is a memorable experience but all 34 rooms are clean and comfortable. The reception service isn't quite as efficient now that the owners have hired outside help, but you can't blame them for wanting a break.
Hotel services *Safe. Internet access.*

Hôtel des Sans Culottes

27 rue de Lappe, 11th (01.48.05.42.92/
fax 01.48.05.08.56). M° Bastille. **Rates** single
€45.73; double €53.36; breakfast included. **Credit**
AmEx, MC,V. **Map** p407 M7.
Slap bang in the middle of the touristy pub crawl
strip, rue de Lappe. Rooms are colourful, clean and
functional, if a little over-Airwicked. The hotel is
named after a group of revolutionaries and its seedy
status has everything to do with its location and
nothing to do with its name.
Room services *Hairdryer. TV.*

The Champs-Elysées & west

Palace

Hôtel de Crillon

10 pl de la Concorde, 8th (01.44.71.15.00/
fax 01.44.71.15.03/www.crillon.com). M° Concorde.
Rates single €460-€550; double €550-€725; suite
€755-€1,200, breakfast €28.20-€41.95. **Credit**
AmEx, DC, MC, V. **Map** p401 F4.
This magnificent neo-classical palace recently
favoured by Madonna groans with marble, mirrors
and gilt. The Michelin-starred Ambassadeurs
restaurant is sublime, the Winter Garden tearoom
has a gorgeous terrace; the Institut Guerlain has its
own beauty salon here.
Hotel services *Fitness centre. Garden. Restaurant.*
Room services *CD-player. Fax. Modem link. TV.*

Four Seasons George V

31 av George V, 8th (01.49.52.70.00/
fax 01.49.52.70.10/www.fourseasons.com).
M° George V. **Rates** single €570-€790; double
€630-€870; suite €1,175 - € 8,000; breakfast €35-
€46. **Credit** AmEx, DC, MC, V. **Map** p400 D4.
While hardcore George V fans may lament the
Disneyfication of the hotel, there is no denying that
the new version churns out serious *luxe:* almost
over-attentive staff, glorious flower arrangements,
divine bathrooms and ludicrously comfy beds.
Hotel services *Bar. Fitness centre. Pool. Restaurant.*
Room services *CD-player. Modem link. PlayStation.*

Hôtel Plaza Athénée

25 av Montaigne, 8th (01.53.67.66.65/
fax 01.53.67.66.66/www.plaza-athenee-paris.com).
M° Alma-Marceau. **Rates** single €460-€488; double
€587-€618; suite €1,190-€1,220; breakfast €30-€43.
Credit AmEx, DC, MC, V. **Map** p401 H5.
The fashion hotel, the Athénée's location allows you
to fall out of bed into the couture shops of avenue
Montaigne. Most rooms are a riot of chandeliers,
gold trimmings and Louis XV furniture but there is
a classy art deco top floor. In summer, the Cour
Jardin becomes a cascade of ivy – a romantic back-
drop for lunch at the Alain Ducasse restaurant.
Hotel services *Bar. Fitness centre. Restaurants.*
Sauna. **Room services** *CD-player. Fax. Internet
connection. Modem link. Wheelchair access.*

Hôtel Royal Monceau

37 av Hoche, 8th (01.42.99.88.00/
fax 01.42.99.89.90/www.royalmonceau.com).
M° Charles de Gaulle-Etoile. **Rates** single €396-€491;
double €442-€537; suite €610-€2,592; breakfast
€27-€40. **Credit** AmEx, DC, MC, V. **Map** p401 H5.
Trompe l'oeil clouds on the ceilings, acres of marble
and four florists arranging a gargantuan display in
the lobby shout *'luxe'* at the Royal Monceau. The
hotel recently amalgamated some rooms into 45 new
suites. One belongs to Omar Sharif, who often enjoys
an *apéro* in the English bar. The Royal Monceau's
other main boast is its fabulous health club Les
Thermes, and there's a romantic garden restaurant.
Hotel services *Fitness club. Pool. Bar. Restaurants.*
Room services *CD-player. Fax. Internet. Modem
link. Radio. Safe. TV. Wheelchair access.*

Hôtel Raphaël

17 av Kléber, 16th (01.44.28.00.28/fax
01.53.64.32.01/www.raphael-hotel.com). M° Kléber.
Rates single or double €420-€505; suite €670-€880;
extra bed €76; breakfast €25-€31. hand **Credit**
AmEx, DC, MC, V. **Map** p400 C4.
The Raphaël, with just 90 rooms, retains a sense of
personal service and privacy. Numerous celebrities
have stayed here since the hotel opened in 1925,
including US presidents Ford and Bush, as well as
Serge Gainsbourg and singer Lenny Kravitz. Superb
360° views from the seventh-floor terrace restaurant.
Hotel services *Bar. Restaurants.* **Room services**
Modem link. Room service (24hr). Radio. TV.

Deluxe

Hôtel François 1er

7 rue Magellan, 8th (01.47.23.44.04/fax
01.47.23.93.43). M° George V. **Rates** single or
double €260-€457; suites €580-€640; breakfast €21.
Credit AmEx, DC, MC, V. **Map** p400 D4.
A portrait of the handsome dude himself smiles
benignly in the foyer of the François 1er. With only
38 rooms and two suites, this is a hotel for those who

Presidents and popstars find privacy at the
plush **Hôtel Raphaël**. *See above.*

want discreet comfort in a surpisingly quiet street in the heart of the Golden Triangle. The smart new decor by Pierre-Yves Rochon combines Renaissance-rich fabrics, oil paintings and marble floors . Guests can use the Royal Monceau health club.

Hotel services *Air con. Baby-sitting. Bar.* **Room services** *Double glazing. Hairdryer. Modem link. TV. Room service (24hr).*

Hôtel Napoléon

40 av de Friedland, 8th (01.56.68.43.21/fax 01.47.66.82.33/www.hotelnapoleonparis.com). M° Charles de Gaulle-Etoile. **Rates** single €250; double €450; suites €480; breakfast €22. **Credit** AmEx, DC, MC, V. **Map** p400 D3.

It may be a mere step away from the Arc de Triomphe but, with its orange awnings and geraniums, the Napoléon has the faded grandeur of a Riviera hotel from the 1920s. Inside, the same elegance pervades, along with a bustling reception. Rooms are very individual and feature Empire furniture, Sèvres vases and framed documents carrying the signature of the Emperor himself.

Hotel services *Air con. Bar. Laundry.* **Room services** *Double glazing. Room service. Fax. Hairdryer. Modem link. Safe. TV.*

K Palace

81 av Kléber, 16th (01.44.05.75.75/ fax 01.44.05.74.74.). M° Trocadéro. **Rates** single €300; double €380; suite €460-€540; breakfast €19. **Credit** AmEx, MC, V. **Map** p400 B5.

A desperately hip hotel for those with an allergy to *belle époque* overload. Sleek lines, leather, marble and a wonderful interior courtyard give a gloriously slick feel and provide a fantastic backdrop for the frequent fashion shoots which take place here. The rooms, staff and clientele all scream understated chic. Don't check in on a bad-hair day.

Hotel services *Air con. Baby-sitting. Bar. Bureau de change. Health club. Laundry. Pool. Safe.* **Room services** *CD player. Double glazing. Fax. Hairdryer. Modem link. Radio. Room service (24hr). Safe. TV. Wheelchair access.*

Hôtel Square

3 rue de Boulainvilliers, 16th (01.44.14.91.90/ fax 01.44.14.91.99/www.hotelsquare.com). M° Passy/RER Kennedy-Radio France. **Rates** single or double €230-€370; suite €450; extra bed €38.11; breakfast €18. **Credit** AmEx, DC, MC, V. **Map** p404 A7.

Though the polished granite curtain wall may look forbidding, the dramatic interior of this courageously modern hotel is welcoming, aided by the personalised service that comes with only 22 rooms. The exotic woods, quality fabrics and paint finishes are striking, with temporary exhibitions in the atrium by leading artists, such as Ben and Viallat.

Hotel services *Air con. Baby-sitting. Bar. Laundry. Restaurant.* **Room services** *CD player. Double glazing. Fax. Hairdryer. Modem link. Radio. Safe. TV/VCR. Wheelchair access.*

Expensive

Hôtel Le Lavoisier

21 rue Lavoisier, 8th (01.53.30.06.06/ fax 01.53.30.23.00/www.hotellavoisier.com). M° St-Augustin. **Rates** single or double €199; suite €245-€385; extra bed €15.24; breakfast €12. **Credit** AmEx, MC, V. **Map** p401 F3.

Reopened in March 99 after a complete refit by designer Jean-Philippe Nuel, the 30-room Le Lavoisier is a classy affair. Decor is refined and warm, and the furniture mixes periods and styles to striking effect.

Hotel services *Air con. Baby-sitting. Bar. Hairdryer. Laundry. Safe.* **Room services** *Double glazing. Internet connection. Modem link. Room service (24hr). TV. Wheelchair access.*

Hôtel de Banville

166 bd Berthier, 17th (01.42.67.70.16/ fax 01.44.40.42.77/www.hotelbanville.fr). M° Porte de Champerret. **Rates** single €127; double €150-€183; suite €244; extra bed €19; breakfast €11. **Credit** AmEx, DC, MC, V. **Map** p400 C1.

Marianne Moreau's mother and grandmother preceded her here and personal touches are proudly maintained. Each of the 38 rooms is individually designed and very feminine, with iron or brass beds and warm Italianate colours. Le Chambre d'Amélie has a great rooftop view from the terrace.

Hotel services *Air con. Airport shuttle. Bar. Laundry.* **Room services** *Double glazing. Hairdryer. Modem link. Radio. Room service (24hr). Safe. TV.*

Hôtel Regent's Garden

6 rue Pierre-Demours, 17th (01.45.74.07.30/ fax 01.40.55.01.42/www.bw-paris-hotels.com). M° Charles de Gaulle-Etoile or Ternes. **Rates** single €124.40; double €134.15-€230.50; triple €180-€243.30; quadruple €252.45; breakfast €10. **Credit** AmEx, DC, MC, V. **Map** p400 C3.

High ceilings and plush upholstery hark back to the Second Empire, when this house was built for Napoléon III's physician. There are 39 large bedrooms, some with gilt mirrors and fireplaces. With its walled garden, this is an oasis of calm ten minutes from the Arc de Triomphe. It is a Best Western, but doesn't feel at all like a chain.

Hotel services *Air con. Baby-sitting. Bureau de change. Garden. Laundry. Parking. Safe.* **Room services** *Double glazing. Hairdryer. Modem link. Room service (24hr). TV.*

Moderate

Hôtel Keppler

12 rue Keppler, 16th (01.47.20.65.05/ fax 01.47.23.02.29/www.hotelkeppler.com). M° Kléber or George V. **Rates** single or double €116.23; breakfast €4.58. **Credit** AmEx, MC, V. **Map** p400 C4.

The high ceilings and spacious rooms are typical of this prestigious neighbourhood but the prices aren't.

There's a charming spiral staircase and a vintage lift. The reception and breakfast room are business-like but subtle lighting adds atmosphere.
Hotel services *Bar. Lift.* **Room services** *Hairdryer. Room service (24hr). Safe. TV.*

Accommodation

Deluxe

Terrass Hôtel
12-14 rue Joseph-de-Maistre, 18th (01.46.06.72.85/ fax 01.42.52.29.11./www.terrass-hotel.com). M° Place de Clichy. **Rates** single €188-€214; double €225-€248; suite €302; breakfast €12. **Credit** AmEx, DC, MC, V. **Map** p401 H1.
Entering the rather dated lobby of the Terrass you may wonder what draws such stars as Pierce Brosnan and MC Solaar to the hotel. Go up to the seventh floor and there's your answer – possibly the best view in the whole of Paris from the rooftop restaurant. Those in the know ask for room 704, from which you can lie in the bath and look out at the Eiffel Tower, or the apartment-sized suite 802. Of 101 rooms, 75 are air-conditioned, and two floors are non-smoking.
Hotel services *Air con. Baby-sitting. Bar. Bureau de change. Laundry. Restaurant.* **Room services** *Double glazing. Hairdryer. Modem link. Room service. TV. Wheelchair access.*

Moderate

Hôtel Ermitage
24 rue Lamarck, 18th (01.42.64.79.22/ fax 01.42.64.10.33). M° Lamarck-Caulaincourt. **Rates** single €72; double €82; triple €104; quad €120; breakfast included. **No credit cards. Map** p401 H1.
This 12-room hotel is only five minutes from the Sacré-Coeur, but on a quiet street far from the tourist madness. The rooms are large and endearingly over-decorated; some on the upper floors have great views and there's a small garden.
Hotel services *Garden.* **Room services** *Double glazing. Hairdryer.*

Prima Lepic
29 rue Lepic, 18th (01.46.06.44.64/fax 01.46.06.66.11). M° Blanche or Abbesses. **Rates** single €99; double €93-€123; suite €150-€170; breakfast €7.50. **Credit** MC, V. **Map** p401 H1.
On the steeply climbing rue Lepic, where leopard-skin pants vie with *tartes Tatins* for shop window space, is the Prima Lepic, which has been a Montmartre hotel for almost a century. The recent renovation did away with its faded charm and spruced up all 38 rooms with over-the-top borders zinging floral prints, but even if you don't go for the '*style anglais*' of the decor, brand new bathrooms and spotlessly clean rooms can't be bad.
Hotel services *Lift. Safe.* **Room services** *Double glazing. TV.*

Royal Fromentin
11 rue Fromentin, 9th (01.48.74.85.93/fax 01.42.81.02.33/www.hotelroyalfromentin.com). M° Pigalle. **Rates** single €98; double €118; triple €149; breakfast included. **Credit** AmEx, MC, V. **Map** p401 H2.
Bargain basement rock-star chic. Only aspiring superstars will fully appreciate the vaguely sleazy feel, views of Sacré-Cœur and illustrious guest book history within staggering distance of some of Paris' major music venues. Previous sleepers include the Spice Girls, Keziah Jones, Blondie and Nirvana – before they made it to the big time. Rock on.
Hotel services *Baby-sitting. Bar. Laundry.* **Room services** *Double glazing. Hairdryer. Room service. TV.*

Budget

Hôtel des Batignolles
26-28 rue des Batignolles, 17th (01.43.87.70.40/ fax 01.44.70.01.04/www.batignolles.com). M° Rome or Place de Clichy. **Rates** single or double €52.50-€102.50; triple €62.50-€110; breakfast €4. **Credit** DC, MC, V. **Map** p401 F2.
This still feels a bit like the girls' boarding house it once was, but provides a good base within easy reach of Montmartre. The Batignolles is simple, quiet and clean, with 33 spacious rooms and a tranquil courtyard.
Room services *Double glazing. Hairdryer. Safe. TV.*

Hôtel Eldorado
8 rue des Dames, 17th (01.45.22.35.21/fax 01.43.87.25.97). M° Place de Clichy. **Rates** single €35; double €53; triple €76; breakfast €5.30. **Credit** AmEx, DC, MC, V. **Map** p401 F2.
Hidden behind place de Clichy is a piece of real bohemia. Owner Anne Gratacos has decorated the 40 rooms individually – leopardskin here, a satin eiderdown there, velvet sofas and flea market finds. Rooms are split between the main house and an annexe across the leafy courtyard. With a billiard room and restaurant, it is a hip address during the fashion shows when agencies use it for hopefuls who aren't yet up to palace hotel status.
Hotel services *Garden. Internet connection. Restaurant. Safe.*

Hôtel Regyn's Montmartre
18 pl des Abbesses, 18th (01.42.54.45.21/ fax 01.42.23.76.69/www.regynsmontmartre.com). M° Abbesses. **Rates** single €61.64- €78; double €72.41-€92.25; breakfast €6.90-€7.60. **Credit** AmEx, MC, V. **Map** p401 G1.
This is a great location opposite the Abbesses Métro in the heart of Montmartre. There's a pretty breakfast room and six of the 22 rooms have superb views.
Hotel services *Laundry. Lift.* **Room services** *Double glazing. Hairdryer. TV.*

Top this: the view from the aptly named **Terrass Hôtel.**

The Latin Quarter & the 13th

Expensive

Hôtel du Panthéon

19 pl du Panthéon, 5th (01.43.54.32.95/
fax 01.43.26.64.65/www.hoteldupantheon.com). RER
Luxembourg/M° Cardinal Lemoine. **Rates** single or
double €183; suite €213; breakfast €9. **Credit**
AmEx, DC, MC, V. **Map** p406 J8.
An elegant, classy hotel with 34 individually
decorated rooms taking their scheme from the *toile
de Jouy* material print on the walls. There's a tasteful basement breakfast room and a pleasant reception with a bar for guests. Some rooms have
impressive views of the Panthéon, others onto a
charming and less imposing courtyard, complete
with chestnut tree. Next door's Hôtel des Grands
Hommes (01.46.34.19.60), is run by the same people
and offers a very similar ambience.
Hotel services *Air con. Baby-sitting. Bar. Bureau
de change. Laundry. Safe.* **Room services** *Double
glazing. Hairdryer. Modem link. TV. Wheelchair
access.*

Moderate

Les Degrés de Notre Dame

10 rue des Grands-Degrés, 5th (01.55.42.88.88/
fax 01.40.46.95.34). M° St-Michel. **Rates** single
€65.55; double €91.47-€137.20; studio €91.47-
€121.96; breakfast included. **Credit** MC,V. **Map** J7
Masses of dark wood and lovingly tended rooms
make this hotel set back from the Seine a real find.
If the ten hotel rooms are taken, ask about their two
studios a few streets away from the hotel, where you
can pretend to be a real Parisian. The studios come
complete with washing machine, power shower and,
in one flat, a conservatory filled with fresh flowers.
Hotel services *Bar. Restaurant.*
Room services *Double glazing. Hairdryer. Modem
link. Room service (24hr). Safe. TV.*

Familia Hôtel

11 rue des Ecoles, 5th (01.43.54.55.27/
fax 01.43.29.61.77/www.hotel-paris-familia.com).
M° Maubert-Mutualité or Jussieu. **Rates** single €66
double €75.50-€110; triple €121; extra bed €18;
breakfast €5.50. **Credit** AmEx, DC, MC, V.
Map p406 J7.
An enthusiastic welcome awaits at this old-fashioned hotel whose balconies are hung with tumbling
plants. Chatty and welcoming owner Eric
Gaucheron will help you get to grips with local lore,
and is immensely proud of the sepia murals and
mahogany furniture that feature in some of the 30
rooms. The Gaucheron family also owns the
Minerve (01.43.26.26.04), just next door and offering
the same fantastic package.
Hotel services *Safe.* **Room services** *Double
glazing. Hairdryer. Minibar. TV.*

Hôtel des Grandes Ecoles

75 rue du Cardinal-Lemoine, 5th (01.43.26.79.23/
fax 01.43.25.28.15/www.hotel-grandes-ecoles.com).
M° Cardinal Lemoine. **Rates** single or double €90-
€120; extra bed €15; breakfast €7. **Credit** MC, V.
Map p406 K8.
A taste of the country in central Paris, this wonderful hotel, with 51 old-fashioned rooms, is built around
a leafy garden where breakfast is served in the summer. The largest of the three buildings houses the
reception area and an old-fashioned breakfast room
with gilt mirror and piano.
Hotel services *Garden. Lift. Parking (€20). Safe.*
Room services *Double glazing. Hairdryer.
Wheelchair access.*

Hôtel Jardins du Luxembourg

5 impasse Royer-Collard, 5th (01.40.46.08.88/
fax 01.40.46.02.28). RER Luxembourg. **Rates** single
or double €130-€140; suite €260; breakfast €9.
Credit AmEx, DC, MC, V. **Map** p408 H8.
It would be hard to find a quieter location than this
cul-de-sac near the Jardins du Luxembourg. Freud
stayed here in 1885 so it's probably a good place to
come to sort out your ego. Kilim rugs, stripped floor-
boards and vivid paintwork and floor tiles should
help keep self-reflective gloom at bay.
Hotel services *Air con. Laundry.* **Room services**
*Double glazing. Hairdryer. Safe. TV. Wheelchair
access.*

La Manufacture

8 rue Philippe de Champagne, 13th (01.45.35.45.25/
fax 01.45.35.45.40/ www.hotel-la-manufacture.com).
M° Place d'Italie. **Rates** single €119; double €128;
triple €145; quad €196; breakfast €7. **Credit**
AmEx, DC, MC, V. **Map** p406 K10.
Revamped from scratch in 1999, and named after the
nearby Gobelins tapestry works, La Manufacture
lives up to its claim to be 'an elegant hotel at affordable rates'. Its designer has got it just right: warm
colours, modern but not too minimalist, squeaky-
clean white-tiled bathrooms and perhaps the nicest
breakfast room in Paris. Place d'Italie may not be in
the heart of the action, but the location is quiet and
not unattractive – plus it's only 15 minutes to Orly.
Hotel services *Air con. Bar.* **Room services.**
Double glazing. Hairdryer. Safe. TV.

Select Hôtel

1 pl de la Sorbonne, 5th (01.46.34.14.80/
fax 01.46.34.51.79/www.selecthotel.fr). M° Cluny-La
Sorbonne. **Rates** double or twin single €131.10;
duplex €190; breakfast €6. **Credit** AmEx, DC, MC,
V. **Map** p406 J7.
Twenty years ago this was a cheap hotel used by
students arriving at the Sorbonne. The owners really went to town on the refurb, introducing a brave
art deco scheme that incorporates a waterfall atrium and a very 1920s basement bar. The deco rooms
are smart with Starck-ish bathrooms, but for the less
adventurous one wing remains more trad.
Hotel services *Air con. Baby-sitting. Bar. Laundry.
Safe.* **Room services** *Double glazing. Hairdryer.
Modem link. Room service. TV.*

Budget

Hôtel Esmeralda

4 rue St-Julien-le-Pauvre, 5th (01.43.54.19.20/
fax 01.40.51.00.68). M° St-Michel or Maubert-
Mutalite. **Rates** single €28-€70; double €75-€80;
triple €90; quad €100; breakfast €6. **No credit**
cards. Map p406 J7.
This 1640 building looks on to a tree-lined square
and over the Seine to Notre-Dame. In the plant-filled
entrance, the resident cat may be curled up in a velvet
chair. Upstairs are 19 floral rooms with antique
furnishings and uneven floors – although fans who
haven't been back for a while should take note that
the Esmeralda is now decidedly shabby chic. This is a
cult address, so book ahead.
Hotel services *Safe. Room service.*

St-Germain, Odéon & Montparnasse

Deluxe

L'Hôtel

13 rue des Beaux-Arts, 6th (01.44.41.99.00/
fax 01.43.25.64.81/www.l-hotel.com). M° St-
Germain-des-Prés. **Rates** double €259-€343; suite
€595-€686; breakfast €16.80. **Credit** AmEx, DC,
MC, V.
Map p405 H6.
Longtime favourite with the fashion pack – Oscar
died here, darlings – L'Hôtel has been taken well in
hand by new owner Jean-Paul Besnard (a biologist,
strangely). Jacques Garcia's revamp has restored the
central stairwell to its former glory; Mistinguett's
chambre retains its art deco mirror bed and Wilde's
former resting place has green peacock murals.
Don't miss the cellar swimming pool and *fumoir.*
Hotel services *Baby-sitting. Bar. Laundry.*
Restaurant. Pool. Steam room. **Room services**
CD-player. Fax. Hairdryer. Room service. Safe. TV.

Hôtel de l'Abbaye

10 rue Cassette, 6th (01.45.44.38.11/
fax 01.45.48.07.86/www.hotel-abbaye.com).
M° St-Sulpice. **Rates** double €180-€253; suite €344;
breakfast included. **Credit** AmEx, MC, V.
Map p405 G7.
This tranquil hotel was originally part of a convent.
Wood panelling, well-stuffed sofas and an open
fireplace make for a relaxed atmosphere but, best of
all, there's a surprisingly large garden where breakfast is served in the warmer months. The 42 rooms
are tasteful and luxurious and the suites have rooftop terraces.
Hotel services *Bar. Bureau de change. Garden.*
Laundry. Lift. Safe. **Room services** *Hairdryer.*
Modem link. Radio. Room service. Safe. TV.

Croissants and contentment in the garden
of the **Hôtel de l'Abbaye.**

Hôtel Bel-Ami

7-11 rue St-Benoît, 6th (01.42.61.53.53/ fax 01.49.27.09.33/www.hotel-bel-ami.com) M° St-Germain-des-Prés. **Rates** single/double €236.30-€388.74, suite €487.84, breakfast €15.24 **Credit** AmEx, MC, V **Map** p405 H6.

With a super-stylish decor and pukka hotel pedigree (Grace-Leo Andrieu also put the *luxe* into The Lancaster and Le Montalembert), this is a favourite during fashion weeks. It's chic, muted minimalism for the most part, but the St-Germain-themed rooms have a warmer decor in memory of the jazz club once housed in the basement.
Hotel services *Baby-sitting. Bar. Laundry. Safe.* **Room services** *CD-player. Fax. Hairdryer. Modem link. Radio. Room service (24hr). Safe. TV. Wheelchair access.*

Hôtel Buci Latin

34 rue de Buci, 6th (01.43.29.07.20/ fax 01.43.29.67.44). M° St-Germain-des-Prés. **Rates** double €190-€300; suite €320; breakfast included. **Credit** AmEx, DC, MC, V. **Map** p405 H7.

Worlds away from the beams 'n' *brocantes* set, the Buci Latin is a bright, modern hotel ideal for stashing the shopping after a hard day in St-Germain. Sculpture galore provides the backdrop for some artful lounging in the lobby, whilst the clean, restful bedrooms guarantee a good night's sleep.
Hotel services *Baby-sitting. Bar. Café. Laundry. Safe.* **Room services** *Hairdryer. Modem link. Radio. Room service (24-hr). TV. Wheelchair access.*

Hôtel Lutétia

45 bd Raspail, 6th (01.49.54.46.46/fax 01.49.54.46.00/www.lutetia-paris.com). M° Sèvres Babylone. **Rates** single or double €290-€442; suite €686; breakfast €120. **Credit** AmEx, DC, MC, V. **Map** p405 G7.

A masterpiece of art nouveau and early art deco architecture, the Lutétia opened in 1910 to accommodate shoppers coming to the Bon Marché. Today its plush bar and lively brasserie are still fine places for resting weary feet. Its 250 rooms, revamped in purple, gold and pearl grey, maintain a '30s feel.
Hotel services *Baby-sitting. Bar. Fitness centre. Laundry. Parking. Restaurants.* **Room services** *Double glazing. Fax. Modem link. Radio. Safe. TV.*

Relais Médicis

23 rue Racine, 6th (01.43.26.00.60/fax 01.40.46.83.39/ www.123france.com). M° Odéon/RER Luxembourg. **Rates** single or double €208-€258; breakfast included. **Credit** AmEx, DC, MC, V. **Map** p406 H7.

Near the Luxembourg Gardens, the very feminine Relais Médicis evokes an era of pennyfarthings and Gibson girls. The spacious bedrooms are decorated with Impressionist floral fabrics and have windowside tables for a romantic breakfast. Piped classical music plays in a little drawing room and there is a courtyard topiary garden.
Hotel services *Baby-sitting. Bar.* **Room services** *Hairdryer. Radio. TV. Safe.*

Deco delight: the **Hôtel Lutétia**. *See left.*

La Villa

29 rue Jacob, 6th (01.43.26.60.00/fax 01.46.34.63.63/ www.villa-stgermain.com). M° St-Germain-des-Prés. **Rates** single/double €225-€352; suites €400; breakfast €13. **Credit** AmEx, MC, V. **Map** p405 H6.

It's been renovated, but the Keith Richards of Paris hotels retains an air of loucheness. Maybe it's the faux crocodile skin on the bedheads or the crinkly taffeta on the taupe-coloured walls. Thankfully, the room numbers are still projected on to the floor in front of your door (in case it's hard to see straight).
Hotel services *Baby-sitting. Bar. Laundry.* **Room services** *Hairdryer. Modem link. Room service (24hr). Safe. TV. Wheelchair access.*

Expensive

Le Clos Médicis

56 rue Monsieur-le-Prince, 6th (01.43.29.10.80/ fax 01.43.54.26.90). M° Odéon/RER Luxembourg. **Rates** single €125; double €150-€180; triple €220; breakfast €10. **Credit** AmEx, DC, MC, V. **Map** p406 H7.

In a 1773 building built for the Medici family is this extremely stylish hotel designed by Jean-Philippe Nuel. The brand-new decor is refreshingly modern and very chic, with taffeta curtains, chenille bedcoverings and antique floor tiles in the bathrooms. Rooms ending in 0 are still to be refurbished.
Hotel services *Air con. Baby-sitting. Bar. Internet access.* **Room services** *Double glazing. Modem link. TV.*

Next to Main Department Stores • 150m from Opéra Garnier
10mn walk to Louvre Museum • 10mn from Eurostar terminal

Grand Hôtel de l'Univers

6 rue Grégoire-de-Tours, 6th (01.43.29.37.00/fax 01.40.51.06.45/www.hotel-paris-univers.com). M° Odéon. **Rates** single €139; double €153. **Credit** AmEx, DC, MC, V. **Map** p406 H7.

15th-century beams, high ceilings and *toile*-covered walls are the trademarks of this hotel, which has just finished a major renovation. *Côté Sud* fans will love the Manuel Canovas fabrics, but there are also mod-cons including a laptop for rent. The same helpful team also runs the Hôtel St-Germain-des Près (36 rue Bonaparte, 6th/01.43.26.00.19/ www.hotel-st.ger.com), which has a medieval-themed room and the sweetest attic in Paris.
Hotel services *Air con.* **Room services** *Double glazing. Hairdryer. Modem point. Safe. TV.*

Hôtel d'Angleterre

44 rue Jacob, 6th (01.42.60.34.72/fax 01.42.60.16.93). M° St-Germain-des-Prés. **Rates** single or double €125-€210; suite €260; breakfast €9.15. **Credit** AmEx, DC, MC, V. **Map** p405 H6.

Low-key elegance prevails at this former British embassy where the US independence treaty was prepared in 1783. Climb the listed staircase or bash away at the grand piano in the salon. Some of the 27 rooms look over the hotel's ivy-strewn courtyard.
Hotel services *Baby-sitting. Bureau de change. Garden. Laundry. Lift (not to all rooms).* **Room services** *Double glazing. Hairdryer. Room service. Safe. TV.*

Hôtel des Marronniers

21 rue Jacob, 6th (01.43.25.30.60/ fax 01.40.46.83.56). M° St-Germain-des-Prés. **Rates** single €110; double €145-€160; triple €200; breakfast €10-€12. **Credit** MC, V. **Map** p405 H6.

An oasis of calm in lively St-Germain, this hotel has a courtyard in front and a lovely conservatory and garden at the back, where you'll find the chestnut trees of the name. The 37 rooms are mostly reasonably sized, with pretty canopies and fabrics.
Hotel services *Air con. Baby-sitting. Bar. Garden. Safe. Tea salon.* **Room services** *Double glazing. Hairdryer. TV.*

Moderate

Hôtel du Danemark

21 rue Vavin, 6th (01.43.26.93.78/ fax 01.46.34.66.06). M° Notre-Dame-des-Champs or Vavin. **Rates** single €110; double €121; double with Jacuzzi €136; breakfast €9. **Credit** AmEx, DC, MC, V. **Map** p405 G8.

Next to Henri Sauvage's 1912 Carreaux Métro building is the newly decorated Danemark. With only 15 rooms, it has a sleek boutique-y look that blends in with the shops along this Montparnasse street. The lobby features leather armchairs and all the rooms have original oil paintings. A recent renovation involved installing a Jacuzzi in one room.
Hotel services *Laundry. Safe.* **Room services** *Double glazing. Hairdryer. Room service (breakfast). TV. Whirlpool.*

Hôtel Istria-Montparnasse

29 rue Campagne-Première, 14th (01.43.20.91.82/fax 01.43.22.48.45). M° Raspail. **Rates** single or double €90-€100; breakfast €8. **Credit** AmEx, DC, MC, V. **Map** p405 G9.

If you're in Montparnasse to revisit its artistic hey-day you can't do better than stay here – Man Ray, Kiki, Marcel Duchamp, Francis Picabia, Erik Satie and Louis Aragon all stayed here. The Istria has been modernised since then but it still has charm with 26 simply furnished, compact rooms, a cosy cellar breakfast room and a comfortable living area. The tiled artists' studios next door featured in Godard's *A Bout de Souffle.*
Hotel services *Garden. Laundry. Lift. Photocopier.* **Room services** *Double glazing. Hairdryer. Room service (24hr). Safe. TV.*

Hôtel Lenox

9 rue de l'Université, 7th (01.42.96.10.95/ fax 01.42.61.52.83/www.lenoxsaintgermain.com). M° St-Germain-des-Près. **Rates** single or double €112-€147; suite €181-€266; breakfast €9-€12. **Credit** AmEx, DC, MC, V. **Map** p405 G6.

This venerable literary and artistic haunt (TS Elliot booked Joyce in on the recommendation of Ezra Pound – or was it the other way round?) has been reborn with a wink at art deco and the jazz age. The Lenox Club Bar, open to the public, is a bravura creation with marquetry scenes of jazz musicians. Bedrooms, reached by an astonishing glass lift, have more traditional decor and ever-so-Parisian views.
Hotel services *Air con. Baby-sitting. Bar. Internet connection. Laundry. Lift. Safe.* **Room services** *Double glazing. Hairdryer. Radio. TV.*

Hôtel du Lys

23 rue Serpente, 6th (01.43.26.97.57/ fax 01.44.07.34.90). M° Odéon or St-Michel. **Rates** single €90; double €105; breakfast included. **Credit** MC, V. **Map** p406 H7.

This is a haven from the *boul'Mich* tourist hell outside and the perfect spot for a bargain romantic weekend. The proprietors are charming and take great pride in maintaining the prevailing calm.
Room services *Double glazing. Hairdryer. Safe. TV.*

Budget

Hôtel du Globe

15 rue des Quatre-Vents, 6th (01.43.26.35.50/ fax 01.46.33.62.69). M° Odéon. Closed August. **Rates** single or double €66-€100; breakfast €9. **Credit** MC, V. **Map** p406 H7.

The Globe is an appealing mix of styles. Gothic wrought-iron doors lead into florid corridors, and an unexplained suit of armour supervises guests from the tiny salon. A small, winding staircase may lead to suitcase trouble.
Room services *Double glazing. Hairdryer. Radio. Room service (24hr). TV.*

Hôtel de Nesle

*7 rue de Nesle, 6th (01.43.54.62.41/fax
01.43.54.31.88/www.hoteldenesle.com). M° Odéon.*
Rates single €50-€79; double €79-€99;
no breakfast. **Credit** AC, MC, V. **Map** p406 H6.
The eccentric Nesle draws an international back-
packer clientele. Madame regales visitors with tales
of the Nesle's hippy past; Monsieur is responsible
for the painted figures on the walls of the 20 rooms
(from colonial to Oriental, Molière to the Knights
Templar). No phones in rooms and no reservations.
Hotel services *Garden. Terrace.* **Room services**
Double glazing.

Hôtel de Nevers

*83 rue du Bac, 7th (01.45.44.61.30/
fax 01.42.22.29.47). M° Rue du Bac.* **Rates** double
€80-€91; extra bed €15; breakfast €6. **No credit
cards. Map** p405 G6.
This characterful 11-room hotel was once part of a
convent. Everything is dinky and dainty, with mini-
wardrobes and neat bathrooms. Rooms are smart,
but the paintwork on the staircase has suffered regular torment as guests have to carry up their luggage. If you can make it up to the fourth floor, two
rooms have tiny, charming terraces.
Hotel services *Safe.* **Room services** *Double
glazing. Hairdryer. TV.*

The 7th & the 15th

Deluxe

Hôtel Duc de St-Simon

*14 rue de St-Simon, 7th (01.44.39.20.20/
fax 01.45.48.68.25). M° Rue du Bac.* **Rates** single or
double €200-€255; suite €315-€320; breakfast €14.
Credit AmEx, MC, V. **Map** p405 F6.
Step off the quiet side street into a pretty courtyard
(where breakfast is served in the summer) – you'll
be following the footsteps of Lauren Baccall, Billy
James and Toni Morisson. The 34 romantically decorated bedrooms include four with terraces above a
leafy garden (sadly not accessible to visitors). A perfect pitch for the glamorous and amorous, though if
you can do without a four-poster bed there are
cheaper and more spacious rooms than the
'Honeymoon Suite'.
Hotel services *Baby-sitting. Bar. Laundry.* **Room
services** *Hairdryer. Modem link. Room service.
Safe. TV (on request).*

Le Montalembert

*3 rue de Montalembert, 7th (01.45.49.68.68/
fax 01.45.49.69.49/www.montalembert.com).
M° Rue du Bac.* **Rates** single or double €300-€440;
suite €640-€760; breakfast €18. **Credit** AmEx, DC,
MC, V. **Map** p405 G6.
A luxury blend of traditional and modern by *très
chic* decorator Christian Liaigre, the Montalembert
is a perfectly executed study in good taste that still
pulls in the same magazine editors, models and
design junkies who rushed here when it opened. The

contemporary rooms are extra slick, the Louis-
Philippe design terribly romantic and even the door
handles are ultra-stylish. Good staff, too.
Hotel services *Baby-sitting. Bar. Laundry.
Restaurant.* **Room services** *Fax. Hairdryer.
Modem link. Radio. Safe. TV/VCR.*

Expensive

Hôtel de l'Université

*22 rue de l'Université, 7th (01.42.61.09.39/
fax 01.42.60.40.84/www.hoteluniversite.com).
M° Rue du Bac.* **Rates** single €80-€125; double
€150-€200; triple €200-€240; breakfast €9. **Credit**
AmEx, MC, V. **Map** p405 G6.
Just a short walk from the Musée d'Orsay, this
spacious 27-room hotel is full of antique wardrobes, warm colours, velvety carpets and soft
furnishings. The elegant vaulted cellar rooms can
be hired for functions.
Hotel services *Air con. Baby-sitting. Bureau de
change. Laundry.* **Room services** *Double glazing.
Hairdryer. Room service. Safe. TV.*

Budget

Hôtel Eiffel Rive Gauche

*6 rue du Gros-Caillou, 7th (01.45.51.24.56/fax
01.45.51.11.77/www.123france.com). M° Ecole
Militaire.* **Rates** single or double €76-€80; triple
€96; quadruple €165; breakfast €7. **Credit** MC, V.
Map p404 D6.
For the quintessential Paris view at a bargain price,
ask for one of the upper floors of this well-situated
hotel – you can see the Eiffel Tower from nine of the
30 rooms. Recently redecorated, they feature
Empire-style bedheads and modern bathrooms and
there is a tiny, tiled courtyard with a bridge. The
owner, Laurent Chicheportiche also has the Villa
Garibaldi on the other side of the Ecole Militaire
(48 bd Garibaldi, 15th; 01.56.58.56.58).
Hotel services *Safe.* **Room services** *Double
glazing. Radio. TV.*

Grand Hôtel Lévêque

*29 rue Cler, 7th (01.47.05.49.15/
fax 01.45.50.49.36/www.hotel-leveque.com).
M° Ecole Militaire.* **Rates** single €50-€53; double
€76-€91; triple €106-€114; breakfast €6.10. **Credit**
AmEx, MC, V. **Map** p404 D6.
Located on a largely pedestrianised market street
near the Eiffel Tower, the Lévêque is good value for
this chic area. The tiled entrance is charming, while
the 50 newly refurbished rooms are well-equipped,
with sparkling white bathrooms in all the doubles;
singles just have a basin.
Hotel services *Lift.* **Room services** *Double
glazing. Hairdryer. Modem link. Safe. TV.*

Techie but tasteful

A few years back, if you wanted an Internet connection in your room you'd have to go for a soulless business hotel with only a trouser press for company. But Paris hotels are waking up to combining the latest mod cons with stylish decor and a bar with a pulse. This new breed of hotel is more likely to attract film producers and ad execs than air-conditioning salesmen, and mod cons don't just mean dedicated modem points but top-of-the-range stereos and DVD players too.

A case in point is the **Hôtel Astor Sofitel Demeure** *(11 rue d'Astor, 8th/ 01.53.05.05.05/fax 01.53.05.05.30/ www.sofitel.com; single or double €335.38-€518.31; AmEx, MC, V)*, recently refurbished by top designer Frédéric Méchiche to give it a luxuriant Proustian ambience. It also boasts a two-Michelin-starred restaurant, so no corporate canteen food here. Turn-of-the-20th-century elegance combines with 21st century technology in the form of Bang & Olufsen stereo TVs with Internet access and a dedicated fax/modem line.

Hotel doyenne Grace Leo-Andreou was behind the restoration of the stunning **Hôtel Lancaster** *(7 rue de Berri, 8th (01.40.76.40.76/ fax 01.40.76.40.00/www.hotel-lancaster.fr; double €400-€545; suite €765-€1615; AmEx, DC, MC, V)*, but it isn't just in terms of

Zen and the art of hotel maintenance: **Pavillon de Paris**.

the decor that every detail has been considered. Here you can get down to some serious business with two phone lines plus a dedicated fax/modem socket, Bang & Olufsen TV and DVD with Internet connection – and the hotel can even lend you a mobile phone.

Hôtel Pergolèse *(3 rue Pergolèse, 16th (01.53.64.04.04/fax 01.53.64.04.40/ www.hotelpergolese.com; single €170-€290; double €185-€320; AmEx, DC, MC, V)* has an interior filled with Philippe Starck and Hilton McConnico furniture that gives the impression of being in a hip designer's apartment. The (yes, you guessed it) Bang & Olufsen hardware is displayed on what the hotel's website calls a 'mahogany sculpture' – but it looks very much like a cupboard to us.

Pershing Hall *(49 rue Pierre-Charron, 8th (01.58.36.58.00/fax 01.58.36.58.01/ www.pershinghall.com; double €381-€500F; suite €724-€1029; AmEx, DC, MC, V)*, Paris' newest luxury hotel, goes one step better than most with not just an Internet link, but a high-speed one to boot, plus Bang & Olufsen TV, DVD and modem line. If you can tear yourself away, the Andrée Putman-designed hotel also has its own DJ bar and a super health club opening this year.

Technophiles on a budget should check into **Pavillon de Paris** *(7 rue de Parme, 9th (01.55.31.60.00/fax 01.55.31.60.01; single €200; double €244; AmEx, DC, MC, V)*, a sleekly designed small hotel that uses the formula of New York's The Hudson with minimal-sized rooms that make it affordable without cutting down on style. Horizontal web-surfing from your bed is quite possible with the Internet-linked TVs, and the Japanese aesthetic extends to a sushi bar and ingenious reception housed in a tiny golden box.

For real technophiles though, there is only one address in Paris – Room 217 at the **Sofitel Paris Arc de Triomphe** *(14 rue Beaujon, 8th/01.53.89.50.50; €534; AmEx, DC, MC,V)*. This 'concept room' is a futuristic fantasy and employs some pretty nifty feng shui. The furnishings are arranged around a triangular space so that you need never turn your back on anybody, and anything you wish to alter in your ambient pad – be it room fragrance, temperature, or lighting – can be modified using the digital touch controls. Choose your bathroom scent, fill the tub, and soak away the stress watching your favourite DVD. What more could you dream of?

Youth accommodation

MIJE

Fourcy 6 rue de Fourcy, 4th (01.42.74.23.45/
fax 01.40.27.81.64/www.mije.com). M° St-Paul.
Fauconnier 11 rue du Fauconnier, 4th
(01.42.74.23.45). M° St-Paul. **Maubisson** 12 rue
des Barres, 4th (01.42.74.23.45). M° Hôtel de Ville.
Open 7am-1am daily. **Rates** dorm €21.80 per
person (18-30s sharing rooms); single €37.40; double
€27.30; triple €24.10; membership €2.30; breakfast
included. **No credit cards. Map** p406 L6, L7, K6.
Two 17th-century aristocratic Marais residences
and a former convent are the most attractive budget
sleeps in Paris. Plain but clean rooms sleep up to
eight; all have a shower and basin. Fourcy has its
own restaurant.

BVJ Paris/Quartier Latin

44 rue des Bernardins, 5th (01.43.29.34.80/
fax 01.53.00.90.91). M° Maubert-Mutualité.**Open** 24
hours. **Rates** dormitory €25 per person; single €30;
double €27; breakfast included. **No credit cards.
Map** p406 K7.
138 beds in bare modern dorms (for up to ten)
and singles, a TV lounge and a work room.
Hostel services Kitchen. Internet access. Safe.
Branch: BVJ Paris/Louvre, 20 rue Jean-Jacques-
Rousseau, 1st (01.53.00.90.90). 200 beds.

Young & Happy Hostel

80 rue Mouffetard, 5th (01.45.35.09.53/
fax 01.47.07.22.24/www.youngandhappy.fr).
M° Place Monge. **Rates** dormitory €19.50 per
person; double €22.50 per person; breakfast
included. **Open** 8am-11am, 4pm-2am daily.
No credit cards. Map p406 J8.
This friendly hostel in the heart of the old student
quarter offers 82 beds in slightly tatty surroundings.
The dorms are a bit cramped but there's a good com-
munity atmosphere.
Hostel services Bar. Bureau de change. Kitchen.
Internet access. Safe.

Auberge Internationale des Jeunes

10 rue Trousseau, 11th (01.47.00.62.00/
fax 01.47.00.33.16/www.aijparis.com).
M° Ledru-Rollin. **Open** 24hrs daily; rooms closed
10am-3pm. **Rates** Nov-Feb €13; Mar-Oct €14;
breakfast included. **Credit** MC, V. **Map** p407 N7.
Cleanliness is a high priority at this large (120 beds)
hostel close to the lively Bastille and within walking
distance of the Marais. There are rooms for two to
six people. Larger rooms have their own bathroom.
Hostel services Vending machine. Internet access.
Safe.

Auberge Jules Ferry

8 bd Jules-Ferry, 11th (01.43.57.55.60/
fax 01.43.14.82.09/www.fuaj.fr). M° République or
Goncourt. **Open** office and hostel 24hrs daily, rooms
closed 10am-2pm. **Rates** €18.50 per person; breakfast
included. **Credit** AmEx, MC, V. **Map** p403 M4.
Friendly IYHF hostel has 100 beds in rooms from two
to six. No advance reservations.
Hostel services Kitchen. Safe. Lockers. Internet access.

Bed & breakfast

Alcove & Agapes

Le Bed & Breakfast à Paris, 8bis rue Coysevox, 18th
(01.44.85.06.05/fax 01.44.85.06.14).
This B&B service offers more than 100 homes
(€45.73-€114.34 for a double). Hosts range from
artists to grandmothers.

Good Morning Paris

43 rue Lacépède, 5th (01.47.07.28.29/
fax 01.47.07.44.45). **Open** 9am-5.30pm Mon-Fri.
Forty rooms throughout the city. Prices range from
€38.11 for one person to €74.70 for three.

Apart-hotels & short-stay rental

A deposit is usually payable on arrival.
Small-ads for private short-term rentals can
be found in the Anglophone magazine Fusac
or on its website www.fusac.fr.

Apparthotel Citadines

Central reservations 01.41.05.79.79/
fax 01.41.05.78.87/www.citadines.com **Rates**
studio from €77; apartment for €90; apartment for
four from €117. **Credit** AmEx, DC, MC, V.
Seventeen modern complexes (Montparnasse,
Montmartre, Opéra, and a new St-Germain branch)
attract a mainly business clientele. Rooms are on the
cramped side, but a kitchenette and table make them
practical for those with children.
Hotel services Lift. **Room services** CD player.
Dishwasher. Double glazing. Hairdryer. Kitchen.
Microwave. TV.

Home Plazza Bastille

74 rue Amelot, 11th (01.40.21.20.00/
fax 01.47.00.82.40/ www.homeplazza.com).
M° St-Sébastien-Froissart. **Rates** single €130;
double €150-€200; suite €215-€268. **Credit** AmEx,
DC, MC, V. **Map** p402 L5.
Aimed at both business people and tourists, this
carefully constructed 'village' of 290 apartments
built around a street is reminiscent of a stage set.
Rooms are clean and modern with well-equipped
kitchenette and spacious bathrooms.
Hotel services Air con. Bar. Business services.
Garden. Parking. Restaurant. **Room services**
Hairdryer. TV.
Branch: Home Plazza St-Antoine, 289bis rue du
Fbg-St-Antoine, 11th (01.40.09.40.00/fax
01.40.09.11.55).

Paris Appartements Services

69 rue d'Argout, 2nd (01.40.28.01.28/
fax 01.40.28.92.01/www.paris.appartements-
services.fr). **Open** 9am-7pm Mon-Fri; 10am-noon Sat.
Rates studio from €790 per week; apartment from
€74 per week. **Credit** MC, V.
Furnished studios and one-bedroom flats in the 1st
to 4th arrondissements, with weekly maid service,
and a 24-hour helpline. Bilingual staff.

Sightseeing

Feature boxes

Introduction

Feel like you're walking in spirals? That'll be the *arrondissement* system.
Follow our lead and you need never lose your bearings again.

Paris is a compact capital city, its urban centre contained by the Périphérique and divided neatly by the Seine into the Left and Right banks, with Ile de la Cité and Ile St Louis in the middle. Parisians speak of their city in terms of *arrondissements*, a system that began with Napoléon and was continued when Baron Haussmann extended the outer limits of the city. Running from one to 20, the *arrondissements* begin at the Louvre and spiral out around the city in a snail-shell-like pattern which, once you can visualise it, does not take long to master. Parisians are more likely to refer to what *arrondissement* they live in than the name of the area itself. Some, such as the 16th (smart residential and embassy land) and the 6th (St-Germain), carry cachet; others are stereotyped (often by people who have never been there) as boring (the 15th) or unsafe (the 20th) – snobbery has a lot to answer for when dealing with *arrondissements*.

We have divided the Sightseeing chapter into five sections: The Seine, The Islands, Right Bank, Left Bank and Beyond the Périphérique. The Right and Left Bank sections are divided into areas which roughly follow *arrondissement*

guidelines, starting from the centre and working outwards in a clockwise direction. *Arrondissements* are given in all addresses. *See p398* **arrondissement map**.

The expressions *Rive Gauche* and *Rive Droite* are well known, but the old adage '*Sur la Rive Gauche on pense, sur la Rive Droite on dépense*' (on the Left Bank one thinks, on the Right Bank one spends money) has all but lost its relevance. While the Left Bank is still home to some of the country's greatest educational establishments, just as much, if not more, spending happens in St-Germain as in the Fbg-St-Honoré and the Marais, while plenty of intellectuals live in the left-wing 19th and 20th *arrondissements*.

A stronger distinction these days is between East and West, western Paris on both sides of the river still being home to the *haute bourgeoisie;* eastern Paris attracting new bohemians and genuine artists with its cheap rents, and pockets of uber-trendiness in the midst of working-class areas.

Getting around is both pleasurable and easy by Métro, bus or on foot (*see p365*, **Directory**), or, for a lazy way to see the sights, what better than a riverboat cruise?

Guided tours

Boat trips

Bateaux-Mouches *pont de l'Alma, Rive Droite, 8th (01.42.25.96.10/recorded info 01.40.76.99.99/www.bateau-mouche.com). Mº Alma-Marceau.* **Departs** *summer* every 30 min 10.15am-11pm daily; *winter* approx every hour from 11am-9pm daily; lasts 1 hour. **Tickets** €6.86, dinner €83.85-€121.96.
Bateaux Parisiens *Tour Eiffel, port de la Bourdonnais, 7th (01.44.11.33.55/ www.bateauxparisiens.com). RER Pont de l'Alma.* **Departs** *summer* every 30 min 10am-11pm daily; *winter* weekdays every hour 10am-1pm, 5-8pm daily, winter weekends call ahead. **Tickets** €8.38, under 12 €4.12, dinner €88.42-€118.91. *Wheelchair access.*
Bateaux Vedettes de Paris *port de Suffren, 7th (01.47.05.71.29). Mº Bir-Hakeim.* **Departs** every 30 min; *summer* 10am-11pm; every hour, *winter* 11am-7pm Sun-Fri, 11am-9pm Sat. **Tickets** €3.05 (for a group of 20),- €7.62 (individuals).

Canal trips

Canauxrama *(01.42.39.15.00/ www.canauxrama.com).* **Departs** *Bassin de la Villette, 13 quai de la Loire, 19th. MºJaurès.* 9.45am, 2.45pm daily. **Departs** *Port de l'Arsenal, opposite 50 bd de la Bastille, 12th. Mº Bastille.* 9.45am, 2.30pm daily. Fewer trips in winter. **Tickets** €7.62-€12.20 (no reductions holidays or weekend pm). Trips last 2-3hrs, live commentary in French; in English if enough demand. *Wheelchair access (call ahead).*
Paris Canal *(Reserve on 01.42.40.96.97/ www.pariscanal.com). Musée d'Orsay (Mº Solférino) to Parc de la Villette (Mº Porte de Pantin) or reverse.* **Departs** mid-Mar to mid-Sept Musée d'Orsay 9.30am daily; Parc de la Villette 2.30pm daily. mid-Nov-Mar Sun only. **Tickets** €16, 12-25 €12, 4-11 €9, no reductions Sun, bank holidays. Three-hour trip with commentary in French and English. Reservation required.

Coach tours

Cityrama *4 pl des Pyramides, 1st (01.44.55.61.00/www.cityrama.com). Mº Palais Royal.* **Departs** *summer* hourly 9.30am-4.30pm daily; *winter* 9.30am,

10.30am, 1.30pm, 2.30pm daily. **Tickets** €22.87; under 12 free. **Les Cars Rouges** *(01.53.95.39.53/www.lescarsrouges.com).* **Departs** 9.30am-7pm *summer* every 10 min Mon-Fri daily; *winter* every 20 min Mon-Fri, every 15 min Sat, Sun. **Tickets** €21, children 4-12 €10. Recorded commentary in English. Hop on hop off at any of nine stops (including Eiffel Tower, Notre-Dame, Louvre, Opéra) tickets valid two days. *Wheelchair access.*
Paris L'Open Tour *(01.43.46.52.06).* **Departs** every 10-15 min *Apr-Oct* 10am-6pm; every 25-30 min *Nov-Mar* 9.30am-4pm,**Tickets** €24, children 4-11 €12, 2-day pass €26. A similar hop on hop off scheme.
Paris Vision *214 rue de Rivoli, 1st (01.42.60.30.01/www.parisvision.fr). Mº Tuileries.* Trips hourly 9.30am-3.30pm daily, extra trips in summer if demand (lasts 2 hours). **Tickets** €22.87, children 4-11 free.

Cycle tours

Maison Roue Libre *95bis rue Rambuteau, Forum des Halles, 1st (01.53.46.43.77/ www.parisvisite.tm.fr/english/rouelib). RER Châtelet-Les Halles.* **Departs** Paris tours May-Oct 11.30am and 3.30pm daily from the Maison Roue Libre. Green tours Apr-Oct Sat, Sun, bank holidays 10am from cycle bus centres. **Tickets** incl bike hire €20, children 4-11 (Green tour) €13.08. 3- and 4-hour long guided rides from RATP-linked bike shop.
Paris à vélo, c'est sympa! *37 bd Bourdon, 4th (01.48.87.60.01/www.parisvelosympa.com). Mº Bastille.* **Departs** 10am, 3pm, 8.30pm. **Tickets** incl bike hire €12.20-€28.20. Multilingual guided tours. Reservation required.

Walking tours

Guided walks in French are listed weekly in *Pariscope* under *Promenades*. Walks in English are usually listed in the *Time Out Paris* section in *Pariscope* and the guides below can organise group walks on request. Prices exclude entrance fees for sights.
Paris Contact Jill Daneels (01.42.51.08.40). **Tickets** €13, students, over-60 €7, under 12 free. 2-hour tours by appointment daily, minimum 4 people.
Paris Walking Tours *Oriel and Peter Caine (01.48.09.21.40/www.pariswalkingtours.com).* Choice of 2-hour tours daily. **Tickets** €10.

Sunday strolls

With traffic outlawed along Seine-side *quais* every Sunday, a walk along the river could almost be classed as fresh air. In fact, the Sunday constitutional is more likely to take place at breakneck speed with pads on as Parisians come out in hordes to worship traffic-free level tarmac on blades, wheels and, occasionally, foot.

Key

🛥 River-boat stops

Suggested walk along the Seine.

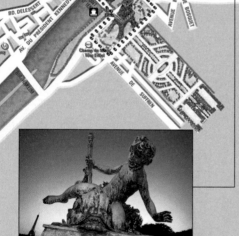

Pont Alexandre III

Built for the 1900 *Exposition Universelle*, the Pont Alexandre III links Les Invalides and the Grand Palais. With its flamboyant flaming torches, it is easily Paris' most ornate bridge.

Nearly nude

On holiday? Or actually hard at it? The *quais* of the Seine are year-long haunts for relaxers, posers, couples and tramps. Summer brings a tautly muscled fleet of sun-seekers and, of course, those people who need your help when it comes to applying their suncream to those hard-to-reach crevices.

Bateaux-mouches

Nothing to do with flies, despite the name, the *bateaux-mouches* that are synonymous with with Seine were in fact started in Lyon in the 19th century by a Monsieur Mouche. These days the craft carry around five million floating spectators every year. Some offer food and entertainment and you can even book them out for parties. Several lines leave from beneath the Eiffel Tower, while Vedettes du Pont Neuf depart from Ile de la Cité and the Batobus makes stops up and down the river. *For booking information see p71.*

The Seine

Some call it the 21st *arrondissement*, others call it the capital's main artery, and still others call it a polluted cess-pit. Most of the city's greatest attractions – palaces, museums, monuments and gardens – sit right by the side of it, and you can live on it, float down it, flirt by it and rave all night on it. Why not go with the flow?

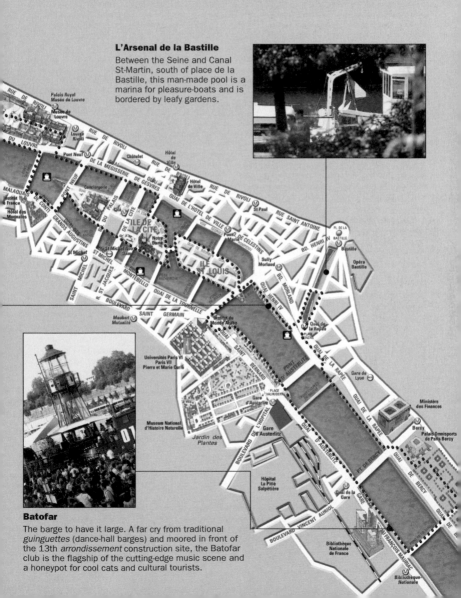

L'Arsenal de la Bastille

Between the Seine and Canal St-Martin, south of place de la Bastille, this man-made pool is a marina for pleasure-boats and is bordered by leafy gardens.

Batofar

The barge to have it large. A far cry from traditional *guinguettes* (dance-hall barges) and moored in front of the 13th *arrondissement* construction site, the Batofar club is the flagship of the cutting-edge music scene and a honeypot for cool cats and cultural tourists.

The Islands

One is the birthplace of the city and the site of Notre-Dame, the other is the neighbourhood where all the posh nobs hang out.

Ile de la Cité

In the 1st and 4th arrondissements.

The settlement that was to grow into Paris was founded on Ile de la Cité around 250 BC by the Parisii. It continued to be a centre of political and religious power into the Middle Ages.

When Victor Hugo wrote *Notre Dame de Paris* in 1831, the Ile de la Cité was still a bustling quarter of narrow medieval streets and tall houses: 'the head, heart and very marrow of Paris'. Baron Haussmann put paid to that; he supervised the expulsion of 25,000 people from the island, razing tenements and some 20 churches. The lines of the old streets are traced into the parvis in front of **Notre-Dame**. The people resettled to the east, leaving behind a few large, official buildings – the law courts, **Conciergerie**, **Hôtel-Dieu** hospital, the police headquarters and, of course, Notre-Dame.

The most charming spot is the western tip, where the **Pont-Neuf** spans the Seine. Despite its name it is the oldest bridge in Paris. Go down the steps to a leafy triangular garden known as the square du Vert-Galant. With a wonderful view of the river, it's a great spot for summer picnics, or you can take a boat trip from the quai with the Vedettes du Pont-Neuf. In the centre of the bridge is an equestrian statue of Henri IV, erected in 1635, destroyed in the Revolution, and replaced in 1818. On the island side of the bridge, the secluded place Dauphine, home to restaurants, wine bars and the seedy **Hôtel Henri IV**, was built in 1607. It was commissioned by Henri IV, who named it in honour of his son, the dauphin Louis, the future King Louis XIII. The red brick and stone houses look out on both *quais* and square, whose third, eastern side was demolished in the 1870s. Malraux had a Freudian analysis of its appeal – 'the sight of its triangular formation with slightly curved lines, and of the slit which bisects its two wooded spaces. It is, without doubt, the sex of Paris.' One wonders what he would have made of the Channel Tunnel.

The towers of the **Conciergerie** (*see p77*) dominate the island's north bank. Along with the Palais de Justice, it was originally part of the Palais de la Cité, residential and administration complex of the Capetian kings. It stands on the site of an earlier Merovingian

fortress and, before that, the Roman governor's house. Etienne Marcel's uprising prompted Charles V to move the royal retinue to the Louvre in 1358, and the Conciergerie was assigned a more sinister role as a prison where people awaited execution. The interior is worth visiting for its Gothic vaulted halls.

Sainte-Chapelle (*see p77*), Pierre de Montreuil's masterpiece of stained glass and slender Gothic columns, is nestled amid the nearby law courts. Surrounding the chapel, the Palais de Justice evolved alongside the Conciergerie. Its Neo-Classical entrance courtyard and fine wrought-iron grille date from the reconstruction by Desmaisons and Antoine after a fire in 1776. After going through security, you can visit the *Salle* des Pas Perdus, busy with plaintiffs and barristers, and sit in on cases in the civil and criminal courts. The Palais is still the centre of the French legal system, although it has long been rumoured that the law courts will be moved out to the 13th or 15th *arrondissement*.

Caged birds are on sale at the market (Sunday only) across the boulevard du Palais, behind the tribunal du Commerce at **place Louis Lépine**. For the rest of the week it's a flower market. The legal theme continues to the south with the Préfecture de Police, known by its address, quai des Orfèvres, and immortalised in Simenon's *Maigret* novels.

The **Hôtel-Dieu**, east of the market place, was founded in the seventh century. During the Middle Ages your chances of survival here were, at best, slim. The hospital was rebuilt in the 1860s on the site of a nearby foundling hospital, and added its morgue to the island's list of popular tourist attractions.

Notre-Dame cathedral (*see p76*), with its twin-towered west front, sculpted portals and buttressed east end dominates the eastern half of the island. In front of the cathedral, the bronze marker known as **Kilomètre Zéro** is the point from which all distances are measured. The **Crypte Archéologique** (*see p77*) under the parvis gives a sense of the island's multi-layered past, when it was a tangle of alleys, houses, churches and cabarets.

The capital's oldest (known) love story unfolded at 9 quai aux Fleurs, where Héloïse lived with her uncle Canon Fulbert, who, rather

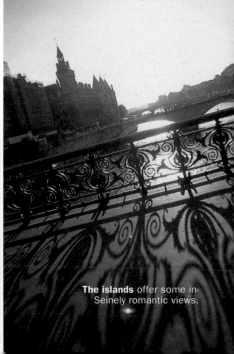

The islands offer some in-Seinely romantic views.

unsportingly, had her lover Abélard castrated. A stone tablet commemorates their doom. A medieval feel persists in the few streets untouched by Haussmann northeast of the cathedral, such as rue Chanoinesse – built to house canons of Notre-Dame – and the narrow rue des Chantres. Steps away from the cathedral at rue du Cloître-Notre-Dame, **Le Vieux Bistro** is one of the best traditional bistros in Paris.

On a more poignant note, the **Mémorial de la Déportation** (10am-noon, 2-5pm daily) on the eastern tip of the island is a tribute to the thousands deported to death camps during World War II. A blind staircase descends to river level, where simple chambers are inscribed with the names of deportees.

Cathédrale Notre-Dame-de-Paris

pl du Parvis-Notre-Dame, 4th (01.42.34.56.10). M° Cité/RER St-Michel. **Open** 8am-6.45pm Mon-Fri, 8am-7.45pm Sat-Sun; towers (01.44.32.16.70) 10am-4.45pm daily. **Admission** free; towers €5.34; €3.81 12-25s; free under-12s. **No credit cards.** **Map** p406 J7

Keen to outdo the new abbey at St-Denis, Bishop Maurice de Sully decided to construct a grandiose new edifice in Paris. Begun in 1163, the Gothic masterpiece was not completed until 1345, straddling two architectural eras – the great galleried churches of the 12th century and the buttressed cathedrals that followed. Among its famous features are the three glorious rose windows and the doorways of the west front, recently cleaned and restored, with their rows of saints and sculpted tympanums depicting the Last Judgement (centre), Life of the Virgin (left), Life of St-Anne (right). In the 1630s Robert de Cotte destroyed the rood screen and choir stalls, making way for the new choir and grille completed only in 1708-25 for Louis XIV. During the Revolution, the cathedral was turned into a temple of reason and a wine warehouse, and the statues of the 28 Kings of Judah higher up the facade were destroyed, having been mistaken for statues of the kings of France – those seen today are replicas. Several of the originals were discovered in 1979 and are now on view at the **Musée National du Moyen Age**. The cathedral regained its ceremonial role for Napoléon's coronation as Emperor in 1804, but by the 19th century had fallen into such dilapidation that artists petitioned Louis-Philippe to restore the cathedral, which was masterfully done by Viollet-le-Duc. During the Nazi occupation the stained-glass was removed, numbered and replaced with sandbags. You can climb the north bell tower to a gallery adorned with ghoulish gargoyles.

Notre-Dame: keep calm, goths, you're home.

La Conciergerie

*1 quai de l'Horloge, 1st (01.53.73.78.50). Mº Cité/
RER Châtelet-Les Halles.* **Open** Apr-Sept 9.30am-
6.30pm daily; Oct-Mar 10am-5pm daily. **Admission**
€5.34; €3.51 12-25s, students; free under-12s; €7.62
with Sainte-Chapelle. **No credit cards.**
Map p406 J6.

Marie-Antoinette was held here during the Revolution
and Danton and Robespierre also did a pre-guillotine
pitstop. The Conciergerie looks every inch the forbidding medieval fortress, yet the pseudo-medieval
facade was added in the 1850s. The 13th-century
Bonbec tower survives from the Capetian palace,
and the Tour de l'Horloge built in 1370, on the corner
of boulevard du Palais, was the first public clock in
Paris. You can visit the kitchens, the Salle des
Gardes and the Salle des Gens d'Armes, an impressive vaulted Gothic hall built in 1301-15. The fortress
became a prison under the watch of the Concierge.
The wealthy had private cells with their own furniture; others were crowded together on beds of straw.
A list of Revolutionary prisoners, including a hair-
dresser, shows that far from all were nobles. Marie-
Antoinette's cell, the Chapelle des Girondins,
contains her crucifix and a guillotine blade.

La Crypte Archéologique

*pl du Parvis-Notre-Dame, 4th (01.43.29.83.51).
Mº Cité/RER St-Michel.* **Open** 10am-6pm; closed
Mon. **Admission** €4.88; €3.35 under 27s, over 60s;
free under-12s. **No credit cards.** Map p406 J7.
The excavations under the parvis span 16 centuries,
from the remains of Gallo-Roman ramparts to a
19th-century drain.

Sainte-Chapelle

*4 bd du Palais, 1st (01.53.73.78.50). Mº Cité/
RER Châtelet-Les Halles.* **Open** Apr-Sept 9.30am-
6.30pm daily; Oct-Mar 10am-5pm daily. **Admission**
€5.34; €3.51 12-25s, students; free under-12s;
€7.62 with Conciergerie. **Credit** (shop) MC, V.
Map p406 J6.
Devout King Louis IX (1226-70), later known as St
Louis, collected holy relics. In the 1240s he bought
the Crown of Thorns, and ordered Pierre de
Montreuil to design a suitable shrine. The result was
the exquisite High Gothic Sainte-Chapelle. The
upper level, intended for the royal family and the
canons, appears to consist almost entirely of stained
glass. The windows depict Biblical scenes, and on
sunny days coloured reflections dapple the stone.
The lower chapel was for the use of palace servants.

Ile St-Louis

In the 4th arrondissement.
The Ile St-Louis is one of the most exclusive
residential addresses in the city. Delightfully
unspoiled, it offers fine architecture, narrow
streets and pretty views from the tree-lined *quais*.

For hundreds of years the island was a
swampy pasture belonging to Notre-Dame and
a retreat for fishermen, swimmers and lovers,

known as the Ile Notre-Dame. In the 14th
century Charles V built a fortified canal through
the middle, thus creating the Ile aux Vaches
('Island of Cows'). Its real-estate potential
wasn't realised until 1614, when speculator
Christophe Marie persuaded Louis XIII to fill in
the canal (now rue Poulletier) and plan streets,
bridges and houses. The island was renamed in
honour of the King's pious predecessor and the
venture proved a huge success, thanks to
society architect Louis Le Vau, who from the
1630s on built fashionable new residences on
quai d'Anjou (including his own at No 3), quai
de Bourbon and quai de Béthune, as well as the
Eglise St-Louis-en-l'Ile. By the 1660s the
island was filled, and unlike the Marais, where
the smart reception rooms were at the rear of
the courtyard, here they were often at the front
to allow their residents riverside views.

The **rue St-Louis-en-l'Ile**, lined with
quirky gift shops, quaint tearooms, lively stone-
walled bars and restaurants and fine historic
buildings, runs the length of the island. The
grandiose Hôtel Lambert (2 rue St-Louis-en-
l'Ile/1 quai d'Anjou) was built by Le Vau in
1641 for Louis XIII's secretary with interiors by
Le Sueur, Perrier and Le Brun. At No 51, Hôtel
Chenizot, look out for bearded faun adorning
the rocaille doorway and the dragons
supporting the balcony. The **Hôtel du Jeu de
Paume**, at No 54 was once a real tennis court.
Ice cream shop **Berthillon**, (No 31) often draws
a queue down the street. There are great views
of the flying buttresses of Notre-Dame at the
western end, where a footbridge crosses to
the Ile de la Cité. Here you will also find the
Brasserie de l'Isle-St-Louis, which draws
Parisians and tourists alike, so don't go if you
fancy a chill-out with your croissant.

Baudelaire wrote part of *Les Fleurs du Mal*
while living at the Hôtel de Lauzun (17 quai
d'Anjou). Earlier, Racine, Molière and La
Fontaine spent time here as guests of La Grande
Mademoiselle, cousin of Louis XIV and mistress
of the dashing Duc de Lauzun. The *hôtel* stands
out for its scaly sea-serpent drainpipes and
trompe l'oeil interiors. There are further literary
associations at 6 quai d'Orléans, where the Adam
Mickiewicz library-museum (01.43.54.35.61/
open 2-6pm Thur) is dedicated to the Polish
Romantic poet who lived in Paris 1832-40.

Eglise St-Louis-en-l'ile

*19bis rue St-Louis-en-l'Ile, 4th (01.46.34.11.60).
Mº Pont-Marie.* **Open** 3-7pm Mon; 9am-noon, 3-7pm
Tue-Sun. **Map** p406 L7.
Built 1664-1765, following plans by Louis Le Vau
and completed by Gabriel Le Duc. The interior follows the classic Baroque model with Corinthian
columns and a sunburst over the altar, and is a popular classical concert venue.

The Right Bank

From guillotine gore to razor-sharp intellects, the glittering areas north of the Seine offer attitude, pulchritude, culture and sleaze.

The Louvre to Concorde

In the 1st arrondissement.

After the monarchs moved from the Ile de la Cité to spacious new quarters on the Right Bank, the Louvre and the secondary palaces of the Tuileries and Palais-Royal became the centre of royal power.

Now a Mecca for art lovers, the **Palais du Louvre** (*see chapter* **Museums**) has huge state rooms, fine courtyards and galleries stretching to the Jardin des Tuileries. Begun as a fortress by Philippe Auguste and turned into a sumptuous Renaissance palace by François 1er, the Louvre was designated a museum by the Revolutionary Convention in 1793. Two hundred years later, Mitterrand's *Grand Louvre* scheme added I M Pei's pyramid in the Cour Napoléon, doubled the exhibition space and

Making an entrance at the **Louvre**.

resulted in the subterranean Carrousel du Louvre shopping mall, auditorium and food halls. The pyramid's steel and glass structure creates mesmerising optical effects with the fountains, especially when floodlit by night.

On place du Louvre, opposite the palace, is **St-Germain-l'Auxerrois**, once the French kings' parish church and home to the only original Flamboyant-Gothic porch in Paris, built in 1435. Mirroring it to the left is the 19th-century neo-Gothic 1st *arrondissement* town hall, alongside chic bar **Le Fumoir**.

Thanks to the *Grand Louvre* scheme, the **Musée des Arts Décoratifs** and the **Musée de la Mode et du Costume** (*see chapter* **Museums** *for more on both*) have been rejuvenated, while the Arc du Carrousel, a mini-Arc de Triomphe built in a fit of modesty by Napoléon in 1806-09, has been restored. The famous Roman bronze horses which surround the arch were taken from St Mark's in Venice. France was obliged to return them in 1815; they were replaced with replicas in 1828. Through the arch you can now appreciate the extraordinary perspective through the **Jardin des Tuileries** all along the Champs-Elysées up to the Arc de Triomphe and beyond to the Grande Arche de la Défense. Originally stretching to the Tuileries palace (burnt down in the Commune), the Tuileries gardens were laid out in the 17th century and remain a living space with cafés, ice-cream stalls and summer fun fair. On the flanks of the Tuileries overlooking **place de la Concorde** stand the **Musée de l'Orangerie**, noted for its series of Monet water lilies (currently closed for renovation), and the **Jeu de Paume**, originally built for playing real tennis, now used for contemporary art exhibitions.

Along the north side of the Louvre, the rue de Rivoli, conceived by Napoléon for military parades and completed by Napoléon III, is remarkable for its uniform, arcaded facades. It runs in a perfect line to place de la Concorde in one direction, and to the Marais in the other, where it becomes rue St-Antoine. Despite the many souvenir shops here, elegant, old-fashioned hotels still remain, along with gentlemen's tailors, bookshops **WH Smith** and **Galignani** and the famous tearoom **Angelina's**. The area formed a little England

> ▶ For detailed museum information and opening times, turn to **Sightseeing: Museums**, starting on page 147.
> ▶ For information on arts events turn to **Arts & Entertainment**, starting on page 275.
> ▶ For shopping information turn to **Shops & Services**, starting on page 235.

in the 1830s-40s as aristocracy, writers and artists flooded across the Channel after the Napoleonic Wars. They stayed at the Hôtel Meurice or in smart new rue de la Paix and rue de Castiglione, dining in the restaurants of the Palais-Royal; at the time the area was described as 'a true quarter of London transposed to the banks of the Seine'.

Do explore the place des Pyramides, at the western end of the Louvre, at the junction of rue de Rivoli and rue des Pyramides. The shiny gilt equestrian statue of Joan of Arc is one of four statues of her in the city. Ancient rue St-Honoré, running parallel to rue de Rivoli, is one of those streets that changes style in different districts – all smart shops towards place Vendôme, local cafés and inexpensive bistros towards Les Halles. At No 296, the Baroque church of **St-Roch** is pitted with bullet holes left by

Napoléon's troops when they crushed a royalist revolt in 1795. With its old houses, rue St-Roch still feels like *vieux* Paris; a couple of shops are even built into the side of the church. Across the road, at 263bis, the 1670-76 Chapelle de l'Assomption has a dome so disproportionately large that contemporaries dubbed it 'dumb dome' (*sot dôme*), a pun on Sodom. Just west of here, much talked-about, pristine-white boutique **Colette** at No 213 has given some oomph to what was a staid shopping area. Opposite is rue du Marché St-Honoré, where Le Rubis wine bar hosts the mob sampling the Beaujolais Nouveau every November. The street formerly led to the covered Marché St-Honoré (on the site of the Couvent des Jacobins, a famous revolutionary meeting place), but that has been replaced by the shiny glass-and-steel offices of the BNP-Paribas bank, designed by Spanish architect Ricardo Bofill.

Further west along rue St-Honoré lies wonderful, eight-sided **place Vendôme**, one of Louis XIV's main contributions, with a perspective that now goes from rue de Rivoli up to Opéra. At the west end of the Tuileries, the **place de la Concorde**, laid out to the glorification of Louis XV, is a masterclass in the use of open space. André Malraux called it 'the

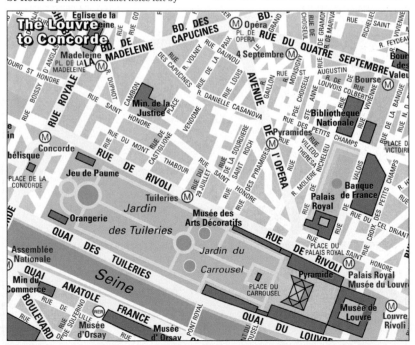

most beautiful architectural complex on this planet' and it's impossible not to be impressed by its grandeur. (It should become even more beautiful from the point of view of pedestrians if current plans to cut down its volume of traffic come to fruition.) The winged Marly horses brought from Venice (these are actually copies of the originals, which are now in the Louvre) frame the entrance to the Champs-Elysées.The smart rue Royale, leading to the Madeleine, boasts superior tearoom **Ladurée** and the legendary but now disappointing **Maxim's** restaurant (featured in Lehár's opera *The Merry Widow*). The rue Boissy d'Anglas offers smart shops and waning fashion-haunt **Buddha Bar**; while the ultimate sporting luxuries can be found at Hermès (note the horseman on its parapet) on rue du Fbg-St-Honoré (westward extension of rue St-Honoré), as well as fashion names Yves Saint Laurent, Gucci, Guy Laroche, Karl Lagerfeld, Chloé, Lanvin and more. More tearooms and fine porcelain can be found in the Galerie Royale and Passage Royale.

Eglise St-Germain-l'Auxerrois

2 pl du Louvre, 1st (01.42.60.13.96). M° Pont Neuf or Louvre. **Open** 8am-8pm Mon-Sat; 9am-10pm Sun. **Map** p401 H6.

This pretty church was for centuries the royal church. Its architecture spans several eras: most striking though is the elaborate Flamboyant Gothic porch. Inside, note the 13th-century Lady Chapel and splendid canopied, carved bench designed by Le Brun in 1682 for the royal family. The church achieved notoriety on 24 August 1572, when the signal for the St-Bartholomew's Day massacre was rung from here.

Eglise St-Roch

296 rue St-Honoré, 1st (01.42.44.13.20). M° Pyramides or Tuileries. **Open** 8.30am-7pm daily. **Map** p401 G5.

Curious rather than beautiful, this surprisingly long church begun in the 1650s was designed mainly by Jacques Lemercier. The area was then the heart of Paris, and illustrious parishioners and patrons left notable funerary monuments: Le Nôtre, Mignard, Corneille and Diderot are all here. Look for busts by Coysevox and Coustou as well as Falconet's statue *Christ on the Mount of Olives*. Paintings include works by Chassériau, Vignon and Le Sueur. There is a kitsch Baroque pulpit and a cherub-adorned retable behind the rear altar. In 1795, a bloody shoot-out occurred in front of the church between royalists and conventionists – look out for the bullet holes which still pit the facade. Thanks to its excellent acoustics concerts are held regularly in the church.

Place de la Concorde

1st/8th. M° Concorde. **Map** p401 F5.

Planned by Jacques Ange Gabriel for Louis XV in 1753, the place de la Concorde is the largest square

Glorious galleries

Built in the early 19th century, Paris's covered *galeries* once bustled with luxury traders. The remaining 20 (over 100 existed in 1840) have an air of faded grandeur.

Galerie Vivienne (*6 rue Vivienne/4 rue des Petits-Champs and 5 rue de la Banque, 2nd, M° Bourse*) is beautiful, with mosaics and stucco arches. Rummage for pulp fiction at **Jousseaume**. **Galerie Vero-Dodat** (*2 rue du Bouloi/19 rue Jean-Jacques-Rousseau, 1st, M° Louvre*) was built in the Restoration and its chequered floor and neo-classical shopfronts are in excellent condition. Choose between antique dolls, then visit lace-fronted **Café de L'Epoque** for refreshment. **Passage Choiseul** (*40 rue des Petits-Champs/23 rue St-Augustin, 2nd, M° Pyramides or Quatre-Septembre*) was the childhood home of the writer Céline. **Passage des Panoramas** (*10 rue St-Marc/11 bd Montmartre, 2nd, M° Richelieu-Drouot*), the oldest passage (opened 1800), has housed refined engravers **Stern** since 1830. Here you'll find old stamps and postcards. Opposite is **Passage Jouffroy** (*10-12 bd Montmartre/9 rue de la Grange-Batelière, 9th, M° Richelieu-Drouot*), constructed in post-Restoration style, replacing wooden structures with iron. Follow-on **Passage Verdeau**, built 1847, has sewing shop **Bonheur des Dames** and its original ornate clock. Refurbished **Passage du Grand-Cerf** (*10 rue Dussoubs/ 145 rue St-Denis, 2nd, M° Etienne Marcel*) is the highest passage. Occupied by contemporary design shops like **La Corbeille**, it also hosts the bi-annual Puces du Design. **Passage Brady** (*46 rue du Fbg-St-Denis/43 rue du Fbg-St-Martin, 16 rue du Fbg-St-Denis/16 bd St-Denis, 10th, M° Château d'Eau or Strasbourg-St-Denis*) is a veritable passage to India, a swirl of colour filled with saris and tempting aromas.

Passage du Grand-Cerf

**Place Vendôme:
the Ritziest roundabout
in Paris.**

in Paris, with grand perspectives stretching east-west from the Louvre to the Arc de Triomphe, and north-south from the Madeleine to the Assemblée Nationale across the Seine. In 1792, the statue of Louis XV was removed from the centre and a revolutionaries' guillotine set up for the execution of Louis XVI, Marie-Antoinette and many more. Gabriel also designed the two colonnaded mansions on either side of rue Royale; the one on the west houses the exclusive Crillon hotel and the Automobile Club de France, the other is the Navy Ministry. The *place* was embellished in the 19th century with sturdy lamp posts, the Luxor obelisk, a present from the Viceroy of Egypt, and the tiered wedding-cake fountains that were recently splendidly restored. The best view is by night, from the terrace by the Jeu de Paume in the Tuileries gardens.

Place Vendôme
1st. M° Tuileries or Opéra. **Map** p401 G4.
Elegant place Vendôme got its name from the *hôtel particulier* built by the Duc de Vendôme previously on this site. Inaugurated in 1699, the eight-sided *place* was conceived by Hardouin-Mansart to show off an equestrian statue of the Sun King. This statue was torn down in 1792, and in 1806 the Colonne de la Grande Armée was erected. Modelled on Trajan's column in Rome and decorated with a spiral comic-strip illustrating Napoléon's military exploits, it was made out of 1,250 Russian and Austrian cannons captured at the battle of Austerlitz, and was built to commemorate the French soldiers who fought in that battle. During the 1871 Commune this symbol of 'brute force and false glory' was pulled down. The present column is a replica, retaining most of the original frieze. Hardouin-Mansart only designed the facades; the buildings behind were put up by various nobles and speculators. Today the square is home to Cartier, Boucheron, Van Cleef & Arpels, Trussardi and other prestigious jewellers and fashion names, as well as banks, the Justice Ministry and the Ritz hotel. Chopin died at No 12, in 1849.

Palais-Royal & Bourse

In the 1st and 2nd arrondissements.
Across the rue de Rivoli from the Louvre, past the **Louvre des Antiquaires** antiques superstore, stands the **Palais-Royal**, once Cardinal Richelieu's private mansion and now the Conseil d'Etat and Ministry of Culture. The **Comédie-Française** theatre stands on the southwest corner. The company, created by Louis XIV in 1680, moved here in 1799 – a spiritual homecoming as Molière died nearby at 40 rue de Richelieu. A fountain commemorates the playwright. The brass-fronted Café Nemours on place Colette is popular with thespians. George Sand used to buy her tobacco across the square at cigar shop A La Civette.

In the 1780s the Palais-Royal was a rumbustious centre of Parisian life, where aristocrats and the financially challenged inhabitants of the *faubourgs* rubbed shoulders. The coffee houses in its arcades attracted radical debate. Here Camille Desmoulins called the city to arms on the eve of Bastille Day. After the Napoleonic Wars, Wellington and Field Marshal von Blücher supposedly lost so much money at the gambling dens that Parisians claimed they had won back their entire dues for war reparations. Only haute cuisine restaurant **Le Grand Véfour** (which was founded as Café Chartres in the 1780s) survives from this era, albeit with decoration from a little later. A more contemporary attraction at Palais-Royal is its new Métro entrance: artist Jean-Michel Othoniel has put a kitsch slant on Guimard's classic art nouveau design by decorating the aluminium struts with glass baubles.

Wander under the arcades to browse in an eccentric world of antique dealers, philatelists and specialists in tin soldiers and musical boxes. Look out for **Galerie Jean de Rohan-Chabot**, filled with contemporary kitsch, and the vintage clothes specialist **Didier Ludot**. Go through the arcades to rue de Montpensier to the west, and the neo-Rococo Théâtre du Palais-Royal. Opposite, next to busy bar

Comédie Française actors commemorated.

L'Entracte, is one of several narrow, stepped passages that run between this road and rue de Richelieu, which, with parallel rue Ste-Anne, is a focus of Paris' Japanese community.

Paris' traditional business district, beating at a considerably less frantic pace than Wall

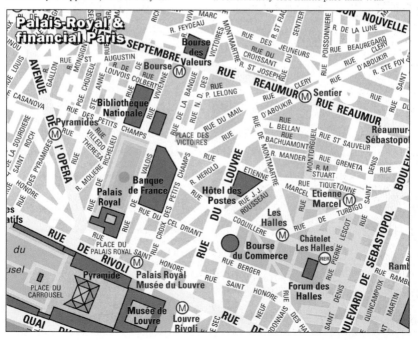

Street, is squeezed between the elegant calm of the Palais-Royal and the frenzied Grands Boulevards. The Banque de France, France's central bank, has occupied the 17th-century Hôtel de Toulouse since 1811. Very little of the original remains, but its long gallery is still hung with old masters. Nearby, the pretty **place des Victoires** was designed, like place Vendôme, by Hardouin-Mansart, forming an intimate circle of buildings today dedicated to fashion. The two worlds now meet in bistro **Chez Georges**, where bankers and fashion moguls rub shoulders. West of the *place*, explore the shop-lined, covered **galerie Vivienne** and **galerie Colbert** and

temporary exhibitions at the **Bibliothèque Nationale Richelieu**. Luxury *épicerie* and wine merchant **Legrand** is on the corner of galerie Vivienne and rue de la Banque. Take a detour along the passage des Petits Pères to see Eglise Notre-Dame-des-Victoires, the remains of an Augustine convent with paintings by Van Loo.

Rue de la Banque now leads to the **Bourse** (stock exchange), behind a commanding neo-Classical colonnade. Otherwise the area has a relaxed feel, at weekends positively sleepy. For business lunches and after-work drinks, stockbrokers and journalists converge on the **Vaudeville** brasserie. Rue des Colonnes is a

Paris, city of lights out

Considering its reputation for stylish living, it is no surprise that Paris has cornered the market in stylish dying. If you've achieved a certain level of showbiz renown, kicking the bucket here can be a shrewd career move. Take the cases of two obviously lost souls who clearly craved peace and quiet but were fated to die here: the Lizard King and the People's Princess.

Paris' three heavyweight cemeteries are teeming with celebrity stiffs. Among the cultural types pushing up the pansies at Montmartre are Berlioz, Truffaut and Nijinsky, while down at Montparnasse rest saucy Serge Gainsbourg and the (presumably now post-) existentialists, Jean-Paul Sartre and Simone de Beauvoir. But it's Père Lachaise that

boasts the city's most-visited grave, and no, it's not Proust's, Piaf's or even Oscar Wilde's. Paris' top tourist tomb contains the body of singer, poet, self-styled erotic politician and convicted flasher, Jim Morrison. The Lizard King arrived in Paris on 11 March 1971 to escape the pressures and temptations of LA. Unfortunately, what he couldn't escape were his addictions: it seems that his principal occupation during his five months in Paris was drinking to toxic levels. You can still meet people who rescued him from bars when he was unable to stand, mistaking him for just another poor guy who'd fallen out with life. Bloated by booze, he was found dead in his bathtub on 3 July 1971.

Three decades after taking that fateful dip, Mr Mojo Risin' is still packing them in at the Père. (Ironically, Jimbo visited the cemetery the week before he died and expressed a wish to be buried there.) The 30th anniversary of his death saw an astonishing 15,000 fans filing past his modest grave (which was rather less modest before somebody nabbed the bust of Jim looking like Apollo in a Dolly Parton wig). Even ordinary days see a constant pilgrimage of portly hippies and wan goths in NHS hornrims at the burial site, which is overseen by two security cameras, perched like pterodactyls, presumably waiting for some zealot to produce a shovel and start digging for glory. But usually the mourners are content to leave beer cans, condoms or a flourish of graffiti by way of tribute. Like the man said, people are strange.

In 2001, rumours circulated (as they do every time a new Doors CD boxed set or quadruple live is released) that the lease on quiet street lined with graceful porticos and acanthus motifs dating from the 1790s. Across the busy rue du Quatre-Septembre is the 1970s concrete and glass HQ of Agence France-Presse, France's biggest news agency. This street and its continuation rue Réaumur were built up by the press barons with some striking art nouveau buildings. Most newspapers have since left, but *Le Figaro* remains in rue du Louvre.

Bibliothèque Nationale Richelieu

58 rue de Richelieu, 2nd (01.53.79.53.79/recorded info 01.53.79.53.79). Mº Bourse. **Open** Galeries Mansart/Mazarine for exhibitions only 10am-8pm Tue-Sat; noon-7pm Sun. Cabinet des Monnaies, Médailles et Antiques 1-7.45pm Mon-Fri; 1-4.45pm Sat; noon-6pm Sun. **Admission** Galerie Mansart/Mazarine €5.40; €3.70 under-26s. Cabinet des Monnaies, Médailles et Antiques free. **Map** p401 H4.

The genesis of the French National Library dates from the 1660s, when Louis XIV's finance minister Colbert brought together the manuscripts of the royal library in this lavish Louis XIII townhouse. The library was first opened to the public in 1692, and by 1724 the institution had received so many new acquisitions that the neighbouring Hôtel de Nevers was added. Some of the original painted decoration can still be seen in Galeries Mansart and Mazarine, now used for exhibitions of manuscripts and prints. Coins, medals and curious royal memorabilia can be seen in the **Cabinet des Monnaies,**

Votive offerings at Mr Morisson's grave.

Jim's grave was up. As news spread, other cities' departments of tourism, the dollar signs flashing in their eyes, contacted the Doors' office with a view to rehousing the remains, but it was all whimsy: Morrison is down there on a perpetual lease, so Mr Mojo won't be risin' any time he doesn't want to.

Rush-hour cars scream at speed from the exit of the Pont de l'Alma underpass, creating a hideous din on the pavement above. A sense of eerie discomfort is palpable here as you shift awkwardly among the people gathered around the fading golden replica of the Flamme de la Liberté, which has recently been tarnished by flashes of pink aerosol. There are too many people in too small an area. Some are pointing video cameras at the static flame; others are asking strangers if this is really the place where it happened; others peer at the hand-written note taped to its base. The note, its letters smudged by rain, is a tribute left by an AIDS sufferer who threatens to haunt anyone daring to steal a flower from the bouquet that was presumably left somewhere nearby. This could quite easily be the least beautiful place in Paris.

A couple of feet below is a focal point in Paris as the city of lights out, the spot where the car carrying Princess Diana hit the thirteenth pillar at a speed of somewhere around 100mph at 24 minutes past midnight on 31 August 1997. By 25 minutes past, the photographers were hungrily snapping away.

Poignantly, the monument that attracts the Diana worshippers was never even intended for her. It's second-hand, having been placed there ten years before the crash to celebrate Franco-American relations. Actually, there is an official memorial to Diana, a children's garden in the Marais. That is irrelevant to the pilgrims; the flame above the place where it all ended is far more popular and somehow more appropriate to the person it now commemorates, not least because, except for very late at night, it seems inconceivable that anyone could ever get any peace in this busy and lonely place.

Médailles et Antiques (*see chapter* **Museums**). The complex was transformed in the 1860s by the innovative circular vaulted reading room designed by Henri Labrouste, but the library is now curiously empty as the books have been moved to the gigantic new Bibliothèque Nationale François Mitterrand.

La Bourse

Palais Brongniart, pl de la Bourse, 2nd (01.49.27.55.55/www.bourse-de-paris.fr). M° Bourse. **Guided tours** call for details. **Admission** €7.70; €4.60 students. **No credit cards. Map** p 402 H4.

After a century at the Louvre, the Palais-Royal and rue Vivienne, the stock exchange was transferred in 1826 to this building, a dignified testament to First Empire classicism designed under Napoléon by Alexandre Brongniart. It was enlarged in 1906 to create a cruciform interior, where brokers buzzed around a central enclosure, the *corbeille* (or crow's nest). Computers have now made the design obsolete, but the atmosphere remains as frenetic as ever.

Louvre des Antiquaires

2 pl du Palais-Royal, 1st (01.42.97.27.00/www.louvre-antiquaires.com). M° Palais Royal. **Open** 11am-7pm Tue-Sun. Closed Sun July-Aug. **Map** p402 H5.

This upmarket antiques centre behind the facade of an old *grand magasin* houses some 250 dealers. Look for Louis XV furniture, tapestries, Sèvres and Chinese porcelain, silver and jewellery, model ships and tin soldiers. Don't expect to find many bargains.

Palais-Royal

main entrance pl du Palais-Royal, 1st (www.palais-royal.org). M° Palais Royal. **Open** Gardens only dawn-dusk daily. **Admission** free. **Map** p402 H5.

Built for Richelieu by Jacques Lemercier, the building was known as the Palais Cardinal. Richelieu left it to Louis XIII, whose widow, Anne d'Autriche, preferred it to the chilly Louvre and gave it its name when she came to live here with her son, the young

The best Night views

The Louvre Pyramid
Well lit, well stunning (*see p78*).

Sacré-Coeur from Pompidou
Ascend the escalators till 9pm, or gaze out from swanky Georges restaurant (*see p190, Eating & Drinking*).

Place de la Concorde
A fantastia of fountains and phallic symbols (*see p81*).

Belleville beauty
Look down on the Eiffel Tower from working-class Belleville (*see p115*).

Louis XIV. In the 1780s the Duc d'Orléans enclosed the gardens in a three-storey peristyle. Housing cafés, theatres, sideshows, shops and apartments, its arcades came into their own as a society trysting place. Today the gardens offer a tranquil spot in the heart of Paris, while many surrounding shops specialise in prints and antiques. The former palace houses the Conseil d'Etat and the Ministry of Culture. Daniel Buren's controversial installation of black and white striped columns of different heights graces the main courtyard.

Place des Victoires

1st, 2nd. M° Bourse. **Map** p402 H5.

Louis XIV introduced the grand Baroque square in the form of circular place des Victoires, commemorating victories against Holland. It was designed in 1685 by Hardouin-Mansart to set off a statue of the king. The original disappeared in the Revolution and was replaced in 1822 with an equestrian statue by Bosio. Today, the sweeping facades shelter fashion names Kenzo and Thierry Mugler.

Opéra & the Grands Boulevards

Mainly in the 2nd, 8th and 9th arrondissements.

The wedding cake of Charles Garnier's **Palais Garnier** opera house, one of Napoléon III's architectural extravaganzas, has just undergone several years of extensive renovation and now has a pristine facade. It evokes the mood of opera at its grandest, and it's not hard to see why the Phantom of the Opera legend started here. Garnier also designed the Café de la Paix, overlooking place de l'Opéra. Behind, in the Jockey Club (now **Hôtel Scribe**), the Lumière brothers held the world's first public cinema screening in 1895. The delightful wood-fronted emporium Old England is opposite on the boulevard des Capucines. Inside, the shop has antiquated wooden counters, Jacobean-style plaster ceilings and equally dated goods and service. The **Olympia** concert hall, at 28 boulevard des Capucines, the legendary venue of Piaf and other greats, was recently knocked down and rebuilt a few metres away. In 2001 it fell into the hands of the Vivendi group. Across the road at No 35, pioneering portrait photographer Nadar opened a studio in the 1860s, soon frequented by writers, actors and artists including Dumas *père*, Doré and Offenbach. In 1874 it was the setting for the first Impressionists' exhibition.

The **Madeleine**, a vaguely religious monument to Napoléon, stands like a classical temple at the end of the boulevard. Its huge Corinthian columns mirror the Assemblée Nationale over the Seine, while the interior is

Sumptous surroundings include a
Chagall ceiling at the **Palais Garnier.**

a riot of marble, cluttered with side altars to saints who look like Roman generals. Most come to the *place* to ogle **Fauchon**, Paris' most extravagant delicatessen, **Hédiard**, **La Maison de la Truffe** and the other luxury foodstores, or for haute cuisine restaurant **Lucas Carton**, with art nouveau interior by Majorelle.

The *grands magasins* (department stores) **Printemps** and **Galeries Lafayette** opened in the late 19th century. Printemps still has an imposing domed entrance and Lafayette (whose controlling company took over France's Marks & Spencer stores in October 2001) a stained-glass dome. Behind the latter, on rue Caumartin, stands the Lycée Caumartin, designed as a convent in the 1780s by Bourse architect Brongniart to become one of Paris' most prestigious lycées under Napoléon. West along Haussmann's boulevard is the small square containing the **Chapelle Expiatoire** dedicated to Louis XVI and Marie-Antoinette. Beyond the Second Empire church of **St-Augustin** is a clever exercise in cast iron by Baltard, architect of the Les Halles pavilions.

Chapelle Expiatoire

29 rue Pasquier, 8th (01.42.65.35.80).
M° Madeleine. **Open** 1-5pm Thur-Sat. **Admission** €2.50. **Map** p401 F3.
The chapel was commissioned by Louis XVIII in memory of his executed predecessors, his brother Louis XVI and Marie-Antoinette. Their remains, along with those of almost 3,000 revolutionary victims, including Philippe-Egalité, Charlotte Corday, Mme du Barry, Camille Desmoulins, Danton, Malesherbes and Lavoisier, were found in 1814 on the exact spot where the altar stands. The year after that, the bodies of Louis XVI and Marie-Antoinette were transferred to the Basilique St-Denis (*see chapter* **Beyond the Périphérique**). The chapel draws ardent (if currently frustrated) royalists for a memorial service in January.

Eglise St-Augustin

46 bd Malesherbes, 8th (01.45.22.23.12).
M° St-Augustin. **Open** 8.45am-noon, 2.45-6pm Mon-Sat; 12.30-4pm Sun. **Map** p401 F3.
Designed by Victor Baltard in 1860-71, St-Augustin is not what it seems. The domed, neo-Renaissance stone exterior, curiously getting wider towards the rear to adapt to the triangular site, is merely a shell. Within, Baltard used an iron vault structure; even the decorative angels are cast in metal. Note the Bouguereau paintings in the transept.

Eglise de la Madeleine

pl de la Madeleine, 8th (01.44.51.69.00).
M° Madeleine. **Open** 9am-7pm Mon-Sat; 7.30am-6pm Sun. **Map** p401 G4.
The building of a church on this site began in 1764. In 1806, Napoléon sent instructions from Poland for Barthélemy Vignon to design a 'Temple of Glory'

Marble marvel: the church of the **Madeleine**.

dedicated to his Grand Army. After the Emperor's fall construction slowed, but the church was finally consecrated in 1845. Inside are three-and-a-half giant domes, a stunning organ and pseudo-Grecian side altars amid a sea of multicoloured marble. The painting by Ziegler in the chancel depicts the history of Christianity, Napoléon (ever the cringeing violet) prominent in the foreground. A favourite location for celebrity weddings and funerals.

Palais Garnier

pl de l'Opéra, 9th (box office 08.34.69.78.68/www. opera-de-paris.fr). M° Opéra. **Open** 12.45-1.45pm daily. Guided tours in English (01.40.01.22.63) 1 and 2pm Tue-Sun €9.20. **Admission** €4.60; €3.20 10-25s, over-60s; free under-10s. **No credit cards.** **Map** p401 G4.
Awash with gilt, satin, red velvet and marble, this is a monument to the Second Empire *haute bourgeoisie*. Designed by Charles Garnier in 1862, it has an auditorium for over 2,000 people. The exterior is opulent in the extreme, with sculptures of music and dance on the facade, Apollo topping the copper dome and nymphs holding torches. Carpeaux's sculpture *La Danse* shocked Parisians with its frank sensuality, and in 1869 someone threw a bottle of ink over its marble thighs. Quite right. The original is safe in the Musée d'Orsay. Since the completion of its interior restoration in 1996, the Garnier has again been hosting lyric productions as well as ballet. Visitors can see the library, museum, Grand Foyer, Grand Staircase and auditorium with its false ceiling, painted by Chagall in 1964. There's occasional talk of returning to the original, still underneath.

Quartier de l'Europe

This area north of Opéra around Gare St-Lazare is *the* Impressionist *quartier*, if hardly a tourist draw now. The exciting new steam age was depicted by Monet in the 1870s in *La Gare St-Lazare* and *Pont de l'Europe*; Caillebotte and Pissaro painted views of the new boulevards, and Manet had a studio on rue de St-Pétersbourg. The area was known for its prostitutes; rue de Budapest remains a thriving red light district, while rue de Rome has long been home to Paris' stringed-instrument makers. Just east of Gare St-Lazare, check out the imposing **Eglise de la Trinité** and art nouveau brasserie Mollard.

Eglise de la Trinité

pl Estienne d'Orves, 9th (01.48.74.12.77). M° Trinité. **Open** 7.15am-8pm Mon-Fri; 9am-8pm Sat; 8.30am-1pm, 4.30-8pm Sun. **Map** p401 G3.
Dominated by the tiered wedding-cake belltower, this neo-Renaissance church was built 1861-67 by Théodore Ballu. Composer Olivier Messiaen (1908-92) was organist here for over 30 years. Guided tours on some Sundays. *Wheelchair access (call ahead).*

The Grands Boulevards

Contrary to popular belief, the string of Grands Boulevards between Madeleine and République (des Italiens, Montmartre, Poissonnière, Bonne-Nouvelle, St-Denis, St-Martin) were not built by Haussmann but by Louis XIV in 1670, replacing the fortifications of Charles II's city wall. This explains the strange changes of level of the eastern segment, as steps lead up to side streets or down to the road on former traces of the ramparts. The boulevards burgeoned after the Revolution, often built on land repossessed from aristocrats or the church. Today they feel rather anonymous, lined with theatres, burger joints and discount stores and the area is up for renovation. Towards Opéra, the grandiose domed banking halls of Crédit Lyonnais (still

being restored after a fire) and the Société Générale reflect the business boom of the late 19th century.

Between boulevard des Italiens and rue de Richelieu is place Boieldieu and the **Opéra Comique** (*see chapter* **Music: Classical & Opera**), where *Carmen* was premiered in 1875. Alexandre Dumas *fils* was born across the square at No 1 in 1824.

The 18th-century *mairie* (town hall) of the 9th *arrondissement* (6 rue Drouot) was once home to the infamous *bals des victimes*, where every guest had to have had a relative lost to the guillotine. The strikingly modern **Hôtel Drouot** auction house stands surrounded by specialist antique shops, coin and stamp dealers and Les Caves Drouot, where auction goers and valuers congregate. There are several grand if a little dilapidated *hôtels particuliers* on rue de la Grange-Batelière, which leads on one side down curious **passage Verdeau** and on the other back to the boulevards via picturesque **passage Jouffroy** and the colourful carved entrance of the **Grévin** waxworks. Across the boulevard look for **passage des Panoramas**. Wander down cobbled Cité Bergère, built in 1825 as desirable residences; though most are now budget hotels, the pretty iron and glass *portes-cochères* remain. The area is home to some wonderful kosher restaurants and the formerly infamous **Folies-Bergère** (currently offering musical entertainment rather than cabaret). The palatial art deco cinema **Le Grand Rex** offers an interesting backstage tour. East of here are Louis XIV's twin triumphal arches, the **Porte St-Martin** and **Porte St-Denis**.

Le Grand Rex

1 bd Poissonnière, 2nd (Cinema info: 08.36.68.70.23/www.legrandrex.com). M° Bonne Nouvelle. **Tour** Les Etoiles du Rex every 50 mins 10am-7pm Wed-Sun, public holidays, daily in school holidays. **Admission** €6.90; €6.10 under-12s; €11.43 tour and film; €10.40 under-12s. **Map** p402 J4.

The best Revolutionary hot-spots

Palais-Royal

Revolutionary Camille Desmoulins called people to arms on the eve of the storming of the Bastille, 13 July 1789 (*see p83*).

Place de la Concorde

It was here that the guillotine that did for Louis XVI and Marie-Antionette was erected in 1792 (*see pp 81-2*).

Place de la Nation

The guillotine was moved here in 1794, the Revolutionaries' busiest summer, following complaints about the stench.

Chapelle Expiatoire

The remains of 3,000 people were found here, including those of Louis XVI, Marie-Antoinette and Camille Desmoulins. (*see left*).

Opened in 1932, the huge art deco cinema was designed by Auguste Bluysen with fantasy Hispanic interiors by US designer John Eberson. See behind the scenes in the wacky 50-minute tour. After a presentation about the construction of the auditorium, visitors are shown the production room, taking in newsreel footage of Rex history and an insight into film tricks with nerve-jolting Sensurround effects. *Wheelchair access (call ahead).*

Hôtel Drouot
9 rue Drouot, 9th (01.48.00.20.20/ recorded information 01.48.00.20.17). Mº Richelieu-Drouot. **Open** 10am-4.30pm Mon-Sat. **Map** p 401 H4.
A spiky aluminium and marble-clad concoction is the unlikely setting for the hub of France's secondary art market. Inside, escalators whizz you up to small salerooms, where medieval manuscripts, 18th-century furniture, Oriental arts, modern paintings and fine wines might be up for sale. Drouot makes a great free exhibition, with pieces of varying quality crammed in together. Details of forthcoming sales are published in the weekly *Gazette de L'Hôtel Drouot,* sold at newsstands. Prestige sales tend to take place at Drouot-Montaigne. *Partial wheelchair access.*
Branches: Drouot-Montaigne 15 av Montaigne, 8th (01.48.00.20.80); Drouot Nord 64 rue Doudeauville, 18th (01.48.00.20.90).

Porte St-Denis & Porte St-Martin
corner rue St-Denis/bd St-Denis, 2nd/10th; 33 bd St-Martin, 3rd/10th. **Map** p402 K4.
These twin triumphal gates were erected in 1672 and 1674 at important entry points as part of Colbert's strategy for the aggrandisement of Paris to the glory of Louis XIV's victories on the Rhine. Modelled on the triumphal arches of ancient Rome, the Porte St-Denis is particularly harmonious, based on a perfect square with a single arch, bearing Latin inscriptions and decorated with military trophies and battle scenes. Porte St-Bernard on the Left Bank has been demolished and a gateway planned for the Fbg-St-Antoine was never built.

Les Halles & Sentier

In the 1st and 2nd arrondissements.
Few places epitomise the transformation of central Paris more than Les Halles, wholesale fruit and veg market for the city since 1181 when the covered markets were established by king Philippe Auguste. In 1969 the trading moved to a new wholesale market in the southern suburb of Rungis, leaving a giant hole – nicknamed *le trou des Halles* (a pun on arsehole). After a long political dispute it was filled in the early 1980s by the miserably designed Forum des Halles mall. One pavilion was saved and reconstructed in the suburbs at Nogent-sur-Marne (*see chapter* **Beyond the Périphérique**). The Forum has become a haunt of drunks, punks and junkies, though the rue Montorgueil market street retains some of the area's former charm. The market crowd and prostitutes of rue St-Denis continue to make this a colourful neighbourhood.

Place des Innocents, now a boarding school for kick-flippers and grinders.

Enjoying a facial at **St-Eustache**.

East of the Forum is the place des Innocents, centred on the Renaissance Fontaine des Innocents. It was moved here from the city's main burial ground, nearby Cimetière des Innocents, which was demolished in 1786 after flesh-eating rats started gnawing into people's living rooms, and the bones transferred to the Catacombes (*see p137* **Subterranean bone-pit views**). Pedestrianised rue des Lombards is a centre for nightlife, with bars, restaurants and the **Baiser Salé**, **Sunset** and **Duc des Lombards** jazz clubs. In ancient rue de la Ferronerie, King Henri IV was assassinated in 1610 by Catholic fanatic François Ravaillac (who had followed the royal carriage held up in the traffic). The street has now become an extension of the Marais gay circuit.

By the Pont-Neuf is **La Samaritaine** department store. It is chaotically organised inside, but has a fantastic art nouveau staircase and *verrière* (grand window). The Toupary restaurant and tearoom at the top also offers great views. From here the quai de la Mégisserie, lined with horticultural suppliers and pet shops, leads towards Châtelet. Les Halles' gardens seem inhabited largely by the homeless. Looming over them is the **Eglise St-Eustache**, with Renaissance motifs inside and chunky flying buttresses without. At the western end of the gardens is the **Bourse du Commerce**. It was built on the site of a palace belonging to Marie de Médicis, who is recalled in the astronomical column outside. Hints of the market past linger in the 24-hour brasserie

Au Pied de Cochon, and the all-night-bistro **La Tour de Montlhéry**.

The area west of Les Halles is packed with clothes shops: **Agnès b**'s empire – along most of rue du Jour – has been joined by more streetwise outlets, and there are further designer names west at place des Victoires (*see above* **Palais-Royal**). East of here, pedestrianised rue Montorgueil, all food shops and cafés, is an irresistible place to while away a few hours. At 20 rue Etienne-Marcel is the **Tour Jean Sans Peur**, a strange relic of the fortified townhouse (1409-11) of Jean, Duc de Bourgogne, which has been greatly restored and is now open to the public.

The ancient easternmost stretch of the rue St-Honoré runs into the southern edge of Les Halles. The Fontaine du Trahoir, rebuilt by Soufflot in 1776 with neo-Renaissance icicles, stands at the corner with rue de l'Arbre-Sec. Opposite, the fine Hôtel de Truden (52 rue de l'Arbre-Sec) was built in 1717 for a wealthy wine merchant. In the courtyard a shop sells historic issues of old papers and magazines. South of the gardens, ancient little streets such as rue des Lavandiers-Ste-Opportune, running towards the Seine, and narrow rue Jean-Lantier, show a human side of Les Halles that has yet to be destroyed in 'cleaning-up' programmes.

Bourse du Commerce

2 rue de Viarmes, 1st (01.55.65.78.41). M° Louvre. **Open** 9am-6pm Mon-Fri, limited access. **Tours** groups of up to 30, reserve in advance, 1h 30 tour, €41.16. **No credit cards**. Map p402 J5.
Now housing some of the offices of the Paris Chamber of Commerce, a world trade centre and commodity market for coffee and sugar, the city's former main grain market was built in 1767 by Nicolas Le Camus de Mézières. It was later covered by a wooden dome and replaced by an avant-garde iron structure in 1809 – then covered in copper, now in glass. *Wheelchair access.*

Eglise St-Eustache

rue du Jour, 1st (01.40.26.47.99). M°/RER-Les Halles. **Open** 9.30am-7.30pm Mon-Sun. Nov-Apr 9.30am-7.30pm daily. **Tour** first Sun of every month 3pm, free (phone ahead). Map p402 J5.
This barn-like church (built 1532-1640) dominates Les Halles. Its elaborately buttressed and mono-lithic vaulted structure is essentially Gothic, but the decoration with Corinthian capitals is distinctly Renaissance. Paintings in the side chapels include a *Descent from the Cross* by Luca Giordano; works by Thomas Couture adorn the early 19th-century Lady Chapel; John Armleder's *Pour Paintings* added in 2000 give a contemporary touch. A favourite with music-lovers, it boasts a magnificent 8,000-pipe organ (free recitals 5.30pm Sun).

Sightseeing

Forum des Halles

1st. M°/RER Châtelet-Les Halles. **Map** p402 J5.
This labyrinthine concrete mall extends three levels underground and includes the Ciné Cité multiplex, the Forum des Images and a swimming pool, as well as mass-market clothing chains, branches of Fnac, Habitat and – a result of empty outlets – the Forum des Créateurs, a section given over to young designers. The first part of the centre was completed in 1979, the second phase by the Bourse du Commerce added in 1986. Both have lost their lustre, but you are bound to end up here sometime, if only to use the vast Métro and RER interchange.

Tour Jean Sans Peur

20 rue Etienne-Marcel, 2nd (01.40.26.20.28/www. jeansanspeur.free.fr). M° *Etienne-Marcel.* **Open** termtime 1.30-6pm, Wed, Sat, Sun; school holidays 1.30-6pm Tue-Sun. **Tour** 2pm; €7.62. **Credit** MC, V. **Map** p402 J5.
This is the remnant of the townhouse of Jean Sans Peur, Duc de Bourgogne. The original *hôtel* spanned Philippe-Auguste's city wall and the base of a turret is still concealed inside. Jean got his nickname (the fearless) from his exploits in Bulgaria. He was responsible for the assassination in 1407 of Louis d'Orléans, his rival and the cousin of Charles VI, which sparked the Hundred Years' War. Jean fled Paris but returned two years later to add this show-off tower to his mansion. The tower was also meant to protect him from any vengeance on the part of the widow of Louis d'Orléans (not so fearless, eh?), but it seems his card was fatally marked: in 1419 he was assassinated by a partisan of the future Charles VII. Today you can climb the multi-storey tower. Halfway up is a remarkable vault carved with naturalistic branches of oak, hawthorn and hops, symbols of Jean Sans Peur and Burgundian power.

Rue St-Denis & Sentier

For years the Sentier district was all crumbling houses, run-down shops and downmarket strip-joints. In recent years the prostitutes and peep-shows have been partly pushed back by energetic pedestrianisation and by the arrival of practitioners of another type of entrepreneurial activity that is prepared to do virtually anything for money – the start-ups.

The tackiness is pretty unremitting along the traditional red-light district of rue St-Denis (and northern continuation rue du Faubourg-St-Denis), which snakes north from the Forum. Kerb-crawlers gawp at the neon adverts for *l'amour sur scène*, and size up defiantly dignified prostitutes in doorways.

Between rue des Petits-Carreaux and rue St-Denis is the site of the Cour des Miracles – a refuge where, after a day's begging, paupers would 'miraculously' regain use of their eyes or limbs. An abandoned aristocratic estate, it was a refuge for the underworld for decades until

cleared out in 1667 by Louis XIV's chief of police. The surrounding Sentier district is the centre of the rag trade, and is correspondingly lively and vivid. Sentier is a delightful island of manufacturing where sweatshops churn out copies of catwalk creations and the streets fill with porters carrying linen bundles over their shoulders. Streets such as rue du Caire, d'Aboukir and du Nil, named after Napoléon's Egyptian campaign, are connected by a maze of passages lined with wholesalers. The area attracts hundreds of illegal and semi-legal foreign workers, trying to make their way in a hostile environment, who line up for work in place du Caire.

Fbg-St-Denis to Gare du Nord

North of Porte St-Denis, which celebrates Louis XIV's victories on the Rhine (*see above* **Grands Boulevards**), along the rue du Fbg-St-Denis, there's an almost souk-like feel, with its food shops, narrow passages and sinister courtyards. The brasserie Julien boasts one of the finest art nouveau interiors in Paris, with wood carved by Majorelle, stunning painted panels and eternally fashionable status, while up dingy cobbled cour des Petites Ecuries, theatre-goers flock to **Brasserie Flo**. Garishly lit passage Brady is a surprising piece of India, full of restaurants and hairdressers. Rue des Petites Ecuries ('stables street') was once known for saddlers but now has Turkish shops and cafés as well as top jazz venue **New Morning**.

The top of rue d'Hauteville affords one of the most unexpected views in Paris. **Eglise St-Vincent de Paul**, with its twin towers and cascading terraced gardens, is about as close as Paris gets to Rome's Spanish Steps. Just behind, on rue de Belzunce, are the excellent modern bistro **Chez Michel** and offshoot Chez Casimir. On boulevard Magenta, the Marché St-Quentin is one of the busiest surviving covered iron markets, built in the 1860s.

Boulevard de Strasbourg was one of Haussmann's new roads, designed to give a grand perspective up to the new Gare de l'Est and soon built up with popular theatres – the mosaic-filled neo-Renaissance Théâtre Antoine-Simone Berriau and the art deco Eldorado. At No 2, another neo-Renaissance creation houses Paris' last fan maker and the **Musée de l'Eventail** (*see chapter* **Museums**). Sandwiched between Gare de l'Est and Canal St-Martin (*see below,* **North-East Paris**) stand the near derelict remains of the **Couvent des Récollets** and its former gardens – now the Square Villemin, a park.

Sweatshop chic in the **Sentier**, centre of the rag trade.

Couvent des Récollets

bd de Strasbourg, 10th. **Map** p402 L3.
This 17th-century Franciscan convent went through
a right-on phase as a women's shelter and hospital
after the Revolution. Today it stands empty, something of a shame for such a charming building,
although an artists' association sometimes holds
Sunday open events in the gardens. The convent's
future is currently under evaluation, with the artists
lending their support to plans for a Cité Européenne
de la Culture.

Eglise St-Vincent de Paul

*pl Franz-Liszt, 10th (01.48.78.47.47). M° Gare du
Nord.* **Open** 8am-noon, 2-7pm Mon-Sat; 4-7pm Sun.
Map p402 K2.
Imposingly set at the top of terraced gardens, the
church was begun in 1824 by Lepère and completed
1831-44 by Hittorff, replacing an earlier chapel to

cater to the newly populous district. The twin towers, pedimented Greek temple portico and evange-
list figures on the parapet are in classical mode. The
interior has a double storey arcade of columns,
murals by Flandrin, and some rather natty church
furniture by Rude.

Gare du Nord

*rue de Dunkerque, 10th (01.53.90.20.20).
M° Gare du Nord.* **Map** p402 K2.
The grandest of the great 19th-century train stations
(and Eurostar terminal since 1994) was designed by
Hittorff in 1861-64. A conventional stone facade,
with Ionic capitals and statues representing towns
of northern France and Europe served by the station,
hides a vast, bravura iron and glass vault.
Impressive on the outside, within it is now something of a dump, and visitors are advised to keep
their hand on their ha'penny at all times.

Beaubourg & the Marais

In the 3rd and 4th arrondissements.
Between boulevard Sébastopol and the Bastille
lies Beaubourg – the historic area in which the
Centre Pompidou landed in 1977 – and the
Marais, built up between the 16th and 18th
centuries and now full of boutiques, museums
and bars that are so trendy they're naff.

Beaubourg & Hôtel de Ville

Contemporary Parisian architecture began with
the **Centre Pompidou**, opened in 1977 in a
formerly run-down area still known by its
medieval name Beaubourg ('beautiful village').
Newly reopened after extensive renovation, this
international benchmark of inside-out high-tech
is as much of an attraction as its contents. Out
on the piazza is the **Atelier Brancusi**, the
sculptor's reconstructed studio. On the other
side of the piazza, peer down rue Quincampoix
for its art galleries, bars and curious passage
Molière. It was here that Scottish financier John
Law ran his speculative venture that crashed
when the South Sea Bubble burst in 1720;
hounded by the mob, he took refuge in the
Palais-Royal. Beside the Centre Pompidou is
place Igor Stravinsky, with the red brick
IRCAM contemporary music institute and the
playful Fontaine Stravinsky, designed by Nikki
de Saint Phalle and Jean Tinguely. On the south
side of the square is the church of St-Merri, with
a Flamboyant Gothic facade complete with an
androgynous demon (don't you find they're
always the worst kind?) leering over the
doorway. Inside are a carved wooden organ loft,
the oldest bell in Paris (1331) and 16th-century
stained glass. There are free chamber music
concerts most weekends.

Beyond Châtelet looms the Hôtel de Ville,
Paris' city hall and home to the mayor. The
centre of municipal rather than royal (or
republican) power since 1260, it overlooks a
square of the same name, once known as place
de Grève, beside the original Paris port. Here
disgruntled workers once gathered – hence the
much-used French word for 'strike' (*grève*).
Protestant heretics were burnt in the *place*
during the Wars of Religion, and the guillotine
first stood here during the Terror, when
Danton, Marat and Robespierre made the Hôtel
their seat of government. Revolutionaries made
it their base in the 1871 Commune, but the
building was set on fire by the Communards
themselves and wrecked in savage fighting. It
was rebuilt on a grander scale in fanciful neo-
Renaissance style with statues representing
French cities along the facade, and could easily
be thought to be a palace.

Centre Pompidou

rue Beaubourg, 4th (01.44.78.12.33).
Mᵒ Hôtel de Ville or Rambuteau/RER Châtelet-Les
Halles. **Open** 11am-9pm Mon, Wed-Fri; 10am-10pm
Sat, Sun, holidays. Closed Tue and 1 May.
Admission €7.70. **Credit** (shop) AmEx, MC, V.
Map p402 K5.
The primary colours and exposed pipes and air
ducts make this one of the most recognisable buildings in Paris. Commissioned in 1968, the centre is
the work of the Italo-British duo Renzo Piano and
Richard Rogers. Their 'inside-out', boilerhouse
approach put air-conditioning and lifts outside, leaving a freely adaptable space within. When the centre opened in 1977, its success exceeded all
expectations. After a revamp the centre reopened in
January 2000 with an enlarged museum, renewed
performance spaces, fashionable Georges restaurant
and a mission to get back to the stimulating inter-
disciplinary mix of old (*see chapter* **Museums**).

Tour St-Jacques

pl du Châtelet, 4th. Mᵒ Châtelet. **Map** p406 J6.
Much-loved by the Surrealists, this solitary
Flamboyant Gothic bell-tower is the remains of the
St-Jacques-La-Boucherie church, built for the power-
ful Butchers' Guild in 1523. Pascal carried out exper-
iments on the weight of air here in the 17th century.
A weather station now crowns the 52-metre-high
tower, which can only be admired from outside.

Pompidou's fashionable Georges restaurant.

The best | Right Bank residents

Mayor Bertrand Delanoë
Hôtel de Ville (4th).

Jim Morrison
17 rue Beautrellis (4th).

Jacques 'President' Chirac
55 rue du Faubourg-St-Honoré (8th).

Victor Hugo
6 place des Vosges (4th).

Colette
9 rue de Beaujolais (1st).

Marcel Proust (with his old mum)
45 rue de Courcelles (8th).

The Marais

East of Roman rue St-Martin and rue du Renard lies the Marais, a magical area whose narrow streets are dotted with aristocratic *hôtels particuliers*, art galleries, fashion boutiques and stylish cafés. The city slows down here, giving you time to notice the beautiful carved doorways and the early street signs carved into the stone. The Marais, or 'marsh', started life as an uninhabited piece of swampy ground used for market gardening, inhabited only by a few religious foundations. In the 16th century the elegant **Hôtel Carnavalet** and **Hôtel Lamoignon** sparked the area's phenomenal rise as an aristocratic residential district; Henri IV began constructing the **place des Vosges** in 1605. Soon nobles started building smart townhouses where famous literary ladies such as Mme de Sévigné and Mlle de Scudéry and influential courtesan Ninon de l'Enclos held court. The area fell from fashion a century later; happily, many of the narrow streets were essentially unchanged as mansions were transformed into industrial workshops, schools, tenements, even a fire station. The current

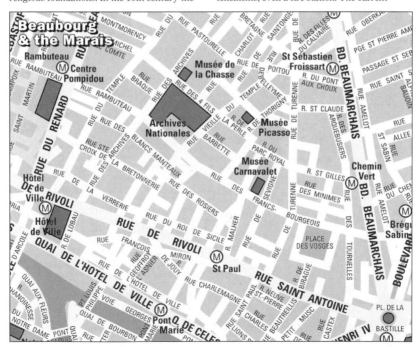

renaissance dates from 1962 when a preservation order from then-Culture Minister André Malraux safeguarded many buildings for use as museums. It is now a lively, international *quartier* and property prices have soared.

The rue des Francs-Bourgeois runs right through the Marais. The street soon forgets its Les Halles legacy in the food shops of rue Rambuteau; further on the street is packed with elegant mansions and original boutiques, such as **Plein Sud** for fashion, **Millefeuilles** for flowers and **Bains Plus** for delectable bathroom accessories. The tearoom **Les Enfants Gâtés** ('spoiled children') sums up the mood. For a little culture, seek out two of Paris' most elegant early 18th-century residences: **Hôtel**

d'**Albret** (No 31) and **Hôtel de Soubise** (No 60), the national archives, where interiors by Boucher and Lemoine can be seen as part of the **Musée de l'Histoire de France** (*see chapter* **Museums**). On the corner of the rue des Francs-Bourgeois and rue Pavée is the austere renaissance **Hôtel Lamoignon**. Built in 1585 for Diane de France, Henry II's illegitimate daughter, it now houses the Bibliothèque Historique de la Ville de Paris.

At the street's eastern end is the stunning place des Vosges. At one corner is **Maison de Victor Hugo**, once occupied by the author. The luxurious Ambroisie restaurant is for special treats, while Ma Bourgogne offers much simpler cuisine. An archway in the southwest corner leads to the elegant **Hôtel de Sully**.

The mob wars: killing in style

27 September 2000. A Wednesday, just after 3pm. Francis Vanverbergh, a middle-aged resident of rue Lord Byron, strolls up to the bar of the Artois Club, just off the Champs-Elysées, and orders a mineral water. He takes a sip before setting the plastic glass down at his usual table. Someone calls his name. He looks up. As he clocks the Colt 45 pointing at his face he realises that, despite having a winning lottery ticket in his pocket, today is decisively not his lucky day. Bing bada boom!

The assassination of Francis 'Le Belge' Vanverbergh was the highest-profile murder in a gangster war that claimed the lives of at least 40 mobsters between 1999 and 2002. As you might expect from Gallic gangsters, they've got taste. No downtown dirt heaps or bleak country lanes for them: all the killings have taken place on or around the most beautiful avenue in the world. Maybe dead hoods go to the Elysian fields along with the heroes. Maybe gangster chic is as much part of the avenue's revival as Ladurée and Louis Vuitton.

We are not talking two-bit punks, and Belgian Frankie was no small fry: being the one-time godfather of the French Connection (the real-

life legendary heroin smugglers, not the trendy threads chain) makes a guy a seriously large *fromage*. In mob terms, his assassination equates to that of Arch Duke Ferdinand. Repercussions have been bloody. So who terminated Frankie, and why?

People on both sides of the law are looking for whoever rubbed him out. The Paris cops believe they could wrap it up if only they could talk to the two prime suspects, Djilali Zitouni and Boualem Talata, but that's gonna be hard without the help of a medium: those guys both checked suddenly into the Wooden Waldorf in the summer of 2001.

As to the why, the cops say that the mob wars are part of a natural evolutionary cycle and that everybody wants a piece of the gaming machine racket. Narcotics and prostitution are already spoken for, but the video poker dough's sitting there waiting to be lapped up by the fastest shooter. They also say it's not over yet. So if you're hanging out after an afternoon's shopping in the Champs and a dapper-looking dude walks towards you carrying a violin case, it's probably safest not to toss him a couple of euros and request a few bars of 'Embraceable You'. You don't want to end up sleeping with the *poissons*.

Even workaday rue du Temple, once the road leading to the Templars' church, is full of surprises. Near rue de Rivoli, the Latina specialises in Latin American films. At No 41 an archway leads into the courtyard of the former Aigle d'Or coaching inn, now the Café de la Gare *café-théâtre*, Le Studio Tex-Mex and dance studios. Further north among bag and accessory wholesalers, the imposing **Hôtel de St-Aignan** at No 71 contains the Jewish museum the **Musée d'Art et d'Histoire du Judaïsme** (*see chapter* **Museums**). Round the corner, **Hôtel de Hallwyll** is a rare domestic building by Ledoux.

The district's two most important museums are also in sumptuous *hôtels*. The **Musée Carnavalet** (*see chapter* **Museums**), dedicated to Paris history, runs across the Hôtel Carnavalet, once home to famous letter-writer Mme de Sévigné, and the later Hôtel le Peletier de St-Fargeau. Curiosities include faithful reconstructions of Proust's bedroom and the Fouquet jewellery shop. The **Hôtel Salé** on rue de Thorigny, built and named in 1656 for a salt tax collector, has been finely restored and extended to house the **Musée National Picasso** (*see chapter* **Museums**). The original ornate staircase remains, as do two fine stone sphinxes in the courtyard.

The Marais is also home to Paris' oldest Jewish community, centred on rue des Rosiers, rue des Ecouffes and rue Pavée (where there's a synagogue designed by Guimard). Originally made up mainly of Ashkenazi Jews who arrived after the pogroms (many were later deported during World War II), the community expanded in the 1950s and 60s with a wave of Sephardic Jewish immigration following French withdrawal from North Africa. As a result, there are now many falafel shops alongside the Jewish bakers and delis, such as Finkelstijn and Paris' most famous Jewish eatery, **Jo Goldenberg**; its exterior still bears the scars of a terrorist attack in the 1980s.

The lower ends of rue des Archives and rue Vieille-du-Temple are the centre of café life and happening bars, including cutesy Petit Fer à Cheval and cosmopolitan Café du Trésor in the neighbouring impasse du Trésor. This area, especially rue Ste-Croix-de-la-Bretonnerie and rue du Temple, is the hub of Paris' gay scene.

Place des Vosges

4th. M° St-Paul. **Map** p406 L6.

The first planned square in Paris was built 1605-12 by Henri IV. The intimate square, with its beautifully harmonious red-brick-and-stone arcaded facades and steeply pitched roofs, is quite distinct from the pomp of later Bourbon Paris. Moreover, it is perfectly symmetrical. Originally the place

Strolling through the centuries in the **Marais**.

Sightseeing

Royale, the square's name dates from the Napoleonic Wars, when the Vosges was the first region of France to pay its war taxes. Mme de Sévigné, salon hostess and letter-writer, was born here in 1626. At that time the garden was a place of duels and romantic trysts; now it attracts hot-shot *boules* players and chaperoned children.

The Temple & Arts et Métiers

The northern, less gentrified half of the Marais towards place de la République is home to tiny local bars, costume-jewellery and rag-trade wholesalers and industrial workshops, alongside art galleries and recently arrived fashion designers. The Quartier du Temple was once a fortified, semi-independent entity under the Knights Templar. The round church and keep have been replaced by Square du Temple and the Carreau du Temple clothes market. The keep became a prison in the Revolution, where the royal family were held in 1792. Rue de Bretagne is crammed with food shops and has the fashionable couscous restaurant **Chez Omar**; rue de Picardie boasts the **Web Bar** which runs exhibitions and concerts.

The St-Paul district

In 1559, Henri II was mortally wounded in a jousting tournament on what is now rue St-Antoine. He is commemorated in a grieving marble Virgin by Pilon in the Jesuit church of **St-Paul-St-Louis**. Towards the Bastille, the heavily domed church of the Visitation Ste-Marie was designed in the 1630s by Mansart. South of rue St-Antoine is a more sedate residential area known as St-Paul. There are still plenty of fine houses, but the overall mood is discreet. The **Village St-Paul**, a colony of antique sellers spread across small interlinked courtyards between rues St-Paul, Charlemagne and quai des Célestins, is a promising source of 1930s and 50s furniture, kitchenware and wine gadgets (open Mon, Thur-Sun). On rue des Jardins-St-Paul is the largest surviving section of the **wall of Philippe Auguste**. The infamous poisoner Marquise de Brinvilliers lived at Hôtel de Brinvilliers (12 rue Charles V) in the 1630s. She killed her father and brothers to inherit the family fortune and was only caught after her lover died... of natural causes.

Two of the Marais' finest mansions are on rue François-Miron, an ancient fork of rue St-Antoine: **Hôtel de Beauvais**, No 68, and **Hôtel Hénault de Cantorbe**, renovated to incorporate the **Maison Européenne de la Photographie**. Down rue de Fourcy towards the river is the **Hôtel de Sens**, a fanciful ensemble of Gothic turrets which now houses

the **Bibliothèque Forney**. Across from the tip of the Ile St-Louis the square Henri-Galli contains a rebuilt fragment of the Bastille prison and the Pavillon de l'Arsenal, built by a timber merchant to put on private art shows and now used for architectural shows.

Eglise St-Paul-St-Louis

99 rue St-Antoine, 4th (01.42.72.30.32). M° Bastille or St-Paul. **Open** 8am-8pm Mon-Fri; 9am-8pm Sat-Sun. **Map** p406 L7.
The domed Baroque Counter-Reformation church, completed in 1641, is modelled, like all Jesuit churches, on the Gesù in Rome, with its single nave, side chapels and three-storey hierarchical facade bearing (replacement) statues of saints Louis, Anne and Catherine. The hearts of Louis XIII and XIV were stolen from here in the Revolution. Most of the original paintings and furnishings were removed then too. In 1802 it became a church again and now houses Delacroix's *Christ in the Garden of Olives*. The shell stoups were a gift from Victor Hugo.

Fortified wall of Philippe Auguste

rue des Jardins-St-Paul, 4th (www.philippe-auguste. com). M° Pont Marie or St-Paul. **Map** p406 L7.
King Philippe Auguste (1165-1223) was the first great Parisian builder since the Romans, enclosing the entire city within a great wall. The largest surviving section, complete with towers, extends along rue des Jardins-St-Paul. Another chunk is at 3 rue Clovis (5th) and odd remnants of towers are dotted around the Marais and St-Germain-des-Prés.

Mémorial du Martyr Juif Inconnu

17 rue Geoffroy-l'Asnier, 4th (01.42.77.44.72). M° St-Paul or Pont-Marie. **Open** 10am-1pm, 2-5.30pm 10am-1pm (library 11am-5.30pm) Mon-Thur; 2-5pm Fri. Closed Jewish holidays. **Admission** €2.30. **No credit cards. Map** p406 K6.
A reminder that many of the Jews rounded up in World War II (first only foreign Jews, later French Jews were taken too) were residents of the Marais, this monument serves as an archive and exhibition centre on the deportations.

The Bastille & eastern Paris

Mainly in the 11th and 12th arrondissements.
Place de la Bastille, traditionally a boundary point between central Paris and the proletarian east, has remained a potent symbol of popular revolt ever since the prison-storming that inaugurated the Revolution. Though still a favourite spot for demonstrations, the area has attracted new cafés, restaurants, galleries and bars since the 1980s.

The site of the prison itself is now a Banque de France office and the gap left by the castle ramparts forms the present-day square, dominated by the massive **Opéra Bastille**. Opened in 1989 on the bicentennial of Bastille Day, it remains highly controversial, but

From dramatic revolution to operatic institution: **the Bastille**

productions sell out and, along with the creation of the Port de l'Arsenal marina to the south, it has contributed to the area's rejuvenation.

The cobbled Rue de Lappe typifies the Bastille's tranformation, as the last remaining furniture workshops, the 1930s Balajo dance hall, old Auvergnat bistro La Galoche d'Aurillac and grocer Chez Teil hold out against

Wass up, Chuck?

Well, you can tell by the way he used his walk, he was a Free French man, no time to talk... except to say an emphatic 'Non' to the UK's application to join the EU. And, yes; viewed from behind, you'd think that the bronze statue represents a big-hipped model huffily vogueing down a catwalk. But take one look at the hooter, and there's no doubt: Paris has finally got a monument to Charles de Gaulle.

There are two reasons why Paris waited so long to put de Gaulle on a plinth: first, the general made it clear that he did not want to be commemorated here; second, Parisians remain unimpressed by his boast of having liberated Paris on his own (a claim to which most of them would react with some approximation of the phrase, 'Oh, yeah? You and whose army?').

And there is one compelling reason why the monument appeared: in 1998 a statue of Winston Churchill was unveiled just down the road. It would be unthinkable, like having Bush without Blair.

a dizzy array of gift shops and theme bars which teem with teens on weekends.

You can still catch a flavour of the old working-class district at the Sunday morning market on boulevard Richard Lenoir or up rue de la Roquette. Rue du Faubourg-St-Antoine still has furniture-makers' *ateliers* and gaudy furniture stores, but is being colonised by clothes shops and bars: one can't help feeling a twinge of regret for when the last neo-Louis XV chair or Nubian slave candelabra disappears. Rue de Charonne has trendy bars and bistros as well as art galleries and shops full of weird 60s furniture. Along with rue Keller, the patch is a focus for record shops, streetwear and, increasingly, young fashion designers. There's still something of a village spirit as the in-crowd hangs out at the **Pause Café** and the Planète Keller committee hold street parties.

However, the main thoroughfares tell only half the story. Behind narrow street frontages are quaintly named cobbled alleys dating back to the 18th century and lined with craftsmen's workshops or quirky bars and bistros. Investigate the cours de l'Ours, du Cheval Blanc, du Bel Air (with hidden garden), de la Maison Brûlée, the passage du Chantier on Faubourg-St-Antoine, or the rustic-looking passage de l'Etoile d'Or and the passage de l'Homme with old wooden shop fronts on rue de Charonne. This area originally lay outside the city walls on the lands of the Convent of St-Antoine (parts of which survive as the Hôpital St-Antoine), where in the Middle Ages skilled furniture makers were free from the city's restrictive guilds, beginning a tradition of independence and free-thinking that made this area a powder keg during the Revolution. Today, many of the workshops are the studios of artists, architects, designers or ad agencies.

Boulevard Beaumarchais separates rowdy Bastille from the elegant Marais. Look out for the polygonal Cirque d'Hiver, designed by Hittorff and still used today (*see chapter* **Cabaret & Circus**). Further east, on rue de la Roquette, a small park and playground surrounded by modern housing marks the site of the prison de la Roquette, where a plaque remembers the 4,000 resistance members imprisoned here in World War II.

Opéra Bastille

pl de la Bastille, 12th (box office 08.36.69.78.68/ guided visits 01.40.01.19.70/www.opera-de-paris.fr). M° Bastille. **Tour** phone for details. **Admission** €9.15; €6.86 students, under-16s, over-60s. **No credit cards. Map** p407 M7.
The Opéra Bastille, opened in 1989, has been controversial for several reasons: the cost, the scale, the architecture, the opera productions. Some thought it a stroke of genius to implant a high-culture edifice

Futuristic footbath at **la Villette** (*see p112* **Meaty culture at la Villette**)

in a working-class area; others thought it typical Mitterrand skulduggery; still others found it patronising. Recent attention has centred on the building itself: netting was put up to stop granite slabs falling, suggesting major repairs are already needed. Although intended as an 'opera for the people', that never really happened; opera and ballet are now shared with the Palais Garnier. (*See chapters* **Dance** and **Music: Classical & Opera**.)

Place de la Bastille

4th/11th/12th. Mº Bastille. **Map** p407 M7.

Nothing remains of the infamous prison which, on 14 July 1789, was stormed by the forces of the plebeian revolt. Though only a handful of prisoners remained, the event provided the rebels with gunpowder, and gave the insurrection momentum. It remains the eternal symbol of the Revolution, celebrated here with a lively street *bal* every 13 July. The prison was quickly torn down, its stones used to build Pont de la Concorde. Vestiges of the foundations can be seen in the Métro; there's part of a reconstructed tower at square Henri-Galli, near Pont de Sully (4th). The Colonne de Juillet, topped by a gilded *génie* of Liberty, is a monument to Parisians killed in the revolutions of July 1830 and 1848.

South of the Bastille

A relatively new attraction here is the **Viaduc des Arts**, a former railway viaduct now containing craft and design boutiques. Atop the viaduct, the **Promenade Plantée** (*see* **Paris Walks: Right Bank refresher,** *p 107*) continues through the Jardin de Reuilly and east to the **Bois de Vincennes**. Further along, avenue Daumesnil is fast becoming a Silicon Valley of computer outlets. At No 186, Eglise du St-Esprit is a curious 1920s concrete copy of the Hagia Sophia in Istanbul. At No 293 the under-appreciated **Musée des Arts d'Afrique et d'Océanie** (*see chapter* **Museums**) contains fantastic tribal art and an aquarium.

It's hard to believe now that, as late as the 1980s, wine was still unloaded off barges at Bercy. This stretch of the Seine is firmly part of redeveloped Paris with the massive Ministère de l'Economie et du Budget and the Palais Omnisports de Paris-Bercy. The ill-fated but dramatic American Center, designed by Frank Gehry, overlooks the Parc de Bercy and the Bercy expo centre. At the eastern edge of the park, in striking contrast to the modern Ciné Cité multiplex, is Bercy Village. Forty-two *chais,* or brick wine warehouses, have been cleaned up and reopened as wine bars and cafés; the result is certainly lively, if somewhat antiseptic. Particularly popular is Club Med World, where the themed bars and juggling barmen are intended to make you think of your next sunshine escape. A further group has been converted as the Pavillons de Bercy, containing the Musée des Arts Forains collection of fairground music and Venetian carnival salons (open to groups by appointment 01.43.40.16.22).

Bois de Vincennes

12th. M° Porte-Dorée or Château de Vincennes.
This is Paris' biggest park. Boats can be hired on
the lake, there are cycle paths, a Buddhist temple, a
racetrack, baseball pitch and flower gardens. It also
contains Paris' main **Zoo** and the **Cartoucherie**
theatre complex. The **Parc Floral de Paris**
(01.43.43.92.95) has horticultural displays, free summer jazz and classical festivals, a picnic area, exhibition space, children's amusements and crazy golf.
Next to the park is the imposing **Château de
Vincennes**, where England's Henry V died in 1422.

Parc de Bercy

rue de Bercy, 12th. M° Bercy or Cour St-Emilion.
Map p407 N9.
On the site of the Bercy warehouses across the river
from the new library, Bercy combines the French
love of geometry with that of food. There's a large
lawn crossed by paths with trees and pergolas and
a grid with square rose, herb and vegetable plots, an
orchard and gardens representing the four seasons.

Le Viaduc des Arts

*15-121 av Daumesnil, 12th (www.viaduc-des-
arts.com). M° Ledru-Rollin or Gare de Lyon.*
Map p407 M8.
Under the arches of a disused railway viaduct, chic
glass-fronted workshops now provide a showroom
for designers and craftspeople. The variety is
fascinating: from contemporary furniture designers
to picture frame gilders, tapestry restorers, porcelain decorators, architectural salvage and a French
hunting horn maker, as well as design gallery VIA
and the late-opening Viaduc Café.

The Champs-Elysées & west

In the 8th, 16th and 17th arrondissements.
The 'Elysian Fields' can be a disappointment
on first, tourist-filled sight, but the avenue
remains the symbolic gathering place of a
nation – for any sporting victory, New Year
or 14 July celebration. After many years'
domination by burger bars, over-priced cafés,
car showrooms and shopping malls, the
Champs-Elysées has gone through an
astonishing renaissance. One of Jacques
Chirac's worthier mayoral efforts was a major
facelift here, with new underground car parks
and smart granite paving. Upmarket shops and
hotels have moved back in the past couple of
years, including branches of Louis Vuitton,
Fnac, the Ladurée tearoom and Marriott hotel,
while a flock of stylish restaurants, such as
Spoon Food & Wine, Man Ray, **Rue Balzac**
and Lô Sushi have drawn a fashionable, and
affluent, crowd back to the surrounding streets.
Most recently, Renault, a long-time resident, has
upped the stakes with its new L'Atelier Renault,

incorporating a super-chic bar and restaurant
within its showroom. At night there is an
impressive vista stretching from floodlit place
de la Concorde to the Arc de Triomphe, with the
crowds lining up for the glitzy **Lido** cabaret,
Queen nightclub and various cinemas.

The great spine of western Paris started life
as an extension to the Tuileries gardens, laid
out by Le Nôtre in the 17th century. By the
Revolution, the avenue had been laid along its
full stretch, but was more a place for a Sunday
stroll than a thoroughfare. Shortly before the
Revolution the local guard worried that its dark
corners offered 'to libertines and people of bad
intentions a refuge that they can abuse'.

It was during the Second Empire that the
Champs-Elysées became a focus of fashionable
society, military parades and royal processions.
Bismarck was so impressed when he arrived
with the conquering Prussian army in 1871 that
he had a replica, the Kurfürstendamm, built in
Berlin. Smart residences and hotels sprung up
along its upper half, together with street lights,
pavements, sideshows, concert halls, theatres
and exhibition centres. The Prussian army in
1871 and Hitler's troops in 1940 both made a
point of marching down it, on both occasions

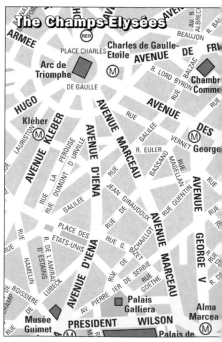

Sightseeing

to a silently hostile reception; but loud celebrations accompanied the allies' victory march along the avenue in 1944.

South of the avenue, the glass-domed **Grand Palais** and **Petit Palais**, both built for the 1900 *Exposition Universelle* and still used for major shows, create an impressive vista across elaborate Pont Alexandre III to Les Invalides. The rear wing of the Grand Palais opening on to avenue Franklin D Roosevelt contains the **Palais de la Découverte** (*see chapter* **Museums**), a fun science museum that's a hit with children. Look out for the statues of Churchill and de Gaulle: Winnie's butcher-than-thou, and Charlie's shows him getting in touch with his feminine side (*see p100* **Wass up, Chuck?**).

To the north are smart shops and officialdom. On circular place Beauvau a gateway leads to the Ministry of the Interior. The 18th-century Palais de l'Elysée, the official presidential residence, is situated at 55-57 rue du Fbg-St-Honoré. Nearby are the equally palatial British Embassy and adjoining ambassadorial residence, once the Hôtel Borghèse.

The lower, landscaped reach of the avenue hides two theatres and haute cuisine restaurants, Laurent and Ledoyen, in fancy

Terrific without traffic: the **Champs-Elysées** in a quiet moment.

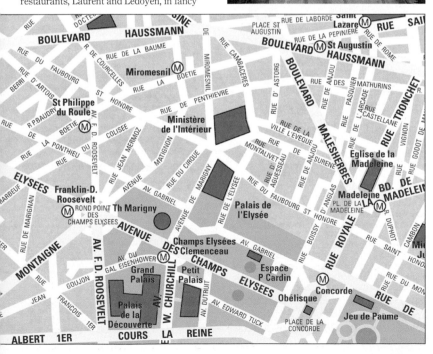

Napoléon III pavilions. At the Rond-Point des Champs-Elysées, Nos 7 and 9 give some idea of the splendid mansions that once lined the avenue. From here, the dress code leaps a few notches as avenue Montaigne reels off its array of fashion houses: Christian Dior, Chanel, Prada, Jil Sander, Loewe, Céline, Ungaro, Calvin Klein and more. Don't miss the lavish **Plaza Athénée** hotel and Auguste Perret's innovative 1911-13 **Théâtre des Champs-Elysées** concert hall topped by the fashionable Maison Blanche restaurant.

At the western end, the **Arc de Triomphe** towers above place Charles de Gaulle, better known as l'Etoile. Begun to glorify Napoléon, the giant triumphal arch was modified after his disgrace to celebrate the armies of the Revolution. The place was commissioned later by Haussmann and most of its facades are well preserved. From the top, look down on great swathes of prize Paris real estate: the swanky mansions along the grassy verges of the avenue Foch – the city's widest street – or the prestige office buildings of avenues Hoche and Wagram.

Arc de Triomphe

pl Charles-de-Gaulle (access via underground passage), 8th (01.55.37.73.77). M° Charles de Gaulle-Etoile. **Open** Apr-Oct 9.30am-11pm daily. Nov-Mar 10am-10.30pm daily. Closed public holidays. **Admission** €6.10; €4.90 18-25s; free under-18s. **Credit** MC, V. **Map** p400 C3.
The Arc de Triomphe forms the centrepiece of Paris' grand east-west axis from the Louvre, through the Arc du Carrousel and place de la Concorde up to the Grande Arche de la Défense. The Arc is 50m tall, 45m wide and decorated with a giant frieze of battle scenes and sculptures, including Rude's *Le Départ des Volontaires*, also known as *La Marseillaise*. Commissioned by Napoléon in 1806 as a tribute to his own military victories, the arch was completed only in 1836. In 1920 the Tomb of the Unknown Soldier was laid at the arch's base and an eternal flame burns to commemorate the dead of World Wars I and II. The manic drivers turn the place into a race track, but fortunately there is a subway. From the top, there's a wonderful view of the 12 avenues spreading out from l'Etoile.

Grand Palais

av Winston-Churchill, av du Général-Eisenhower, 8th (01.44.13.17.17/01.44.13.17.30). M° Champs-Elysées-Clemenceau. **Map** p401 E5.
Built for the 1900 *Exposition Universelle*, the Grand Palais was the work of three different architects, each of whom designed a facade – which goes some way to explain its extravagantly eclectic style. The famous golden horses are currently being restored, part of a major programme of work that will keep the building closed until 2005, when it will continue its role as a venue for international exhibitions. (*See chapter* **Museums**).

Petit Palais

av Winston-Churchill, 8th (01.42.65.12.73). M° Champs-Elysées-Clemenceau. **Map** p401 E5.
This was also built for the 1900 *Exposition Universelle*, only here the style is rather more charmingly Rococo. The Petit Palais closed in February 2001 for interior renovations which are estimated to last two years; some of the medieval exhibits are displayed in the Louvre.

Monceau & Batignolles

At the far end of avenue Hoche is intimate Parc Monceau (main entrance bd de Courcelles), with its neo-Antique follies and large lily pond. The park is usually full of neatly dressed children and nannies, and surrounded by some of the most costly apartments in Paris, part of the planned late 19th-century expansion of the city over the *plaine* Monceau. There are three museums which give an idea of the extravagance of the area when it was newly fashionable. These are **Musée Jacquemart-André** on boulevard Haussmann, **Musée Nissim de Camondo** (18th-century decorative arts) and **Musée Cernushi** (Chinese art). (*See chapter* **Museums**.) There are some nice exotic touches, such as the unlikely red lacquer Galerie Ching Tsai Too (48 rue de Courcelles, 8th), near the fancy wrought-iron gates of Parc Monceau, or the onion domes of the Russian Orthodox **Alexander Nevsky Cathedral** on rue Daru. Built in the mid 19th century when a sojourn in Paris was an essential part of the education of every Russian aristocrat, it is still at the heart of an emigré little Russia.

Famed for its stand during the Paris Commune, the Quartier des Batignolles to the northeast is much more working class, with the lively rue de Lévis street market, tenements overlooking the deep railway canyon and the attractive square des Batignolles park with its pretty church overlooking a small semi-circular *place*.

Alexander Nevsky Cathedral

12 rue Daru, 8th (01.42.27.37.34). M° Courcelles. **Open** 3-5pm Tue, Fri, Sun. **Map** p400 D3.
The edifice has enough onion domes, icons and incense to make you think you were in Moscow. This Russian Orthodox church was built 1859-61 in the neo-Byzantine Novgorod-style of the 1600s, on a Greek-cross plan by the Tsar's architect Kouzmine, architect of the St-Petersburg Beaux-Arts Academy. Services, on Sunday mornings and Orthodox saints' days, are in Russian.

Cimetière des Batignolles

rue St-Just, 17th (01.53.06.38.68). M° Porte de Clichy. **Open** 8am-6pm Mon-Fri, 9am-6pm Sat-Sun, Oct-Apr; 8.30am-5.30pm Sat; 9am-5.30pm Nov-Mar; 8am-5.45pm Mon-Fri; 8.30am-5.45pm Sat; 9am-5.45pm Sun Apr-Sept.

The Tomb of the Unknown
Soldier at the **Arc de Triomphe**.

Stony faced at the **Palais de Chaillot**.

Squeezed between the Périphérique and the boulevard des Amiraux lie the graves of poet Paul Verlaine, Surrealist André Breton and Léon Bakst, costume designer of the Ballets Russes.

Trocadéro

South of the Arc de Triomphe, avenue Kléber leads to the monumental buildings and terraced gardens of the Trocadéro, with spectacular views over the river to the Eiffel Tower. The vast symmetrical 1930s **Palais de Chaillot** dominates the hill and houses four museums and the Théâtre National de Chaillot. Across place du Trocadéro is the small **Cimetière de Passy**. The Trocadéro gardens below are a little dilapidated, but the bronze and stone statues showered by powerful fountains form a spectacular ensemble with the Eiffel Tower and Champ de Mars across the river.

The slightly dead area behind Trocadéro holds a few surprises. Hidden among the shops on avenue Victor-Hugo, behind a conventional-looking apartment block, is No 111, the Galerie Commerciale Argentine, a brick and cast-iron apartment block and shopping arcade, now mostly empty, designed by ever-experimental Henri Sauvage and Charles Sarazin in 1904.

Cimetière de Passy

2 rue du Commandant-Schloesig, 16th (01.47.27.51.42/www.findagrave.com). M° Trocadéro. **Open** 8am-5.14pm Mon-Fri; 8.30am-5.45pm Sat; 9am-5.45pm Sun. **Map** p400 B5.
Since 1874 this has been considered one of the most

elegant places in Paris to be laid to rest. Maybe only Parisians could take an interest in matters of after-death chic. Tombs here include those of composers Debussy and Fauré, painters Manet and his sister-in-law Berthe Morisot, designer Ruhlmann and writer Giraudoux, as well as numerous generals and politicians.

Palais de Chaillot

pl du Trocadéro, 16th. M° Trocadéro. **Map** p400 C5.
Looming across the river from the Eiffel Tower, the immense pseudo-classical Palais de Chaillot was built by Azéma, Boileau and Carlu for the 1937 international exhibition and actually stands on the foundations of an earlier complex put up for the 1878 World Fair. It is home to the **Musée de la Marine** (dedicated to marine and naval history) and the **Musée de l'Homme** (ethnology, anthropology, human biology) in the western wing. The ex-**Musée des Monuments Historiques**, which used to be housed in the eastern wing, is due to reappear in 2003 as Cité de l'Architecture. The **Théâtre National de Chaillot** still lurks cosily in the eastern wing.

Passy & Auteuil

West of l'Etoile, most of the 16th *arrondissement* is pearls-and-poodle country, dotted with curios, avant-garde architecture and classy shops.

When Balzac lived at 47 rue Raynouard (now **La Maison de Balzac**), Passy was a country village where people came to take cures for anaemia at its mineral springs – a name reflected in the rue des Eaux. Nearby the **Musée du Vin** is of interest for its location in the cellars of a wine-producing monastery destroyed in the Revolution. Passy was absorbed into the city in 1860 and today is full of smart Haussmannian apartment blocks but readily available building land also meant that Passy and adjoining Auteuil were prime territory for experimental architecture.

West of the Jardins du Ranelagh (originally high-society pleasure gardens, modelled on the bawdy 18th-century London version) is the **Musée Marmottan**, which features a fabulous collection of Monet's late water lily canvases, other Impressionists and Empire furniture (*see chapter* **Museums**).

Next to the Pont de Grenelle is **Maison de Radio-France**, the giant Orwellian home to the state broadcasting bureaucracy opened in 1963. You can attend concerts or take guided tours (*see chapters* **Museums** *and* **Music: Classical & Opera**) round its endless corridors; employees nickname the place 'Alphaville' after the Godard film.

From here, in upmarket Auteuil, go up rue Fontaine, the best place for specimens of art

Paris Walks: Right Bank refresher

Even the most beautiful city can produce mild cases of burnout. Partying, shopping and prolonged exposure to high culture can leave the chi channels blocked. This Right Bank refresher is a 20-minute constitutional, aimed at chilling you out, taking you that crucial one beat back in tempo from the rest of the city, so that you can rejoin the fray revitalised. (It's a straight-liner, so minimal map reading skills are required.)

Start at Métro Bastille, which is served by lines 5, 8 and 10. Emerge on to place de la Bastille and walk around the front of the Opéra Bastille on rue de Lyon. Take avenue Daumesnil on your left. After a couple of paces, you'll reach some steps (clearly marked Promenade Plantée), 44 in total; here's your cardiovascular exercise for the day. Upstairs you'll be walking along the top of a former railway line that has been transformed into an inner-city haven. This is the Promenade Plantée.

As you go through the double wrought-iron green archways, the roses, trees and shrubs will bring an immediate sensation of peace. And, as you progress, looking to your right, you'll soon see that you can gaze directly into some very chic apartments. The people who

rustling, and butterflies dancing on the air, the effect is magical.

At the end of the promenade you'll find two ponds and a conglomeration of lavender bushes, leading you directly into the Jardin de Reuilly. This park presents you with tiers of greenery and flowerbeds layered in explosions of colour, along with a beautiful waterfall. Curving over the park is a wooden bridge. This crossing point seems to have been designed for people-watching: you can stand on it and observe activities unfold or rest beneath it on a hot day and let peace descend around you.

live in them are used to passers-by, and they tend to go about their business regardless of voyeurs, so prepare to glimpse Parisian domestic life in the raw. Another advantage of being a little way up is that you can stop to inspect delightful architectural flourishes on windows and corners of buildings that you just wouldn't see at ground level.

Every few yards you'll pass through green arches covered in plant life. Pausing beneath them gives an impression of being under a completely green canopy, and if there happens to be a breeze to set the leaves

A knee's up in the **Bois de Boulogne**.

nouveau architecture by Hector Guimard. Despite extravagant iron balconies, **Castel Béranger** at No 14 was originally low-rent lodgings; Guimard designed outside and in, right down to the wallpaper and stoves. He also designed the less-ambitious Nos 19, 21 and tiny Café Antoine at No 17.

The area around Métro Jasmin is the place to pay homage to the area's other prominent architect, Le Corbusier. The **Fondation Le Corbusier** occupies two of his avant-garde houses in the square du Dr-Blanche, while a little further up rue du Dr-Blanche, rue Mallet-Stevens is almost entirely made up of refined houses by Robert Mallet-Stevens. Most have been rather altered, but one has a fantastic stained glass stairwell.

West of the 16th, across the Périphérique, sprawls the **Bois de Boulogne**, a royal hunting reserve turned park.

Bois de Boulogne

16th (www.boisdeboulogne.com), M° Porte-Dauphine or Les Sablons.
Covering 865 hectares, the Bois was the ancient hunting Forêt de Rouvray. A series of gardens with scrubby woodland, cut through by roads and footpaths, it was landscaped in the 1860s when grottoes and cascades were created around the Lac Inférieur, where you can hire rowing boats in summer. The Jardins de Bagatelle (route de Sèvres à Neuilly, 16th/ 01.40.67.97.00/open 9am-5.30pm summer), surrounding a château that belonged to the Marquis de Hertford, are famous for their roses, daffodils and water lilies. The **Jardin d'Acclimatation** is a children's amusement park. The Bois has two race-

courses (Longchamp and Auteuil), sports clubs, the **Musée National des Arts et Traditions Populaires** and a restaurant. Packed at weekends with dog walkers, picnickers and joggers, despite clean-up attempts it remains seedy at night.

Castel Béranger

14 rue La Fontaine, 16th. M° Jasmin. Closed to the public. **Map** p404 A7.
Guimard's masterpiece of 1895-98 is the building that epitomises art nouveau in Paris. Guimard sought not just a new aesthetic but also explored new materials. Here you can see his love of brick and wrought-iron, asymmetry and renunciation of harsh angles not found in nature. Along with the whiplash motifs characteristic of art nouveau, there are still many signs of Guimard's earlier taste for fantasy and the medieval. Green seahorses climb up the facade and the faces on the balconies are supposedly a self portrait, inspired by Japanese figures to ward off evil spirits.

Fondation Le Corbusier

Villa La Roche, 10 square du Dr-Blanche, 16th (01.42.88.41.53/www.fondationcorbusier.asso.fr). M° Jasmin. **Open** 10am-12.30pm, 1.30-6pm Mon-Thur (library 1.30-6pm); 10am-12.30pm, 1.30am-5pm Fri. Closed Aug. **Admission** €2.30; €1.60 students.
This house, designed by Le Corbusier in 1923 for a Swiss art collector, shows the visionary architect's ideas in practice, in drawings, paintings, sculpture and furniture. Adjoining Villa Jeanneret – also by Le Corbusier – houses the Foundation's library.

Les Serres d'Auteuil

3 av de la Porte d'Auteuil, 16th (01.40.71.75.23). M° Porte d'Auteuil. **Open** 10am-6pm (summer); 10am-6pm (winter). **Admission** €0.80.
Occasional guided tours in French and English. **No credit cards.**
These romantic glasshouses were opened in 1895 to cultivate plants for Parisian parks and public spaces. Today there are seasonal displays of orchids and begonias. Best of all is the steamy tropical central pavilion with palm trees, birds and a pool of Japanese ornamental carp.

Montmartre & Pigalle

Mainly in the 9th and 18th arrondissements.
Montmartre, away to the north on the tallest hill in the city, is the most unabashedly romantic district of Paris. Despite the onslaught of tourists who throng Sacré-Coeur and place du Tertre, it's surprisingly easy to get away from the main drag. Climb and descend quiet stairways, peer into little alleys and deserted squares or explore streets like rue des Abbesses, with its young, arty community.

For centuries, Montmartre was a quiet, windmill-packed village. As Haussmann sliced through the city centre, working-class families began to move out in search of accommodation and peasant migrants poured into industrialising Paris from across France. The hill was absorbed into Paris in 1860, but remained fiercely independent. In 1871, after the signing of an armistice with Prussia, the new right-wing French government sought to disarm the local National Guard by taking away its cannons installed in Montmartre. An angry crowd led by teacher and radical heroine Louise Michels drove off the government troops, killing two generals and taking over the guns, thus starting the Paris Commune, commemorated by a plaque on rue du Chevalier-de-la-Barre.

From the 1880s artists moved in to the area. Toulouse-Lautrec patronised Montmartre's bars and immortalised its cabarets in his posters; later it was frequented by artists of the Ecole de Paris, Utrillo and Modigliani.

The best starting point is the Abbesses Métro, one of only two in the city (along with Porte Dauphine) to retain its original art nouveau glass awning designed by Hector Guimard. Across place des Abbesses as you emerge from the station is the art nouveau church of St-Jean de Montmartre, with its turquoise mosaics around the door. Along rue des Abbesses and adjoining rue Lepic, which winds its way up the *butte* (hill), are many excellent food shops, wine merchants, busy cafés, including the heaving Sancerre, and offbeat boutiques. Along impasse Marie-Blanche there's a strange neo-Gothic house. The famous Studio 28 cinema, opened in 1928, is on rue Tholozé. Buñuel's *L'Age d'Or* had a riotous première here in 1930; you can still see footprints made by him and Cocteau in the foyer.

In the other direction from Abbesses, at 11 rue Yvonne-Le-Tac, is the Chapelle du Martyr where, according to legend, St Denis picked up his head after his execution by the Romans in the third century. Montmartre means 'hill of the martyr' in his memory, but its original derivation is probably from temples to Mars and Mercury in Roman times.

Around the corner, the cafés of rue des Trois Frères are popular for an evening drink. The street leads into place Emile-Goudeau, whose staircases, wrought-iron street lights and old houses are particularly evocative, as is the unspoiled bar **Chez Camille**. At No 13 stood the Bateau Lavoir. Once a piano factory, it was divided in the 1890s into a warren of studios where artists lived in penury, among them Braque, Picasso and Juan Gris. Among the ground-breaking works of art created here was Picasso's *Demoiselles d'Avignon*. The building burned down in 1970, but its replacement still rents out space to artists. Further up the hill on rue Lepic are the village's two remaining windmills. The Moulin du Radet was moved

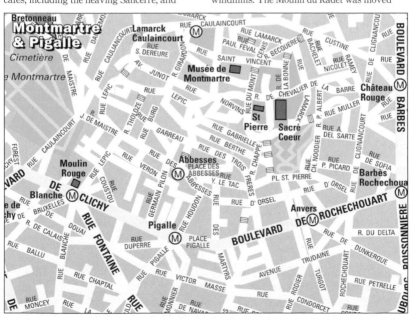

here in the 17th century from its hillock in rue des Moulins near the Palais-Royal. The Moulin de la Galette, made famous by Renoir's painting, is a replica now topping a restaurant.

On top of the hill, the area round place du Tertre is all that's worst about Montmartre. Dozens of so-called artists compete to sketch your portrait or try to flog lurid sunset views of Paris; **Espace Dalí** on rue Poulbot offers a slighly more illustrious alternative. The streets are packed with souvenir shops and tacky restaurants. According to legend it was here that the French '*bistro*' has its origins – from the occupying Russian soldiers who demanded to be served 'quickly' in their native tongue.

Just off the square is the oldest church in the district, St-Pierre-de-Montmartre, whose columns have grown bent with age. Founded by Louis VI in 1133, it is a fine example of early Gothic, and a striking contrast to its extravagant neighbour and Montmartre's most prominent landmark, **Sacré-Coeur**, standing on the highest point in the city. If you are climbing up from square Willette, avoid the main steps and try the less-crowded steps of rue Foyalter or rue Maurice-Utrillo on either side.

On the north side of place du Tertre in rue Cortot is the quiet manor housing the **Musée de Montmartre**, devoted to the area and its former inhabitants, with original Toulouse-Lautrec posters. Dufy, Renoir and Utrillo all had studios here. Nearby in rue des Saules is the Montmartre **vineyard**, planted in 1933 in memory of the vineyards that covered the hillside ever since the Gallo-Roman period. The grape-picking each autumn is an annual ritual (*see chapter* **Paris by Season**). As for the wine itself, a local song proclaims that for every glass you drink, you pee twice as much out.

Further down the hill amid rustic, shuttered houses is the Lapin Agile cabaret at 22 rue des Saules, another legendary meeting point for Montmartre artists which is still going strong today. A series of pretty squares leads to rue Caulaincourt, towards the **Cimetière de Montmartre**, a curiously romantic place. Winding down the back of the hill, the wide avenue Junot is lined with exclusive houses, among them the one built by Adolf Loos for Dadaist poet Tristan Tzara at No 15, a monument of modernist architecture.

Cimetière de Montmartre

20 av Rachel, access by stairs from rue Caulaincourt, 18th (01.43.87.64.24/www.findagrave.com).
M° Blanche. **Open** 8am-6pm Mon-Sat; 9am-6pm Sun (summer); 8am-5.30pm Mon-Sat; 9am-5.30pm Sun (winter). **Map** p401 G1.

Here you will find the graves of Sacha Guitry, Truffaut, Nijinsky, Berlioz, Degas, Greuze, Offenbach, Feydeau, Dumas *fils* and German poet Heine, reflecting the area's theatrical and artistic past. There's also La Goulue, whose real name was Louise Weber, first great star of the cancan and model for Toulouse-Lautrec, celebrated beauty Mme Récamier and the consumptive heroine Alphonsine Plessis, inspiration for Dumas' *La Dame aux Camélias* and Verdi's *La Traviata*. Mementoes are still left daily for Egyptian pop diva Dalida.

Sacré-Coeur

35 rue du Chevalier-de-la-Barre, 18th (01.53.41.89.00). M° Abbesses or Anvers. **Open** Crypt/dome 6am-10.30pm daily. **Admission** Crypt and dome €4.60; €2.45 6-16s, students; free under-6s. **No credit cards. Map** p402 J1.

The sugar-white dome is one of the most visible landmarks in Paris. Begun as an act of penance after the nation's defeat by the Prussians in 1870, Sacré-Coeur wasn't finished until 1914; consecration was finally in 1919. A jumble of architects worked on the mock Romano-Byzantine edifice. The view from the dome is breathtaking.

Pigalle

Straddling the 9th and 18th *arrondissements*, Pigalle has long been the sleaze centre of Paris. By the end of the 19th century, of the 58 houses on rue des Martyrs, 25 were cabarets (a few such as Michou and Madame Arthur remain today); others were dubious hotels used for

---

Don't miss Boney's braggadocio

Eglise de la Madeleine
Just a little pseudo-Grecian temple (*see p88*).

Arc de Triomphe
The boy done good at Austerlitz (*see p104*).

Arc de Triomphe du Carrousel
Pretty, pink. Pretentious, moi? (*see p78*).

Place Vendôme column
If it's good enough for Nelson... (*see p82*).

Pont d'Iéna
To Prussia, with love (*see p72*).

Père Lachaise
Dig this: Boney built the boneyard (*see p115*).

Montmartre takes on an eerie hue after dark.

illicit liaisons. The **Moulin Rouge**, once the image of naughty *fin-de-siècle* Paris, has become a cheesy tourist draw. Its befeathered dancers still cancan across the stage but are no substitute for La Goulue and Joseph Pujol – the *pétomane* who could pass wind melodically.

This brash area has recently become a trendy night spot. The Moulin Rouge's old restaurant has become the **MCM Café**, while the **Folies Pigalle** cabaret is a hip club. What was once the Divan Japonais, depicted by Toulouse-Lautrec, has been transformed into **Le Divan du Monde**, a nightclub and music venue, while the old **Elysée Montmartre** music hall puts on an eclectic array of one-nighters.

La Nouvelle Athènes

Just south of Montmartre and bordered by the slightly seedy area around Gare St-Lazare (*see above*, **Quartier de l'Europe**) lies this mysterious, often overlooked *quartier* once beloved of artists and artistes of the Romantic era. Long-forgotten actresses and *demi-mondaines* had bijoux mansions built there. Some of the prettiest can be found in tiny rue de la Tour-des-Dames, which refers to one of the many windmills owned by the once-prosperous Couvent des Abbesses. The windmill stood until 1822; by then superstars such as the legendary Mlle Mars had moved in. She had a splendid place built at No 1, replete with

skylight and deliciously lurid fake marble, which can be glimpsed through the glass door. Well-known academic painters Horace Vernet and Paul Delaroche also had houses built here. Wander through the adjoining streets and passageways to catch further angles of these miniature palaces and late 18th-century *hôtels particuliers*, especially on rue de La Rochefoucauld.

The area round the neo-Classical Eglise Notre-Dame-de-Lorette, which includes rue Taitbout, haunt of Balzac's fallen heroine in *Splendeurs et Misères des Courtisanes*, was built up in Louis-Philippe's reign and famous for its courtesans, known as *lorettes*. From 1844 to 1857, Delacroix had his studio at 58 rue Notre-Dame-de-Lorette (next to the house, at No 56, where Gauguin was born in 1848). The painter later moved to place de Furstenberg in the 6th *arrondissement* (now Musée Delacroix).

Just off rue Taitbout stands square d'Orléans, a remarkable housing estate built in 1829 by English architect Edward Cresy. This ensemble of flats and artists' studios attracted the glitterati of the day, including Taglioni, Pauline Viardot, George Sand and her lover Chopin. The couple each had first-floor flats and could wave at each other from their respective drawing rooms. The **Musée de la Vie Romantique** (*see chapter* **Museums**) in nearby rue Chaptal displays the writer's mementoes in a perfect setting. Take in place Gustave-Toudouze, with pleasant tearoom Thé folies, and glorious circular place St-Georges, home to the true Empress of Napoléon III's Paris, the notorious Païva, who lived in the neo-Renaissance No 28, thought outrageous at the time of its construction (before she moved to an equally extravagant house on the Champs-Elysées).

The **Musée Gustave Moreau**, meanwhile, is grounds alone for a visit. Originally the artist's studio, it was actually planned by him to become a museum to house several thousand works that he bequeathed to the nation. Fragments of *la bohème* can still be gleaned in the area, though the Café La Roche, where Moreau met Degas for drinks and rows, has been downsized to the forgettable La Jaconde on the corner of rues de La Rochefoucault and La Bruyère. Degas painted most of his memorable ballet scenes round the corner in rue Frochot and Renoir hired his first decent studio at 35 rue St-Georges. A few streets away in

Cité Pigalle, a charming collection of studios, stands Van Gogh's last Paris house (No 5), from where he moved to Auvers-sur-Oise. There is a plaque here, but nothing on the building in rue Pigalle where Toulouse-Lautrec drank himself to death in 1903.

La Goutte d'Or

For a very different experience, head for Barbès-Rochechouart Métro station and the area north of it. In Zola's day this was (and it still is) one of the poorest working-class districts in the city. Zola used it as a backdrop for *L'Assommoir*, his novel set among the district's laundries and absinthe cafés.

Now it is primarily an African and Arab neighbourhood, and it can seem like a colourful slice of Africa or a state under constant police siege, with frequent sweeps on *sans-papiers* (illegal immigrants or those without

Meaty culture at La Villette

If you had 50 hectares of land that used to house France's national meat market and abattoir going spare and a billion francs of taxpayers' money, what would you do with it? Create an urban space made up of abstract structures in a design that expressly challenged the common conception of a park as a mere open space of greenery? Theme that space as a catalyst for cultural democratisation, the kind of place where art and society hold a dialogue?

You would? Funnily, enough, that's exactly what they did at parc de la Villette. The Park is now established as a leading cultural centre. Before its conception everybody associated north-east Paris with one thing – industry. This project took shape in the 1970s, after the final cow was slaughtered.

La Villette attracts an average of four million visitors per year, despite – or thanks to – its off-beat vibe. Throwing together a mish-mash of art and culture to create a disjointed experience was the key aim of the park's designer, Swiss architect Bernard Tschumi; he scored a bullseye there. A walk in this park is no, er, mere walk in the park. A wander round exposes your receptors to rap, experimental classical music, bits of bikes sunk into concrete, obscure art, heavy metal, space cinema, huge funnels that produce weird noises and technological psychedelia. There are even green areas with that could conceivably pass as a park.

Although La Villette is host to film and music festivals, the four structural jewels in

its crown are **la Cité de la Musique, la Cité des Sciences, la Géode** and **Le Zénith**. Every variety of pop music gig takes place here, but the Zénith (with an audience capacity of over 6,000) is best known as the centre of the Paris' thriving rap scene. La Géode is a hemispherical cinema whose polished metallic exterior acts as a giant mirror of its surroundings: this can make for some cloud-bending vistas. Inside you can see natural-science films on a giant hemispheric screen. Things take a more rigidly scientific – but no less impressive – turn at la Cité des Sciences et de l'Industrie, a technology museum identification papers). Down rue Doudeauville, you'll find African music shops, rue Polonceau has African grocers and Senegalese restaurant Chez Aïda, while Square Léon is the focus for la Goutte d'Or en Fête every June, which tries to harness some of the local talent. Some bands, such as Africando and the Orchestre National de Barbès, have become well known across Paris. There is a lively street market under the Métro tracks (Mon, Wed, Sat morning), with stalls of exotic vegetables and rolls of African fabrics. From here rue d'Orsel leads back to Montmartre via **Marché St-Pierre**. The covered market hall is now used for exhibitions of naïve art, but in the street, outlets such as Dreyfus and Moline vie with discount fabrics.

On the northern edge of the city at Porte de Clignancourt is Paris' largest flea market, the **Marché aux Puces de St-Ouen** (*see chapter* **Shops & Services**).

housed in a stunning renovation of a slaughterhouse building created by Adrien Fainsilber. This showroom of all things scientific opened, with sublime timing, at the very moment in March 1986 when Halley's Comet was passing by. That's style.

La Cité de la Musique is another astonishing building, this time designed by Christian de Portzamparc. As well as staging a varied repertoire of concerts, it houses a multi-media centre and a museum of music including a vast collection of antique instruments.

North-east Paris

In the 10th, 11th, 19th and 20th arrondissements.
The old working-class area north and east of République is in transformation, mixing pockets of charm with grotty or even dangerous areas. The main attraction is **Père Lachaise** cemetery. Ménilmontant, the area around it, and neighbour Belleville, once villages where Parisians escaped at weekends, were absorbed into the city in 1860.

Canal St-Martin to La Villette

Canal St-Martin, built 1805-25, begins at the Seine at Pont Morland, disappears underground at the Bastille, then re-emerges at rue du Faubourg-du-Temple east of place de la République. This stretch has the most charm, lined with shady trees and crossed by iron footbridges and locks. Most of the warehouses have closed, but the area is still semi-industrial and a bit shabby, with the odd barge puttering into view. Designers have begun snapping up old industrial premises and unusual bars including **Chez Prune** have multiplied.

You can take a boat up the canal between the Port de l'Arsenal and the Bassin de la Villette. Between the fifth and sixth locks at 101 quai de Jemmapes is the **Hôtel du Nord**, which inspired Marcel Carné's 1938 film. The hotel has reopened as a lively bar, used for Laughing Matters comedy evenings. East of here is the Hôpital St-Louis (main entrance rue Bichat), founded in 1607 to house plague victims and built as a series of isolated pavilions to stop disease spreading. A mishmash of buildings has been added to the original brick and stone pavilions, but an effort at restoration is now being made. Behind the hospital, the rue de la Grange-aux-Belles housed the infamous Montfaucon gibbet, built in 1233, where victims were hanged and left to the elements. Much of the area has been redeveloped, but today the street contains music cafés **Chez Adel** (No 10) and Apostrophe (No 23). Only the inconspicuous Le Pont Tournant, on the corner with quai de Jemmapes overlooking the swing bridge, still seems to hark back to canal days of old.

To the east is the Parti Communiste Français, on the place du Colonel-Fabien, a surrealistic, curved glass curtain raised off the ground on a concrete wing, built in 1968-71 by Brasilian architect Oscar Niemeyer with Paul Chemetov and Jean Deroche.

To the north, place de Stalingrad was landscaped in 1989 to expose the Rotonde de la Villette, one of Ledoux's grandiose toll houses which now houses exhibitions and

Sightseeing

archaeological finds. Here the canal widens into Bassin de la Villette, built for Napoléon in 1808, bordered by new housing developments, as well as some of the worst of 1960s and '70s housing. At the eastern end of the basin is an unusual 1885 hydraulic lifting bridge, the Pont de Crimée. Thursday and Sunday mornings inject some vitality with a canalside market, place de Joinville. East of here, the Canal de l'Ourcq (created in 1813 to provide drinking water, as well as for freight haulage) divides: Canal St-Denis runs north through St-Denis towards the Seine, Canal de l'Ourcq runs through La Villette and suburbs east. The area has been revitalised since the late 1980s by the **Cité des Sciences et de l'Industrie** science museum, the activity-filled postmodern **Parc de la Villette** and **Cité de la Musique** concert hall and music museum (*see* **Villette: parky, innit?**, *p114*).

Ménilmontant & Charonne

Once just a few houses on a hill where vines and fruit trees were cultivated, Mesnil-Montant (uphill farm) expanded with bistros, workers' housing, balls and bordellos. It became part of Paris in 1860 with Belleville, and has a similar history: workers' agitation, resistance in the

Commune, large immigrant population. Today it's a thriving centre of alternative Paris, as artists and young Parisians have moved in. Flanking boulevard de Ménilmontant, the **Cimetière du Père Lachaise** is generally thought to be the most illustrious burial site in Paris.

The area mixes 1960s and 70s monster (raving loony, in terms of their social effects) housing projects with older dwellings, some gentrified, some derelict. Below rue des Pyrénées, the Cité Leroy or Villa l'Ermitage are calm houses with gardens. At its junction with rue de Ménilmontant there is a bird's-eye view into the centre of town. Follow rue Julien-Lacroix to place Maurice-Chevalier and 19th-century Notre-Dame-de-la-Croix church.

For a restful glass, try Lou Pascalou (14 rue des Panoyaux), La Buvette (same street) or Le Soleil on the boulevard (No 136). While side streets still display male-only North African cafés, old *parigot* locals and half-bricked-up houses, the rue Oberkampf has had a meteoric rise. Five years ago the area consisted largely of grocers and bargain stores; now it is home to some of the city's hippest bars. The cutting edge may already be moving elsewhere, but international trendies have followed the artists and Le Mécano, Mercerie

Rue de Ménilmontant, a rue with a true Pompidou view.

and Scherkhan bars have succeeded the success of **Café Charbon** and **Le Cithéa** club. Offbeat art shows are put on at **Glassbox**, while a more cultural concentration has evolved on rue Boyer with the Maroquinerie literary café.

East of Père-Lachaise is Charonne, which joined Paris in 1859. The medieval Eglise St-Germain de Charonne, place St-Blaise, is the city's only church, apart from St-Pierre de Montmartre, still to have its own graveyard. The rest of Charonne, centred on rue St-Blaise, is a prettified backwater of quiet bars and bistros. Cross the Périphérique at Porte de Montreuil for the suburban **Puces de Montreuil** (*see chapter* **Shops & Services**), probably the most junky of the Paris fleamarkets.

Cimetière du Père Lachaise

main entrance bd de Ménilmontant, 20th (01.55.25.82.10). M° Père-Lachaise. **Open** 9am-5.30pm daily. **Map** p407 P5.

With thousands of tightly packed tombs arranged along cobbled lanes and tree-lined avenues, this is said to be the world's most visited cemetery. Named after the Jesuit Père de la Chaise, Louis XIV's confessor, it was laid out by the architect Brongniart in 1804. It was never meant to be 'just' a cemetery, and was designed as somewhere for talking a walk or having a quiet ponder. The presumed remains of medieval lovers Abélard and Héloïse were moved here in 1817, along with those of Molière and La Fontaine, in a bid to gain popularity for the site. Famous inhabitants soon multiplied: Sarah Bernhardt, Egyptologist Champollion (marked, appropriately, with an obelisk), Delacroix, Ingres, Bizet, Balzac, Proust, Chopin (his tomb is empty – his remains were returned to Poland), Colette and Piaf. Jim Morrison, buried here in 1971 (although the same type of person who claims that Elvis Presley is alive and holding knitting workshops in South Africa would maintain that Jim is knocking about alive and well on the Rimbaud trail), managed to resist eviction in 2000 and still attracts a flow of spaced-out pilgrims (*see* **Paris, city of lights out,** *pages 84-5*). Oscar Wilde's headstone, carved by Epstein, is a winged, naked, male angel which was considered so offensive that it was neutered by the head keeper, who showed generosity of spirit by using the offending member as a paper-weight. The Mur des Fédérés got its name after 147 members of the Paris Commune of 1871 were lined up and shot against it.

Belleville

This fashionable area was incorporated into the city in 1860 and became a work and leisure place for the poorer classes. Despite attempts to dissipate workers' agitation by splitting the former village between 11th, 19th and 20th

Altitude training in Parc de Belleville.

arrondissements, it was the centre of opposition to the Second Empire. Cabarets, artisans, and workers' housing typified *fin-de-siècle* Belleville.

On the boulevard de Belleville, Chinese and Vietnamese shops rub shoulders with Muslim and Kosher groceries, butchers and bakers, couscous and felafel eateries.

On the small streets off the rue de Belleville, old buildings hide courtyards and gardens. Rue Ramponneau mixes new housing and relics of old workers' Belleville. At No 23, down a crumbling alley, an old iron smithy has become La Forge, a squat for artists, many of whom are members of La Bellevilloise association, which is trying to save the area from redevelopment and preserve its original charm.

Up the avenue Simon Bolivar is the eccentric **Parc des Buttes-Chaumont**, one of the most attractive landscaping feats of Baron Haussmann's designers. East of the park, between place des Fêtes and place de Rhin et Danube, are a number of tiny, hilly streets lined with small houses and gardens that still look positively provincial.

Parc des Buttes-Chaumont

rue Botzaris, rue Manin, rue de Crimée, 19th. M° Buttes-Chaumont. **Map** p403 N3.

This wonderland is possibly the perfect meeting of nature and the artificial, with its meandering paths and vertical cliffs. It was designed by Haussmann in the 1860s on the distinctly unpromising site of a granite quarry, rubbish tip and public gibbit. With all that froth and mania safely in the past, waterfalls now cascade out of a man-made cave, which even has its own fake stalactites.

The Left Bank

Grab an eiffel of the monuments, spend a packet on a designer jacket or come over all existential in the café noir *quartiers* south of the Seine.

The Latin Quarter

In the 5th arrondissement.

This section of the Left Bank east of boulevard St-Michel is probably so named because students here spoke Latin until the Revolution. Another theory is that it alludes to the vestiges of Roman Lutétia, of which this area was the heart. The first two Roman streets were on the site of present-day rue St-Jacques (later the pilgrims' route to Compostella) and rue Cujas. The area still boasts many medieval streets, scholarly institutions and the city's most important Roman remains: the Cluny baths, now part of the **Musée National du Moyen Age**, and the **Arènes de Lutèce** amphitheatre.

Quartier de la Huchette

The boulevard St-Michel, at one time symbolic of student rebellion (*see p119* **May 68 & all that**), has been taken over by fast-food giants and downmarket shoe and clothes chains. You'll find more Greek restaurants and cafés than evidence of medieval learning down rue de la Huchette and rue de la Harpe. Look out for 18th-century wrought-iron balconies and carved masks on the latter street. Find, too, rue du Chat-Qui-Pêche, supposedly Paris' narrowest street, and rue de la Parcheminerie, named after the parchment sellers and copyists who once lived here. Sticking up amid the tourist paraphernalia is Paris' most charming medieval church, the **Eglise St-Séverin**, which has an exuberant Flamboyant Gothic interior.

Across the ancient rue St-Jacques is **Eglise St-Julien-le-Pauvre**, built as a resting place for pilgrims in the 12th century. The area still attracts a dedicated crowd: amid the over-hanging medieval buildings on rue Galande

Rocky Horror fans get their weekly fix at **Studio Galande** cinema.

By the river, back from the *bouquinistes*, or booksellers, lining the *quais*, expats congregate at second-hand English bookshop **Shakespeare & Co** (37 rue de la Bûcherie).

A medieval garden is the latest attraction at the **Musée National du Moyen Age – Thermes de Cluny**, across boulevard St-Germain. A Gothic mansion built over ruined Roman baths, the museum houses a magnificent collection of medieval art.

East of here place Maubert, now a morning marketplace (Tue, Thur, Sat), was used in the 16th century to burn books and hang Protestant heretics. The little streets between here and the *quais* are among the city's oldest. Rue de Bièvre charts the course of the river Bièvre, which flowed into the Seine in the Middle Ages. Religious foundations once abounded; remnants of the Collège des Bernardins can be seen in rue de Poissy. On quai de la Tournelle there's food for all budgets, from the illustrious **Tour d'Argent** (No 17) to the Tintin shrine *café-tabac* Le Rallye (No 11). Below, numerous houseboats are moored at a former dock for hay and wood.

Eglise St-Julien-le-Pauvre

rue St-Julien-le-Pauvre, 5th (01.43.54.52.16).
M° Cluny-La Sorbonne. **Open** 9.30am-noon, 3-6.30pm Mon-Sat; 9.30am-6.30pm Sun. **Map** p406 J7.
Formerly a sanctuary for pilgrims en route for Compostella, the present church dates from the late 12th century. Originally part of a priory, it became the university church when colleges left Notre-Dame for the Left Bank. Since 1889 it has been used by the Greek Melchite church. Ignore the poorly maintained exterior; the interior is well worth a visit. One of the trees in the garden is said to be the oldest in Paris.

Eglise St-Séverin

1 rue des Prêtres-St-Séverin, 5th (01.42.34.93.50).
M° Cluny-La Sorbonne. **Open** 11am-7.30pm Mon-Sat; 11am-8pm Sat; 9am-8pm Sun. **Map** p406 J7.
Primitive and Flamboyant Gothic styles merge in this complex little church, built mostly between the 13th and 15th centuries. The double ambulatory is famed for its 'palm tree' vaulting and unique double spiral column. Next door the remains of the charnel house can be seen.

▶ For detailed museum information and opening times, turn to **Sightseeing: Museums**, starting on page 147.
▶ For information on arts events turn to **Arts & Entertainment**, starting on page 275.
▶ For shopping information turn to **Shops & Services**, starting on page 235.

It's not George, but it is gorgeous: **Cluny**.

The museum is famed for its Roman remains and medieval art, most notably the Lady and the Unicorn tapestry cycle. The museum itself, commonly known as the Cluny, is also a rare example of 15th-century secular architecture. It was built – atop a Gallo-Roman baths complex dating from the second and third centuries – by Jacques d'Amboise in 1485-98 for lodging priests at the request of the Abbé de Cluny. With its main building behind a courtyard, it set new standards for domestic comfort and was a precursor of the Marais *hôtels particuliers*. The baths are the finest Roman remains in Paris: the vaulted frigidarium (cold bath), tepidarium (warm bath) and caldarium (hot bath) are visible. A printer, a laundry and cooper set up here in 1807, before it became a museum in 1844. The new medieval garden is inspired by courtly and saintly love and planted with species found in medieval treatises, tapestries and paintings. (*See chapter* **Museums.**)

Musée National du Moyen Age – Thermes de Cluny

6 pl Paul-Painlevé, 5th
(01.53.73.78.00/www.musee-moyenage.fr).
M° Cluny-La Sorbonne. **Open** 9.15am-5.45pm
Mon, Wed-Sun. **Admission** €5.50; €4 18-25s,
all Sun; free under-18s, CM. **Credit** (shop) V.
Map p406 J7.

The Sorbonne & the Montagne Ste-Geneviève

An influx of well-heeled residents has pushed up prices; accommodation in this warren of narrow streets is now beyond most students' reach. However, the intellectual tradition persists: the Montagne Ste-Geneviève has a concentration of academic institutions, from the

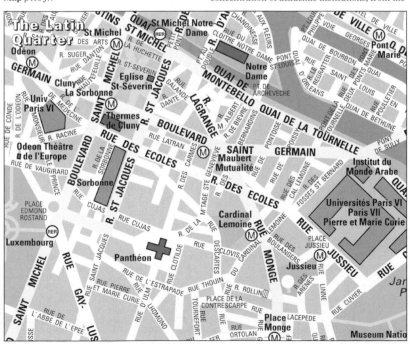

Sorbonne to research centres to Grandes
Ecoles such as the Ecole Normale Supérieure;
students throng in countless specialist book
stores and the art cinemas of rue Champollion
and rue des Ecoles.

The district began its long association with
learning in about 1100, when a number of
scholars, including Pierre Abélard, began to live
and teach on the Montagne, independent of the
established Canon school of Notre-Dame. This
loose association of scholars began to be
referred to as a university. The Paris schools
soon attracted scholars from all over Europe,
and the 'colleges' – really just student
residences – multiplied, until the University of
Paris was given official recognition with a
charter from Pope Innocent III in 1215.

By the 16th century, the university – now
known as the **Sorbonne**, after the most
famous of its colleges – had been co-opted by
the Catholic establishment. A century later,
Cardinal Richelieu rebuilt it, but it slid into
decay again. After the Revolution, when the
university was forced to close, Napoléon revived
the Sorbonne as the cornerstone of his new,
centralised education system. The university
participated enthusiastically in the uprisings of
the 19th century, and was also a seedbed of the
May 1968 revolt. Nowadays the Sorbonne is
decidedly less turbulent. The present buildings
are mostly 19th century; only the Baroque
Chapelle de la Sorbonne, where Richelieu is
buried, survives from his rebuilding.

Look out for the independent **Collège de
France**, also on rue des Ecoles, which was
founded in 1530 by a group of humanists led
by Guillaume Budé with the patronage of
François 1er. For intellectual fodder,
neighbouring Brasserie Balzar attracts a
fascinatingly varied clientele.

Climb up rue St-Jacques, winding rue de la
Montagne-Ste-Geneviève or take rue des
Carmes, with the Baroque chapel of the Syrian
church, and rue Valette past the brick and stone
entrance of the Collège Ste-Barbe, where
Ignatius Loyola and later Montgolfier and Eiffel
studied, to place du Panthéon. The huge domed
Panthéon, originally commissioned by Louis
XV as a church to honour the city's patron
Ste-Geneviève, was converted in the Revolution
into a secular temple for France's *grands
hommes*. *Grandes femmes* (kicking off with
Marie Curie) were only admitted from 1995,
suggesting, perhaps, that women's lib(erté) was
not high on the list of revolutionary priorities.
In the surrounding square, conceived by the
Panthéon's architect Soufflot, is the elegant
classical *mairie* (town hall) of the 5th
arrondissement, mirrored by the law faculty.
On the north side, the Bibliothèque Ste-

May 68 & all that

The Left Bank may house the comfortingly
sedate buildings of one of Europe's most
revered universities, but the riots of 3 May
1968, when 1,500 police faced 2,000
students at the Sorbonne, came close to
throwing France into revolution once again.
The conflict had begun on the out-of-town
campus of Nanterre, where students
began protesting against the archaic
education system. When police tried to
break up a meeting in the courtyard of the
Sorbonne thousands joined in to protest
against police brutality. Conflicts erupted
all over the Latin Quarter. 10 May saw the
tumultuous 'nuit des barricades', after
which trade unions joined in. By 20 May,
six million French workers were on strike.

And then? Nothing. Within a fortnight the
strikers were going back to work and the
students were looking forward to their
summer break. The rapid collapse of the
uprising had a lot to do with the perceived
association between revolution and
communism; de Gaulle's ploy of announcing
that communists were conspiring to
overthrow the government caused a surge
in nationalist feeling that overwhelmed that
of rebellion. France was for the French;
foreign Marxism had gate crashed, and
rather ruined, the party. However, '*les
événements*', as they became known,
shook people's beliefs and became a
reference point for a generation. 'Soixante-
huitards' crop up in all sorts of top places
and the events are a salutary reminder of
the volatility of the French people.

Geneviève, built 1844-50 by Labrouste, has medieval manuscripts and a magnificent iron-framed reading room. Opposite is **Hôtel des Grands-Hommes**, where Surrealist André Breton invented 'automatic writing' in the 1920s.

Pascal and Racine, and the remains of Paris' patron saint, Ste Geneviève, are buried at **St-Etienne-du Mont**, on the northeast corner of the square. Jutting up behind is the Gothic-Romanesque Tour de Clovis. Further along rue Clovis is a chunk of Philippe-Auguste's 12th-century city wall. Hemingway lived on both rue du Cardinal-Lemoine and rue Descartes (plaque at No 74 rue du Cardinal-Lemoine). James II resided at No 65 in the severe buildings of the former Collège des Ecossais, founded in 1372 to house Scottish students. At No 75 hides the charming **Hôtel des Grandes-Ecoles**.

Collège de France
11 pl Marcelin-Berthelot, 5th (01.44.27.12.11). Mº Cluny-La Sorbonne. **Map** p406 J7.
Built in 1530 with the patronage of François 1er, the college's purpose is to teach knowledge in the making rather than established knowledge. Lectures – which are free and open to the public – can include such eminent names as Claude Lévi-Strauss, Emmanuel Le Roy Ladurie, Jean-Claude Pecker and Jacques Tits.

Eglise St-Etienne-du-Mont
pl Ste-Geneviève, 5th (01.43.54.11.79). Mº Cardinal-Lemoine/RER Luxembourg. **Open** 9am-noon, 2-7pm Mon-Sat; 9am-noon, 2.30-7pm Sun. **Map** p406 J8.
Ste-Geneviève saved the city from Attila the Hun in 451; her shrine here has been a popular pilgrimage place since the Dark Ages. The present church was built in an amalgam of Gothic and Renaissance styles between 1492 and 1626, and originally adjoined the abbey church of Ste-Geneviève. The facade mixes Gothic rose windows with classical

columns. The stunning Renaissance roodscreen, with its double spiral staircase and ornate stone strapwork, is the only one left in Paris. Ste-Geneviève's elaborate brass-covered shrine is to the right of the choir, surrounded by plaques giving thanks for miracles she has performed.

Le Panthéon
pl du Panthéon, 5th (01.44.32.18.00). RER Luxembourg. **Open** 10am-6.15pm daily.
Admission €7; €4.50 18-25s; free under-18s. **Credit** MC, V. **Map** p406 J8.
Soufflot's neo-classical megastructure was the architectural *Grand Projet* of its day, commissioned by a grateful Louis XV to thank Ste-Geneviève for his recovery from illness. But events caught up with its completion in 1790, and post-Revolution it was re-dedicated as a 'temple of reason' and the resting-place of the nation's great men. The crypt of greats includes Voltaire, Rousseau, Victor Hugo and Zola. New heroes are added rarely: Pierre and Marie Curie's remains were transferred here in 1995, she being the first woman to be interred in her own right. André Malraux, de Gaulle's culture minister, arrived to keep her company in 1996. Inside you can admire the Greek columns and domes, as well as 19th-century murals by symbolist painter Puvis de Cha vannes. Do brave the steep spiral stairs up to the colonnade, and you'll be rewarded with some truly wonderful views across the city. Also offers the chance to experience Foucauld's pendulum.

La Sorbonne
17 rue de la Sorbonne, 5th (01.40.46.22.11/ www.sorbonne.fr). Mº Cluny-La Sorbonne. **Map** p406 J7.
Founded in 1253 by Robert de Sorbon, the University of the Sorbonne was at the centre of the Latin Quarter's intellectual activity from the Middle Ages until the dramatic events of May 1968, when it was occupied by students and stormed by the CRS (riot police). The authorities subsequently splintered the University of Paris into several less-threatening outposts, but the Sorbonne remains home to the Faculté des Lettres. Rebuilt by Richelieu and reorganised by Napoléon, the present buildings mostly date from 1885 to 1900 and include a labyrinth of classrooms and quaint lecture theatres, as well as an observatory tower. Officially, the courtyards are not open to the public but if you look the part it is easy enough to walk in. Attitude is often all you need in Paris. The elegant dome of the 17th-century chapel dominates place de la Sorbonne; Cardinal Richelieu is buried inside.

The Best Chill outs

Musée Rodin
Hit the garden, dig the talent (*see p130*).

Jardin des Plantes
Tip-toe through those tulips (*see p124*).

Mur Pour la Paix
Give it a chance (*see p134*).

Parc André Citroën
Something funky in the 15th? (*see p134*).

Cimetière du Montparnasse
Dead calm (*see p135*).

The rue Mouffetard area

Place de la Contrescarpe has been a famous rendezvous since the 1530s, when writers Rabelais, Ronsard and Du Bellay frequented the Cabaret de la Pomme de Pin at No 1. It is still known for its lively cafés. **Rue Mouffetard,**

Time for reflection in the **Jardin des Plantes**.

originally the road to Rome and one of the oldest streets in the city, winds off to the south. Cheap bistros, ethnic knick-knack shops and crowds of tourists have somewhat eroded what Hemingway described as 'that wonderful narrow crowded market street' beloved of bohemians. There is a busy street market (Tue-Sat and Sun morning) on the lower half. It's particularly seething at weekends when the market spills on to the square and around the cafés in front of the **Eglise St-Médard**. There's another busy market at place Monge (Wed, Fri, Sun morning). From 1928-29 George Orwell stayed at 6 rue du Pot-de-Fer. Then an area of astounding poverty, it is now lined with cheap bars and restaurants. Orwell deigned to work as a *plongeur* (washer-upper), and his experiences are vividly depicted in *Down and Out in Paris and London*. The restored houses along **rue Tournefort** bear no relation to the cheap garrets of Balzac's *Le Père Goriot* (*see p31* **Never Mind the Balzacs**).

Beyond rue Soufflot is one of the most picturesque stretches of the rue St-Jacques containing several ancient buildings. Note the elegant *hôtel* at No 151. There are also good food shops, the vintage bistro Perraudin and Aussie bar Café Oz. Rue d'Ulm houses the elitist Ecole Normale Supérieure, which was occupied

▶ Many of the Left Bank's churches hold classical and gospel concerts (often free on Sundays). For details turn to p321 **Music: Classical & Opera**.

by the unemployed in January 1998; in an echo of 1968, several students joined in. Turn off up hilly rue des Fossés-St-Jacques to discover place de l'Estrapade, tucked behind the Panthéon. The square has a dark past: the estrapade was a wooden tower from which deserters were dropped in the 17th century. To the west, broad rue Gay-Lussac leads to the **Jardins du Luxembourg**. Further down rue St-Jacques is another eminent landmark, the **Val-de-Grâce**, the least-altered and most ornate of all Paris' Baroque churches.

Eglise St-Médard

141 rue Mouffetard, 5th (01.44.08.87.00). Mº Censier-Daubenton. **Open** 9am-noon, 2.30-7pm Tue-Sat; 4-7pm Sun. **Map** p406 K9.
The original chapel here was a dependency of the Abbaye de Ste-Geneviève; rebuilding at the end of the 15th century created a much larger, late Gothic structure. Some of the capitals were fluted to suit 1780s neo-classical fashion.

Eglise du Val-de-Grâce

pl Alphonse-Laveran, 5th (01.40.51.47.28). RER Port-Royal. **Open** Call to arrange guided visits noon-6pm, Tue, Wed, Sat, Sun. **Admission** €4.57, €2.29 6-12s, free under-6s. **No credit cards. Map** p406 J9. Anne of Austria vowed to erect 'a magnificent temple' if God blessed her with a son. He presented her with two. The resulting church and its Benedictine monastery – now a military hospital and the **Musée du Service de Santé des Armées** devoted to military medecine (*see chapter* **Museums**) – were built by François Mansart and Jacques Lemercier. Expensive and built over decades, this is the most luxuriously Baroque of the city's 17th-century domed churches. The dome paintings' swirling colours are meant to prefigure heaven.

The Jardin des Plantes district

The quieter eastern end of rue des Ecoles is a focus for Paris' Muslim community, major academic institutions and home to several Roman relics. Old-fashioned bistros on rue des Fossés-St-Bernard contrast with the brutal 1960s-70s slab architecture of Paris university's campuses VI and VII (known as Jussieu), now the subject of a major regeneration project (*see chapter* **Architecture**). Between the Seine and Jussieu is the strikingly modern glass **Institut du Monde Arabe**, which has a busy programme of concerts and exhibitions. The **Jardin Tino Rossi,** along the river,

Baroque beauty: **Val-de-Grâce**.

Paris people: Bertrand Burgalat

Any hip Parisian aged between 20 and 40 will tell you that Bertrand Burgalat can stake a claim – not that he ever would – to being the coolest man in Paris. They will also tell you that this composer, producer, arranger, mixer, multi-instrumentalist and record company mogul does his thing in a recognisably 'St-Germain' style: that is to say that he makes his art by collaborating with artists from all sorts of creative spheres (the term was coined in the early 1950s and related to the groups of jazz musicians and writers who lived and worked together on the Left Bank). Parisians, who are quite often genealogical in their analysis of entertainers, see Burgalat in terms of his approach as a direct descendant of Maurice Chevalier and Serge Gainsbourg.

A strong contributory factor to Burgalat's success is his impeccable choice of influences: he frequently cites the work of such artists as the Rubettes, Roxy Music and that legendary trouser-splitter PJ Proby as having been crucial in the formation of his oeuvre. Burgalat has mixed their theatrical art-school attitude with the painstaking production methodology of Phil Spector and Brian Wilson to produce the music and the image that kick-started the renaissance – or should we say *naissance* – in French pop. His electrolounge sound, which he calls kitsch-pop, has influenced everybody who's somebody.

The main outlet for Burgalat's work is the Tricatel label, which he founded in 1995 and is now the most successful independent set-up in France. Foremost among his roster of artistes are the author Michel Houellebecq (*see p33*, **Weller-weller-weller ooh!**), ultra-cool Swedish band Eggstone and April March from the US. The label holds parties at various Left Bank venues, which are a magnet for the city's glitterati.

The St-Germainesque refusal to be pigeonholed has meant that Burgalat can be a wealthy businessman and still have enough cred points in the bank to play bass and keyboards in Air's touring band. These days, references to 'BB' conjure up images not of a pouting sex grenade but of a *Rive Gauche* popinjay who has achieved a status most of us secretly crave but so rarely achieve, 'la coolitude', coupled with a decidedly bulging bank account.

Sightseeing

contains the dilapidated **Musée de la Sculpture en Plein Air**.

The Paris mosque is not far away up rue Linné. You may want to stop off at the **Arènes de Lutèce**, the Roman amphitheatre. The central arena and many tiers of stone seating were discovered in 1869 during the building of rue Monge. They started to be excavated in 1883, due to the archaeological zeal of Victor Hugo. The green-roofed **Mosquée de Paris** was built in 1922, partly inspired by Granada's Alhambra, though its popular Moorish tearoom is a very Parisian experience.

The mosque looks out on to the **Jardin des Plantes**, Paris' superb botanical garden. Established in 1626 as a garden for medicinal plants, it features an 18th-century maze, a winter garden brimming with rare species and the brilliantly renovated Grande Galerie de l'Evolution of the **Muséum National d'Histoire Naturelle**. There's also the *ménagerie*, an unlikely by-product of the Revolution, when royal and noble collections of wild animals were impounded.

Arènes de Lutèce

entrances rue Monge, rue de Navarre, rue des Arènes, 5th. Mº Cardinal-Lemoine or Jussieu.
Open 8am-5.30pm winter; 8am-10pm summer.
Map p406 K8.
The Roman arena, where roaring wild beasts and wounded gladiators met their deaths, sat 10,000. The site was discovered in 1869 and now incorporates a romantically planted garden. It attracts skateboarders and *boules* players; concerts and theatre are also sometimes staged here.

Institut du Monde Arabe

1 rue des Fossés-St-Bernard, 5th (01.40.51.38.38/www.imarabe.org). Mº Jussieu.
Open Museum 10am-6pm Tue-Sun. Library 1-8pm Tue-Sat. Café noon-6pm Tue-Sun. **Admission** roof terrace, library free. Museum €3.81; €3.05 12-25s, students; free under-12s, CM. Exhibitions €6.86; €5.34 students, over-60s. **Map** p406 K7.
A clever blend of high-tech steel, glass architecture and Arab influences, this wedge-shaped *Grand Projet* was designed by French architect Jean Nouvel in 1980-87. Nouvel took his inspiration from the screens of Moorish palaces. Inside is a collection of

Papa got a brand new plaque at **Les Deux Magots.**

Middle Eastern art, archaeological finds, exhibition spaces, a library and café. The institute runs a programme of dance and classical Arab music. There are great views from the roof, and a fine restaurant.

Jardin des Plantes

pl Valhubert, rue Buffon or rue Cuvier, 5th (01.40.79.30.00). M° Gare d'Austerlitz or Jussieu. **Open** Mon, Wed-Sun, summer 10am-6pm; winter 10am-5pm (Alpine garden Apr-Sept 8am-11am, 1.30-5pm; greenhouses summer 1-5pm Mon, Wed-Fri; 10am-5pm Sat, Sun; winter 1-5pm Mon, Wed-Sun; *ménagerie* summer 9am-6pm; winter 9am-5pm). **Admission** free; greenhouses €2.29; *ménagerie* €4.57-€3.05. **Map** p406 L8.

Although small and slightly run-down, the Paris botanical garden contains more than 10,000 species, and includes tropical greenhouses, rose, winter and Alpine gardens. Begun by Louis XIII's doctor as the royal medicinal plant garden in 1626, it opened to the public in 1640. It also contains the **Ménagerie**, a small zoo, and the **Muséum National d'Histoire Naturelle**, including the magnificently renovated 1880s Grande Galerie de l'Evolution. Several ancient trees include a false acacia planted in 1636 and a cedar planted in 1734. A tablet on the former laboratory announces that this is where Henri Becquerel discovered radioactivity in 1896. *See also chapters* **Museums** *and* **Children**.

La Mosquée de Paris

1 pl du Puits-de-l'Ermite, 5th (01.45.35.97.33/ tearoom 01.43.31.38.20/Turkish baths 01.43.31.18.14/www.mosquee-de-paris.com). M° Censier-Daubenton. **Open** tours 9am-noon, 2-6pm Mon-Thur, Sat, Sun (closed Muslim holidays); tearoom 9am-11.30pm daily; restaurant noon-3pm, 7-10.30pm daily; baths (women) 10am-9pm Mon, Wed, Sat; 2-9pm Fri; (men) 2-9pm Tue; 10am-9pm Sun. **Admission** €2.29; €1.52 7-25s, over-60s; free under-7s; tearoom free; baths €12.96-€30.49. **Credit** MC, V. **Map** p406 K8.

The mosque's green-and-white minaret oversees the centre of the Algerian-dominated Muslim community in France. Built 1922-26 in Hispano-Moorish style, with elements inspired by the Alhambra and Fez's Mosque Bou-Inania, the mosque is a series of buildings and courtyards in three sections: religious (grand patio, prayer room and minaret); scholarly (Islamic school and library); and, entered from rue Geoffroy-St-Hilaire, commercial (domed *hammam* or Turkish baths and relaxing Moorish tearoom).

St-Germain & Odéon

St-Germain-des-Prés is where the great legend of Paris café society and intellectual life grew up. Verlaine and Rimbaud drank here; a few generations later, Sartre, Camus and de Beauvoir scribbled their first masterpieces and musicians congregated around writer, critic and trumpeter Boris Vian in Paris' postwar jazz boom.

Earnest types (and Ernest types) still stride along with weighty tomes and the literati still gather on terraces – to give TV interviews – but the area is so expensive that any writers here are either well-established or rich (though not necessarily in talent). Luxury fashion groups have moved in: Armani took over the old Drugstore, Dior a bookshop, Cartier a classical record shop and Louis Vuitton unpacked its bags at place St-Germain; since the All Jazz

Club and La Villa Jazz Club closed, musicians have crossed the river. It didn't happen without a fight: in 1997 a band of intellectuals founded SOS St-Germain in an attempt to save the area's soul. Even some of the fashionistas seemed to jump camp – Sonia Rykiel joined the campaigners and Karl Lagerfeld opened his own photography gallery on rue de Seine. Nevertheless, St-Germain now almost rivals the avenue Montaigne for its designer boutiques.

From the boulevard to the Seine

Hit by shortages of coal during World War II, Sartre descended from the ivory tower of his apartment on rue Bonaparte to save a bundle in heating bills. 'The principal interest of the **Café de Flore**,' he noted, 'was that it had a stove, a nearby Métro and no Germans.' Although

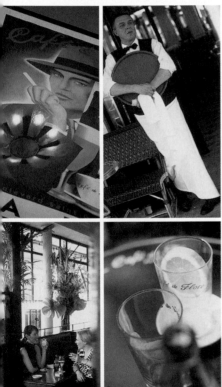

you can now spend more on a few coffees there than on a week's heating, the Flore (172 bd St-Germain) remains an arty favourite and hosts *café philo* evenings in English. Its rival, **Les Deux Magots** (6 pl St-Germain-des-Prés), now provides for an interesting cross-section of tourists. At No 151 is politicians' favourite Brasserie Lipp; at No 170 is the late-night bookshop and intelligentsia pick-up venue **La Hune**. Art nouveau fans should look out for the brasserie Vagenende (No 140).

Traces of the cloister and part of the Abbot's palace remain behind the church on rue de l'Abbaye. Built in 1586 in red brick with stone facing, it prefigures the place des Vosges. The charming place Furstenberg (once the stableyard of the Abbot's palace), now shades upmarket furnishing fabric stores and the house and studio where the painter Delacroix lived (*see chapter* **Museums**). Rue de l'Echaudé shows a typical St-Germain mix: cutting-edge fashion at **L'Eclaireur** (No 24) and bistro cooking at L'Echaudé-St-Germain (No 21). Ingres, Wagner and Colette lived on rue Jacob; its elegant 17th-century *hôtels* now contain specialist book, design and antiques shops, pleasant hotels and bohemian throwbacks including *chansonnier* bistro Les Assassins.

Further east, the rue de Buci hosts a street market, running into rue de Seine with a lively scene centred around the **Bar du Marché** and Chai de l'Abbaye cafés. Rue Bonaparte (where Manet was born at No 5 in 1832), rue de Seine and rue des Beaux-Arts are still packed with small art galleries specialising in 20th-century abstraction, tribal art and art deco furniture (*see chapter* **Galleries**). Oscar Wilde died 'beyond his means' at what was then the Hôtel d'Alsace, now the renovated and still fashionably over-the-top **L'Hôtel** in rue des Beaux-Arts. La Palette and Bistro Mazarin are good stopping-off points with enviable terraces on rue Jacques-Callot. Rue Mazarine, with shops of lighting, vintage toys and jewellery, is now home to Conran's brasserie **L'Alcazar** (No 62) in a former cabaret. The **Ecole Nationale Supérieure des Beaux-Arts**, Paris' main fine-arts school and a former monastery, is at

Wild fauna at the **Flore.**

the northern end of rue Bonaparte. On the quai de Conti is the **Institut de France**, recently cleaned to reveal its crisp classical decoration. Next door stands the neo-classical Hôtel des Monnaies, formerly the mint (1777-1973) and now the **Musée de la Monnaie**, a coin museum. Opposite, the iron Pont des Arts footbridge leads across to the Louvre.

Coffee was first brought to Paris in 1686 at Café Procope on rue de l'Ancienne-Comédie. Frequented by Voltaire, Rousseau, Benjamin Franklin, revolutionary Danton and later Verlaine, it is now an attractive restaurant aimed at tourists; it contains some remarkable memorabilia, including Voltaire's desk and a postcard from Marie-Antoinette. The back opens on to the twee cobbled passage du Commerce St-André, home to toy shops, jewellers and chintzy tearooms. In the 18th century, Dr Joseph-Ignace Guillotin first tested out his notorious execution device – designed to make public executions more humane – in the cellars of what is now the Pub St-Germain. The first victim was reputedly a sheep. Jacobin

regicide Billaud-Varenne was one of those who felt the blade of Dr Guillotin's invention. His former home (45 rue St-André-des-Arts) was an incongruous location for the first girls' *lycée* in Paris, the Lycée Fénelon, founded in 1883. Formerly a 'des res', today rue St-André-des-Arts is lined with gift shops, crêperies and an arts cinema. Escape the main thoroughfare and make for the quiet side streets, such as rue des Grands-Augustins, rue de Savoie and rue Séguier, home to printers, bookshops and dignified 17th-century buildings. On the corner of rue and quai des Grands-Augustins, the restaurant Lapérouse still boasts a series of private dining rooms, while Les Bookinistes offers contemporary flavours. The turreted Hôtel de Fécamp, at 5 rue de Hautefeuille, was the medieval townhouse of the abbots of Fécamp, begun in 1292. Rue Gît-le-Coeur ('here lies the heart') is so-called, legend has it, because one of Henri IV's mistresses lived here. At No 9 is the now rather luxurious Hôtel du Vieux Paris, or the 'Beat Hotel', where William Burroughs revised *The Naked Lunch*.

Mind your language

You can say what you like about Cardinal Richelieu – but he took the long view. In 1635 he founded an organisation, the Académie Francaise, whose specific purpose was to look after the well-being of the French language. Its mission statement was, 'to take every possible care to impose definitive rules on the language, to make it pure, eloquent and capable of serving the sciences and the arts'. Its members were dubbed, like some band of comic book superheroes, the Immortals, a title their successors retain to this day.

There is no mention in the history books of Richelieu's having been visited by Nostradamian premonitions of Hollywood, MTV, the Internet and the other perceived vehicles of American English cultural imperialism. Perhaps he was just a born worrier. Whatever, his prescience is impressive and his concern well founded, for French has become, despite the protective attention of the Immortals, the Norma Desmond of once-great international languages.

No longer the language of Europe, no longer even the language of diplomacy, the language of Molière has slumped to ninth position in the league of international languages. A touch of the *vocé fala Inglêse?* will get you a lot further on the planet in 2002 than the old *parlez-vous* routine, and more than a few people exit

Anglophone universities these days believing that Molière was Jane Eyre's sister.

The plucky denizens of the Académie do not take things lying down (except, maybe, their heart pills), and in 1994 they hassled the French government into passing a law discouraging the use of English on TV and radio, and also in advertising. Eight years later, there's an advert running on French TV that bangs on about the amount of '*le family space*' available in a certain car.

It is undoubtedly the information superhighway that poses the biggest threat to the work of the Immortals. In houses and cybercafés all over France, vulnerable young minds are exposed to such corrupting terms as 'cool', 'web', 'chat room' and 'start-up'. 'Surfer' is the verb they use for browsing the net. The Académie has reacted to this in its usual way; it has tried to replace words that have passed naturally into usage with francophonic variations (this is the institution, let us not forget, that reacted to the word 'bra' with '*soutien-gorge*', literally, 'breast support' – how erotic). Thus came their suggestions for what we (but not they) might call e-French: having '*plugiciel*' for 'plug-in' is fine, and how could anybody object to '*épépineur*' for 'debugger'? But surely the snappy and succinct replacement for 'virus' – '*fragment*

Ecole Nationale Supérieure des Beaux-Arts (Ensb-a)

13 quai Malaquais, 6th (01.47.03.52.15). M° Odéon or St-Michel. **Open** courtyard 8.30am-8pm Mon-Fri; exhibitions Tue-Sun, times vary. **Admission** exhibitions €3.81; €2.29 students, children, free under-12s. **Credit** V. **Map** p406 H6.

Paris' most prestigious fine-art school is installed in what remains of a 17th-century convent, the 18th-century Hôtel de Chimay and some later additions. After the Revolution, the buildings were transformed into a museum of French monuments, then in 1816 into the *Ecole*. Today it is often used for exhibitions (*see chapter* **Museums**).

Institut de France

23 quai de Conti, 6th (01.44.41.44.41/www.institut-de-france.fr). M° St-Germain-des-Prés. **Guided tours** Sat, Sun (call ahead for times). **Admission** €3.05. **No credit cards**. **Map** p406 H6.

The institute was founded by Mazarin as a school. In 1805 the five academies of the Institut (Académie Française, Académie des Inscriptions et Belles-Lettres, Académie des Sciences, Académie des Beaux-Arts, Académie des Sciences Morales et Politiques),

were transferred here. Inside is Mazarin's ornate tomb by Hardouin-Mansart, and the Bibliothèque Mazarine. Access to the library is open to anyone over 18 who turns up with ID, two photos and €15.24 for a one-year library card.

Eglise St-Germain-des-Prés

3 pl St-Germain-des-Prés, 6th (01.43.25.41.71). M° St-Germain-des-Prés. **Open** 8am-7pm daily. **Map** p405 H7.

This is the oldest church in Paris. On the advice of Germain (later bishop of Paris), Childebert, son of Clovis, had a basilica and monastery built towards 543; it was known as St-Germain-le-Doré because of its copper roof. During the Revolution the abbey was burnt and a saltpetre refinery installed; the spire was added as part of a clumsy 19th-century restoration. Despite all this most of the present structure is 12th-century, and some ornate carved capitals and the tower remain from the 11th. Interesting tombs include that of Jean-Casimir, deposed king of Poland who became abbot of St-Germain in 1669, and Scottish nobleman William Douglas. Under the window in the second chapel is Descartes' funeral stone; his ashes (bar his skull) have been here since 1819.

Sightseeing

L' Institut de France.

infectieux de code nécessitant un programme hôte' – adequately illustrates the naked ludicrousness of trying to apply committee rules to organic growth.

In July 2001 even the European Commission tried to put the boot into La Desmond, with a sneaky proposal to save translation costs by presenting official documents in the language most members would understand; the admission of Sweden and Finland into the Union means that that language would certainly turn out to be English. The plan had the blessing of Commission President Romano Prodi, who is a fanatical supporter of the

adoption of the English language, in which, bizarrely, he has only a basic level of competence. Maybe he applies objective logic to his decision-making process. The proposal was only scuppered when the German and French foreign ministers realised what was afoot and fired off outraged letters of protest at the thought of English becoming the *lingua franca* of the Union.

So what now for the Immortals as they meet every Thursday in their Institut de France (*see above*) lair and discuss the state of the language? Has the Académie degenerated into just an anachronism, now that the French language is richly garnished with English, and Paris in particular is increasingly *un melting pot culturel*? And what about the perceived threat from 'immigrant' languages? Is it finally time for the Immortals to fall on their quills?

The continued existence of the Académie and the challenges it faces illustrate a paradox that runs throughout French society: most of the population positively wants modernisation and change, if for no other reason than to compete with other countries; but the nation is much under the influence of reactionary groups that refer back constantly to tradition rather than gearing up to make France's future cultural contribution as glorious as that of its past.

St-Sulpice & the Luxembourg

South of boulevard St-Germain between Odéon and Luxembourg is a quarter that epitomises civilised Paris, full of historic buildings and interesting shops. Just off the boulevard lies the covered market of St-Germain, once the site of the St-Germain Fair. Following redevelopment it now houses an underground swimming pool, auditorium, food hall and a shopping arcade. There are bars and bistros along rue Guisarde, nicknamed *rue de la soif* (street of thirst) thanks to its regular swarm of merry carousers. Rue Princesse and rue des Canettes are a beguiling mix of lively bistros, including **Mâchon d'Henri** and Brasserie Fernand, budget eateries, Italian pizzerias and late-night haunts known to a determined few: the Birdland bar, Bedford Arms and notoriously elitist nightspot **Club Castel**.

Pass the fashion boutiques, antiquarian book and print shops and high-class patisseries and you come to St-Sulpice, a surprising 18th-century exercise in classical form with two uneven turrets and a colonnaded facade. Delacroix painted the frescoes in the first chapel on the right. The square contains Visconti's imposing, lion-flanked Fontaine des Quatre Evêques and is used for an antiques fair and a poetry fair every summer. The **Café de la Mairie** remains a favourite with intellectuals and students, while between shops of religious artefacts, the chic boutiques along place and rue St-Sulpice include Yves Saint Laurent, Christian Lacroix, **Agnès b**, Vanessa Bruno, Muji, perfumier Annick Goutal, the furnishings of Catherine Memmi and milliner **Marie Mercié**. Prime shopping territory continues to the west: clothes shops on rue Bonaparte and rue du Four and leather, accessory and fashion shops on rue du Dragon, rue de Grenelle and rue du Cherche-Midi. If you spot a queue in the latter street, it's most likely for **Poilâne**'s designer bread. **Au Sauvignon**, at the busy carrefour de la Croix-Rouge, is a perfect place for people watching. One hundred and fifteen priests were killed

Groping and godliness in place St-Sulpice:

in 1792 in the chapel of St-Joseph des Carmes (70 rue de Vaugirard), once a Carmelite convent, now hidden within the Institut Catholique. To the east lies wide rue de Tournon, lined by some grand 18th-century residences, such as the elegant Hôtel de Brancas (now the **Institut Français de l'Architecture**) with figures of Justice and Prudence over the door. This opens up to the **Palais du Luxembourg**, which now serves as the Senate, and its adjoining park.

Returning towards boulevard St-Germain, you pass the neo-classical **Odéon, Théâtre de l'Europe** built in 1779 and a leading theatre. Beaumarchais' *Marriage of Figaro* was first performed here in 1784. The semi-circular place in front was home to revolutionary hero Camille Desmoulins, at No 2, now La Méditerranée restaurant, decorated by Jean Cocteau. Another hangout among the antiquarian bookshops on rue de l'Odéon is Le Bar Dix. Joyce's *Ulysses*

The best Intellectual hangouts

Café de Flore
Does existentialist translate into English? Find out at a *café philo* session (see p229).

Les Deux Magots
Enjoy a mandarin or two. Simon de Beauvoir did (see p229).

La Hune
Their eyes met across a crowded bookshelf (see p264).

L'Entrepôt
Cinecafé and restaurant perfect for deconstructing the *septième art* (see p233).

Sightseeing

posers' paradise the **Café de la Mairie** (left) and the prayerful **Eglise St-Sulpice**.

was first published next door (No 12) by Sylvia Beach at the legendary, original **Shakespeare & Co** in 1922.

Up the street at 12 rue de l'Ecole-de-Médecine is the colonnaded neo-classical Université René Descartes (Paris V) medical school, now home to the **Musée d'Histoire de la Médicine** (*see chapter* **Museums**). The Club des Cordeliers cooked up revolutionary plots across the street at the Couvent des Cordeliers (No 15), a Franciscan priory founded by St Louis in the Middle Ages. Marat, one of the club's leading lights, met a rather undignified end in the tub at his home in the same street, when he was stabbed up the tap end in 1793 by Charlotte Corday. Look out for the doorway of the neighbouring *hôtel* and the domed building at No 5, once the barbers' and surgeons' guild. Climb up rue André-Dubois to rue Monsieur-le-Prince for the popular budget restaurant Polidor at 41, which has been feeding students and tourists since 1845 and, near the boulevard St-Michel, the **3 Luxembourg** arts cinema.

Eglise St-Sulpice

pl St-Sulpice, 6th (01.46.33.21.78). M° St-Sulpice.
Open 8am-7pm daily. **Map** p405 H7.
If you look closely you will notice that one of the church's two towers is shorter (actually a good five metres) than the other: it is, in fact, unfinished. The grandiose Italianate facade – and the towers – were designed by Jean-Baptiste Servandoni, although he died (in 1766) before the other tower was completed. Altogether, it took 120 years (starting from 1646)

and six architects to finish the church; the *place* in front of the building and the fountain were designed in the 19th century by Visconti. Look for three paintings by Delacroix in the first chapel: *Jacob's fight with the Angel, Heliodorus chased out of the Temple* and *St Michael killing the Dragon*.

Jardins and Palais du Luxembourg

pl Auguste-Comte, pl Edmond-Rostand or rue de Vaugirard, 6th. M° Odéon/RER Luxembourg.
Open dawn-dusk daily. **Map** p405 H8.
The *palais* was built in the 1620s for Marie de Médicis, widow of Henri IV, by Salomon de Brosse, on the site of the former mansion of the Duke of Luxembourg. Its Italianate style was intended to remind her of the Pitti Palace in her native Florence. In 1621, she commissioned Rubens to produce for the palace the 24 huge paintings celebrating her life (in various stages of undress) that are now in the Louvre. Reworked by Chalgrin in the 18th century, the *palais* now houses the Senate. The gardens are the real draw today: part formal, with terraces and gravel paths, part 'English garden' of lawns, they are the quintessential Paris park. The garden is peopled with diverse sculpted *dramatis personae,* from the looming Cyclops on the 1624 Fontaine de Médicis, to queens of France, a mini Statue of Liberty and a monument to Delacroix. There are orchards, con-taining over 300 varieties of apples, and an apiary where you can take courses in beekeeping. The **Musée du Luxembourg** in the former Orangerie is used for art exhibitions such as the recent presti-gious Raphael exhibition. Most interesting, though, are the people: chess players, joggers and martial arts practitioners; children on ponies, in sandpits, on

roundabouts and playing with the old-fashioned sailboats on the lake. There are the chicest tennis courts on the Left Bank, *boules* pitches, a café and a bandstand, while the park chairs are beloved of book lovers, those looking for love and those who seem to have found it.

The monumental 7th & west

Mainly 7th arrondissement, parts of 6th and 15th.
Townhouses spread west from St-Germain into the 7th *arrondissement*, as the vibrant street and café life subsides in favour of residential blocks and government offices. The 7th easily divides into two halves: the more intimate Faubourg St-Germain to the east, with its historic mansions and fine shops and, to the west of Les Invalides, an area of windswept wide avenues and, of course, the Eiffel Tower.

The Faubourg St-Germain

Often written off by Proust as a symbol of staid, *haute bourgeoise* and aristocratic society, this area remains home to some of Paris' oldest and grandest families, though most of its 18th-century *hôtels particuliers* have now been taken over by embassies and government ministries. You can admire their stone gateways and elegant courtyards, especially on rues de Grenelle, St-Dominique, de l'Université and de Varenne. Among the most beautiful is the Hôtel Matignon (57 rue de Varenne), residence of the Prime Minister; the facade is sometimes visible through the heavily guarded entrance portal. Used by the French statesman Talleyrand for lavish receptions, it boasts the biggest private garden in Paris. The Cité Varenne at No 51 is a lane of exclusive houses with private gardens. You'll have to wait for the open-house *Journées du Patrimoine* to see the decorative interiors and private gardens of others such as the Hôtel de Villeroy (Ministry of Agriculture, 78 rue de Varenne), Hôtel Boisgelin (Italian Embassy, 47 rue de Varenne), Hôtel d'Estrées (residence of the Russian ambassador, 79 rue de Grenelle), Hôtel d'Avaray (residence of the Dutch ambassador, 85 rue de Grenelle) or Hôtel de Monaco (Polish Embassy, 57 rue St-Dominique).

Continuing westward along the Seine, facing the Pont de la Concorde and the place de la Concorde across the river, is the **Assemblée Nationale**, the lower house of the French parliament. Beside the Assemblée is the Foreign Ministry, often referred to by its address, the quai d'Orsay. Beyond it stretches the long, grassy esplanade leading up to the golden-domed **Invalides**, the vast military hospital

A merry dance in the **Luxembourg Gardens.**

complex which now houses the **Musée de l'Armée** and **Napoléon's tomb**. The two churches inside – St-Louis-des-Invalides and the Eglise du Dôme – glorify French monarchs. Stand with your back to the dome and you'll see that the esplanade gives a striking perspective across cherubim-laden **Pont Alexandre III** to the Grand and Petit Palais, all three constructed for the 1900 *Exposition Universelle*.

Just beside Les Invalides, a far cosier place to visit is the **Musée Rodin**, housed in the

charming 18th-century Hôtel Biron and its romantic gardens. Rodin was invited to move here in 1908 on the understanding that he would bequeath his work to the state. As a result, you can now see many of his great sculptures, including *The Thinker* and *The Burghers of Calais*, in a beautiful setting. Not far from here on rue de Babylone, an interesting architectural oddity is **La Pagode** cinema, a replica of a Japanese pagoda.

Assemblée Nationale

33 quai d'Orsay, 7th (01.40.63.60.00/ www.assemblee-nat.fr). Mº Assemblée Nationale. **Guided tours** 10am, 2pm, 3pm Sat when Chamber not in session; ID required. **Map** p405 F5.

The Palais Bourbon has held parliament's lower house since 1827. Built in 1722, the palace was extended by the Prince de Condé, who added the Hôtel de Lassay, now official residence of the Assembly's president. Inside, the library is decorated with Delacroix's *History of Civilisation*. Visitors can attend debates.

Chapelle de la Médaille Miraculeuse

Couvent des Soeurs de St-Vincent-de-Paul, 140 rue du Bac, 7th (01.49.54.78.88). Mº Sèvres-Babylone. **Open** 8am-12.30pm, 2.30-7pm Mon, Wed-Sun; 8am-7pm Tue. **Map** p405 F7.

In 1830 saintly nun Catherine Labouré was visited by the Virgin, who gave her a medal which performed many miracles. Attracting over two million faithful every year, the kitsch chapel – an extraordinary concoction of statues, mosaics and murals, and the embalmed bodies of Catherine and her mother superior – continues to be one of France's most visited pilgrimage sites. Reliefs to the left of the entrance recount the story of the nun's life.

Les Invalides

esplanade des Invalides, 7th (01.44.42.54.52/Musée de l'Armée 01.44.42.37.67/www.invalides.org). Mº Invalides. **Open** Apr-Sept 10am-6pm daily; Oct-Mar 10am-5pm daily. **Admission** courtyard free. Musée de l'Armée & Eglise du Dôme €6; €4.50 12-18s, students under 26; free under-12s, CM. **Credit** MC, V. **Map** p401 E6.

Despite its imposing gilded dome, the Hôtel des Invalides was (and in part, still is) a hospital. Commissioned by Louis XIV to care for the war-wounded, at one time it housed up to 6,000 invalids – hence the name. Now the *hôtel* contains the **Musée de l'Armée** (*see chapter* **Museums**), with its staggering display of wartime paraphernalia, and Musée de l'Ordre de la Libération. Since 1840 the Baroque Eglise du Dôme (designed by Hardouin-Mansart) has been dedicated to the worship of Napoléon, whose body was brought here from St Helena 19 years after he died. The church of St-Louis, known

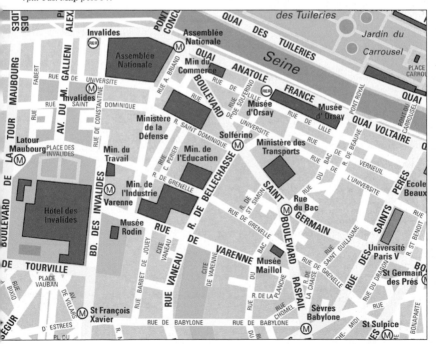

Sightseeing

as the Church of the Soldiers, is decorated with captured flags and its crypt filled with the remains of military men. Cannon barrels are littered everywhere but, even if you're not interested in military history, it's worth a wander through the gardens and the principal courtyard to get an idea of the power of royal patronage.

Musée d'Orsay

1 rue de la Légion d'Honneur, 7th (01.40.49.48.14/ recorded information 01.45.49.11.11/www.musee-orsay.fr). Mº Solférino/ RER Musée d'Orsay. **Open** 9am-6pm Tue-Sun. **Admission** €6.86; €5.03 18-25s, over-60s, Sun; free under-18s; free first Sun of month. **Credit** (shop) AmEx, MC, V. **Map** p405 G6.

Originally a train station designed by Victor Laloux to coincide with the 1900 *Exposition Universelle*, the Orsay is now home to masterpieces by Monet, Degas, Renoir, Pissarro and Van Gogh. Look out for the statues representing Toulouse, Bordeaux and Nantes, the towns the station originally served. By the 1950s, the platforms were too short for modern trains and the station was threatened with demolition. At this point, it became home to a theatre (the Renault-Barrault), and Orson Welles' version of *The Trial* was shot here. It was saved in the late 70s when President Giscard d'Estaing decided to turn it into a museum spanning the fertile art period 1830-1914. The interior was redesigned by Italian architect Gae Aulenti, and the main attraction is the skylit Impressionist gallery on the upper floor. *See chapter* **Museums**.

West of Les Invalides

To the west of the Invalides is the massive **Ecole Militaire,** the military academy built by Louis XV which would later train Napoléon.

The best Domes

Les Invalides
17th-century perfection (*see p131*).

Panthéon
Inspired by St Paul's in London (*see p120*).

Ecole Militaire
Where Boney boned up on the battle biz (*see above*).

Le Dôme
Montparnasse fish palace (*see p135*).

Institut de France
The Baroque cupola winks at the Palais du Louvre while the doughty Immortals guard the French language (*see pages 126-7*).

Still used by the army, it is closed to the public. Opposite its south entrance are the Y-shaped **UNESCO** building, constructed in 1958, and the Modernist Ministry of Labour. But it's not all officialdom and bureaucracy: there's the old-fashioned bistro Thoumieux at 79 rue St-Dominique; at No 129, an arcaded square featuring the attractive **Fontaine de Mars**; smart food shops in rue Cler and one of Paris' prettiest street markets on the **avenue de Saxe**.

This area was once far more industrial. The corner of rue Surcouf and rue de l'Université is the site of the Manufacture du Gros Caillou, where France's first cigarettes were made in 1845. From the north-western side of the Ecole Militaire begins the vast **Champ de Mars**, a market garden converted into a military drilling ground in the 18th century. It's a popular place for Bastille Day celebrations. The Champ also houses the quietly beautiful **Mur pour la Paix** (*see p134* **The Writing's on the Wall**) and forms a backdrop to the **Eiffel Tower**.

Les Egouts de Paris

entrance opposite 93 quai d'Orsay, by Pont de l'Alma, 7th (01.53.68.27.81). Mº Alma-Marceau/ RER Pont de l'Alma. **Open** May-Sept 11am-5pm, Sat-Wed; Oct-Apr 11am-4pm Sat-Wed. Closed three weeks in Jan. **Admission** €3.81; €2.29 5-12s, over 60s; free under 5s, CM. **Map** p400 D5.

For centuries the main source of drinking water in Paris was the Seine, which was also the main sewer. Thankfully, construction of an underground sewerage system began in 1825. Today, the Egouts de Paris is perhaps the smelliest museum in the world; each sewer in the 2,100km system is marked with a replica of the street sign above.

Eiffel Tower

Champ de Mars, 7th (01.44.11.23.45/recorded information 01.44.11.23.23/www.tour-eiffel.fr). Mº Bir-Hakeim/RER Champ-de-Mars. **Open** Sept-9 June 9.30am-11pm daily; 10 June-Aug 9am-midnight. **Admission** By lift 1st level €3.66; €2.13 3-12s; 2nd level €6.86; €3.81 3-12s; 3rd level €9.91; €5.32 3-12s; free under-3s. By stairs 1st & 2nd levels €3.05. **Wheelchair access (1st & 2nd levels only). Credit** AmEx, MC, V. **Map** p404 C6.

It's hard to miss the Eiffel Tower, even if you choose not to visit it. At 300m tall, when built in 1889 for the *Exposition Universelle* it was the tallest building in the world. Now, with its aerial, it reaches 321m. The view of it from Trocadéro across the river is monumental, but the distorted aspect from its base most dramatically shows off the graceful ironwork of Gustave Eiffel and brings home its simply massive scale. Be prepared for a long wait for the lifts (which travel 100,000km a year); in 2001 the tower received a record 6.4 million visitors. In fact the number of visitors has led to a plan to add five levels of exhibition space by excavating beneath the tower. For now, save time and money by stopping at the first or second platform. Those who go on to the top

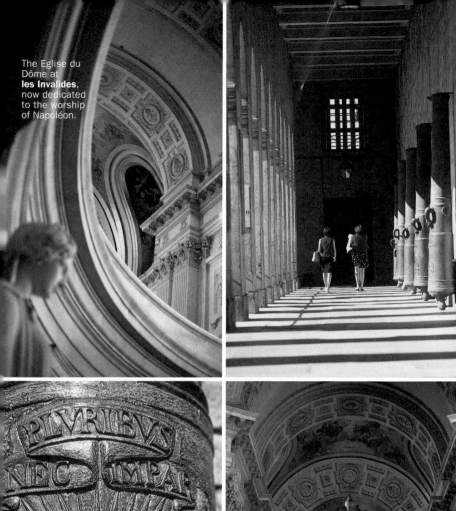

The Eglise du Dôme at **les Invalides**, now dedicated to the worship of Napoléon.

The writing's on the wall

Peace is the word, and it's written all over the wall. In fact it's there in 32 languages and 14 alphabets. The Mur pour la Paix is one of Paris' most quietly beautiful and dignified monuments.

Designed by artist Clara Halter and built by architect Jean-Michel Wilmotte, the wall for peace went up in 2000 (aptly enough, on the Champ de Mars and in full view of the Ecole Militaire) to celebrate the hopes brought by the new millennium. Based thematically on the Wailing Wall in Jerusalem, and inspired by graffiti on the old Berlin Wall, the Mur is an astonishing tripartite arch. Two vertical partitions in glass and stainless steel are covered in etched messages in calligraphic scripts; between them a wooden passageway holds banks of computer monitors.

The monitors' existence shows that the Mur pour la Paix is not a memorial but a call to action: it invites people to write their own messages for peace, either directly on to the structure, or via the website www.murpourlapaix.com. The mail messages are displayed on the monitors in an attempt to create an eternal reminder of the state that the world has never managed to reach and which, particularly in the year 2001, seemed more elusive than ever.

can view Eiffel's cosy salon and enjoy amazing panoramas: over 65km on a good day. In December 2001, a team of 25 painters started the job of giving the tower a lick of new paint (its 18th touch-up), a redecoration that should be finished by February 2003. At night the city lights against the Seine live up to their romantic image – and the queue is shorter. You can eat at the Altitude 95 bistro on the first level or the super-smart Jules Verne on the second.

UNESCO

pl de Fontenoy, 7th (01.45.68.10.00/www.unesco.org). M° Ecole-Militaire. **Open** 9am-6pm Mon-Fri. **Map** p404 D7.

The Y-shaped UNESCO headquarters was built in 1958 by a multinational team. A giant construction in concrete and glass, it's worth visiting for the sculptures by Picasso, Arp, Giacometti and Calder in the lobbies. Inside it buzzes with palpable post-war idealism. Behind there's a Japanese garden, with a concrete contemplation cylinder by Japanese minimalist architect Tadao Ando.

Village Suisse

38-78 av de Suffren/54 av de la Motte-Picquet, 15th (01.43.06.44.18). M° La Motte-Picquet-Grenelle. **Open** 10.30am-1pm; 2-7pm Mon, Thur-Sun. **Map** p404 D7.

The mountains and waterfalls created for the Swiss Village at the 1900 *Exposition Universelle* have long since gone, but the village lives on. Rebuilt as blocks of flats, the street level has been colonised by some 150 boutiques offering high-quality antiques and collectables. The village and its gardens are particularly popular on Sundays.

Fronts de Seine

Downstream from the Eiffel Tower, the 15th *arrondissement* is rarely high on the tourist agenda. The high-tech **Maison de la Culture du Japon** stands near the Pont Bir-Hakeim on quai Branly. The riverfront, with its tower block developments, was the scene of some of the worst architectural crimes of the 1970s. Further west there is hope: the sophisticated headquarters of the Canal+ TV channel (2 rue des Cévennes) are surrounded by fine modern housing, and the **Parc André Citroën**, on the site of a former car factory, opened in 1992.

Parc André Citroën

rue Balard, rue St-Charles, quai Citroën, 15th. M° Javel or Balard. **Open** dawn-6pm Mon-Fri; 9am-6pm Sat, Sun, holidays. **Map** p404 A9.

This park is a fun, 21st-century take on a French formal garden. It comprises glasshouses, computerised fountains, waterfalls, a wilderness and gardens with different-coloured plants and even sounds. Modern-day Le Nôtres (Gilles Clément and Alain Provost) have been at play: stepping stones and water jets prove that this is a garden for pleasure as well as philosophy.

No fat cats at **UNESCO**.

Maison de la Culture du Japon
101 bis quai Branly, 15th (01.55.33.51.90).
M° Bir-Hakeim. RER Champ de Mars Tour Eiffel.
Open noon-7pm Tue, Wed, Fri, Sat; noon-8pm Thur.
Admission free. **Map** p404 C6.
Built in 1996 by the Anglo-Japanese architectural
partnership of Yamanaka and Armstrong, this
opalescent glass cultural centre reflects Paris' large
Japanese community. There is a full programme of
exhibitions, theatre and film, plus a library, authentic Japanese tea ceremony and a shop.

Montparnasse & beyond

*Mainly 6th and 14th arrondissements, parts of 13th
and 15th.*
The legend of Montparnasse began in the early
1900s, when artists such as Picasso, Léger and
Soutine fled to 'Mount Parnassus' from the
rising rents in Montmartre. They were joined
by Chagall, Zadkine and other escapees from
the Russian Revolution and also by Americans,
including Man Ray, Henry Miller, Ezra Pound
and Gertrude Stein. Between the wars the
neighbourhood symbolised modernity.

Today, Montparnasse is a less festive place.
The high-rise **Tour Montparnasse**, Paris'
tribute to Manhattan, is the most visible of
several infelicitous projects of the 70s; at least

there are good views from the top. The old
Montparnasse railway station witnessed two
events of historical significance: in 1898 a
runaway train went out of control and burst
through its facade; the Germans surrendered
Paris here on 25 August 1944. It has been
transformed into a maze of steel and glass, with
the **Jardin de l'Atlantique** suspended over
the TGV tracks.

Nearby rue de la Gaîté, once renowned for its
cabarets, has fallen prey to strip joints, but
boulevard Edgar-Quinet has pleasant cafés and
a street market (Wed, Sat mornings). The
boulevard du Montparnasse still buzzes at
night, thanks to its many cinemas and
legendary brasseries: the Dôme at No 108, now
a luxurious fish restaurant and bar; giant art
deco brasserie **La Coupole** at No 102, which
opened in 1927; and opposite, classic late-night
café **Le Select**. Further east, legendary literary
café **La Closerie des Lilas**, opened as a
dance hall in the 1840s, was a favourite with
everyone from Lenin and Trotsky to Picasso
and Hemingway. Le Nègre de Toulouse and the
Dingo are long gone but there's still a sense of
the *louche* at the Rosebud in rue Delambre.
Look out for Rodin's 1898 *Balzac* on boulevard
Raspail; his rugged, stubbornly virile rendition
of the novelist caused such a furore that it
wasn't displayed in public for 40 years.

A more recent addition is the glass and steel
Fondation Cartier by Jean Nouvel on
boulevard Raspail, an exhibition centre for
contemporary art. Inexpensive clothes can be
found on rue de Rennes. There are shoe, food
and children's shops on rues Vavin and Bréa,
which lead to the **Jardins du Luxembourg**.
Stop for a coffee at Café Vavin and look at Henri
Sauvage's white tiled apartment building at
6 rue Vavin, built in 1911-12.

Cimetière du Montparnasse
3 bd Edgar-Quinet, 14th (01.44.10.86.50).
M° Edgar-Quinet or Raspail. **Open** 16 Mar-5 Nov
8am-6pm Mon-Fri; 8.30am-6pm Sat; 9am-6pm Sun;
6 Nov-15 Mar 8am-5.30pm Mon-Fri; 8.30am-5.30pm
Sat; 9.30am-5.30pm Sun. **Map** p405 G9.
The cemetery roll-call reads like a who-was-who of
Left Bank cultural life. Pay homage to writers Jean-
Paul Sartre and Simone de Beauvoir, Baudelaire,
Maupassant, Tzara, Beckett, Ionesco and Duras;
composers César Frank and Saint-Saëns; sculptors
Dalou, Rude, Bartholdi, Laurens (with his own sculpture *Douleur* on the tomb) and Zadkine; the unfortunate Captain Alfred Dreyfus, André Citroën of car
fame, and Mr and Mme Pigeon forever reposing in
their double bed. From cinema and showbiz are
Jean Seberg, waif-like star of *A bout de souffle*,
beloved comic Coluche and *provocateur* Serge Gainsbourg. Brancusi's sculpture *Le Baiser* (The Kiss),
adorns a tomb in the north-east corner.

Sightseeing

Jardin de l'Atlantique

entry from Gare Montparnasse or pl des Cinq-Martyrs-du-Lycée-Buffon, 15th. Mº Montparnasse-Bienvenüe. **Open** dawn-dusk daily. **Map** p405 G9.
Perhaps the hardest of all Paris' new gardens to find, the Jardin de l'Atlantique, opened in 1995, takes the Parisian quest for space airbound with an engineering feat suspended 18 metres over the tracks of Montparnasse station. It is a small oasis of granite paths, trees and bamboo in an urban desert of modern apartment and office blocks. Small openings allow you to peer down on the trains below.

Tour Maine-Montparnasse

33 av du Maine, 15th (01.45.38.52.56). Mº Montparnasse-Bienvenüe. **Open** 9.30am-10.30pm daily. **Admission** exhibition/terrace €7.55; €6.40 students, over-60s; €5.18 5-14s; free under-5s. **No credit cards.** **Map** p405 F9.
Most would agree that the only good thing about the tower is the view. Built in 1974 on the site of the former Gare Montparnasse, this steel-and-glass monster, at 209m high, is lower than the Eiffel Tower, but more central. A lift whisks you up to the 56th floor, where you'll find a display of aerial views of Paris, allowing you to see how the city has changed since 1858; there is a terrace on the 58th floor. Fortunately, you will rarely find a queue.

Denfert-Rochereau & Montsouris

A spookier kind of burial ground can be found at place Denfert-Rochereau, entrance to the **Catacombs** (*see* **Subterranean bone-pit views**, *page 137*). The bones of six million people were transferred here just before the Revolution from overcrowded Paris cemeteries to a network of underground tunnels that spreads under much of the 13th and 14th *arrondissements*. The entrance is next to one of the toll gates of the Mur des Fermiers-Généraux built by Ledoux in the 1780s. A bronze lion, sculpted by Bartholdi of Statue of Liberty fame, dominates the traffic junction. It is a replica of the Lion de Belfort in eastern France, symbol of resistance against Germany in 1870 under Colonel Denfert-Rochereau.

One of the big draws here is a lovely large park, the **Parc Montsouris**. On its opening day in 1878 the man-made lake suddenly and inexplicably emptied and the engineer responsible promptly committed suicide. Around the western edge of the park are small streets such as rue du Parc Montsouris and rue Georges-Braque that were built up in the early 1900s with charming villas and artists' studios, including the Villa Ozenfant (53 av Reille), designed in 1922 by Le Corbusier for painter Amédée Ozenfant, and the Villa Guggenbuhl (14 rue Nansouty) designed in 1926-27 by Lurçat. On the southern edge of Montsouris the

Cité Universitaire, home to 6,000 foreign students, is worth visiting for its themed pavilions, designed by eminent architects.

Cité Universitaire

bd Jourdan, 14th. RER Cité Universitaire (www.ciup.fr).
Founded in the 1920s in a fervent wave of interwar internationalism and a desire to attract foreign students, the Cité Universitaire is an odd mix. The 40 pavilions, inspired by Oxbridge and US/UK campuses (although here purely residential) were designed in supposedly national style, some by architects of the country like the De Stijl Collège Néerlandais by Willem Dudok; others in exotic pastiche like the Asie du Sud-Est pavilion with its Khmer sculptures and bird-beaked roof. The Swiss (1935) and Brazilian (1959) pavilions by Le Corbusier reflect his early and late styles. You can visit the Swiss one (01.44.16.10.16; 10am-noon, 2-5pm daily).

Parc Montsouris

bd Jourdan, 14th. RER Cité-Universitaire.
The most colourful of the capital's parks. Commissioned by Haussmann and laid out by Alphand, its gently sloping lawns descend towards an artificial lake, with turtles and ducks and a variety of trees and flowerbeds. Spot the bed planted with different roses for French newspapers and magazines.

15th arrondissement

Tranquil and residential, the 15th, centred on the shopping streets of rue du Commerce and rue Lecourbe, is Paris' largest *arrondissement* and the one that probably has the least for the tourist. Having said that, it's worth making a detour to visit **La Ruche** ('beehive'), designed by Eiffel as a wine pavilion for the 1900 exhibition and resituated here as artists' studios. Nearby on rue des Morillons the **Parc Georges Brassens** was opened in 1983.

Parc Georges Brassens

rue des Morillons, 15th. Mº Porte de Vanves. **Map** p404 D10.
Built on the site of the former Abattoirs de Vaugirard, Parc Georges Brassens prefigured the industrial recuperation of Parc André Citroën and La Villette. The gateways crowned by bronze bulls have been kept, as have a series of iron meat market pavilions, which house a busy antiquarian and second-hand book market at weekends. The interesting Jardin des Senteurs is planted with aromatic species while, in one corner, a small vineyard produces 200 bottles of Clos des Morillons every year.

La Ruche

passage de Dantzig, 15th. Mº Convention. **Map** p404 D10.
Peek through the grille or sneak in behind an unsuspecting resident to see the former wine pavilion, rebuilt here by philanthropic sculptor Alfred Boucher to be let out as studios for struggling

Sightseeing

Subterranean bone-pit views

Dig, if you will, the picture: you're ferreting around looking for the box with the Christmas decorations in, when suddenly eight or nine corpses come hurtling through the wall. Not pleasant, but it happened to 18th-century Parisians when the communal ditch of the Cimetière des Innocents burst in 1725, torpedoing hundreds of cadavers into people's cellars. Not pleasant, but not surprising when you consider that being laid to rest in Paris usually meant being hurled into the nearest public burial pit. (There are reports of the ground level of church yards having risen by as much as five metres by the time the Cimetière des Innocents let it all hang out.)

With hundreds of dead bodies lying about the place, disease began to spread and the civic authorities had to act. In 1785, they had the brainwave of parking the bones in the old quarries at La Tombe-Issoire. The tramps who had called the quarries home were evicted, and deliveries began. The first batch took 15 months to shift (the operation was only ever carried out at night), and fresh deliveries continued to be made until 1870, by which time the remnants of six million people from 17 different cemeteries had been rehoused.

The overwhelming sensation left by a visit to the Catacombs today (not recommended for claustrophobes or those who feel unequal to the 85-step spiral staircase that takes you 20m below ground level) is not, as you might

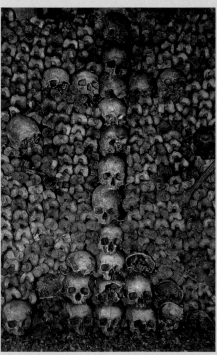

suppose, spookiness but simply awe at the volume of body parts they contain. The warning at the entrance to the ossuary is as camply melodramatic as anything you'd see in a Hammer horror film: 'Stop! This is the empire of death!', it reads; but don't stop – you'd miss the unique and astonishing sight of the decorative bone walls. Each one is brown with age and has a lower section composed of about 75cm-worth of femurs, some of which still have shrivelled slivers of dry skin clinging to them. On top there is a row of skulls, then a mix of various bony elements, all finished off with another row of skulls. These walls can be as much as three metres deep. You'd also miss the poems and legends carved in stone, most of which have a strong *carpe diem* vibe. The Catacombs also have such eye-catching oddities as a sepulchral lamp, an underground spring and natural bell-shaped ceilings.

There are two practicalities visitors need to bear in mind. One – a torch is essential for picking out details. Two – don't fall prey to the temptation of lifting any ossified souvenirs or filching a new prop for the ventriloquism act: bags and coats are searched at the exit.

Les Catacombs *1 pl Denfert-Rochereau, 14th (01.43.22.47.63). Mº Denfert-Rochereau.* **Open** 11am-4pm Tue; 9am-4pm Wed-Sun. Closed public holidays. **Admission** €5.03; €3.35 8-25s, over-60s; free under-8s, CM. **No credit cards**. Map p405 H10.

Don't walk on the grass? Lie on it instead at **Parc Montsouris.**

artists. Chagall, Soutine, Brancusi and Modigliani all spent periods here, and the 140 studios are still much sought after by artists.

The 13th arrondissement

A working-class area that became one of the most industrialised parts of Paris in the 19th century, the 13th has been one of the most marauded areas of Paris since World War II, from the tower blocks of Chinatown to the new national library and the burgeoning development zone around it.

Gobelins & La Salpêtrière

Its image may be of tower blocks, but the 13th also contains some historic parts, expecially where it borders on the 5th (*see pp116-124*). The **Manufacture Nationale des Gobelins** is home to the French state weaving companies. The tapestries and rugs produced here continue a tradition dating back to the 15th century, when Jean Gobelin set up his dyeing works by the river Bièvre. Followed by tanneries and other industries, the river became notorious for its pollution until covered over in 1912, while the slums were depicted in Hugo's *Les Misérables*. The area was tidied up in the 30s, when the Square Réné Le Gall, a small park, was laid out on former tapestry-workers' allotments. On rue des Gobelins, where Gobelin lived, the so-called **Château de la Reine Blanche** is a curious medieval relic.

On the western edge of the *arrondissement*, next to the Gare d'Austerlitz, is the Hôpital de la Pitié-Salpêtrière, one of the oldest hospitals in Paris. Founded in 1656 by Louis XIV to round up vagrant and unwanted women, ironically it was here that Princess Diana was brought after her fatal crash. It is also known for the beautiful **Chapelle St-Louis-de-la-Salpêtrière**.

The busy road intersection of place d'Italie has seen more developments with, opposite the town hall, the Centre Commercial Italie 2, a bizarre high-tech confection designed by Japanese architect Kenzo Tange, which contains the **Gaumont Grand Ecran Italie** cinema. There's a good food market on boulevard Auguste-Blanqui (Tue, Fri, Sun mornings) and the sharply contrasting attractions of Chinatown and the Butte aux Cailles.

Chapelle St-Louis-de-la-Salpêtrière

47 bd de l'Hôpital, 13th (01.42.16.04.24).
M° Gare d'Austerlitz. **Open** 8.30am-6.30pm daily.
Map p406 L9.
In order to separate the sick from the insane and the destitute from the debauched, the chapel had to be build with eight naves. Designed by Libéral Bruand in 1657-77 with an octagonal dome in the centre, this austerely beautiful chapel is now sometimes used for art exhibitions. Around the chapel are some of the buildings of the Hôpital de la Pitié-Salpêtrière, founded on the site of a gunpowder (saltpetre) factory by Louis XIV, specifically to house unwanted women. In the 1790s it became a research centre for the insane. Charcot pioneered neuro-psychology here, and even received a famous visit from Freud. It is now one of Paris' main teaching hospitals.

For 'interdit' read 'don't forget your cozzie' at **Parc André Citroën**.

Château de la Reine Blanche

17 rue des Gobelins, 13th. M° Gobelins. **Map** p406 K10.
Through a gateway you can spot the turret and first floor of an ancient house. The curious relic is named after Queen Blanche of Provence who had a *château* here, but was probably rebuilt in the 1520s for the Gobelins. Blanche was also associated with the Couvent des Cordeliers, of which a fragment survives on the corner of rue Pascal and rue de Julienne.

Manufacture Nationale des Gobelins

42 av des Gobelins, 13th (01.44.08.52.00).
M° Gobelins. **Open** visits by guided tour only, 2.15 and 2.30pm Tue-Thur (1.5 hours); reserve in advance on 01.44.54.19.33 **Admission** €7.62; €6.10 7-24s.
No credit cards. Map p406 K10.
Tapestries have been woven here since 1662. Known as the Gobelins after Jean Gobelin, a dyer who previously owned the site, the factory was at its wealthiest during the *ancien régime* when tapestries were produced for royal residences under artists such as Le Brun and Oudry. Today tapestries are still woven and visitors can watch weavers at work. The guided tour (in French) through the 1912 factory helps you to understand the weaving process and takes in the 18th-century chapel and the Beauvais tapestry workshops. Arrive 30 minutes before the tour.

Chinatown

South of the rue de Tolbiac is Paris' main Chinatown, centred between the 60s tower blocks along avenues d'Ivry and de Choisy, and home to a multi-Asian community. The bleak modern architecture could make it depressing, yet it's a fascinating piece of South-East Asia, lined with kitsch restaurants, Vietnamese *pho* noodle bars and Chinese patisseries, as well as the large Tang Frères supermarket on avenue d'Ivry. Less easy to find is the Buddhist temple hidden in an underground car park beneath the

Don't miss | Hemingway's hot spots

74 rue du Cardinal-Lemoine
His first address in Paris.

Quai des Grands Augustins
Where he browsed among the bouquinistes.

Closerie des Lilas
He wrote here. He wrote fine and well and good. And then he had a beer, and he drank deep...

27 rue de Fleurus
The studio apartment where he would visit Gertrude Stein.

Rue Jacob
Where F Scott Fitzgerald asked Ernie to appraise his penis. The verdict: OK, but not great, Gatsby.

tallest tower block (Autel de la culte de Bouddha, av d'Ivry, opposite rue Frères d'Astier-de-la-Vigerie, open 9am-6pm daily). Come here for the traditional lion and dragon dances at Chinese New Year (*see chapter* **By Season**).

La Butte aux Cailles

In contrast to Chinatown, the villagey Butte aux Cailles is a neighbourhood of old houses, winding cobblestone streets and funky bars and restaurants. This workers' neighbourhood, home in the 1800s to many small factories, was one of the first to fight during the 1848 Revolution and the Paris Commune. The Butte has preserved its insurgent character and has resisted the aggressive forces of city planning and construction companies. The cobbled rue de la Butte-aux-Cailles and the rue des Cinq-Diamants are the HQ of the arty, *soixante-huitard* bohemian forces. The cottages built in 1912 in a mock-Alsatian style at 10 rue Daviel were one of the earliest public housing schemes in Paris. Further south, explore passage Vandrezanne, the square des Peupliers, the rue Dieulafoy and the streets of the Cité Florale.

The Butte offers a selection of relaxed, inexpensive bistros: Le Temps des Cérises, run as a cooperative, busy **Chez Gladines** and more upmarket Chez Paul. Several feisty bars, including **La Folie en Tête** and Le Merle Moqueur, provide music and cheap beer on tap to a youthful crowd spilling on to the pavement.

The developing east

Dominique Perrault's Bibliothèque Nationale de France François Mitterrand began the massive redevelopment of a desolate area formerly taken up by railway yards. The ZAC Rive Gauche project, which has employed 50 architects and 30 urbanists, centres around the University of Paris VII Denis Diderot which will open next year, accommodating 30,000 students and lecturers. It is envisaged as a 'new Latin Quarter', where students will interact with local small businesses, hospitals and industry. Existing industrial buildings in the area, such as Les Frigos former refrigerated warehouses (now containing artists' studios), and the majestic Grands Moulins de Paris, partly burnt down in 1996, will be incorporated. Currently much of the area resembles a building site as new tower blocks appear overnight, shops open and roads change names. Happily, a growing flotilla of music bars moored on the Seine – the **Batofar, Péniche Blues Café** and **Péniche Makara** – provides signs of new life in the air. Across the railway, a pioneering art nucleus called ScèneEst is burgeoning among the offices

and housing developments. Overlooking the boulevards des Amiraux, Le Corbusier's Armée du Salut hostel (12 rue Cantagrel, 13th/01.53.61.82.00) points to earlier urban planning.

Bibliothèque Nationale de France François Mitterrand

quai François-Mauriac, 13th (01.53.79.53.79). M° Bibliothèque or Quai de la Gare. **Open** 10am-8pm Tue-Sat; noon-7pm Sun. Closed two weeks in Sept/Oct and two weeks in Aug. **Admission** day €3.05; annual €30.49; student €15.24. **Credit** MC, V. **Wheelchair access. Map** p407 M10.

Opened in December 1996, the new national library (dubbed 'TGB' or *Très Grande Bibliothèque*) was the last of Mitterrand's *Grands Projets* and also the most expensive. Perrault was criticised for his curiously dated-looking design, which hides readers underground and stores the books in four L-shaped glass towers. In the central void is a garden (open only to researchers) filled with 140 trees, uprooted from Fontainebleau at a cost of 40 million francs. The research section opened in autumn 1998, whereupon the computer system failed to get the right books to the right person and staff promptly went on strike. The library houses over ten million volumes, and has room for 3,000 readers. Books, newspapers and periodicals are on public access to anyone over 18. There are regular concerts and exhibitions. (*See chapters* **Museums**, **Directory**.)

Lapping it up in **La Butte aux Cailles**.

Beyond the Périphérique

From ghettos with junkies and in-yer-face monkeys to leafy suburbia where
nothing disturbs ya, the *banlieues* offer a stunning contrast of lifestyles.

Boulogne & the west

Paris' most desirable suburbs lie to the west,
where the middle classes built expensive
properties between the wars. Decentralisation
also means that La Défense, Neuilly, Boulogne,
Levallois and Issy-les-Moulineaux have become
work locations for Paris residents, notably in
the advertising, media and service industries.

Neuilly-sur-Seine is the most sought-after
residential suburb. Smart apartment blocks
have gradually replaced the extravagant
mansions built around the Bois de Boulogne.

Boulogne-Billancourt is the main town in
the region outside Paris. In 1320 the Gothic
Eglise Notre Dame was begun in tribute to a
statue of the Virgin washed up at Boulogne-sur-
Mer. By the 18th century, Boulogne was known
for its wines and laundries and, early in the 20th
century, for its artist residents (Landowski,
Lipchitz, Chagall, Gris), while Billancourt was
known for industry (cars, aviation and cinema).
The former Renault factory has been sitting like
a beached whale in the Seine since it closed in
1992, but looks set for a prestigious future as the
Fondation Pinault contemporary art museum,
which it is predicted to become in 2004. Near the
Bois de Boulogne are elegant villas, and some
fine examples of 1920s and 30s architecture by
Le Corbusier, Mallet-Stevens, Perret and Lurçat,
well pinpointed by plaques. The Musée des
Années 30 focuses on artists and architects who
lived in the town at the time.

Across the Seine, the **Parc de St-Cloud** is
surrounded by villas. South of St-Cloud is
Sèvres, site of the Musée National de Céramique.

The Château de Malmaison at Rueil-
Malmaison was loved by Napoléon and
Joséphine, who transformed its interior in
Empire style. The eccentric Château de Monte
Cristo (01.30.61.61.35) at Port Marly was built
for Alexandre Dumas with a tiled Moorish
room. In the grounds, the Château d'If is
inscribed with the titles of his many works.

St-Germain-en-Laye is a smart suburb with a
château, where Henri II lived in rip-roaring
style with his wife Catherine de Médicis and
his mistress Diane de Poitiers. Here Louis XIV
was born, Mary Queen of Scots grew up, and
the deposed James II lived for 12 years.
Napoléon III turned the château into the Musée

Sightseeing

des Antiquités Nationales. The Musée
Départemental Maurice Denis has a collection
of Nabi and Post-Impressionist art.

Further west, the town of Poissy merits a
visit for its Gothic Collégiale Notre Dame (8 rue
de l'Eglise), much restored by Viollet-le-Duc,
and Le Corbusier's avant-garde Villa Savoye.

Les Jardins Albert Kahn

*14 rue du Port, 92100 Boulogne (01.46.04.52.80).
M° Boulogne-Pont St Cloud.* **Open** May-Sept 11am-
6.30pm; Oct-Apr 11am-5.30pm Tue-Sun. **Admission**
€3.35; €2.29 13-25s, over-60s; free under-13s,
disabled. **Credit** V.

With red bridges, Japanese shrines, Alsatian forests
and cascading streams, the gardens created by
financier Albert Kahn (1860-1940) should be twee,
yet somehow never are. There's an enormous -
variety crammed in a small space. Water and ever-
greens dominate the gardens, making them
interesting even in winter. *Wheelchair access.*

Drancy

In the summer of 2001 the French government made the remains of Drancy, the camp five miles north of Paris in which prisoners were held before being transferred to Auschwitz, an historic monument.

This marked a major step in France's emergence from its denial of responsibility for what happened to persecuted minorities during the wartime occupation. It was not until 1995 that Chirac admitted that the French state was responsible for assisting the Nazis in committing atrocities. Before that, governments had argued that there was a real distinction between the Vichy regime and France.

The facts are these: Drancy originally contained Spanish refugees fleeing from Franco, all of whom were handed over by the French to the Nazis – few survived; the rounding up of French Jews was ordered by the Nazis but carried out by the French police; until July 1943 Drancy was run by the French on behalf on the Nazis; some 70,000 people were held there on their way to Auschwitz; in a ten-week period in 1942, 6,000 French Jewish children were moved from Drancy to Auschwitz; one-quarter of France's wartime Jewish population was murdered (it should be noted that those who survived were, in most cases, protected by French Catholics); in total, the Vichy regime passed over 160 anti-Semitic laws.

In 1997 the French Roman Catholic church apologised to the Jewish people for having turned a blind eye to French collaboration in the holocaust. In 1998 Maurice Papon, a Vichy official, was sentenced to serve ten years in a Paris prison for crimes against humanity. Perhaps one of the legacies of the Chirac years will be a readiness to reflect maturely on the mistakes of the past.

Parc de St-Cloud

92210 St-Cloud (01.41.12.02.90). M° Pont de St Cloud. **Open** Mar-Oct 7.30am-9pm daily; May-Aug 7.30am-10pm daily; Nov-Feb 7.30am-8pm daily. **Admission** free; €3.05 cars. **No credit cards.**
You can play football or frisbee, walk or picnic on the grass, yet this is another classic French park laid out by Le Nôtre, and all that remains of a royal château that belonged to 'Monsieur', brother of Louis XIV. There are complex avenues that meet in stairs, long perspectives, a great view over Paris from the Rond-Point du Balustrade and a series of pools and fountains: most spectacular is the Grande Cascade, a multi-tiered feast of dolphins and sea beasts (switched on 2pm, 3pm, 4pm Sun in June).

Villa Savoye

82 rue de Villiers, 78300 Poissy (01.39.65.01.06/ www.fondationlecorbusier.asso.fr). RER Poissy + 15 min walk. **Open** Apr-Oct 9.30am-12.30pm, 1.30-6pm Mon, Wed-Sun; Nov-Mar 9.30am-12.30pm, 1.30-4.30pm Mon, Wed-Sun. **Admission** €3.96; €2.44 18-25s; free under-18s. **Credit** MC, V.
Built in 1929 for a family of rich industrialists, this luxury house with its sculpted spiral staircase and roof terraces is perhaps Le Corbusier's most successful work. Inside are some seminal pieces of Modernist furniture. *Wheelchair access.*

La Défense

La Défense's skyscrapers and walkways create the feeling of another world (*see p145* **A banlieusard rain's a-gonna fall**). The area is lively, though: businessy in the week, and filled with visitors at the weekend.

La Défense (named after a stand against the Prussians in 1870) has been a showcase for French business since the mid-50s, when the triangular CNIT exhibition hall (01.46.92.11.11/ open 9am-6pm Mon-Sat) was built for trade shows, but it was the **Grande Arche** that gave the district a true monument. Over 100,000 people work here, and another 35,000 live in the futuristic blocks of flats on the southern edge. None of the skyscrapers display any great architectural distinction, although together they make an impressive sight. A recent wave of development has seen westward growth and includes a new 40-storey tower by Pei Cobb Freed and a church by Franck Hammoutène. The Info-Défense kiosk (01.47.74.84.24/ open Apr-Oct 10am-6pm, Nov-Mar 9.30am-5.30pm Mon-Fri) in front of CNIT has maps and guides of the area.

La Grande Arche de la Défense

92400 Paris la Défense (01.49.07.27.57/ www. grandearche.com). M° La Défense. **Open** 10am-7pm daily (last ride to the rooftop 6.30pm). **Admission** €7.01 summer; €6.10 winter; €5.35 under-17s, students. **Credit** AmEx, MC, V.

Completed for the bicentenary of the Revolution in 1989 the Grande Arche, designed by obscure Danish architect Johan Otto von Spreckelsen, is now a major tourist attraction. Only from close up do you realise how vast it is. A stomach-churning ride in high-speed glass lifts soars up through the 'clouds' to the roof where there is a fantastic view into Paris. Outside on the giant forecourt are fountains and sculptures by artists including Miró, Serra, Calder and César's Thumb. *Wheelchair access.*

St-Denis & the north

Amid the suburban sprawl stands one of the treasures of Gothic architecture: the Basilique St-Denis, where most of France's monarchs were buried. St Denis also boasts the innovative Musée de l'Art et d'Histoire de St-Denis in a scrupulously preserved Carmelite convent, a busy covered market, and some fine modern buildings, such as Niemeyer's 1989 HQ for Communist newspaper *L'Humanité* and Gaudin's extension to the town hall. Across the canal is the elegant **Stade de France**, designed for the 1998 Football World Cup. The département of Seine St-Denis also has a lively cultural life, with a buzzing theatre scene and prestigious jazz and classical music festivals. Le Bourget, home to Paris' first airport (still used for VIPs and private aircraft) contains the **Musée de l'Air et de l'Espace**. North of Sarcelles, Ecouen, noted for its Renaissance

château, now the Musée National de la Renaissance, gives glimpses of a rural past. Enghien-les-Bains, set around a large lake where you can hire rowing boats and pedalos, provided a pleasure haven in the 19th century with the development of its spa, a casino (the only one in the Paris region) and a racecourse.

Basilique St-Denis

6 rue de Strasbourg, 93200 St-Denis (01.48.09.83.54). M° St-Denis-Basilique. **Open** Apr-Sept 10am-7.30pm Mon-Sat; noon-7pm Sun. Oct-Mar 10am-5pm Mon-Sat; noon-5pm Sun. **Admission** nave free. Royal tombs €5.49 per person (€4.05 per person in a group); €3.51 18-25s, students; free under-18s. Guided tours 11.15am, 3pm Mon-Sat, 12.15pm Sun (€3.81 audio guide in English). **No credit cards.**

Legend has it that when St-Denis was beheaded, he picked up his head and walked to Vicus Catulliacus (now St-Denis) to be buried. Now, *that's* magic. The first church, parts of which can be seen in the crypt, was built over his tomb in around 475. The present edifice is the first example of true Gothic architecture. The basilica was begun by Abbot Suger in the 12th century. In the 13th, master mason Pierre de Montreuil erected the spire and rebuilt the choir, nave and transept. This was the burial place for all but three French monarchs between 996 and the end of the *ancien régime*, so the ambulatory is a museum of French funerary sculpture. During the Revolution in 1792, the tombs were desecrated and the royal remains thrown into a pit nearby.

Limbo down to **La Défense** for some of the best views in town.

Cimetière des Chiens

4 pont de Clichy, 92600 Asnières (01.40.86.21.11).
M° Mairie de Clichy. **Open** 16 Mar-14 Oct 10am-6pm
Mon, Wed-Sun; 15 Oct-15 Mar 10am-4.30pm, Mon,
Wed-Sun. **Admission** €2.59; €1.22 6-12s. **No**
credit cards.
Many of Paris' dogs end up here on a slightly for-
lorn island in the Seine. A decaying neo-Byzantine
entrance points to a grander past: just within lies a
grand monument, a small girl draped over a large
dog: Barry the St Bernard 'who saved the lives of 40
people. He was killed by the 41st.' RIP, Bazza.

Eglise Notre Dame du Raincy

av de la Résistance, 93340 Le Raincy
(01.43.81.14.98). SNCF/RER E Raincy-Villemomble.
Open 10am-noon, 2-6pm Mon-Sat; 10am-noon Sun.
Auguste Perret's little-known modernist masterpiece was built 1922-23 as a modest war memorial.
In place of conventional stained glass, the windows
are coloured glass blocks that create fantastic reflections on the interior.

Stade de France

rue Francis de Pressensé, 93200 St-Denis
(01.55.93.00.00/www.stadefrance.fr). M° St-Denis
Porte de Paris/RER B La Plaine-Stade de
France/RER D-Stade de France St-Denis. **Open**
10am-6.00pm daily (except during events).
Admission €6 adults; €4.50 children; free under 6s.
Coulisses du Stade (10am, 2pm, 4pm) €14; €10 6-17s,
students; free under-6s (visit in English 2pm). **Credit**
MC, V.
The Stade de France, designed by Zubléna, Macary,
Regembal and Constantini, was built in a record 31
months – just in time for the 1998 football World
Cup. Its spectacular flying saucer-like steel and alu-
minium roof has become a landmark.

Vincennes & the east

The more upmarket residential districts in the
east surround the Bois de Vincennes, such as
Vincennes, dominated by its medieval castle
and home to Paris' main zoo. Joinville-le-Pont,
famous for being the place where Marcel Carné
shot *Les Enfants du Paradis*, and Champigny-
sur-Marne draw weekend crowds along the
banks of the Marne. In Champigny-sur-Marne,
the Musée de la Résistance Nationale tells the
history of the French Résistance.

Château de Vincennes

av de Paris, 94300 Vincennes (01.48.08.31.20).
M° Château de Vincennes. **Open** Oct-Mar 10am-
noon, 1.15pm-5pm daily; Apr-Sept 10am-noon, 1.15 -
6pm daily. **Admission** €4.88, €3.20 18-25s; €3.81,
€2.29. **No credit cards.**
An imposing curtain wall punctuated by towers
encloses this medieval fortress. Few traces remain
of Louis VII's first hunting lodge, or the fortified
manor built by Philippe-Auguste. The square keep
was begun by Philippe VI and completed by

defence-obsessed Charles V, who also began rebuilding the newly-renovated Flamboyant-Gothic Sainte-
Chapelle. Louis XIII had the Pavillon du Roi and
Pavillon de la Reine built by Louis Le Vau (completed 1658). The castle was transformed into bar-
racks in the 19th century.

Pavillon Baltard

12 av Victor Hugo, 94130 Nogent-sur-Marne
(01.43.24.76.76/www.pbpa.net). RER Nogent-sur-
Marne. **Open** during salons/exhibitions only.
In the 1970s when Les Halles was demolished someone had the foresight to save one of Baltard's iron
and glass market pavilions (No 8: the egg and poultry shed), and resurrect it in the suburbs.

Sceaux & the south

Interwar and postwar urbanisation transformed
villages and defensive fortresses into areas of
workers' housing. Bordering Paris, the 'red' (left
wing) suburb of Malakoff is home to many artists.
Sceaux was formerly the setting for a château
built for Louis XIV's finance minister Colbert.
The present building housing the Musée de l'Ile
de France (01.46.61.06.71) dates from 1856 but
the park follows Le Nôtre's original design; the
Orangerie is used for summer chamber music.
At Châtenay-Malabry, the 1930s Cité de la
Butte-Rouge garden-city estate was a model of
its time for social housing. Chateaubriand,
forced to leave Paris for criticising Napoléon,
lived in a pretty villa (Maison de Chateaubriand)
in Vallée-aux-Loups, where the landscaped park
is evidence of his passion for gardening.
   The south-eastern suburbs boomed during
19th-century industrialisation, witness Ivry-sur-
Seine with its warehouses and the Manufacture
des Oeillets, a former rivet factory that is now a
theatre. Ivry is famed for its social policies, such
as the 1970s L'Atelier housing projects.
   The bleak new town of Evry, 30km south of
Paris, created in 1969, is of note for then-radical
housing estates like Les Pyramides and the
modern **Cathédrale de la Résurrection**.

Arcueil Aqueduct

Spanning the Bièvre valley through Arcueil and
Clamart, this impressive double-decker structure
brings water from Wissous to Paris. A Roman structure existed a few metres from this one. In 1609
Henri IV decided to reconstruct the aqueduct, and
by 1628 it provided water for 16 Paris fountains.

Cathédrale de la Résurrection

1 clos de la Cathédrale, 91000 Evry (01.64.97.93.53).
SNCF Evry-Couronnes. **Open** 10am- 6pm Mon-Fri;
10am-noon, 2-6pm Sat; 2.30-7pm Sun.
Completed in 1995, this was the first new cathedral
in France since the war. Mario Botta's rather heavy,
truncated, red-brick cylindrical form seeks to establish a new aesthetic for religious architecture.

A banlieusard rain's a-gonna fall

Somebody has got to do something about the violence in certain suburbs of Paris; in 2001, President Chirac said as much himself. Sometimes it seems that the Périphérique separates two completely different societies (indeed the *banlieue* problem is referred to here as *la fracture sociale*).

To illustrate the difference: just five miles north-east of the beauty of the Louvre there is a suburb called Aubervilliers. Here illegally imported apes are trained to attack people, and to go for the face when they do. Whole areas of other suburbs are no-go zones for first-aid services, though some will go in if they are accompanied by the police. One Saturday in the spring of 2001, a shopping centre in the suburb of La Défense was chosen as the forum for a two-hour battle between 400 rival gang members from other manors. In September, news of the destruction of the World Trade Center brought jubilation to La Cité des 4,000, a run-down estate that is home primarily to Muslim immigrants.

A key cause of the social tension that results in these reactions (although poor housing, unemployment and heavy-handed policing hardly help) is the failure of French society to assimilate immigrants from former colonies. There is a strong expectation from the host society that newcomers should leave their old culture behind and endeavour to become French; the very notion of multiculturalism can be at odds with the centralising tendency of the French state.

This expectation is often frustrated, and there is now a significant number of young people who were born in France and speak French but feel that they fit into neither the French culture nor that of their immigrant parents.

More sinister has been the harsh treatment of certain immigrants by the authorities (anthropologist Paul Silverstein has drawn parallels between the urban apartheid of colonial North Africa and that of the Paris suburbs). Patrols of riot police and soldiers walk around the suburbs with sub-machine guns and enforce stop-and-search laws.

The presence of Muslims in the suburbs (Islam is the second-most practised religion in France) also reveals a paradox in the way society is structured: state education has to be free and secular, but in a multi-cultural society the rhetoric of nationality and secularism can often shield racism and religious discrimination. This is a real danger. In 1998, *Le Monde* published a report on racism in France in which one in every five French citizens admitted to being xenophobic; 40% said that there were too many black and Arab people in the country.

So, as the President has pointed out, something must be done. Since 1995 the National Urban Integration Plan and the Urban Revival Pact have tried to boost the suburbs' economies, but changes need to take place at a far deeper social level before *banlieusards* from immigrant families can legitimately feel that they are part of France.

Museums

Delicate ancient relics, astonishing specimens of surrealism and grisly shrunken heads. No, not members of the Sénat: things you can see in Paris' museums.

Paris is the most museumy of all museum cities. Where else can you get the **Musée du Louvre**, the **Musée d'Orsay**, the **Centre Pompidou** and the **Musée Edith Piaf**? The museum scene is buzzing, and the city is a hive of ground-breaking exhibitions and sites.

In 2002 major exhibitions include numerous tie-ins to the Victor Hugo bicentenery *(see p177,* **Happy birthday, dear Victor***)*, while a France-wide Czech season will see temporary exhibitions of Czech fine and decorative art and photography at several Paris museums.

Note that most museums are closed on Monday or Tuesday. Try to visit major museums and shows on weekdays, especially at lunch time or evening; reduced rates on Sunday often generate big crowds. Reduced admission charges apply often to pensioners or students, but bring an identity card or passport to prove your status. Most ticket counters close 30-45 minutes before closing time. Prebooking is now essential before 1pm at the **Grand Palais**. It's also possible to prebook for the **Louvre** and selected major exhibitions at other museums. National museums are free on the first Sunday of the month. Municipal-run museums are free except for temporary exhibitions.

Paris Carte Musées et Monuments (CM)

Price one day €12.20, three days €24.39, five days €36.59.

This card gives free entry into 70 museums and monuments all over Paris (indicated below by CM), and allows you to jump queues. It's very good value if you're in Paris for a few days and plan on intensive museum visiting, although you have to pay extra for special exhibitions. It can be bought at museums, tourist offices, branches of Fnac and main Métro and RER stations.

The Louvre

entrance through Pyramid, Cour Napoléon, 1st (01.40.20.50.50/ recorded information 01.40.20.51.51/www.louvre.fr). M° Palais Royal. **Open** 9am-6pm Thur-Sun; 9am-9.45pm Mon, Wed. Closed Tue. Temporary exhibitions, Medieval Louvre 10am-9.45pm Mon, Wed-Sun. **Admission** €7.01 (until 3pm); €4.57 after 3pm, Sun; free under-18s first Sun of month. **Credit** MC, V. **Map** p402 H5.

The Louvre is Paris' museum to end all museums: just when you think you've mastered it, you turn a corner and discover another awesome staircase or whole series of unsuspected rooms. Its sheer breadth can be mind-boggling but it also means there's something for everyone: Renaissance painting, grandiose battle scenes, Antique sculpture, Egyptian mummies, intimate medieval jewels. Both royal palace and art collection, it's a bit like knocking the contents of the National Gallery, the Victoria & Albert Museum and the British Museum all together and placing them in a cross between Westminster Palace and Buck Pal for good measure. And while IM Pei's

glass entrance Pyramid is a stunning piece of contemporary architecture, there are whole chunks of medieval castle hidden away inside, and many items are displayed in state rooms under coffered, painted ceilings.

The Palace

The palace was home to generations of French monarchs from the 14th century. In the 1190s Philippe Auguste built a massive keep as part of his new Paris defences, which was turned into a royal residence in the mid-14th century by Charles V. Some imposing chunks of curtain wall and turrets, including Charles V library tower, for centuries literally buried underneath the later palace, can now be seen within the underground complex. The vaulted Salle St-Louis, discovered in the 19th century, with its central supporting column and a carved grotesque head is the only remnant from the core of Philippe Auguste's fortress.

In the 1540s, François 1er asked Pierre Lescot to begin a Renaissance palace (now the western wing of enclosed Cour Carrée). Continued by his successors, the different facades are carved with royal monograms – H interlaced with C and D for Henri II, his queen Catherine de Médicis and favourite Diane de Poitiers. Henri IV and Louis XIII completed the Cour Carrée and built the wing along the Seine. The pedimented facade along rue du Louvre was added by Perrault under Louis XIV, who also brought in Le Vau and Le Brun to refurbish the interior, with a sumptuous suite for his mother Anne of Austria (now housing Roman antiquities). After the court left for Versailles under Louis XIV, the royals abandoned the palace and the apartments were often occupied by artists and state servants. After the Revolution, Napoléon added the grand stairway by his architects Percier and Fontaine (only the ceilings of the former landing, now Salles Percier et Fontaine, remain) and built the galleries along rue de Rivoli, complete with imperial figures. His nephew Napoléon III added the Cour Napoléon.

The art collection was first opened to the public in 1793, but the Ministry of Finance remained in the palace until the 1980s, when the Louvre's latest great transformation, the *Grand Louvre* project, began with the opening of the Richelieu Wing in 1993, doubling the exhibition area. IM Pei's glass pyramid in the Cour Napoléon, opened in 1989, now serves as the dramatic main entrance.

Users' Tips

• tickets can be bought in advance at Fnac, Carrefour, Auchan and Virgin ticket offices or on the web. If buying on the spot, credit card ticket machines can be quicker than the tills.
• tickets are valid all day: you can leave the museum and re-enter if you wish.
• if there's a huge queue in the Cour Napoléon (or it's raining), enter via the Carrousel from rue de Rivoli or from Palais-Royal Métro (advance tickets can also be bought to queue jump at the Virgin Megastore inside the Carrousel).

• the museum is divided into three wings: Denon and Richelieu down the Seine and Rivoli sides respectively, Sully which joins them up and runs around the Cour Carrée at the end.
• do pick up a plan at the information desk.
• staff shortages mean that some rooms are closed on a weekly schedule, check on 01.40.20.51.51 or www.louvre.fr.
• there plenty of places to eat within the museum itself: elegant Café Richelieu, the Café Denon and Café Mollien, which has an outdoor terrace in summer. Under the pyramid are a sandwich bar, café and the Grand Louvre restaurant serving classic French cuisine. Outside the museum, Café Marly overlooks the pyramid and serves trendy brasserie-style food, while the Restorama in the Carrousel du Louvre offers multiple self-service outlets ranging from Lebanese and pizza to cheese and wine.
• shopaholics shouldn't worry either. The Louvre

has excellent art book, postcard, poster and gift shops (with reproductions of many Louvre items), a special children's art bookshop, as well as several stalls around the museum where you can acquire museum guides. If this won't do, there's always the Carrousel shopping centre...

• DON'T try to see everything on one visit. DO let yourself be beguiled – you're bound to get lost or diverted at some point, use it as an excuse to discover the unexpected.

The Collections

Ancient Egypt

Sully: ground and 1st floors; Richelieu: ground floor.
The Egyptian department has its origins in Napoléon's Egyptian campaign of 1798-99 and the work of Champollion, the Egyptologist who decyphered hieroglyphics in 1824. The pink granite Giant Sphinx leads to two routes. The Thematic Circuit presents Nile culture (fishing, agriculture, hunting, daily and cultural life, religion and death) through sculptures, painted scenes and artefacts, notably the Mastaba of Akhethetep, from Sakkara, a richly decorated burial chamber dating from c2,400BC. Six small sphinxes from Saqqara, a row of apes from Luxor and the lion-headed goddess Sekhmet recreate elements of temple complexes. Massive stone sarcophaguses, precious mummy cases and a bandaged-up mummy, amulets, jewellery and jars of entrails, along with mummified cats, dogs, ibises, fish and a crocodile are all part of a vivid display on funeral rites and the journey to resurrection in the next world.

The Pharoanic Circuit takes a chronological approach from Ancient Empire stone figures, such as the Seated Scribe, via elongated painted wood figures of the Middle Empire to the New Empire with its pharaonic statues, cat goddesses, painted papyrus scrolls and hieroglyphic tablets. Note the double statue of the God Aman protecting Tutankhamen and the lovely, black diorite 'cube statues' of squatting priests and intendants.

Oriental Antiquities & Islamic art

Sully: 1st floor; Richelieu: lower-ground floor; 1st floor.

Less well-known than the Egyptian collection, but every bit as well worth the visit, the department of Oriental Antiquities spans the Eastern Mediterranean basin. Amid Cypriot animalistic vases and carved reliefs from Byblos, don't miss the Statue of Ain Ghazal, a 7,000-year-old Neolithic statue that is the earliest item in the Louvre – here on long-term loan from Jordan.

The highlight, though, are two stupendous palace reconstructions: the great court, 713BC, from the palace of Sargon II at Khorsabad (in present-day Iraq) with its giant bearded and winged bulls and friezes of warriors and civil servants, and the palace of Darius I at Susa (now Iran), c510 BC, with its fantastic glazed brick reliefs depicting rows of archers, lions and gryphons, along with all sorts of bowls, statues and other artefacts. A column with bull-shaped capital gives some sense of the palace's scale.

Islamic decorative arts include early glass, fine 10th-12th-century dishes decorated with birds and calligraphy, Iranian blue and white wares, Iznik ceramics, intricate inlaid metalwork from Syria, carpets, screens, weapons and funerary stele.

Greek, Roman & Etruscan antiquities

Denon: lower ground floor, ground floor; Sully: ground floor, 1st floor

The *Winged Victory of Samothrace*, a 2nd-century BC Hellenistic statue, stands sentinel at the top of the Daru staircase, just part of a huge collection that reflects western collecting in pieces amassed by François 1er and Richelieu, the Borghèse collection acquired in 1808 and the Campana collection of thousands of painted Greek vases and small terracottas.

Many Greek classical sculptures have only come down via later Roman copies, including the graceful *Artemis à la Biche* and curious *Hermaphrodite*, male on one side, female the other (lying on a mattress sculpted by Bernini), both displayed in the Salle des Caryatids, which still has its grandiose Renaissance entrance sculpted by Jean Goujon. Look also for the 2.3m-high *Athena Peacemaker* and the *Venus de Milo*, renowned for her serene expression and seriously sensuous pose.

Etruscan civilisation of central Italy spans roughly 7th century BC until submission to the Romans in the 1st century AD. The highlight is the *Sarcophagus of the Cenestien Couple*, c 530-510BC, in painted terracotta, which charmingly depicts a smiling couple reclining at a banquet. Roman antiquities include a vivid relief of sacrificial animals

from a temple in Rome, intricately carved sarcophaguses and portraits of Augustus, small bronze statues and helmets, mosaic floors from Roman colonies in North Africa and early Christian Syria and the Boscoreale Treasure, fabulous silverwork excavated at a villa near Pompeii.

French painting

Richelieu: 2nd floor; Sully: 2nd floor; Denon: 1st floor.

An anonymous portrait of *Jean Le Bon*, c1350, is the earliest known free-standing French portrait (as opposed to the donor portraits in religious paintings). Paintings from the Dijon and Provençal schools, including the powerfully expressive *Pièta de Villeneuve-lès-Avignon* attributed to Enguerrand Quarton, show how powerful regional courts rivalled that of Paris as cultural patrons.

Jean Clouet's *Portrait of François 1er* marks the influence of the Italian Renaissance on portraiture, although most remained intimate, precious objects, seen in a room of small portraits by François Clouet and Corneille de Lyon. Works from the Ecole de Fontainebleau, which developed when François 1er invited Italian artists to his court, include the anonymous *Diana the Huntress*, an elegant Mannerist nude, perhaps a likeness of Henri II's mistress, legendary beauty Diane de Poitiers, and the curious double portrait *Isabelle d'Estrée and her Sister*.

Poussin's religious and mythological subjects epitomise the balance of composition and colour of 17th-century French classicism, in works full of erudite references for an audience of cognoscenti. Also working in Italy, Claude Lorraine painted golden-lit, idealised landscapes. The reduced palette, simplified lines and fascination with lighting effects of Georges de la Tour look modern now but overturned convention as he used peasant figures in his religious night scenes like *Mary Magdelene with an Oil Lamp* and *St-Joseph Carpenter with Young Christ*.

Philippe de Champaigne elevated the art of the official portrait but was also responsible for the austerity and reduced palette of his *Ex Voto*, a double portrait of two Jansenist nuns at the Abbaye de Port Royal. Look also at Charles Le Brun's wonderfully pompous Chancellier Seguier and his four grandiose battle scenes, in which Alexander the Great stands in for Louis XIV.

The 18th century begins with Watteau's large *Gilles* and delicate *Embarkation for Cythera*. Boucher's fantasies typify the high Rococo, while his more intimate *Le Déjeuner* is a light, 18th-century take on the genre painting. Works by Chardin include sober still lifes, but also delicate figure paintings. If you're used to the sugary images of Fragonard, don't miss the set of *Fantaisies* which forego sentimentality for wonderfully fluent, broadly painted fantasy portraits, intended to capture moods rather than particular likenesses.

Also in the Sully wing are sublime Neo-Classical portraits by David and his gifted pupils Guérin, Gros, Girodet and Benoist, Ingres' *La Baigneuse* and

Le Bain Turc, small paintings by Delacroix and Géricault, portraits and Orientalist scenes by Chassériau and landscapes by Corot, Théodore Rousseau and the Barbizon school.

Large format, late 18th-to mid-19th-century paintings hang in the Grand Galerie in the Denon wing. Here are David's giant Neo-Classical history paintings, *Rape of the Sabine Women, Oath of the Horatii* extolling Republican virtues, and *Sacré de Napoléon,* as well as his portrait of celebrated beauty *Mme Récamier,* along with Gros' *Napoléon at the Battle of Eylau,* Delaroche's *Napoléon Crossing the Alps,* Ingres' *Oedipus Explaining the Enigma* and Chassériau's disquieting double portrait *The Two Sisters.* Art continues to mix with politics as Delacroix espouses the Revolutionary cause in the stirring, flag-flying *Liberty Leading the People,* 1830, tribute to the Trois Glorieuses of the July Revolution, or the Massacres of Scio, championing the Greek struggle for independence. The quintessential Romantic painting with its combination of anguished, expressive suffering and masterly composition is *The Raft of the Médusa,* Géricault's masterpiece which shocked with its subject matter of a real shipwreck, widely reported in the press in 1816, in which the survivors resorted to cannibalism.

French sculpture
Richelieu: ground floor.
French sculpture is displayed in and around the two glazed sculpture courts created as part of the *Grand Louvre.* A medieval tour round the different regional schools takes in capitals from Cluny, Virgins from Alsace, 14th-century figures of Charles V and Jeanne de Bourbon that originally adorned the exterior of the Louvre and the late 15th-century *Tomb of Philippe Pot,* the effigy of Burgundian knight carried by eight black-clad mourners. Fine Renaissance memorials, fountains and portals include Jean Goujon's friezes from the Fontaine des Innocents.

In the Cour Marly, pride of place goes to Coustou's *Chevaux de Marly,* two rearing horses being restrained by their grooms, as well as two slightly earlier equestrian pieces by Coysevox, all originally sculpted for the favourite royal château at Marly-le-Roi. In Cour Puget are the four bronze captives by Martin Desjardins, from a statue in place des Victoires, Clodion's Rococo frieze and Pierre Puget's twisting, Baroque *Milo of Croton.* Amid 18th-century heroes and allegorical subjects, look for Pigalle's *Mercury* and *Voltaire.*

Italian painting
Denon: 1st floor.
Two rooms of fragile Renaissance frescoes by Botticelli, Fra Angelico and Luini open the Italian department. Cimabue's *Madonna of the Angels,* c1270, carries on the hieractic composition of Byzantine icons but looking ahead to the Renaissance's modelling of form in a sensitive treatment of faces and shadowing of drapery that prefigures Giotto. Fra Angelico's *Coronation of the Virgin,* c1435, shows harmony of composition and colour. Mantegna's *Calvary, St-Sebastian* and bacchanale scenes are a return to classical antique models. Highlights of the Sienese school include Simone Martini's *Christ Carrying the Cross* and Piera della Francesa's *Portrait of Sigismondo Malatesta.* There's a tiny predella possibly by Di Credo or an early Leonardo, both pupils of Verrocchio.

Florentine High Renaissance treasures include Raphael's *Belle Jardinière* Virgin and child, and two lovely small paintings depicting dragon slayers St George and St Michael, works by Ghirlandaio and Leonardo's *Virgin of the Rocks* and *Virgin, Child and Ste-Anne*. As for the *Mona Lisa* (known in France as *La Joconde*), almost impossible to look at both because of her familiarity and the camera-clicking crowds in front, she is currently in the Salle Rosa, but will have her own room from December 2002.

Venetian paintings are also currently displaced. Veronese's monumental, richly coloured *Noces de Cana* is a typically Venetian lavish, worldly treatment of a Biblical subject. Other highlights include the celebrated *Fête Champêtre* attributed to a young Titian and/or his mysterious master Giorgione, Titian's strictly profile portrait of *François 1er*, and paintings by Tintoretto, Paris Bordone and Lotto.

The long gallery continues with Mannerist portraits by Bronzino, and works by Nicolas dell'Abate and Pontormo, the fruit and leaf heads of Arcimboldo's *Four Seasons*. Baroque masterpieces include Caravaggio's *Fortune Teller*.

Italian sculpture

Denon: ground floor, lower ground floor.
Renaissance treasures include Donatello's painted marble relief, works by Duccio, della Quercia and Mino de Fiesole and the glazed earthenware reliefs of the Della Robbia family. Don't miss Michelangelo's *Dying Slave* and *Captive Slave*, two of the captives originally planned for the tomb of Pope Julius II in Rome, Adrien de Vriesse's elongated bronze *Mercury and Psyche* and Giambologna's *Mercury*. On the Mollien staircase, look at Benevenuto Cellini's *Nymphe of Fontainebleau* relief.

Northern schools

Richelieu: 2nd floor; Denon: lower ground floor.
The northern Renaissance includes Flemish altarpieces by Memling and Van der Weyden, Bosch's fantastical, proto-Surrealist *Ship of Fools*, Metsys' *The Moneylender and his Wife*, which combines a complex moral message, lively everyday detail and visual games, as well as the northern Mannerism of Cornelius van Haarlem.

The Galerie Médicis is devoted to Rubens' Médicis cycle. The 24 canvases commissioned in the 1620s for the Palais de Luxembourg by Marie de Médicis, widow of Henri IV, mix actual events and classical mythology for the glorification of the queen. But look also at Rubens' more personal, glowing portrait of his second wife *Hélène Fourment and her Children*, along with Van Dyck's *Charles I & his Groom* and peasant-filled townscapes by Teniers.

Dutch paintings include early and late self-portraits by Rembrandt, his *Flayed Ox* and the warmly glowing nude *Bathsheba at her Bath*. There are Vermeer's *Astronomer* and *Lacemaker* amid interiors by De Hooch and Metsu, and the meticulously finished portraits and trompe l'oeil framing devices of Dou. Works from the Haarlem school include Hals, Judith Leyster and Van Goyen.

German paintings hung over several small side galleries include portraits by Cranach, Durer's *Self-Portrait* and Holbein's *Anne of Cleves*.

Recently opened rooms of later northern and Scandinavian paintings include Caspar David Friedrich's *Trees with Crows*, the sober, classical portraits of Christian Købke and pared back views of Peder Balke. A small British collection includes landscapes by Wright of Derby, Constable and Turner and portraits by Gainsborough, Reynolds

and Lawrence. Northern sculpture (Denon, lower-ground floor), ranges from Erhart's Gothic *Mary Magdalene*, possibly after an engraving by Durer, to the Neo-Classical work of Thorvaldsen.

Decorative Arts
Richelieu: 1st floor; Sully: 1st floor
The decorative arts collection runs from the Middle Ages to the mid-19th century, often with royal connections. Many of the finest medieval items came from the treasury of St-Denis amassed by the powerful Abbot Suger, counsellor to Louis VI and VII, among them *Suger's Eagle*, an antique porphyry vase with gold mounts and two other cups made for Suger, a serpentine plate surrounded by precious stones and the sacred sword of the kings of France, also dubbed 'Charlemagne's sword', as the Capetian monarchs sought to legitimise their line.

Renaissance galleries take in ornate carved chests, German silver tankards, cases brimming with Italian maiolica, small bronzes, large-scale Limoges enamel portraits by 16th-century master Léonard Limousin, Palissy plates modelled in relief with surprisingly realistic lizards, fish and shells and the *Hunts of Maximilien*, 12 16th-century Brussels tapestries, depicting months, the zodiac and noble hunting scenes (possibly of Emperor Charles V) in the forests around Brussels.

17th and 18th-century French decorative arts are displayed in fine panelled rooms. There are pieces by Boulle in his characteristic brass and tortoiseshell inlay with ormolu mounts. Later furniture includes the elaborate Rococo 'monkey commode' of Crescent and parquetry by Leleu. There is French faience and porcelain, silverware, watches and scientific instruments. Napoléon III's opulent apartments, used until the 1980s by the Ministry of Finance, have been preserved with chandeliers and upholstery intact.

Tribal Art
Denon: ground floor.
A small display in the Pavillon de Flore augurs what is to come in the future Musée des Arts Premiers. Items range from Benin bronze heads from Nigeria and Polynesian carved wood statues to pot-bellied terracotta figures from Mexico.

Other museums

Fine art

Centre Pompidou (Musée National d'Art Moderne)
rue St-Martin, 4th (01.44.78.12.33/ www.centrepompidou.fr). M° Hôtel-de-Ville or Rambuteau/RER Châtelet-Les Halles. **Open** 11am-9pm Mon, Wed-Sun. Closed Tue, 1 May. **Admission** €5.05; €3.05 18-26s; free under-18s. **Exhibitions** (includes museum) €4.05-€8.05; €4.57-€6.10 18-26s; one day ticket €9.15, €7.62 18-26s. **Credit** MC, V. **Map** p406 K6.

The Musée National d'Art Moderne reopened in 2000 after major renovation of the Centre Pompidou, with enlarged galleries that now incorporate architecture and design, as well as the unparalleled collection of fine art. The vast scale of the Centre's holdings means that only a tiny proportion can be seen at any one time, with a partial rehang, in particular of the installation-heavy contemporary section, every year (Ben's *Shop* in 2000, Beuys' *Plight* in 2001). The route now starts on level four with the contemporary (post 1960 to today) period. The 2001 rehang favoured abstraction and minimalism – Stella, Ryman, Morellet, André, Judd et al – as well as a room of 'Klein blue' canvases and art actions by Yves Klein, the Support-Surface artists Viallat, Dezeuze and Jacquard, 60s and 70s happenings, body, performance and video art and Fluxus, going on to recent photography by Bustamente and Jouve and installations by Penone, Raynaud, Rondinone and Boltanski. The Centre also has plenty of Pop art, Arte Povera and *nouveau réalisme* that may well reappear next time around. Level five covers the historic period from roughly 1905 (Fauves and Cubism) to 1960, taking a historic route with Matisse, Picasso, Delaunay, Léger, Kandinsky, Malevich, Schad and Dix up to American colour-field painting and Abstract Expressionists in the 50s, and artists like Bacon, Fautrier and Dubuffet who worked between figuration and abstraction. An extensive section on Dada and Surrealism includes Duchamp ready-mades, Haussmann's *The Spirit of Our Time*, paintings by Ernst, Magritte, Miró et al, and a fascinating reconstruction of one wall of André Breton's studio in rue Fontaine where he juxtaposed drawings by fellow artists alongside tribal art, crystals and objects he picked up at the fleamarket. In a pluri-disciplinary approach, temporary exhibitions are often linked to performances, concerts and debates. Major shows in 2002 include 'La Révolution surréaliste' (Mar-June), designer Philippe Starck (May-July), Daniel Buren (June-Sept), Max Beckmann (Sept-Dec) and 'Sonic Process' (Oct-Jan) on electronic music and contemporary art. *See also chapters* **Architecture, Right Bank, Children** and **Film**.
Shops. Children's workshops. Cinema. Auditorium. Café. Restaurant. Wheelchair access. Guided Visits.

Musée d'Art Moderne de la Ville de Paris/ARC
11 av du Président-Wilson, 16th (01.53.67.40.00). M° Iéna or Alma-Marceau. **Open** 10am-5.30pm Tue-Fri; 10am-7pm Sat, Sun (collection); 10am-6.30pm Tue-Sun (temporary exhibitions). Closed Mon, some public holidays. **Admission** collection free; temporary exhibitions €6.10-€8.38, free under-13s. **Credit** (shop) AmEx, DC, MC, V. **Map** p400 D5.

This monumental museum was built for the 1937 *Exposition Universelle* (Dufy's vast mural *La Fée Electricité* originally painted for the electricity pavilion hangs in a special curved room, but will be closed for much of 2002). Today the building holds the municipal collection of modern art, arranged in roughly chronological order. The collection is particularly strong on the Cubists, Fauves, the Delaunays (including Robert Delaunay's 1912 *L'Equipe de Cardiff*), Rouault, Schwitters and Ecole de Paris artists Soutine, Modigliani and Van Dongen. The postwar section goes from Support-Surface, the torn-poster works of Villegle and compressions by César and Arman, 70s conceptual art (Boltanski, Messager, Gette, Gilbert & George) and arte povera to videos by young artists (Huyghe, Bournigault) and Tania Mourad's humming, white-domed meditation room, which opens the collection. Don't miss the Salle Matisse, where an unfinished version of Matisse's *La Danse*, rediscovered in 1993, hangs alongside *La Danse de Paris*, as the artist resolved the composition of his mural for the Barnes Foundation, along with a recent donation of early (striped, of course) canvases by Daniel Buren. The museum is most visited, however, for its dynamic temporary exhibitions, with major names of modern art (Fauvism and *Die Brücke* to Rothko), plus adventurous, often experimental, contemporary shows put on by ARC (Animation, Recherche, Confrontation). Shows in 2002 include Picabia and Bertrand Lavier. *Bookshop. Café. Concerts. Wheelchair access.*

Musée Cognacq-Jay

*Hôtel Donon, 8 rue Elzévir, 3rd (01.40.27.07.21). M°
St-Paul.* **Open** 10am-6.15pm Tue-Sun. Closed Mon, some public holidays. **Admission** collection free;

Top Celebrity Connections

Marcel Proust's bedroom...
Musée Carnavalet (*See p171*).

Charlemagne's sword...
Musée National du Louvre (*See p149*).

André Breton's wall...
Centre Pompidou (*See p153*).

Balzac's coffee pot...
Maison de Balzac (*See p160*).

Louis XIV's hunting dogs...
Musée de la Chasse et de la Nature (*See p164*).

Edward III's saddle cloth...
Musée National du Moyen Age (*See p165*).

Napoléon's barge...
Musée de la Marine (*See p173*).

Louis XVI's rhinoceros...
Muséum National d'Histoire Naturelle (*See p165*).

temporary exhibitions €4.57; €3.05 over-60s; €2.29 13-26s; free under-13s. **No credit cards.**
Map p406 L6.
This intimate museum in a carefully restored *hôtel particulier* houses the collection put together in the early 1900s by Ernest Cognacq, founder of La Samaritaine, and his wife Louise Jay. Their tastes stuck mainly to the French 18th century, focusing on outstanding French Rococo artists such as Watteau, Fragonard, Boucher, Greuze and pastellist Quentin de la Tour, although some English (Reynolds, Lawrence, Romney), Dutch and Flemish (an early Rembrandt, Ruysdael, Rubens), and a sprinkling of Canalettos and Guardis have slipped in too. Pictures are displayed in panelled rooms alongside furniture, porcelain, tapestries and sculpture of the same period.
Bookshop. Children's workshops.

Musée Départemental Maurice Denis, 'Le Prieuré'

*2bis rue Maurice Denis, 78100 St-Germain-en-Laye
(01.39.73.77.87). RER A St-Germain-en-Laye.* **Open**
10am-5.30pm Wed-Fri; 10am-6.30pm Sat, Sun. Closed 1 Jan, 1 May, 25 Dec. **Admission** €3.81; €2.29 12-25s, students, over-60s; free under-12s, CM (€5.34 and €3.81 during exhibitions). **No credit cards.**
Out in the elegant commuterland of St-Germain-en-Laye, this former royal convent and hospital became home and studio to Nabi painter Maurice Denis in 1915, who also decorated the chapel in the garden. The remarkable collection comprises paintings, prints and decorative objects by the Nabis (a group that also included Sérusier, Bonnard, Vuillard, Roussel and Valloton), who sought a renewed spirituality in painting. There are also paintings by their forerunners Gauguin and the Pont-Aven school, and by Toulouse-Lautrec.
Bookshop.

Musée Jacquemart-André

*158 bd Haussmann, 8th (01.42.89.04.91/
www.musee-jacquemart-andre.com). M° Miromesnil
or St-Philippe-du-Roule.* **Open** 10am-6pm daily.
Admission €7.62; €5.79 7-17s, students; free under-7s. **Credit** MC, V. **Map** p401 E3.
The magnificent collection gathered by Edouard André and his wife Nélie Jacquemart is as worth visiting for its illustration of the life of the 19th-century *haute bourgeoisie*, as for the treasures they unearthed. The ground floor reception rooms take in the circular Grand Salon, rooms of tapestries and French furniture, Boucher mythological fantasies, a lovely Nattier portrait, the library (with Dutch paintings including Rembrandt's *The Pilgrims of Emmaus*), the Moresque smoking room hung with English portraits, and the magnificent polychrome marble winter garden with double spiral staircase. Up on the stairway three recently restored Tiepolo frescoes from the Villa Contarini depict the arrival of Henri III in Venice. Upstairs, what was to have been Nélie's studio became their 'Italian museum': an exceptional small Early Renaissance collection

All you need's at the **Centre Pompidou.** *See p153.*

that includes Uccello's *St George and the Dragon*, Virgins by Perugino, Botticelli and Bellini, Mantegna's *Ecce Homo*, a superb Schiavone portrait, a Carpaccio panel and Della Robbia terracottas. The audioguide (in English) is very informative, and there's another Tiepolo in the elegant tea room.
Audio guide in six languages. Bookshop. Café (11.30am-6pm). Partial wheelchair access.

Musée Marmottan – Claude Monet

2 rue Louis-Boilly, 16th (01.42.24.07.02/www.marmottan.com). M° La Muette. **Open** 10am-6pm Tue-Sun. Closed Mon, 1 May, 25 Dec. **Admission** €6.50; €4 8-25s, over-60s; free under-8s. **Credit** MC, V. **Map** p400 A6.
Michel Monet bequested 165 of his father's works, plus sketchbooks, his palette and family photos, to the Musée Marmottan, including a breathtaking series of late water-lily canvases, 1916-19, displayed in a special circular room, where the artist no longer seems intent on the impressions of the 1870s but in pure colour sensation. The collection also contains Monet's *Impression Soleil Levant*, which gave the Impressionist movement its name, and canvases by Sisley, Renoir, Pissarro, Manet, Caillebotte and Berthe Morisot as well as some by the 19th-century Realists. The rest of the collection should not be ignored: there's a room containing the Wildenstein collection of medieval illuminated manuscripts and the recently restored ground- and first-floor salons house smaller Monets, early 19th-century gouaches, an extraordinary Sèvres porcelain geographical clock and fine First Empire furniture adorned with pharaohs' busts and sphinxes, inspired by Napoléon's Egyptian campaigns.
Shop. Partial wheelchair access.

Musée de l'Orangerie

Jardin des Tuileries, 1st (01.42.97.48.16). M° Concorde. **Open** in 2004. **Map** p403 F5.
Monet's eight, extraordinarily fresh, huge, late *Nymphéas* (water lilies) (*see also above* **Musée Marmottan**), conceived especially for two oval rooms in the Orangerie, were left by the artist to the nation as a 'spiritual testimony'. The museum is closed until 2004 for a major overhaul. On reopening the Jean Walter and Paul Guillaume collection of Impressionism and the Ecole de Paris will also go on show again, plus furniture and decorative objects.

Musée National d'Orsay

1 rue de la Légion d'Honneur, 7th (01.40.49.48.14/ recorded information 01.45.49.11.11). M° Solférino/ RER Musée d'Orsay. **Open** 10am-6pm Tue, Wed, Fri, Sat; 10am-9.45pm Thur; 9am-6pm Sun. Closed Mon, 1 Jan, 1 May. **Admission** €7.62; €5.79 18-25s, all on Sun; free under-18s; CM. **Credit** (shop) AmEx, MC, V. **Map** p401 G6.
Opened in 1986, the Musée d'Orsay fills a Beaux-Arts train station built for the 1900 *Exposition Universelle*, saved from demolition to become Paris' museum devoted to the pivotal years 1848-1914. Architect Gae Aulenti remodelled the interior, keeping the iron-framed coffered roof and creating galleries off either side of a light-filled central canyon. The drawbacks of her conversion are now apparent but the museum still draws long queues. Much of the problem is that the Impressionists and Post-Impressionists are knee-deep in tourists upstairs, while too much space is given downstairs to *art pompier* – Couture's languid nudes or Meissonier's history paintings. The museum follows a chronological route, starting on the ground floor, running

up to the upper level and finishing on the mezzanine, thus both highlighting continuities between the Impressionists and their forerunners and their revolutionary use of light and colour.

Running down the centre of the tracks a central sculpture aisle takes in monuments and maidens by artists including Rude, Barrye and Carrier-Belleuse, but the outstanding pieces are by Carpeaux, including his controversial *La Danse* for the facade of the Palais Garnier, which shocked 19th-century moralists with its naked dancers.

The right Lille side of the central aisle is dedicated to the Romantics and history painters. Cool portraits by Ingres and his follower Amaury-Duval contrast with the Romantic passion of Delacroix's North African period. The sugary cupids of Cabanel's *Birth of Venus* are the sort of official *art pompier* that was wildly popular at the time before sinking into later ignominy. Further on are examples of early Degas, and mystical works by the Symbolists Gustave Moreau and Puvis de Chavannes, who privileged allegory and symbolic meaning rather than the focus on contemporary life of the Impressionists.

The first rooms to the Seine side of the central aisle are given over to the Barbizon landscape painters Corot, Daubigny and Millet. Don't miss Daumier's clay bust caricatures. One room is dedicated to Courbet, with *The Artist and his Studio* and his monumental *Burial at Ornans*. His sexually explicit *L'Origine du Monde* still shocks today. This floor also covers pre-1870 works by the Impressionists (Monet, Pissarro, Van Gogh, Manet's *Olympia*) and precursor Boudin, several of whom are portrayed in Fantin-Latour's *Un atelier aux Batignolles*. Other side galleries treat 19th-century decorative arts, including an extraordianary wardrobe with bronzes of charging Merovingian warriors by Fremiet.

Upstairs you can see masterpieces by Pissarro, Renoir and Caillebotte, Manet's controversial *Déjeuner sur l'Herbe*, several of Monet's paintings of Rouen cathedral and depictions of his garden at Giverny, and paintings, pastels and sculptures by Degas. The riches continue with the Post-Impressionists. Among the boiling colours and frantic brushstrokes of Van Gogh are his *Church at Auvers* and his last painting, *Crows*. There are Cézanne still lifes, Gauguin's Breton and Tahitian periods, Toulouse-Lautrec's depictions of Montmartre lowlife, the Pointillists Seurat and Signac, the mystical works of Redon and the primitivist jungle of the Douanier Rousseau.

On the mezzanine are the Nabis painters – Vallotton, Denis, Roussel, Bonnard and Vuillard – who treated religious and domestic scenes in a flat, decorative style. Several rooms are given over to the organic, flowing forms of Art Nouveau decorative arts, including furniture by Majorelle, silverware and Gallé and Lalique ceramics, along with paintings by Klimt and Burne-Jones, as well as architectural drawings and early photography. The sculpture terraces include busts and studies by Rodin, heads by Rosso and bronzes by Bourdelle and Maillol. *See also chapter* **Left Bank**.
Audioguide. Bookshop. Café-restaurant. Cinema. Guided tours. Library (by appointment). Wheelchair access.

Musée du Petit Palais

av Winston-Churchill, 8th (01.42.65.12.73).
M° Champs-Elysées-Clemenceau. **Open** in 2004.
Map p403 E5.
Standing across the road from the Grand Palais (*see below* **Exhibition Centres**), the Petit Palais was likewise constructed for the 1900 *Exposition Universelle*. Since then it has been home to the eclectic municipal art collection that ranges from Antique Greek vases to French decorative arts, though its chief interest is in 19th-century French art, including Couture, Courbet and studies for public sculpture, as well as putting on exhibitions. The museum is currently under renovation; a few of the medieval exhibits are on display at the Louvre.

One-man shows

Atelier Brancusi

piazza Beaubourg, 4th (01.44.78.12.33). M° Hôtel de Ville or Rambuteau/RER Châtelet-Les Halles. **Open** 1-7pm Sat, Sun. **Admission** (included with Centre Pompidou – Musée National d'Art Moderne) €7.62; €5.79 18-26s; free under-18s, first Sun in month. **Credit** AmEx, MC, V. **Map** p406 K6.
When Constantin Brancusi died in 1956 he left his studio in the 15th *arrondissement* and all its contents –work, tools, photos, bed and wardrobe – to the state. Rebuilt outside the Centre Pompidou, the studio has since been faithfully reconstructed. His fragile works in wood and plaster, including his celebrated endless columns and streamlined bird forms, show how Brancusi revolutionised sculpture.

Atelier-Musée Henri Bouchard

25 rue de l'Yvette, 16th (01.46.47.63.46/www.musee-bouchard.com). M° Jasmin. **Open** 2-7pm Wed, Sat. Closed last two weeks of Mar, June, Sept and Dec. **Admission** €3.81; €2.29 students under-26; free under-6s. **No credit cards.**
Prolific sculptor Henri Bouchard moved here in 1924. Lovingly tended by his son and daughter-in-law, his dusty studio, crammed with sculptures, casts and moulds, sketchbooks and tools, gives an idea of the official art of the time. Bouchard began with Realist style peasants and maidens, but in around 1907-09 Bouchard moved to a more stylised, pared-down, linear modern style, as seen in his reliefs for the Eglise St-Jean-de-Chaillot and the monumental *Apollo* for the Palais de Chaillot.

Espace Dalí Montmartre

11 rue Poulbot, 18th (01.42.64.40.10). M° Anvers or Abbesses. **Open** 10am-6.30pm daily; 10am-9pm July-Aug. **Admission** €7; €6 teachers; €5.34 over-60s; €5 8-25s, students; free under-8s. **Credit** (shop) AmEx, DC, MC, V. **Map** p401 H1.

Loft glory at **Atelier Brancusi**. *See left.*

The black-walled interior, artistically programmed lighting and specially composed soundtrack make it clear that this is a high-marketing presentation of the artist's work. Don't expect to see Dali's Surrealist paintings; the museum concentrates on his sculptures (mainly bronzes) often taking elements in the paintings from the tacky end of his career and his book illustrations (La Fontaine's fables, Freud, de Sade, Dante, *Alice in Wonderland*).
Shop.

Fondation Dubuffet

137 rue de Sèvres, 6th (01.47.34.12.63/ www.dubuffet-fondation.com). M° Duroc. **Open** 2-6pm Mon-Fri. Closed Aug, public holidays.
Admission €4. **No credit cards. Map** p405 E8.
You must literally travel up a (very charming, so it's not too traumatic) garden path to reach the museum tucked away in an old three-storey mansion. Set up by the artist (1901-85) in 1974, the foundation ensures that there is a significant body of his works permanently accessible to the public. There is a changing display of Dubuffet's playful and exuberant drawings, paintings and sculptures, plus *maquettes* of the architectural sculptures from the Hourloupe cycle.
Archives (by appointment). Bookshop.

Musée Bourdelle

16-18 rue Antoine-Bourdelle, 15th (01.49.54.73.73). M° Montparnasse-Bienvenüe or Falguière. **Open** 10am-5.40pm Tue-Sun. Closed Mon, public holidays. **Admission** collection free; temporary exhibitions €4; €3 students, over-60s; free under-13s. **No credit cards. Map** p405 F8.

An interesting museum devoted to Rodin's pupil, sculptor Antoine Bourdelle, who produced monumental works, like the Modernist relief friezes at the Théâtre des Champs-Elysées. Housed around a small garden, the museum includes the artist's studio and apartments, a 1950s extension revealing the evolution of Bourdelle's equestrian monument to General Alvear in Buenos Aires, and bronzes and *maquettes* – notably studies of Beethoven in various guises that embody different aspects of creative genius – in a new wing by Christian de Portzamparc. Other artists, including Eugène Carrière and, briefly, Chagall also had studios here.
Bookshop. Children's workshops. Reference library (by appointment). Wheelchair access.

Musée National Delacroix

6 pl Furstenberg, 6th (01.44.41.86.50). M° St-Germain-des-Prés. **Open** 9.30am-5pm Mon, Wed-Sun. Closed Tue, some public holidays. **Admission** €3.90; €2.59 18-25s; €4.57, €3.51 during exhibitions; free under-18s, first Sun of month, CM. **Credit** MC, V. **Map** p405 H6.
Eugène Delacroix moved to the pretty place Furstenberg in 1857 to be nearer to the Eglise St-Sulpice where he was painting murals. The Louvre and the Musée d'Orsay house his major paintings, but the collection displayed in his apartment and the studio includes small oil paintings, some free pastel studies of skies and sketches, and still maintains some of the atmosphere of the studio as it must have been when he was beavering away like a wild thing at the canvas. Other displays relate to his friendships with Baudelaire and George Sand.
Bookshop.

Musée National Hébert

85 rue du Cherche-Midi, 6th (01.42.22.23.82). M° St-Placide or Vaneau. **Open** 12.30-6pm Mon, Wed-Fri; 2-6pm Sat, Sun and public holidays. Closed Tue, 1 Jan, 1 May, 25 Dec. **Admission** €3; €2.44 18-25s; free under-18s, first Sun of month, CM. **No credit cards. Map** p405 F7.
Ernest Hébert (1817-1908) was a painter of Italian landscapes and figurative subjects, who bent to the fashion of the time with hilariously uptight pious portraits and lachrymose depictions of sentimental shepherdesses during the mid-century, and brightly coloured, Symbolist-influenced muses and Impressionist-tinged ladies towards the end of his career. The endless watercolours and oils are unremarkable and do begin to drag a bit after a while, but they're an interesting testament to 19th-century taste – though the run-down house, built in 1743, has a certain completely knackered appeal.
Bookshop.

Musée National Jean-Jacques Henner

43 av de Villiers, 17th (01.47.63.42.73). M° Monceau or Malesherbes. **Open** 10am-noon, 2-5pm Tue-Sun. Closed Mon, some public holidays. **Admission** €4; €2.06 18 25s; free under-18s, first Sun of month, CM. **No credit cards. Map** p401 E2.

A passion for fashion

Style has been bred in French bone since the creation of Versailles, but it is largely thanks to the fashion infrastructure established in 1882, and such design associations as the Union Françaises des Arts du Costume, that Paris remains the lynchpin of fashion. The Union, founded in 1948, helped change our vision of clothing as it's aim was to create the very first fashion museum. The Musée de la Mode et du Textile, opened in 1986, is run by professionals directly involved in the industry. This proximity to creators has allowed it to amass the richest collection of 20th-century fashion worldwide, including the entire archives of Vionnet and 5,000 original drawings by Schiaparelli.

The museum doesn't see itself merely as an archive, but as piecing together 'the collective memory' of contemporary fashion. Curator Lydia Kamitsis says, 'My title *conservatrice* literally means "keeper", but keeper for what reason? No matter how beautiful a piece of clothing is, it is not a piece of art; clothes live in relation to the body and their rapport with society.'

Considering the break-neck pace of consumerism today, Kamitsis has set herself quite a task. Still, you couldn't imagine anyone more suited to gripping the coat tails of the clothing industry. Dressed in skin-tight fake snakeskin trousers, a boyish black jacket by Marc Bihan and sporting a punkish hairdo and a bunch of knucklebuster silver rings, Kamitsis looks all fired-up for fashion action. With zest, she says, 'There is one absolute rule here: we never stop re-evaluating our strategy on what to exhibit in the museum. I am interested in designs that don't have an immediate commercial value but pave the way for the future. An example might be a piece by Comme des Garçons or Junya Watanabe. I also choose pieces that initiate a huge consumer response. In the 80s it was essential to have a piece in Lycra by Azzedine Alaia whose designs were a way of rethinking the body. A body stocking was also a must, be it from Naf Naf or another mass brand. It is important for the museum to show the two fashion extremes – highly researched, experimental pieces along with clothing and accessories with universal appeal.'

Regarding the 90s and the first decade of the 21st century, Kamitsis has yet to make a move, although she did acquire a few pieces from a Vivienne Westwood auction recently. In any event, her choices are the fruit of exhaustive research and contact with people in all areas of the industry. She finds working as a lecturer an advantage in pinning down fashion moods: 'I am very attentive to young people's perception of fashion as they are the most difficult public to capture.'

Indeed, the bottom line is refreshingly unprecious: it's all about keeping the museum's visitors entertained. 'My role is to create programmes that help the public make up their own minds about fashion. For me an exhibition succeeds when the public goes away rethinking received ideas about fashion and seeing it through new perspectives.'

Musée de la Mode et du Textile
Palais du Louvre, 107 rue de Rivoli, 1st (01.44.55.57.50). M° Palais Royal. **Map** 402 H5.

Very popular in his day (critic Véron called him 'a 19th-century Leonardo'), Henner (1829-1905) now seems less interesting than his Post-Impressionist contemporaries. His sketches, drawings and letters give an insight into his creative process and appeal more than his society portraits, nymphs and naïads.

Musée-Jardin Paul Landowski

14 rue Max Blondat, 92100 Boulogne-Billancourt (01.46.05.82.69). M° Boulogne-Jean Jaurès. **Open** 10am-noon, 2-5pm Wed, Sat, Sun. **Admission** €2.29; €1.52 18-25s, over-60s. **No credit cards**.
Sculptor Landowski (1875-1961) won the *Prix de Rome* in 1900, and thereafter was kept busy with state commissions. Most of his work was on a monumental scale, treating both classical and modern themes. His most intriguing work was *Temple*: four sculpted walls depicting 'the history of humanity'. This was not a man who thought small.

Musée Maillol

59-61 rue de Grenelle, 7th (01.42.22.59.58/www.museemaillol.com). M° Rue du Bac. **Open** 11am-6pm Mon, Wed-Sun. Closed Tue. **Admission** €6.10; €4.57 students; free under-16s. **Credit** (shop) AmEx, MC, V. **Map** p405 G7.
Dina Vierny met sculptor Aristide Maillol (1861-1944) at the age of 15, and for the next ten years was his principal model, idealised in such sculptures as *Spring, Air and Harmony*. In 1995 she opened this museum displaying his drawings, pastels, engravings, tapestry panels, ceramics and his early Nabis-related paintings, as well as sculptures and terracottas, displayed over the renovated 18th-century Hôtel Bouchardon. Maillol's sculptures are a search for harmony and purity and his rounded, serene, stylised figures epitomise his ideal of nature and womanhood. Of course, they're not much like the real thing. There are also works by Picasso, Rodin, Gauguin, Degas and Cézanne, a whole room of Matisse drawings, some rare Surrealist documents and multiples by Marcel Duchamp and Jacques Duchamp-Villon, and naive painters like Camille Bombois and André Bouchart. Vierny has also championed Russian artists from Kandinsky and Poliakoff to Ilya Kabakov, whose installation *The Communal Kitchen* recreates the atmosphere and sounds of a shared Soviet kitchen. Interesting temporary exhibitions have ranged from Bonnard to Basquiat. The highlight of 2002 promises to be the Toulouse-Lautrec poster exhibition (Feb-May). *Bookshop. Café. Wheelchair access.*

Musée Gustave Moreau

14 rue de la Rochefoucauld, 9th (01.48.74.38.50). M° Trinité. **Open** Mon, Wed-Sun; 10am-12.45pm, 2-5.15pm. Closed Tue, some public holidays. **Admission** €3.35; €2.29 18-25s, Sun; free under-18s, CM. **Credit** (bookshop) MC, V. **Map** p401 G3.
Most eccentric of all the one-man museums, this is not only where Symbolist painter Gustave Moreau (1825-98) lived, worked and taught, but was also designated by the artist to become a museum after his death. Clearly, he was not encumbered by an excess

of modesty. But, boy, was he fecund. The enormous double-storey studio is crammed with Moreau's paintings, many unfinished (though one gets the gist), and there are thousands more of his drawings and watercolours to pull out from shutters on the walls – go gently, body-builders. His mind in retreat, Moreau developed a personal mythology, filling his detailed canvases with images of *St John the Baptist*, *St George* and the divinely lascivious *Salomé*, griffins and unicorns, strange plants and fantastical architecture, using jewel-like colours that owed much to the rediscovery of the early Italian masters, as well as to medieval art and Indian miniatures, in phallic compositions full of domineering women. What a nightmare. Don't miss the dinky private apartment where he lived with his parents, which he arranged symbolically in their memory. This was no pipe-and-slippers man. *Bookshop.*

Musée National Picasso

Hôtel Salé, 5 rue de Thorigny, 3rd (01.42.71.25.21). M° Chemin-Vert or St-Paul. **Open** 9.30am-5.30pm (9.30am-6pm Apr-Oct) Mon, Wed-Sun. Closed Tue, 25 Dec, 1 Jan. **Admission** €5.49; €3.96 18-25s, all on Sun €3.96; free under-18s, first Sun of month, CM. **Credit** (shop) AmEx, MC, V. **Map** p404 L6.
An unparalleled collection of paintings and sculpture by Pablo Picasso (1881-1973), acquired by the state in lieu of inheritance tax and housed in one of the grandest Marais mansions. Are you drooling yet? You should be, for the collection represents all phases of the master's long and varied career, showing Picasso's continual inventiveness and – rare in great artists – sense of humour. Masterpieces include a gaunt, blue-period self-portrait, studies for the *Demoiselles d'Avignon*, *Paolo as Harlequin*, his Cubist and classical phases, the surreal *Nude in an Armchair*, lively beach pictures of the 1920-30s, portraits of his favourite models Marie-Thérèse and Dora Maar, and the unabashedly ribald pictures he produced in later years, the naughty old dauber that he was. The unusual, intriguingly named wallpaper collage, *Women at their Toilette*, gets its own small room. The drawings for the pivotal *Demoiselles d'Avignon* are here, as well as prints and ceramics. But it is the sculpture which really grabs your attention by the lapels and gives it a good shake, from the vast plaster head on the staircase and the spiky *Project for Monument to Apollinaire* to the *Girl on a Swing*. Look closely at the sculpture of an ape – you'll see that its face is actually made out of a toy car. You don't see many of those on *Antiques Roadshow*. Also here are minotaur etchings, ceramics, Picasso's collection of tribal art – juxtaposed with allegedly 'primitive' wood figures that he actually carved himself – and paintings by Matisse and Douanier Rousseau. What can you say? This excellent museum is an astonishing testament to one man's energetic and bewilderingly inventive genius. Respect to the bald guy.
Audiovisual room. Bookshop. Outdoor café May-Oct. Wheelchair access.

Musée National Rodin

Hôtel Biron, 77 rue de Varenne, 7th
(01.44.18.61.10/www.musee-rodin.fr). M° Varenne.
Open *Apr-Sept* 9.30am-5.45pm Tue-Sun; *Oct-Mar*
9.30am-4.45pm Tue-Sun. Closed Mon, 25 Dec, 1 Jan, 1
May. **Admission** €5; €3 18-25s, all on Sun; free
under-18s, art students, CM, first Sun of month.
Gardens only €1. **Credit** MC, V. **Map** p405 F6.
The Rodin museum occupies the *hôtel*
particulier where Rodin lived and sculpted at
the end of his life. The famous *Kiss, Cathedral,*
the *Walking Man,* and *maquettes* showing how
complex compositions such as the *Burghers*
evolved, studies for *Balzac,* portraits and early
terracottas are indoors, accompanied by several
works by Rodin's mistress and pupil Camille
Claudel, and paintings by Van Gogh, Monet,
Renoir, Carrière and Rodin himself. In the
gardens are the *Burghers of Calais,* the
elaborate *Gates of Hell,* the final proud portrait
of *Balzac,* the eternally absorbed – and
absorbing – *Thinker,* Orpheus under a shady
stretch of trees, several unfinished nymphs
seemingly emerging from the marble and 40
restored marbles behind glass including *Victor*
Hugo. Fans can also visit the Villa des Brillants
at Meudon (01.41.14.35.00; May-Oct, 1-6pm Fri-
Sun, museum and gardens €1.98, gardens only
€1.07), where he worked from 1895.
Bookshop. Garden café. Partial wheelchair access. Visits
for visually handicapped (by appointment).

Musée Zadkine

100bis rue d'Assas, 6th (01.43.26.91.90). M° Notre-
Dame-des-Champs or Vavin/RER Port Royal. **Open**
10am-5.40pm Tue-Sun. Closed Mon, public holidays.
Admission collection free; temporary exhibition
prices vary; free under-13s. **No credit cards.**
Map p405 G8.
Works by the Russian-born Cubist sculptor Ossip
Zadkine are displayed around the garden and tiny
house in Montparnasse where he lived from 1928
until his death in 1967. Zadkine's compositions
include musical, mythological and religious subjects
and his style varies with the materials: bronzes tend
to be geometrical, wood more sensuous flowing with
the grain. Sculptures are cleverly displayed at eye
level, along with drawings by Zadkine and some
paintings by his wife Valentine Prax. The studio is
used for temporary exhibitions of contemporary art.

Exhibition centres

Most open only during exhibitions. Various
cultural centres also mount shows, including:
Centre Culturel Calouste Gulbenkian (Portugal
– 51 av d'Iéna, 16th/ 01.53.23.93.93); Centre
Culturel Suisse (32-38 rue des Francs-Bourgeois,
3rd/01.42.71.38.38); Centre Wallonie-Bruxelles
(127 rue St-Martin, 4th/01.53.01.96.96); Goëthe
Institut (Germany – 17 av d'Iéna/16th/
01.44.43.92.30/and Galerie Condé, 31 rue de

Condé, 6th/01.40.46.69.60); Institut Finlandais
(60 rue des Ecoles, 5th/01.40.51.89.09); Institut
Néerlandais (121 rue de Lille, 7th/
01.53.59.12.40); Maison de l'Amérique Latine
(217 bd St-Germain, 7th/01.49.54.75.00).

Bibliothèque Forney

Hôtel de Sens, 1 rue du Figuier, 4th
(01.42.78.14.60). M° Pont-Marie. **Open** 1.30-8.30pm
Tue-Fri; 10am-8pm Sat. Closed Mon, Sun, public hols.
Admission €3.05; €1.52 students under 28, over-
60s; free under-12s. **No credit cards. Map** p406 L7.
Set in the turrets of the oldest mansion in the Marais,
the library specialises in the applied and graphic arts
and has a wing given over to temporary displays.

Bibliothèque Nationale de France –
Richelieu

58 rue de Richelieu, 2nd (01.53.79.81.26/
www.bnf.fr). M° Bourse. **Open** 10am-8pm Tue-Sat;
noon-7pm Sun. Closed Mon, two weeks in Sept,
public holidays. **Admission** €3.05; free under-12s.
Crypte free. **Credit** MC, V. **Map** p401 H4.
Within the old Bibliothèque Nationale, the Galeries
Mansart and Mazarine take in all works on paper
from medieval manuscripts and historic watercolours to photography and contemporary prints. A
new gallery, La Crypte, is used for contemporary
and graphic art. *See also* chapter **Right Bank.**

Bibliothèque Nationale de France –
François Mitterrand

quai François-Mauriac, 13th (01.53.79.59.59/
www.bnf.fr). M° Bibliothèque or Quai de la Gare.
Open 10am-7pm Tue-Sat; noon-7pm Sun. Closed
Mon, two weeks in Sept, public holidays.
Admission €5; €4 12-26s, students; free under-12s.
Credit MC, V. **Map** p407 M10.
The gigantic new library could not be more differ-
ent from its historic parent but shares a similarly
erudite programme, which includes photography,
artists' books and an ongoing cycle related to writ-
ing. Mar-June 2002 celebrates Victor Hugo's bicen-
tenary with his letters, manuscripts and drawings.
See chapters **Left Bank** *and* **Directory.**
Café. Wheelchair access.

Chapelle St-Louis de la Salpêtrière

47 bd de l'Hôpital, 13th (01.42.16.04.24). M° Gare
d'Austerlitz. **Open** 8.30am-6.30pm daily.
Admission free. **No credit cards. Map** p406 L9.
Libéral Bruand's austere 17th-century chapel provides a fantastic setting for contemporary art,
notably installations by Viola, Kawamata, Kapoor
and Holzer for various Festivals d'Automne.
Wheelchair access.

Ensb-a (Ecole Nationale Supérieure
des Beaux-Arts)

13 quai Malaquais, 6th
(01.47.03.50.00/www.ensba.fr). M° St-Germain-des-
Prés. **Open** 1-7pm Tue-Sun. Closed Mon, public
holidays. **Admission** €3.81; €2.29 students; free
under-12s. **Credit** MC, V. **Map** p406 H6.

Exhibitions at France's central art college vary from the pick of the previous year's graduates or theme shows of contemporary art, to Ensb-a's rich holdings of prints and drawings (nude studies, Géricault, Italian drawing). Worth going to spot new talent. *See also chapter* **Left Bank**. *Bookshop.*

Espace Paul Ricard

9 rue Royale, 8th (01.53.30.88.00/www.espacepaulricard.com). M° Concorde. **Open** 10am-7pm Mon-Fri. **Admission** free. **No credit cards. Map** p401 F4.

The purveyor of *pastis* here promotes contemporary art, notably with the Prix Paul Ricard – young French artists shortlisted by an indepedent curator for an annual prize – held to coincide with FIAC each autumn. Other shows have included new German painters and contemporary design.

Fondation Cartier pour l'art contemporain

261 bd Raspail, 14th (01.42.18.56.72/recorded info 01.42.18.56.51/www.fondation.cartier.fr). M° Raspail. **Open** noon-8pm Tue, Wed, Fri-Sun; noon-10pm Thur. Closed Mon. **Admission** €4.57; €3.05 under-25s, students, over-60s; free under-10s. **Credit** (shop) MC, V. **Map** p405 G9.

Jean Nouvel's 1990s glass and steel building, which combines exhibition centre with Cartier's offices up above, is as much a work of art as the quirky installations inside. Monographic shows by contemporary artists and photographers (Panamarenko, Pierrick Sorin, Keita, Eggleston) alternate with wide-ranging multicultural, century-crossing themes, such as

'Birds' or 'the Desert'. That saves one the effort of trying to work out what the hell's going on. Takashi Murakami and other Japanese artists invade the gallery from June to October 2002. Experimental music, dance and video are presented in '*Soirees Nomades*' (June-September 8pm Thur). *Bookshop. Wheelchair access.*

Hot Ossip at **Musée Zadkine.** *See left.*

Fondation d'Entreprise Coprim

46 rue de Sévigné, 3rd (01.44.78.60.00/
www.fondation-coprim.com). M° St-Paul. **Open**
10am-6pm Mon-Fri; 2-6pm Sat. Closed Sun, two
weeks in Aug, public holidays. **Admission** free.
No credit cards. Map p406 L6.
The gallery belonging to property developer Coprim
moved recently to a former print workshop in the
Marais; the new environment is most attractive. The
bent is mostly towards contemporary figurative
painting – Gérard Garouste, Combas, et al – including a prestigious annual prize for young artists.
Bookshop.

Fondation EDF-Espace Electra

6 rue Récamier, 7th (01.53.63.23.45/www.edf.fr). M°
Sèvres-Babylone. **Open** noon-7pm every day. Closed
public holidays, March, Aug. **Admission** €1.52, free
students, over-60s, under-10s. **No credit cards.**
Map p405 G7.
This former electricity substation, owned by the
French electricity board, is used for varied fine art,
graphic and design exhibitions, from garden designer Gilles Clément to Latin American art – some with
an appopriately electric connection.

Fondation Icar

159 quai de Valmy, 10th (01.53.26.36.61). M°
Colonel Fabien or Château Landon. **Open** 1-7pm
Wed-Sun. **Admission** free.
American-funded Icar puts on occasional, but
always intriguing, exhibitions of American conceptual art, plus related music and lectures, in a strikingly converted, light-filled former industrial
premises beside the Canal St-Martin.

Fondation Mona Bismarck

34 av de New-York, 16th (01.47.23.38.88). M° Alma-
Marceau. **Open** 10.30am-6.30pm Tue-Sat. Closed
Mon, Sun, Aug, public holidays. **Admission** free.
No credit cards. Map p400 C5.
The Fondation provides a chic setting for eclectic
exhibitions of everything from Etruscan antiquities
to North American Indian art, often lent by presti-
gious foreign collections.

Galéries Nationales du Grand Palais

3 av du Général-Eisenhower, 8th (01.44.13.17.17/
www.rmn.fr). M° Champs-Elysées-Clemenceau. **Open**
10am-8pm Mon, Thur-Sun; 10am-10pm Wed. Prebooking compulsory before 1pm. Closed Tue, 1 May,
25 Dec. **Admission** €7.62; €5.34 18-26s, all on Mon
(€8.68 and €6.25 with prebooking); free under-13s.
Credit MC, V. **Map** p401 E5.
Paris' premier venue for blockbuster exhibitions is
a striking leftover from the 1900 *Exposition*
Universelle. It still has plenty of life left in it. The
glass-domed central hall is closed for restoration, but
two other exhibition spaces remain. Highlights of
2002 include Chassériau, Louis XIII decorative arts,
and John Constable.
See also chapter **Right Bank.**
Audioguides. Shop. Café. Cinema. Wheelchair access.

Halle St-Pierre – Musée d'Art Naïf Max Fourny

2 rue Ronsard, 18th (01.42.58.72.89/
www.hallesaintpierre.org). M° Anvers. **Open** 10am-
6pm daily. Closed 1 Jan, 1 May, 25 Dec, Aug.
Admission €6; €5 students 12-26; free under-4s.
Credit (shop) AmEx, DC, MC, V. **Map** p402 J2.
The former covered market specialises in *art brut* (a
term coined by Dubuffet to describe self-taught *sin-*
guliers, including the mentally ill, who used poor or
idiosyncratic materials) and *art-naïf* (self-taught
artists who use more traditional techniques) from its
own and other collections. Two shows run until 28
July 2002: Jephan de Villiers and Oeil pour oeil.
Bookshop. Café/restaurant. Children's workshops.

Jeu de Paume

1 pl de la Concorde, 8th (01.47.03.12.50).
M° Concorde. **Open** noon-9.30pm Tue; noon-7pm Wed-
Fri; 10am-7pm Sat, Sun. Closed Mon, some public
holidays. **Admission** €6; €4.50 students, over-60s;
free under-13s. **Credit** MC, V. **Map** p401 F5.
When the Impressionist museum moved from here
to the Musée d'Orsay, the former royal real tennis
court was intelligently redesigned for modern and
contemporary art shows. Retrospective-style shows
held here have included César, Arman and Morellet
with occasional excursions into architecture including Oscar Niemeyer at the start of 2002, with an
exhibition of Picasso's erotic art slotted in as a sure-
fire crowdpuller.
Bookshop. Café. Cinema. Wheelchair access.

The eye-popping exterior of the
**Fondation Cartier pour l'art
contemporain. See p161.**

Musée-atelier Adzak

3 rue Jonquoy, 14th (01.45.43.06.98). M° Plaisance.
Open depends on show.
The eccentric house and studio built by the late Roy Adzak resounds with traces of the conceptual artist's plaster body columns and dehydrations. Now a registered charity, it gives (mainly foreign) artists a first chance to exhibit in Paris.

Musée National du Luxembourg

19 rue de Vaugirard, 6th (01.42.34.25.95).M° St-Sulpice/RER Luxembourg. **Open** 10am-11pm Mon and Fri, 10am-7pm Tue-Thur, 10am-8pm Sat and Sun. **Admission** €7.62; €5.34 students; €2.29 under 12s. **Credit** MC,V. **Map** p405 F7.
This small museum was the first public gallery in France when it opened in 1750 and was later a forerunner of the Musée National d'Art Moderne. After several years in the wilderness, a more coherent policy is now in evidence under the control of the national museums and French Senate.

Palais de Tokyo: Site de Création Contemporaine

13 av de New-York, 16th (01.47.23.54.01/ www.palaisdetokyo.com). M° Iéna or Alma-Marceau. **Open** noon-midnight Tue-Sun. Closed Mon, some public holidays. **Admission** €5, €3. **Map** p400 B5.
In the opposite wing of the Palais de Tokyo to the Musée d'Art Moderne de la Ville de Paris, this adventurous venture, curated by Jérôme Sans and Nicolas Bourreaud, has added an important new venue to the contemporary art scene and hopes to gain a wider audience with long opening hours and stylish restaurant. Proclaimed 'a laboratory for contemporary art', it kicked off in January 2002 with a hip list of artists including Wang Du, Franck Scurti, Matthew Ritchie, Virginie Barré and solo shows by Mélik Ohanian, Navin Rawanchaikul and Monica Bonvicini. The building has been stripped back to its concrete shell, revealing a skylit central hall, and permitting the coexistence of exhibitions and installations or one-off fashion shows or performances.
Bar. Restaurant. Shop. Wheelchair access.

Passage de Retz

9 rue Charlot, 3rd (01.48.04.37.99). M° Filles du Calvaire. **Open** 10am-7pm Tue-Sun. **Admission** €6; €4 students under 26, over-60s; free under-12s. **Credit** (shop) MC, V. **Map** p402 L5.
This Marais mansion has been resurrected as a gallery. Along with survey-style shows that have taken in Latin American and Asia, look out for contemporary design and offbeat theme offerings.
Bookshop. Café. Partial wheelchair access.

Pavillon des Arts

101 rue Rambuteau, 1st (01.42.33.82.50/ www.pavillondesarts.com). **M° Châtelet-Les Halles.** **Open** 11.30am-6.30pm Tue-Sun. Closed Mon, public holidays. **Admission** €5.50; €4 students, over-60s; €2.50 14-26s; free under-13s. **No credit cards.** **Map** p402 K5.

This gallery in the Forum des Halles hosts varied exhibitions from contemporary photography to Turner to Paris history. *Wheelchair access.*

Le Plateau

corner of rue du Plateau and rue Carducci, 19th (01.53.19.88.10). M° Buttes Chaumont. **Open** 2-7pm Wed-Fri, 11am-7pm Sat- Sun. **Admission** €3; free under-18s, students.
This new contemporary art space opened in spring 2002 arose out of a campaign by local associations for a community-based arts centre in northeast Paris and the search for an exhibition space for the FRAC (Fonds Régional d'Art Contemporain) d'Ile de France. Exhibitions from the FRAC collection alternate with artist-curated shows and projects with local artists' groups, complemented by experimental cinema, contemporary music and dance.

Renn 14/16 Verneuil

14/16 rue de Verneuil, 7th (01.42.61.25.71). M° Rue du Bac. **Open** noon-7pm Tue-Sat. Closed Mon, Sun, public holidays. **Admission** free. **Map** p405 G6.
The gallery owned by film director Claude Berri has changed address and style – rather than abstract painting it now concentrates on photography. *Wheelchair access.*

Photography

Centre National de la Photographie

Hôtel Salomon de Rothschild, 11 rue Berryer, 8th (01.53.76.12.32/www.cnp-photographie.com). M° Charles de Gaulle-Etoile. **Open** noon-7pm Mon, Wed-Sun. Closed Tue, 1 May, 25 Déc. **Admission** €4.60; €2.30 10-25s, over-60s; free under-10s. **Credit** MC, V. **Map** p400 D3.
The National Photography Centre takes a contemporary line. Major retrospectives have included Hannah Collins, Sophie Calle and Thomas Struth, with Sam Taylor-Wood in 2001. In two basement levels, the Atelier gives space to young artists exploring photography and new media, while short video programmes are screened in the café.
Wheelchair access (call ahead). Café.

Maison Européenne de la Photographie

5-7 rue de Fourcy, 4th (01.44.78.75.00/www.mep-fr.org). M° St-Paul or Pont-Marie. **Open** 11am-7.45pm Wed-Sun. Closed Mon, Tue, public holidays. **Admission** €5; €2.50 students, over-60s; free under-8s, all 5-8pm Wed. **Credit** (over €9.15) MC, V. **Map** p406 L6.
This institution, based in a restored Marais mansion and minimalist modern extension, usually runs several shows at once. Solo shows have included Cartier-Bresson, Weegee and Depardon. The cellars are used for more experimental and multimedia works. This energetic venue organises the citywide biennial *Mois de la Photo* (next in November 2002) and the Art Outsiders (new media art on the web) festival in September.
Auditorium. Café. Library. Wheelchair access.

Sightseeing

Patrimoine Photographique

Hôtel de Sully, 62 rue St-Antoine, 4th
(01.42.74.47.75/www.patrimoine-photo.org).
Mº Bastille. **Open** 10am-6.30pm Tue-Sun. Closed
Mon, some public holidays. **Admission** €3.81;
€2.29 students, under-25s, over-60s; free under-10s.
No credit cards. Map p406 L7.

Historic photographic shows feature figures such as
Cecil Beaton, Jacques-Henri Lartigue, Lucien Hervé,
or themes (The Egyptian pyramids, crime photog-
raphy). Exhibitions in 2002: The American Dream
(Mar-June); Arnold Newman (June-Sept); Corpus
Christie, the representation of Christ in photography
(Oct-Jan 03).

Decorative arts

Musée des Antiquités Nationales

Château, pl du Château, 78100 St-Germain-en-Laye
(01.39.10.13.00). RER A St-Germain-en-Laye. **Open**
9am-5.15pm Mon, Wed-Sun. Closed 25 Dec, 1 Jan.
Admission €3.81; €2.59 students 18-25; free under-
18s, first Sun of month. **Credit** (shop) MC, V.

Thousands of years spin by from one cabinet to the
next in this awe-inspiring museum tracing France's
rich archaelogical heritage: some of the early
Paleolithic animal sculptures existed long before the
Ancient Egyptians. Artefacts from the Romans in
Gaul are more familiar but fine quality. The
redesigned Neolithic galleries feature statue-men-
hirs, female statues and an ornate tombstone from
Cys-la-Commune. Exhibits are well presented and
not short of curiosities: massive antlers from a prehistoric Irish deer and a set of 18th-century cork
models of ancient sites.
Guided visits. Shop. Wheelchair access.

Musée des Arts Décoratifs

Palais du Louvre, 107 rue de Rivoli, 1st
(01.44.55.57.50/www.ucad.fr). Mº Palais Royal.
Open 11am-6pm Tue, Thur, Fri; 11am-9pm Wed;
10am-6pm Sat, Sun. Closed Mon, some public
holidays. **Admission** €5.34; €3.81 18-25s; free
under-18s, CM. **Credit** MC, V. **Map** p402 H5.

This rich collection of decorative arts is currently
undergoing a major facelift as part of the *Grand
Louvre* project, but unlike the Louvre proper, where
many works boast royal origin, this is essentially a
representation of bourgeois life and continues right
up to modern and contemporary design. So far only
the Renaissance and Middle Ages galleries are open;
the remaining departments are scheduled for completion in 2004. In addition to 16th-century Venetian
glass and Flemish tapestries, there are two reconstructions of period rooms: a panelled Gothic Charles
VIII bedchamber and a Renaissance room. The religious art collection includes a wonderful altarpiece
of the life of John the Baptist by Luis Borassa.
Temporary exhibitions often feature aspects of 20th-
century design or contemporary artist-designers,
such as Miguel Barcelo and Nikki de Saint-Phalle.
Library. Shop. Wheelchair access (105 rue de Rivoli).

Musée National de la Céramique

pl de la Manufacture, 92310 Sèvres
(01.41.14.04.20). Mº Pont de Sèvres. **Open** 10am-
5pm Mon, Wed-Sun. Closed Tue, public holidays.
Admission €4; €2.60 18-25s; free under-18s, CM,
all on Sun. **Credit** (showroom) MC, V.

Founded in 1738 as a private concern, the porcelain
factory moved to Sèvres from Vincennes in 1756 and
was soon taken over by the state. Finely painted, delicately modelled pieces that epitomise French
Rococo style, together with later Sèvres, adorned
with copies of Raphaels and Titians, demonstrate
extraordinary technical virtuosity. The collection
also includes Delftware, Meissen, Della Robbia
reliefs, Hispano-Moorish pieces and wonderful
Ottoman plates and tiles from Iznik.
Shop and showroom. Wheelchair access.

Musée de la Chasse et de la Nature

Hôtel Guénégaud, 60 rue des Archives, 3rd
(01.53.01.92.40). Mº Rambuteau. **Open** 11am-6pm
Tue-Sun. Closed Mon, public holidays. **Admission**
€4.60; €2.30 16-25s, students under 26, over-60s;
€0.75 5-16s; free under 5s. **No credit cards.**
Map p406 K5.

Housed on three floors of a beautiful mansion, this
museum presents a range of objects from Stone Age
arrow heads to Louis XV console tables, Sèvres
porcelain and carved ivory tankards under the common theme of hunting; nature, unless in the form of
an alarming array of stuffed animals, doesn't get
much of a look-in. The highlight are the wonderfully ornate weapons: crossbows inlaid with ivory and
mother-of-pearl, rifles decorated with hunting
scenes, swords engraved with masks; all reminders
that hunting was a luxury sport and its accou-
trements important status symbols. There's a huge
display of bird and animal studies by France's first
great *animalier* painter Alexandre-François
Desportes, as well as his portrait of Louis XIV's
favourite hunting dogs and hunting scenes and still
lifes by De Dreux, Chardin and Oudry.
Bookshop.

Musée du Cristal Baccarat

30bis rue de Paradis, 10th
(01.47.70.64.30/www.baccarat.fr).Mº Poissonnière.
Open 10am-6pm Mon-Sat. Closed Sun, public
holidays. **Admission** €3; €2 12-25s, students; free
under-12s. **Credit** (shop) AmEx, DC, MC, V. **Map**
p402 H5.

This is the showroom of celebrated glassmaker
Baccarat, with a museum attached. The main attraction is in seeing which fallen head of state or deposed
monarch used to drink out of Baccarat glasses.
Many a champion of the people seems to have
sloshed via a Baccarat. There are also some kitsch
but technically magnificent pieces produced for the
great exhibitions of the 1800s and the superb Art
Deco services designed by Georges Chevalier.
Baccarat transferred its workshops here in 1832; the
street remains full of glass and china outlets.

Musée de l'Eventail

2 bd de Strasbourg, 10th (01.42.08.90.20).
Mº Strasbourg-St-Denis. **Open** 2-6pm Mon-Wed.
Workshop 9am-12.30pm, 2-6pm Mon-Fri. Closed
Aug, public holidays. **Admission** €5; €2.50 under
12s. **No credit cards. Map** p402 K4.

The fan-making Hoguet family's collection is housed
in the workshop and neo-Renaissance showroom,
and you may well see fans being made (now generally for fashion shows) as you walk around. Exhibits
go from 18th-century fans with mother-of-pearl and
ivory sticks to early 20th-century advertising fans
and contemporary designs by Karl Lagerfeld.
There's also a display on the techniques and materials used to make these luxury items – which, until
the French Revolution, only the nobility were per-
mitted to use.
Shop.

Musée de la Mode et du Costume

Palais Galliéra, 10 av Pierre 1er de Serbie, 16th
(01.56.52.86.00). Mº Iéna or Alma-Marceau. **Open**
during exhibitions 10am-6pm Tue-Sun. Closed Mon,
public holidays. **Admission** €6.86; €4.88 over-60s;
€3.51 13-26s; free under-13s. **Credit** MC, V. **Map**
p400 C5.

Opposite the Musée d'Art Moderne de la Ville de
Paris (*see above* **Fine Art**), is this fanciful 1890s
mansion. Exhibitions range from historical periods
or themes to individual dress designers.

Musée National du Moyen Age –
Thermes de Cluny

6 pl Paul-Painlevé, 5th (01.53.73.78.00/www.musee-
moyenage.fr). Mº Cluny-La Sorbonne/RER St-Michel.
Open 9.15am-5.45pm Mon, Wed-Sun. Closed Tue,
some public holidays. **Admission** €4.73; €3.05 18-
25s, all on Sun; free under-18s, first Sun of month,
CM. **No credit cards. Map** p406 J7.

Occupying the Paris mansion of the medieval abbots
of Cluny (*see chapter* **Left Bank**) and the remains
of a Roman bathing establishment, the museum of
medieval art and artefacts retains a domestic scale
suitable for the intimacy of many of its treasures.
Most famous is the *Lady and the Unicorn* tapestry
cycle: six, late 15th-century Flemish *mille-fleurs*
tapestries depicting convoluted allegories of the five
senses, which are beautifully displayed in a special
circular room. Other textiles include fragile Coptic
embroidery and Edward III's emblazoned saddle
cloth. Elsewhere there are enamel bowls and caskets
from Limoges, ornate gold reliquaries, stained glass,
carved ivory, medieval books of hours, wooden
chests and locks, Nottingham alabasters, and
Flemish and German wood carving. One of the most
fascinating rooms is devoted to chivalry and everyday life at the end of the Middle Ages. The heads of
the kings of Judah from Notre-Dame, mutilated in
the Revolution under the mistaken belief that they
represented the kings of France (how's that for poor
image spin-doctoring?), and rediscovered (minus
their noses, but that could have been worse, and a
small effort of imagination can make up for the nasal

Heads, they lost – **Museé de
la Chasse et de la Nature.**
See p164.

deficiencies) in 1979, are the highlight of a sculpture collection that also includes capitals and statues from the abbey of St-Germain-des-Prés, St-Denis and the Sainte Chapelle.
Bookshop. Concerts. Guided tours in English 2pm Wed; 11.45 Sat.

Musées des Parfumeries-Fragonard

9 rue Scribe, 9th (01.47.42.93.40) and 39 bd des Capucines, 2nd (01.42.60.37.14). Mº Opéra. **Open** 9am-5.30pm Mon-Sat. Closed Sun, 25 Dec. (Apr-Oct rue Scribe open daily). **Admission** free. **Credit** AmEx, MC, V. **Map** p401 G4.

Get on the scent at the two museums showcasing the collection of perfume house Fragonard. Don't worry: it's not one big PR exercise. The five rooms at rue Scribe range from Ancient Egyptian ointment flasks to Meissen porcelain scent bottles, while the second museum contains, among others, bottles by Lalique and Schiaparelli. Both have displays on scent manufacture and an early 20th-century 'perfume organ' (which sounds a lot saucier than it actually is, so don't get your hopes up) with rows of the ingredients used by 'noses' when creating those stimulating concoctions. *Shop.*

The best Sculpture

La Danse...
Carpeaux's naked controversy at Museé d'Orsay (*See p155*).

Streamlined birds...
taking flight at Atelier Brancusi (*See p156*).

Spanish Surrealism...
Dali's so daring, dahling, at Espace Dali Montmartre (*See pp156-7*).

Temple...
four walls telling a great big story at Museé-Jardin Paul Landowski (*See p159*).

Girl on a swing...
art doesn't so much evolve as go into hyperdrive at Museé National Picasso (*See p159*).

The Kiss...
superior puckering among the treasures at Musée National Rodin (*See p160*).

Music, myth and religion...
in a blaze of virtuosity at Musée Zadkine (*See p160*).

Neolithic menhirs...
art going back to its roots at Musée des Antiquités Nationales (*See p164*).

Hindu and Buddhist pieces...
awesomely serene at Musée des Arts Asiatiques – Guimet (*See p169*).

Musée de la Publicité

Palais du Louvre, 107 rue de Rivoli, 1st (01.44.55.57.50/www.ucad.fr). Mº Palais Royal. **Open** 11am-6pm Tue, Thur, Fri; 11am-9pm Wed; 10am-6pm Sat-Sun. Closed Mon, some public holidays. **Admission** €5.34; €3.81 18-25s; free under-18s, CM. **Credit** MC, V. **Map** p401 H5.

Only a tiny proportion of its 50,000 posters from the 13th century to World War II, another 50,000 since 1950, promotional objects and packaging are on show at one time. Instead, the museum serves for temporary exhibitions that go from individual graphic designers to the history of Citroën advertising, while the multimedia space allows you to access historic posters by artists like Toulouse-Lautrec. Thus, this is a museum you can visit again and again (and again). A vital element is collaborations with young French artists, intended to reflect the ad world as a realm of creativity. Its distressed interior by architect Jean Nouvel was inspired by the city: the result is contemporary yet respectful. An exhibition on the history of avertising publicity from 1842-1920 promises to be a real highlight of the 2002 attractions (27 March-22 Sept).
Café. Shop. Wheelchair access.

Musée Nissim de Camondo

63 rue de Monceau, 8th (01.53.89.06.40/ www.ucad.fr). Mº Villiers or Monceau. **Open** 10am-5pm Wed-Sun. **Admission** €4.57; €3.05 18-25s; free under-18s, CM. Closed Mon, Tue, some public holidays. **Credit** MC, V. **Map** p401 E3.

The collection put together by Count Moïse de Camondo is named after his son Nissim, killed in World War I. Moïse replaced the family's two houses near Parc Monceau with this palatial residence in 1911-14, and lived here in a style more akin to his love of the 18th century. Grand first-floor reception rooms are absolutely crammed with furniture by leading craftsmen of the Louis XV and Louis XVI eras, including Oeben, Riesener, Weisweiler and Leleu, huge silver services and sets of Sèvres and Meissen porcelain, set off by Savonnerie carpets and Aubusson tapestries in loudly colourful, good condition. There are also rooms for daily use, including Nissim de Camondo's bedroom and, for those interested in how the other half lived, the recently opened kitchens and servants' quarters.
Bookshop.

Musée National de la Renaissance

Château d'Ecouen, 95440 Ecouen (01.34.38.38.50). SNCF from Gare du Nord to Ecouen-Ezanville, then bus 269. **Open** 9.30am-12.30pm, 2-5.15pm Mon, Wed-Sun. Closed Tue, 1 Jan, 1 May, 25 Dec. **Admission** €3.81; €2.59 18-25s Sun; free under-18s, first Sun of month, CM. **No credit cards.**

Overlooking an agricultural plain, yet barely outside the Paris suburbs, the Renaissance château built 1538-55 for Royal Constable Anne de Montmorency and his wife Margaret de Savoie is the authentic setting for a wonderful collection of 16th-century decorative arts. There are some real treasures arranged

The treasures of Thermes de Cluny.
See p165.

Architecture & urbanism

Cité de l'Architecture et du Patrimoine
Palais de Chaillot, pl du Trocadéro, 16th (01.44.05.39.10/www.archi.fr/IFA-CHAILLOT). M° Trocadéro. **Open** 2003. **Map** p400 B5.
The former Musée des Monuments Français was founded by Gothic revivalist Viollet-le-Duc to record the architectural heritage of France. It reopens in 2003 with an enlarged and updated collection, amalgamated with the Institut Français d'Architecture (*see below*). The medieval and classical section retains the stupendous plaster casts of great monuments from all over France, while the new modern and contemporary galleries use drawings, photos and models in thematic presentations of achitecture and the urban landscape.

Musée des Années 30
Espace Landowski, 28 av André-Morizet, 92100 Boulogne-Billancourt (01.55.18.46.45). M° Marcel Sembat. **Open** 11am-6pm Tue-Sun. Closed Mon, 15-31 Aug, public holidays. **Admission** €4; €3 students, over-60s; free under-16s. **No credit cards**.
The Musée des Années 30 is a reminder of what an awful lot of second-rate art was produced in the 1930s. There are decent Modernist sculptures by the Martel brothers, graphic designs and Juan Gris still lifes and drawings, but the highlights are the designs by avant-garde architects including Perret, Le Corbusier, Lurçat and Fischer.
Guided visits 2.30pm Sun. Shop. Wheelchair access.

Institut Français d'Architecture
6 rue de Tournon, 6th (01.46.33.90.36/ www.archi.fr/IFA-CHAILLOT). M° Odéon. **Open** (during exhibitions) 12.30-7pm Tue-Sun. **Admission** free. **No credit cards**. **Map** p406 H7.
Exhibitions examine 20th-century architects or aspects of the built environment, with an emphasis on modernist pioneers and current projects. IFA is due to move into the Cité de l'Architecture (*see above*) in 2003.
Lectures. Library. Partial wheelchair access (call ahead).

Pavillon de l'Arsenal
21 bd Morland, 4th (01.42.76.33.97/www.pavillon-arsenal.com). M° Sully-Morland. **Open** 10.30am-6.30pm Tue-Sat; 11am-7pm Sun. Closed Mon, 1 Jan. **Admission** free. **Credit** (shop) MC, V. **Map** p406 L7.
This centre presents imaginative exhibitions on urban design and architecture, in the form of drawings, plans, photographs and models, often looking at Paris from unusual perspectives, be it that of theatres, hidden courtyards or the banks of the Seine. There's a 50m² model of Paris, and a permanent exhibition '*Paris, la ville et ses projets*' on the historic growth of the city. From October 2002 the exhibition 'Paris, as in the cinema', will detail aspects of city life which are familiar but rarely focused upon. The exhibition will touch on various themes, including the changing urban environment.

over three floors of the château (some parts only open in the morning or afternoon, so do make sure to phone ahead of time if you have things you particularly want to see). Best of all are the original painted chimneypieces, decorated with caryatids, grotesques, Biblical and mythological scenes. Complementing them are Limoges enamels, armour, embroideries, rare painted leather wall hangings, and a magnificent tapestry cycle depicting the story of David and Bathsheba. This is the sort of museum in which aesthetes might well swoon with pleasure, so the easily moved should bring their smelling salts or a thermos of rose water.
Bookshop. Wheelchair access (call ahead).

Musée de la Serrurerie – Musée Bricard
Hôtel Libéral Bruand, 1 rue de la Perle, 3rd (01.42.77.79.62). M° St-Paul. **Open** 2-5pm Mon; 10am-noon, 2-5pm Tue-Fri. Closed Sat, Sun, two weeks in Aug, public holidays. **Admission** €4.57; €2.29 students, over-60s; free under-18s. **No credit cards**. **Map** p406 L6.
This museum, belonging to Bricard locksmiths, is housed in the cellars of the elegant mansion that architect Libéral Bruand built for himself in 1685. The collection focuses on locks and keys (Freud would have had a field day) from Roman times to the end of the last century, finely wrought or engraved in the style of the time, but also takes in window fastenings, hinges, tools and elaborate, gilded door handles from Versailles, complete with Louis XIV's personal sunburst.

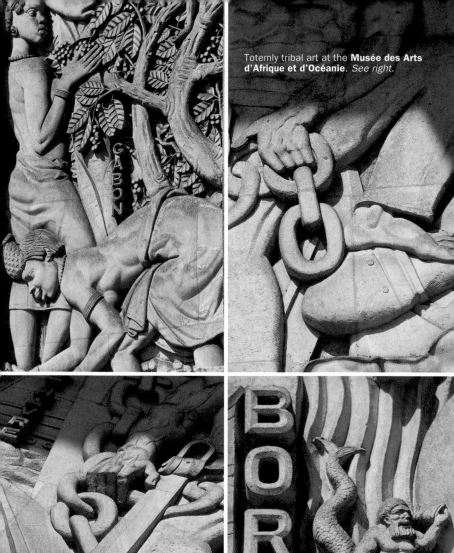

Totemly tribal art at the **Musée des Arts d'Afrique et d'Océanie**. *See right.*

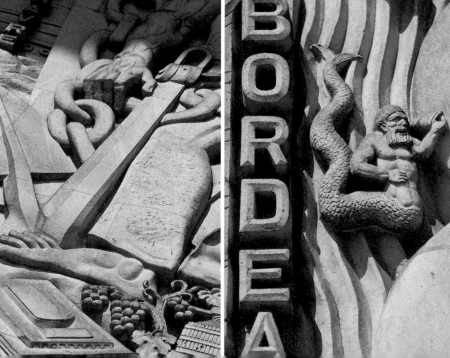

Ethnology, folk & tribal art

Musée des Arts d'Afrique et d'Océanie

293 av Daumesnil, 12th (01.44.74.84.80/recorded information 01.43.46.51.61/www.afric-network.fr).
Mº Porte Dorée. **Open** 10am-5.20pm Mon, Wed-Sun. Closed Tue, 1 May. **Admission** €5.70; €4.30 18-25s, all on Sun; free under-18s, first Sun of month, CM. **Credit** (shop) MC, V.

A winning combination of tropical fish and live crocs in the basement, tribal art up above. The building was designed for the 1931 *Exposition Coloniale*, with an astonishing bas-relief on the facade and two Art Deco rooms by Ruhlmann. On either side of a vast reception room are Aboriginal and Pacific island art, including carved totems from Vanuatu and hook figures from Papua New Guinea. Upstairs, African masks and statues include Dogon statues from Mali, pieces from Côte d'Ivoire and Central Africa, Benin bronzes and other Nigerian art. There are also jewellery and embroidery from the Maghreb. The second floor is used for temporary displays. The tribal art will eventually become part of the Musée des Arts Premiers. As for the crocs... *Aquarium. Shop.*

Musée National des Arts et Traditions Populaires

6 av du Mahatma-Gandhi, 16th (01.44.17.60.00/www.musee-mnatp.art.dz).
Mº Les Sablons. **Open** 9.30am-5pm Mon, Wed-Sun. Closed Tue, some public holidays. **Admission** €4; €2.60 10-25s, over-60s, students; free under-10s, first Sun of month, CM. **No credit cards.**

In contrast with its 1960s buiding, this centre of French folk art in the Bois de Boulogne spotlights the traditions and popular culture of pre-industrial France. Rural life is depicted through agricultural tools, household objects, furnitúre and costumes. The liveliest sections are those devoted to customs and beliefs – where you'll find a crystal ball, tarot cards, thunder stones and early medicines – and popular entertainment, with displays on the circus, sport and puppet theatres. The museum may move to Marseille.
Auditorium. Shop. Library/sound archive (by appointment). Wheelchair access.

Musée Dapper

35bis rue de Paul Valéry, 16th (01.45.00.01.50).
Mº Victor-Hugo. **Open** 11am-7pm Wed-Sunday,. closed Mon and Tue. **Admission** €4.60; €2.30 students, 16s-25s, large families; free under-16s, journalists. **Map** p400 B4.

This small specialist museum makes a refreshing change from the conventional Paris pit stops. The Fondation Dapper began in 1983 as an organisation dedicated to preserving sub-saharan art. Reopened in 2000 after a renovation, the new Alain Moatti-designed museum includes a performance space, bookshop and café. A glass bridge leads you into the reception, underneath is the café, a mixture of red lacquer and brown hues. The exhibition space houses two themed exhibitions every year covering Africa and the African diaspora.

Musée de l'Homme

Palais de Chaillot, pl du Trocadéro, 16th (01.44.05.72.72). Mº Trocadéro. **Open** 9.45am-5.15pm Mon, Wed-Sun. Closed Tue, public holidays. **Admission** €4.57; €3.05 under-18s, over-60s, groups. **Credit** (shop) MC, V. **Map** p400 B5.

Hiving off the human biology, anthropology and ethnology sections of the Muséum National d'Histoire Naturelle, the Musée de l'Homme begins with world population growth, going on to consider birth control, death, disease, genetics and racial distinction before turning to tribal costumes, tools, idols and ornaments from all over the world. Displays are arranged by continent, and while the Americas have been modernised, the African and European content doesn't seem to have changed for half a century. The displays could do with some labelling in English, but the variety of the collections (parts of which are to be controversially transferred to Chirac's Musée des Arts Premiers), including a shrunken head, a stuffed polar bear and a reconstruction of a Mayan temple, makes for ideal escapism on a rainy day.
Café. Cinema. Lectures. Library. Photo Library. Wheelchair access (call ahead).

Oriental arts

Musée National des Arts Asiatiques – Guimet

6 pl d'Iéna, 16th (01.56.52.53.00/www.museeguimet.fr). Mº Iéna. **Open** 10am-6pm Mon, Wed-Sun. **Admission** €5.05; €3 students 18-25; free under-18s, first Sun of month. CM. **Credit** (shop) MC, V. **Map** p401 E5.

The reopened museum of Asian art was the success story of 2001, as it emerged enlarged and rejuvenated from five years of renovation. Founded by Lyon industrialist Emile Guimet in 1889 to house his collection tracing Chinese and Japanese religious history and later incorporating the Oriental collections from the Louvre, Musée Guimet boasts some 45,000 objects from Neolithic times on, in a voyage to Asia that conveys the flow of religions and civilisations. Downstairs galleries focus on India and Southeast Asia, centred on the stunning collection of Hindu and Buddhist Khmer sculpture from Cambodia. Amid legions of calmly smiling Buddhas and the striking seventh-century *Harihara*, a half-Shiva, half-Vishnu figure, you can't miss the massive *Giant's Way*, part of the entrance to a temple complex at Angkor Wat, where two female demi-goddesses hold a seven-headed cobra. Upstairs, Chinese antiquities include mysterious jade discs probably used in fertility rites, an elephant-shaped Shang dynasty bronze pot, lively terracotta figures, horses and camels found in tombs, fragile paintings from Dunhuang and later Chinese celadon wares and porcelain. Other rooms contain Afghan and

Sightseeing

Pakistani glassware and sculpture, Tibetan mandalas and statues, Nepalese ritual items, Japanese Buddhist sculpture, paintings and lacquer and ceramics, as well as an array of Moghul jewellery, caskets, fabrics and miniatures.
Auditorium. Guided visits. Library. Restaurant. Shop. Wheelchair access.

Musée Cernuschi

7 av Velasquez, 8th (01.45.63.50.75). M° Villiers or Monceau. **Open** 2004. **Map** p401 E2.
Currently closed for renovation, the nucleus of this collection of Chinese art was amassed by erudite banker Henri Cernuschi on a long voyage to the Far East in 1871. It ranges from Neolithic terracottas and legions of Han and Wei dynasty funeral statues to refined Tang celadon wares, Sung porcelain, fragile paintings on silk, bronze vessels and jade amulets.
Wheelchair access (call ahead).

Musée de l'Institut du Monde Arabe

1 rue des Fossés-St-Bernard, 5th (01.40.51.38.38/www.imarabe.org). M° Jussieu. **Open** 10am-6pm Tue-Sun. Closed Mon, 1 May. **Admission** €4; €3 18-25s, students, over-60s (prices vary for exhibitions: ring to check); free under-18s, CM. **Credit** MC, V. **Map** p406 K7.
Opened in 1987 as a *Grand Projet*, the institute of the Arab world brings together a library, cultural centre, exhibitions and the 'Museum of Arab Museums', displaying items on long-term loan from museums in alternating Arab countries alongside its own permanent collection. The objects cover a huge geographical (India to Spain) and historical (prehistoric to contemporary) span. Particularly strong are the collections of early scientific instruments, 19th-century Tunisian costume and jewellery and contemporary fine art. Temporary exhibitions have ranged from ancient Syrian sculpture to Matisse's Moroccan paintings.
Bookshop. Cinema. Lectures. Library. Tearoom. Wheelchair access.

History

Mémorial du Maréchal Leclerc de Hauteclocque et de la Libération de Paris & Musée Jean Moulin

23 allée de la 2e DB, Jardin Atlantique (above Grandes Lignes de Gare Montparnasse), 15th (01.40.64.39.44). M° Montparnasse-Bienvenüe. **Open** 10am-6pm Tue-Sun. Closed Mon, public holidays. **Admission** collection free; temporary exhibitions €4; €3 students, over 60s, groups; €2 under 25s. **No credit cards. Map** p405 F9.
A slightly academic approach to World War II and the Résistance characterises this double museum, dedicated to Free French Forces commander General Leclerc and left-wing Résistance martyr Jean Moulin. Temporary exhibitions and extensive documentary material are backed up by film archives; in the first part captions are translated into English,

though the translations disappear in the Résistance room. An impressive 270° slide show relates the liberation of Paris. Memorable documents include a poster exhorting Frenchmen in occupied France to accept compulsory work service in Germany – to act as 'ambassadors of French quality'.
Bookshop. Lectures. Research centre. Wheelchair access (call ahead).

Musée de l'Armée

Hôtel des Invalides, esplanade des Invalides, 7th (01.44.42.37.72). M° Varenne or Latour-Maubourg. **Open** *Apr-Sept* 10am-6pm daily; *Oct-Mar* 10am-5pm daily. Closed 1 Jan, 1 May, 1 Nov, 25 Dec. **Admission** €5.79; €4.27 under-18s, students under 26; free under-12s, CM. **Credit** MC, V. **Map** p405 E6.
After checking out Napoléon's tomb under the vast golden dome of Les Invalides, many tourists don't bother to pursue their visit with the army museum, included in the ticket. If you are interested in military history, the museum is a must, but even if sumptuous uniforms and armour are not your thing, the building is in itself a splendour. Besides military memorabilia, the rooms are filled with fine portraiture (don't miss Ingres' masterpiece of Emperor Napoléon on his throne), some well-recreated interiors, as well as the newly reopened museum of *maquettes* of fortifications. The World War I rooms are particularly immediate and moving, the conflict brought vividly to life by documents and photos. The General de Gaulle wing, opened in 2000, at last gives World War II the coverage it deserves, taking in not only the Free French forces and the Résistance but also the Battle of Britain and war in the Pacific, and alternating weaponry, uniforms and curious artefacts with some blood-chilling film footage. *See also* **Les Invalides**, *chapter* **Left Bank**.
Café. Films. Concerts. Lectures. Shop.

Musée d'Art et d'Histoire de St-Denis

22bis rue Gabriel-Péri, 93200 St-Denis (01.42.43.05.10). M° St-Denis Porte de Paris. **Open** 10am-5.30pm Mon, Wed-Fri; 2pm-6.30pm Sat and Sun. Closed Tue, public holidays. **Admission** €3.05; €1.52 students, over-60s; free under-16s. **No credit cards.**
This prizewinning museum in the suburb of St-Denis is housed in the former Carmelite convent that in the 18th century numbered Louise de France, daughter of Louis XV, among its incumbents. Although there are displays of local archaeology, prints about the Paris Commune, Modern and post-Impressionist drawings and documents relating to the poet Paul Eluard who was born in the town, the most vivid part is the first floor where the nuns' austere cells have been preserved.

Khmer quick and dig the **Musée National des Arts Asiatiques – Guimet.** *See p169.*

Musée du Cabinet des Médailles

Bibliothèque Nationale Richelieu, 58 rue de Richelieu, 2nd (01.53.79.81.26). Mº Bourse. **Open** 1pm-6pm daily. Closed one week in Sept, public holidays. **Admission** free. **Credit** MC, V. **Map** p402 H4.

With attention now focused on the new Bibliothèque François Mitterrand, the original building cuts a rather melancholy figure. On the first floor is the anachronistic Cabinet des Médailles: the extensive collection of coins and medals is actually for specialists, but efficient sliding magnifying glasses help bring exhibits to life. Probably the most interesting aspect for the general public are the museum's parallel Greek, Roman and medieval collections, where oddities include the Merovingian King Dagobert's throne and Charlemagne's chess set, (wht a fun guy he must have been) nestling among Greek vases and miniature sculptures from all periods. The attendants seem ever so slightly put out by the mere existence of visitors.

Shop. Partial wheelchair access.

Musée Carnavalet

23 rue de Sévigné, 3rd (01.44.59.58.58/www.paris-france.org/musees). Mº St-Paul. **Open** 10am-6pm Tue-Sun. Closed Mon, some public holidays. **Admission** collection free; prices vary for exhibitions: ring to check; €3 14-26; free under-13s; **Credit** (shop) AmEx, MC, V. **Map** p406 L6.

The museum of Paris history owes its origins to Baron Haussmann who, in 1866, persuaded the city to buy the Hôtel Carnavalet to house some of the interiors from buildings destroyed to make way for his new boulevards. Since then the museum has added a second *hôtel* and built up a huge collection which tells the history of the city from pre-Roman Gaul to the 20th century. The newly opened orangery, the only surviving one in Paris dating from the 17th century, features Neolithic dug-out canoes excavated at Bercy.

The Hôtel Carnavalet contains the main collection and retains much of its old atmosphere, with an attractive *cour d'honneur* and a formal garden.

Carnavalet's most famous resident was Mme de Sévigné, whose letters to her daughter bring alive aristocratic life under Louis XIV (and whose desk is in the museum). Portraits of the author and her circle, her Chinese-export, lacquered desk and some of her letters are displayed in the panelled first-floor gallery and salon. All that remains of the adjoining 17th-century Hôtel Le Peletier de St-Fargeau, linked since 1989, is the elegant grand staircase and one restored, panelled cabinet.

Displays are chronological. The original 16th-century rooms house the Renaissance collections with portraits by Clouet, and furniture and pictures relating to the Wars of Religion. The first floor covers the period up to 1789 with furniture, applied arts and paintings displayed in restored, period interiors. The bold colours, particularly in the oval boudoir from the Hôtel de Breteuil (1782), may come as a shock to those with pre-conceived ideas about subdued 18th-century taste. Interesting interiors include the Rococo cabinet painted for engraver Demarteau by his friends Fragonard, Boucher and Huet in 1765 and the Louis XIII-style Cabinet Colbert.

The collections from 1789 on are housed in the *hôtel* next door. The Revolutionary items are the best way of getting an understanding of the convoluted politics and bloodshed of the period. There are portraits of all the major players, prints, objects and memorabilia including a bone model of the guillotine, Hubert Robert's gouaches and a small chunk of the Bastille prison. Those of a sentimental bent should look at the pathetic souvenirs from the Temple prison where the royal family were held, among them the Dauphin's lead soldiers.

Highlights of the later collections include items belonging to Napoléon, views of Paris depicting the effects of Haussmann's programme, the ornate cradle given by the city to Napoléon III on the birth of his son, the Art Nouveau boutique designed by Mucha in 1901 for jeweller Fouquet and the Art Deco ballroom of the Hôtel Wendel painted by Catalan artist José-Maria Sert. Rooms devoted to French literature finish the tour with portraits and room settings, including Proust's cork-lined bedroom.
Bookshop. Guided tours. Reference section (by appointment). Lectures. Wheelchair access.

Musée de l'Histoire de France

Hôtel de Soubise, 60 rue des Francs-Bourgeois, 3rd (01.40.27.62.18/www.archivesnationales.culture.gouv .fr/chan). M° Hôtel-de-Ville or Rambuteau. **Open** 10am-5.45pm Mon, Wed-Fri; 1.45-5.45pm Sat, Sun. Closed Tue, public holidays. **Admission** €3.05; €2.29 18-25s; free under-18s. **No credit card**s. **Map** p406 K6.

Housed in one of the grandest Marais mansions, this museum is part of the National Archives. The museum is being renovated with a view to new presentation that favours the plurality of possible historical interpretations. In the meantime, a changing selection of historical documents and artefacts cover not just major political events – the Wars of Religion, the French Revolution – but also social issues and

Horticulture vultures gather at **Musée Carnavalet**. *See p171.*

quirky aspects of daily life, from the founding of the Sorbonne to an ordonnance about umbrellas or World War I postcards. If this all sounds slightly dry, then there's another reason to visit the Hôtel de Soubise: the finest Rococo interiors in Paris. The apartments of the Prince and Princesse de Soubise were decorated in the 1730s with superb plasterwork, panelling and paintings by artists including Boucher, Natoire, Restout and Van Loo.
Shop.

Musée National de la Légion d'Honneur

2 rue de la Légion d'Honneur, 7th (01.40.62.84.25).
M° Solférino/RER Musée d'Orsay. **Open** 11am-5pm Tue-Sun. Closed Mon, 1 Jan, 1 May, from July/Sep 2001-2002/3. **Admission** €3.81; €2.29 students 18-25; free under-18s, CM. Credit (shop) MC, V.
Map p405 G6.
The museum devoted to France's honours system is housed in the stables of the superb Hôtel de Salm, bought by Napoléon in 1804. The museum itself has undergone a facelift in time for the bicentenary of the Ordre de la Légion d'Honneur. The wonderful array of official gongs and lookalike mayoral chains is enlivened by some superb portraiture, including a display which combines the cloak of the Ordre du St-Esprit and a portrait by Van Loo of the creation of the Order, featuring the same costume. A new gallery evokes World War I through sketches, portraits and medals.
Shop.

Musée de la Marine

Palais de Chaillot, pl du Trocadéro, 16th
(01.53.65.69.69/www.musee-marine.fr). M°
Trocadéro. **Open** 10am-6pm Mon, Wed-Sun. Closed Tue. **Admission** €5.79; €3.81 under-26s, over-60s; free under-5s, CM. **Credit** (shop) AmEx, MC, V.
Map p400 B5.
The ideal place to find your sealegs, the maritime museum concentrates on French naval history from detailed carved models of battleships and Vernet's imposing series of paintings of the ports of France (1754-65) to a model of a nuclear submarine, as well as the Imperial barge, built when Napoléon's delusions of grandeur were reaching their zenith in 1810. There are also carved bows, old maps, antique and modern navigational instruments, ships in bottles, underwater equipment and romantic maritime paintings plus a new area devoted to the modern navy. The museum is currently undergoing construction work, although all rooms remain open.
Shop.

Musée de la Monnaie de Paris

11 quai de Conti, 6th (01.40.46.55.35). M° Odéon
or Pont-Neuf. **Open** 11am-5.30pm Tue-Fri; noon-5.30pm Sat, Sun. **Admission** €3.05; €2.29 students 18-25; free under-18s, over-60s, CM, all on Sun.
Credit (shop) MC, V. **Map** p406 H6.
Housed in the handsome Neo-Classical mint built in the 1770s by Jacques-Denis Antoine, this high-tech museum tells the story of France's coinage from pre-

Roman origins to the present day through a series of sophisticated displays and audiovisual presentations. The history of the French state is directly linked to its coinage, and the museum is informative about both. If your French is sufficient for the tour, a visit to the still-functioning *ateliers*, taking in foundry, engraving and casting of coins and medals, is fascinating. It remains to be seen how the introduction of the euro will affect the collection.
Shop. Visit to atelier (2.15pm Wed, Fri reserve ahead).

Musée de Montmartre

12 rue Cortot, 18th (01.46.06.61.11). M° Lamarck-Caulaincourt. **Open** 11am-5pm Tue-Sun. Closed Mon, 1 Jan, 1 May, 25 Dec. **Admission** €3.81; €3.05 students, over-60s; free under-8s. **Credit** (shop) MC, V. **Map** p401 H1.
At the back of a peaceful garden, this 17th-century manor is a haven of calm after touristy Montmartre. The museum is administered by the Société d'Histoire et d'Archéologie du Vieux Montmartre, which since 1886 has aimed to preserve documents and artefacts relating to the historic hilltop. The collection consists of a room devoted to Modigliani, who lived in rue Caulaincourt, the recreated study of composer Gustave Charpentier, some original Toulouse-Lautrec posters, porcelain from the short-lived factory at Clignancourt and a tribute to the local cabaret, the Lapin Agile. The studios above the entrance pavilion were occupied at various times by Renoir, Emile Bernard, Raoul Dufy and Suzanne Valadon with her son Maurice Utrillo.

Musée du Montparnasse

21 av du Maine, 15th (01.42.22.91.96).
M° Montparnasse-Bienvenüe or Falguière. **Open** *during exhibitions* Wed-Sun. **Admission** €3.81; €3.05 students under-26, over-60s; free under-15s.
No credit cards. Map p405 F8.
The Musée du Montparnasse opened in 1998 in one of the last remaining alleys of artists' studios in Montparnasse. In the 1930s and 40s it was home to Marie Vassilieff who opened her own academy and canteen where penniless artists – such as regulars Picasso, Modigliani, Cocteau, Matisse and Zadkine – came for cheap food. Trotsky and Lenin were also among her guests. Exhibitions tracing various facets of Montparnasse's artistic past have included Foujita and Japanese artists and Jean Cocteau. *See chapter* **Left Bank.**

Musée de la Préfecture de Police

1bis rue des Carmes, 5th (01.44.41.52.54).
M° Maubert-Mutualité. **Open** 9am-5pm Mon-Fri; 10am-5pm Sat. Closed public holidays. **Admission** free. **No credit cards. Map** p406 J7.
Rather spookily located upstairs in a hideous police station, the history of Paris is viewed via crime and its prevention since the founding of the Paris police force in the 16th century. You need to read French to best appreciate the assorted warrants and ordonances, but there are plenty of evocative murder weapons. Among eclectic treasures are prisoners'

expenses from the Bastille, including those of dastardly jewel thief the Comtesse de la Motte, the exploding flowerpot planted by Louis-Armand Matha in 1894 in a restaurant on the rue de Tournon, and the gory *Epée de Justice*, a 17th-century sword blunted by the quantity of noble heads chopped.

Musée de la Résistance Nationale

Parc Vercors, 88 av Marx Dormoy, 94500 Champigny-sur-Marne (01.48.81.00.80/www.musee-resistance.com). RER A Champigny-St-Maur then bus 208. **Open** 9am-12.30pm, 2-5.30pm Tue-Fri; 2-6pm Sat, Sun. Closed Mon, weekends in August. **Admission** €3.81; €1.91 students; free schoolchildren, war veterans. **No credit cards.**
Occupying five floors of a 19th-century villa, the Résistance museum starts at the top with the pre-war political background and works down, via defeat in 1940, German occupation and the rise of the maquis, to victory. Given the universal appeal of the Résistance movement, it's slightly odd that no effort is made for foreign visitors: hundreds of photographs aside, the bulk of the material consists of newspaper archives, both from official and clandestine presses, with no translations. Three short archive films and a few solid artefacts are more accessible, with a sobering wall of machine guns and pistols, a railway saboteur's kit (cutters to chop through brake pipes, sand to pour into gearboxes and logs to lay across tracks) and a homemade device for scattering tracts. Displays steer clear of wallowing in collaborationist disgrace and of Résistance hero tub-thumping.

Literary

Maison de Balzac

47 rue Raynouard, 16th (01.55.74.41.80). M° Passy. **Open** 10am-6pm Tue-Sun. Closed Mon, public holidays. **Admission** collection free; temporary exhibitions €3.30; €2.20 over-60s, €1.60 14-26; free under-13s. **No credit cards. Map** p404 B6.
Honoré de Balzac (1799-1850) rented a flat at this address in 1840 to avoid his creditors and established a password to sift friends from bailiffs. The museum now spread over several floors gives a rather dry presentation of his work and life, but the garden is pretty and gives an idea of the sort of country villa that lined this street when Passy was a fashionable spa. A wide range of memorabilia includes first editions, letters, corrected proofs, prints, portraits of friends and Polish mistress Mme Hanska, plus a 'family tree' of Balzac's characters that covers several walls. The study houses his desk, chair and the monogrammed coffee pot that fuelled all-night work on much of *La Comédie humaine*.
Library (by appointment).

Maison de Chateaubriand

La Vallée aux Loups, 87 rue de Chateaubriand, 92290 Chatenay-Malabry (01.47.02.08.62). RER B Robinson + 20min walk. **Open** (guided tours only except Sun) *Apr-Sept* 10am-noon, 2-6pm Wed, Fri-Sat, Sun; *Oct-Mar* 2-5pm Tue-Sun. Closed Mon, Jan, 25 Dec. **Admission** €4.50; €3 students, over-60s; free under-8s. **No credit cards.**
In 1807, attracted by the quiet Vallée aux Loups, Chateaubriand (1768-1848), author of *Mémoires d'outre tombe*, set about transforming a simple 18th-century country house into his own Romantic idyll and planted the park with rare trees as a reminder of his travels. Most interesting are the over-the-top double wooden staircase, based on a maritime design, a reminder of the writer's noble St-Malo birth, and the portico with two white marble Grecian statues supporting a colonnaded porch. Anyone familiar with David's *Portrait of Mme Récamier* in the Louvre will find the original chaise longue awaiting the sitter, who was one of Chateaubriand's numerous lovers – no doubt to the discomfort of his stern wife, Céleste. After a politically inflammatory work Chateaubriand was ruined and in 1818 had to sell his beloved valley.
Concerts/readings (spring, autumn). Shop. Tearoom.

Musée de la Vie Romantique

16 rue Chaptal, 9th (01.48.74.95.38). M° Blanche. **Open** 10am-6pm Tue-Sun. Closed Mon, public holidays. **Admission** free; temporary exhibitions €9, €4.50 over-60s, students under 26; free under-13s, CM. **No credit cards. Map** p401 G2.
When artist Ary Scheffer lived in this villa, this area south of Pigalle was known as the New Athens because of the concentration of writers, composers and artists living here. Baronne Aurore Dupin, alias George Sand (1804-76), was a frequent guest at Scheffer's soirées, and the house is now devoted to the writer, her family and her intellectual circle, which included Chopin, Delacroix (art tutor to her son) and composer Charpentier. Quietly charming, the museum reveals little of her writing or proto-feminist ideas, nor her affairs with Jules Sandeau, Chopin (represented by a marble bust) and Alfred de Musset; rather it presents a typical bourgeois portrait in the watercolours, lockets and jewels she left behind. In the courtyard, Scheffer's studio is used for exhibitions.
Bookshop. Concerts.

Musée Mémorial Ivan Tourguéniev

16 rue Ivan Tourguéniev, 78380 Bougival (01.45.77.87.12). M° La Défense, plus bus 258. **Open** *Apr-Oct* 10am-6pm Sun; by appointment for groups during the week. **Admission** €4.60; €3.80 12-26s; free under-12s. **No credit cards.**
The proverbial Russian soul persists in unexpected places like tranquil, Seine-side Bougival. The sumptuous datcha where novelist Ivan Turgenev lived for several years until his death in 1883 was a gathering spot for composers Saint-Saëns and Fauré, opera divas Pauline Viardot and Maria Malibran, and writers Henry James, Flaubert, Zola and Maupassant. As well as letters and editions (mainly in Russian), there's the music room where Viardot held court.
Bookshop. Concerts. Guided Tours for groups, 5pm Sun, all year round.

Palais de Chaillot, home of the
Musée de l'Homme. *See p169.*

Music & media

Musée Edith Piaf

5 rue Crespin-du-Gast, 11th (01.43.55.52.72).
Mº Ménilmontant. **Open** by appointment 1-6pm
Mon-Thur (call two days ahead). Closed Sept.
Admission donation. **No credit cards.**
Map p403 N5.
Les Amis d'Edith Piaf run this tiny two-room museum in a part of Paris familiar to the singer, who was
in many ways the French Shirley Bassey. The memorabilia exudes love for the 'little sparrow', her
diminutive stature graphically shown by a lifesize
cardboard cut-out. Her little black dress and tiny
shoes are particularly moving, and letters, posters
and photos provide a personal touch. There's a
sculpture of the singer by Suzanne Blistène, wife of
Marcel, who produced most of Piaf's films, and CDs
and books on sale for the devoted fan.
Library. Shop.

Musée de la Musique

Cité de la Musique, 221 av Jean-Jaurès, 19th
(01.44.84.44.84/www.cite-musique.fr). Mº Porte de
Pantin. **Open** noon-6pm Tue-Thur, Sat; noon-7.30pm
Fri; 10am-6pm Sun. Closed Mon, some public
holidays. **Admission** €6.10; €4.57 18s-25s; €2.29 6-
18s; free under-6s, over-60s, CM. **Credit** MC, V.
Map p403 insert.
Alongside the concert hall in the striking modern
Cité de la Musique, the innovative music museum
houses the gleamingly restored collection of instruments from the old Conservatoire, interactive computers and scale models of opera houses and concert
halls. On arrival you are supplied with an audioguide in a choice of languages. Don't be a precious
old luvvie and spurn this offer, for the musical commentary is an essential part of the enjoyment, playing the appropriate music or instrument as you
approach the exhibit. Alongside the trumpeting
brass, curly woodwind instruments and precious
strings are more unusual items, such as the
Indonesian gamelan orchestra, whose gurgling, percussive sounds so influenced the work of both
Debussy and Ravel. Some of the concerts in the
museum's amphitheatre use historic instruments
from the collection. *See also chapters* **Right Bank**
and **Music: Classical & Opera**.
Audioguide. Library. Shop. Wheelchair access.

Musée de l'Opéra

Palais Garnier, 1 pl de l'Opéra, 9th (01.40.01.24.93).
Mº Opéra. **Open** 10am-6pm daily. **Admission** €6;
€4 10-25s, students, over-60s; free under-10s. **No**
credit cards. Map p401 G4.
The magnificently restored Palais Garnier houses
small temporary exhibitions relating to current
opera or ballet productions, and a permanent collection of paintings, scores and bijou opera sets
housed in period cases. Not the place where you'll
find yourself mingling with too many leery White
Stripes or Slipknot fans, then. The picture gallery is
a sort of National Portrait Gallery for musicians and
allows many an enthralling gazing session. The
entrance fee includes a visit to the auditorium (if
rehearsals permit).

Religion

Musée d'Art et d'Histoire du Judaïsme

Hôtel de St-Aignan, 71 rue du Temple, 3rd (01.53.01.86.53). M° Rambuteau. **Open** 11am-6pm Mon-Fri; 10am-6pm Sun. Closed Sat, some Jewish holidays. **Admission** €6.10; €3.81 18-26s, students. **Credit** (shop) AmEx, MC, V. **Map** K5

Opened in 1998 in a Marais mansion, the Jewish museum gives Jewish heritage a showcase. Focusing on migrations and communities, exhibits bring out the importance of ceremonies, rites and learning, and show how styles were adapted across the globe. A silver Hannukah lamp made in Frankfurt, finely carved Italian synagogue furniture, painted wooden sukkah cabin from Austrian, embroidered Bar Mitzvah robes, Torah scrolls and North African dresses put the emphasis on fine craftsmanship but also on religious practice, for which a certain familiarity with the decorative arts is helpful. There are also documents and paintings relating to the emancipation of French Jewry after the Revolution, and the Dreyfus case, from Zola's *J'Accuse* to anti-Semitic cartoons. An impressive array of paintings by the early 20th-century avant-garde and the Ecole de Paris includes El Lissitsky, Mané-Katz, Modigliani, Soutine and Chagall. The Shoah (holocaust) is side-stepped – with the exception of a work by Christian Boltanski that commemorates the Jews who were living in the Hôtel St-Aignan in 1939, 13 of whom died in concentration camps.

Auditorium. Café. Library. Shop. Wheelchair access.

Musée de la Franc-Maçonnerie

16 rue Cadet, 9th (01.45.23.20.92). M° Cadet. **Open** 2-6pm Tue-Sun. Closed Mon, Sun, public holidays, 14 July-15 Aug. **Admission** €2; free under-12s. **No credit cards. Map** p401 H3.

At the back of the Grand Orient de France (French Masonic Great Lodge), a school-hall type room traces the history of freemasonry from medieval stone masons' guilds to the present via prints of famous masons (General Lafayette and 1848 revolutionary leaders Blanc and Barbès).

Bookshop. Wheelchair access (call ahead).

Science, medicine & technology

La Cité des Sciences et de l'Industrie

La Villette, 30 av Corentin-Cariou, 19th (01.40.05.80.00/01.40.05.12.12/www.cite-sciences.fr). M° Porte de la Villette. **Open** 10am-6pm Tue-Sat; 10am-7pm Sun. Closed Mon, public holidays. **Admission** €7.62; €5.34 7-16s, students under 25, over-60s; free under-7s; all on Sat; Cité/Géode pass (Tue-Fri) €14.03; €12.04 children, students under 25, over-60s. **Credit** MC, V. **Map** p403 insert.

The ultra-modern science museum at La Villette has been riding high since its opening in 1986 and pulls in over five million visitors a year. Originally intended as an abattoir, the expensive project was derailed mid-construction and cleverly transformed into a gigantic, state-of-the-art science museum. **Explora**, the permanent show, occupies the upper two floors, whisking visitors through 30,000 m2 of 'space, life, matter and communication', where scale models of satellites including the Ariane space shuttle, planes and robots make for an exciting journey. There's an impressive array of interactive exhibits on language and communication enabling you to learn about sound waves and try out different smells. Put on your Michael Fish act and pretend to be a weatherman in the Espace Images, try out the delayed camera and other optical illusions in the Jeux de lumière, or draw 3D images on computer. The Serre 'garden of the future' investigates futuristic developments in agriculture and bio-technology. The Espace section, devoted to man's conquest of space, lets you experience the sensation of weightlessness. Other sections feature climate, ecology and the environment, health, energy, agriculture, the ocean and volcanoes. The Automobile gallery looks at the car both as myth and technological object, with driving simulator and displays on safety, pollution and future designs. The lower floors house temporary exhibitions, a documentation centre and children's sections. The Louis Lumière cinema shows films in 3-D, and there's a restored submarine moored next to the Géode. *See also chapters* **Right Bank**, **Film** and **Children**.

Bookshop. Café. Cinema. Conference centre. Library (multimedia). Wheelchair access & hire.

Musée de l'Air et de l'Espace

Aéroport de Paris-Le Bourget, 93352 Le Bourget Cedex (01.49.92.71.99/recorded information 01.49.92.71.71/www.mae.org). M° Gare du Nord then bus 350/M° La Courneuve then bus 152/RER Le Bourget then bus 152. **Open** *May-Oct* 10am-6pm; *Nov-Apr* 10am-5pm Tue-Sun. Closed Mon, 25 Dec, 1 Jan. **Admission** €6; €4.05 8-16s, students; free under-8s. **Credit** MC, V.

The air and space museum is a potent reminder that France is a technical and military as well as cultural power. Housed in the former passenger terminal at Le Bourget airport, the collection begins with the pioneers, including fragile-looking biplanes, the contraption in which Romanian Vivia succeeded in flying 12 metres in 1906, and the strangely nautical command cabin of a Zeppelin airship. Outside on the runway are Mirage fighter planes, a Boeing 707, an American Thunderchief with painted shark-tooth grimace and Ariane launchers 1 and 5. Within a vast hangar, walk through the prototype Concorde 001 and view wartime survivors, a Spitfire and German Heinkel bomber. Further hangars are packed with military planes, helicopters, commercial jets and bizarre prototypes like the Leduc, designed to be launched off the back of another plane, stunt planes, missiles and satellites. A section is devoted to hot

Happy birthday, dear Victor

2002 is the 200th anniversary of the birth of Victor Hugo. The prolific Hugo looms large in the pantheon of French writers, having produced two of the most popular novels of the 19th century, the historical romance *Notre Dame De Paris* (better known to Anglophones as *The Hunchback of Notre Dame*), and the massive social historical work *Les Misérables* (mercifully, Hugo did not live to see them turned into musicals). Those represent just the twin peaks of his high-protein career, which spanned Romantic costume dramas, lyrical and satirical poetry and a veritable mountain of journalism. Hugo's works are characterised by their blending historical reality with wild, imaginative drama, and his life was as dramatic as anything you'll find in his books: he was raised by parents who both spent their married life bed-hopping and living through the resulting domestic crises; his winning the hand of Adèle le Foucher produced in his brother a fit of jealousy-fuelled insanity that put the poor man straight into a mental hospital; Hugo's first child, Léopold, died as a baby; his beloved daughter Léopoldine drowned and, in the same year (1845), he became a figure of scandal by being caught with his trousers round his ankles in the company of his mistress; Napoléon III's coup d'état forced the actively republican Hugo into 20 years of exile on Guernsey, where he worked standing upright at a lectern, morosely gazing across the sea towards the coastline of France and turning out an average of 20 pages of prose each day; plagued by ill health in his twilight years (the elderly Hugo was described by André Maurois as being like an ageing faun) he took to such pursuits as carving furniture with his teeth; he finally returned to Paris as a hero – two million people attended his funeral, and he was laid to rest in the Panthéon. Not bad for a man whose middle name was Marie.

La Maison de Victor Hugo, Paris' museum of the man, is itself 100 years old. Hugo lived here from 1832 to 1848 (the building is early 17th century and spent its formative years as a hotel), and visitors can see first editions of his works, his sometimes bizarre, self-designed furniture, and nearly 500 of his drawings. The house was closed for five months in late 2001 in order to gear up for two major exhibitions to mark the bicentennial year: *Voir des étoiles* runs from

April until July and has been organised in partnership with the Bibliothèque Nationale and the Comédie Française. This exhibition concentrates on Hugo's work as a playwright and illustrates it in its historical context, showing how it paved the way for modern French theatre. *Aubes* runs from October until January 2003, and revolves round the intriguing notion of allowing the art historian Harald Szeeman to take Hugo's drawings and sketches and arrange them alongside works by 20th-century artists. (Hugo groupies should note that the exhibitions stretch across the Channel to Vic's pad during his exile on Guernsey, Hauteville House – the *Exilium vitae est* show, running from April until September, features his vision of Europe and the place of the sea in his various works).

The Maison de Victor Hugo is a good place to celebrate the life of this astonishing man, who invested his literature with the same quality that hallmarked his life: oomph.

Hôtel de Rohan-Guéménée, 6 pl des Vosges, 4th (01.42.72.10.16). Mº Bastille. **Open** 10am-5.40pm Tue-Sun. Closed Mon, public holidays. **Admission** until 15 Aug €3.35; €2.29 students; free under-26s, over-65s, CM; collection free from 15 Aug 2002. **Credit** (shop) MC, V. **Map** p406 L6.

air balloons, invented in 1783 by the Montgolfier brothers and swiftly adopted for military reconnaissance. Recent additions to the musem include a new and improved planetarium and the 'Espace' section, dedicated to space travel. Most captions are summarised in English.

Shop. Wheelchair access (except new 'Espace' building).

Musée des Arts et Métiers

60 rue Réaumur, 3rd (01.40.27.22.20). M° Arts et Métiers. **Open** 10am-6pm Mon, Wed, Sat, Sun; 10am-7.30pm Thur. Closed Tue. **Admission** €5.34; €3.81 students under-26; over-60s;-5s free. **Credit** call for details. **Map** p402 K5.

The successful combination of 12th-century structure and 21st-century technology and design reflects the museum's aim – to demonstrate the history and future of the technical arts. A new permanent exhibition looking at seven aspects of science and technology has been created from the museum's vast collection of over 80,000 machines and models. Throughout, videos and interactive computers explain the science behind the exhibits and at the end of each section there is a workshop for budding young scientists and technophobes alike to get to grips with what is on display. Most impressive is the chapel where an elaborate glass and steel staircase enables you to climb right up into the nave. There amid the stained glass you can gaze down upon the wonders of man's invention, which include Bleriot's plane and the first steam engine.

Musée d'Histoire de la Médecine

Université René Descartes, 12 rue de l'Ecole-de-Médecine, 6th (01.40.46.16.93). M° Odéon. **Open** 15 July-Sept 2-5.30pm Mon-Fri; Oct-13 July 2-5.30pm Mon-Wed, Fri, Sat. Closed Sun, public holidays. **Admission** €3.05; free under-12s. **No credit cards**. **Map** p406 H7.

The medical faculty collection covers the history of medicine from ancient Egyptian embalming tools through to a 1960s electrocardiograph. There's a gruesome array of serrated-edged saws and curved knives used for amputations, stethoscopes and syringes, the surgical instruments of Dr Antommarchi, who performed the autopsy on Napoléon and the scalpel of Dr Félix, who operated on Louis XIV.

Muséum National d'Histoire Naturelle

57 rue Cuvier, 5th (01.40.79.30.00); Grande Galerie (01.40.79.54.79). M° Jussieu or Gare d'Austerlitz. **Open** Grande Galerie 10am-6pm Mon, Wed, Fri-Sun; 10am-10pm Thur. Closed Tue. **Admission** *Grande Galerie* €6.10; €4.57 5-16s, students, over-60s; free under-5s. *Other pavilions* each €4.57; free under-5s. **No credit cards**. **Map** p406 K9.

The brilliantly renovated Grande Galerie de l'Evolution has taken Paris' Natural History Museum out of the dinosaur age. Architect Paul Chemetov successfully integrated modern lifts, stairways and the latest lighting and audiovisual techniques into the 19th-century iron-framed structure. As you enter, you will be confronted with the 13.66m-long skeleton of a whale: the rest of the ground floor is dedicated to other sea creatures. On the first floor are the mammals, mostly in the open – with the exception of Louis XVI's rhinoceros, stuffed on a wooden chair frame.

Videos and interactive computers give information on life in the wild. Glass-sided lifts take you up through suspended birds to the second floor, which deals with man's impact on nature and considers demographic problems and pollution. The third floor traces the evolution of species, while a gallery at the side, deliberately retaining old-fashioned glass cases, displays endangered and extinct species. There's a 'discovery' room for the under-12s and laboratories for teenagers. *See also chapters* **Left Bank** *and* **Children**.

Auditorium. Bookshop. Café. Library. Wheelchair access (Grande Galerie).

Musée Pasteur

Institut Pasteur, 25 rue du Dr-Roux, 15th (01.45.68.82.83/www.pasteur.fr). M° Pasteur. **Open** 2-5.30pm Mon-Fri. Closed weekends, public holidays, Aug. **Admission** €3; €1.50 students. **Credit** V. **Map** p405 E9.

The apartment where the famous chemist and his wife lived for the last seven years of his life (1888-95) has hardly been touched since his death; you can still see their furniture and possessions, family photos and a room of scientific instruments. The highlight is the extravagant, Byzantine-style mausoleum on the ground floor housing Pasteur's tomb, decorated with mosaics of his scientific achievements.

Musée de la Poste

34 bd de Vaugirard, 15th (01.42.79.23.45/www.laposte.fr). M° Montparnasse-Bienvenüe. **Open** 10am-6pm Mon-Sat. Closed Sun. **Admission** €4.57; €3.05; free under 12s. **Credit** V. **Map** p405 E9.

Although belonging to the state postal service, this is more than just a company museum. Amid uniforms, pistols, carriages, bicycles, letter boxes, portraits, official decrees, cartoons and fumigation tongs emerge some fascinating snippets of history: during the 1871 Siege of Paris, hot-air balloons and carrier pigeons were used to get post out of the city and *boules de Moulins*, balls containing hundreds of microfiche letters, were floated down the Seine in return, mostly to never arrive. The second section gives a survey of French and international philately. Philately will get you nowhere.

Musée de Radio-France

Maison de Radio-France, 116 av du Président-Kennedy, 16th (01.56.40.15.16/01.56.40.21.80/www.radio-france.fr). M° Ranelagh/RER Kennedy-Radio France. **Open** guided tours 10.30am, 11.30am, 2.30pm, 3.30pm, 4.30pm Mon. **Admission** €3.80; €3 8s-25s, students, over-60s. **No credit cards**. **Map** p404 A7.

Join hordes of schoolkids (which really adds to the fun) at Paris' original science museum, housing designs from Leonardo da Vinci's extraordinary inventions onwards. Replicas, models, audiovisual material and real apparatus are used to bring displays to life. Permanent displays cover biology, astronomy, chemistry, physics and earth sciences. The Planète Terre space takes account of developments in meteorology, while one room is dedicated to the sun.

Café. Experiments. Shop. Wheelchair access.

Eccentricities

Musée de la Contrefaçon

16 rue de la Faisanderie, 16th (01.56.26.14.00). M°
Porte-Dauphine. **Open** 2-5.30pm Tue-Sun. Closed Mon, public holidays. **Admission** €2.30; free under-12s. **No credit cards.** **Map** p400 A4.

The small museum set up by the French anti-counterfeiting association puts strong emphasis on the penalties involved in forgery (the law in France applies to the receivers of forged goods, too). Although the oldest known forgery is displayed (vase covers from c200 BC), the focus is on contemporary copies of well-known brands – Reebok, Lacoste, Vuitton, Ray Ban – with the real thing displayed next to the fake. Even Babie doll, Barbie's illicit clone, gets a look-in. Definitely an oddity among oddities.

Musée de la Curiosité

11 rue St-Paul, 4th (01.42.72.13.26). M° St-Paul or
Sully Morland. **Open** 2-7pm Wed, Sat, Sun (longer during school holidays). Closed Mon, Tue, Thur, Fri. **Admission** €6.86, €4.57 3-12s; free under-3s. **No credit cards.** **Map** p406 L7.

The museum of magic gives you a show of card tricks, a talk on the history of magic going as far back as Ancient Egypt and a fine selection of the tools of the trade, such as wands, a cabinet for cutting people in half, optical illusions and posters. The welcome is enthusiastic and friendly, and the guides are passionate about their art.

Musée du Vin

5 square Charles-Dickens, 16th
(01.45.25.63.26/www.museeduvinparis.com). M°
Passy. **Open** 10am-6pm Tue-Sun. Closed Mon, 24 Dec-2 Jan. **Admission** €6; €5.40 over-60s; €5.25 students. **Credit** (shop/restaurant) AmEx, DC, MC, V. **Map** p404 B6.

Unless you are a total oenophile, the main appeal of the museum is the beauty of the building itself: the vaulted cellars of a wine-producing monastery that was destroyed in the Revolution. The ancient bottles, vats, corkscrews and cutouts of medieval peasants making wine are quickly seen, but at the end your patience is rewarded with a *dégustation* (tasting), which isn't as disgusting as it sounds, and the wine that's on sale isn't forced down your throat. You could go in clueless and come out legless. *Restaurant (noon-3pm). Shop. Wheelchair access.*

A corking time at **Musée du Vin**. *See right.*

Audio-visual history is presented with an emphasis on French pioneers such as Branly and Charles Cros, including documentary evidence of the first radio message between the Eiffel Tower and the Panthéon. Particularly interesting is the London broadcast of the Free French with its delightfully obscure coded messages. From the museum you can see people recording radio programmes below.

Musée du Service de Santé des Armées

pl Alphonse-Laveran, 5th (01.40.51.40.00). RER
Port-Royal. **Open** noon-6pm Tue, Wed for groups; 1.30-6pm Sat, Sun for individuals. **Admission** €4.60; €2.30 6-12s; free under-6s. **No credit cards.** **Map** p406 J9.

The museum traces the history of military medicine, via recreations of field hospitals and ambulance trains, and beautifully presented antique medical instruments and pharmacy jars. World War I brings a chilling insight into the true horror of the conflict, when many buildings were transformed into hospitals and, ironically, medical science progressed in leaps and bounds.

Palais de la Découverte

av Franklin D Roosevelt, 8th (01.56.43.20.21/
www.palais-decouverte.fr). M° Franklin D Roosevelt.
Open 9.30am-6pm Tue-Sat; 10am-7pm Sun. Closed Mon, 1 Jan, 1 May, 14 July, 15 Aug, 25 Dec. **Admission** €4.57; €3.05 5-18s, students under 26; free under-5s. Planetarium €2.29. **Credit** AmEx, MC, V. **Map** p405 E5.

EDOKKO

回転寿司 江戸っ子

sushi • yakitori

The most
entertaining
revolving
sushi bar
in Paris...

Take-Away Service available

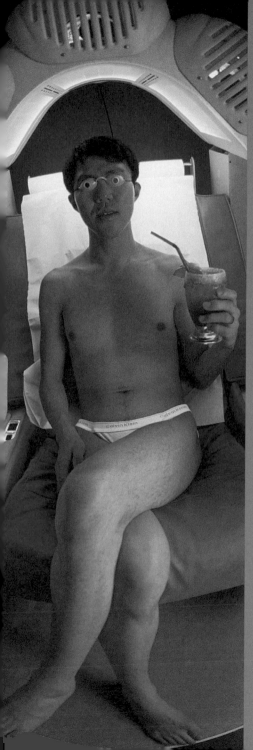

Eat, Drink, Shop

Restaurants

Peckish, are we? You've come to the right place. Whether you want to pleasure your palate or simply fill your boots, here's a selection that will make you drool.

Recently, chefs have dared to ask the question 'Is French food finished?' (*see p28*) and a new style has been emerging, led by a handful of iconoclasts. The fashion restaurant is here to stay – led this year by **Nobu, La Maison Blanche** and **Market** (*see p197*) – but the real buzz has been about chefs who are daring to do their own thing, sometimes in unlikely settings.

The most talked-about chef of the past year has been Pascal Barbot of **L'Astrance** (*see p28*). After working with Alain Passard, Barbot opened a rather serious grey dining room in the 16th, where he has shown that cutting-edge cuisine doesn't have to come at a crippling cost. Sharing this philosophy is the rather more casual **Café des Délices** (*see p28*), where chef Giles Choukroun's priority is putting customers at ease – all the better to enjoy his imaginative cooking. Nicolas Vagnon is inventing a style all his own at **La Table de Lucullus** (*see p201*).

Except for the very simplest restaurants, it is wise to book ahead. For most places, this can be done the same day as your visit. More time should be allowed for haute cuisine restaurants, which need to be booked weeks in advance and checked the day before. On the clothing front, anything bar your gym gear should be fine, but you'll find that Parisians look smart when they go out, so denim could make you stick out. By law, all bills include a service charge, so only tip if you're happy with your experience. In this chapter, we use the terms *prix fixe* and *menu* to indicate a meal where you get a starter, main course and dessert for a set price.

For further listings see the *Time Out Paris Eating and Drinking Guide*.

The Islands

Brasseries

Brasserie de l'Isle St-Louis
55 quai de Bourbon, 4th (01.43.54.02.59).
M° Pont-Marie. **Open** noon-1am Mon, Tue, Fri-Sun; 5pm-1am Thur. Closed Aug. **Average** €30.
Credit MC, V. **Map** p406 K7.
A rustic world of dark wood and mounted animal heads transports you a very long way from the city. Food, in keeping with the setting, is earthy and sat-isfying rather than refined. Expect richly flavoured sauces and dreamy, dollopy desserts.

The Louvre, Palais-Royal & Les Halles

Bistros

Chez La Vieille
1 rue Bailleul/37 rue de l'Arbre Sec, 1st
(01.42.60.15.78). M° Louvre-Rivoli. **Open** noon-2pm Mon-Wed, Fri; noon-2pm, 7.30-9.30pm Thur.
Average €38. **Prix fixe** €24.39. **Credit** AmEx, DC, MC, V. **Map** p402 J5.
If you ever despair over how Paris is changing, let a meal in this splendid bistro cure you. The starters are brilliant – lentils, courgettes stuffed with veal and a sublime *céléri rémoulade*. Mains are homely and appealing, too – veal braised with green olives and cannelloni stuffed with ewe's milk cheese.

Willi's Wine Bar
13 rue des Petits-Champs, 1st (01.42.61.05.09/
www.williswinebar.com). M° Pyramides. **Open** noon-2.30pm, 7-11pm Mon-Sat. **Average** €30. **Prix fixe** €29.73. **Lunch menu** €24.09. **Credit** MC, V. **Map** p402 H5.
There's an atmosphere of low-key stylishness at this long-running and very popular *bistrot à vins* near the Palais-Royal. The plentiful bread nibbles are excellent, and the main courses include lamb from the Corrèze and tuna steak with sun-dried tomatoes. The desserts are particularly sublime.

You can resist anything but temptation at **Atelier Berger**. *See p183.*

Le Gavroche

19 rue St-Marc, 2nd (01.42.96.89.70). M° Bourse or Richelieu-Drouot. **Open** 7am-2am Mon-Sat. **Average** €23. **Prix fixe** €17.53 (until 10pm). **Credit** MC, V. **Map** p402 H3.

This wine bistro near the Bourse continues to pack 'em in. Slabs of roast lamb, plates of black pudding, platters of thick beef, extra extra rare, are carried past in a whirl of activity. The wine is specially bottled by reliable Burgundy contacts. Booking is recommended for lunch.

Mimosa

44 rue d'Argout, 2nd (01.40.28.15.75). M° Sentier. **Open** noon-3pm Mon-Sat (evenings for private parties by arrangement). **Average** €15. **Prix fixe** €11.43, €14.48. **Credit** MC, V. **Map** p402 J4.

Hats off to Xavier Trauet and Thierry Soulat, who have replaced Cedric Eng at this little gem. Xavier runs things out front, warmly greeting his customers. Thierry cooks simple, thoughtful food with a Mediterranean bias. The omelettes are groovy, especially the *paysanne*, loaded with potatoes and smoky bacon, sprinkled with chives, beautifully soft and served with green salad. Salads are generous, too.

Brasseries

Au Pied de Cochon

6 rue Coquillière, 1st (01.40.13.77.00/ www.pieddecochon.com). M° Les Halles. **Open** 24 hours daily. **Average** €34. **Credit** AmEx, DC, MC, V. **Map** p402 H5.

Once your crispy trotter arrives, accompanied by fries, watercress, sauce Béarnaise, it may not be immediately obvious what to do next; don't hesitate to ask for a bit of advice. Le Pied de Cochon has all the usual brasserie food for those who refuse to partake in the foot-fest. *Wheelchair access.*

Contemporary/funky

L'Atelier Berger

49 rue Berger, 1st (01.40.28.00.00/ www.atelierberger.com). M° Louvre-Rivoli. **Open** noon-2.30pm, 7-11pm Mon-Sat. Closed 23-25 Dec. **Average** €38. **Prix fixe** €30.18. **Lunch menu** €22.11. **Credit** AmEx, MC, V. **Map** p402 J5.

Jean Christiansen's style is imaginative seasonal cooking, as surprising to look at as it is to eat. A deep-fried oyster starter comes with a pale green asparagus *panna cotta*, just-cooked asparagus and crunchy celery in a vividly flavoured vinaigrette. Mains are served on yellow and blue floor tiles.

Cabaret

2 pl du Palais-Royal, 1st (01.58.62.56.25). M° Palais Royal. **Open** noon-6am Mon-Fri. **Average** €69. **Credit** AmEx, DC, MC, V. **Map** p402 H5.

Cabaret offers quality food overlooking either exhibition rollerblading on the *place* or exhibition posing in the Jacques Garcia-decorated basement. The sizeable booths have quickly become some of the top tables in town. The menu is Costes-like and house specials such as grilled duck and cod with spices are well-executed. *Wheelchair access.*

Fish

Iode

48 rue d'Argout, 2nd (01.42.36.46.45). M° Sentier. **Open** 12.30-3pm, 8.30-11.30pm Mon-Fri; 8.30-11.30pm Sat. **Average** €34. **Credit** MC, V. **Map** p402 J4.

Something fishy has been going on in this new-wave Breton bistro. Big hits are the creamy, carefully seasoned tartare of grenadier and a pile of crisp deep-fried baby squid. If the fare fills you up, finish with a berry and citrus salad in a light mint syrup; heartier appetites could try *crêpes Suzette* with a glass of cloudy draught cider.

Menu Lexicon

Agneau lamb. **Aiguillettes** (*de canard*) thin slices of duck breast. **Aïoli** garlic mayonnaise. **Aligot** mashed potatoes with melted cheese and garlic. **Aloyau** beef loin. **Anchoïade** spicy anchovy and olive paste. **Andouillette** sausage made from pig's offal. **Anguille** eel. **Asperge** asparagus. **Aubergine** aubergine (GB); eggplant (US).

Ballotine stuffed, rolled up piece of meat or fish. **Bar** sea bass. **Bavarois** moulded cream dessert. **Bavette** beef flank steak. **Béarnaise** sauce of butter and egg yolk. **Beignet** fritter or doughnut. **Belon** smooth, flat oyster. **Biche** venison. **Bifteak** steak. **Bisque** shellfish soup. **Blanc** breast. **Blanquette** 'white' stew made with eggs and cream. **Boudin noir/blanc** black (blood)/white pudding. **Boeuf** beef; **– bourguignon** beef cooked Burgundy style, with red wine, onions and mushrooms; **– gros sel** boiled beef with vegetables. **Bouillabaisse** Mediterranean fish soup. **Bourride** a *bouillabaisse*-like soup, without shellfish. **Brochet** pike. **Bulot** whelk.

Cabillaud fresh cod. **Caille** quail. **Canard** duck. **Cannelle** cinnamon. **Carbonnade** beef stew with onions and stout or beer. **Carré d'agneau** rack of lamb. **Carrelet** plaice. **Cassis** blackcurrants, also blackcurrant liqueur used in *kir*. **Cassoulet** stew of haricot beans, sausage and preserved duck. **Céleri** celery. **Céleri rave** celeriac. **Cèpe** cep mushroom. **Cervelle** brains. **Champignon** mushroom; **– de Paris** button mushroom. **Chateaubriand** thick fillet steak. **Chaud-froid** a sauce used to glaze cold dishes. **Chevreuil** young roe deer. **Choucroute** sauerkraut, served *garnie* with cured ham and sausages. **Ciboulette** chive. **Citron** lemon. **Citron vert** lime. **Citronelle** lemongrass. **Civet** game stew. **Clafoutis** batter filled with fruit, usually cherries. **Cochon de lait** suckling pig. **Coco** large white bean. **Colin** hake. **Confit de canard** preserved duck. **Contre-filet** sirloin steak. **Coquelet** baby rooster. **Coquille** shell. **Coquilles St-Jacques** scallops. **Côte** chop; **côte de boeuf** beef

rib. **Crème brûlée** creamy custard dessert with caramel glaze. **Crème Chantilly** sweetened whipped cream. **Crème fraîche** thick, slightly soured cream. **Cresson** watercress. **Crevettes** prawns (GB), shrimp (US). **Croque-madame** sandwich of toasted cheese and ham topped with an egg; **croque-monsieur** sandwich of toasted cheese and ham. **En croûte** in a pastry case. **Cru** raw. **Crudités** assorted raw vegetables. **Crustacé** shellfish.

Daube meat braised in red wine. **Daurade** sea bream. **Désossé** boned. **Dinde** turkey. **Duxelles** chopped, sautéed mushrooms.

Echalote shallot. **Eglefin** haddock. **Endive** chicory (GB), Belgian endive (US). **Entrecôte** beef rib steak. **Epices** spices. **Epinards** spinach. **Escabèche** sautéed and marinated fish, served cold. **Escargot** snail. **Espadon** swordfish. **Estouffade** meat that's been marinated, fried and braised.

Faisan pheasant. **Farci** stuffed. **Faux-filet** sirloin steak. **Feuilleté** 'leaves' of (puff) pastry. **Filet mignon** tenderloin. **Fines de claire** crinkle-shelled oysters. **Flambé** flamed in alcohol. **Flétan** halibut. **Foie** liver; **foie gras** fattened goose or duck liver. **Forestière** with mushrooms. **Au four** baked. **Fricassé** fried and simmered in stock, usually with creamy sauce. **Frisée** curly endive. **Frites** chips (GB); fries (US). **Fromage** cheese; **– blanc** smooth cream cheese. **Fruits de mer** shellfish. **Fumé** smoked.

Galette round flat cake of flaky pastry, potato pancake or buckwheat savoury *crêpe*. **Garni** garnished. **Gelée** aspic. **Gésiers** gizzards. **Gibier** game. **Gigot d'agneau** leg of lamb. **Gingembre** ginger. **Girolle** wild mushroom. **Glace** ice cream. **Glacé** frozen or iced. **Goujon** breaded, fried strip of fish; also a small catfish. **Gras** fat. **Gratin dauphinois** sliced potatoes, baked with milk, cheese and garlic. **Gratiné** browned with breadcrumbs or cheese. **A la Grecque** vegetables served cold in the cooking liquid with oil and lemon juice. **Cuisses de grenouille** frogs' legs. **Grillé** grilled. **Groseille** redcurrant. **Groseille à maquereau** gooseberry.

Haché minced. **Hachis Parmentier** shepherd's pie. **Hareng** herring. **Haricot** bean; **– vert** green bean. **Homard** lobster. **Huître** oyster.

Ile flottante whipped egg white floating in vanilla custard.

Jambon ham; **– cru** cured raw ham. **Jarret de porc** ham shin or knuckle. **Julienne** vegetables cut into matchsticks.

Langoustine Dublin Bay prawns, scampi. **Lapin** rabbit. **Lamelle** very thin slice. **Langue** tongue. **Lard** bacon; **lardon** small cube of bacon. **Légume** vegetable. **Lièvre** hare. **Limande** lemon sole. **Lotte** monkfish.

Mâche lamb's lettuce. **Magret** duck breast. **Maison** of the house. **Maquereau** mackerel. **Marcassin** wild boar. **Mariné** marinated. **Marmite** small cooking pot. **Marquise** mousse-like cake. **Merguez** spicy lamb/beef sausage. **Merlan** whiting. **Merlu** hake. **Meunière** fish floured and sautéed in butter. **Miel** honey. **Mignon** small meat fillet. **Mirabelle** tiny yellow plum. **Moelle** bone marrow; **os à la – marrow** bone. **Morille** morel mushroom. **Moules** mussels; **– à la marinière** cooked with white wine and shallots. **Morue** dried, salted cod; **brandade de –** cod puréed with potato. **Mousseline** *hollandaise* sauce with whipped cream.

Navarin lamb and vegetable stew. **Navet** turnip. **Noisette** hazelnut; small round portion of meat. **Noix** walnut. **Noix de coco** coconut. **Nouilles** noodles.

Oeuf egg; **– en cocotte** baked egg; **– en meurette** egg poached in red wine; **– à la neige** see *Ile flottante*. **Oie** goose. **Oignon** onion. **Onglet** cut of beef, similar to *bavette*. **Oseille** sorrel. **Oursin** sea urchin.

Palourde type of clam. **Pamplemousse** grapefruit. **Pané** breaded. **en Papillote** cooked in a packet. **Parfait** sweet or savoury mousse-like mixture. **Parmentier** with potato. **Paupiette** slice of meat or fish, stuffed and rolled. **Pavé** thick steak. **Perdrix** partridge. **Persil** parsley. **Petit salé** salt pork. **Pied** foot (trotter). **Pignon** pine kernel. **Pintade/pintadeau** guinea fowl. **Pipérade**

Basque dish of green peppers, white onions and tomatoes, often served with scrambled egg. **Pistou** pesto-like basil and garlic paste. **Plat** dish; main course; **– du jour** daily special. **Pleurotte** oyster mushroom. **Poire** pear. **Poireau** leek. **Poisson** fish. **Poivre** pepper. **Poivron** red or green (bell) pepper. **Pommes lyonnaises** potatoes fried with onions. **Potage** soup. **Pot au feu** boiled beef with vegetables. **Poulet** chicken. **Poulpe** octopus. **Pressé** squeezed. **Prune** plum. **Pruneau** prune.

Quenelle light, poached fish (or poultry) dumpling. **Quetsche** damson. **Queue de boeuf** oxtail.

Ragoût meat stew. **Raie** skate. **Râpé** grated. **Rascasse** scorpion fish. **Réglisse** liquorice. **Ris de veau** veal sweetbreads. **Riz** rice. **Rognons** kidneys. **Rôti** roast. **Rouget** red mullet.

St Pierre John Dory. **Salé** salted. **Sandre** pike-perch. **Sanglier** wild boar. **Saucisse** sausage. **Saucisson** small dried sausage. **Saumon** salmon. **Seiche** squid. **Suprême** (*de volaille*) fillets (of chicken) in a cream sauce. **Supion** small squid.

Tapenade Provençal black olive and caper paste, often with anchovies. **Tartare** raw minced steak (also tuna or salmon). **Tarte aux pommes** apple tart. **Tarte Tatin** warm, caramelised apple tart cooked upside-down. **Timbale** dome-shaped mould, or food cooked in one. **Tisane** herbal tea. **Tournedos** small slices of beef fillet, sautéed or grilled. **Tourte** covered pie or tart, usually savoury. **Travers de porc** pork spare ribs. **Tripes** tripe. **Tripoux Truffes** truffles. **Truite** trout.

Vacherin cake of layered meringue, cream, fruit and ice cream; a soft, cow's milk cheese. **Veau** veal. **Velouté** stock-based white sauce; creamy soup. **Vichyssoise** cold leek and potato soup. **Volaille** poultry.

Cooking time requests (La cuisson)

Cru raw. **Bleu** practically raw. **Saignant** rare. **Rosé** pink (said of lamb, duck, liver, kidneys). **A point** medium rare. **Bien cuit** well done. **Très bien cuit** very well done.

Eat, Drink, Shop

Haute Cuisine

L'Espadon

Hôtel Ritz, 15 pl Vendôme, 1st (01.43.16.30.80/
www.ritzparis.com). M° Madeleine or Concorde.
Open noon-3pm, 7.30-11pm daily. **Average** €183.
Prix fixe €141 (dinner only). **Lunch menu** €63.
Credit AmEx, DC, MC, V. **Map** p401 G4.
With the return of chef Michel Roth, one of the most
sumptuous dining rooms in the world is again one
of the best restaurants in Paris. This place purrs
luxury. The service is perfect, and the food is outstanding. Case in point: Breton lobster salad with
mesclun dressed with raspberry vinegar, hazelnut
oil, lobster coral and salmon eggs, or the luscious
crayfish tail brochette with powdered pistachios and
a creamy shellfish soup. For dessert, the best *millefeuille* in Paris. The wine list has been intelligently
revised, too. *Wheelchair access.*

International

Chinese: Chez Vong

10 rue de la Grande Truanderie, 1st
(01.40.26.09.36). M° Etienne-Marcel. **Open** noon-
2.30pm, 7-11.30pm Mon-Sat. **Average** €38. **Credit**
MC, V. **Map** p402 J5.
This is the place to sample traditional ingredients
you might otherwise hesitate over. There are no
shortcuts: the seafood salad is heaped with real,
freshly shredded crab, mushrooms and jellyfish
strips have exactly the right consistency, and even
simple dumplings contain firm whole prawns. To
contrast with the fine sizzling fish plates, choose at
least one duck dish. Of the classic dessert options,
the sesame-covered nougat is a nice conclusion.

Indonesian: Djakarta Bali

*9 rue Vauvilliers, 1st (01.45.08.83.11). M° Louvre-
Rivoli.* **Open** 7-11pm Tue-Sun. **Average** €30.
Prix fixe €15-€40. **Credit** MC, V.
Map p402 J5.
This superb restaurant offers a splendid opportunity to discover the cuisine of the islands of the
Indonesian archipelago. Start with the *soto ayam*, a
delicious soup of chicken broth, rice noodles and
vegetables. Outstanding main courses include
rendang daging, tender slices of beef in coconut milk
seasoned with Indonesian herbs.

Italian: Bio.It

*15 rue des Halles, 1st (01.42.21.10.21). M° Châtelet-
Les Halles.* **Open** 10am-10.30pm Mon-Sat. **Average**
€18. **Credit** DC, MC, V. **Map** p402 J5.
Fresh buffalo mozzarella and ricotta are flown in
from Italy every fortnight. The restaurant works like
a canteen: you take a tray and choose from a buffet
in front of an open kitchen. Everything is homemade
using quality seasonal produce, and is predominantly vegetarian. There are assorted hot dishes,
including a fine mushroom risotto, penne with

artichokes, and stuffed tomato and aubergine.
Organic Italian wine is sold by the glass or bottle.

Japanese: Kinugawa

9 rue du Mont-Thabor, 1st (01.42.60.65.07).
M° Tuileries. **Open** noon-2.30pm, 7-10pm Mon-Sat.
Prix fixe €77, -€106 (dinner only). **Lunch menu**
€25, €41. **Credit** AmEx, DC, MC, V.
Map p401 G5.
Everything here breathes excellence. The food follows the highly refined *kaiseki-ryori* tradition,
embodying the virtues of *wabi* (simplicity) and *sabi*
(unstudied elegance). From the classic (but stun-
ningly fresh) sashimi to the original lime-scented
fish consommé, everything slides down a treat.

Thai: Baan-Boran

43 rue Montpensier, 1st (01.40.15.90.45).
M° Palais Royal. **Open** noon-3pm, 6pm-1am Mon-Fri;
6pm-1am Sat (last orders 11.30pm). **Average** €30.
Lunch menu €11. **Credit** AmEx, DC, MC, V.
Map p402 H5.
Fans of Thai food will be delighted by this reasonably priced new spot specialising in regional cooking. Try the grilled chicken with green papaya salad,
or shellfish cooked in a banana leaf with coconut
milk. Unusually, there is also a list of 'light' dishes
prepared without sugar or added fat, including
grapefruit salad with dried prawns, braised crab and
fish steamed with herbs.

Opéra & the Grands Boulevards

Bistros

Le Bistrot du Sommelier

97 bd Haussmann, 8th (01.42.65.24.85).
M° St-Augustin. **Open** 7.30-11pm Mon-Fri.
Average €61. **Prix fixe** €74, €99 (dinner only).
Credit AmEx, V. **Map** p401 F3.
'Bistrot' is perhaps a misnomer for this small but
luxurious restaurant. Chef Jean-Michel Descloux's
menu découverte, served only to the whole table, is
indeed a voyage of discovery of wines and food.
How's about thick slices of salt-cured salmon, served
with chicory and a goat's cheese mousse?

Chez Catherine

65 rue de Provence, 9th (01.45.26.72.88).
M° Chaussée d'Antin-La Fayette. **Open** noon-3pm
Mon; noon-3pm, 8-10.30pm Tue-Fri. Closed Aug.
Average €38. **Credit** MC, V. **Map** p401 G3.
Catherine Guerraz's menu is a selection of sturdy
bistro classics. Starters run from a mousse-like
mushroom timbale garnished with crayfish tails to
roasted red peppers, while main courses include a
first-rate *steak au poivre* and a stylish rendition of
tagliata. Superb crème brûlée and cardamom-
scented cheesecake are among the excellent desserts.
Book at least a week ahead.

Eat, Drink, Shop

Brasseries

Brasserie Flo

7 cour des Petites-Ecuries, 10th (01.47.70.13.59).
M° Château d'Eau. **Open** noon-3pm, 7pm-1.30am
daily. **Average** €38. **Prix fixe** €30 (dinner only).
Lunch menu €21. **Credit** AmEx, DC, MC, V.
Map p402 K3.

Brasserie Flo is the foundation of Jean-Paul Bucher's
Flo empire. Main courses are beyond reproach: tender Scottish salmon with chunks of bacon, baked
whole garlic cloves and bright-green spinach, and
juicy roast veal with morels, served with a crisp and
creamy rice galette. Hedonists can finish their meal
with the decadent *coupe* Flo, cherry ice cream
drowned in cherry liqueur, or a potent prune and
Armagnac *vacherin. Wheelchair access.*

Chartier

7 rue du Fbg-Montmartre, 9th. (01.47.70.86.29).
M° Grands Boulevards. **Open** 11.30am-3pm, 6pm-
10pm daily. **Average** €12. **Prix fixe** €13.
Credit MC, V. **Map** p402 J4.

There's a seat for everyone at Chartier, and the entire
menu is reassuringly inexpensive. Highlights
include rollmops (pickled herring), generous green
salads and the whole roasted fennel which accompanies a good pork plate. Save room for that most
traditional of French desserts: chestnuts with cream.

Garnier

*111 rue St-Lazare, 8th (01.43.87.50.40). M° St-
Lazare.* **Open** noon-3pm, 7-11.30pm daily. **Average**
€46. **Credit** AmEx, DC, MC, V. **Map** p401 G3.

This is one of the two or three best brasseries in
Paris. Outstanding main courses include tuna steak
a la plancha, served with tangy carrots and a decorative reduction of balsamic vinegar and pine nuts.
Desserts are remarkably good, too, including *baba
au rhum* – spongy cake doused with Martinique rum
at the table, or a delicate vanilla *millefeuille.* The wine
list, however, is rather expensive.

Haute Cuisine

Lucas Carton

*9 pl de la Madeleine, 8th (01.42.65.22.90/
www.lucascarton.com). M° Madeleine.* **Open** 8-10.30pm
Mon, Sat; noon-2.30pm, 8-10.30pm Tue-Fri. Closed
Aug. **Average** €183. **Lunch menu** €64.
Credit AmEx, DC, MC, V. **Map** p401 G4.

Amuse-bouches such as spiced squid perk up the
palate before adventurous starters: a carpaccio of
tuna, flavoured with shallot, pink ginger, aromatic
oil and a crunchy spiced *tuile*; and ravioli, each filled
with a small scallop and a slice of courgette, served
in a buttery sauce. Alain Senderens' signature duck
à l'Apicius is available only *à la carte*, but you can
always plump for another dish of roast duck served
with an enjoyable combination of sautéed leek and
diced mango. Lucas Carton never fails to deliver a
hard-to-equal luxury eating experience.

Chill out at room temperature
at **Chez Catherine.** See p187.

International

Caribbean: La Paillotte des Iles

*16 rue Thorel, 2nd (01.45.08.58.22). M° Bonne
Nouvelle.* **Open** 12.30-2.30pm 7.30pm-midnight
daily. **Average** €24. **Prix fixe** €14-€28.
Lunch menus €8-€12. **No credit cards.**
Map p402 J4.

Starters such as a salad of *patates douces* are followed by joys like *colombo de capitaine*, a meaty,
big-boned fish lightly curried and served with fluffy
rice and a pot of red beans in thick gravy. *Tourment
d'amour* (a kind of gâteau), banana flambé and rum
and raisin and coconut ice cream finish off the edible heaven. At weekends there is a disco, so you can
dance off one or two of the thousands of calories
you'll enjoy ingesting here.

Regional

Alsatian: L'Alsaco

*10 rue Condorcet, 9th (01.45.26.44.31/
www.alsaco.net). M° Poissonnière.* **Open** 7-11pm
Mon, Sat; noon-2.30pm, 7-11pm Tue-Fri. Closed last
two weeks in July, Aug. **Average** €30. **Prix fixe**
€19, €29 (dinner only). **Lunch menu** €19.
Credit MC, V. **Map** p402 J2.

All the Alsatian favourites are here and this is one
of the best places in Paris to try them. There is little
point in ordering *à la carte* – the *menus* incorporate
most dishes and are much better value. If things are
getting wintry outside, do try *bäckaofa*, a warming,
hearty beef and potato stew which is not dissimilar
to the Irish version. *Wheelchair access.*

Eat, Drink, Shop

Breton: Ty-Coz

35 rue St-Georges, 9th (01.48.78.42.95).
M° St-Georges. **Open** noon-2pm, 7-10pm Tue-Sat.
Average €46. **Prix fixe** €25.92 (dinner only).
Credit AmEx, MC, V. **Map** p402 H3.
Ty-Coz is the place for superlative seafood: the problem is what to choose; a whole fresh crab glistening on a bed of iodine-packed seaweed is as much of a must as the fillet of golden smoked haddock with a side dish of beautifully cooked mushrooms and courgettes with colourful strips of carrot, beans and a sprinkling of parsley. And, for a faultless dessert, try a *crêpe* that oozes melted chocolate.

Beaubourg & the Marais

Bistros

Baracane

38 rue des Tournelles, 4th (01.42.71.43.33).
M° Bastille or Chemin Vert. **Open** noon-2.30pm,
7pm-midnight Mon-Fri; 7pm-midnight Sat. **Average**
€23. **Prix fixe** €22, €36 (also available at lunch).
Lunch menu €8, €13. **Credit** MC,V.
Map p406 L6/L7.
This venue affords a welcome respite from the Bastille and Place des Vosges crowds. Starters include a smoky Jerusalem artichoke soup with bacon. Mains keep the positive momentum going: a fresh trout pan-fried with hazelnuts, parsley and butter, and a hearty pastry-wrapped *croustade* of roasted feta, mushrooms and green vegetables. Generous desserts arrive as part of the €22.56 *menu*. Fine service and fabulous value.

Fontaines d'Elysabeth

1 rue Ste-Elysabeth, 3rd (01.42.74.36.41).
M° Arts et Métiers. **Open** noon-2.30pm, 8pm-midnight Mon-Fri; 8pm-midnight Sat. Closed Aug.
Average €12. **Prix fixe** €9-€11. **No credit
cards. Map** p405 K5.
This bistro, with its floral curtains and dark wood furniture, feels like the heart of the countryside – with cuisine to match. The short menu, jotted down in blue felt-tip pen in what looks like Sumerian script, tells tempting tales of homespun cooking: no pretensions, no let-downs. From a range of mainly charcuterie-based starters, the potato mayonnaise salad with tomatoes and gherkins could not taste fresher. The *cassoulet* is succulent, with pieces of lamb simply melting off the bone. A good bottle of Côtes du Rhône for €9.90 underlines the unbeatable value of this establishment.

Le Hangar

12 impasse Berthaud, 3rd (01.42.74.55.44).
M° Rambuteau. **Open** 6.30pm-midnight Mon;
noon-3pm, 6.30pm-midnight Tue-Sat. Closed three weeks in Aug. **Average** €27. **No credit cards.
Map** p402 K5.
The Hangar treats its visitors to imaginative classical cuisine. Starters such as salmon tartare and an inspired chilled avocado soup are fabulous. Main courses include pan-fried foie gras accompanied by mashed potatoes puréed with olive oil, and a good, herb-filled rendition of steak tartare. Those with a chocolate addiction will be hard-pressed Hamlet-style to choose between the oozing hot chocolate cake and the airy *soufflé au chocolat*. The answer is, of course, to have both.

Le Pamphlet

38 rue Debelleyme, 3rd (01.42.72.39.24). M° Filles du Calvaire. **Open** noon-2.30pm, 7.30-11pm daily. **Average** €34. **Prix fixe** €25.92. **Lunch menu** €19.82. **Credit** V. **Map** p402 L5.

This auberge on the northern fringes of the Marais was a well-kept secret for years. If you're reading this, we can asume that word has now got out. Main courses include a protein-packed tuna steak on a *pipérade*-inspired bed of scrambled eggs, and juicy chicken breast with a crust of toasted hazelnuts. Desserts such as strawberries roasted in salted butter and served with celery ice cream should deal with any lingering hunger pangs. *Wheelchair access.*

Haute Cuisine

L'Ambroisie

9 pl des Vosges, 4th (01.42.78.51.45). M° Bastille or St-Paul. **Open** noon-1.30pm, 8-9.30pm Tue-Sat. Closed Aug. **Average** €200. **Credit** AmEx, MC, V. **Map** p406 L6.

The fact that a meal here can easily head beyond €460 a couple must be addressed before any trilling over the beauty of the dining rooms or the magnificent food. Just the facts: sublime appetisers, feather-light first courses, and main courses such as a turban of perfectly cooked sea bass on a bed of *duxelles* (finely chopped mushrooms) and petals of cep, and turbot with preserved citrus rind, mustard seeds and braised chicory. Spectacular, once you're sure you can afford it. *Wheelchair access.*

International

Jewish: L'As du Fallafel

34 rue des Rosiers, 4th (01.48.87.63.60). M° St-Paul. **Open** 11am-midnight Mon-Thur, Sun; noon-sunset Fri. **Average** €5.30. **Credit** MC, V. **Map** p406 K6/L6.

L'As has morphed in the past few years into a noisy eatery. The tables are close together, the plates and forks are plastic, yet a meal here is a great experience. Falafel is what it's all about. Don't miss out on the *spécial*, which comes with extras of sautéed aubergine and a dollop of houmous. Freshly-squeezed orange or carrot juice makes a fine accompaniment. Booze is, of course, even finer.

Latin American: A la Mexicaine

68 rue Quincampoix, 3rd (01.48.87.99.34). M° Rambuteau or Les Halles. **Open** 8-11pm Mon; noon-3pm, 8-11pm Wed-Sat. **Average** €23. **Prix fixe** €16, €31. **Credit** AmEx, MC, V. **Map** p406 J6/K5.

Yurira Iturriaga, the proprietor, leads a one-woman crusade against Tex-Mex mediocrity in Paris. The guacamole is wonderful, as are tacos stuffed with cheese or chicken, marinated pork with black beans, chicken *pipau*, and all of the dishes made from delicious Argentine beef. Finish with the rich cake made from chocolate, maize flour and eggs, and do try some Mexican wine. *Wheelchair access.*

North African: 404

69 rue des Gravilliers, 3rd (01.42.74.57.81). M° Arts et Métiers. **Open** noon-2.30pm, 8pm-midnight Mon-Fri; noon-2.30pm (brunch), 8pm-midnight Sat, Sun. Closed two weeks in Aug. **Average** €27. **Lunch menu** (Mon-Fri only) €13.57; brunch €20.58 (Sat, Sun). **Credit** AmEx, DC, MC, V. **Map** p402 K5.

404 is a restaurant with great atmosphere. The chicken *tagines* are impressive, but it's with the desserts that things really start to rock here: we're talking such gastronomic groovers as mini *crêpe Berbère* with honey and nuts, and an outstanding sweet mound of semolina called *saffae*, topped with toasted almonds, which crumbles as you dig in and is doused with a milky sauce. Ooh, matron!

North African: Chez Omar

47 rue de Bretagne, 3rd (01.42.72.36.26). M° Arts et Métiers. **Open** noon-2.30pm Mon-Sat; 7pm-midnight Sun. **Average** €23. **No credit cards. Map** p402 L5.

Affluent and arty thirtysomethings continue to crowd into Chez Omar. The traditional bistro setting exercises a sentimental charm; the waiters are cheekily frenetic; the couscous and vegetables seemingly limitless. But before you launch into your grilled lamb brochette, your enormous barbequed *méchoui* (grilled lamb) or your spicy *merguez* sausage, have a care: make sure you have a mint tea – not only is it delicious, but it is believed to help digestion. **Branch:** Café Moderne, 19 rue Keller, 11th (01.47.00.53.62).

Regional

Au Bourguignon du Marais

52 rue François-Miron, 4th (01.48.87.15.40). M° St-Paul. **Open** noon-3pm, 7.30-11pm Mon-Fri; noon-5pm (brunch) Sat. **Average** €38. **Prix fixe** €22.10 (brunch only). **Credit** AmEx, DC, MC, V. **Map** p406 K6.

This stylish dining room with exceptionally friendly and efficient staff serves delightfully pleasing food. Try a starter of tender sautéed *girolles* with cured ham and parmesan shavings on a bed of rocket. An unmissable main is the seared tuna steak, glistening wantonly in an herb vinaigrette with steamed spinach on the side. Fans of Burgundy will relish a journey through the wine list.

Contemporary/trendy

Georges

Centre Pompidou, 6th floor, rue Rambuteau, 4th. (01.44.78.47.99). M° Rambuteau. **Open** noon-2am Mon, Wed-Sun. **Average** €46. **Credit** AmEx, DC, MC, V. **Map** p402 K5.

Here is another of the Costes brothers' successful scene centrals. Daytime sees exhibition escapees and casual diners while night-time is more a Gucci groove. The food is fine, but prices are on the high side. The cup-full of gazpacho is chilled and spicy, and the artichoke hearts with salmon slices are perfect for a hot summer's day. *Wheelchair access.*

Vegetarian

Le Potager du Marais
22 rue Rambuteau, 3rd (01.44.54.00.31).
M° Rambuteau. **Open** noon-3pm, 7-11pm Mon-Sat.
Average €15. **Prix fixe** €14.48. **Lunch menu**
€9.91. **Credit** AmEx, MC, V. **Map** p402 K5.
The chef turns out lovely fresh pastas, soups, and
daily specials with quality ingredients and flavour-
ful yet light seasonings. For main dishes, try the
stuffed tomato, the curried tofu penne, or a superbly
soft and succulent cep ravioli with olive oil and
herbs. The specials hardly leave room for dessert,
but be brave and try the poached pear, smothered
in chocolate, or the flower-scented crème brûlée.

La Verte Tige
13 rue Ste-Anastase, 3rd (01.42.77.22.15).
M° St-Sébastien-Froissart. **Open** noon-2.30pm, 7.30-
10.30pm Tue-Sat, 12.30-4pm Sun. Closed Aug.
Average €15. **Prix fixe** €16.62 (evenings, Sat and
Sun lunch). **Credit** MC, V. **Map** p402 L5.
This vegetarian restaurant is in a class of its own.
The chef has taken traditional Iranian dishes and
subtracted the meat elements: thus the espinada – a
spinach purée with fried onions, garlic and yoghurt
that has just the right tang. Mains include a varied
vegetarian platter and couscous with tofu sausage
– there is also a different €7.93 plat du jour each
weekday. The €16.62 menu offering three generous
courses is particularly good value.

The Bastille & eastern Paris

Bistros

A la Biche au Bois
45 av Ledru Rollin, 12th (01.43.43.34.38).
M° Gare de Lyon. **Open** noon-2.30pm, 7-10.30pm
Mon-Fri. Closed end July to third week in Aug.
Average €20. **Prix fixe** €19.51. **Credit** AmEx,
DC, MC,V. **Map** p407 M8/N6.
It's a game kind of place. Why not go all countrified
and kick off with homemade terrines – rabbit, fish,
duck and deer – a simple tomato salad or eggs
poached in red wine, but leave lots of room for the
robust mains. Then have a tussle with the tray of
ripe cheeses or a pillowy apple tart with custard.
And the wine list with lots of bottles under €15
ensures further contentment. Don't forget to book.

Chez Paul
13 rue de Charonne, 11th (01.47.00.34.57).
M° Bastille. **Open** noon-2.30pm, 7pm-12.30am daily.
Average €24. **Credit** AmEx, MC, V. **Map** p407 M7.
You'll notice Chez Paul because it's the one that has
a queue out the door – all year round. This is a fantasy French restaurant; the waiters and waitresses
are frenetic and (mostly) friendly. The menu groans
with traditional recipes: the steak is excellent, as is
the foie gras with lentils. Servings are satisfying and
tasty. Make sure you book.

Michelin man

French chefs are not known for their warm
embrace of British foodies, especially as
UK cuisine gets about as much respect in
this town as a bad French accent. So raise
your glasses to an event that should put
many a Gallic gastronome in a spin – for
the first time ever, France's food Bible, the
Michelin *Guide Rouge*, has a Brit at its
helm. His name: Derek Brown.

Many French people have seen his
appointment as a crime against all things
tasty, and there is much disgruntled
scepticism surrounding the prospect of a
rosbif passing comment on their cooking.
French food critic Gilles Pudlowski fumed,
'Is this an April fool? An Englishman will
bring nothing good.' Michelin officials
defended Brown's appointment, however,
claiming audaciously that even certain
Brits can be connoisseurs.

So what of this mysterious new boy?
Brown started working for Michelin as a
humble inspector in 1971, scouring the
Anglo restaurant scene. He was quickly
promoted to chief editor of the UK guide,
and followed this with a spell in South-East
Asia, before braving the land of the garlic
munchers. With more than thirty years'
experience, this is a man well-equipped to
hush his critics. Since arriving in Paris, he
has lauded the openness of French fusion
cooking, a trend he welcomes, 'providing
the chef doesn't get too complicated.' His
buzzword is simplicity and he is reticent
when pressed to reveal a favourite nibble
or tipple – proving his commitment to
traditional Michelin tight-lipped secrecy.

Le Grand Colbert

... a first rate, typically French Brasserie, open until late and affordable for all budgets. Meals vary from simple dishes to the most exquisite cuisine. Whatever takes your fancy, you can savour a relaxing moment in a lovely Parisian atmosphere.

Menu: 24.39€ (including coffee)
Open daily from noon-1am (with last orders taken up until 1am)

2 rue Vivienne, 2nd. Tel: 01.42.86.87.88. M° Bourse

...Comme Cochons

135 rue de Charenton, 12th (01.43.42.43.36).
Mº Reuilly-Diderot. **Open** noon-2.30pm, 8-11.30pm
Mon-Sat. **Average** €27. **Lunch menu** €12.20.
Credit AmEx, DC, MC, V. **Map** p407 P9/Q10.
Dishes are simple but appetising and carefully prepared. The lunch *menu* is a financial miracle, offering three courses and wine. Main courses change depending on the market, and desserts like chocolate cake or fluffy coffee mousse are scrummy.

La Connivence

1 rue de Cotte, 12th (01.46.28.46.12). Mº Ledru-Rollin or Gare de Lyon. **Open** noon-2.30pm, 7.45-11pm Mon-Sat; noon-2.30pm Sun. Closed Aug. **Prix fixe** €16.76, €21.34 (dinner only). **Lunch menus** €12.19, €15.24. **Credit** MC, V. **Map** p407 N7.
What a find: an imaginative take on comfort food. Lunch choices are a little more limited than in the evening, but the dishes are just as complex. Try the *terrine de la mer, sauce grelette* – a cool and light seafood concoction with a whipped cream sauce – and a lovely *fraîcheur de crevettes* from the *carte*. Main courses are meatier, and larger appetites might have room to bow out with *crêpes* with candied orange or a chocolate Charlotte. *Wheelchair access.*

Brasseries

Le Train Bleu

Gare de Lyon, Place Louis-Armand, 12th (01.43.43.09.06). Mº Gare de Lyon. **Open** 11.30am-3pm, 7-11pm daily. **Average** €49. **Prix fixe** €39.64. **Credit** AmEx, DC, MC, V. **Map** p407 M8.
This has long been one of the most romantic restaurants in Paris; and that's saying something. The fare consists of fine renderings of French classics and first-rate produce. Lobster served on a bed of walnut-oil-dressed salad leaves or pistachio-studded *saucisson* de Lyon with a warm salad of small *ratte* potatoes are meals in themselves. A large *baba au rhum*, doused with good Martinique fire water and slathered with cream will reward anyone with a bit of room for afters. *Wheelchair access.*

Classic

L'Oulette

15 pl Lachambeaudie, 12th (01.40.02.02.12). Mº Cour St-Emilion. **Open** noon-2.15pm, 8-10.15pm Mon-Fri; 8-10.15pm Sat. **Average** €46. **Prix fixe** €25.15, €42.69. **Credit** AmEx, DC, MC, V. **Map** p407 P10.
The *menus* are what you should explore, such as the €44 evening effort which includes as much red and white wine as you can drink (up to a bottle of each per person). Then come mains such as duck terrine, girdled in Jurançon jelly and studded with large nuggets of foie gras. To bring the curtain down on the gastronomic experience, choose from the extensive selection of coffees.

Au Pressoir

257 av Daumesnil, 12th (01.43.44.38.21). Mº Michel Bizot. **Open** noon-2.30pm, 7.30-10.30pm Mon-Fri. **Average** €76. **Prix fixe** €65.54. **Credit** AmEx, MC, V. **Map** p 407 M8/Q9.
Appetisers are sublime; starters are often specials of the day, such as foie gras terrine with the contrasting texture of artichokes. Mains such as *tournedos aux cèpes* surpass all expectations and then you are confronted by desserts such as wild strawberries magically held in thrall by spun sugar, accompanied by homemade vanilla ice cream.

International

Italian: Sardegna a Tavola

1 rue de Cotte, 12th (01.44.75.03.28). Mº Ledru-Rollin. **Open** 7.30-11.30pm Mon; noon-2.30pm, 7.30-11.30pm Tue-Sat. **Average** €30. **Lunch menu** €14.94. **Credit** AmEx, MC, V. **Map** p407 N7.
This Sardinian restaurant gets better and better. The good-value lunch *menu* includes thinly sliced charcuterie and chunky vegetables. Then comes ravioli stuffed with ricotta and mushrooms in thick, tomato-mushroom sauce, and farfalle pasta with a combination of mint, crushed almonds, fresh chilli pepper and plenty of olive oil.

Thai: Bali Bar

9 rue St-Sabin, 11th (01.47.00.25.47). Mº Bastille. **Open** noon-3pm, 7.30pm-11.30am Tue-Fri; noon-3pm, 7.30pm-2am Sat, Sun. **Average** €30. **Prix fixe** €33.54. **Lunch menu** €14.48. **Credit** DC, MC, V. **Map** p407 M6.
You'll love the Bali Bar. Lubricate yourself with a cocktail and then hit starters such as a basket of steamed pork and prawn dumplings. Among classic Thai fare is the *yam neua*, a spicy salad of rare beef, shallots, mint and coriander. Service is occasionally haphazard, but staff are good-humoured and good fun. *Wheelchair access.*

The Champs-Elysées and west

Bistros

Les Ormes

8 rue Chapu, 16th (01.46.47.83.98). Mº Exelmans. **Open** 12.15-2pm, 7.30-10pm Tue-Sat. **Average** €34. **Prix fixe** €28.97. **Lunch menu** €21.34, €25.91. **Credit** AmEx, MC, V. **Map** p404 A10.
The lusty cooking of talented young chef Stéphane Molé is worth a nibble. The brief, good-value *prix-fixe* changes almost daily, but typical dishes include *quenelles de brochet* (pike-perch) with *sauce américaine*, snails and wild mushrooms with a sorrel *timbale* and pumpkin soup garnished with morsels of sautéed lamb sweetbreads. Desserts are excellent, and the wine list offers many bargains.

Eat, Drink, Shop

Savy

23 rue Bayard, 8th (01.47.23.46.98). Mº Franklin D. Roosevelt. **Open** noon-2.30pm, 7.30-11pm (bar 7.30am-12.30pm, 3-8pm) Mon-Fri. **Average** €38. **Prix fixe** €25. **Lunch menu** €16, €20. **Credit** AmEx, MC, V. **Map** p401 E4.
Be sure to start with the *farçou averyonnais*, surprisingly light fried herb and chard patties, while other favourites include Puy lentils and *salade gourmande*. For main courses, go the meat route, such as the thick tender rump-steak *pavé* with Béarnaise sauce and crispy *frites*, or fish brought in daily from the Breton port of Guilvinec. Desserts are mainly age-old favourites suited to the cultivation of business girths.

Brasseries

Le Fouquet's

99 av des Champs-Elysées, 8th (01.47.23.70.60/ www.lucienbarriere.com). Mº George V. **Open** 8am-2am (last order 11.30pm) daily. **Average** €73. **Credit** AmEx, DC, MC, V. **Map** p400 D4.
The staff are charming and the food reliable. *Plats du jour* such as roasted tuna are particularly munchable. Of course, prices reflect the location and the popularity of the place, but the wine list can still produce a mild panic attack with its mark-ups and little available under €30 a bottle. *Wheelchair access.*

Restaurant Cap Vernet

82 av Marceau, 8th (01.47.20.20.40). Mº Charles de Gaulle-Etoile. **Open** Mon-Fri noon-2.30pm, 7-11pm Mon-Fri; 7-11pm Sat. **Average** €42. **Lunch menu** €32.78. **Credit** AmEx, DC, MC, V. **Map** p400 C4.
This fine brasserie has a predominantly seafood menu. Mains such as a thick slab of salmon in a pleasant, herby green sauce (is that the sound of you drooling?), also garnished with mashed potatoes, should really float your boat. The only drawbacks are the relatively stiff prices and consistently inefficient and indifferent service.

Classic

Lasserre

17 ave Franklin D. Roosevelt, 8th (01.43.59.53.43). Mº Franklin D. Roosevelt. **Open** noon-2.30pm, 7.30-10.30pm daily. **Average** €47. **Prix fixe** €24.35, €15.24. **Credit** AmEx, DC, MC, V. **Map** p401 E4.
This is a place you must visit; if you do, you'll never forget it and you'll be planning your return before the dessert's arrived. Bernard Joinville's joint epitomises Parisian dining excellence. Before a spoonful has so much as entered your delicate cakehole, you know you've died and gone to paradise. Tinkling piano, philanthropic waiters, banks of flowers and – steady your beating heart – a roof that can open out and give you that sitting-'neath-the-Paris-sky feeling on beautiful days. All the food is impeccable, but if the chance presents itself, do have a bash at the duck in orange sauce.

Contemporary/funky

L'Angle du Faubourg

195 rue du Faubourg St-Honoré, 8th (01.40.74.20.20). Mº Ternes or George V. **Open** noon-2.30pm, 7-11pm Mon-Fri. Closed 27 July-21 Aug. **Average** €61. **Prix fixe** €42.69 (dinner only). **Lunch menu** €35.06. **Credit** AmEx, DC, MC, V. **Map** p400 D3.
Start with the vegetable salad to see how shrewdly and deliciously chef Cosnier has updated traditional bistro dishes. Even the humble lettuce gets an injection of attitude here and is transformed into a sexy little veg that's a million miles away from that limp green thing that used to sit shame-facedly on your plate. Mains are wonderful, too, including a snowy slab of roasted cod with a small salad and a 'condiment' of *brandade de morue* with fresh herbs, and roast lamb shoulder with black olives and garlic. Desserts are fresh and appealing: pineapple ravioli filled with mascarpone cheese, a passionfruit milkshake and raspberry *clafoutis*.

Virtuoso cooking in sumptuous surroundings at **Lasserre**. *See left.*

L'Astrance

4 rue Beethoven, 16th (01.40.50.84.40). M° Passy.
Open noon-2pm, 8-10.30pm Wed-Sun; 8-10.30pm
Mon, Tue. Closed one week in Feb. **Average** €52.
Prix fixe €57.17, €65.55. **Lunch menu** €28.20.
Credit AmEx, DC, MC, V. **Map** p404 B6.

More good news: this is one of the best restaurants
to open in Paris for a long time. The slight damp-
ener is that good news travels fast, so this place is
quite often crowded. To business: the exquisite
effects of Pascal Barbot's sojourn in Sydney show
up in delicious dishes like 'ravioli' of avocado and
crab, baked mussels with a Moroccan-style salad of
grated carrots, a soup of milk and toast crumbs, and
luscious scallops in peanut cream sauce – and these
are just the starters. The stellar performance continues through main courses: whatever you choose,
you won't go wrong. Desserts are excellent, too,
including a divine deconstructed apple crumble and
milk ice cream with French toast smeared with
caramelised milk; it certainly deconstructs your ability to say no. But who wants to?

Korova

33 rue Marbeuf, 8th (01.53.89.93.93).
M° Franklin D Roosevelt. **Open** noon-3pm, 7.30pm-
2am Mon-Fri, Sun; 7.30pm-2am Sat. **Average** €53.
Lunch menu €30.49 (Mon-Fri). **Credit** AmEx, DC,
MC, V. **Map** p400 D4.

Owned by TV presenter Jean-Luc Delarue, this slick
new restaurant is pulling in trendy punters like
clockwork – Orange, that is, since it's named after
the bar in the Anthony Burgess novel. But you knew
that. A lot of thought has gone into this place. The
decor by architect-designer Christian Biecher has
60s white plastic pod chairs and dramatic lighting.
Service is rather friendlier than at most fashion
restaurants (staff have been known to smile), and
the food is actually pretty good, though the most
talked-about dish, the chicken roasted with Coca-
Cola, is probably best avoided. Desserts, created by
star pâtissier Pierre Hermé, are original and delicious, especially *pom, pomme, pomme*, an apple
fantasia. *Wheelchair access.*

La Maison Blanche

15 ave Montaigne, 8th (01.47.23.55.99). M° Alma-Marceau. **Open** noon-2.30pm, 8pm-midnight daily. Closed Aug. **Average** €76. **Credit** AmEx, MC, V. **Map** p401 E4.

It's the starters that star, with dishes as visually interesting as they are appetising: try sea urchins stuffed with dressed crab and garnished with caviar; raw and cooked vegetables with beetroot caramel; *tarte Tatin* of shallots with grilled red mullet; and foamy chestnut soup. The best of the mains is sea bass baked with preserved lemons. Desserts are brilliant: a raspberry-filled *dacquoise* with wild peach sorbet will sort you out. And they have the best selection of Languedoc-Roussillon wines in town.

Market

15 av Matignon, 8th (01.56.43.40.90). M° Champs-Elysées Clemenceau. **Open** noon-3pm, 6.30-10.30pm Mon-Thur, Sun; noon-3pm, 6.30-11.30pm Fri, Sat. **Average** €80. **Lunch menu** €39. **Credit** AmEx, MC, V. **Map** p401 E4.

Bankrolled by movie mogul Luc Besson and sporting a terribly glam if rather OTT '90s decor, this has become the most fashionable place in town. What's more, widely-travelled big-name chef Jean-Georges Vongerichten turns out some wonderful food: dazzling starters like scallops marinated in citrus juice, garnished with roast peppers, or cep, onion, walnut and garlic oil pizza. Then come main courses like lobster with Thai herbs, duck breast with sesame juice and a crispy *confit* with tamarind sauce. Finish with the runny chocolate tart or *panna cotta* with an exotic fruit salad and choose one of the reasonably priced Côtes du Rhônes.

Nobu

15 rue Marbeuf, 8th (01.56.89.53.53). M° Franklin D. Roosevelt. **Open** noon-3pm, 6.30pm-12.30am Mon-Fri; 6.30-12.30pm Sat, Sun. Bar 6.30pm-2am daily. Closed 25 Dec. **Average** €69. **Prix fixe** €68.60. **Lunch menu** €53.36. **Credit** AmEx, DC, MC, V. **Map** p400 D4.

Intriguing dishes such as tempura of Florida rock shrimp (rather like a langoustine but from the Gulf of Mexico), a tomato '*ceviche*', sublime sushi and sashimi, miso-marinated black cod cooked until it's more or less lacquered, and wonderful *à la carte* tempura all hit the spot. The wine list includes some wonderful bottles such as the South African Neethlingshof *sauvignon blanc* (€36.59), and service is patient and efficient. Nobu is that rarest of things in Paris – a non-smoking restaurant.

Rue Balzac

3-5 rue Balzac, 8th (01.53.89.90.91). M° Franklin D. Roosevelt or George V. **Open** 12.15-2.15pm, 7.15-11pm Mon-Thur; 12.15-2.15pm, 7.15-11.30pm, Fri; 7.15-11.30pm Sat, Sun. Closed three weeks in Aug. **Average** €61. **Credit** AmEx, DC, MC, V. **Map** p400 D4.

Not as rock'n'roll as you might expect from a restaurant owned by Johnny Hallyday, this is a class joint with Michel Rostang as executive chef. The menu

offers four options in each category (eggs, starters, pasta and rice, fish and meat). The cooking is quite inventive, with starters such as rice-paper-thin slices of aubergine layered with a crab and aubergine filling, and good fish mains such as sea bass fillet *a la plancha* with an artichoke and fresh coriander *confit*. Don't miss the chocolate *fondant* for puds. *Wheelchair access.*

Shozan

11 rue de la Tremoille, 8th (01.47.23.37.32). M° Franklin D. Roosevelt or Alma-Marceau. **Open** Mon-Fri noon-2.30pm, 7-10.30pm. **Average** €61. **Prix fixe** €60, €75 (dinner only). **Lunch menu** €22, €29. **Credit** AmEx, DC, MC, V. **Map** p400 D4.

Shozan shows how good 'fusion' cuisine can be. Appetisers are elegant, and two starters not to be missed are the sushi of grilled foie gras on seaweed-wrapped rounds of rice filled with rhubarb and apple chutney, and the langoustine tempura with a white asparagus mousse. Desserts run from sesame-caramel wafers layered with pink grapefruit, served with a verbena infusion on a grapefruit jelly to rhubarb compote dotted with tiny meringues in a thyme-flavoured caramel sauce.

Spoon, Food and Wine

14 rue de Marignan, 8th (01.40.76.34.44). M° Franklin D. Roosevelt. **Open** noon-2pm, 7-11pm Mon-Fri. Closed last week in July and first three weeks in Aug. **Average** €50. **Credit** AmEx, DC, MC, V. **Map** p401 E4.

When Alain Ducasse's world-food bistro opened several years ago, it had the effect of a fire alarm going off in a wax museum. Since then, Paris has changed – and, impressively, so has Spoon. Ducasse plays a sensuous game for assiduous gourmets. One could start with a sublime *mousse d'étrilles* (velvet swimming crab) and a brilliant and original casserole of cod, aubergine and tomatoes with sesame cream. Continue with spare ribs with *sauce diable* and potato chips, and a sublime grilled loin of rabbit with its liver and kidneys. Finish with the best cheesecake in town and chocolate-dipped ice cream.

Tanjia

23 rue Ponthieu, 8th (01.42.25.95.00). M° Franklin D. Roosevelt. **Open** noon-3pm, 8pm-1am Mon-Fri; 8pm-1am Sat, Sun. Closed Aug. **Average** €46. **Prix fixe** €53.35. **Credit** AmEx, DC, MC, V. **Map** p401 E4.

The food's better than you'd expect at this trendy Moroccan, and the staff are pleasantly attitude-free. The assorted starters for two – pricey at €15.24 a head but sufficient to feed a small army – include *briouats* (turnovers) of gambas, chicken and chèvre, aubergine caviar, and salads. Then it's on to pigeon *pastilla* (crispy pastry with ground pigeon and almonds) and generous servings of mild lamb *tagine* (cooked ten hours with 25 spices) or couscous with organic veggies. Try the fig ice cream and order mint tea – just to see the waiters pour it deftly from a great height.

Eat, Drink, Shop

Alain Ducasse at the Plaza Athénée, a magical dining experience. *See below.*

Haute

Alain Ducasse au Plaza Athénée

Hôtel Plaza Athénée, 25 av Montaigne, 8th (01.53.67.65.00/www.alain-ducasse.com). M° Alma-Marceau. **Open** 8-10.30pm Mon-Wed; 1-2.30pm, 8-10.30pm Thur, Fri. Closed 21 Dec-31 Dec, 14 Jul-20 Aug. **Average** €153. **Prix fixe** €190, €250. **Credit** AmEx, DC, MC, V. **Map** p400 D5.
Eating here is guaranteed event as this is one of the finest restaurants in Europe. The dining room offers a beautiful setting, service is superb, and so is the food. As well as classics such as the langoustines in a creamy *nage* topped with Oscietra caviar, Ducasse also offers vegetarian main courses and an innovative *menu* that allows you to sample three half-portions of any dish of you choose, plus cheese and dessert for €190. A sumptuous wine list, celebrated cheeses and excellent desserts round out the glamour here. If you want to give somebody a treat, this is the place to come. *Wheelchair access.*

Les Ambassadeurs

Hôtel de Crillon, 10 pl de la Concorde, 8th (01.44.71.16.16/www.crillon.com). M° Concorde. **Open** noon-2.30pm, 7-10.30pm daily. **Average** €153. **Prix fixe** €135. **Lunch menu** €62 (Mon-Fri). **Credit** AmEx, DC, MC, V. **Map** p401 F5.
Les Ambassadeurs is the exclusive residence of VIPs. Dominique Bouchet's cooking oozes classical technique. A main course of *supions farcis à la basquaise* produces the most tender baby squid, stuffed with finely shredded peppers and served with a not-bad risotto. A crab-and-apple charlotte and *brandade de morue* with a *sauce vierge* are flawless. The wine list has some very grand bottles at even grander prices. *Wheelchair access.*

Ghislaine Arabian

16 av Bugeaud, 16th (01.56.28.16.16). M° Victor Hugo. **Open** noon-2.30pm, 7.30-11pm Mon-Fri. **Average** €61. **Lunch menu** €45. **Credit** AmEx, DC, MC, V. **Map** p400 B4.
Ghislaine Arabian, one of the most talented chefs in France, has opened this superb new restaurant. It's interesting to encounter her northern French cooking since it seems directional at a time when Parisians appear to be tiring of Provençal cuisine. Following an appetiser of a potato with a smoked spratt in a light cream sauce, try her grey shrimp croquettes with fried parsely – a true Belgian classic – and a spectacular *millefeuille* of fresh vegetables. Try not to resist desserts like rhubarb *speculoos* biscuit with a strawberry compote and whole-milk ice cream. Prices are reasonable for this level of cooking. *Wheelchair access.*

Pierre Gagnaire

6 rue Balzac, 8th (0158.36.12.50/ www.pierre-gagnaire.com). M° George V. **Open** noon-2pm, 7.30-10pm Mon-Fri; 7.30-10pm Sun (Oct-Apr only). Closed mid July-mid Aug. **Average** €152. **Prix fixe** €182.94. **Lunch menu** €79.27. **Credit** AmEx, DC, MC, V. **Map** p400 D4.
Superb. The *amuse-bouches* could be mistaken for Zen art, and starters are bold: cold, raw gambas in deeply flavoured olive sauce; bok choy with foie gras and a rooster's *sot-l'y-laisse* (a tantalising morsel also known as the 'oyster'); and risotto with frogs' legs, anybody? Main courses are intriguing: pink suckling lamb rubbed with ewe's milk curd and *nicchia* capers, served with toasted rice, Shanghai cabbage with *petit gris* snails and fennel shoots. Sounds obscene, tastes great. Then there is *le grand dessert*, Gagnaire's seven-plate extravaganza. France definitely needs at least one chef like this dude.

International

Indian: Kirane's

85 av des Ternes, 17th (01.45.74.40.21). M° Porte Maillot. **Open** noon-2.30pm, 7-11pm Tue-Sat. **Average** €27. **Prix fixe** €26.68 (dinner only). **Lunch menu** €12.04. **Credit** AmEx, DC, MC, V. **Map** p400 B3.

One of the few places in Paris where'll you find authentic Indian fare. A good way to start is the mixed tandoori featuring juicy chunks of chicken, fat prawns, moist salmon and succulent pieces of lamb. The lamb rogan josh is a masterpiece of finely balanced spices while royal salmon *hara* is an attractive coral wedge of grilled, marinated fish in an aromatic green sauce. The pleasure can be concluded and the palate calmed with fruit salad and a heavily pistachioed kulfi.

Regional

Le Graindorge

15 rue de l'Arc de Triomphe, 17th (01.47.54.00.28). M° Charles-de-Gaulle-Etoile. **Open** noon-2.30pm, 7.30-11pm Mon-Fri; 7.30-11pm Sat. Closed two weeks in Aug. **Average** €38. **Prix fixe** €30.18 (dinner only). **Lunch menu** €26.67. **Credit** AmEx, MC, V. **Map** p400 C3.

The regional card isn't overplayed, since you could easily have a meal here without heading north, but it would be a shame to miss such beautifully done Franco-Belgian specialties as *potjevleesch*, a jellied terrine of rabbit, pork and veal, or a delicate and generously served *waterzooi*. The mains are excellent, Finish with an outstanding crème brûlée with rhubarb preserves. *Wheelchair access.*

Le Maquis

3 rue du Commandant Rivière, 8th (01.42.56.68.03). M° St-Philippe du Roule. **Open** noon-2.30pm, 7.30-10.30pm Mon-Fri; 7.30-10.30pm Sat. **Average** €28. **Credit** AmEx, MC, V. **Map** p401 E4.

This restaurant favours a sober expression of Corsican culture. The *à la carte* menu includes a selection of the island's charcuterie. To follow, the aubergines *bonifacio* is a combination of sweet oven-roasted tomatoes smothered in herbs and garlic with succulent, spicy strips of aubergine.

Montmartre & Pigalle

Bistros

Casa Olympe

48 Georges, 9th (01.42.85.26.01). M° Saint Georges. **Open** noon-2pm, 8-11pm Mon-Fri. **Prix fixe** €32.10. **Credit** AmEx, MC, V. **Map** p402 H3.

Main courses of guinea hen with a single, large wild-mushroom-stuffed ravioli, and pork fillet with home-made sauerkraut in a sauce of vinegar, sugar, spices and veal stock are great. Desserts include the Paris Brest – *choux* pastry filled with hazelnut cream.

Chez Toinette

20 rue Germain-Pilon, 18th (01.42.54.44.36). M° Abbesses. **Open** 8-11pm Tue-Sat. **Average** €20. **No credit cards. Map** p402 H2.

Try a sublimely aromatic *côtelette de marcassin*, baby wild boar cutlet smothered in wild mushrooms, bay leaves and coriander, complemented by a fruity Côtes de Thau red *vin de pays* recommended by the waiter. The baked chocolate and pear tart merits a full-page review to itself. Reserve even on weekdays.

La Table de Lucullus

129 rue Legendre, 17th (01.40.25.02.68).
M° La Fourche. **Open** 12.30-2pm, 7.30-11pm Tue-Fri;
7.30-11pm Sat. Closed Aug, one week in Feb/Mar.
Average €38. **Credit** MC, V. **Map** p401 F1.
Excellent bread gets gets the drooling groove in
place, and starters of langoustine carpaccio and brilliantly garnished foie gras are delicious. Main
courses were excellent, too. Finish with a wonderful
cheese course and fresh figs with raspberries. It's
essential to reserve. *Wheelchair access.*

Brasseries

La Mascotte

52 rue des Abbesses, 18th (01.46.06.28.15).
M° Abbesses. **Open** noon-2.30pm, 7-11pm Tue-Sun.
Average €17. **Prix fixe** €12-€24. **Credit** AmEx,
V. **Map** p402 H2.
Ever since the highly calorific (and some would say
saccharin) *Amélie Poulain* made everyone curious
about Montmartre again this good neighbourhood
brasserie has been crowded. Here you find quality
escargots and really first-rate oysters, delicious *fruits
de mer*, and main courses such as *sole meunière* with
chive-and-tarragon brightened mash, *petit salé* and
steaks. The simple wine list is full of good buys, too,
but be patient with the service – your reward is a
good meal with a gentle bill. *Wheelchair access.*

International

African: Le Mono

*40 rue Véron, 18th (01.46.06.99.20). M° Blanche or
Abbesses.* **Open** 7-11.30pm Mon-Tue, Thur-Sun.
Closed Aug. **Average** €20. **Credit** MC, V.
Map p402 H1.
Le Mono offers a refreshing break from typical West
African cuisine with its variety of grilled fish and
uncommon side dishes, served single-handedly by
the easy-going host. Begin with stuffed crab, prawn
fritters or *léle*, tasty bean cakes smothered in tomato
sauce, then launch into generous mains. There are
two plates for vegetarians plus other side dishes; fish
lovers should try the sea bream, mullet, grouper,
capitaine or *akpavi*, an African carp, cooked whole
with *ablo* rice, tomatoes and onions.

North-east Paris

Bistros

Astier

44 rue Jean-Pierre-Timbaud, 11th (01.43.57.16.35).
M° Parmentier. **Open** noon-2pm, 8-11pm Mon-Fri.
Closed Easter, Aug, Christmas. **Prix fixe** €23.52.
Lunch menu €19.82. **Credit** V. **Map** p403 M4.
Four courses for an incredible €23.52. There's meat
and cream, as one might expect, but also plenty of
fish and seasonal ideas: on one hand, a tangy
anchovy 'gâteau' starter (marinated anchovies on a

Dainty desserts at **Astier**. *See left.*

base of potato and herbs) on the other, baked egg in
a cream and morel sauce. Then on to one of the best
cheese trays in the business – a generous basket that
gets left on the table for you to help yourself.
Restrain yourself enough for the summery desserts.
The wine list is famous and voluminous. *Wheelchair
access (ring in advance).*

La Boulangerie

15 rue des Panoyaux, 20th (01.43.58.45.45).
M° Ménilmontant. **Open** noon-2pm, 7.30-11.30pm
Mon-Fri; 7.30pm-midnight Sat; noon-3pm, 7.30-
11.30pm Sun. **Prix fixe** €17.99. **Lunch menu**
€8.08, €11.43. **Credit** MC, V. **Map** p403 P4.
La Boulangerie offers just about everything you
could ask of a restaurant: a warm setting in a former bakery, helpful waiters, and imaginative cooking at a very reasonable price. The *croustillant de
grenadier* shows the chef's creativity – a *brandade*-
like potato and white fish purée wrapped in crisp
brik pastry and served with a creamy Noilly butter
sauce. Rearrange your taste buds with a freshly
made apple sorbet with apple liqueur.

Café Noir

15 rue St-Blaise, 20th (01.40.09.75.80).
M° Porte de Bagnolet. **Open** 7pm-midnight daily.
Average €30. **Credit** MC, V. **Map** p403 Q5.
Café Noir has a compact but blissfully quiet terrace
in summer, and the interior is quirky, too. This is a
restaurant that has hit its stride. Star starter is

Specialities:

Duck confit • Stuffed cabbage

Aligot • Salers Beef

Duck magret with honey and cêpes

Foie gras terrine

Set - menu for lunch

choice of 14€ or 20€

Set - menu for dinner 20€

Restaurant Aveyronnais
5 rue Mandar, 2nd. M° Sentier/Etienne Marcel
Tel: 01.40.26.70.55 Fax: 01.40.26.70.22
Open Tues-Sun12pm-2.30pm and 7.30pm-11.30pm

Free House Apéritif for Time Out readers

Restaurant
Le Porokhane
African Specialities

Maffé - Yassa
Braised Fish /Chicken

Live Music

3 rue Moret, 11th
M° Ménilmontant
Tel: 01.40.21.86.74
Open Daily 7pm-2am

refreshing pinwheels of smoked salmon and avocado, served with a nicely dressed salad. For mains, try tasty plaice with pesto, served with lightly cooked bean sprouts and salicorne seaweed. Blue-and-white check tablecloths and neon strip lights take you back in time, but the wine list is modern.

Restaurant L'Hermès
23 rue Mélingue, 19th (01.42.39.94.70).
M° Pyrénées. **Open** noon-2.30pm, 7.30-10.30pm
Tues-Sat. Closed Aug. **Average** €30. **Prix fixe**
€22.10. **Lunch menu** €12.20. **Credit** MC, V.
Map p403 P3.
The south-western-inspired food shows inventiveness. A langoustine, foie gras and veggie medley, stuffed into a crispy *crêpe*, keeps pace with the other starter, a slice of silky-smooth eggplant custard with tomato. For dessert, try the expertly crafted desserts like prune, Armagnac and orange flowerwater cake. Wines are on the pricey side but well-selected.

Le Zéphyr
1 rue du Jourdain, 20th (01.46.36.65.81). M°
Jourdain. **Open** noon-2pm, 8-11pm Mon-Fri; Sat 8-11pm. Closed Aug. **Average** €26. **Prix fixe**
€24.39. **Credit** AmEx, DC, MC, V. **Map** p403 P3.
It would be easy to come for the art deco setting alone, but this bistro does wicked food. Pumpkin flan topped with quivery pan-fried foie gras and a citrusy vinaigrette, maybe? Or a soup of chicory and maroilles (a potent northern cheese) with curry, elegantly served in a big white bowl. Dessert-wise, take whatever the day's special is. There are plenty of affordable wines. *Wheelchair access.*

Brasseries

Terminus Nord
23 rue Dunkerque, 10th (01.42.85.05.15).
M° Gare du Nord. **Open** 11am-1am daily. **Prix fixe**
€30.18 (dinner only). **Lunch menu** €21.04. **Credit**
AmEx, DC, MC, V. **Map** p402 K2.
The towering shellfish platters – oysters, prawns, mussels, crabs *et al* – are probably the menu's safest bets, but try to have a look at the reactions of those further ahead in their dining as standards do vary; the salmon with creamed lentils is fresh and well seasoned, and the smoked fish platter is generous with at least a half-dozen offerings. Desserts like *tarte Tartin* and profiteroles are agreeable, and the wines are well-priced.

International

North American: Blue Bayou
111-113 rue St-Maur, 11th (01.43.55.87.21).
M° Parmentier or St-Maur. **Open** noon-2pm,
7.30pm-midnight Mon-Sat; 11am-5pm (brunch) Sun.
Average €21. **Prix fixe** €12.96, €18.14 (brunch).
Credit MC, V. **Map** p403 M3/N6.
It's impossible to go too far wrong in a place named after a Roy Orbison track, and this place is more than alright for more than a while. What makes the

Blue Bayou more authentically American than many pretenders is size. The dining room feels airy and spacious, and portions are satisfyingly unfinishable. Sometimes, only the greatest effort prevents one slapping one's thighand letting rip with a joyous 'Yee-har!' In the heart of the Oberkampf bar scene, this restaurant is busiest in the evenings and for its Sunday brunches. This is the place for jambalaya, a hearty plate of nicely spiced sausage, chicken, peppers and rice.

Regional

Au Casque d'Or
51 rue des Cascades, 20th (01.43.58.44.55/
www.aucasquedor.com). M° Jourdain. **Open** noon-2.30pm, 7-11pm Mon-Fri; 7-11pm Sat. **Average** €26.
Credit MC, V. **Map** p403 P3.
At this cosy neighbourhood restaurant you'll find Auvergnat cooking with a modern touch, matched with well-selected regional wines. Dig the *entrecôte truffade*, melting meat cooked perfectly to order and served with a golden cake of potatoes with fresh tomme cheese, or the superb suckling pig. A few traditional desserts are available but everyone orders the homemade ice creams: do likewise, and you won't refret it.

Les Fernandises
19 rue de la Fontaine-au-Roi, 11th (01.48.06.16.96).
M° République. **Open** noon-2.30pm, 7.30-10.30pm
Tue-Sat. Closed one week in May, Aug. **Average**
€33.54. **Prix fixe** €21. **Lunch menu** €16.77.
Credit MC, V. **Map** p403 M4/N4.
Definitely one for the *fromage*-ophiles. Here, there are eight varieties of excellent camemberts. Pre-cheese treats include poultry-laden starters – a salad laced with strips of tender duck and chicken livers on warm lentils – a nicely crisped duck breast paired with *gratin dauphinois*, and a tasty roast pigeon. If you've still got room for dessert, there's a *tarte aux pommes flambée* that's well worth ordering. The wine list is reasonably priced and there is a good selection of Calvados. Book ahead.

The best Choc puds

Rue Balzac
Chocolate *fondant* that rocks. *See p197.*

... Comme Cochons
Pig out on the chocolate cake. *See p193.*

Le Hangar
Soufflés like swamps of dark brown naughtiness. *See p189.*

Ty-Coz
Choc oozes from their crêpes. *See p189.*

The Latin Quarter & the 13th

Bistros

L'Avant-Goût

26 rue Bobillot, 13th (01.53.80.24.00). M° Place d'Italie. **Open** noon-2pm, 8-11pm Tue-Sat. **Average** €27. **Prix fixe** €24.39. **Credit** MC, V. **Map** p406 K10.
This popular bistro is getting quite a name for itself. The blackboard menu is designed to reflect the best seasonal produce, such as the refreshing, chilled cucumber soup laced with tiny clams and a hot, asparagus gratin with an egg on top, both proof of how Beaufront can marry different textures and flavours. The well-seared calf's liver comes with a hint of spice in the *jus* and a luscious gratin dauphinois, while the meringue and chocolate fondant concoction with orange sorbet is an example of the desserts. You can expect to be satisfied, not stuffed. Book at least a week ahead in the evening.

Bistro Jef

9 rue Cujas, 5th (01.43.29.20.20). M° Cluny-La-Sorbonne/RER Luxembourg. **Open** noon-2pm, 8-11pm Mon-Sat. Closed 29 July-17 Aug. **Average** €30. **Lunch menu** €12.20, €15.24. **Credit** AmEx, DC, MC, V. **Map** p406 J8.
A carefully prepared *cuisine du terroir* with a south-western edge. A lentil salad comes with a well-judged dressing and a heap of warm, perfectly sautéed chicken livers; the *verdure du jour* is a herby, mixed green salad. A good main is slices of rosy roast beef with puréed potato or pike-perch in saffron sauce with rice, both served with sautéed courgettes. For dessert, two variants on the crème brûlée: have them both.

La Rôtisserie de Beaujolais

19, quai de la Tournelle, 5th (01.43.54.17.47). M° Jussieu. **Open** noon-2.15, 7.30-10.30pm Tues-Sun. **Average** €30. **Credit** MC, V. **Map** p406 K8.
Lashings of traditional favourites such as onion soup, snails in garlic, *coq au vin*, Lyonnaise sausage, *confit de canard* and grills are the order of the day in this jolly bistro overlooking the Seine. The country-comfort tinge means warm leeks in a creamy vinaigrette that give off dreamy vapours, oyster mushrooms with garlic and parsley as starters, and super mashed spuds partnering plump chicken legs hot from the rôtisserie. Desserts run from *tarte Tartin* to titanic floating islands.

Classic

La Truffière

4 rue Blainville, 5th (01.46.33.29.82). M° Place Monge. **Open** noon-2pm, 7-10.30pm Tue-Sun. **Prix fixe** €48.78, €67.07. **Lunch menu** €21.34 (Tue-Sat), €24.39 (Sun). **Credit** AmEx, DC, MC, V. **Map** p406 K8.

Balmy summer night sipping at **Café Noir**. *See p201.*

There's a good-value set menu, or you can choose from such delights as scrambled eggs, or a salad with nuts and slivers of fresh truffle. Main courses such as quail and rabbit with rich foie gras and truffle sauces are delicious. A generous selection of cheeses and desserts includes a superb caramelised sweet potato concoction and the well-named *puits d'amour*, a 'well' from which spring berries and crème pâtissière like lambs skipping in a vernal field. Warning: the quality of the food here can make you come over all poetic. *Wheelchair access.*

Haute

La Tour d'Argent

15-17 quai de la Tournelle, 5th (01.43.54.23.31/ www.tourdargent.com). M° Pont Marie or Cardinal Lemoine. **Open** noon-1.30pm, 7.30-9.30pm Tue-Sun. **Average** €137. **Lunch menu** €59.45. **Credit** AmEx, DC, MC, V. **Map** p406 K7.

Don't let the classy (and glassy) surroundings and the views-to-die-for make you think you can't afford this. The lunch *prix fixe* offers some Tour d'Argent classics, plus contemporary dishes and a selection of wine. Starters are a 'mosaic' of foie gras and rabbit flavoured with Sauternes wine, and langoustine tails in a tangy curry sauce with salad will get you going, and follow your instincts for the main. For afters, a *millefeuille* of fresh raspberries and strawberries, perhaps? *Wheelchair access.*

International

Chinese: La Chine Masséna

Centre Commercial Masséna, 13 pl de Vénétie, 13th (01.45.83.98.88). M° Porte de Choisy. **Open** 9am-11.30pm Mon-Thur; 9.30am-1.30am Fri-Sun. **Average** €14. **Lunch menu** €7.93. **Credit** MC, V.

This 500-seater with stage and dance floor is a mainstay for Chinese and Cambodian community events, but the place is most welcoming to those who don't belong to either of those communities. The setting provides a lot of non-food-related entertainment. On Saturday nights you might see a shy newlywed couple have their first dance, followed by a working man's club-type of live music, ranging from Chinese pop to Dalida, Elvis, Doris Day and Cher. But we're here to talk about food: the fare is authentic Chinese, Thai and Vietnamese. You won't get any culinary surprises, nor will you come away disappointed. Book on Friday and Saturday nights.

Greek: Les Délices d'Aphrodite

4 rue de Candolle, 5th (01.43.31.40.39). M° Censier-Daubenton. **Open** noon-2.30pm, 7-11.30pm Mon-Sat. **Average** €26. **Prix fixe** €27.45 (dinner only), €10.35-€28.65 (selection of mezedes). **Lunch menu** €18.30. **Credit** MC, V. **Map** p406 K9.

This is the place for a real taste of Greece. Start by sharing *dolmades*, and you'll be on the way to forgetting any grey Paris skies. Main courses are

Appetising views at **Tour d'Argent**. *(See left).*

satisfying: roast cod with tomato, fennel and Kalamata olives; chicken kebabs marinated in turmeric with sesame sauce; and *soulva*, spit-roasted lamb. Moussaka and *pastitso* keep traditionalists happy. You can finish your meal with feta in olive oil and oregano, or sweet, sticky desserts like baklava.

Korean: Han Lim

6 rue Blainville, 5th (01.43.54.62.74). M° Place Monge. **Open** noon-2.30pm, 7-10.30pm Tue-Sun. **Average** €18. **Lunch menu** €11.13. **Credit** MC, V. **Map** p406 K8.

The Han family serves homestyle fare, which has long been a favourite among the expatriate Asian community and is now well integrated into the wider demographic. That's a bit of a shame, because this is the sort of place one wants to keep for oneself. There are no pre-selected dinner menus and the plates arrive in the order that they are ready. Look out for the *panchan*, small bowls of assorted vegetable side dishes that come with the tableside grilled beef barbecue, and for the *bibimbap*, a medley of vegetables, fried egg, meat and rice mixed with a dollop of sweet hot sauce. Booking is advised.

Spanish: Fogon Saint-Julien

10 rue St-Julien-le-Pauvre, 5th (01.43.54.31.33). M° St-Michel. **Open** noon-3pm, 8pm-1am Mon-Sat. **Average** €35. **Prix fixe** €28.20. **Lunch menu** €18.29. **Credit** MC, V. **Map** p406 J7.

When it comes to Spanish cooking, you'll probably eat far better at this little Iberian restaurant than in most major Spanish resorts. Of course, the tenth *arrondissement* doesn't have all the charms of Ibiza. Start with an assortment of tapas, then choose your rice – paella is the house speciality and comes in six different cooked-to-order versions. The best idea is to come in a group and order several different versions to share.

Regional

Savoie: Alexandre

24 rue de la Parcheminerie, 5th (01.43.26.49.66).
M° St-Michel or Cluny-La Sorbonne. **Open** 6-11.30pm
daily. **Average** €15. **Credit** MC, V. **Map** p406 J7.
There are only three items on the menu and no
desserts. Each selection is accompanied by lumber-
jack portions of salad, bread, potatoes and a trio of
squirt bottles containing ketchup, mayonnaise, and
Béarnaise sauces. Each table is obliged to order the
same dish, so go with people who share your tastes.
Large portions mean you can stuff yourself endlessly with comforting gooey mouthfuls, hardly
making a dent in the pile of slightly dry dipping
bread. Goodbye hunger, hello spare tyre.

Pays Basque: Chez Gladines

30 rue des Cinq-Diamants, 13th (01.45.80.70.10).
M° Corvisart. **Open** 9am-2am daily. **Average** €9.
Lunch menu €9.15. **No credit cards. Map** p406
K10.
Chez Gladines is lucky enough to be in the Butte-
aux-Cailles – a series of villagey streets hidden
among the huge housing blocks of the 13th. In this
little oasis, you could almost pretend to be somewhere in the French Pays Basque. Most diners go
for the giant salads served in earthenware bowls
with a choice of ingredients such as fried potatoes,
jambon de Bayonne and just about any duck part
you can imagine. This is a no-frills experience, but
it is completely enjoyable.

St-Germain & Odéon

Bistros

Allard

41 rue St-André-des-Arts, 6th (01.43.26.48.23).
M° Odéon or RER St-Michel. **Open** 12.30-2.30pm,
7.30-11pm Mon-Sat. **Prix fixe**
€22.87, €30.49. **Lunch menu** €22.87. **Credit**
AmEx, DC, MC, V. **Map** p406 H7.
Way back in time, before anyone in this neighbourhood had ever seen a kebab or mime artists who
don't move, there was Allard. And, comfortingly,
there still is. Nothing has changed. Definitely not the
wallpaper. Nor the long aprons and impeccable service by the waiters. Nor a few venerable fixtures on
the menu, including a number of dishes for two. The
duck of a thousand olives, for example, is deeply
impressive. The food is not cheap, but everybody
should come here at least once. *Wheelchair access.*

Au 35

35 rue Jacob, 6th (01.42.60.23.24). M° St-Germain-
des-Prés. **Open** noon-2pm, 7-11pm daily. **Average**
€30. **Lunch menu** €13.72, €14.48. **Credit** MC, V.
Map p405 H6.
You might expect St-Germain to be full of bistros
such as this and yet they've become a surprisingly
rare breed. Tweedy publishers and local ladies pile

in to the endearingly cramped interior for the
lunchtime *menu*, so you won't find many knife fights
or bullshitting competitions. The food is simple,
French home cooking with plenty of personalised
touches, such as a crisp green bean salad with
parmesan, chicken in a tarragon cream sauce with
basmati rice and a steamed cod fillet with a purée of
potatoes and black olives. *Wheelchair access.*

Contemporary/funky

Restaurant Hélène Darroze

4 rue d'Assas, 6th (01.42.22.00.11). M° Sèvres-
Babylone. **Open** 12.30-2.15pm, 7.30-10.15pm Mon-
Sat. **Average** €122. **Prix fixe** €88.42, €117.39.
Lunch menu €36.59. **Credit** AmEx, MC, V.
Map p405 G7/H9.
Hélène Darroze, one of the most talented young
female chefs in France, gives us a flash of her gastronomic credentials. Basque and South-western
flavours are combined. The comparison of goose
and duck foie gras is in almost-too-lavish helpings,
the former *au naturel*, the latter *confit* and gently
spiced, served with an exotic fruit chutney and small
mesclun. A *moelleux au chocolat* with a bitter chocolate ice cream and rum baba flambéed in Armagnac
with berries is followed by a trolley laden with
caramels, marshmallow, macaroons and *pet-de-*
nonne to completes one's sense of joy.

International

Belgian: Bouillon Racine

3 rue Racine, 6th (01.44.32.15.60). M° Cluny-La
Sorbonne. **Open** noon-3pm, 7pm-midnight daily.
Average €32. **Prix fixe** €28.81. **Lunch menu**
€15.09 (Mon-Fri). **Credit** AmEx, MC, V.
Map p406 H7.
The two-floor space, trimmed in mirrors, wrought-
iron chandeliers and pale green decorative flourishes
envelops you in bygone elegance. After downing one
of the 50-odd Belgian beers at the bar, head upstairs
to the more formal dining room. The fare is refined
and offers a twist: each dish is coupled with a recommended beer. Chef Jean-Claude L'honneur took over
in early 2000, and the quality of the food is as good
as (or even better than) previously.

Latin American: Fajitas

15 rue Dauphine, 6th (01.46.34.44.69). M° Odéon.
Open noon-11pm Tue-Sun; 7-11pm Mon. **Average**
€24. **Prix fixe** €17.53. **Credit** AmEx, MC, V.
Map p406 H7.
A Mexican/American husband-and-wife team run
this colourful new restaurant in St-Germain, but
there is very little Tex in the Mex. Miguel cooks deliciously fresh northern Mexican dishes with some
southern specials among the starters. The guacamole gets the thumbs-up for its homemade consistency and the addition of small tomato pieces.
The signature *fajitas* with beef and chicken are a
magnificent main. Miguel is a champion of the *faji-*

Eat, Drink, Shop

ta's untapped potential. In an effort to hook the French he has devised the mini-wrap – miniature *fajitas* with wildly adventurous fillings including tandoori chicken. Lightly fried, they make a fine take-away lunch and a selection of them can be ordered as a main. The only problem is that once you start... well, you know the rest. These versatile nibbles can also feature as puddings – the banana and caramel version is ambrosial.

The 7th & the 15th

Bistros

Au Bon Accueil

14 rue Monttessuy 7th (01.47.05.46.11). M° Alma-Marceau. **Open** noon-2.15pm, 7-10.30pm Mon-Fri. **Prix fixe** €28.20. **Lunch menu** €25.15. **Credit** MC, V. **Map** p400 D5.

This is a good place to lunch after a bracing canter up the Eiffel Tower (or even after a mere wander round the base). The food is refined peasant: an excellent-value lunch menu offers a very good *fricassée* of *girolle* mushrooms and *petit gris* snails. The puds (walnut and quince crumble, roast figs, warm *moelleux* with chocolate sauce) are good.

L'Os à Moëlle

3 rue Vasco-de-Gama, 15th (01.45.57.27.27). M° Lourmel. **Open** 12.15-2pm, 7.30-11.30pm Tue-Sat. Closed Aug. **Prix fixe** €32 (dinner only). **Lunch menu** €26.68. **Credit** MC, V. **Map** p404 B9.

The lacy-curtained aspect of this place and the sleepy location does attract lunching *Madames d'un certain âge*, and why not? You'll see plenty of fine specimens preserved in blue hair rinse. By evening, there's a six-course *menu dégustation* which is glorious gluttony. Start with a flavoursome pheasant broth sprinkled liberally with fresh coriander. If you're still functioning four or five courses down the line, round off with a slice of ewe's milk tomme, and a good selection of desserts. *Wheelchair access.*

Classic

Violon d'Ingres

135 rue St-Dominique, 7th (01.45.55.15.05). M° Ecole-Militaire or RER Pont de l'Alma. **Open** 7-11pm Mon-Sat. **Average** €76. **Prix fixe** €90. **Credit** AmEx, MC, V. **Map** p405 D7.

Details such as the bread, canapés and amazing *petits fours* all indicate that Christian Constant's banjo is perfectly tuned. Starters include a tomato and seafood *millefeuille*, prepared with such culinary dexterity that it seems a shame to bring a knife to bear on it. Desserts can be spectacular if souffléed potatoes lightly caramelised and filled with a coffee crème pâtissière, served beside a fluffy liquorice mousse, and the whole dish topped with piping hot chocolate sauce, is your sort of spectacular.

Contemporary/funky

Restaurant Petrossian

18 bd de La Tour-Maubourg, 7th (01.44.11.32.32) M° Invalides or La Tour-Maubourg. **Open** noon-2pm, 7.30-10.30pm Tue-Sat. Closed Aug. **Average** €61. **Prix fixe** €90 (dinner only). **Credit** AmEx, DC, MC, V. **Map** p405 E6.

This is an intriguing restaurant for anyone after delicious and creative cooking. A meal starts with wonderful *beignets* of taramasalata and moves on to dishes such as smoked salmon with white salmon sorbet, risotto with foie gras and carrots, or smoked swordfish with a corn compote and turnip ragoût, all beautifully presented and offering contrasts of taste, texture and temperature. Desserts are stunning, the most amazing being the 'Teaser, five explosions of taste' – a mixture of fruit coulis, jellies, and creams garnished with sugared pistachios. That's a beast of a dessert; well worth a grapple.

Thiou

3 rue Surcouf, 7th (01.40.62.96.50). M° Invalides. **Open** noon-2pm, 8-11pm Mon-Fri; 8-11pm Sat. Closed Aug. **Average** €38. **Lunch menu** €26. **Credit** AmEx, DC, MC, V. **Map** p405 E5.

Let's just start by saying that Madame Thiou serves the best Thai food in Paris. Hers is a simple mantra: super-fresh, high quality ingredients prepared with care and flair. It works wonderfully well. Starters such as juicy chicken satays and peanut sauce are followed with impressive main courses such as the terrifyingly named *kae phad prik wan*, tender cubes of lamb sautéed with red and green pepper and served with fried rice. Desserts are mainly fruit based, so weight watchers can kid themselves that they're being virtuous. The wine list is reasonable – from €22.10 – the service is attentive, and the setting is elegant and cosy.

Fish

Le Divellec

107 rue de l'Universite, 7th (01.45.51.91.96). M° Invalides. **Open** noon-2pm, 7.30pm-9.30pm Mon-Fri. **Average** €107. **Lunch menu** €44.21, €59.46. **Credit** AmEx, DC, MC, V. **Map** p405 E5.

This well-mannered dining room is an exceptionally pleasant place for a nosh up. Often in restaurants of this calibre, you get the proverbial fish eye when you opt for the cheapest *menu*, but that's not the case here. Delicious appetisers are followed by such mains as sautéed salmon on a bed of spinach. Le Divellec offers a superb dessert trolley, brimming with chocolate mousse, fresh raspberries and strawberries, fruit tarts, *oeufs à la neige*, poached blood oranges and other delicious choices. This is the place to visit when you are gripped by one of those take-no-prisoners desires for good food right now.

The dessert laboratory
that is **Petrossian.** *See left*.

Haute Cuisine

L'Arpège

84 rue de Varenne, 7th (01.45.51.47.33/ www.alain-passard.com). M° Varenne. **Open** 12.30-2pm, 8-10pm Mon-Fri. **Average** €213. **Prix fixe** €213. **Credit** AmEx, DC, MC, V. **Map** p405 F6.

Chef Alain Passard announced in 2001 that he was abandoning meat in favour of a new *haute cuisine* based almost exclusively on vegetables and seafood. It's a bold move. That brave decision has paid off handsomely. Diners love excellent new dishes such as sea urchins with (get this) nasturtium flowers and leaves, a very delicate vegetable couscous and a brilliant dish of lobster sautéed in mustard with a garnish of tiny red onions from Roscoff. A main course of scallops wrapped in bay leaves and served on a bed of young leeks is superb, unless, of course, you believe that flora feels pain every time you plunge the fork in... *Wheelchair access.*

International

Chinese: Chen

15 rue du Théâtre, 15th (01.45.79.34.34). M° Charles Michels. **Open** noon-2.30pm, 7.30-10.30pm Mon-Sat. **Average** €69. **Prix fixe** €74.70. **Lunch menu** €39.64. **Credit** AmEx, MC, V. **Map** p404 B7/C8.

An intriguing approach makes this a place you simply have to visit: the finest French produce, much of it *appellation d'origine contrôlée*, is blended with Chinese technique. Star dishes include elegant Eurasian starters like courgette flowers stuffed with crab mousse in a sauce of fresh crab meat, and frogs' legs sautéed in salt and Szechuan pepper, plus main courses like rock lobster in ginger. Even the desserts are good, including the *tan yuang aux fleurs de laurier*, gummy rice dumplings stuffed with sugar and bay leaf in a 'broth' infused with laurel flowers. You don't have to be daring to eat here – just a lover of good, inventive food.

Vietnamese: Kim Ahn

49 av. Emile Zola, 15th (01.45.79.40.96). M° Charles Michels. **Open** 7.30-11pm Tue-Sun. **Average** €40. **Prix fixe** €33.53. **Credit** AmEx, MC, V. **Map** p404 A8/C8.

Caroline Kim Ahn emphasises quality and authenticity in everything she lays before you. The spring rolls bursting with chicken, prawns, vermicelli and Vietnamese mint are standouts. Mains of lacquered, sliced duck with a sweet orange and soy sauce, and langoustines caramelisées, two giant prawns in a sticky combo of onions, sugar, soy and fish are typical of the refined, careful cooking. Fresh tropical fruits such as mangostan, a plum-brown fruit with a marshmallowy white centre and a taste akin to a sweet mini banana, are good bets for dessert.

Regional

D'Chez Eux

2 av de Lowendal, 7th (01.47.05.52.55). M° Ecole-Militaire. **Open** noon-2.30pm, 7.30-10.30pm Mon-Sat. Closed three weeks in Aug. **Average** €46. **Lunch menu** €28.05, €33.54. **Credit** AmEx, DC, MC, V. **Map** p405 E7.

Begin with the trolley of salads or the equally tempting range of charcuterie, with hams and pâtés to satisfy the heartiest pork lover. Main courses include a guinea fowl grand-mère, served in a copper pan and carved at the table on its comfortable bed of potatoes, bacon and mushrooms. Let's not kid ourselves – we're here for the dessert trolley: chocolate mousse, creamy homemade vanilla ice cream and a collection of stewed fruits. Heady. *Wheelchair access.*

Montparnasse & beyond

Bistros

Josephine 'Chez Dumonet'

117 rue du Cherche-Midi, 6th (01.45.48.52.40). M° Duroc. **Open** 12.30-2.30pm, 7.30-11pm Mon-Fri. **Average** €42. **Credit** AmEx, MC, V. **Map** p405 F7. What a treat. Behind crisp white curtains lies an interior with cracked-tile floor, frosted tulip lamps, huge mirrors and acres of warm wood ministered by a handful of courteous waiters. Black truffles

Delicacy at **Kim Ahn**. *See above.*

from Quercy star in the line-up of winter dishes and the creamy omelette generously studded with this earthy tuber is a great starter. For mains, try scallops *à la provençale*, a duck confit or a creamy, warming *boeuf bourguignon*. For a grand finale, try the Grand Marnier soufflé.

La Régalade
49 av Jean-Moulin, 14th (01.45.45.68.58). M° Alésia. **Open** noon-2pm, 7pm-midnight Tue-Fri; 7pm-midnight Sat. Closed Aug. **Prix fixe** €29.73. **Credit** MC, V. **Map** p405 G10.
The provincial-style dining room is as lively as ever (don't go for a quiet natter) and reservations remain notoriously hard to obtain – two weeks for a week-night table, so do make sure you've booked in good time. Starters are typically south-western, such as chilled raw oysters, and mains are wintery, for example, juicy roasted capon, served with chestnuts. Don't expect big portions or generous accompaniments here – flavour is the thing, as in the towering Grand Marnier soufflé, Camdeborde's signature dessert. Nobody does it better.

Wadja
10 rue de la Grande-Chaumière, 6th (01.46.33.02.02). M° Vavin. **Open** noon-2.30pm, 7.30-11pm Mon-Fri. Closed Aug. **Average** €30. **Prix fixe** €13.57. **Credit** MC, V. **Map** p405 G9.
Service is friendly and the food a pleasant reminder of how exciting and varied bistro cooking can be when it draws on French regions and seasonal produce. The €13.57 daily *menu* is remarkable: three courses of whatever chef Didier Panisset has decided on for that day. The wine list combines produce from all over France, maps and quite useful descriptions of producers for those who want to impress their date with oenophilia.

Brasseries

La Coupole
102 bd du Montparnasse, 14th (01.43.20.14.20). M° Vavin. **Open** 8.30am-1am Mon-Thur; 8.30am-1.30am Fri, Sat. **Average** €34. **Prix fixe** €30.18 (dinner only). **Lunch menu** €15.54. **Credit** AmEx, DC, MC, V. **Map** p405 F8/H9.

Mince and the revolution

Mad cow really hit the French consciousness in late 2000, when the first victims of CJD were shown on television. Since then, organic food has lost its dope-head hippy image. Organic shopping used to mean paying triple the normal price for earthy carrots at the boulevard Raspail market on a Sunday; now, most of the 29% of French consumers who regularly eat organic foods need look no further than their local supermarkets.

If organic food has hit the mainstream, serving it in a Paris restaurant remains an under-appreciated labour of love. Carole Sinclair, who opened her bistro **Le Safran** (*29 rue d'Argenteuil, 1st/01.42.61.25.30*) in 1999, negotiates with merchants at the markets to buy the organic ingredients for her reasonably priced dishes. She finds it cheaper to do most of the shopping herself.

'I tell the market guys that it's good publicity for their products. If I wait until the end of the market they're often willing to give me a deal. The other day I persuaded a merchant to let his red peppers go at €2.75 a kilo, which is still far higher than the price of ordinary peppers.'

Le Safran immediately caught on with British and American tourists, who make up 80% of her clientele. 'People seem much more aware of organic food abroad. My foreign customers are so grateful that they often hug me as they leave. They ask for dishes such as my starter of raw beetroot with orange slices and olives. I need to develop my French clientele.' Unfortunately, the slump in travel following the attack on the World Trade Center has dealt a real economic blow to the organic restaurateurs.

Jesus Tounsi is trying to appeal to as broad a customer base as possible with his restaurant **Le Potager du Marais** (*see p191*), open since early 2000 – his aim is 'to bring organic and vegetarian cooking out of its ghetto'. Though he attracts people 'of all ages and customs' with dishes such as avocado with seaweed, and organic smoked fish, organic food is a hard sell in France.

'One customer looked at the bread basket and said, what's this? The waiter explained to him that we serve organic bread. He went across the street and bought a baguette – if I had been there, I would have thrown him out. The French don't like to change their habits; the English are far ahead of us.'

Like all the restaurateurs we spoke to on this subject, Tounsi opened his restaurant out of personal conviction rather than any hope of getting rich quick. 'I've been eating organic products for 26 years and I believe in doing as much as I can to preserve the environment. I grew up in Algeria where I was raised on organic food, so really I'm just going

This restaurant is always buzzing with an eclectic crowd of Parisians, suburbanites and tourists. Service is good-natured, with plenty of corny jokes from the wise-cracking waiters. Truffled scrambled eggs make a good starter and for mains you should think seafood: you could spend an hour tackling a plate-sized crab. Fun, rather than a gastronomic experience, a meal at La Coupole is a people-watching treat.

Fish

Le Bar à Huîtres

112 bd du Montparnasse, 14th (01.43.20.71.01/ www.lebarahuitres.fr). M° Vavin. **Open** noon-2pm, 7-11pm daily. **Average** €30. **Prix fixe** €22, €38. **Credit** AmEx, DC, MC, V. **Map** p405 F8/H9.
This little chain does good seafood and has a great atmosphere. Among the delights are a dozen superbly fresh and perfectly opened oysters. For mains, you can do worse than a tender, cooked-exactly-as-ordered tuna steak with *haricots verts* and

roasted tomato garnish and a similarly generous sauté of sliced *encornets* (squid) with garlic and olive oil, plus rice. Desserts are fine, too.

Vegetarian

Aquarius

40 rue de Gergovie, 14th (01.45.41.36.88). M° Pernety or Plaisance. **Open** noon-2.15pm, 7-10.30pm Mon-Sat. **Average** €15. **Lunch menu** €9.90. **Credit** AmEx, DC, MC, V. **Map** p405 F10.
This popular vegetarian eatery has friendly staff and relaxed customers. It's basic, bright and cheery, and gives the impression of having expanded over time to accommodate an increasing demand. There are several impressive-looking salads and, when it comes to main course, they really know how to do a vegetarian lasagne. All the meals are served with good sourdough bread. About a third of the ingredients used are organic, and organic wine is on the menu. There are over a dozen desserts on offer, ranging from fruit salad to a *fondant au chocolat*.

back to my roots. People are surprised because I'm not charging a lot – our lunch menu is at €10.'

Raphaël Bembaron, chef and owner of the restaurant **Il Baccello** (*33 rue Cardinet, 17th/01.43.80.63.60*) also says he is simply serving the type of food he likes to eat. 'I lived in Italy for five years and worked with products of exceptional quality. Working at the vegetarian restaurant Joia in Milan had the greatest impact on me – the style of cooking was exactly what I was seeking.'

Bembaron puts the emphasis on vegetables, fruit and herbs, plus organically farmed fish and a little meat. 'Vegetables have an important place in traditional Italian cooking. In France we often think of the vegetable as a garnish. I also use a lot of olive oil and no butter. My oil comes from Tuscany but it isn't labelled organic – though many producers basically use organic methods, the label is expensive and complicated to get.'

Bembaron concedes that most of his French customers come for his creativity and the quality of the products, regardless of whether they are organic. 'The French don't go out of their way to eat organic. Since the opening two years ago, I've probably had ten tables of customers who came here specifically for that.' Well, it's a start.

Carole Sinclair at her bistro **Le Safran**.

Bars, Cafés & Tearooms

Admit it: posing seductively in a bar, slaying them all with your wit in a café and pigging out on cakes in a tea room are among your top Paris fantasies.

If you can get to know Paris' cafés and bars, you can get to know Paris. These are the city's sitting rooms, the places where everybody comes for a natter, a drink, and – more often than you might think – a canoodle; this *is* Paris. Legendary after-hours boozer magnet Polly Magoo is no more (*see p231* **Red-eye refuges**), but don't listen to the scaremongers who bemoan the decline of the '*zincs*' (the old-style cafés with their impressive array of irregular regulars); there's plenty left for traditionalists, and lots of great new places, too. Parisian cafés and bars are fantastic for a spot of people-watching: you'll see the sozzled old Gainsbourg-alikes, the pretty young things who fall out of bed looking like film stars, the dazed and confused and those gangs of middle-aged ladies who look for all the world like they've been bingeing on gorilla biscuits and are ready for a punch-up. Note that prices are generally lowest standing at the bar, slightly higher seated inside and highest on the terrace outside. And don't forget that while you're drinking in the sights and sounds, people will be having a look at you, too. *Santé!* For further listings see the *Time Out Paris Eating and Drinking Guide*.

The Islands

Cafés

L'Escale
1 rue des Deux-Ponts, 4th (01.43.54.94.23). M° Pont Marie. **Open** Tue-Sun 7.30am-9pm. Closed three weeks in Aug. Beer **Credit** MC, V.
Map p406 K7.
With an idyllic Ile St-Louis location and grumpy regulars reading *L'Equipe* at the counter, L'Escale remains a real neighbourhood café/wine bar. There is no prix fixe, but a meal will cost about €18. Expect all the veg to be cooked in olive oil and garlic, and the small portions of meat to be tender. The *vins du mois* are often worth a slurp.

Tearooms

La Charlotte en l'Ile
24 rue St-Louis-en-Ile, 4th (01.43.54.25.83).
M° Pont Marie. **Open** noon-8pm Thur-Sun. Tea and puppet show by reservation only, Wed; piano tea Fri 6-8pm. Closed July and Aug. **Credit** V.

Poetess and chocolatier Sylvie Langlet has been spinning sweet fantasies here for years. In the miniscule front room she sells superb dark chocolate and candied fruit sticks, while at six round tables she offers 36 teas of quality.

The Louvre, Palais-Royal & Les Halles

Bars

Flann O'Brien's
6 rue Bailleul, 1st (01.42.60.13.58/ www.irishfrance. com/flannobrien). M° Louvre-Rivoli. **Open** 4pm-2am daily. **No credit cards. Map** p401 3F.
If you think one Irish pub is pretty much the same as the next, order a pint of Guinness here. Flann O'Brien's is a cut above the rest. Competition on the pool table is fierce, but the live Irish band keeps the atmosphere congenial. *Wheelchair access.*

Le Fumoir
6 rue de l'Amiral-de-Coligny, 1st (01.42.92.00.24/ www.lefumoir.com). M° Louvre-Rivoli. **Open** 11am-2am daily. Closed one week in Aug. **Credit** AmEx, MC, V. **Map** p406 H6.
Even the bar staff seem to have been included in the interior decorator's sketches. A sleek crowd sipping martinis or browsing the papers at the bar gives way to young professionals in the restaurant. The real pearl is the 3000-book library. *Wheelchair access.*

Harry's New York Bar
5 rue Daunou, 2nd (01.42.61.71.14/ www.harrys-bar.fr). M° Opéra. **Open** 11am-3am daily. **Credit** AmEx, DC, MC, V. **Map** p401 G4.
Harry's claims to have invented the Bloody Mary; it's certainly been the origin of some bloody awful hangovers. White-coated waiters engage in banter with tourists, local businessmen and American alumni. Just don't ask for a soft drink. Ever.

Le Tambour
41 rue Montmartre, 2nd (01.42.33.06.90). M° Les Halles. **Open** 24 hours daily. Credit MC, V.
Map p402 J4.
Châtelet is hardly lacking in all-night bars, but this place is a welcome alternative to the generally tacky boozers. Despite the statuettes on the shelves, this is not the home of the intellectual elite: although many of the drinkers have strongly expressed opinions, they are not often of the genre 'coherent'.

Hot gossip and cool drinks at La **Fourmi**. See p225.

Cafés

Bar de l'Entr'acte
47 rue Montpensier, 1st (01.42.97.57.76). M° Palais Royal. **Open** 10am-2am Tue-Fri; noon-midnight Sat, Sun. **Credit** AmEx, MC, V. **Map** p402 H5.
Finding a table can be tricky during peak hours as this casual drinking hole is popular with theatre goers and the local boho chic. The *jardin d'hiver*, a cellar done up with theatre scenery and red curtains, is best visited after several drinks.

Le Café
62 rue Tiquetonne, 2nd (01.40.39.08.00). M° Etienne-Marcel. **Open** 10am-2am Mon-Sat; noon-midnight Sun. **Credit** MC, V. **Map** 402 J5.
This joint buzzes with loud and funky music. The interior is a fusion between Ali Baba's cavern and an explorer's attic, filled with African statuettes, antique globes, a Lenin bust and browning maps of exotic locations. The food is less adventurous.

Café Marly
93 rue de Rivoli, cour Napoléon du Louvre, 1st (01.49.26.06.60). M° Palais Royal. **Open** 8am-2am daily. **Credit** AmEx, DC, MC, V. **Map** p401 H5.
Opened in 1994 as part of the Grand Louvre project, Café Marly is another Costes-brothers success. The terrace has a privileged view of the glass pyramid. Waiters glide between tables delivering gazpacho and €89.94 sevruga caviar to customers who sip cocktails (€9.91) and spot celebs.

La Coquille
30 rue Coquillière, 1st (01.40.26.55.36). M° Les Halles. **Open** 7am-10pm Mon-Sat. **Credit** MC, V. **Map** p402 J5.
This down-to-earth, vintage '50s shoebox café is a local favourite. The bar has a good selection of cheap wines, €0.91-€1.52 a glass. The budget food, fast and fresh, runs from *entrecôtes* to giant salads (the *salade coquille* is particularly nice). Admire the Portuguese owner's gravy boat collection as you sip a glass of *vinho verde*.

Tea rooms

Angelina's
226 rue de Rivoli, 1st (01.42.60.82.00). M° Tuileries. **Open** 9.45am-7pm daily. Wed-Mon in July and Aug. **Credit** AmEx. V. **Map** p405 G5.
Between the two world wars, the smart set needed only to say, 'meet you on the rue de Rivoli' when arranging a tea date, such was the fame of this neo-rococo tearoom. The specialities have always been the mont blanc: soft and chewy meringue with whipped cream and chestnut cream topping, though the mont has diminished in size over the years. Still, Angelina's is currently in its element, with an excellent lunch menu.
Branches: Galeries Lafayette (3rd floor), 40 bd Haussmann, 9th (01.42.32.30.32); Palais des Congrès, 2 pl de la Porte-Maillot, 17th (01.40.68.22.50).

Opéra & the Grands Boulevards

Bars

Le Barramundi
3 rue Taitbout, 9th (01.47.70.21.21). M° Richelieu-Drouot. **Open** noon-3pm, 7.30pm-2am Mon-Fri; 8pm-5am Sat. Closed two weeks in Aug. **Credit** AmEx, DC, MC, V. **Map** p405 G5.
Relaxed, pretty young things disappear into vast squishy sofas while nursing potent cocktails and looking faintly bored. The Indian-inspired DJ box pumps out decent chill-out music on Friday nights (there is a 'dance party' on Saturdays) and the drinks list is 'reassuringly' expensive. *Wheelchair access.*

De la Ville Café
34 bd Bonne Nouvelle, 10th (01.48.24.48.09). M° Bonne Nouvelle. **Open** 11am-2am Mon-Sat; 3pm-2am Sun. **Credit** MC, V. Map p402 J4.
De la Ville is a new addition to the art-squat-as-style-statement gang. The upstairs looks like a turn-of-the-century church hall and the apothecary-and-cobbler-sharing-office-space corner is a weird design concept. The comfy rattan sofas, brilliant service, and genial punters make this a top place to *apéro*.

Tea rooms

Ladurée
16 rue Royale, 8th (01.42.60.21.79). M° Madeleine or Concorde. **Open** 8.30am-7pm Mon-Sat; 10am-7pm Sun. **Credit** AmEx, DC, MC, V. **Map** p401 F4.
Avoiding someone's eye when they're desperately seeking yours is an art that French waiters have perfected, and Ladurée staff do it exceptionally well. Once you accept this, you can settle back and enjoy one of Paris' favourite institutions. It's the maca-roons that regulars devour by the mound, whether coffee, coconut, chocolate, pistachio or mint.

The best For ambiance

Café Marly
Caviar cool, with views of the Louvre pyramid. *See left.*

Ladurée
If you haven't been, you haven't really been to Paris. *See above.*

Fu Bar
Full of Anglos quaffing massive cocktails. Bliss, eh? *See p229.*

La Tour de Pierre
Left Bank atmospherics. *See p231.*

Eat, Drink, Shop

Beaubourg & the Marais

Bars

Chez Richard
37 rue Vieille-du-Temple, 4th (01.42.74.31.65).
Mᵒ Hôtel-de-Ville or St-Paul. **Open** 6pm-2am daily.
Closed two weeks in Aug. **Credit** AmEx, MC, V.
Map p406 K6.
A real gem that pulls in a mix of first-daters, people
looking for a quiet night out and pre-party gangs
gathering strength. The long squishy bar begs
elbows and pissed philosophising, while the friendly staff, well-mixed cocktails and perfectly chilled
champagne bring Chez Richard close to heaven.

L'Enoteca
25 rue Charles V, 4th (01.42.78.91.44). Mᵒ St-Paul.
Open noon-2.30pm, 7.30-11.30pm daily. Closed one
week in Aug. **Credit** MC, V. **Map** p406 L7.
If you like Italian wine, then this classy Marais trat-
toria is a must. The list is astounding, with hard-to-
find wines from all the best producers: Gaja, Aldo
Conterno, Vajra, Felsina Berardenga and a stack of
vintages. The food is delicious too.

All for one for the road at
De la Ville Café. *See p217.*

The Lizard Lounge
18 rue du Bourg-Tibourg, 4th (01.42.72.81.34/
www.hip-bars.com). Mᵒ Hôtel-de-Ville. **Open** noon-
2am daily. Closed one week in Aug. **Credit** MC, V.
Map p406 K6.
The Anglophone/phile crowd indulges in serious
flirting over lethal cocktails. Trip hop and house
music help everything along and from 8pm you can
shake your stuff on the small dance floor in the cellar. Brunch is an institution at The Lizard Lounge;
come early for the Sunday papers, cheap Bloody
Marys and a mean eggs Benedict (€9.15-€15.24).

Stolly's
16 rue Cloche-Perce, 4th (01.42.76.06.76/www.hip-
bars.com). Mᵒ Hôtel de Ville or St-Paul. **Open**
4.30pm-2am daily. **Credit** MC, V. **Map** p406 K6.
Proving that size really doesn't matter, Stolly's
packs a large crowd into a small space. The hardcore cocktails, friendly staff and loud music create
a welcoming atmosphere. Always full of expats getting steadily trolleyed, Stolly's is a great place to
watch the football or the rugby.

Cafés

L'Apparemment Café
18 rue des Coutures-St-Gervais, 3rd
(01.48.87.12.22). Mᵒ Filles du Calvaire or St-Paul.
Open noon-2am Mon-Fri ; 4pm-2am Sat; noon-
midnight Sun. **Credit** MC, V. **Map** p406 L6.
This cosy café across from the Picasso museum is
decorated like the front room of an eccentric booze
fiend. All the comforts of home with, of course, a bill.
Drinks are a little steep but will keep you fuelled for
longer than most. The food is simple and popular;
arrive early for meals.

Baz'Art Café
36, bd Henri IV, 4th (01.42.78.62.23). Mᵒ Sully
Morland or Bastille. **Open** 8am-midnight daily.
Credit AmEx, MC, V. **Map** 406 L7.
This light, airy and very spacious café attracts
everyone. It offers good-quality café fare and a
relaxed, stylish atmosphere in which to linger. The
sandy yellow walls, red velvet chairs and jazzy
soundtrack make a fabulosa backdrop and the service couldn't be friendlier. Plenty of market-fresh
salads to choose from – or check out the great-value
Sunday brunch for €17.53.

Café Beaubourg
43 rue St-Merri, 4th (01.48.87.63.96). Mᵒ Hôtel-de-
Ville or RER Châtelet-Les Halles. **Open** 8am-1am
Mon-Fri; 8am-2am Sat, Sun. **Credit** AmEx, DC, MC,
V. **Map** p406 K6.
The waiters, in tailored black suits (the Costes brothers' standard), are better-dressed than most clients.
No small feat as this dimly-lit hang-out, like its sibling restaurant Georges atop the Centre Pompidou,
is frequented by the rich and the beautiful – but it
doesn't spurn the rest of us. The terrace is ideal for
sipping the generous, frothy *café crème.*

Eat, Drink, Shop

Café du Trésor

7-9 rue du Trésor, 4th (01.42.71.78.34). M° Hôtel de Ville or St-Paul. **Open** noon-2am daily.
Credit MC, V. **Map** p406 K6.

Le Trésor has one of the bigger Marais terraces and the kids dig it, maaaan. The interior wears its colours on its sleeve: bold and primary. Knowing grins and eyebrow theatre will have to do as the music is decibelmungous. Some little nooks and crannies are comfortable and private.

L'Etoile Manquante

34 rue Vieille-du-Temple, 4th (01.42.72.48.34/ www.cafeine.com). M° Hôtel de Ville or St-Paul.
Open 9am-2am daily. **Credit** MC, V. **Map** p406 K6.

Xavier (Petit Fer à Cheval) Denamur's latest art-work-filled endeavour is worth a visit even if you only use the loo. As you relieve yourself, an electric train circulates beneath a photo of a block of flats by night. Then don't forget to smile as you wash your hands and see yourself recorded on the screen reflected in the mirror. By the way, the food's OK.

Web Bar

32 rue de Picardie, 3rd (01.42.72.66.55/ www.webbar.fr). M° République. **Open** 8.30am-2am Mon-Fri; 11am-2am Sat; 11am-midnight Sun.
Credit MC, V. **Map** p402 L6.

The net-plus ultra of Paris cyberspace is more than a computer geek's lair. Industrial vibes intensify as you pass through its wicker-chaired terrace, its mellow-lit bar slamming with speed chess, and the impressive triple-height atrium (a former silversmith's atelier). Web activities extend to live web painting and on-line DJ links.

The Bastille, eastern & north-eastern Paris

Bars

Bar des Ferailleurs

18 rue de Lappe, 11th (01.48.07.89.12). M° Bastille. **Open** 5pm-2am Mon-Fri; 3pm-2am Sat, Sun. **Credit** MC, V. **Map** p407 M7.

Decorated with the old junk from a French grandad's garage, this quirky little bar is one of the few places on the rue de Lappe where you're likely to find genuine Parisians hanging out with hard-drinking out-of-towners.

China Club

50 rue de Charenton, 12th (01.43.43.82.02/ www.chinaclub.cc). M° Ledru-Rollin or Bastille. **Open** 7pm-2am Mon-Thur, Sun; 7pm-3am Fri-Sat. Closed 20 Jul-20 Aug. **Credit** AmEx, MC, V. **Map** p407 M7.

With huge Chesterfields, low lighting and a sexy long bar, it's impossible not to feel glamorous here. It's like an extremely relaxed gentleman's club with a distinctly colonial Cohibas-and-cocktails feel. This is ideal seduction territory, but equally good for a raucous gossip session.

L'Entre-potes

14 rue de Charonne, 11th (01.48. 06.57.04). M° Ledru-Rollin. **Open** 5pm-2am daily. **Credit** AmEx, MC, V. **Map** p407 M7.

Rather than nervous groups of boys and girls hoping to pull (as can be the case in some of the block-buster Bastille bar/clubs), intimate groups of friends enjoy each other's company here. Curiously, the front window of the bar proclaims 'American Bar', but the place feels utterly French.

La Flèche d'Or

102bis rue de Bagnolet, 20th (01.43.72.04.23/www. flechedor.com). M° Alexandre Dumas. **Open** 10am-2am Tue-Sun. **Credit** AmEx, DC, MC, V.

Music fans flock to this funky venue, in a former station on the defunct Petite Ceinture railway line, to catch local groups or dig the decidedly alternative media scene that runs from Télébocal community TV and salsa *bals* to impassioned debates on terrifyingly tedious subjects. *Wheelchair access.*

Lou Pascalou

14 rue des Panoyaux, 20th (01.46.36.78.10). M° Ménilmontant. **Open** 9am-2am daily.
Credit MC, V. **Map** p403 P4.

Dress down for a visit to this Ménilmontant mainstay, where a bohemian crowd hangs out until the small hours, and spills onto the pavement on warm evenings. Chess matches roll on and on for hours as regulars settle scores over a *pression* or two. Chunky sets and a roll-out board are available from behind the bar for free, as well as a timer for the real pros. Not the wildest place in Paris.

Le Sanz Sans

49 rue du Fbg-St-Antoine, 11th (01.44.75.78.78). M° Bastille or Ledru-Rollin. **Open** 9am-2am Mon-Thurs; 9am-5am Fri, Sat; 11am-2am Sun. **Credit** DC, MC, V. **Map** p407 M7.

The Sanz Sans draws in a huge, usually non-local crowd on the weekends. The place is always packed then, and invariably there are a couple of girls in hot pants gyrating on the bar to the DJ's beats. What more could anyone possibly want? It has a number of faces, depending on the hour and your condition, although the crowd tends toward young and bouncy whatever the time. As do the chicks in hot pants. *Wheelchair access.*

Les Trois Têtards

46 rue Jean Pierre Timbaud, 11th (01.43.14.27.37). M° Oberkampf or Parmentier. **Open** 8pm-2am Mon-Fri; 5pm-2am Sat-Sun. **Credit** MC, V. **Map** p403 M4/N4.

A familiar interior of rickety chairs and murals is presided over by genial staff and a raucous crowd. Everyone seems to know everyone else, or maybe they're just very good with strangers. The eponymous house speciality is an intoxicating (if weird) combination of vodka, grapefruit juice, mint and a 'secret' ingredient.

Coolest shaker

Colin Peter Field is officially superlative: jet-set glossy *Forbes* magazine has proclaimed the supremo of the **Ritz's Hemingway Bar** (15 pl Vendome, 1st/01.43.16. 32.96) to be the world's best bartender, and those who have been privileged to be on the receiving end of, well, not just his cocktails but his whole presentational art, have no reason to begrudge him that accolade. So what better man's opinions to seek on the subject of what makes a great bartender?

'Discretion, bonhomie, the understanding ear and, of course, technical brilliance in the art of mixing drinks do not make you great,' states the charismatic Mr Field in the snug, evocative atmosphere of his bar. 'All of those should be taken for granted in anyone who dares to serve you a drink.' One wonders if that philosophy has made any impression on the consciousness of the bar staff of one's local boozer, but do go on, Colin. 'A great bartender should make a contribution to the world of cocktails.' How? 'By creativity: by making the art evolve.

'We have a lot to learn from the world of *haute cuisine*. For example, the creation of dishes focuses around the availability of seasonal and regional products; the same should apply to cocktails'. Field is serious about giving each of his drinks a unique identity: he will tailor the composition of his mixtures after keen observation of the body language and mood of his customer; the colour of the freshly-cut flower petal with which he garnishes a woman's drink will be selected to enhance her hair colour and skin tones. This aesthetic approach is not surprising from a man who believes that a cocktail is drunk first by the eyes.

There is another vital factor in great bartending: 'Showmanship. It's absolutely imperative, and let's face it: every bartender in the world wants to be famous.' And what, according to the world's finest bartender, are the secrets of a successful bar? 'That's simple: soul and history.'

The Hemingway Bar (which started its existence as a waiting room for ladies whose better halves were getting sloshed elsewhere) has plenty of history. The walls are hung with photos of the great Ernest doing his thing: hunting, fishing, tippling, occasionally even writing. Field enhances the historical vibe by insisting that the only music that's heard in

his domain should come via the interaction of the needle of his gramophone with the grooves on his collection of 78s. The dress code is liberal – 'Try to look good so that you'll feel good, and I don't think I'd let anyone in if they were trying to dress like a rapper.' And, of course, all of that adds to the soul of the bar, which is not so much traditional as respectful of tradition; at any rate, it is certainly very welcoming. Colin Field wants people to come to his bar and let the atmosphere of the place ooze into them. And if you do, not only will you relax, not only will you have the chance to taste the work of the world's best bartender, but you'll also find the sum total effect of the experience will be to give you some deliciously wicked ideas.

Cafés

Ba'ta'clan Café
50 bd Voltaire (01.49.23.96.33) 11th.
M° Oberkampf. **Open** 7am-2am daily. **Credit** MC, V.
Map p407 M5/N6.
The Ba'ta'clan café, next door to the theatre of the same name, attracts a varied clientele. The open-plan bar spills out onto a huge terrace, which starts to get really busy around 11pm. Inside, big leather armchairs make for a cosy evening's drinking under the watchful gaze of a statue of a Greek god. Psychedelic paintings, heavy metal chandeliers and fairy lights complete the ensemble. A wide range of food is on offer, and pots of wine are cheap and plentiful. *Wheelchair access.*

Le Bistrot du Peintre
116 av Ledru-Rollin, 11th (01.47.00.34.39).
M° Ledru-Rollin. **Open** 7am-2am Mon-Sat; 9am-midnight Sun. Closed Christmas. Credit DC, MC, V.
Map p407 M8/N6.
This is a fine example of a sophisticated, well-restored art nouveau café, with luscious carved wood, painted vineyard scenes, frosted-glass partitions, tall mirrors and a long zinc bar. Hot dishes such as pot-au-feu or baked sea bream change daily, while Salers beef, salads and plates of charcuterie are always available, along with good wines.

Chez Prune
71 quai de Valmy, 10th (01.42.41.30.47).
M° République. **Open** 7am-2am Mon-Sat; 10am-2am Sun. **Credit** MC, V. **Map** p402 L4.
If Oberkampf is too mainstream, then this vibrant Canal St-Martin hotspot may be just the place for a *pastis* or a well-cooked lunch. Everyone seems to know each other, but it's far from cliquey: as long as you look suitably street and have a screenplay to talk about you'll fit right in.

Pause Café
41 rue de Charonne, 11th (01.48.06.80.33). M°
Ledru-Rollin. **Open** 7am-2am Mon-Sat; 9am-8.30pm Sun. **Credit** AmEx, MC, V. **Map** p407 M7/P6.
Mime school graduates have the best chance of getting a waiter's attention. Still, the setting's funky and bright and the kitchen makes an effort with hot specials, a selection of filling *tourtes*, and goat's cheese in brik pastry with sweet sautéed pears. Seats on the heated terrace are coveted even in winter.

Le Rendez-vous des Quais
MK2 sur Seine, 10-14 quai de la Seine, 19th
(01.40.37.02.81). M° Stalingrad or Jaurès. **Open** noon-midnight daily. **Credit** AmEx, DC, MC, V.
Map p403 M1/M1.
You can easily while away hours at this relaxed café on the esplanade of the Bassin de la Villette. Film buffs can't miss with the €22.71 *menu ciné*. The food is a cut above typical café fare, and desserts tend towards the rich and gooey. The clients, thankfully, do not. *Wheelchair access.*

Le Soleil
136 bd de Ménilmontant, 20th (01.46.36.47.44).
M° Ménilmontant. **Open** 9am-2am daily. **No credit cards. Map** p403 N4/P5.
Aptly named, as the terrace catches most of the afternoon sun, café is a standby for local artists, musicians and hipsters and always an interesting place to strike up a conversation. Totally unexceptional inside, but you want to be outside anyway.

Le Viaduc Café
43 av Daumesnil, 12th (01.44.74.70.70). M° Ledru-Rollin or Gare de Lyon. **Open** 9am-4am daily.
Credit AmEx, DC, MC, V. **Map** p407 M8/Q9.
If you're not a regular, the unique setting and pretty good food can be let down by occasionally aloof service, but it's nonetheless a fine place for a sophisticated apéritif or nightcap. Jazz brunch on Sunday.

Tea rooms

Les Petits Plus
20 bd Beaumarchais, 11th (01.48.87.01.40/
www.lespetitsplus.com). M° Bastille. **Open** 11am-7pm
Mon-Sat; 11am-7.30pm Sun. **Credit** AmEx, DC, MC,
V. **Map** p403 M4.
This is 'Goldilocks and the Three Bears' territory: scrubbed wood floor, tables and chairs, and dressers set against pristine white walls. The 21 teas, served in transparent teapots, include the poetic *sonate d'automne, voyage d'hiver, secret tibétain* and Etna.

The Champs-Elysées & west

Bars

The Bowler
13 rue d'Artois, 8th (01.45.61.16.60). M° St-Philippe du Roule. **Open** 11am-2am daily. Hot food served noon-2.30pm daily; curry 7.30-10.30pm Sun. **Happy hour** 5-6.30pm Mon-Fri, 7-9pm Sat, Sun. **Credit** AmEx, MC, V. **Map** p401 E4.
The Bowler is the refuge of the love-France-loathe-the-French expat. It's full of ruggerbuggers, students and bankers shooting weak-chinned smiles at pashmina 'n' pearls girls. Sunday's pub quiz is legendary. Plan hen nights for Saturdays when drinks are cheaper for 'ladies'.

L'Endroit
67 pl du Dr-Félix-Lobligeois, 17th (01.42.29.50.00).
M° Villiers. **Open** noon-2am daily. Closed 1 Jan-15
Feb. **Credit** MC, V. **Map** p401 F2.
L'Endroit is a slick café on a charming square, where well-dressed, well-behaved 30-somethings lounge. Movie-set lamps diffuse soft light over an art deco-style interior featuring spring-loaded barstools that keep the barflies bouncing while the barmen serve cocktails like chihuahua pearls and purple rains from a motorised carousel of bottles.

Eat, Drink, Shop

The James Joyce

71 bd Gouvion-St-Cyr, 17th (01.44.09.70.32).
M° Porte-Maillot. **Open** 7am-2am daily. **Credit**
AmEx, DC, MC, V. **Map** p400 B3.
A friendly Irish corner pub (is there such a thing as
an *un*friendly Irish pub?) where there's always a
football game to catch and a pint of Guinness to be
had. Joyceian memorablia covers the dark wood
panelling and fills the display cases, and the stained-
glass windows show scenes from *Ulysses*.

Latina Café

114 av des Champs-Elysées, 8th (01.42.89.98.89).
M° George V. **Open** noon-5am daily. **Credit** MC, V.
Map p402 D4.
The Latina Café is a sexy place. But the most important element is the music. And the dancing. Run in
partnership with Radio Latina, the music – including live concerts on Tuesday and Thursdays – is
streets away from the Ricky Martin/Enrique Iglesias
crap peddled at ersatz 'Latino' joints across town.

Polo Room

3 rue Lord-Byron, 8th (01.40.74.07.78/
www.poloroom.com). M° George V. **Open** noon-3pm,
5pm-1am Mon-Thur; Fri, noon-3pm, 5pm-2am Sat;
7pm-1am Sun. **Credit** AmEx, DC, MC, V.
Map p400 D3.
The 'posh' decor here mixes ye olde colonial club
pieces with net curtains, laser lights and low tables
that make it look like a drinking den for leprechauns.
The suave and sophisticated drinks list features
variations on the martini theme – but avoid the man-
darintini, a mix of hair-curling vodka and fizzy
orange. *Wheelchair access.*

Cafés

Granterroirs

30 rue de Miromesnil, 8th (01.47.42.18.18).
M° Miromesnil. **Open** Mon-Fri 8.30am-8pm. Food
served all day. Closed three weeks in Aug. **Credit**
AmEx,V, MC. **Map** p401 F3.
Welcome to snack-time, luxury-style. This gourmet
delicatessen-cum-café is always packed out at
lunchtime with gaggles of local office workers. Don't
be deterred, you cool dudes, you – even if you have
to be shoe-horned onto the benches alongside the
two large picnic tables, it's always worth sinking
your fangs into a snackette here. Sensational tarts.
Wheelchair access.

Handmade

19 rue Jean-Mermoz, 8th (01.45.62.50.05). M°
Franklin D Roosevelt or Miromesnil. **Open** 8am-5pm
Mon-Fri. **Credit** MC, V. **Map** p401 E4.
Englishman Hugh Wilson has created a temple to
chic, and he's done it with missionary zeal. Stone
floor, pale wood tables and minimalist white walls
set the tone, while help-yourself packs of homemade
sandwiches, inventive mini-salads, water or fruit
juice are all carefully packaged, and tea is imported
direct from Delhi. *Wheelchair access.*

Hendrix on the wall at **Les Trois**
Têtards. *See p220.*

Montmartre & Pigalle

Bars

Chào-Bà-Café

22 bd de Clichy, 18th (01.46.06.72.90). M° Pigalle.
Open 8.30am-2am Mon-Wed, Sun; 8.30am-4am Thur;
8.30am-5am Fri, Sat. **Credit** MC, V. **Map** p401 G2.
The former Café Pigalle is now a French Indochina
theme bar that blends in seamlessly with the neon
peep show parlours flanking it on the Pigalle strip.
A bust of Ho Chi Minh looks on approvingly as the
thirsty toast and the hungry dine in fine capitalist
style on Franco-Vietnamese food. Oh, the decadence!

La Fourmi

74 rue des Martyrs, 18th (01.42.64.70.35).
M° Pigalle. **Open** 8am-2am Mon-Thur; 8am-4am Fri-
Sat; 10am-2am Sun. **Credit** MC, V. **Map** p402 H2.
With a retro-industrial decor, long zinc bar and
trademark Duchampian bottle-rack chandelier, this
spacious bar in happening Pigalle buzzes all day and
night with a young, arty crowd and even artier staff,
joined by the odd person from the lower orders.

Cafés

Le Chinon

49 rue des Abbesses, 18th (01.42.62.07.17). M°
Abbesses. **Open** 7am-2am daily. **Map** p402 H1/H2.
The old vino's a bit dodgy, but as long as you stick
to coffee or beer you should be fine, especially if you
follow the lead of the mostly-French clientele and
avoid eating here (watching the bartender eat pasta
should just about put you off anyway). Simply meet
your friends here and appreciate the renovated loo.

CAFE PUCE

BAR • RESTAURANT

This new restaurant in the exciting 11th arrondissement of Paris invites anglophones to come and taste its traditional and inventive cuisine.
Average price: 23 € Sunday brunch

68 avenue de la République, 11th - Tel: 01.43.58.03.03 - M° Saint Maur

Le Sancerre

*35 rue des Abbesses, 18th (01.42.58.47.05). M°
Abbesses.* **Open** daily 7am-2am. Food served all day.
Credit MC, V. **Map** p402 H1/H2.

Don't let the slighty crazy-old-weirdo-of-the-woods
appearance of the staff or the premises fool you.
Service here is always efficient and professional, and
the kitchen crew serves up an appetising selection
of omelettes, salads and sandwiches. The beverage
menu offers an extensive choice of wines or
whiskies. The people-watching possibilities are
every bit as savoury as the food.

The Latin Quarter & the 13th

Bars

La Folie en Tête

*33 rue de la Butte-aux-Cailles, 13th (01.45.80.65.99).
M° Corvisart or Place d'Italie.* **Open** 5pm-2am Mon-
Sat. Closed 25 Dec-2 Jan. **Credit** MC, V. **Map** p406
K10.

On lazy, hazy, crazy summer evenings this throbbing bar is reminiscent of a mobile-phone-and-sun-
glasses Mediterranean student hangout where
carefree tenderlings congregate around their
Vespas, shooting the breeze outside. The four
Belgian beers on tap are good value and happy hour
is unbeatable – not only does it make you extremely happy, but it lasts more than an hour.

The best For hot dates

Le Barramundi

Disappear into the squishy sofas and check
our your date's upholstery. *See p217.*

Chez Richard

The chilled champagne keeps your ardour
harder longer. *See p219.*

China Club

The lights are low, and so are the comfy
chairs. *See p220.*

Les Petits Plus

Create that fairytale atmosphere for your
Little Bow Peep. *See p223.*

Latina Café

The perfect setting in which to unleash your
suave Latin lover routine. *See p225.*

Au Vieux Colombier

Candle-lit and positively throbbing with
promise. *See p229.*

Le Pantalon

*7 rue Royer-Collard, 5th (01.40.51.85.85). RER
Luxembourg.* **Open** 5.30pm-2am Mon-Sat. No credit
cards. **Map** p406 J8.

A bastion of self-consciously anarchic kook. An
ancient hoover attached to a dustbin lid hangs
from the ceiling but manages to seem run-of-the-
mill next to the disembodied arm holding a sun
umbrella and beautifully patterned naked body-
casts. A wild and crazy student crowd downs
drinks to funked-up bagpipe music (we're not
jiving with you here) while a mangy stuffed
sheep overlooks from a miniature balcony. And
all of that before you've had so much as a sip.

Cafés

Le Comptoir du Panthéon

*5 rue Soufflot, 5th (01.43.54.75.36). RER
Luxembourg.* **Open** 7.30am-1am Mon-Sat; 9am-7pm
Sun. **Credit** MC, V. **Map** p406 J8.

This café has been stylishly renovated with contrasting dark wood and crimson velvet furniture,
funky coloured walls and abstract art. The bourgeois, well-dressed students are more likely to be discussing *affaires du coeur,* the right approach to
make to papa for another hand-out or the PSG score
sheet than engaging in political discourse or organising the next demo; and it's all the better for it. The
terrace gives a stunning view of the Panthéon, the
Law Faculty and the Mairie du Vème.

La Route du Cacao

*Quai de la Gare, 13th (01.53.82.10.35/
www.larouteducacao.com). M° Quai de la Gare or
Bibliothèque.* **Open** 10am-7pm Mon-Fri, Sun.
Credit MC, V. **Map** p407 M9/N10.

This *péniche* specialises in decades of the chocolate variety. Each of the six hot chocolate variations
is made to order, so you can choose the level of coag-
ulation. The chocolate chip cookies knocked up on
the premises are always worth a nibble. The rather
functional decor features benches upholstered in car-
pet, but all that is made up for by the view of the sun
setting over the Seine. What a way to add a couple
of kilos to that already-bulging waist-line!
Wheelchair access.

Le Verre à Pied

*118bis rue Mouffetard, 5th (01.43.31.15.72). M°
Censier-Daubenton.* **Open** 8.30am-9pm Tue-Sat; 9am-
2.30pm Sun. No credit cards. **Map** p406 J9.

The buzz of rue Mouffetard can wear you out –
thankfully there are places like this where you can
slow things down with a cold drink. Le Verre à Pied,
open since 1870, recently featured in the smasheroo
film *Le Fabuleux Destin d'Amélie Poulain* (whaddya
mean, you've never heard of it? Don't you read the
film chapter?). Locals and street performers crowd
in at the small tables for homely fare as the market
shuts down for lunch; there is usually just one hot
special. The conversation is great, even if you don't
understand one syllable of it.

Eat, Drink, Shop

Brasil Tropical
Montparnasse

Dinner – Performances
Gives you the new show
"YES BRAZIL"

Tuesday to Saturday from 8pm

Set menus from 50€ during the week (drinks not included)

70€ & 85€ on Fridays and Saturdays (drinks included)

36 rue du Départ, 15th
Reservations: 01.42.79.94.94

Tea rooms

Le Café Maure de la Mosquée de Paris

39 rue Geoffroy-St-Hilaire, 5th (01.43.31.38.20). Mº Censier-Daubenton. **Open** 9am-11.30pm daily. Tea €1.52. Pâtisseries €1.52. **Credit** MC, V. **Map** p406 K9.

Most people make a beeline for the terrace with its landscaped garden and luminous, cobalt-blue pebbles. The interior tearooms decorated in elaborate Moorish style are more comfortable, and air-conditioned, which improves everyone's humour no end.

St-Germain & Odéon

Bars

Le Bar Dix

10 rue de l'Odéon, 6th (01.43.26.66.83). Mº Odéon. **Open** 5.30pm-2am daily. **No credit cards.** **Map** p402 H5.

If you want to converse with the natives, this is the place to do it. Students and oldies merge into a convivial, laid-back melée. Faded posters cover shabby walls but a precariously steep staircase leads down to a much larger, but equally packed cellar. Spot a space, make a bolt for it, order a pitcher of the set drink and settle in for the duration.

Le Comptoir des Canettes

11 rue des Canettes, 6th (01.43.26.79.15). Mº Mabillon. **Open** noon-2am Tue-Sat. Closed Aug, Christmas. **Credit** MC, V. **Map** p405 G7.

The heart of St-Germain still runs red as wine in this historic *bar à vins* (aka Chez Georges), despite the recent, tragic demise of old Georges himself. Street-level is filled with local shop owners and residents while downstairs is host to a younger, student crowd huddled at long tables. RIP, Georgie.

Fu Bar

5 rue St-Sulpice, 6th (01.40.51.82.00). Mº Odéon. **Open** 4pm-2am daily. Happy hour 4-9pm Mon, Wed-Sat; 4pm-2am Tue; 4pm-midnight Sun. Beer 25cl €2.74. Cocktails €6.10-€6.86. **Credit** MC,V. **Map** p405 H7.

The tiny Fu Bar is a brilliant addition to any serious bar hopper's itinerary; it's full of up-for-it Anglos making inroads into the cocktail list. Obscene measures and plenty of punter interaction make this a top choice for a huge night out.

Cafés

Bar de la Croix-Rouge

2 carrefour de la Croix-Rouge, 6th (01.45.48.06.45). Mº St Sulpice. **Open** 6am-10pm Mon-Sat. Food served all day. Beer 25cl €3.2-€4.26. **No credit cards.** **Map** p405 G7.

The Bar de la Croix-Rouge is at the heart of shopping Mecca. It's ideal to stop mid-spend for a quick espresso or kir, as the beautiful ones stroll past. On a sunny afternoon, you'd be hard-pushed to bag one of the pavement tables on the terrace. The dark brown interior is fairly cramped, but buzzing, and the simple food is good value. *Wheelchair access*

Café de Flore

172 bd St-Germain, 6th (01.45.48.55.26). Mº St-Germain-des-Prés. **Open** 7am-1.30am daily. Food served all day. **Credit** AmEx, MC, V. **Map** p405 H7.

The haunt of the Surrealists in the 1920s and '30s is smokier and both rougher and more stylish than Les Deux Magots nearby, with a perpetual buzz and insouciant yet charming waiters. Although it has had no shortage of illustrious customers – Dali, Miró, Breton and Eluard were regulars – the Flore's internationally spun crowd still contains its share of writers, 'intellectuals', filmmakers and artists. Don't worry – the occasional real person pops in, too.

Les Deux Magots

6 pl St-Germain-des-Prés, 6th (01.45.48.55.25/ www.lesdeuxmagots.com). Mº St-Germain-des-Prés. **Open** 7.30am-1.30am daily. **Credit** AmEx, DC, MC, V. **Map** p405 H7.

This is the epitome of the Paris literary haunt (since 1933, it has been awarding its own literary prize — how's that for naff?). Dishes include the usual suspects – charcuterie and *rosbif froid* – as well as more indulgent foie gras and Sevruga caviar. With past regulars such as Sartre and de Beauvoir, Picasso, Verlaine and Hemingway, this was the place to have an Existential crisis; now, however, it's better suited for a financial one.

Les Editeurs

4 carrefour de l'Odéon, 6th (01.43.26.67.76/ www.lesediteurs.fr). Mº Odéon. **Open** 8am-2am daily. Food served noon-2am daily. **Credit** AmEx, MC, V. **Map** p406 H7.

This is a great spot to sip an apéritif and watch the world go by. You don't need to be feeling sociable to come here; the shelves are stacked with books from nearby publishers, which customers are free to peruse if you fancy a bit of a literary pose. Should hunger strike, you can order *choucroute* or lighter dishes such as a club sandwich or roast cod.

La Tour de Pierre

53 rue Dauphine, 6th (01.43.26.08.93/ www. latouredepierre.com). Mº Odéon. **Open** 8am-9pm Mon-Sat. Closed two weeks in Aug. **Credit** MC, V. **Map** p406 H7.

Time stands still in this tiny, award-winning tabac/wine bar on the Left Bank. OK, so it might take an age to get served, but what atmosphere! Where else would you meet an Appeals Court judge dressed in tweeds and quoting Oscar Wilde and a member of the jury for one of France's most notorious serial-killer trials? *Wheelchair access.*

OPEN EVERY DAY AT 12.30 PM EXCEPT MONDAY LUNCH
WEEKEND BRUNCH FROM 12.30 PM TO 3.30 PM
41 RUE DU TEMPLE, 4TH - TEL: 01 42 74 10 38

BAR ᴀ TAPAS
Happy Hour
from 5.30pm to 7.30pm

Au Vieux Colombier

65 rue de Rennes, 6th (01.45.48.53.81).
M° St-Sulpice. **Open** 8am-midnight Mon-Sat; 11am-
8pm Sun. **Credit** MC, V. **Map** p405 G7.
With a long, varnished wood bar, teardrop chandeliers and other art nouveau touches, Au Vieux
Colombier attracts a demographic cross-section of
the area. Making colourful cocktails and serving
cheapish beer and refreshing snacks with blinding
speed, the young staff are friendly and efficient. A
great place to get sloshed, in fact. Full-wall mirrors
combat any feelings of claustrophobia in the small
room and create lovely reflections when the candles
come out at dusk.

Tea rooms

L'Artisan de Saveurs

*72 rue du Cherche-Midi, 6th (01.42.22.46.64). M° St-
Placide.* **Open** noon-6.30pm Tue-Sun. **Credit** MC, V.
Map p405 F8.
From a deep red banquette one can study the inviting menu; the black *thé des lettrés*, 'both spicy and
malty with hints of honey and chocolate', and
Bourbon, 'a South African Roibosch tannin-free tea
flavoured with vanilla' maybe? The mini scones and
apple and walnut muffins come with redcurrant
jelly, butter and whipped cream.

The 7th & the 15th

Cafés

Café du Marché

38 rue Cler, 7th (01.47.05.51.27). M° Ecole-Militaire.
Open 7am-midnight Mon-Sat; 7am-5.30pm Sun.
Credit MC, V. **Map** p405 E6.
You don't really expect to find a relaxed place like
this sandwiched between the Eiffel Tower and
Invalides. This is a perfect place to rest the tootsies
during tourist duties, to have a cheap drink or three
or to enjoy one of the copious *salades composées*
(€7.62) or daily specials that tempt you knowingly
from the blackboard menu (€9.15). *Wheelchair access.*

Au Dernier Métro

70 bd de Grenelle, 15th (01.45.75.01.23/
www.auderniermetro.com). M° Dupleix. **Open** 6am-
2am daily. **Credit** AmEx, DC, MC, V. **Map** p404
C7/D8.
A gem of a café; nay, a treasure. Colourful paintings
and old advertising hoardings line the walls and the
bar has designated elbow space for each of the
habitués, with corresponding floor space for their
faithful and drowsy hounds. The enormous salads
and *plats du jour* are always good choices, and the
welcoming atmosphere means that you're likely to
end up talking to the guy next to you about the cause
of his broken heart or your plans for world domination. Then you can both discuss whether your novels are commercial enough to be accepted by an
agent or simply too high-brow for mass appeal.

Red-eye refuges

Polly Magoo has gone, leaving a gap on
the hangover tour and a bereft crowd
mourning the loss of Paris' worst loo. But
fear not, serious dipsos, the city still has
after-hours oases for those who like to
booze way after the last métro.

Le Crocodile (6 rue Royer-Collard,
5th/01.43.54.32.37) disproves the theory
that locals' bars are full of gummy old men
dribbling into beer; the twenty-somethings
who congregate here prefer to dribble over
each other. Fab table-hopping can be
found at **Mathis** (3 rue de Ponthieu, 8th/
01.53.76.01.62), a cool salon hidden in a
grotty hotel. Expect to be pampered by the
staff, exchange daring witticisms, sit back
and look sensuous. Or just plain drunk.

If you need minimal lighting, **Le Bar** (27
rue de Condé, 6th/01.43.29.06.61) is
perfect. Head to the back of the bar for
subterranean chic in the tunnel section
and lay into the pricey but potent cocktails.
Resolutely alternative, **La Patache** (60 rue
de Lancry, 10th/ 01.42.08.14.35) is the
unlikely but welcoming haunt of local
lushes and slummers. An interesting mix
of Hemingway-loving Americans and French
poseurs and penseurs gather at the
nameless bar at 20 rue des Quatre-Vents
(6th/01.43.26.06.61). Listen to tall
stories at the bar and play weird variations
of backgammon until the early hours, you
wild, tempestuous beasts.

Le Bar: hiccoughs and pick-ups.

La Frégate

*1 rue du Bac, 7th (01.42.61.23.77/www.la-
fregate.com). M° Rue du Bac.* **Open** 7am-midnight
daily. **Credit** AmEx, MC, V. **Map** p405 F7/G6.
Next to the Musée d'Orsay, with a view over the
Seine to the Louvre, there's plenty to look at from
the orderly terrace here. The interior has been
revamped with a curving bar at the front and a second room with larger restaurant tables, more
accommodating for the fish-focused menu.

No Stress Café

27 rue Balard, 15th (01.45.58.45.68). M° Javel.
Open 10am-2am Mon-Fri; 8pm-2am Sat, Sun.
Credit MC, V. **Map** p404 A8/A9.
Although the adverts for massages and other stress-
relieving activities may suggest an upmarket St-
Denis-style pleasure parlour, this is in fact a bona
fide chill-out zone. The tense exhibitionist in you can
be treated to a ten-minute shiatsu massage (fully
clothed). Should pollution levels be at the root of
your stress, you can inhale oxygen-in-a-can à la
Michael Jackson. Or, relieve stress the orthodox way
by having a few beers or cocktails at the bar.

Le Roi du Café

*59 rue Lecourbe, 15th (01.47.34.48.50). M° Sèvres-
Lecourbe.* **Open** 7am-2am daily. **Credit** MC, V. **Map**
p404 B10.
This is the perfect address for lazy, warm summer
evening. Just sitting on the terrace chills you out in
record time. The range of liquor behind the bar
means you'll never run out of fancy drinks to try,
but the real reason for hanging out here is the worn
art deco elegance. OK, maybe it's the drinks, too.

Montparnasse & beyond

Cafés

Café de la Place

*23 rue d'Odessa, 14th (01.42.18.01.55). M° Edgar-
Quinet.* **Open** 7.30am-2am Mon-Sat; 10am-11pm
Sun. **Credit** MC, V. **Map** p405 G9.
This pavement café has a warm feel with a wood-
panelled interior, vintage Ricard jugs and battered
1950s ads. There is also a vast selection of wines on
offer. The real draw, however, is the lively terrace,
a perfect location for a summertime *apéro*.

L'Entrepôt

*7-9 rue Francis-de-Pressensé, 14th (01.45.40.60.70).
M° Pernéty.* **Open** 11.30am-2am Mon-Sat. **Credit**
AmEx, MC, V. **Map** p405 F10.
Something for every taste: a restaurant with leafy
outdoor courtyard, an independent arts cinema, and
a café. The ceilings are high and the matt black walls
are covered with film posters. You can relax on the
couches and listen to music several nights a week.

Le Select

*99 bd du Montparnasse, 6th (01.42.22.65.27).
M° Vavin.* **Open** 8am-3am daily. **Credit** MC, V.
Map p405 F8/H9.
As the setting of events in biographies of writers
such as Hemingway and Fitzgerald, you might think
Le Select would have little need to blow its own
trumpet. But no: this '*bar américain*' is swimming
in its own nostalgia. It's good, but it won't be great
again until it forgets who it used to be.

RECIPROQUE
～ Nicole Morel ～

photo: Pascal Faligot

Featured above are clothes from: CHANEL, DIOR, HERMÈS, CHRISTIAN LACROIX, HERVE LEGER, VUITTON, GUCCI, MOSCHINO, PRADA, VERSACE, VIVIENNE WESTWOOD.

HIGH FASHION
CLOTHING
WOMEN
MEN

CONSIGNMENT SHOP
800m² Retail Space

TRINKETS-GIFTS
ACCESSORIES
JEWELLERY
FURS

The best and biggest second-hand boutique in Paris. Ladies' and men's clothing by famous fashion designers, all in perfect condition.

ALAIA - ARMANI - BOSS - CERRUTI- CHURCH'S - FAÇONNABLE - FERAUD
GALLIANO - GAULTIER - GIVENCHY - DONNA KARAN - KENZO - RALPH LAUREN
LOBB - MIYAKE - MUGLER - MONTANA - REVILLON - ROCHAS - SAINT-LAURENT
PAUL SMITH - TOD'S - WESTON - YAMAMOTO and a lot more...

We buy Hermes, Vuitton, Dior, Chanel, Prada & Gucci for cash. Open all year round.

88, 89, 92, 93, 95, 97, 101, 123 Rue de la Pompe, 16th. M° Pompe.
Tel: 01.47.04.82.24 / 01.47.04.30.28 / Gift: 01.47.27.93.52

photo: Pascal Faligot

Shops & Services

It's time to check your credit limit, throw your inhibitions to the wind and do some Paris purchasing. What do you mean, you only want a carrier bag?

It's easy to feel overwhelmed by the shopping Mecca that is Paris. If you follow the more obvious routes of boulevard St Michel, Les Halles and the Champs-Elysées you run the risk of pushing through crowds all day only to come home with with high stress levels and nothing that you couldn't have bought back home.

Paris has far more specialised shopping areas than many other cities. For non-stop designer labels go to avenue Montaigne and its offshoots or rue du Faubourg St-Honoré. Equally crammed with exclusive retailers is St-Germain, which has all the major chains as well as more small-time treasure troves. Its history of literary greats still gives the Left Bank the edge for books as well as children's clothes and toys.

For a laid-back browse, head to the Marais in the 4th and explore its hip shoe, jewellery, gift and lifestyle boutiques. For ultra-street accessories try rue Française and neighbouring streets around Etienne Marcel in the 2nd. On a sunny day, stroll along the Canal St Martin in the 10th, where you'll find second-hand bookshops and eccentric clothing outlets. For devoted foodies, first stop is place de la Madeleine in the 8th, home to Maison de la Truffe and Fauchon. Antique-lovers should scout out the 7th, and Imelda Marcos wannabes can bolster their collection on rue de Grenelle.

But before you get so laden with bags you can no longer totter on your Gucci heels, there is one serious fact to remember. Crime has risen sharply in Paris in the past year, so watch out for pickpockets on escalators, Métro stations and busy shopping districts. Happy shopping!

Fashion

Concept stores

Over the past few years the art, craft and fashion worlds have fused together, resulting in a fascinating cross-breeding of ideas. The fruits of this creative mix can be found in Paris' new concept stores.

Beauty By Et Vous

25 rue Royale, 8th (01.47.42.31.00). M° Madeleine. **Open** 10.30am-7.30pm Mon-Sat. **Credit** AmEx, DC, MC, V. **Map** p401 F4.

The French fashion chain Et Vous opened this 450-square-metre store devoted to cutting-edge clothes, accessories and beauty in spring 2000. Now it's an essential stop-off for international fashion editors sizing up the latest French designer fantasies. Note in particular the beaten-up, beautifully cut creations of the label Changement de Propriétaire.

Bleue comme Bleu Vendôme

2 rue de Castiglione, 1st (01.58.62.54.54). M° Concorde/Tuileries. **Open** 9.30am-7pm Mon-Sat. **Credit** AmEx, DC, MC, V. **Map** p401 G5.

Following the success of their hair, beauty and tea salon at 47bis avenue Hoche, proprietors Sophie Séguela and Valérie Gérin have taken client pampering a step further with this 'Personal Store'. The ground floor spotlights fashion and beauty brands for women and men, plus babywear, and also has a sleek restaurant. Upstairs, covering 420 square metres, are a men's and women's hair salon, a colour studio and beauty treatment area.

Castelbajac Concept Store

26 rue Madame, 6th (01.45.48.40.55). M° St-Sulpice. **Open** 10am-7pm Mon-Sat. **Credit** AmEx, DC, MC, V. **Map** p405 G7.

The large slabs of white tiling throughout this spacious store give the surreal impression of looking at clothes in a public toilet. Whatever next. Although one of the first designers to combine fashion with furniture and houseware, Jean-Charles de Castelbajac has not lost his passion for Seventies futurism. Hence the predictable rows of white suits, along with utility wear in painfully bright shades. **Branch:** 31pl du Marché-St Honoré, 1st (01.42.60.41.55).

Colette

213 rue St Honoré, 1st (01.55.35.33.90/ www.colette.fr). M° Tuileries. **Open** 10.30am-7.30pm Mon-Sat. **Credit** AmEx, DC, MC, V. **Map** p401 G4.

Truly, madly minimalist accessories are displayed under glass casing in this clinical lifestyle store, as if their WOW factor might be a hazard to customers. Clock the hair and beauty brands själ, Kiehl's, Bumble & bumble, Bliss, Aesop as you enter the store and the ultra-cool reviews and photo albums on the mezzanine. What to wear? Don't despair: find inspiration from the headless dummies (that's the mannequins, not the sales assistants) on the first floor draped with work by new and established fashion artistes. Don't forget to cool off in the famous water bar in the basement.

Upla

17 rue des Halles, 1st (01.40.26.49.96). M° Châtelet.
Open 10.30am-7pm Mon-Sat. **Credit** AmEx, DC,
MC, V. **Map Map** p405 J5.

Proprietor Catherine Barade offers an intriguing
array of independent fashion, accessories, beauty,
condiments and incense in her spacious stores, with
the accent on natural living. Cutest finds are the
Sigitoys stuffed animals. As for your wardrobe,
there are masterfully cut trousers by Angeline
Kingsley (€266.76), Italian merino men's sweaters
in delectable shades (€301.82), along with Upla's
own collection of classics for women and men.
Branch: 5 rue St-Benoît, 6th (01.40.15.10.75).

Department stores

In the scramble to attract a younger clientele,
the major department stores are focusing on
fashion and beauty for women and men.

BHV (Bazar de l'Hôtel de Ville)

*52-64 rue de Rivoli, 4th (01.42.74.90.00/
www.bhv.fr). Tile shop 14 rue du Temple
(01.42.74.92.12); DIY hire annexe 40 rue de la
Verrerie (01.42.74.97.23); M° Hôtel de Ville.* **Open**
9.30am-7pm Mon, Tue, Thur, Sat; 9.30am-8.30pm
Wed, Fri. **Credit** AmEx, MC, V. **Map** p401 G5.

DIY (*bricolage*) fiends spend hours in the basement
of this sprawling hardware store drooling over
hinges, screws, nuts and bolts. There is even a
Bricolage Café, decked out like an old tool shed,
offering hefty salads and a computer to surf DIY
sites. The store has a good choice of men's outdoor
wear, and surprisingly upmarket bedlinen. The
newly opened 2,000-square-metre space Box & Co
section devoted to every type of storage utility imag-
inable will appeal to Parisians squeezed for space.

Le Bon Marché

*24 rue de Sèvres, 7th (01.44.39.80.00). M° Sèvres-
Babylone.* **Open** 9.30am-7pm Mon-Sat.
Credit AmEx, DC, MC, V. **Map** p405 G7.

Le Bon Marché is the most swish and user-friendly
of the major department stores thanks to an extensive redesign by LVMH. The prestigious Balthazar
men's section offers a cluster of designer 'boutiques',
while the major comfort zone for women is the
Theatre of Beauty. Escalators designed by Andrée
Putman take you up to the fashion floor, which
includes the store's own label of well-cut cotton
shirts. In the basement, among toys and books, are
152 pillars designed by Gustave Eiffel. The Grande
Epicerie food hall is in the adjoining building with
an antiques gallery, bar and restaurant above.

Galeries Lafayette

*40 bd Hausmann, 9th (01.42.82.34.56/fashion show
reservation 01.42.82.30.25/fashion advice
01.42.82.35.50/www.galerieslafayette.com).
Cigar cellar 99 rue de Provence. M° Chaussée
d'Antin/RER Auber.* **Open** 9.30am-7pm Mon-Wed,
Fri, Sat; 9.30am-9pm Thur. **Credit** AmEx, DC, MC,
V. **Map** p401 H3.

This vast wedding cake of a department store has
revamped its fashion, beauty and accessories sections. Le Labo on the first floor introduces progressive international creators. Ninety established
designers are spread over the first and second floors
and the store has five fashion and beauty consultants to guide you through the sartorial maze. As for
the household goods labyrinth on the low-ceilinged
upper floors, save yourself the headache. The new
men's fashion space on the third floor of Lafayette
Homme is a must, with its natty designer corners
and 'Club' space with fax and Internet access. The
biggest wine cellar in Paris, with over 3,000 labels,
is on the first floor and there is a cigar counter offering 60 varieties on ground level.

Monoprix

Branches all over Paris. **Open** generally 8am-8pm
Mon-Sat; some branches open till 10pm, including
Roquette, Commerce and Opéra. **Credit** MC, V.

Every *arrondissement* has a couple of these practical stores stocking everything from paper clips to
pâté. The most representative, with its wet fish
counter, cheese and charcuterie displays, bread shop
and fashion department, is on the Champs-Elysées.

Au Printemps

*64 bd Haussmann, 9th (01.42.82.50.00/
www.printemps.com). M° Havre-Caumartin/ RER
Auber.* **Open** 9.35am-7pm Mon Wed, Fri, Sat;
9.30am-10pm Thur. **Credit** AmEx, DC, MC, V.
Map p401 G3.

In October 2001 the Printemps de la Mode store
opened its new 3,000-square-metre luxury area.
Watches take centre stage, but most impressive is
the array of 41 women's shoe brands in the sleek
white space furnished by Ron Arad and Mies Van
der Rohe. Check out, too, the funky makeup artist
brands in the Printemps de la Maison store, along
with its well-stocked home decoration and furnishings departments. For a breather, zoom to the 9th
floor terrace restaurant and take in the art nouveau
cupola. Alternatively, plunge to the basement and
pick out an English thriller on the book shelves in
the 'literary café'.

La Samaritaine

*19 rue de la Monnaie, Ist (01.40.41.20.20). M° Pont
Neuf.* **Open** 9.30am-7pm Mon-Wed, Fri, Sat; 9.30am-
10pm Thur. **Credit** AmEx, DC, MC, V. **Map** p402 J6.

This giant four-store complex covering a total of
48,000 square metres takes its name from the bas-
relief of the Good Samaritan situated on the Pont
Neuf. And today, given the out-dated look of its
departments, you could almost mistake the interior
for a giant charity store. Yet the main building with
its elaborate turquoise and gold wrought-iron work
and magnificent atrium is one of the jewels of the
belle époque, crying out to be restored. Thankfully
its new owner LVMH is planning to do just that,
with a big accent on fashion. In the meantime this
behemoth is worth visiting for its art nouveau
decoration alone.

Shopping in vitro at **Colette**.
See p235.

Collected designerwear

One-stop shops for the hottest clothes, shoes and conversation-piece accessories.

Camerlo

4 rue Marignan, 8th (01.47.23.77.06). M° Franklin D Roosevelt. **Open** 10am-7pm Mon-Sat. **Credit** AmEx, DC, MC, V. **Map** p401 E4.

Exuberant dressers who frequent this swanky area rely on Dany Camerlo to fit them out in head-turning style. Hence her selection of wild ideas from Russian duo Seredin et Vassiliev or Frenchman Laurent Mercier. For more low-key happenings she might suggest Pascal Humbert, Alberta Ferretti or Van der Straeten, with sleek shoes by Bruno Frisoni.

Kabuki Femme

25 rue Etienne Marcel, 1st (01.42.33.55.65). M° Etienne Marcel. **Open** 10.30am-7.30pm Mon-Sat. **Credit** AmEx, DC, MC, V. **Map** p402 G5.

On the ground floor there's intrepid footwear by Costume National, Miu Miu and Prada and bags by the same designers, along with Fendi's cult creations. Burberry belts and Miu Miu sunglasses are also stocked here. Upstairs houses no-flies-on-me suits by Helmut Lang and Véronique Leroy, Prada and Costume National.

Kokon To Zai

48 rue Tiquetonne, 2nd (01.42.36.92.41). M° Etienne Marcel. **Open** 11.30am-7.30pm Mon-Sat. **Credit** AmEx, DC, MC, V. **Map** p402 J5.

The neon lights and club atmosphere in this tiny, mirrored space are in keeping with the dark glamour of its designs. Wickedly *provocateur* T-shirts by Yazbukey hang beside Viktor & Rolf and Bernhard Willhelm, and owner Marjan Pejoski's own designs.

L'Eclaireur

3ter rue des Rosiers, 4th (01.48.87.10.22) M° St-Paul. **Open** 10.30am-7pm Mon-Sat. **Credit** AmEx, DC, MC, V. **Map** p406 L6.

Set in a dandified warehouse with iron girders, L'Eclaireur contains the most uncompromising of the über labels' designs, including pieces by Comme des Garçons, Helmut Lang, Martin Margiela and Prada. On a softer note, succumb to the sorbet-coloured knitwear by Portofino, and the delicious pumps of Angelo Figus.

Branches: for men and women 10 rue Herold, 1st (01.40.41.09.89); for men only (see Mainly Men's Wear) 12 rue Malher, 4th (01.44.54.22.11); and Galerie 26, ave-des-Champs Elysées, 8th

L'Espace Créateurs

Porte Bergere, Niveau–1, Forum des Halles, 1st (times vary; for all info phone 06.21.02.69.65).

Nine boutiques that are a great source of fledgling talent. Names tipped to soar are Belgian Hans de Foer (formerly Jean-Paul Gaultier's assistant) and Cypriot Erotokritos in Boutique des 5; Yao Souka from Laos and award-winning Turkish designer Yesim Chambrey in boutique des 10.

Hunt the treasure at **Kokon To Zai**. *See left.*

Maria Luisa

2 rue Cambon, 1st (01.47.03.48.08). M° Concorde. **Open** 10.30am-7pm Mon-Sat. **Credit** AmEx, DC, MC, V. **Map** p401 G4.

Venuzulean Maria Luisa Poumaillou was one of Paris' first stockists of Galliano, McQueen and the Belgian fashion elite, and has an unflagging eye for stars in the making. A series of shops cover fashion labels (Olivier Theyskens, Diego Dolcini, Jose Enrique Ona Selfa, Rick Owens), shoes and accessories (notably Carel&Rubio's brilliantly inventive gloves), streetware (at 38 rue du Mont Thabor) and men's suits (at 19bis rue du Mont Thabor).

Onward

147 bd St-Germain, 6th (01.55.42.77.56). M° St-Germain des Prés. **Open** 11am-7pm Mon, Sat; 10am-7pm Tue-Fri. **Credit** AmEx, DC, MC, V. **Map** p405 G6.

Ever hungry for the most far out design, Onward has a rapid turnover of young talent. Flavours of the season are Karim Bonnet's paint-splashed cotton concoctions, Bernhard Willhelm's tangled wraps, the floaty chiffon of Markus Lurfer, Boyd's Union Jack linings and the Hello Kitty pumps of Yomeda.

Onze

11 rue Oberkampf, 11th (01.43.55.32.11). M° Filles du Calvaire or Oberkampf. **Open** 11am-7.30pm Mon-Sat. **Credit** AmEx, DC, MC, V. **Map** p403 M5.

Need a break from the designer hot spots? Then head up to the 11th, twice as cool since Canadian Chantal Fortin opened Onze in late 2000. Her choice of experimental young creators rivals Maria Luisa's for filed-down chic – and prices. Look for the laser-printed *trompe l'oeil* skirts of Belgian Christoph Broich, the cardigan jackets of A.T. Shirt and neat Est-ce-que separates. The reading lamps by Tio made from scrap metal are equally irresistible.

Eat, Drink, Shop

Shine

30 rue de Charonne, 11th (01.48.05.80.10).
Mº Bastille. **Open** 11am-7.30pm Mon-Sat.
Credit AmEx, DC, MC, V. **Map** p407 M7.
If you are looking for what some might see as a funkier, more youthful batch of cutting-edge clothes than Maria Luisa's selection, then Vinci D'Elia has just the schmutter you need at Shine. You'll find the lacy creations of Preen and eighties styles of Blaak, both English labels, incidentally. Of course, there are French designs and these French include Anne Valerie Hasch's elegant separates made with traditionally masculine fabrics, and cashmere sweaters by Mathilde. From the US there are supremely feminine silk dresses (€304.90) by Diane Von Furstenberg and Earl Jeans (from €182.94).

Designer focus

A selection of independent designers and established names whose work is intimately bound up with Paris.

Amin Kader

2 rue Guisarde, 6th (01.43.26.27.37). M Mabillon.
Open 2-7.30pm Mon; 10.30am-7.30pm Tue-Sat.
Credit AmEx, MC, V. **Map** p406 H7.
This tiny boutique is a best-kept secret of fashion pros (until now, that is). What keeps them coming back are the Berber couturier's superbly soft Arran-knit cashmere pullovers, fluid crêpe-de-chine trousers and raincoats dripping with elegance. As for Kader's entirely hand-stitched travel bags, they are whisked away in pairs by the happy few. In keeping with his aestheticism-at-all-costs approach, Kader stocks the divine Florentine church Santa Maria Novella's beauty products.

Apoc

47 rue des Francs-Bourgeois, 4th (01.44.54.07.05).
Mº St-Paul. **Open** 10.30am-7.30pm Tue-Sat.
Credit AmEx, DC, MC, V. **Map** p406 L6.
Short for 'A Piece of Cloth', Issey Miyake's lab-style boutique takes a conceptual approach to how clothes are manufactured. Along with ready-to-wear Lycra cotton clothes are great rolls of tubular wool jersey which is cut *sur mesure*. Miyake's assistants will advise you on a unique ensemble.

Balenciaga

10 av George V, 8th (01.47.20.21.11). Mº Alma-
Marceau or George V. **Open** 10am-7pm Mon-Sat.
Credit AmEx, Dc, MC, V. **Map** p400 D4/D5.
Venerable fashion houses have become a stepping stone to stardom for a number of designers, Nicolas Ghesquière included. His style fits Cristobal Balenciaga's like a glove, hence his intention to stick with the Spanish master. Still, since Gucci took over the house in summer 2001, his brooding, sharp-edged ready-to-wear has given way to a looser, more street-easy style for summer.

Barbara Bui

23 rue Etienne Marcel, 1st (01.40.26.43.65). Mº
Etienne Marcel. **Open** 1-7.30pm Mon; 10.30-7.30pm
Tue-Sat. **Credit** AmEx, DC, MC, V. **Map** p402 J5.
Businesspeople who like to cut to the chase have a sartorial ally in Barbara Bui. Dressed in her lean, impeccably cut trousers, figure-hugging shirts and jackets and dagger heels, your wish is the board's command. T-shirts and swimwear come in vacuum packs for hoarding. Naturally.
Branches: 43 rue des Francs-Bourgeois, 4th (01.53.01.88.05); accessories 12 rue des Saints Pères, 6th; 35 rue de Grenelle, 7th (01.45.44.05.14); 50 av Montaigne, 8th (01.42.25.05.25).

Power dressing without stressing at
Barbara Bui. *See above.*

Comme des Garçons
*54 rue du Fbg-St-Honoré, 8th (01.53.30.27.27). M°
Madeleine or Concorde.* **Open** 11am-7pm Mon-Sat.
Credit AmEx, DC, MC, V. **Map** p400 D3.
Rei Kawakubo's juxtaposed design ideas and revolutionary mix of materials have greatly influenced
fashion over the past two decades. The art brut store
also stocks clothes by protégé Junya Watanabe.

Galerie Gaultier
*30 rue du Fbg-St-Antoine, 12th (01.44.68.84.84).
M° Bastille.* **Open** 11am-7.30pm Mon, Sat; 10.30am-
7.30pm Tue-Fri. **Credit** AmEx, DC, MC, V.
Map p407 M7.
There are two Jean Paul Gaultiers, the one that
impregnates his designs with street style, inspired
by his art student years in London, found here; and
the other Gaultier, pretender to the great French couture tradition. Ready to wear is available at both.

Lagerfeld Gallery
40 rue de Seine, 6th (01.55.42.75.51). M° Odéon.
Open 11am-7pm Tue-Sat. **Credit** AmEx, MC, V.
Map p407 H6.
Fans of King Karl can check out the latest cuts of
his cloth at the designer's style laboratory, and tour
a photography exhibition – very probably his own
work. Alternatively, you could just sneak in to
browse the latest fashion, beauty and art press scattered over the handsome round table at the front of
the gallery. All browsers are welcome.

Marcel Marongiu
*203 rue St-Honoré, 1st (01.49.27.96.38).
M° Tuileries.* **Open** 10.30am-7.30pm Mon-Sat.
Credit AmEx, MC, V. **Map** p401 G4.
As if expressing his roots, this part-French, part-
Swedish designer's clothes mix sensuality with
spareness. He is fascinated by opposites, seen in his
ineffably poised jersey wool dresses (€205.81) with
a jagged hemline. Most impressive are his black
evening bustier dresses made of dozens of organza
squares that swish like a mermaid's tail.

Martin Grant
32 rue des Rosiers, 4th (01.42.71.39.49) M° St-Paul.
Open 1-7.30pm Tue-Sat. **Credit** AmEx, MC, V.
Map p406 L6.
The beautiful, chipped tiled floor and worn velvet
chairs in this little boutique give the impression of
a retrofied Prada advert. This is couture, though, as
interpreted by Australian designer Martin Grant. If
you're a stickler for steady cutting and pure textiles
devoid of fussy designs, check him out.

Martine Sitbon
*13 rue de Grenelle, 7th (01.44.39.84.44). M° Rue du
Bac or Sèvres Babylone.* **Open** 10.30am-7pm Mon-
Sat. **Credit** AmEx, MC, V. **Map** p405 G7.
The scent of orange and mimosa lures you deep into
Sitbon's vault-like store. Beneath the vast ceiling,
few pieces hang on the railings, but each appears to
have a secret history, born of the originality of the
fabric and cut and its singular harmony. The men's

clothes will tickle you pink, too. If the prices are out
of your reach (around €700 for a jacket), she has cute
leather mittens at €48.78, her mimosa-scented candles at €28.97 and minute watches in aluminium
cases (€343.01) that slide onto leather bands.

Paule Ka
20 rue Malher, 4th (01.40.29.96.03). M° St-Paul.
Open 10.30am-1pm, 2-7.30pm Mon, Wed; 10.30am-
7.30pm Tue, Thur-Sat. **Credit** AmEx, MC, V.
Map p406 L6.
If Jackie Onassis is your style icon then allow Serge
Cajfinger to make your day. Just the touch of his
satin, organza or taffeta pieces on your fingertips is
enough to make you afraid for your wallet. Console
yourself, these clothes are made to last.
Branches: 192 bd St-Germain, 6th (01.45.44.92.60);
45 rue Francois 1er, 8th (01.47.20.76.10).

Plein Sud
*21 rue des Francs-Bourgeois, 4th (01.42.72.10.60).
M° St Paul.* **Open** 11am-7pm Mon-Sat. **Credit**
AmEx, MC, V. **Map** p406 L6.
Fayçal Amor's glove-tight designs are meant for the
Twiggys of this world, but don't let that faze you if
you're into spiky stilettos, skirts slit to show off your
fishnet tights and a very black, or brown, wardrobe.
Branches: 2 place des Victoires, 2nd (01.42.36.75.
02); 70bis rue Bonaparte, 6th (01.43.54.43.06).

Severine Peraudin
*5 place St-Sulpice, 6th (01.43.54.23.16) M° St-
Sulpice.* **Open** 11am-7.30m Mon-Sat. **Credit** AmEx,
DC, MC, V. **Map** p406 H7.
The French designer works with superfine layers of
stretch polyamide to create delicious evening wear
in two or three tones, such as turquoise and tangerine, pistachio and terracotta, or black, pink and grey.
Prices start at around €150 for a long sleeved top
with a silk V-neck border.

Sonia Rykiel
*175 bd St-Germain, 6th (01.49.54.60.60). M° St-
Germain-des-Prés.* **Open** 10.30am-7pm. **Credit**
AmEx, DC, MC, V. **Map** p406 G6.
Even if her fabrics aren't as super-soft as they once
were, the queen of stripes is still producing skinny
rib knitwear evoking the Left Bank babes of Sartre's
time. True, she is stuck on rhinestones, which do little more than spell out SONIA.

Victoire
*12 place des Victoires, 2nd (01.42.61.09.02)
M° Bourse or Palais Royal.* **Open** 10am-7pm Mon-
Sat. **Credit** AmEx, DC, MC, V. **Map** p405 H5.
This colour-loving designer is as clever at creating
classic separates with quirky edges as she is bagging a neat address. Along with her own designs,
she stocks crowd-pullers such as Macintosh with its
new-look rainwear, and handbag wizards Mirà, Lulu
Guinness and Marie Bouvero.
Branches: women and men 4 rue Duphot, 1st
(01.55.35.95.05); 1 rue Madame, 6th (01.45.44.28.14);
16 rue de Passy, 16th (01.42.88.20.84).

Eat, Drink, Shop

Yohji Yamamoto

3 rue de Grenelle, 7th (01.42.84.28.87). M° Sèvres Babylone or St-Sulpice. **Open** 10.30am-7.30pm Mon-Sat. **Credit** AmEx, DC, MC, V. **Map** p405 G7.

One of the few true pioneers working in the fashion industry today, Yohji Yamamoto's masterful cuts and finish are greatly inspired by the kimono and traditional Tibetan costume. His dexterity with form makes for unique shapes and styles, largely in black, but when he does colour, it's a blast of brilliance. **Branches:** 47 rue Etienne Marcel, 1st (01.45.08. 82.45); Y's 25 rue du Louvre, 1st (01.42.21.42.93), 69 rue des Saints Pères, 6th (01.45.48.22.56).

Lingerie & swimwear

Sheer and transparent fabrics are so much in vogue right now that it's show time for underwear. Paris' slinky lingerie virtuosos will make sure you're well laced up.

Alice Cadolle

14 rue Cambon, 1st (01.42.60.94.94). M° Concorde. **Open** 9.30am-1pm Mon-Sat. Ready-to-wear only on Sat. All *sur mesure* by appointment only. **Credit** AmEx, MC, V. **Map** p401 G4.

Five generations of lingerie *sur mesure* are embodied in this boutique, founded in 1889 by Herminc Cadolle, the inventor of the *brassière*. Her great, great, granddaughter, the suitably Barbie-like Poupie Cadolle, continues the tradition on the belle époque third floor. Poupie's ready-to-wear speciality are bodices and corsets so soigné that Christian Lacroix and Thierry Mugler have made the garments an intrinsic part of their collections. The machine-made bras are impeccably executed, too.

Fifi Chachnil

26 rue Cambon, 1st (01.42.60.38.86). M° Madeleine. **Open** 11am-7pm Mon-Sat. **Credit** AmEx, MC, V. **Map** p401 G4.

Fifi Chachnil offers a modern take on *frou frou* underwear in the pin-up tradition. It's about time someone did, we hear you cry. Her ingeniously chic colour mixes, such as deep red silk bras with boudoir pink bows and pale turquoise girdles with orange trim, will have you purring with pleasure. Transparent black babydoll negligees with a pleated border and empire-line bust are another favourite. **Design studio:** 68, rue Jean-Jacques Rousseau, 1st (01.42.21.19.93).

Sabbia Rosa

73 rue des Saints Pères, 6th (01.45.48.88.37). M° St-Germain-des-Prés. **Open** 10am-7pm Mon-Sat. **Credit** AmEx, MC, V. **Map** p405 G7.

Settle yourself on the soft green leather sofa in this lingerie heaven and let Moana Moatti slip on feather-trimmed satin mules or spread before you satin, silk and chiffon negligées in delicious shades of tangerine, lemon, mocha, pistachio. All sizes are medium, others are made *sur mesure*; prices range from €121.96 for a bra to €335.39 for a peignoir.

Erès

2 rue Tronchet, 8th (01.47.42.28.82). M° Madeleine. **Open** 10am-7pm Mon-Sat. **Credit** AmEx, DC, MC, V. **Map** p401 G4.

Don't be misled by the demure interior of this boutique: the label's beautifully cut, minimalist bikinis and swimsuits are red hot and designed to cause a sensation. They're thoroughly recommended if you want to make a splash. A big advantage for the natural woman is that the top and bottom can be purchased in different sizes, or you can buy just one piece of a bikini – should you lose half somehow, or decide that you don't want all your bases covered. **Branches:** 4bis rue du Cherche-Midi, 6th (01.45.44.95.54); 40 av Montaigne, 8th (01.47.23.07.26); 6 rue Guichard, 16th (01.46.47.45.21).

Izka

140 rue du Fbg-St-Honoré, 8th (01.43.59.07.07). M° Saint Philippe du Roule. **Open** 10am-7pm Mon-Sat. **Credit** AmEx, MC, V. **Map** p400 D3.

Launched in 1999, Gerard Petit's brand of sporty, seamless lingerie has already been snapped up by Warners, who are very big in underwear. The ten skimpy sets of bras and pants in microfibre (one is tempted to collect the whole collection, for fear of being caught short) have accompanying vests and you can mix and match the colours and models to cause gasps of admiration. Prices run from €30.76 for a seamless bra to €85.68 for the seriously wired model. And let's face it, most models appear to be seriously wired. **Branch:** 74 rue de Rennes, 6th (01.45.49.25.85).

Sophie S

15 rue Boissy d'Anglas, 8th (01.42.65.02.52). M° Concorde. **Open** 10am-7pm Mon-Sat. **Credit** AmEx, MC, V. **Map** p401 F4.

Situated opposite the Crillon hotel, this boutique is frequented by VIPs with wives back home to mollify or girlfriends in situ to keep happy. Hubbies and sugar daddies might choose a custom-made satin and chantilly lace slip (€564.06) by in-house designer Karine Gilson. The more fashion-conscious (or even just plain conscious) can make their choice between Dolce et Gabbana, Roberto Cavalli, Dior and Nina Ricci for lingerie and swimwear.

Laurence Tavernier

7 rue du Pré-aux-Clercs, 7th (01.49.27.03.95). M° Rue du Bac. **Open** 10am-7pm Mon-Sat. Closed Aug. **Credit** AmEx, MC, V. **Map** p405 G6.

Laurence Tavernier's beautiful cotton and satin bathrobes and night gowns are so elegant they deserve to be worn outdoors (but don't try it, unless you want to spend a night in the cells – or worse). As for staging a pretty if rather prim bedroom scene, you couldn't do better – handily, the designer is the sister of film director Bertrand Tavernier, so there's plenty of advice on close-ups and key grips. **Branches:** 5 rue Cambon, 1st (01.40.20.44.23); 3 rue Benjamin Franklin, 16th (01.46.47.89.39).

RIP Marks & Spencer

One of the greatest *causes célèbres* – one might even say *scandales* – of the 2001 Paris shopping scene concerned a corner of this foreign field that we had all assumed would remain forever England. What corner? That fruit corner with a much-adored heat-in-the-micro tagliatelle and some unrivalled lingerie was Marks & Spencer. More specifically, the thunderbolt news was that the 18 French branches of that bastion of English retail were to close by the end of the year.

The outrage that followed – well, you really had to be there. It was not simply a question of disgruntled ex-pats lamenting the loss of the chance to rifle through racks of beige trenchcoats, big pants and oh-so-British woolen separates, although there were many snivelling female 30-somethings to be found on street corners, wailing over missed purchases of some of the store's amazing range of all-singing, all-bulge-smoothing hosiery. No, the impact went much deeper, in fact it went right to the heart of the French belief in how people should be treated. It is a fundamental affront to the intrinsically socialist French to see 1,700 jobs cut if there is any viable way of saving them. Should this be filed under cultural difference, or was it just a very tough break?

Whatever the reasons behind the closure, the French were certainly on reliably volatile form to show their displeasure at the demise of the British department giant. Condolence books appeared in the main Paris branch on bd Haussmann. Anti-fat-cat slogans were plastered on shop windows. Customers rioted and started ransacking the shelves, while staff burst into tears. The Prime Minister, Lionel Jospin, employed his best Gallic grimace and called the affair a scandal. And then, in July, the M&S boys suddenly announced that they had decided against simply closing the stores and would, in fact, try to find a buyer to protect people's jobs. Help was at hand in the chivalrous form of French group Galeries Lafayette, who declared that they would take over and save as many jobs as possible. So now you'll see posters of Laetitia Casta wearing little more than a cheeky grin where once was a soft-focus gran sporting thermals in the Lake District. Sadly, Galeries Lafayette is doing little to save the faithful Marks and Sparks brand. The stores will have different names, different layouts and different identities. They won't be M&S any more.

Adieu, M&S. Bye-bye, piped cream profiteroles; so long, little cartons of juice that explode when you poke the straw in; and bonjour yet more high-street uniformity. Stands the Church clock at ten-to-three? And is there chicken tikka still for tea?

Parisian chic

The most Parisian and accessibly priced labels, along with weekend mufti.

Agnès b

2, 3, 6, 10, 19 rue du Jour, 1st (women 01.45.08.56.56/ men 01.42.33.04.13). Mº Les Halles or Etienne–Marcel. **Open** 10am-7pm Mon-Wed, Fri, Sat; 10am-9pm Thur. **Credit** AmEx, MC, V. **Map** p402 J5
Fashions come and ago but Agnès b rarely wavers from her own design vision: pure lines in excellent quality cotton, merino wool and silk. More power to her dainty little elbow for that. Best buys are her shirts, pullovers and cardigans that keep their shape for years. To get the most out of the label, the cool plan of attack is to tour her mini-empire of women, men, children, travel and accessories outlets.
Branches: 83 rue d'Assas (baby/child), 6th (01.43.54.69.21); 13 rue Michelet (women), 6th (01.46.33.70.20); 22 rue St-Sulpice (children), 6th (01.40.51.70.69); 6, 10, 12 rue du Vieux-Colombier (women/beauty/children/men), 6th (01.44.39.02.60); 17, 25 av Pierre 1er de Serbie (women/men), 16th (01.47.20.22.44/01.47.23.36.69).

Antik Batik

18 rue de Turenne, 4th (01.44,78.02.00). Mº Bastille. **Open** 11am 7pm Tue-Sat; 2-7pm Sun. **Credit** AmEx, DC, MC, V. **Map** p402 L5.
This thoroughly chilled-out boutique offers an African take on boho chic, with delicately embroidered dresses and tops and silk blouses in ethnic prints. It does a great line in jazzy bonnets and bandanas, too, along with bejewelled T-shirts of the Eiffel Tower (€83.85) and Arabian-nights slippers. Even if you don't buy anything, it's worth going in just to recharge your buying batteries.

A.P.C.

3, 4 rue de Fleurus, 6th (01.42.22.12.77). Mº St Placide. **Open** 10.30am-7pm Mon-Sat. **Credit** AmEx, MC, V. **Map** p405 G8.
Think of Muji crossed with a rough-cut Agnès b and you get an idea of A.P.C. This gear is much sought after by the Japanese in-crowd. Look out for Londoner Jessica Ogden's wacky shirts and tops: each month designer Jean Toitou gives her 75 A.P.C. items to rework as she likes. Men's clothes are at No 4, along with quirky accessories; cross the road to No 3 for the women's collection.

Claudie Pierlot

1 rue Montmartre, 1st (01.42.21.38.38). Mº Sentier. **Open** 11am-7pm Mon-Sat. **Credit** AmEx, MC, V. **Map** p402 H4.
For true Parisian chic a black beret is essential, and Claudie Pierlot can always oblige no matter what the season. Wear it with her simple, elegant tank tops and cardigans and little black suits so right for the office. Next door Mon Ami Pierlot (01.40.28.45.55) houses a sportier, weekend collection.
Branch: 23 rue du Vieux Colombier, 6th (01.45.48.11.96).

Corinne Sarrut

4 rue du Pré aux Clercs, 7th (01.42.61.71.60). Mº Rue du Bac or St-Germain-des-Prés. **Open** 10am-7pm Mon-Sat. **Credit** AmEx, MC, V. **Map** p405 F7.
Fans of *Amélie Poulain* will be charmed by the work of Corinne Sarrut, who dressed Audrey Tautou for the part. In fact anyone with a weakness for the 40s silhouette will love her trapeze creations in silk-like viscose. Most recent, timeless designs include devoré bias-cut dresses and skirts, skinny rib shirts and mini tweed trench coats.
Branches: (previous season) 24 rue du Champ de Mars, 7th (01.45.56.00.65); 7 rue Gustave Courbet, 16th (01.55.73.09.73); (wedding and evening) 42 rue des Saints Pères, 7th (01.45.44.19.92).

Comptoir des Cotonniers

59ter, rue Bonaparte, 6th (01.43.26.07.56). Mº St-Germain-des-Prés. **Open** 11am-7pm Mon; 10am-7.30pm Tue-Sat. **Credit** MC, V. **Map** p405 H6.
Sturdy cotton and wool basics for mothers and daughters who like to keep in step with fashion. Trendy touches include ruffles on classic cotton jackets (€144.83), zips on velvet coats (€160.97) and fitted leather belts on trousers for a hip silhouette.
Branches include: 29 rue du Jour, 1st (01.53.40.75.77); 18 rue St Antoine, 4th (01.40.27.09.08); 53 rue de Passy, 16th (01.42.88.06.30).

Diapositive

42 rue du Four, 6th (01.45.48.85.57). Mº Sèvres Babylone. **Open** 10.30am-7pm Mon-Sat. **Credit** AmEx, MC, V. **Map** p406 H7.
A practical yet soigné range of grown-up business suits and evening wear that is good value (suits around €380). For a touch of office glamour, and to avoid changing for an evening out, there are gold lamé-speckled fine wool pullovers and sequin-patterned long-sleeved T-shirts.
Branches: 12 rue du Jour, 1st (01.42.21.34.41); 33 rue de Sèvres, 7th (01.42.44.13.00); 20 avenue Ternes, 17th (01.43.80.05.87).

Irié Wash

8 rue Pré-aux-Clercs, 6th (01.42.61.18.28). Mº Rue du Bac or St-Germain-des-Prés. **Open** 10.15am-7pm Mon. Closed 3 weeks in Aug. **Credit** MC, V. **Map** p405 F7.
Elegantly avant-garde Parisians love this Japanese designer who is constantly researching new methods and materials, including laser cutting, hologram prints and most recently a polyester and elastane mix like an ultra-supple suede (€190 for a dress).

Isabel Marant

16 rue de Charonne, 11th (01.49.29.71.55). Mº Ledru-Rollin. **Open** noon-7pm Mon; 10.30am-7.30pm Tue-Sat. **Credit** AmEx, MC, V. **Map** p407 M7.
Marant's clothes are easily recognisable by their ethno-babe brocades, blanket-like coats and heavily decorated sweaters, and the in-crowd is in hot pursuit. Abou Dhabi Bazar stocks her streetwear range.
Branch: 1 rue Jacob, 6th (01.43.26.04.12).

Just the ticket at **Isabel Marant**. *See below.*

Stella Forest

*76 rue Réaumur, 2nd (01.40.26.76.96). Mº
Réaumur-Sébastopol.* **Open** 11am-7pm Mon-Sat.
Credit MC, V. **Map** p402 K4.

Forest's windswept and interesting renegade style,
mixing denim and lace, fake fur and nylon, wool and
pearls, will appeal to wayward teenagers who want
to be hip with class. Isn't that all of us? Tomboys
should clock the funky ties over striped poplin shirts
(€89.84), while glamour kittens might well find
themselves attracted by the floor-length patched
(thankfully) fake furs.
Branch: 61 rue Bonaparte, 6th (01.40.26.76.96).

Tara Jarmon

18 rue du Jour, 6th (01.46.33.26.60). Mº Mabillon.
Open 10.30am-7.30pm Mon-Sat. **Credit** AmEx, MC,
V. **Map** p406 H7.

Shoppers with sunny dispositions shouldn't miss
this charming boutique where black is a rare sight.
The Canadian designer could have had Audrey
Hepburn in mind when designing her freshly-
coloured, no-fuss dresses in natural fabrics. But no:
it was *you* she was thinking of.
Branches: 73 av des Champs-Elysées, 8th
(01.45.43.45.41); 51 rue de Passy, 16th (01.45.24.45.20).

Vanessa Bruno

25 rue St-Sulpice, 6th (01.43.54.41.04). Mº Odéon.
Open 10.30am-7pm Mon-Sat. **Credit** AmEx, DC,
MC, V. **Map** p406 H7.

Vanessa Bruno's very individual clothes have a cool
and steady Zen-like quality that no doubt comes
from her stay in Japan. Working girl skirts and
trousers in faded pink pinstripe (€99.09 and
€144.83) are matched with skinny tops and
sweaters in a rare and refreshing choice of colours.

Zadig et Voltaire

*1 rue de Vieux Colombier, 6th (01.43.29.18.29).
Mº St Sulpice.* **Open** 1-7.30pm Mon; 10.30am-7.30pm
Tue-Sat. **Credit** AmEx, DC, MC, V.
Map p405 G7.

Grungy casual wear in moody shades, besides the
odd flare of neon pink or other eye-blinking tone
of sweater. A regular turnover of cutting edge
designers deposit work here including Moon
Young Hee and Jean Colonna.
Branches: 9 rue du 29 Juillet, 1st (01.42.92.00.80);
4, 12 rue Ste Croix de La Bretonnerie, 4th
(01.42.72.09.55/01.42.72.15.20).

Paul et Joe

*62 rue des Saints Pères, 7th (01.40.28.03.34). Mº
Rue du Bac or St Germain-des-Prés.* **Open** 11am-
7.30pm Mon-Sat. **Credit** AmEx, DC, MC, V.
Map p405 G6.

Fashion victims have taken a great shine to French
designer Sophie Albou's weathered Forties look
creations, so much so that she has opened this
new flagship boutique and a men's wear branch
(Paul and Joe are her sons). The main store aims
to be noticed with its large bubblegum pink
gramophone.
Branches: 46 rue Etienne Marcel (01.40.28.03.34);
men 40 rue du Four, 6th (01. 45.44.97.70).

Street, club & sports wear

There are two ways of following the urban
street wear faith: you can either tail the kids
hip hopping out of Urban Music near Les
Halles, or head up to Etienne Marcel where the
trailblazers of rock chic have their flagship
stores.

Cop. Copine

89 rue Rambuteau, 1st (01.40.28.03.72/www.cop-copine.com). M° Les Halles. **Open** 10.30am-7.30pm Mon, Wed-Sat; 11am-7pm Tue. **Credit** AmEx, MC, V. **Map** p402 K5.

The poor girl's Jean-Paul Gaultier (and, of course, there's no shame in being poor) in sporty, ultra-light polyamide. Prices range from €44.21 for a trashy long-sleeved T-shirt to €106.19 for a long-length, graffiti smeared dress. The question is, are the mauve-haired sixtysomethings in Cop. for themselves or their granddaughters?
Branch: 3 rue Montfaucon, 6th (01.42.34.70.25).

Diesel

21 rue Montmartre, 2nd (01.42.21.87.75). M° Etienne Marcel. **Open** 10.30am-7.30pm Mon-Sat. **Credit** AmEx, DC, MC, V. **Map** p402 K4.

After 20 years in the jeans business, Renzo Rossi is still tapping into teen dreams with brio, and managing to hit the spot with older generations, too. Tripping through the Bettina Rheims-style setting of his flagship Paris store is every bit as supernatural as a trip to South Beach.

Kiliwatch

64 rue Tiquetonne, 2nd (01.42.21.17.37). M° Etienne Marcel. **Open** 2-7pm Mon; 11am-7pm Tue-Thur; 11am-8.30pm Fri; 11am-7.30pm Sat. **Credit** AmEx, MC, V. **Map** p402 J5.

This vast clothes hangar is filled to bursting with hoodies, casual shirts and washed-out jeans. It attracts Paris' hippest crowd, mainly for its latest disco sounds, magazines and club flyers.

Le Shop

3 rue d'Argout, 2nd (01.40.28.95.94). M° Etienne Marcel. **Open** 1-7pm Mon; 11am-7pm Tue-Sat. **Map** p402 J5.

Street-savvy teenagers hang out at this sprawling covered market with its collection of around 25 brands. The male rapper homies and hip-hoppers go for Homecore, Tribal, Body Cult and Triiad (also at 7 rue de Turbigo, 1st), while the girls slip into Lady Soul, Misolka and Oxyde (also at 12 rue de Turbigo).

Le Vestibule

3 place St-Opportune, 1st (01.42.33.21.89). M° Châtelet. **Open** 10.30am-7pm Mon-Sat. Open one Sun in every month. **Credit** AmEx, DC, MC, V. **Map** p402 J5.

An eye-popping showcase for the wildest creations of the vintage street wear and club gear genre, including exhibits by mainstream labels such as Dolce et Gabbana, Bikkembergs and Castelbajac. For effortless flash and panache, Cultura, Diesel StyleLab, Replay and its Coca-Cola Ware label are hard to beat. *Le Vest* is definitely worth a visit, just for the tog-spotting. You don't have to buy.

Marithé et François Girbaud Inside

38 rue Etienne Marcel, 2nd (01.53.40.74.20). M° Etienne Marcel. **Open** noon-7pm Mon; 10am-7pm Tue-Sat. **Credit** AmEx, DC, MC, V. **Map** p402 J5.

This soixantehuitard couple are as pioneering as ever, producing complex street wear in high-tech fabrics using laser cutting and welding.
Branches: 7 rue du Cherche-Midi, 6th; 8 rue de Babylone, 7th (01.45.48.78.86); 49 av Franklin Roosevelt, 8th (01.45.62.49.15).

Murphy & NYE

18 rue du Vieux Colombier, 6th (01.42.22.04.84). M° St Sulpice. **Open** 11am-7pm Mon; 10am-7pm Tue-Sat. **Credit** AmEx, MC, V. **Map** p405 G7.

A specialist in sailing gear, Murphy & NYE can be relied on for classic, lightweight and resilient outdoor clothing with a lean cut to jackets and trousers for men and women; there's even a section for babies. The casual wear items are rarely over €300.

The writing's on the wall at way cool **Le Shop**. *See left.*

Replay

36 rue Etienne Marcel, 1st (01.42.33.16.00).
M° Etienne Marcel. **Open** 10.30am-7.30pm Mon-Sat.
Credit AmEx, DC, MC, V. **Map** p402 J5.
Aficionados of stone-washed, tea-soaked, deeply distressed jeans must hit Replay. Claudio Buziol's store,
resembling a huge recycled, metal-hinged cardboard
box, lies opposite Renzo Rossi's Diesel – once design
partners, the two Italians are now rivals in fashion
sedition. E Play, the label's more radical sibling, is
at 33 rue Etienne Marcel.
Branch: 12 rue Pierre Lescot, 1st (01.40.42.94.88).

Stealth

42 rue du Dragon, 6th (01.45.49.24.14). M° St-
Germain-des-Prés or St Sulpice. **Open** 2-7.30pm
Mon; 10.30am-7.30pm Tue-Sat. **Credit** AmEx, MC,
V. **Map** p406 H7.
Marcus Klosseck, a New York-based indie record
producer and designer is the mastermind behind this
super-cool boutique. His men's label Aem Kei (the
phonetic rendering of his initials) melds New York
street style with European refinement, and his
women's line Aem Aya has fresh ideas. Other urban
underground names to discover here are Tsumori
Chisato, Fake London, Haseltine and the hilariously named Poetry of Sex. Not only that but you can
plug in to unreleased cuts of groovoid R'&'B,
Electronic Grooves and UK Garage.

The Village

22 rue des Halles, 1st (01 40 39 09 06). M° Châtelet.
Open 11am-7.30pm Mon-Sat. **Credit** AmEx, DC,
MC, V. **Map** p406 J5.
In this slickly designed concession store the chaps
will find corners for hot US men's street labels Ecko,
Stussy and North Face and Brit gear Full Circle (a
sort of Paul Smith gone awry in the wash). As for
the girls, there's the trippy, zippy, Mandarin-style
creations of Misolka and vintage trashy chic from
Cultura of Italy. A collection of 50s vintage apparel
is downstairs, *fripe*-freaks.

Vintage, designer cast-offs and discount fashion

The craze for vintage fashion has seen second-
hand clothes shops flourish across the city.
However, given the demand, it's hard to
uncover a good bargain.

Alternatives

18 rue du Roi-de-Sicile, 4th (01.42.78.31.50). M° St-
Paul. **Open** 11am-1pm, 2.30-7pm Tue-Sat. Closed 15
July-15 Aug. **Credit** V. **Map** p402 K6.
This is one of the most stylish, if rather cramped,
boutiques for designer cast-offs in surprisingly good
condition. A men's Burberry coat will set you back
€373.50; you might find women's Miu Miu high-
heels for €120.84, as well as wearable pieces by Jean-
Paul Gaultier, Comme des Garçons and Dries Van
Noten. Well worth a rummage.

La Clef des Marque

124-126 bd Raspail, 6th (01.
M° Vavin. 12.30-7pm Mon; 1
Credit MC, V. **Map** p405 G7
Parents will most certainly
ing discount warehouse for
outdoor, sport and dance wear. Adults are catered
for too, of course. Best bargains in the menswear section are the cashmere and wool Italian sweaters at
€43.94, Lacoste tennis shoes (€28.34) and Adidas
and Superga trainers. For women (or simply fans of
women's clothing) there are naughty sheepskin jackets at €107.66, Christian Dior stockings for €6.37
and jogging and sportswear.
Branch: 86 rue du Fbg St-Antoine, 12th
(01.40.01.95.15).

Le Depôt-Vente de Buci-Bourbon

6 rue de Bourbon-le-Château, 6th (01.46.34.45.05).
M° Mabillon. **Open** 11am-8pm daily. **Credit** MC, V.
Map p405 H7.
What a great name for a shop, eh? Cool is the word
all-round here. These two side-by-side boutiques
have an exuberant mix of high-quality vintage jewellery, coffee services, wild 50s sunglasses and men's
ties. Good-condition women's retro couture items are
mixed with second-hand modern designer clothes
and shoes, all at reasonable prices. You'll leave this
joint with a smile on your face and something fabulously funky in your carrier.

Didier Ludot

19, 20 23, 24 galerie Montpensier, 1st
(01.42.96.06.56). M° Palais-Royal. **Open** 10.30am-
7pm Mon-Sat. *125 galerie Valois, 1st*
(01.40.15.01.04). **Open** 11am-7pm Mon-Sat.
Credit AmEx, DC, V. **Map** p402 H5.
Didier Ludot's series of mini temples to *haute cou-*
ture, including a boutique (galerie Valois) devoted
entirely to little black dresses, have been so successful that he now has a concession in Le
Printemps, his own line (more little black dresses;
mourn or exalt as the mood takes you) and a perfume. There's success for you. Ludot's prices are
exorbitant, but then again he has stunning pieces –
Molyneux, Balenciaga, Fath, Dior, Pucci, Feraud,
Stern et al from the 1940s onwards.

L'Habilleur

44 rue de Poitou, 3rd (01.48.87.77.12). M° St-
Sébastien-Froissart. **Open** 11am-8pm Mon-Sat.
Credit MC, V. **Map** p402 L5.
Urban warriors prowl in that cool way they have
through this slick store for its severely cut men's and
women's wear by John Richmond, Plein Sud,
Martine Sitbon and Bikkembergs, and dagger-toed
shoes by Patrick Cox. All the pieces, which are end-
of-line or off-the-catwalk, are half price. However,
when you compare the original price with
L'Habilleur's mark-down you wonder who would be
fool enough to pay full whack. One presumes that
it's those who can afford to be foolish.

Eat, Drink, Shop

Duck blinds? No, just the changing rooms at **Mandarina Duck**. *See below.*

Accessories

Most fashion boutiques offer a snappy selection of accessories. Rue du Dragon in the 6th is crammed with boutiques offering young designers' creations.

Bags

Jamin Puech

61 rue d'Hauteville, 10th (01.40.22.08.32).
Mº Poissonnière. **Open** 10am-2pm, 3-7pm Mon-Sat.
Credit MC, V. **Map** p402 K3.
The full collection of Isabelle Puech and Benoit Jamin's dazzling handbags are on show here, complete with antler horn chairs and torn-up sofa. Choose from Arran knit and leather bags (€297.28),

densely embroidered holdalls, evening bags covered in tiny metal trinkets and more complex designs.

Jérome Gruet,

9 rue St-Roch, 1st (01.42.92.03.20). Mº Pyramides.
Open 10am-7.30pm Mon-Fri; noon-7.30pm Sat.
Credit AmEx, DC, MC, V. **Map** p401 G5.
Gruet has a style entirely his own, making his boutique a refreshing find. His signature – and brilliantly inspired – material is *toile de jouy*. Slip on beautifully finished espadrilles in the material (€60.98), or pick a matching handbag, makeup pouch or purse slashed with turquoise ribbon.

Mandarina Duck

219 rue St-Honoré, 1st (01.42.60.76.20).
Mº Tuileries. **Open** 10am-7pm Mon-Sat. **Credit**
AmEx, DC, MC, V. **Map** p401 G4.
The Italian label's flagship store attracts visitors as

much for its interior by the Dutch team Droog Design as its travel-light handbags and luggage. The label's speciality is its mix of leather, plastic and nylon resulting in functional pieces at reasonable prices.
Branches: 7 bd de la Madeleine, 1st (01.42.86.08.00); 51 rue Bonaparte, 6th (01.43.26.68.38).

Mériau
81 rue du Bac, 7th (01.45.48.90.65). M° Rue du Bac.
Open 10.30am-7pm Mon-Sat. **Credit** AmEx, MC, V. **Map** p405 G6.
Don't be put off by the deeply retro window displays of this accessories store. Mériau brings three generations of *savoir faire* resulting in infinitely fine leather gloves, umbrellas and silk scarves.

MH Way
17 rue des Saints Pères, 6th (01.42.60.81.65). M° St-Germain des Prés. **Open** 2-7pm Mon; 10.30am-1.15pm, 2-7pm Tue-Sat. **Credit** AmEx, DC, MC, V. **Map** p405 H7.
Looking for solutions for sorting paperwork, travelling light and stowing the wallet? Makio Hasuika, the Japanese designer behind this brand, has all-in-one answers. His briefcase-style handbags (and vice versa), portfolios, shoulder pouches and backpacks come in dozens of forms and are super-light, with pure couture lines.
Branch: 135 bd St-Germain, 6th (01.43.26.27.12).

Peggy Huyn Kinh
11 rue Coëtlogon, 6th (01.42.84.83.83). M° St-Sulpice. **Open** 10am-7pm Mon-Sat. **Credit** AmEx, MC, V. **Map** p405 G7.
This street may not be a flash point for fashion locusts, but that doesn't concern Peggy Huyn Kinh, star designer for Cartier and other luxury heavyweights. Her own label includes a boar skin baguette bag (€419.23) that folds in one twist like a mini accordeon, or a crumpled python skin holdall. She does minimalist silver jewellery, too.

Sisso's
27 rue St-Sulpice, 6th (01.44.07.11.40). M° Odéon. **Open** 10am-2pm, 3-7pm Mon-Sat. **Credit** AmEx, MC, V. **Map** p405 H7.
The selection of glamorous limited-edition accessories in Florence Sisso's boutique ooze cachet. Centrepiece designs include blue suede motorbike helmuts (€221.05), Fendi's delicious baguette bags and logo-spattered raincoats (€347.58).
Branch: 20 rue Malher, 4th (01.44.61.99.50).

Ursule Beaugeste
15 rue Oberkampf, 11th (01.48.06.71.60). M° Oberkampf. **Open** 11am-2.30pm, 3-7pm Tue-Fri; 11.30am-2.30pm, 3-7pm Sat. Closed Aug. **Credit** MC, V. **Map** p403 M5.
Funky name for a shop, or what? Japanese and American style fiends have become so attached to Anne Grand Clément's trademark tweed handbags (€150.92) that she now has a skirt and 'Jeffrey' hat to match. Things just get better and better. She also

stocks calf skin bowling bags, beautifully stitched gloves and beaded purses.

Eyewear

These boutiques showcase eyewear as design objects, focusing on French optic know-how, madcap Los Angeles ideas and Japanese assembly skills.

Traction
6 rue du Dragon, 6th (01.42.22.28.77). M° St-Germain-des-Prés. **Open** 2-7pm Mon, 10.30-7pm Tue-Sat. **Credit** AmEx, DC, MC, V. **Map** p406 H7.
This brand, owned by the Gros family, marries four generations of know-how with a keen sense of modernity. Ask Takeno Fujimine to show you the heavy metal specs that are super-light when worn, or the frames with quirky details on the shaft, if you really want your specs to be conversation pieces. Gone are the days when glasses where mere derision-attracting devices to help you see.

Alain Mikli
74 rue des Saints Pères, 7th (01.53.63.87.40). M° St-Sulpice. **Open** 10am-7pm Mon-Sat. **Credit** AmEx, DC, MC, V. **Map** p405 G7.
This wizard French spectacle designer was among the first to inject some red-hot vroom into prescription peepers. Yes, ladies and gentlemen, this is the dude who made bins sexy. His signature material is cellulose acetate, a wood and cotton mix that is sliced from blocks. The Starck-designed boutique has a central glass counter where the colourful frames are laid out like designer sweeties, while upstairs Mikli's collection of 'travel wear' is displayed in an 18th-century setting.

Lafont
11 rue Vignon, 8th (01.47.42.25.93). M° Madeleine. **Open** 10am-7pm Mon-Sat. **Credit** AmEx, MC, V. **Map** p401 G4.
Philippe Lafont carries on the impeccable, hand-finished work of his grandfather, who founded this optician in 1923. The speciality of his designer wife (that's as in: wife who works as a designer) Laurence is small oval frames that tilt upwards like cat's eyes, perfect, of course, for those small, elfin faces.
Branches: 2 rue Duphot, 1st (01.42.60.01.02); 17 bd Raspail, 7th (01.45.48.24.23).

Hats

Tasteful titfers are freely available in Paris. So are weird creations that are only identifiable as hats because they're worn on the head. Le Bon Marché and Au Printemps stores have extensive hat collections by lots of innovative young creators and international names; millinery maniacs should also check out what's available in the designer boutiques.

Eat, Drink, Shop

Get framed at **Alain Mikli**. *See p247.*

Jacques Le Corre

193 rue St-Honoré, 1st (01.42.96.96.40).
M° Tuileries. **Open** 10am-7pm Mon-Sat. **Credit**
AmEx, MC, V. **Map** p401 G4.
This flamboyant Breton experiments with textures
and pigments to create daywear hats and berets in
unusual fabrics. The shopper reaps the rewards of
these experiments. Some of his large lamb skin bags
have bead patterns stamped on them like braille,
others are dyed in fiery red or warm terracotta.

Philippe Model

33 place du Marché St-Honoré, 1st (01.42.96.89.02).
M° Pyramides. **Open** 10am-7pm Mon-Sat. **Credit**
AmEx, DC, MC, V. **Map** p401 H5.
Since the early 1980s Philippe Model has been performing hat tricks for his Parisian clients. Exuberant
colours and two-tone designs are his signature skills.
So if you're determined to stand out in the wedding,
racing, boating, or golfing crowd, Model is your
man. Prices from €53.36 for a beret to €3811.23 for
a sumptuous *sur mesure* headdress.

Marie Mercié

23 rue St-Sulpice, 6th (01.43.26.45.83). M° Odéon.
Open 11am-7pm Mon-Sat. **Credit** AmEx, DC, MC,
V. **Map** p405 H7.
Mercie's inspirations make you wish you were in an
era when hat wearing was *de rigueur*. What fun to
step out in a Schiaparelli-style creation shaped like
curved fingers complete with shocking pink nail varnish and a pink diamond ring, or a little beret like a
face with huge turquoise eyes and red lips. Ready-
to-wear ranges from €30.49-€68.60. Hats made-to-
measure take 10 days.

Divine

39 rue Daguerre, 14th (01.43.22.28.10). M° Denfert-
Rochereau. **Open** 10.30am-1pm, 3-7.30pm Tue-Sat.
Closed three weeks in Aug. **Credit** AmEx, MC, V.
Map p405 G10.

Hundreds of ready-to-wear hats by milliners across
Europe are united in this boutique, which has
become something of a titferville. There are straw
boaters, Basque berets, deer stalkers, trilbies,
cloches, top hats and floppy ones, so no one is disappointed; even the prices aren't too shocking:
€7.62-€457.35. Proprietor Pascale Testart also has
a selection of vintage millinery in mint condition by
appointment.

Tête en l'Air

65 rue des Abbesses, 18th (01.46.06.71.19).
M° Abbesses. **Open** 10.30am-7.30pm Mon-Sat.
Closed Aug. **No credit cards. Map** p402 H1.
Couture duo Thomas and Anana have been creating wayward hats for attention-seeking Parisians
for eight years. Anana's favourite creation was a
Bacchus-style overflowing goblet worn by a client
at Longchamps. Prices from €53.36 to €533.57 for
the wildest client ideas.

Jewellery

In this city of artisans there is certainly no lack
of jewellery designers. Here is a small selection
of the best to suit all tastes and pockets.

Cérize

380 rue St-Honoré, 1st (01.42.60.84.84).
M° Concorde. **Open** 10am-7pm Mon-Sat. **Credit**
AmEx, DC. MC V. **Map** p401 G4.
Don't be misled by the slightly gaudy window displays: this boudoir-pink boutique has impressively
crafted costume jewellery. Look out, too, for the
evening bags with embroidery by François Lesage,
godfather of Christian Lacroix and embroider to all
the star couturiers. There are also some excellent,
eye-popping T-shirts showing blondes wearing little else besides strass. It's worth a visit if only to
check those out.

Galerie Hélène Porée

1 rue de l'Odéon, 6th (01.43.54.17.00) Mº Odéon.
Open Tue-Sat 11am-7pm; Dec 11am-7pm daily.
Credit AmEx, MC, V. **Map** p406 H7.
Around 40 international ultra-minimalist designers
are represented in this starch-white gallery. You can
expect temptation to be placed firmly in your path.
The French contingent includes Chavent, with his
trompe l'oeil pieces, and Schotard who creates an
intriguing mousse effect with precious metals. Prices
start at €12.20 for a porcelain amulet by Belgian
Pete Stockmans and run into hundreds and thousands, whatever your currency reference.

Kathy Korvin

13 rue de Tournon, 6th (01.56.24.06.66) Mº Odéon.
Open 10am-7pm Mon-Fri; 11am-7pm Sat. **Credit**
AmEx, MC, V. **Map** p406 H7.
This Franco-American jeweller specialises in spider's web-thin silver necklaces and bracelets encir-
cling semi-precious stones, feathers and Swarovksi
crystals, which give an even airier quality to the
pieces. Her necklaces with nests of fine crocheted
gold or silver are particularly elfin. Prices start at
€22.87 for simple silver earrings to €365.88 for a
heavy gold pendant.

La Licorne

38 rue de Sévigné, 4th (01.48.87.84.43). Mº St-Paul.
Open 11.30am-6.30pm daily. **Credit** AmEx, DC,
MC, V. **Map** p406 L6.
The musty smell at La Licorne is perhaps not surprising given it harbours the contents of a costume
jewellery factory dating from 1925-30s. Anyway,
don't be put off by the whiff (how many times have
you heard that, girls?). Besides the abundance of art
deco Bakelite, there is a veritable treasure trove of
50s diamanté, as well as some 19th-century jet.

Mi Amor & Sicamor

*10 & 20 rue du Pont Louis-Philippe, 4th
(10.42.71.79.29/01.42.76.02.37). Mº St-Paul or Pont
Marie.* **Open** 11am-7pm daily. **Credit** AmEx, MC,
V. **Map** p406 K7.
City bohos gravitate to these two jewellery and
accessories shops with their psychedelic installations and curtains of funky necklaces and earrings
made from multi-coloured recycled glass, iron filings
and cotton coils (€15.24-€121.96). The remarkably
stylish headgear includes pretty, wrapped-around
silk scarves and playful – some would even say
cheeky – berets from €13.18.

La Reine Margot

7 quai de Conti, 6th (01.43.26.62.50). Mº Pont Neuf.
Open 10.30am-1pm, 2pm-7pm Mon-Sat. **Credit**
AmEx, DC, MC, V. **Map** p406 H6.
Gilles Cohen, proprietor of this beautiful antiques
gallery, invites international jewellers to create mod-
ern pieces using ancient stones, amulets and seals.
This approach results in some truly exquisite pieces
designed by masters of their craft. Prices are sur-
prisingly reasonable, starting at €274.41 for a
Francisca Miro 22 carat gold ring.

Satellite

*10 rue Dussoubs, 2nd (01.55.34.95.70). Mº Reamur-
Sébastopol.* **Open** 10am-7pm Mon-Sat. **Credit**
AmEx, MC, V. **Map** p402 K5.
Stylist Sandrine Dulon uses only the best quality
material from the Czech Republic and Bavaria. The
brilliance of the stones and intricacy of the work
results in enchanting earrings, bracelet and necklace
ensembles. Prices are from €9.89 to €659.11.
Branches: 15 rue du Cherche-Midi, 6th
(01.45.44.67.06); 23 rue des Francs-Bourgeois, 4th
(01.40.29.45.77).

Shoes

Au Printemps' luxury floor (*see p236*) is an
excellent source of designer labels, including
Hermès shoemaker Pierre Hardy, who is
making a name for himself solo.

Alain Tondowski

*13 rue de Turbigo, 2nd (01.42.36.44.34). Mº Etienne
Marcel.* **Open** 10.30am-7.30pm Mon-Sat. **Credit**
AmEx, MC, V. **Map** p402 J5.
Tondowski's shoes bring to mind the footnotes of a
fashion illustration – a few perfectly executed
squiggles. Besides being super elegant, his designs
(from around €300) have a taut, urban edge, highlighted by the boutique with the models framed in
polished metal and Plexiglas cubes.

Pleasure treasure at **La Licorne**. *See left.*

Anatomica

14 rue du Bourg Tibourg, 4th (01.42.74.10.20).
Mº Hôtel de Ville. **Open** 10.30am-7pm Mon-Sat;
3-7pm Sun. **Credit** AmEx, DC, MC, V. **Map** p406 K6.
Sensible footwear backers and fashion victims (you
can be both) love this store devoted to natural form
shoes; it has the Paris franchise for Birkenstocks –
every model and colour are represented. Other
brands include Trippen and Cydwoq.

Christian Louboutin

19 rue Jean-Jacques Rousseau, 1st (01.42.36.05.31).
Mº Palais Royal. **Open** 10.30am-7pm Mon-Sat.
Closed Aug. **Credit** AmEx, DC, MC, V.
Map p402 J5.
Each of Louboutin's creations, with their hallmark
red soles, are displayed in individual frames, like
Cinderella's slipper. His Trash mules – incorporat-
ing used Métro tickets, glitter, torn letters and
postage stamps – are particularly coveted.
Branch: 38 rue de Grenelle, 7th (01.42.22.33.07).

Free Lance

30 rue du Four, 6th (01.45.48.14.78). Mº St-
Germain des Prés. **Open** 10am-7pm Mon-Sat.
Credit AmEx, MC, V. **Map** p405 H7.
Guy and Yvon Rautureau design for women who
walk on the wild side. How else do you explain red
PVC Prince of Wales check ankle boots with ice-pick
toes and heels (€320.14), thigh-length white boots
with splashes of lime green and pink paint or
spindly pink pony skin stilettos?
Branches: 22 rue Mondétour, 1st 42.33.74.70; for
men 16 rue Bourg Tibourg, 4th (01.42.77.01.55); 22
rue de Sèvres, 7th (01.42.22.94.02)

Gelati

6 rue St-Sulpice, 6th (01.43.25.67.44) Mº Odéon.
Open 10am-7pm Mon-Sat. **Credit** MC, V.
Map p405 H7.
If you want your feet to be always in vogue but can't
afford designer prices then go for Gelati. The once-
Italian (now French) company offers a stylish range
of court and evening shoes in the hippest shapes and
colours. Prices start at around €115.

Iris

28 rue de Grenelle, 7th 01.42.22.89.81) Mº Rue du
Bac. **Open** 10.30am-7pm Mon-Sat. **Credit** AmEx,
MC, V. **Map** p405 F7.
Iris is the Italian manufacturer of shoes by Marc
Jacobs, Ernesto Esposito, Alessandro Dell'Acqua and
Veronique Branquino, which is why you'll find these
designers' whole footwear range in its dazzlingly
white boutique. Esposito's pieces are recognisable
by their flower patterns (€381.12), inspired by his
late chum Andy Warhol's work. Dell'Acqua's fetish
is hand-pleated leather pumps (€373.50).

Michel Perry

4 rue des Petits Pères, 2nd (01.42.44.10.07).
Mº Etienne Marcel. **Open** 10.30am-7pm Mon-Sat.
Credit AmEx, MC, V. **Map** p402 J5.
If you like your shoes high and colourful, then Perry

Pierre Victoire offers the *crème de la crème* of vintage couture. *See p254.*

is most assuredly your man. You can also tell a
Perry by its width: he designs Westons, the classic
shoe for Frenchmen, perhaps why his women's models are on the broad side. They are not so broad that
you'll feel your feet rattling around within and hitting the sides, however. The real draw of this boutique is the fantastic selection of hot labels including
Chloé, Olivier Theyskens, Boyd, Gilles Rosier and
Julien McDonald.
Branch: previous season's collection only at L'autre
boutique, 42 rue de Grenelle, 7th (01.42.84.12.45).

Robert Clergerie

5 rue du Cherche-Midi, 6th (01.45.48.75.47). Mº St-
Sulpice. **Open** 10am-7pm Mon-Sat. **Credit** AmEx,
MC, V. **Map** p405 G7.
Clergerie has thankfully settled back into designing
his exquisitely practical daywear. The maestro has
even revived that two-tone loafer he created at the
start of his career in 1981. Not that he is out of the
fashion ring: his stylised 'boxing trainer' Tatoute
(€301.85) knocks the socks off other models. True,
prices are high, but the mark-up for Clergerie in
Britain will take your breath away.
Branches: 46 rue Croix des Petits Champs, 1st
(01.42.61.49.24); 18 ave Victor Hugo, 16th
(01.45.01.81.30).

Rodolphe Menudier

14 rue de Castiglione, 1st (01.42.60.86.27)
Mº Concorde. **Open** 10.30am-7.30pm Mon-Sat.
Credit AmEx, MC, V. **Map** p401 G5.
This silver and black cylinder of a boutique is a perfect setting for Menudier's racy designs that mix
moods and materials. Dozens of open silver-handled
drawers display his stilettos laid flat in profile. Mini
shopping trolleys are filled with wayward shades of
exclusive hosiery made by Gerbé and Chantal
Thomass. If that's not pampering enough, then slip

Eat, Drink, Shop

upstairs for a RM pedicure or a spot of reflexology and let your feet know just how much you love them.

Men

Admirers of the *BCBG* style of dressing should check out branches of Vercourt and Berteil, or Phist and Alain Figaret for shirts. For the best international overview of male clothing and footwear pick **Le Bon Marché** and **Galeries Lafayette Homme**. As for the hip Parisian, here are a few pointers.

L'Eclaireur Homme
12 rue Malher, 4th (01.44.54.22.11). M° St-Paul.
Open 11am-7pm Mon-Sat. **Credit** AmEx, DC, MC, V. **Map** p406 L6.
Among the exposed ducts of this former printing works you'll find the usual designer suspects: Prada, Comme des Garçons, Dries Van Noten, Martin Margiela. The star label, though, is Italian Stone Island, whose radical technical clothing features parkas with a 'steel outer shell' to fight pollution.

Façonnable
9 rue du Fbg-St-Honoré, 8th (01.47.42.21.18.04). M° Concorde. **Open** 10.30am-7pm Mon-Sat. **Credit** AmEx, DC, MC, V. **Map** p401 F4.
Façonnable may be largely the domain of the BCBG male, but its timeless city slicker suits and country-gent cords are of too good a quality to be bypassed. Particularly tempting are soft suede jackets (€754.62) and checked shirts (€83.85).

Jack Henry
54 rue des Rosiers, 4th (01.44.59.89.44). M° St-Paul. **Open** 2.30-8pm daily. **Credit** AmEx, DC, MC, V. **Map** p406 K6.

This thirtysomething New Yorker has been honing his sartorial skills in Paris for over a decade. The spare, dark suits (around €560) in his tiny boutique offer a fine, elongated silhouette, enhanced by chest-hugging knitwear. It is inspired by US combat gear, but this means discipline in hidden details rather than pockets in unlikely places.
Branch: Henry's women's wear is at 1 rue Montmartre, 1st (01.42.21.46.01).

Lanvin
15 rue du Fbg-St-Honoré, 8th (01.44.71.33.33). M° Concorde. **Open** 10am-6.45pm Mon-Sat. **Credit** AmEx, DC, MC, V. **Map** p401 F4.
If you feel all shopped out, then Lanvin will restore your faith in consumerism. The exquisite business suit fabrics, such as meltdown Prince of Wales checks, will have shareholders mesmerised, while the numerous ply cashmere sweaters will soften up any resistance.

Loft Design
12 rue du Fbg-St-Honoré, 8th (01.42.65.59.65). M° Madeleine or Concorde. **Open** 10am-7pm Mon-Sat. **Credit** AmEx, DC, MC, V. **Map** p401 F4.
Thirteen years ago Patrick Freche decided to produce clothes colour-coordinated with the Paris skyline, ie, grey and black. It turned out to be not such a dull idea as Loft now has a cult following with the Paris media and fashion crowd.

Madelios
23 bd de la Madeleine, 1st (01.53.45.00.00). M° Madeleine. **Open** 10am-7pm Mon-Sat.
Credit AmEx, DC, MC, V. **Map** p401 G4.
Soulless it may be, but men on the move will find what they need in this 4,500-square-metre emporium. For the fashion aware there is Dirk Bikkembergs, Paul Smith, Helmut Lang and Comme des

Garçons; for hunting and shooting look for Holland & Holland and Barbour, while city wear specialists include Daks, Dormeuil and Givenchy.

Anthony Peto

56 rue Tiquetonne, 2nd (01.40.26.60.68).
M° Etienne Marcel. **Open** 11am-7pm Mon-Sat.
Credit AmEx, MC, V. **Map** p402 J5.
Ubiquity is not for men of the world, which is why gents appreciate the creations of British *chapelier* Mr Peto. Expect *sur mesure* and ready-to-wear hats from Panamas to sexy trilbies and Rasta berets (€106.71-€152.45) from this subtle colourist. Complementing his singular designs are scarves by Vivienne Westwood, ties by Duchamp and cufflinks by Paul Smith.

Soy!

22 rue Cambon, 1st (01.47.03.02.02). M° Concorde.
Open 10am-7pm Mon-Sat. **Credit** AmEx, MC, V.
Map p401 G4.
The funky selection here includes colourful high-cotton shirts by discreet Paris designer Eric Bergere, subtle *tromple l'oeil* pullovers by New York Industries, chill-out gear by Dirk Bikkembergs and Italian suits by Trend Collection. It's just a pity the sales assistant was helpful as a tailor's dummy.

Victoire Hommes.

15 rue du Vieux Colombier, 6th (01.45.44.28.02/
www.victoire-paris.com). M° St-Sulpice. **Open**
10.30am-7pm Mon-Sat. **Credit** AmEx, DC, MC, V.
Map p405 G7.
Cloth and wool connoisseurs choose Victoire for her relaxed business and outdoor wear. Regulars whisk away the raincoat, jacket or trousers they fancy double-quick as she only stocks one example for each size in most designs. Her shirts come in lots of groovy shades and stripes, and some have Liberty patterns inside the cuffs, to reveal only when you're in the mood (are you ever not? Be honest). There are dandy accessories, too.
Branches: 10-12 rue du Colonel-Driant, 1st (01.42.97.44.87); 4 rue Duphot, 1st (01.55.35.95.01).

Children

Children's clothes & shoes

Young urban sophisticates head straight for Baby Gap, Gap Kids, Agnès b, Zara and **Bill Tornade Enfants** (or Baby Dior and Gucci if you've got the bank balance). For the classic French *BCBG* look, rush to **Bonpoint** or **Jacadi**; for cheap-and-cheerful try **Du Pareil au Même**, Dipaki and Tout Compte Fait. Natalys caters for expectant mums and kids. Monoprix's good-value children's sections are worth a look too. There are clusters of kids' shops on the Faubourg St-Antoine and in rues Bréa and Vavin in Montparnasse.

Bill Tornade Enfants

32 rue du Four, 6th (01.45.48.73.88).
M° St-Germain des Prés. **Open** 10.30am-7pm
Mon-Fri, 10.30am-7.30pm Sat. Closed Aug. **Credit**
AmEx, MC, V. **Map** p405 H7.

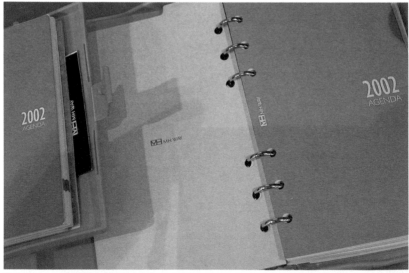

Suave accessories at **MH Way**. *See p249.*

Designer Sylvia Rielle's sophisticated children's wear is more for trendy parties than everyday rolling around on the floor and fighting. Lots of shiny, sparkly modern fabrics.

Jean Bourget
167 rue St-Jacques, 5th (01.44.07.03.48). RER Luxembourg. **Open** 10am-7pm Mon-Sat. **Credit** MC, V. **Map** p406 J8.
Stylish, well-made clothes for children under 15, with plenty of the fancy buckles, funky pockets, Velcro and clever details that appeal to kids.

Jacadi
76 rue d'Assas, 6th (01.45.44.60.44/www.jacadi.fr). M° Vavin. **Open** 10am-7pm Mon-Sat. **Credit** MC, V. **Map** p405 G8.
Jacadi's child and babywear – especially pleated skirts, smocked dresses, dungarees and fair isle knits – are a favourite with well-to-do parents. But the clothes are well made and there's funky stuff too. Some branches stock shoes and baby equipment. **Branches include:** 9 av de l'Opéra, 1st (01.49.27.06.29; 4 av des Gobelins, 5th (01.43.31.43.90).

Du Pareil au Même
15-17 rue des Mathurins (Maison at 23), 8th (01.42.66.93.80). M° Havre-Caumertin/RER Auber. **Open** 10am-7pm Mon-Sat. **Credit** MC, V. **Map** p401 G3.
Colourful, hard-wearing basics (three months to 14 years) at remarkably low prices; although note that sizing tends to be small. 18 basic shops have been joined by DPAM Maison or DPAM Bébé shops, which are great for gifts. **Branches include:** 122 rue du Fbg-St-Antoine (Maison at 120), 12th (01.43.44.67.46); 6 rue de l'Ouest (Maison at 15), 14th (01.43.20.59.51).

Petit Bâteau
26 rue Vavin, 6th (01.55.42.02.53). M° Vavin. **Open** 10am-7pm Mon-Sat. **Credit** MC, V. **Map** p405 G8.
Petit Bateau is the place for undies, bodies and the famous cotton T-shirts. **Branches:** 81 rue de Sèvres, 7th (01.45.49.48.38); 116 av des Champs-Elysées, 8th (01.40.74.02.03).

Les Petits Bourgeois
35 rue de Turenne, 3rd (01.48.04.38.88). M° St Paul. **Open** 10am-7pm daily. **Credit** AmEx, MC. **Map** p406 L6.
Classy clothes and shoes (Burberry, Timberland, Charabia etc). Prices range from expensive to extortionate, with a few cheaper (and funkier) options.

Six Pieds Trois Pouces
223 bd St-Germain, 7th (01.45.44.03.72). M° Solférino. **Open** 10am-7pm Mon-Sat. Closed Mon in Aug. **Credit** AmEx, V. **Map** p405 F6.
An excellent range of children's and teens' shoes goes from classics by Startrite, Aster and Little Mary to trendy Reeboks and Timberland, as well as shoes under its less expensive own label. **Branches include:** 85 rue de Longchamp, 16th (01.45.53.64.21); 78 av de Wagram, 17th (01.46.22.81.64).

Bill Tornade Enfants. *See p254.*

Toy & book shops

Cosy traditional toyshops abound in Paris, while the new chains offer multimedia. The gadgets at Pier Import are a favourite with pre-teens. Department stores all provide animated windows and gigantic toy floors at Christmas. The best sources of children's books in English are WH Smith and Brentano's (*see pp262-3*).

Apache
84 rue du Fbg-St-Antoine, 12th (01.53.46.60.10/ www.apache.fr). M° Ledru Rollin. **Open** 10am-8pm Mon-Sat. **Credit** MC. V. **Map** p407 M7.
The shape of toyshops to come. A brightly lit, colourful two-storey space with an activities studio and cyber-café. Equally colourful goodies go from marbles and soft toys to fancy dress, space hoppers and videos. There's also furniture and bath gear.

Chantelivre
13 rue de Sèvres, 6th (01.45.48.87.90). M° Sèvres-Babylone. **Open** 1-7pm Mon; 10am-7pm Tue-Sat. **Credit** MC, V. **Map** p405 G7.
This specialist children's bookshop leads from teen reads to picture books and a baby section. There are publications on children's health and psychology for parents, a small English-language section, plus CDs, videos, paints, stationery and party supplies. Books are arranged sometimes by theme and sometimes by publisher, which can be confusing.

How to be a boho Goddess

Coming to Paris can be an unsettling experience for any female with curves. Walking along the city's narrow streets you notice the people are narrow and pointy too, which can leave you slightly nervous when it comes to looking stylish. However, help is at hand in the form of the original Parisian look: the boho. This term is applied to anyone looking vaguely (and artfully) dishevelled, or like a wealthy, image-conscious gipsy. Bohemian chic can be pulled off by virtually anyone, and the good news is it allows you to have a bum and a bust.

'Vintage' has become a buzzword for Hollywood stars, and it's what the boho look is all about: mixing second-hand and classic pieces and wearing the result with panache. The trick is to look like you don't care what you're wearing even though you've planned it meticulously. Follow our guide and you'll have effortless style in minutes.

The essential item in any bohemian's wardrobe is the totally impractical skirt. Think lace, think billowing, think high, dry cleaning bills. A good place to start is cheap and chic Spanish label **Zara** (128 rue de Rivoli, 1st, 01.44.82.64.00/Mº Chatelet; and branches), which puts twists on wardrobe basics. You'll find ruffled shirts, sassy takes on Edwardian blouses and elegant floor length coats. Marais boutique **Abou Dhabi** (10 rue des Francs-Bourgeois, 3rd, 01.42.77.96.98/Mº St-Paul) has gorgeous mid-calf skirts in denim and wool with lace fringes and unusual cuts. Slightly more expensive is Japanese boutique **Fengge** (3 rue Française, 1st, 01.42.33.90.03/Mº Etienne Marcel), just behind Forum des Halles. Run by Joan Kong, this tiny shop stocks designer labels such as Yesim Chambrey and Elsa Esturgie, and is crammed with spider-web knitted separates, felt skirts and quirky Perspex wrist-cuffs to give your look that eclectic edge.

Secondly, every boho must have the perfect bag. It must be worn nonchalantly, and should ideally be outrageous. Your first port of call is **Lollipops** (60 rue Tiquetonne, 2nd, 01.42.33.15.72/Mº Etienne Marcel and branches), a fast-growing bag outlet that caters for every possible taste, colour and material. There are Manga-inspired retro shoppers with Lichtenstein car prints, crunchy green leather purses and lacy red clutch bags for extra Moulin Rouge flounce. Lollipops also have great badges, hatpins and brooches or customising your more ordinary clothes.

Finally you need to attend to your feet, which don't have to be overly comfortable as the boho girl spends most of her time sipping coffee and reading books. Pop into kooky favourite **Antoine et Lili** (95 quai Valmy, 10th, 01.40.37.41.55/Mº Jacques Bonsergent and branches), where you'll find Chinese clogs or felt slippers. For colder days, try **L'Est Rose** (9, rue de Turbigo, 1st, 01.40.39.07.00/Mº Etienne Marcel) for soft Victorian boots. After that you can browse **Antoine et Lili's** very pink shops for some funky fairy lights and candles, to set off that artistic ambience in your Parisian garret. You can also try **Le Chant des Sirènes** (31 rue Beaurepaire, 10th, 01.42.08.80.51/Mº Republique) for those funkadelic sea-shell lamps and mermaid mirrors.

Now that you're snug in your furry shoes, floaty skirt and laissez-faire attitude, all that's left is to purchase some boho literature. For contemporary photography, architecture, film and art books head down to **La Librairie de la Creation (artazart)** (83 quai Valmy, 10th, 01.40.40.24.00/Mº République), and choose from such bizarre gems as *The Illustrated Penis*, *The Larger Illustrated Penis*, *Ronnie Reason's Guide to Life*, *This is Blythe* and *Taxi Driver Wisdom*.

In the pink **Antoine & Lili**. ⟩

Les Cousines d'Alice

36 rue Daguerre, 14th (01.43.20.24.86). M° Denfert-Rochereau. **Open** 10am-1.30pm, 2.30-7.15pm Mon; 10am-7.15pm Tue-Sat; 11am-1pm Sun. Closed 3 weeks in Aug. **Credit** MC, V. **Map** p405 G10.

This shop is crammed with soft toys, well-selected books and construction games. There are also plenty of inexpensive pocket-money treats.

Fnac Junior

19 rue Vavin, 6th (01.56.24.03.46). M° Vavin. **Open** 10am-7.30pm Mon-Sat. **Credit** AmEx, MC, V. **Map** p405 G8.

The Fnac group has turned its hand to books, toys, videos, CDs and CD-roms for under-12s. Many things take an educational slant but there are fun basics, too. The shop lays on storytelling and activities (mainly Wed, Sat) for 3s-up, from makeup, magic and mime to multimedia. Helpful staff, good layout, and games that can be tried out. **Branches**: Bercy Village, cours St-Emilion, 12th (01.44.73.01.58); 148 av Victor-Hugo, 16th (01.45.05.90.60).

La Grande Récré

27 bd Poissonnière, 2nd (01.40.26.12.20). M° Grands Boulevards. **Open** 10am-7.30pm Mon-Sat. **Credit** AmEx, MC, V. **Map** p402 J4.

The French toy supermarket (local rival to Toys R Us) may lack the charm of more trad compatriots but its shelves are packed high: pink and plastic for girls, guns and cars for boys, plus craft sets and Playdoh, Gameboys, Pokémon spin-offs and the like.

La Maison du Cerf-Volant

7 rue de Prague, 12th (01.44.68.00.75). M° Ledru-Rollin. **Open** 10am-7pm Tue-Sat. **Credit** V. **Map** p407 M7.

Spend anything from €6 to €1,067 on every kind of kite: dragons, galleons, scary insects and acrobatic stunt kites. If it flies, it's here.

Au Nain Bleu

406-410 rue St-Honoré, 8th (01.42.60.39.01). M° Concorde. **Open** 9.45am-6.30pm Mon-Sat. **Credit** AmEx, MC, V. **Map** p401 G4.

Dating from 1836, France's most prestigious toy shop is the nearest you'll get to London's Hamley's only stuffier and more old-fashioned. Toys from all around the world range from furry animals to electronic games. No lifts.

Pain d'Epices

29 passage Jouffroy, 9th (01.47.70.08.68). M° Grands Boulevards. **Open** 12.30-7pm Mon; 10am-7pm Tue-Thur; 10am-9pm Fri, Sat. **Credit** MC, V. **Map** p402 H4.

Everything a self-respecting doll would need, from tiny cutlery to toothpaste. There are also dolls' house kits or the finished thing, and a selection of traditional dolls, teddies, marionettes and wooden toys.

Les Petits Plus

23 bd Beaumarchais, 4th (01.48.87.01.40). M° Bastille. **Open** 10am-7.30pm daily. **Credit** DC, MC, V. **Map** p406 L5.

This bright and funky shop stocks fantastic household gifts and loads of toys (look out for Babar, Hello Kitty and the occasional Tellytubby). Upstairs you'll find a tearoom with light bites, cooking and guide books and novelty foodstuffs to take home.

Pylones

57 rue St-Louis-en-l'île, 4th (01.46.34,05.02). M° Pont Marie. **Open** 10.30am-7.30pm daily. **Credit** AmEx, MC, V. **Map** p406 K7.

Hilarious gadgets and knick-knacks for kids and kids-at-heart. Furry pencil cases, animated postcards and Wallace and Gromit toothbrushes.

Health & Beauty

Makeup & perfume

L'Artisan Parfumeur

24 bd Raspail, 7th (01.42.22.23.32). M° Rue du Bac. **Open** 10.30am-7pm Mon-Sat. **Credit** AmEx, DC, MC, V. **Map** p405 G7.

Among scented candles, potpourri and lucky charms you will find the best vanilla perfume Paris can offer – Mûres et Musc, a bestseller for more than 20 years. L'Artisan also offers the unusual Dzing!, a powerful scent for women.

Editions de Parfums Frédéric Malle

37, rue de Grenelle, 7th (01.42.22.77.22/fax 01.42.22.77. 33/www.editionsdeparfums.com) M° Rue de Bac. **Open** 11am-7pm Mon-Sat. **Credit** AmEx, MC, V. **Map** p405 E6/F7.

Designed by Olivier Lempereur and Andrée Putman, Editions de Parfums is quite a showcase. Choose from eight exclusive perfumes made by top creators commissioned by Frédéric Malle, a former consultant for Christian Lacroix, Chaumet and Hermès.

Guerlain

68 av des Champs-Elysées, 8th (01.45.62.52.57). M° Franklin D Roosevelt. **Open** 10.30am-8pm Mon-Sat; 3-7pm Sun. **Credit** AmEx, MC, V. **Map** p401 E4.

This bijou boutique is one of the last vestiges of the golden age of the Champs-Elysées, although the family sold the company to LVMH some years ago. Head 'nose', Jean-Paul Guerlain is still producing outstanding creations, such as the Aqua Allegorica range, including the sublime Eau de Pamplun.

L'Occitane

55 rue St-Louis-en-l'Ile, 4th (01.40.46.81.71). M° Pont-Marie. **Open** 10.30am-7.30pm Mon-Sat. **Credit** AmEx, DC, MC, V. **Map** p406 K7.

The 22 branches of this Provençal chain in Paris proffer natural products in artistic packaging. Soap rules, but there's also essential oils and perfumes.

Eat, Drink, Shop

Make Up For Ever Professional

5 rue La Boétie, 8th (01.42.66.01.60).
M° Miromesnil. **Open** 10am-7pm Mon-Sat. Closed
Sat in Aug. **Credit** AmEx, DC, MC, V. **Map** p401 E3.
Despite the name, this is a French outfit. With loads
of glitter, hair spray, nail varnish, lipstick, fake
eyelashes and stick-on tatoos, prepare for a colour
explosion.
Branch: 22 rue de Sèvres, 7th (01.45.48.75.97).

Parfums Caron

*34 av Montaigne, 8th (01.47.23.40.82). M° Franklin
D. Roosevelt.* **Open** 10am-6.30pm Mon-Sat.
Credit AmEx, DC, MC, V. **Map** p401 E4.
In its elegant art deco boutique, Caron sells re-
editions of its classic favourites from 1911-54,
including the spicy, eastern rose scent Or et Noir.

Séphora

70 av des Champs-Elysées, 8th (01.53.93.22.50).
M° Franklin D Roosevelt. **Open** 10am-midnight
Mon-Sat; noon-midnight Sun. **Credit** AmEx, MC, V.
Map p401 E4.
The flagship of this cosmetic chain carries 12,000
French and foreign brands of scent and slap.

Beauty salons & spas

The city's legendary beauty salons are as
sought-after as ever, but two younger
generation brands, Anne Sémonin and Samuel
Par, have a more personalised cachet.

Anne Sémonin

*2 rue des Petit Champs, 2nd (01.42.60.94.66). M°
Bourse or Pyramides.* **Open** 10am-7pm Mon, Wed,
Fri, Sat; 10am-8pm Tue, Thur. **Credit** AmEx, DC,
MC, V. **Map** p402 H5.

This is a very Zen salon; very cool, very relaxed,
very dungaree-and-organic digestives in feel.
Aromatherapy oils, creams and lotions made from
natural ingredients are juggled to create the perfect
elixir for each client. Had a late night? Jump-start the
body with a mask of algae and essential oils of ylang
ylang (try saying that when you've had a few),
cypress, lavender and palmarosa (€22.11 for 50ml);
or ask for Sémonin's Jet Lag Treatment, a volcanic
mud bath incorporating iron elements of seawater.
Branch: Le Bristol, 108 rue du Fbg St Honoré, 8th
(01.42.66.24.22).

Les Bains du Marais

*31-33 rue des Blancs-Manteaux, 3rd
(01.44.61.02.02). M° Rambuteau.* **Open** 11am-8pm
Mon, Tue; 11am-7pm Wed. **Credit** V. **Map** p402 K6.
This shop offers a luxurious modern take on the
hammam experience with spotless steam rooms. For
a full day's indulgence, lunch in the sleek café and
choose from beauty treatments such as facials and
essential oils massages. It's a tough life.

Carita

11 rue du faubourg St Honoré, 8th (01.44.94.11.29).
M° Concorde or Madeleine. **Open** 9.30am-6.45pm
Mon-Sat. **Credit** AmEx, MC, V. **Map** p401 F4.
Brace yourself. Gird up those loins. Beauty requires
some sacrifice. Be prepared for an unforgiving
microscopic study of your skin. After that, you'll be
shamelessly pampered with treatments starting
with Rénovateur – a defoliation scrub with a base
sunflower seed oil, Carita's trademark ingredient.
Scissors superstar Jean-Claude Gallon keeps the
hairdressing salon a veritable hot spot.
Branch: Carita Tyala, 39 rue du Cherche Midi, 6th
(01.45.49.13.57); Carita Montaigne, 3 rue Boccador,
8th (01.47.23.76.79).

Be thoroughly cleansed at **Carita**.
See right.

Guerlain Institut de Beauté
68 av des Champs-Elysées, 8th (01.45.62.11.21).
Mº Franklin D Roosevelt. **Open** 9.30am-6.45pm Mon-
Sat. **Credit** AmEx, MC, V. **Map** p401 E4.
An air of luxe and exclusivity reigns here, even if
the opulence is somewhat faded. The beauticians are
very agreeable and the repertoire of treatments is
excellent, using all-natural products, usually plant
based, just the job for slapping a load of goo all over
your face and feeling fresh and relaxed. A facial
includes a fabulously fantastic face massage, fee
€105.04 for 90 minutes.
Branch: 29 rue de Sèvres, 6th (01.42.22.46.60).

Lancôme Institut
29 rue du faubourg St Honoré, 8th (01.42.65.30.74).
Mº Concorde or Madeleine. **Open** 10am-7pm Mon-
Sat. **Credit** AmEx, DC, MC, V. **Map** p401 F4.
If you're a fan of Lancôme products, a trip to its
beauty institute is the ideal way to learn exactly
which creams, tonics and sebums are best for you.
Not only that, but you'll also discover the most effective way to apply them. Best of all, you will be in the
fairy hands of top-notch beauticians. Try one of their
rejuvenating one-hour facials for a mere €67.99.

Samuel Par
46 rue Madame, 6th (01.45.49.22.21). Mº St Sulpice.
Open 10am-7pm Tue-Sat. **Credit** MC, V.
Map p405 G7.
You can sense the work of an artist on entering this
orange-scented salon, once the studio of Poliakoff
and now of Patrick Sounigo, the proprietor of
Samuel Par. It positively exudes creative inspiration,
and the medium will be you. But don't worry – it's
all done painlessly. Hot towels laid on the face or
body are the first step to decompression. A facial
Revitaliser (€64.03 for 90 minutes) of plant extracts
from the South of France is almost as good as actually being there.

Home

Antiques

If you're after antiques and retro it helps to
know who specialises in what: traditional
classy antiques in the **Carré Rive Gauche** of
the 7th, **Village Suisse** and Fbg-St-Honoré, art
deco in St-Germain, 1950s-70s retro plastic
around rue de Charonne in the 11th, antiquarian
books and stamps in the covered passages, in
the *bouquinistes* along the *quais*, or at **Parc
Georges Brassens**. Then, of course, there are
the **Marchés aux Puces de St-Ouen**,
Montreuil and **Vanves**, and auction house
Drouot, now joined by Sotheby's and
Christie's. There are also frequent *brocantes* –
antiques and collectors' markets, especially in
summer. Look for notices in listings magazines
and advertising banners hung in the streets.

The nose how

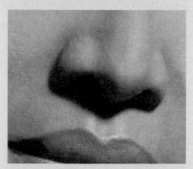

Emilie Coppermann is a professional nose.
Not a gossip columnist, nor a model, she
belongs to an elite group of individuals
who are paid to sniff things. Noses are the
connoisseurs of the world of smell, highly
sensitive to the subtleties of every odour
around them. Emilie is a brave woman –
there is no natural smell she doesn't like.
Whatever flares this lady's nostrils usually
ends up in a chic bottle and sells for big
bucks: she's the lady who turns your bog
standard Charlie into Chanel No.5.
  Ms.Coppermann discovered her passion
for aromas as a child. Quickly progressing
to graduate from the prestigious Versailles
Nose Academy, she went on to schmooze
with the creators of such esteemed pongs
as Opium, Dune and Amarige. She now
runs her own company, split between Paris
and New York. Her nose is, perhaps
unwisely, uninsured. What if she got it
caught in a métro door?
  Anyone looking to break into the world of
nosedom should heed Emilie's advice.
First, you must be able to recognise all the
primary ingredients, of which there are
around four hundred. Next you must match
them harmoniously, then copy floral scents
and finally reproduce existing perfumes.
Sensitive hooters can improve with
training, but most professionals have a
natural gift. The creative process is all
about finding new ideas and new
materials. So if your dinner guest happens
to writhe with joy at the combination of
pumpkin and parsley, take out your
notebook and set to work – no odour is
too strange, all whiffs hold inspiration.
As for Emilie, her favourite smell is,
ironically, unperfumed skin.

Eat, Drink, Shop

Design, furniture & tableware

Le Bihan

41 rue du Fbg-St-Antione, 11th (01.43.43.06.75).
Mº Bastille. **Open** 2-7pm Mon; 10am-7pm Rue-Sat.
Credit AmEx, V. **Map** p407 M7.
In case you thought the Faubourg was now entirely clothes shops or mock Louis XV, check out Le Bihan, a three-floor showcase for the best of modern design. Furniture and lighting go from re-editions of Perriand, Gray and Van der Rohe to top contemporaries like Pesce, Pillet, Santachiara, Morrison, Arad et al.

Bô

8 rue St-Merri, 4th (01.42.72.84.64). Mº Hôtel de Ville. **Open** 11am-8pm Mon-Sat; 2-8pm Sun.
Credit AmEx, MC, V. **Map** p406 K6.
Chic, pared-back contemporary style. Candlesticks, vases, unusual lights, new-agey incense burners and elegant grey Limoges porcelain are all *très bô*.

Christophe Delcourt

125 rue Vielle-du-Temple, 3rd (01.42.78.44.97).
Mº Filles du Calvaire. **Open** 10am-7pm Mon-Fri;
11am-7pm Sat. **Credit** MC, V. **Map** p402 L6.
The French furniture designer has moved into a larger shop laid out as a series of rooms where Delcourt's designs can be seen alongside contemporary ceramics. Art deco-influenced geometrical lines are given a contemporary edge as stained wood is often combined with waxed black steel in elegant low dressers, dining tables and lamps.

CFOC

170 bd Haussmann, 8th (01.53.53.40.80).
Mº St-Philippe-du-Roule. **Open** 10am-7pm Mon-Sat.
Credit AmEx, DC, MC, V. **Map** p401 E3.
La Compagnie Française de l'Orient et de la Chine is full of eastern promise, from Chinese teapots and celadon bowls, lacquerware, Mongolian pottery and Iranian blown glass to slippers and silk jackets. Downstairs is an art deco interior by Ruhlmann.
Branches include: 163, 167 bd St-Germain, 6th (01.45.48.00.18); 65 av Victor-Hugo, 16th (01.45.00.55.46).

Dîners en Ville

27 rue de Varenne, 7th (01.42.22.78.33). Mº Rue du Bac. **Open** 2-7pm Mon; 10.30am-7pm Tue-Sat.
Closed 2 weeks in Aug. **Credit** MC, V. **Map** p405 F6.
New and antique tableware stylishly displayed: colourful glasses, Italian earthenware, fancy cutlery and luxurious tablecloths.

Etat de Siège

1 quai Conti, 6th (01.43.29.31.60). Mº Pont Neuf.
Open 10.30am-7pm Mon-Sat. **Credit** AmEx, MC, V.
Map p405 H6.
Packed with stylish seating arrangements, from Philippe Starck gnome stools to understated classics. Puts a firm emphasis on funky *fauteils*.

Kartell Flagship Shop

242 bd St-Germain, 7th (01.45.48.68.37).
Mº Rue du Bac. **Open** 10am-1pm, 2pm-7pm Tue-Sat
Credit MC, V. **Map** p405 G6.
Kartell, something of a futuristic warehouse, stocks the work of designers such as Philippe Starck, Piero Lissoni and Antonio Citterio. Sophisticated office lines are presented upstairs; downstairs, a lollipop-coloured feast goes from Ron Arad's Bookworm to Philippe Starck's gnome stools and Ero/s armchairs.

Muriel Grateau

131 Galerie de Valois, Jardins du Palais-Royal, 1st (01.40.20.90.30). Mº Palais Royal. **Open** 11am-12.30pm, 1-7pm Mon-Sat. **Credit** AmEx, MC, V.
Map p401 H5.
If your taste is for sobriety, then you'll love Grateau's contemporary minimalist chic. Biscuitware, linen tablecloths, porcelain and glasses and towels are elegantly displayed. Serious stuff at serious prices.

Potiron

57 rue des Petits-Champs, 1st (01.40.15.00.38).
Mº Quatre Septembre. **Open** 10am-8pm Mon-Sat.
Credit V. **Map** p401 H4/H5.
Ethnic knick-knacks, sparkly cushions, fake-fur throws and fab, affordable tableware. Stock changes regularly to keep up with trends and there's always something to make your studio a little more *soigné*.

Yves Delorme

8 rue Vavin, 6th (01.44.07.23.14). Mº Vavin.
Open noon-7pm Mon; 10.30am-1.30pm, 2.30-7pm
Tue-Sat. **Credit** AmEx, MC, V. **Map** p405 G8.
Extravagant thread-counts with prices to match. The ludicrously soft sheets in tastefully muted tones

The best Shops

For the pick of catwalk cool

Concept store **Beauty By Et Vous** *(see p235)* to schmooze with the fashion editors.

For made-to-measure underwear

Bodices and corsets at luxurious boutique **Alice Cadolle** *(see p242)*.

For one-stop shopping

Crockery to clothing at price-friendly **Au Printemps** *(see p236)*.

For wannabe buskers

Find yourself a new squeeze at **Paris Accordéon** *(see p264)*.

For a little light reading

Browse through French literature and theory at **La Hune** *(see p264)*.

To liven up your daily bread

A natural at **L'autre Boulange** *(see p267)*.

Get your table well and truly laid at **Dîners en Ville** *See left.*

are ideal for four-posters and futons alike.
Branch: 96 rue St-Dominique, 7th (01.45.55.51.10).

Fabrics & trimmings

Maison de la Fausse Fourrure
34 bd Beaumarchais, 11th (01.43.55.24.21).
Mº Bastille. **Open** 11am-7pm Mon-Fri. Closed Aug.
Credit AmEx, MC, V. **Map** p407 M6.
The 'House of Fake Fur' pays tribute to our furry friends. Synthetic animal-print coats, bags and hats in a choice of chic 'leopard' or cheeky 'monkey', as well as furniture and bolts of fake fur fabric.

Marché St-Pierre
pl St-Pierre, 18th. Mº Anvers or Barbès
Rochechouart. **Dreyfus** *2 rue Charles-Nodier, 18th*
(01.46.06.92.25). **Open** 10am-6.30pm Tue-Sat;
Tissus Reine *5 pl St-Pierre, 18th (01.46.06.02.31).*
Open 2-6pm Mon; 9.30am-6.30pm Tue-Sat.
Moline *1 pl St-Pierre, 18th (01.46.06.14.66).*
Open 1.30-6.30pm Mon; 9.30am-6.45pm Tue-Sat.
Credit AmEx, MC, V. **Map** p402 J2.
These three shops have the best selections of fabrics. Reine has selections of discounted silks and luxury fabrics. Moline specialises in upholstery fabrics. Dreyfus is a crowded, five-floor warehouse, with home furnishing fabrics and discounted bolts.

Flea markets

One man's trash is another man's treasure trove, and nowhere can you delve deeper (and in more rubbish) than at the capital's flea

markets. Dealers will generally come down by 10 to 15 per cent, though don't expect too much of a concession as most are well aware of what they are selling. Watch out for pickpockets.

Marché aux Puces d'Aligre
pl d'Aligre, 12th. Mº Ledru-Rollin.
Open 9am-noon daily.**Map** p407 N7.
The only puces within the Paris walls has origins going back before the French Revolution. Remaining true to its junk tradition, you'll find a handful of *brocanteurs* peddling books, kitchenwares, phone cards and knick-knacks at what seem optimistically astronomical prices.

Marché aux Puces de Vanves
av Georges Lafenestre and av Marc-Sangrier, 14th.
Mº Porte de Vanves. **Open** 7.30am-7pm Sat, Sun.
Begun in the 1920s, this is the smallest and friendliest of the Paris flea markets. Conviviality and civility reign, and a stroll through the colourful stands here makes for a peaceful, gently stimulating Sunday morning outing. If you get here early enough, there are decent buys for collectors of dolls, 1950s costume jewellery, glass, crystal, old photographs, magazines (*Picture Post, Life*) and prints, eau de cologne bottles, biscuit tins, lace, linens and buttons.

Marché aux Puces de Montreuil
93100 Montreuil-sous-Bois, Mº Porte de Montreuil.
Open 7.30am-7pm Sat, Sun, Mon.
The monster of all flea markets – less in terms of size than pure anarchy. In this sense, it is the mar-

ket that remains closest to its origins. Like one vast car boot sale, it disgorges mountains of second-hand clothing, indistinguishable parts for cars, showers and sundry machines, and a jumble of miscellaneous rubbish from its dusty not to say downright grungy bowels. You'll find little pre-1900, but there are fun collectables like *pastis* jugs. Stallholders shout out their prices above the din; feisty women push their prams over your toes, but the *souk*-like soul of the place will win you over in the end.

Florists

Christian Tortu
6 carrefour de l'Odéon, 6th (01.43.26.02.56).
M° Odéon. **Open** 10am-8pm Mon-Sat. Closed 2 weeks in Aug. **Credit** AmEx, DC, MC, V. **Map** p405 H7.
Paris' most celebrated florist is famous for combining flowers, twigs, bark and moss into still lifes. You can buy his accessories at 17 rue des Quatre-Vents.

Mille Feuilles
2 rue Rambuteau, 3rd (01.42.78.32.93).
M° Rambuteau or Hôtel de Ville. **Open** 2-9pm Mon; 10am-9pm Tue-Sat. Closed 2 weeks in Aug. **Credit** AmEx, MC, V. **Map** p406 K6
Wonderfully scented Mille Feuilles mixes genres, with fresh flowers, garden statuary, ceramics, pots and chandeliers all cluttered together. 2 Mille Feuilles, across the road at 59 rue des Francs-Bourgeois, has painted wrought-iron garden furniture, glasses and lead planters.

Kitchen & bathroom

Bains Plus
51 rue des Francs-Bourgeois, 4th (01.48.87.83.07).
M° Hôtel de Ville. **Open** 11am-7.30pm Tue-Sat; 2.30-7pm Sun. **Credit** AmEx, MC, V. **Map** p406 K6.
The ultimate gentleman's shaving gear, duck-shaped loofahs, seductive dressing gowns, chrome mirrors and Provençal bath oils and soaps.

E Déhillerin
18 rue Coquillière, 1st (01.42.36.53.13).
M° Les Halles. **Open** 8am-12.30pm, 2-6pm Mon; 8am-6pm Tue-Sat. **Credit** MC, V. **Map** p402 J5.
Suppliers to great chefs since 1820, this no-nonsense warehouse has every kitchen utensil from gigantic ladles to stacks of Le Creuset. It's excellent for knives, the best and cheapest shop in Paris for copper pots and one of the few places in the world you can buy a special razor blade for slitting baguettes.

Kitchen Bazaar
11 av du Maine, 15th (01.42.22.91.17).
M° Montparnasse-Bienvenüe. **Open** 10am-7pm Mon-Sat. **Credit** AmEx, MC, V. **Map** p405 F8.
A festival of chrome gadgetry and modish accessories, Kitchen Bazaar is perfect for buying a few luxury items after sorting out the essentials. 1950s -throwback KitchenAid blenders join space-age kettles, graphite cutlery, and (insofar as pepper grinders

can be sexy) sexy pepper grinders. Bath Bazaar Autrement (6 av du Maine, 15th/ 01.45.48.89.00), across the street, sells bathroom goodies.
Branches: 23 bd de la Madeleine, 1st.

A Simon
48, 52 rue Montmartre, 2nd (01.42.33.71.65).
M° Etienne-Marcel. **Open** 1.30-6.30pm Mon; 8.30am-6.30pm Tue-Sat. **Credit** AmEx, MC, V. **Map** p402 J5.
This professional kitchen supplier mixes quality goods and cheery tat. Chefs' briefcases of knives sit next to Tefal woks and beautiful glassware shares a shelf with cheekily phallic salt cellars. Sabatier, Au Nain and Culineer knives are reasonably priced and their cake-making selection is excellent.

Leisure

Books

See also Fnac and Virgin Megastore in **Music & CDs** below.

Attica (Language Learning Bookshop)
64 rue de la Folie Méricourt, 11th (01.49.29.27.27/www.attica.fr). *M° Oberkampf.*
Open 10am-2pm Mon; 10am-7pm Tue-Sat. **Credit** MC, V. **Map** p403 M5.
Having problems with your French, or fancy twisting your tongue on a new language altogether? Choose from one of 320 covered by Attica's range of books, CD-roms, dictionaries and video/audio cassettes. There's a solid body of European language learning tools (with a leaning towards English) and a great but eclectic mix of the more obscure.

Bouquinistes
Along the quais, especially quai de Montebello, quai St-Michel, 5th. M° St-Michel. **Open** times depend on stall, Tue-Sun. **No credit cards.** **Map** p406 J7.
The green boxes along the *quais* are a Paris institution. Ignore the nasty postcards and rummage through the stacks of ancient paperbacks for something existential. Pick & mix for bibliophiles – be sure to haggle.

Brentano's
37 av de l'Opéra, 2nd (01.42.61.52.50). M° Opéra.
Open 10am-7.30pm Mon-Sat. **Credit** AmEx, MC, V. **Map** p401 G4.
A good address for American classics, modern fiction and bestsellers, plus an excellent array of business titles. The children's section is in the basement.

La Chambre Claire
14 rue St-Sulpice, 6th (01.46.34.04.31). M° Odéon.
Open 2-7pm Mon; 10am-7pm Tue-Sat. **Credit** MC, V. **Map** p406 H7.
Specialises in photography, with plenty of titles in English and a photography gallery downstairs.

Puces d'Aligre – one person's rubbish is
another person's, er, rubbish. *See p261*.

Galignani

224 rue de Rivoli, 1st (01.42.60.76.07). M° Tuileries.
Open 10am-7pm Mon-Sat. **Credit** AmEx, MC, V.
Map p401 G5.
Opened in 1802, Galignani was reputedly the first
English-language bookshop in Europe, and at one
point even published its own daily newspaper.
Today it stocks fine- and decorative-arts books and
literature in both French and English.

Gibert Joseph

26, 30 bd St-Michel, 6th (01.44.41.88.88).
M° St-Michel. **Open** 10am-7.30pm Mon-Sat.
Credit AmEx, MC, V. **Map** p406 J7.
Best known as a bookshop serving the Left Bank
learning institutions, as well as a place to flog text
books. Some titles in English.

La Hune

170 bd St-Germain, 6th (01.45.48.35.85).
M° St-Germain des Prés. **Open** 10am-11.45pm Mon-
Sat. **Credit** AmEx, DC, MC, V. **Map** p405 G7.
A Left Bank institution, La Hune boasts an interna-
tional selection of art and design books and a superb
collection of French literature and theory.

Institut Géographique National

*107 rue La Boétie, 8th (01.43.98.85.00). M° Franklin
D. Roosevelt.* **Open** 9.30am-7pm Mon-Fri; 11am-
12.30pm, 2-6.30pm Sat. **Credit** AmEx, MC, V.
Map p401 E4.
Paris' best cartographic shop stocks international
maps, detailed guides to France, wine, cheese, walking and cycling maps and historic maps of Paris.

Librairie Gourmande

4 rue Dante, 5th (01.43.54.37.27). M° St-Michel.
Open 10am-7pm daily. **Credit** MC, V. **Map** p406 J7.
Chefs from all over the world hunt out Geneviève
Baudon's bookstore dedicated to cooking, wine and
table arts. Lashings of *bonhomie* from the staff
makes shopping here an experience to savour.

Librarie Scaramouche

161 rue St-Martin, 3rd (01.48.87.78.58).
M° Rambuteau. **Open** 11am-1pm, 2-7.30pm Mon-Sat.
Credit MC, V. **Map** p402 K5.
This shrine to celluloid, from the most obscure
movies to box-office blockbusters, is packed with
film posters, stills and books in French and English.

Shakespeare & Co

37 rue de la Bûcherie, 5th (01.43.26.96.50).
M° Maubert-Mutualité/RER St-Michel. **Open** noon-
midnight daily. **No credit cards. Map** p406 J7.
Sylvia Beach's famous shops live on in name only,
although Shakespeare & Co still attracts wannabe
Hemingways. The chaotic collection isn't particularly cheap and the staff's rudeness is bewildering.

Village Voice

6 rue Princesse, 6th (01.46.33.36.47). M° Mabillon.
Open 2-8pm Mon; 10am-8pm Tue-Sat; 2-7pm Sun.
Credit AmEx, DC, MC, V. **Map** p406 H7.
The city's best selection of new fiction, non-fiction

and literary magazines in English. The literary
events and poetry readings are a welcome respite
from the *faux*-intellectualism which frequently pervades book-lovers' haunts.

WH Smith

248 rue de Rivoli, 1st (01.44.77.88.99).
M° Concorde. **Open** 9am-7.30pm Mon-Sat; 1-7.30pm
Sun. **Credit** AmEx, MC, V. **Map** p401 G5.
Just like being back in Blighty; over 70,000 titles and
a huge crush around the magazine section.

Gifts & eccentricities

Deyrolle

46 rue du Bac, 7th (01.42.22.30.07). M° Rue du Bac.
Open 10am-6.45pm Mon-Sat. **Credit** AmEx, MC, V.
Map p405 G6.
A taxidermist's dream. This dusty shop, established
1831, overflows with stuffed animals, from a polar
bear to exotic birds. Have your own pets lovingly
stuffed from €579.31(for a cat) or even hire a beast
for a few days. Fab maps and posters, too.

Diptyque

34 bd St-Germain, 5th (01.43.26.45.27).
M° Maubert-Mutualité. **Open** 10am-7pm Mon-Sat
Credit: AmEx, MC, V. **Map** p405 G6/K7.
Diptyque's scented candles in 48 different varieties
are the best you'll ever come across. They smell
and look divine and are long-lasting; try the
chèvrefeuille (honeysuckle) or jasmine and you can't
fail to agree. A smaller range of scents includes
freesias and figs in the recipies.

Nature et Découvertes

*Carrousel du Louvre, 99 rue de Rivoli, 1st
(01.47.03.47.43). M° Palais Royal.* **Open** 10am-8pm
daily. **Credit** AmEx, MC, V. **Map** p401 H5.
This chain sells useful (and less so) camping and
stargazing accessories, musical instruments, art
supplies, divining rods and games. It has a kids' play
space (workshops Wed afternoon).
Branches include: Forum des Halles, rue Pierre
Lescot, 1st (01.40.28.42.16).

Papeterie Moderne

12 rue de la Ferronerie, 1st (01.42.36.21.72).
M° Châtelet. **Open** 9am-noon, 1.30-6.30pm Mon-Sat.
No credit cards. Map p402 J5.
Source of those enamel plaques that adorn Paris
streets and forbidding gateways. Here you can find
that Champs-Elysées sign or the guard-dog with a
twist *(attention chien bizarre)* for a mere €6.10.

Paris Accordéon

80 rue Daguerre, 14th (01.43.22.13.48).
M° Denfert-Rochereau or Gaîté. **Open** 9am-noon,
1-7pm, Tue-Fri; 9am-noon, 1-6pm Sat.
Credit AmEx, MC, V. **Map** p405 G10.
This yellow-painted shop has shelves laden with the
French national instrument, the accordion, from sim-
ple squeeze-box to the most beautiful tortoiseshell,
new and second-hand. Sheet music also sold here.

Paris-Musées

29bis rue des Francs-Bourgeois, 4th
(01.42.74.13.02). M° St-Paul. **Open** 2-7pm Mon;
11am-7pm Tue-Sat; 11am-6.30pm Sun.
Credit AmEx, DC, MC, V. **Map** p406 L6.
Run by the Ville de Paris museums, this shop showcases funky lamps and ceramics by young designers, along with reproductions of jewellery, glassware
and other items in the city's museums.
Branch: Forum des Halles, 1 rue Pierre-Lescot, 1st
(01.40.26.56.65).

Robin des Bois

15 rue Ferdinand-Duval, 4th (01.48.04.09.36).
M° St-Paul. **Open** 10.30am-7.30pm Mon-Sat;
2-7.30pm Sun. **Credit** MC, V. **Map** p406 L6.
Robin Hood is linked to an ecological organisation
of the same name. Everything is made with recycled
or ecologically sound products, including bottle-top
jewellery, natural toiletries and recycled notepaper.

Music & CDs

There are clusters of specialist record shops
around Les Halles (1st) and rue Keller (11th);
second-hand outlets are concentrated in the 5th.

Bimbo Tower

5 passage St-Antoine, 11th (01.49.29.76.71).
M° Ledru-Rollin. **Open** noon-7pm Tue-Sat.
Credit V. **Map** p406 L6/L7.
Not for those looking for the latest mainstream hit,
or bimbos either. You'll find all manner of new
underground, counter-culture music here: from con-

Hitting the books at **Gibert Joseph**.
See p266.

crete music to sonic poetry and performance, rare
discs, independent labels, auto-produced records
and the latest Japanese imports.

Born Bad

17 rue Keller, 11th (01.48.06.34.17). M° Ledru-Rollin.
Open 12pm-8pm Mon-Sat. **Credit** AmEx, DC, MC, V.
Map p407 M6.
You can buy anything from punk, rock and hardcore to ska and soul in this indie record shop. There
are also rock videos, T-shirts, stickers, etc plus a
shelf of anarchistic books and fanzines. New and
second-hand CDs and vinyl sell for around €10-€12.

Crocodisc

42 rue des Ecoles, 5th (01.43.54.47.95).
M° Maubert-Mutualité. **Open** 11am-7pm Tue-Sat.
Closed 2 weeks Aug. **Credit** MC, V. **Map** p406 J7/K8.
An excellent albeit slightly expensive range includes
pop, rock, funk, Oriental, African, country music and
classical. For jazz, blues and gospel try its spe-
cialised branch Crocojazz (64 rue de la Montagne
Ste-Geneviève, 5th/ 01.46.34.78.38).

Fnac

74 av des Champs-Elysées, 8th (01.53.53.64.64/
www.fnac.com). M° George V. **Open** 10am-midnight
Mon-Sat; noon-midnight Sun. **Credit** AmEx, MC, V.
Map p400 D4.
Almost a French institution, Fnac's musical range
is tame but certainly wide-reaching – the African
section is particularly reliable. Fnac also stocks books,
computers, stereo, video and photography equipment, as well as being Paris' main concert box office.
Branches: Forum des Halles, 1st (01.40.41.40.00);
136 rue de Rennes, 6th (01.49.54.30.00); 4 pl de la
Bastille, 12th (01.43.42.04.04) music only.

Eat, Drink, Shop

Gibert Joseph

34 bd St-Michel, 6th (01.44.41.88.55). M° St-Michel.
Open *10am-7pm Mon-Sat.* **Credit** MC, V.
Map p405 H9/J7.
This huge bookstore and stationer has a music section which fills three floors. A large stock of videos and CDs with a particularly good Indie section.

Monster Melodies

9 rue des Déchargeurs, 1st (01.42.33.25.72).
M° Les Halles. **Open** 11am-7pm Mon-Sat. **Credit**
AmEx, MC, V. **Map** p402 J5.
The owners will help you hunt out treasures, and with over 10,000 second-hand CDs (59F/€8.99-89F/€13.57) of all species, it's just as well.

Virgin Megastore

52-60 av des Champs-Elysées, 8th (01.49.53.50.00).
M° Franklin D. Roosevelt. **Open** 10am-midnight
Mon-Sat; noon-midnight Sun. **Credit** AmEx, DC, MC,
V. **Map** p401 E4.
In addition to great views from the top-floor café, the luxury of perusing the latest CDs till midnight makes this a choice spot. The store also sells videos and books, with a strong selection of music titles.
Branch: Carrousel du Louvre, 99 rue de Rivoli, 1st
(01.49.53.50.00)

Sport & fitness

Bicloune

*7 rue Froment, 11th (01.48.05.47.75). M° Bréguet
Sabin.* **Open** 9am-1pm Tue-Wed, Fri, Sat; 9am-1pm,
2-8pm Thurs. **Credit** AmEx, MC, V. **Map** p407 M6.
A good range of spanking new bikes, from special hi-tech multi-gear numbers to standard wheels about town. Full range of accessories for cycling

fiends and repairs by appointment. Branch down the road at 93 bd Beaumarchais (01.42.77.58.06) specialises in old and made-to-measure bikes.

Citadium

*50-55 rue Caumartin, 9th (01.55.31.74.00). M° Havre
Caumartin.* **Open** 10am-8pm Mon-Wed, Fri, Sat; 10am-9pm Thurs. **Credit** AmEx, MC, V. **Map** p401 G3.
One of France's biggest sports stores and fast becoming cult. The latest surf 'n' skater vids blast out into the four huge themed floors ('urban street', 'glide', 'athletic' and 'outdoor') all manned by expert staff and stocking everything from designer watches to cross-country skis and travel books.

Décathlon

*26 av de Wagram, 8th (01.45.72.66.88/
www.decathlon.fr). M° Charles de Gaulle-Etoile.*
Open 10am-8pm Mon-Wed, Fri; Thur 10am-9pm; Sat
9am-8pm. **Credit** MC, V. **Map** p400 C3.
The closest thing to sport supermarkets. The chain's popularity is based largely on its extensive selection of inexpensive, good-quality, own-brand clothing and equipment.
Branches include: La Défense, Centre Commercial
les Quatre Temps, Niveau 1, rue des Arcades
(01.47.74.57.79).

Go Sport

*Forum des Halles Niveau -3, Porte Lescot, 1st
(01.40.13.73.50/www.go-sport.fr). RER Châtelet-Les
Halles.* **Open** 10am-7.30pm Mon-Sat; Sun 10am-7pm.
Credit AmEx, DC, MC, V. **Map** p402 J5.
Go Sport has a large selection (albeit chaotically arranged) of equipment and brands.
Branches include: Centre Commercial Italie 2,
30 av d'Italie, 13th (01.53.62.91.91); 10 pl de la
République, 11th (01.49.05.71.85).

Au Vieux Campeur

main shop 48 rue des Ecoles, 5th (01.53.10.48.48/
www.au-vieux-campeur.com). M° Maubert-Mutualité.
Open: 11am-7.30pm Mon-Tue, Thur-Fri; Wed 11am-
9pm; Sat 9.30-7.30pm. **Credit** MC, V. **Map** p406 J7/K8.
A Parisian institution, Au Vieux Campeur runs 19
specialist shops between rue des Ecoles and the bd
St-Germain. The group deals with just about all
sports you can do in public, from scuba diving to
skiing – except golf, which it considers too bourgeois! Despite such rampant thought policing, staff
are knowledgeable and friendly.

Stationery & art supplies

Calligrane

4-6 rue du Pont Louis-Philippe, 4th (01.48.04.31.89).
M° Pont Marie. **Open** 11am-7pm Tue-Sat. Closed
2 weeks in Aug. **Credit** MC, V. **Map** p406 K6.
Three shops devoted to handmade paper from all
over the world, including encrusted papers, designer
office supplies, writing paper and Filofaxes.

Sennelier

3 quai Voltaire, 7th (01.42.60.72.15).
M° St-Germain-des-Prés. **Open** 2-6.30pm Mon;
9.30am-12.30pm, 2-6.30pm Tue-Sat. **Credit** AmEx,
DC, MC, V. **Map** p406 H6.
Old-fashioned colour merchant Sennelier has been
supplying artists since 1887. Oil paints, watercolours and pastels include rare pigments, along
with primered boards, varnishes and paper.

Food & drink

Every Parisian neighbourhood has its market
and speciality shops where the faithful wait
patiently in slow-moving queues for rustic corn-
fed chicken, farmhouse camembert or briny
oysters fresh from Brittany. Supermarkets and
suburban *hypermarchés* are indeed a force to be
reckoned with but the latest food scares have
produced a renewed attention to quality and a
willingness to pay a little extra. The Mairie has
plans to open roving markets in the afternoons
and evenings, complete with child-care facilities
and delivery service, to make them more
accessible to working Parisians.

Bakeries

L'Autre Boulange

43 rue de Montreuil, 11th (01.43.72.86.04).
M° Nation or Faidherbe-Chaligny. **Open** 7.30am-
1.30pm, 4-7.30pm Mon-Fri; 7.30am-12.30pm Sat.
Closed Aug. **No credit cards. Map** p403 P3.

Plenty of leg-over opportunities at
Bicloune. *See left.*

Bread-worshipping baker Michel Cousin rustles up
23 mouth-watering kinds of organic bread in his
wood-fired oven including the *flutiot* (rye bread with
raisins, walnuts and hazelnuts), the *sarment de
Bourgogne* (sourdough and a little rye) and a spiced
cornmeal bread ideal for foie gras. Great croissants
and *chaussons* for superior snacking.

Max Poilâne

87 rue Brancion, 15th (01.48.28.45.90/
www.max-poilane.fr). M° Porte de Vanves.
Open 7.30am-8pm Mon-Sat, 10am-7pm Sun.
No credit cards. Map p404 D10.
Using the venerable Poilâne family recipe, the lesser-known Max produces bread that easily rivals that
of his more famous brother Lionel. So it's true what
they say: make bread not war.
Branches: 29 rue de l'Ouest, 14th (01.43.27.29.91);
42 rue du Marché-St-Honoré, 1st (01.42.61.10.53).

Moisan

5 pl d'Aligre, 12th (01.43.45.46.60). M° Ledru-Rollin.
Open 7am-1.30pm, 3-8pm Tue-Sat; 7am-2pm Sun.
No credit cards. Map p407 N7.
An organic baking pioneer, Michel Moisan lovingly
turns out crunchy *boules de levain*, a mouthwater-
ing selection of *petits pains*, gorgeous orange-scented brioches and those scrummy flaky apple tarts.
Branch: 4 av du Général Leclerc, 14th
(01.43.22.34.13).

Moulin de la Vierge

*166 av de Suffren, 15th (01.47.83.45.55). M° Sèvres-
Lecourbe.* **Open** 7am-8pm Mon-Sat. **No credit
cards. Map** p404 C6.
Basile Kamir learned breadmaking after falling in
love with an old abandoned bakery. His naturally
leavened country loaf is thick, dense and fragrant.
Branches include: 82 rue Daguerre, 14th
(01.43.22.50.55); 105 rue Vercingétorix, 14th
(01.45.43.09.84); 77 rue Cambronne, 15th
(01.44.49.05.05).

Au Noisetier

33 rue Rambuteau, 4th (01.48.87.68.12).
M° Rambuteau. **Open** 8am-7.45pm Mon, Tue, Fri-
Sun. Closed July or Aug. **No credit cards.**
Map p402 K5.
Veteran baker Jean-Pierre Malzis has seen the neighbourhood change in his 28 years here, but his delicious speciality, the *noisetier*, remains the same:
twisty or round, with a crunchy crust and nutty-
coloured, naturally leavened crumb.

Poilâne

8 rue du Cherche-Midi, 6th (01.45.48.42.59/
www.poilane.com). M° Sèvres Babylone or St-Sulpice.
Open 7.15am-8.15pm Mon-Sat. **No credit cards.**
Map p405 F8.
You can now buy the dark-crusted, chewy-centred
Poilâne loaf in many supermarkets but if you want
it fresh out of the oven this tiny, old-fashioned bak-
ery is the place to go for the real thing. The buttery
apple tarts almost better the bread.
Branch: 49 bd de Grenelle, 15th (01.45.79.11.49).

(vertical tab) **Eat, Drink, Shop**

René-Gérard St-Ouen

111 bd Haussmann, 8th (01.42.65.06.25).
M° Miromesnil. **Open** 7.30am-7.30pm Mon-Sat.
Closed Aug. **No credit cards. Map** p401 E3.
Celebrated for his edible 'bread sculptures' shaped
like cats, horses, bicycles and the Eiffel Tower, this
baker also does more conventional breads.

Pâtisseries

A Lerch

4 rue du Cardinal Lemoine, 5th (01.43.26.15.80).
M° Cardinal Lemoine. **Open** 8am-7.30pm Wed-Sun.
No credit cards. Map p406 K8.
With its wedding cake ceiling, this is a dream pâtisserie for those who like their cakes rustic. The speciality is Alsatian fruit tarts, with five or six seasonal
varieties on display at any given time (apple,
quetsch plum, pear and rhubarb-meringue).

Gérard Mulot

76 rue de Seine, 6th (01.43.26.85.77). M° Odéon.
Open 6.45am-8pm Mon, Tue, Thur-Sun. Closed Aug.
No credit cards. Map p406 H7.
Picture-perfect cakes – bitter chocolate tart and the
mabillon, caramel mousse with apricot marmalade
– attract local celebrities.

Maison Rollet Pradier

6 rue de Bourgogne, 7th (01.45.51.78.36).
M° Assemblée Nationale. **Open** 8am-8pm Sun;
8am-7pm Mon-Sat. Closed three weeks in Aug.
Credit AmEx, DC, MC, V. **Map** p405 F6.
Enjoy sumptuous gâteaux laden with chocolate curls
or hazelnuts, or bread specialities *flûte rollet* and
boule de levain. Upstairs, there is a sandwich counter
and tea room.

Démoulin

6 bd Voltaire, 11th (01.47.00.58.20/
www.chocolat-paris.com). M° République. **Open**
8.30am-7.30pm Tue-Sat; 8am-1.30pm, 3-7pm Sun.
Closed Aug. **Credit** MC, V. **Map** p403 M5.
Chocolate maker and pastry chef Philippe
Démoulin's Ali Baba, filled with vanilla custard, rum
and raisins, is not to be missed. Nor, his bitter chocolate and meringue Negresco.

Cheese

The sign *maître fromager affineur* denotes
merchants who buy young cheeses from farms
and age them on their premises. *Fromage
fermier* and *fromage au lait cru* signify farm-
produced and raw milk cheeses respectively.

Alléosse

13 rue Poncelet, 17th (01.46.22.50.45). M° Ternes.
Open 9am-1pm, 4-7pm Tue-Fri; 9am-1pm, 3.30-7pm
Sat; 9am-1pm Sun. **Credit** MC, V. **Map** p400 C2.
People cross town for the cheeses – wonderful farm-
house camemberts, delicate st-marcellins, a choice
of *chèvres* and several rarities.

Marie-Anne Cantin

12 rue du Champ-de-Mars, 7th
(01.45.50.43.94/www.cantin.fr). M° Ecole Militaire.
Open 8.30am-7.30pm Mon-Sat; 9am-1pm Sun.
Credit MC, V. **Map** p404 D6.
Cantin, a vigorous defender of unpasteurised cheese,
is justifiably proud of her dreamily creamy st-marcellins, aged *chèvres* and nutty beauforts. The
cheeses are ripened in her cellars.

Alain Dubois

80 rue de Tocqueville, 17th (01.42.27.11.38).
M° Malesherbes or Villiers. **Open** 9am-1pm, 4-8pm
Tue-Fri; 8.30am-8pm Sat; 9am-1pm Sun. Closed first
and two weeks in Aug. **Credit** MC, V. **Map** p401 E2.
Dubois, who stocks some 70 varieties of goat's
cheese plus prized, aged st-marcellin and st-félicien,
is the darling of the superchefs. Fortunately, he will
ship orders to his world-wide fanbase.
Branch: 79 rue de Courcelles, 17th (01.43.80.36.42).

Laurent Dubois

2 rue de Lourmel, 15th (01.45.78.70.58). M° Dupleix.
Open 9am-1pm, 4-7.45pm Tue-Fri; 8.30am-1pm, 3.30-
7.45pm Sat; 9am-1pm Sun. Closed Aug. **Credit** MC,
V. **Map** p404 C7.
Nephew of the famous cheese specialist Alain
Dubois, Laurent Dubois is a master in his own right
and may be beginning something of a Dubois cheese
dynasty. Especially impressive are his nutty two-
year-old comté and crackly vieille mimolette.

Chocolate

Cacao et Chocolat

29 rue de Buci, 6th (01.46.33.77.63). M° Mabillon.
Open 10.30am-7.30pm Tue-Sat. **Credit** AmEx, MC,
V. **Map** p405 H7.
Opened in 1998, this shop decorated in burnt-orange
and ochre recalls chocolate's ancient Aztec origins
with spicy fillings (honey and chilli, nutmeg, clove
and citrus), chocolate masks and pyramids.
Branch: 63 rue St Louis en l'Ile, 4th (01.46.33.33.33).

Christian Constant

37 rue d'Assas, 6th (01.53.63.15.15). M° St-Placide.
Open 8.30am-9pm Mon-Fri; 8am-8.30pm Sat, Sun.
Credit MC, V. **Map** p405 G8.
A true master chocolate maker and *traiteur,*
Constant is revered by *le tout Paris.* Trained in the
arts of pâtisserie and chocolate, he scours the globe
for new and delectable ideas. Ganaches are subtly
flavoured with verbena, jasmine or cardamom.

Debauve & Gallais

30 rue des Saints-Pères, 7th (01.45.48.54.67).
M° St-Germain-des-Prés. **Open** 9am-7pm Mon-Sat.
Closed Aug. **Credit** MC, V. **Map** p405 G7.
This former pharmacy, with a facade dating from
1800, once sold chocolate for medicinal purposes. Its
intense tea, honey or praline-flavoured chocolates
do, indeed, heal the soul.
Branches: 33 rue Vivienne, 2nd (01.40.39.05.50); 107
rue Jouffroy d'Abbans, 17th (01.47.63.15.15).

All crescent and accounted for

Forget candlelit dinners, croissants are the essence of Parisian romance – only the most dedicated city-dwellers brave drizzly mornings to savour this warm and crunchy luxury. But the swell crescent pastry can be very deflating if it fails to make the grade. Made of yeasty dough layered with butter, the traditional *croissant au beurre* is notoriously hard to get right.

Our blind taste test of freshly baked croissants proved once again that looks aren't everything. The squat and endearingly misshapen fare from **Au Levain du Marais** won top marks for superior crunch and flavour. Croissants from the frozen food shop Picard infiltrated the test, and predictably took last place. Our panel of four rated the croissants for visual appeal, aroma, flakiness, crunch and flavour. Personal tastes varied but the winner's vote was unanimous.

Au Levain du Marais *32 rue de Turenne, 3rd (01.42.78.07.31)* – **7/10**. Dark-crusted with a toasty aroma, Thierry Rabineau's small and oddly-shaped croissants had a soft and rather dense interior. They were admired for remarkable flakiness and balanced flavour.

Pierre Hermé *72 rue Bonaparte, 6th (01.43.54.47.77)* – **6.5/10**. Gleaming chocolate cakes outshine humble breakfast rolls in this pastry shrine, but Hermé still ranks among the city's croissant kings. Dark golden on top with a pale base, the croissants had a buttery scent which one taster found 'nondescript' and another

'lingering and fresh'. Dense and beautifully flaky, these were the sweetest of the lot.

Poujaran *20 rue Jean-Nicot, 7th (01.47.05.80.88)* – **6.5/10**. Celebrity baker Jean-Luc Poujaran's croissants were burnt at the tips; perhaps hailing from an overcooked batch. Despite their chargrilled appearance, they were impressively springy, with well-defined shape.

Le Triomphe *95 rue d'Avron, 20th (01.43.73.24.50)* – **6/10**. Well-known among pastry aficionados, this bakery produces a surprisingly pale croissant with dense, barely cooked layers. 'Looks like Dracula's had a go at them', grumbled one taster. These had good crunch and great, elasticky tips.

J.P. Cosnier *8 rue Gay-Lussac, 5th (01.43.54.31.69)* – **6/10**. This neighbourhood bakery stood up reasonably well to its more prestigious rivals. Puffy with a slightly burnt centre tip, the croissants smelled enticing but the texture was too airy.

Kayser *79 rue du Commerce, 15th (01.44.19.88.54)* – **5.5/10**. Kayser, a classy chain, failed to wow tasters. The pastries were 'too soft', 'limp' and 'dry' and they looked 'insipid and charmless'.

Picard *(branches throughout Paris)* – **5.5/10**. After 30 minutes in the oven, these ready-to-bake croissants emerged almost burnt underneath. One taster dubbed them 'the perfect blend of yeast and butter'. Others were sceptical, finding the smell 'sharp', the texture 'chewy' and the taste 'funny'.

Jean-Paul Hévin

3 rue Vavin, 6th (01.43.54.09.85). M° Vavin. **Open** 10am-7.30pm daily. Closed 6-27 Aug. **Credit** MC, V.**Map** p405 G8.

A stylish window display tempts you to test florentines, and ganaches scented with smoked tea, or honey, and bitter chocolate-orange. If you love pure chocolate, try the intriguing Trinité or smoky Chuao. **Branches:** 231 rue St-Honoré, 1st (01.55.35.35.96); 16 av de La Motte-Picquet, 7th (01.45.51.77.48).

La Maison du Chocolat

89 av Raymond-Poincaré, 16th (01.40.67.77.83/www.lamaisonduchocolat.com). M° Victor-Hugo. **Open** 10am-7pm Mon-Sat. **Credit** AmEx, MC, V. **Map** p400 B4.

Robert Linxe opened his first Paris shop in 1977 and has been inventing new chocolates ever since. Using Asian spices, fresh fruits and herbal infusions he has won over the most demanding chocolate-lovers. **Branches:** 19 rue de Sèvres, 6th (01.45.44.20.40); 225 rue du Fbg-St-Honoré, 8th (01.42.27.39.44); 52 rue François 1er, 8th (01.47.23.38.25); 8 bd de la Madeleine, 9th (01.47.42.86.52).

Richart

258 bd St-Germain, 7th (01.45.55.66.00/ www.richart.com). M° Solférino. **Open** 10am-7pm Mon-Sat. Closed one week in Aug. **Credit** MC, V. **Map** p405 F6.

Each chocolate ganache has an intricate design, packages look like jewel boxes and each purchase comes with a tract on how best to savour chocolate.

Hot choc at **Constant**. *See p268.*

Regional specialities

La Cigogne

61 rue de l'Arcade, 8th (01.43.87.39.16). M° St-Lazare. **Open** 8.30am-7pm Mon-Fri. Closed Aug. **Credit** MC, V. **Map** p401 F4.

Hearty Alsatian fare at La Cigogne includes scrumptious tarts, strüdel, beravecka fruit bread plus sausages laced with pistachios.

Charcuterie Lyonnaise

58 rue des Martyrs, 9th (01.48.78.96.45). M° Notre-Dame de Lorette. **Open**8.30am-1.30pm, 4-7.30pm Tue-Sat; 9am-12.30pm Sun. Closed 15 July-15 Aug. **Credit** MC, V. **Map** p401 H2.

Jean-Jacques Chrétienne prepares Lyonnais delicacies *quenelles de brochet*, *jambon persillé* and *hure* (pistachio-seasoned tongue).

Treats & traiteurs

Allicante

26 bd Beaumarchais, 11th (01.43.55.13.02/ www.allicante.com). M° Bastille. **Open** daily 10am-7.30pm **Credit** V AmEx DC **Map** p406 M6.

A paradise of oily delights, including rare olive oils from Liguria, Sicily and Greece, fragrant pine nut, pistachio and almond varieties, and oils extracted from apricot, peach and avocado pits. Wow your guests with pricey argania oil, pounded by hand by Berber women in Morocco.

L'Epicerie

51 rue St-Louis-en-l'Ile, 4th (01.43.25.20.14). M° Pont Marie. **Open** 10.30am-8pm daily. **Credit** MC, V. **Map** p406 K7.

A perfect delicatessen gift shop crammed with pretty bottles of blackcurrant vinegar, five-spice mustard, orange sauce, tiny pots of jam, honey with figs and indulgent boxes of chocolate snails.

Fauchon

26-30 pl de la Madeleine, 8th (01.47.42.60.11). M° Madeleine. **Open** 9.30am-7pm Mon-Sat. **Credit** AmEx, DC, MC, V. **Map** p401 F4.

Paris' most famous food store is like every specialist deli rolled into one with windows as much for gawping as buying. There's a museum-like prepared-food section, cheese, fish and exotic fruit counters, an Italian deli, fine wines in the cellar, chocolates and a plush tea room for refreshment.

Jean-Paul Gardil

44 rue St-Louis en l'Ile, 4th (01.43.54.97.15). M° Pont Marie **Open** 8.30am-12.30pm, 4-7.30pm Tue-Sat; 8.30am-12.30pm Sun. **Credit** MC,V. **Map** p406 K7.

Rarely has meat looked so beautiful as in this fairytale shop, where geese hang in the window and a multitude of plaques confirm the butcher's skill in selecting the finest meats, such as milk-fed veal and lamb, *coucou de Rennes* chickens, Barbary free-range ducklings, and Bresse poulard and geese. Staff are pleasant, unlike the fur-coated clients.

The spice of life at **L'Epicerie**. *See p245.*

Goutmanyat

3 rue Dupues, 3rd. No telephone number. M° Temple
Open 2-8pm Mon-Sat. **Credit** AmEx, DC, MC, V.
Map p402 L5.

Jean-Marie Thiercelin's family has been in the spice
business since 1809, and his little shop is a treasure
trove of flavourings which are sorted, cleaned and
stored in his own temperature-controlled warehouses. Star chefs come here for Indonesian *cubebe*
pepper, gleaming fresh nutmeg, long pepper (an
Indian variety) and Spanish and Iranian saffron.

Hédiard

21 pl de la Madeleine, 8th (01.43.12.88.88/
www.hediard.fr). M° Madeleine. **Open** shop 9.30am-
8pm Mon-Sat; traiteur 9am-10pm Mon-Sat. **Credit**
AmEx, DC, MC, V. **Map** p401 F4.

The first establishment to introduce exotic foods to
the Parisians, Hédiard specialises in rare teas and
coffees, unusual spices, imported produce, jams and
candied fruits. The original shop, dating from 1880,
has a posh tea room upstairs.
Branches include: 126 rue du Bac, 7th
(01.45.44.01.98); 70 av Paul-Doumer, 16th
(01.45.04.51.92); 106 bd des Courcelles, 17th
(01.47.63.32.14).

Huilerie Artisanale Leblanc

*6 rue Jacob, 6th (01.46.34.61.55). M° St-Germain-
des-Près.* **Open** 2.30-7.30pm Mon; 11am-7.30pm Tue-
Sat. Closed three weeks in Aug. **No credit cards.**
Map p405 H6.

The Leblanc family started out making walnut oil
from its family tree in Burgundy and selling to its
neighbours before branching out to skillfully press
pure oils from hazelnuts, almonds, pine nuts, grilled
peanuts, pistachios and olives.

La Maison de la Truffe

19 pl de la Madeleine, 8th (01.42.65.53.22/
www.maison-de-la-truffe.com). M° Madeleine.
Open 9am-8pm Mon; 9am-9pm Tue-Sat. **Credit**
AmEx, DC, MC, V. **Map** p401 F4.

Come here for truffles worth more than gold –
Piedmontese white truffles from Alba cost a cool
€4573 a kilo – or for the more affordable truffle oils,
sauces and vinegars.

Poissonerie du Dôme

4 rue Delambre, 14th (01.43.35.23.95). M° Vavin
Open 8am-1pm, 4-7pm Tue-Sat; 8am-1pm Sun.
Credit MC, V. **Map** p405 G9.

Jean-Pierre Lopez' tiny shop is probably the best
fishmonger in Paris. His fish are individually selected, many coming straight from small boats off the
Breton coast. Each one is bright of eye and sound of
gill. Try the drool-inducing (but bank-breaking) turbot, the giant crabs or the scallops, when in season.

Markets

Market streets open 8am-1pm and 4-7pm Tue-
Sat; 8am-1pm Sun. The roving markets set up
at 8am and vanish at 1pm. Arrive early for the
best selection, late for fresh food bargains.

Market streets

Rue Mouffetard

5th. M° Censier-Daubenton.
Wind your way up from medieval St-Médard to prod
peaches, sample the flûte Gana at Steff le Boulanger
(No 123) or take a pit stop at the butterfly-themed
Bar des Papillons (No 129).

Mexi & Co: everything for living *la vida loca*, at your fingertips.

Marché d'Aligre

rue and pl d'Aligre, 12th. M° Ledru-Rollin. Open mornings only.

One of the cheapest markets in Paris offers North African and Caribbean produce, herbs, unusual potatoes and onions and cheap fruit. The covered market next door, although more expensive, is open in the afternoon.

Rue Daguerre

14th. M° Denfert-Rochereau.

A good local market with products from the Aveyron region, the Vacroux cheese stall and the Daguerre Marée fishmonger.

Rue Poncelet

rue Poncelet and rue Bayen, 17th. M° Ternes.

Take in the coffee aromas at the Brûlerie des Ternes on this classy street which also boasts cheese shop Alléosse and a German deli.

Roving markets

Marché Biologique

bd Raspail, 6th. M° Sèvres-Babylone. Open Sun.

Très chic organic market with produce direct from the farm at far from rustic prices. Other organic markets: boulevard des Batignolles, 17th (Sat) and rue St-Charles, 15th (Tue, Fri).

Saxe-Breteuil

av de Saxe, 7th. M° Ségur. Open Thur, Sat.

Possibly the most scenic of Paris' markets, with the Eiffel Tower poking up between tree-lined rows of impeccable stalls.

Marché Bastille

bd Richard-Lenoir, 11th. M° Bastille. Open Thur, Sun.

A big daddy which seems to go on for miles. Look out for Provençal olives and oils, game, cheese, fish and wild mushrooms.

Cour de Vincennes

12th. M° Nation. Open Wed, Sat.

A classy kilometre-long market reputed for fruit, veg and free-range poultry.

International

Le Mille-Pâtes

5 rue des Petits-Champs, 1st (01.42.96.03.04). M° Palais Royal. Open 9am-3.15pm Mon; 9.30am-3.15pm, 4.40-7.30pm Tue-Thur; 9.30am-7.30pm Fri, Sat. Closed Aug. Credit AmEx, DC, MC, V. Map H4.

A treasure trove of Italian delicacies: amaretti biscuits, charcuterie, white truffles in season, and takeaway panini and hot pastas.

Kioko

46 rue des Petits-Champs, 2nd (01.42.61.33.65). M° Pyramides. Open 10am-8pm Tue-Sat; 11am-7pm Sun. Credit MC, V. Map H4.

Everything you need to make sushi (or good ready-made sushi for the lazy), plus sauces, snacks, sake, Japanese beer, tea and kitchen utensils. Ten per cent off on weekends.

Izraël

30 rue François-Miron, 4th (01.42.72.66.23). M° Hôtel de Ville. Open 9.30am-1pm, 2.30-7pm Tue-Fri; 9-7pm Sat. Closed Aug. Credit MC, V. Map K6.

Spices and other delights from as far afield as Mexico, Turkey and India – juicy dates, feta cheese, tapenades and lots of spirits.

Mexi & Co
10 rue Dante, 5th (01.46.34.14.12). M° Maubert-Mutualité. **Open** noon-midnight daily. **No credit cards. Map** J7.
Everything you need for a fiesta, including marinades for fajitas, dried chillies, South American beers, cachaça and tequilas.

Jabugo Iberico & Co.
11 rue Clément Marot, 8th (01.47.20.03.13). M° Alma-Marceau, Franklin D. Roosevelt. **Open** 10am-8pm Mon-Sat. **Credit** AmEx, DC, MC, V. **Map** E4.
This shop specialises in Spanish hams with the Bellota-Bellota label, meaning the pigs have feasted on acorns. Manager Philippe Poulachon compares the complexity of his cured hams (at nearly €92 a kilo) to the delicacy of truffles.

Sarl Velan Stores
87 passage Brady, 10th (01.42.46.06.06). M° Château d'Eau. **Open** 9.30am-8.30pm Mon-Sat. **Credit** MC, V. **Map** K4.
Situated in an passage of Indian cafés and shops, this is an emporium of spices and vegetables, shipped from Kenya and India.

Tang Frères
48 av d'Ivry, 13th (01.45.70.80.00). M° Porte d'Ivry. **Open** 9am-7.30pm Tue-Fri; 8.30am-7.30pm Sat, Sun. **Credit** MC, V.
Chinatown's biggest Asian supermarket is great for flat, wind-dried duck and all sorts of unidentifiable fruit and veg to get your hands on.

Les Délices d'Orient
52 av Emile Zola, 15th (01.45.79.10.00). M° Charles-Michels. **Open** 8.30am-9pm Tue-Sun. **Credit** MC, V. **Map**
Shelves here brim with houmous, stuffed aubergines, halva, fava beans, stuffed vine-leaves, Lebanese bread, felafel, olives and all manner of Middle Eastern delicacies.
Branch: 14 rue des Quatre-Frères Peignot, 15th.

Wine, beer & spirits

Most *cavistes* happily dispense advice, so ask if you have a specific wine or menu in mind. To buy direct from producers, visit the Salon des Caves Particulières at Espace Champerret in March and December.

Legrand Filles et Fils
1 rue de la Banque, 2nd (01.42.60.07.12). M° Bourse. **Open** 9am-7pm Mon, Wed-Fri; 9am-9pm Thur; 9am-7pm Sat. **Credit** AmEx, MC, V. **Map** H4.
This old-fashioned shop offering fine wines and brandies, chocolates, teas, coffees and bonbons has just opened a new showroom for its huge selection of tasting glasses and gadgets, housed within Galerie Vivienne. Free wine tastings take place on Thursday evenings, with visiting experts to show you what to sip and what to spit.

Ryst Dupeyron
79 rue du Bac, 7th (01.45.48.80.93/ www.dupeyron.com). **Open** 12.30-7.30pm Mon; 10.30am-7.30pm Tue-Sat. Closed one week in Aug. **Credit** AmEx, MC, V. **Map** F7.
The Dupeyron family has sold Armagnac for four generations. You'll find bottles dating from 1868 (and nearly every year since) in this listed shop. Treasures include some 200 fine Bordeaux, vintage Port and rare whiskeys. Labels can be personalised on the spot, which may be helpful when your purchases send you into oblivion.

Les Caves Augé
116 bd Haussmann, 8th (01.45.22.16.97). M° St-Augustin. **Open** 1-7.30pm Mon; 9am-7.30pm Tue-Sat. **Closed** Mon in Aug. **Credit** AmEx, MC, V. **Map** E3.
The oldest wine shop in Paris – Marcel Proust was a regular customer – is serious and professional, with sommelier Marc Sibard advising.

Les Caves Taillevent
199 rue du Fbg-St-Honoré, 8th (01.45.61.14.09/ www.taillevent.com). M° Charles-de-Gaulle-Etoile or Ternes. **Open** 2-8pm Mon; 9am-8pm Tue-Fri; 9am-7.30pm Sat. Closed first three weeks in Aug. **Credit** AmEx, DC, MC, V. **Map**
Half a million bottles make up the Taillevent cellar. Saturday tastings with the three head sommeliers. Wines start from €3.65 a bottle.

La Maison du Whisky
20 rue d'Anjou, 8th (01.42.65.03.16/ www.whisky.fr). M° Madeleine. **Open** 9.30am-7pm Mon; 9.15am-8pm Tue-Fri; 9.30am-7.30pm Sat. **Credit** AmEx, MC, V. **Map** F4.
Jean-Marc Bellier is fascinating as he explains which whisky matches which food or waxes lyrical about different flavours such as honey and tobacco. He also hosts a whisky club.

Bières Spéciales
77 rue St-Maur, 11th (01.48.07.18.71). M° St-Maur. **Open** 4-9pm Mon; 10:30am-1pm, 4-9pm Tue-Sat. **Credit** AmEx, DC, MC, V. **Map** M3.
Single bottles and cans from 16 nations (at last count) neatly cover the walls. Belgium might dominate but you'll also find Polish, Scottish, Corsican, Portuguese and Chinese brews.

Les Domaines qui Montent
136 bd Voltaire, 11th (01.43.56.89.15). M° Voltaire. **Open** 10am-8pm Tue-Sat. Lunch served noon-2.30pm. **Credit** MC, V. **Map** M5.
This is not only a wine shop but a convivial place to have breakfast, lunch or tea. Wines cost the same as they would at the producer's and there is no extra charge for drinking them on the premises (with food). Saturday tastings with up-and-coming producers are featured in the shop.

Eat, Drink, Shop

Moulin BAL du **Rouge**

NEW SHOW!

Féerie

BAL DU
Moulin Rouge PARIS

DINNER & SHOW AT 7PM FROM 125€
SHOW AT 9PM: 89€, AT 11PM: 79€
MONTMARTRE - 82, BD DE CLICHY - 75018 PARIS
RESERVATIONS: 01 53 09 82 82 - WWW.MOULIN-ROUGE.COM

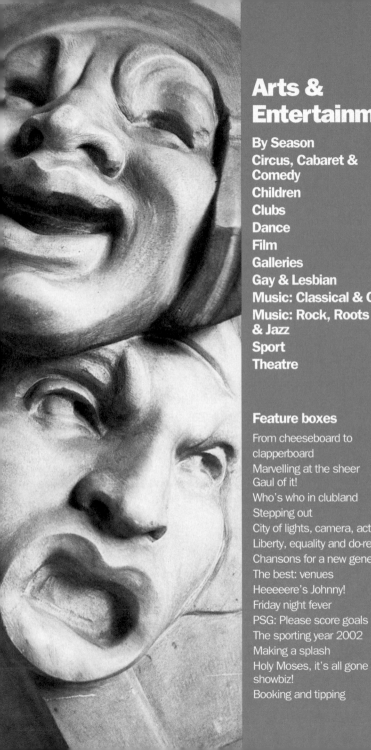

Arts & Entertainment

Paris by Season

Celebrating the arts, history and just about everything else under the sun is a year-long affair for Paris, a city with a packed cultural calendar.

The French do not take their festivities lightly. Historic events like Bastille Day are still big – and a great excuse for a knees-up – while there are also plenty of new ideas on the scene. Summer is a great time to explore the city by foot, but from mid-July to the end of August Parisians de-camp to the provinces and the serious arts season closes down, resuming in the autumn. Over Christmas and New Year, arts venues are open as usual.

Look out for two-for-one promotions, such as 'La Mairie de Paris vous invite au concert' and 'La Mairie de Paris vous invite au théâtre' (information on 01.42.78.44.72). The *Time Out Paris* section inside *Pariscope* covers events each week. Selected museum shows are previewed in chapter **Museums**; further annual events and festivals are covered in the **Arts & Entertainment** chapters.

Public holidays

On *jours fériés* banks, many museums, most shops and some restaurants close; public transport runs as on Sunday. New Year, May Day, Bastille Day and Christmas are the most fully observed holidays. New Year's Day (Jour de l'An) 1 Jan; Easter Monday (Lundi de Pâques); May Day (Fête du Travail) 1 May; VE Day (Victoire 1945) 8 May; Ascension Day (Jour de l'Ascension); Whit Monday (Lundi de Pentecôte); Bastille Day (Quatorze Juillet) 14 July; Feast of the Assumption (Jour de l'Assomption) 15 Aug; All Saints' Day (Toussaint) 1 Nov; Remembrance Day (L'Armistice 1918) 11 Nov; Christmas Day (Noël) 25 Dec.

Spring

end Mar: Salon de l'Agriculture
Paris-Expo, pl de la Porte de Versailles, 15th. Mº Porte de Versailles. **Information** 01.49.09.60.00/ www.salon-agriculture.com. **Admission** €6-€10.
Farmers from all over France meet to show-off prize livestock and crops. There's also a fishing-tackle exhibition and a vast hall of regional food and wine.

Mar-Apr: Banlieues Bleues
Seine St-Denis area (01.49.22.10.10/ www.banlieuesbleues.org). **Admission** €11.43-€22.87.
This five-week long festival held in the Paris suburbs draws French and international names in jazz, blues, R&B, soul, funk, flamenco, world and gospel.

early Mar: Festival EXIT
Maison des Arts et de la Culture de Créteil, pl Salvador Allende, 94000 Créteil (01.45.13.19.19/ www.maccreteil.com). Mº Créteil-Préfecture. **Tickets** €6.10-€30.49.
This modern, international festival sets contemporary dance and theatre against new technology.

mid - Mar: La Nuit des Publivores
Grand Rex, 1 bd Poissonnière, 2nd. Mº Bonne-Nouvelle. **Information** 01.44.88.98.00/ www.miko.fr/publivores/ **Admission** €34.00.
While most people might see a commercial break as an opportunity to nip to the loo (my darling), the organisers of this all-night ad-fest elevate these mini-films to cult status. A pantomime atmosphere pervades as viewers chant slogans and boo cheesy ads.

end Mar-early May: Foire du Trône
pelouse de Reuilly, 12th (01.46.27.52.29/ www.foiredutrone.com). Mº Porte Dorée. **Admission** free; rides €1.52-€3.05.
France's biggest funfair boasts over 350 attractions, including plenty of stomach-churning rides, bungee jumping, freak-shows and candy floss.

Good Friday: Le Chemin de la Croix
square Willette, 18th. Mº Anvers or Abbesses. **Information** Sacré-Coeur (01.53.41.89.00).
A crowd follows the Archbishop of Paris from the bottom of Montmartre up the steps to the Sacré Coeur, as he performs the stations of the cross.

early Apr: Festival du Film de Paris
Cinéma Gaumont Marignan, 27 av des Champs-Elysées, 8th. Mº Franklin D. Roosevelt. **Information** 01.45.72.96.40/www.festival.wannadoo.fr. **Admission** day €5.34; week €22.87.
The public can preview unreleased international films and mingle with directors, actors and technicians. A luvvie fest.

1 Apr: Poisson d'Avril
Watch your back and try not to retaliate too violently, as pranksters attempt to stick paper fish on to each other as an April Fool's gag.

7 Apr: Marathon de Paris
starts around 9am, av des Champs-Elysées, first runners finish around 11am, av Foch. **Information** 01.41.33.15.68/www.parismarathon.com.
The Paris marathon takes in many of the sites of Paris, but will you enjoy them as they load you into the oxygen tent. For those with less puff, there's a half-marathon in March.

The annual knees-up of the **Marathon de Paris**.

30 Apr-12 May: Foire de Paris
Paris-Expo, pl de la Porte de Versailles. M° Porte de Versailles. **Information** 01.49.09.60.00/ www.comexpo-paris.com. **Admission** €9.15.
This enormous salon covers all areas of the charade we call modern living, including house, garden, travel and technology.

1 May: Fête du Travail
Labour Day is more ardently maintained than Christmas or New Year. All museums and sights (except the Eiffel Tower) close while unions stage a colourful march through working-class eastern Paris via the Bastille. Lilies of the valley are sold on street corners and given (or sold, if you want to get your euros back, kids) to mum.

18 - 20 May: Le Printemps des rues
A weekend of street performance, exhibitions, and free concerts around the Bastille, Bercy, République, Nation and La Villette.

8 May-29 June: Festival de St-Denis
Various venues in St-Denis. M° St-Denis Basilique. **Information** 01.48.13.06.07/www.festival-saint-denis.fr. **Admission** €9.15-€42.69.
The Gothic St-Denis Basilica and other historic buildings host classical concerts.

Summer

27 May-9 June: French Tennis Open
Stade Roland Garros, 2 av Gordon-Bennett, 16th (01.47.43.48.00/www.frenchopen.org). M° Porte d'Auteuil. **Admission** €21-€53.

Showbiz stars fill the stands at the glitzy Grand Slam tournament to watch the balls fly.

29 May-2 June: Les Cinq Jours de l'Objet Extraordinaire
rues du Bac, de Lille, de Beaune, des Sts-Pères, de l'Université, de Verneuil, quai Voltaire, 7th. M° Rue du Bac or St-Germain-des-Prés. **Information** 01.42.60.70.10/www.carrerivegauche.com. **Admission** free.
Over 100 chic antique dealers each showcase one exciting find. Special evening and Sunday openings.

5 June-7 July: Foire St-Germain
pl St-Sulpice and other venues in St-Germain-des-Prés, 6th. M° St-Sulpice. **Information** 01.43.29.61.04/www.foiresaintgermain.org.
Concerts, theatre, lectures and workshops. In the square there's an antiques fair and poetry salon.

16 June-14 July: Festival Chopin à Paris
Orangerie de Bagatelle, parc de Bagatelle, Bois de Boulogne, 16th. M° Porte Maillot, then bus 244. **Information** 01.45.00.22.19/www.frederic-chopin.com. **Admission** €12.20-€22.87.
The romance of the piano is promised, with candle-lit evening concerts complementing the mood.

21 June: Fête de la Musique
All over France. **Information** 01.40.03.94.70/ www.fetedelamusique.fr. **Admission** free.
Free concerts all over the city. Expect rock, ragga and fusion at Denfert-Rochereau, Arab musicians at the Institut du Monde Arabe and classical at the Sainte-Chapelle and Musée d'Orsay.

mid-June: Feux de la St-Jean

quai St-Bernard, 5th
Mº Gare d'Austerlitz. **Admission** free.
Parisians celebrate the feast of St John the Baptist
with fireworks along the Seine.

23 June: Gay Pride March

Information Centre Gai et Lesbien (01.43.57.21.47/
www.gaypride.fr).
The parade of colourful floats and outrageous costumes fill the streets around the Bastille. Followed
by an official *fête* and numerous club events.

29 June-7 July: La Goutte d'Or en Fête

square Léon, 18th. Mº Barbès-Rochechouart.
Information 01.53.09.99.22. **Admission** free.
Established names play raï, rap and reggae alongside up-and-coming local talent in the largely Arab
and African Goutte d'Or neighbourhood.

13, 14 July: Le Quatorze Juillet (Bastille Day)

The French national holiday commemorates the
storming of the Bastille prison on 14 July 1789, start
of the French Revolution and a foretaste of bloodier
events to come (*see chapter* **History**). On the
evening of 13 July, Parisians dance at place de la
Bastille. More partying takes place at firemen's
balls: the stations of rue de Sévigné, rue du Vieux-
Colombier, rue Blanche and bd du Port-Royal are
particularly renowned (usually 13 and 14 July).
There's a big gay ball on quai de la Tournelle (5th).
At 10am on the 14th, crowds line the Champs-
Elysées as the President reviews a military parade
from the Arc de Triomphe to Concorde. (Note: Métro
stops on the Champs are closed.) In the evening,
thousands gather on the Champ-de-Mars for fireworks at Trocadéro.

mid July-mid Aug: Paris, Quartier d'Eté

Various venues. **Information** 01.44.94.98.00/
www.quartierdete.com. **Admission** free-100F/€15.24.
Classical and jazz concerts, dance and theatre performances are given all over the city in this lively
series. Outdoor venues include the Tuileries, the
Palais-Royal and the Jardins du Luxembourg.

16 July-25 Aug: Le Cinéma en Plein Air

Parc de la Villette, 19th (01.40.03.76.92/www.la-
villette.com). Mº Porte de Pantin. **Admission** free.
Settle back in a deckchair as night falls over the park
and take in a classic film projected onto the big
screen in the Prairie du Triangle.

6-28 July: Le Tour de France

finishes av des Champs-Elysées, 8th. **Information**
01.41.33.15.00/www.letour.fr.

Fancy dressing and fun vibes at the **Fête de
la Musique.**

Spot the yellow jersey as the cyclists speed along the
Champs-Elysées towards the finish line to complete
the final stage of the epic bike race.

15 Aug: Fête de l'Assomption

Cathédrale Notre-Dame de Paris, pl Notre-Dame, 4th
(01.42.34.56.10). Mº Cité. **Admission** free.
Notre Dame becomes again a place of religious
rather than touristic pilgrimage, with a parade
around the Ile de la Cité behind a statue of the
Virgin. A national public holiday.

Autumn

Sept: Fêtes de La Seine

Quais de la Seine (01.42.76.67.00).
Fireworks, power boats, water skiing, a *brocante*
and other events on and beside the river.

mid Sept: Jazz à La Villette

211 av Jean-Jaurès, 19th (08.03.07.50.75/
01.44.84.44.84/www.la-villette.com). Mº Porte de
Pantin. **Admission** €24.39.
Once limited to the Grande Halle, the La Vilette jazz
fest now also takes over the park, the Cité de la
Musique and even local bars. The line-up is stacked
with big names and up and coming talents.

mid-Sept: Rendez-vous Electroniques

It's a wikkid, hap'nin', mash-head cool and vibey
typa thang 'bout everything electronic. The
central meeting point for the festival hosts
debates, video projections, films and installations,
as well as concerts and DJ sets.

13, 14, 15 Sept: Fête de L'Humanité

Probably Parc de La Corneuve, Seine-St-Denis.
Information 01.49.22.72.72/www.fete2002.
humanite.presse.fr. **Admission** €9.15.
L'Humanité, French Communist Party newspaper,
has run this festival since 1930, interrupted only by
the Occupation. Its mix of world music, jazz and
heated debate (how Parisian is that?) is more popular than ever.

3rd weekend in Sept: Journées du Patrimoine

All over France. **Information** CNMHS, Hôtel de
Sully, 62 rue St-Antoine, 4th (01.44.61.20.00)
This is the weekend when thousands queue for
hours to see the parts the public cannot reach. It's
an exercise in faux state glasnost and perestroika,
but no less interesting for that. The longest waits
are for the Palais de l'Elysée (home of the President),
Matignon (home of the PM), Palais-Royal (Ministry
of Culture, Conseil d'Etat) and Palais du Luxembourg (Senate). If you don't like waiting, seek out the
more obscure embassies, ministries or opulent corporate headquarters: the Marais and Fbg-St-Ger-
main are particularly ripe for historic mansion
hopping. *Le Monde* and *Le Parisien* publish info.

Wigging out at the **Gay Pride March**.

mid Sept-end Dec: Festival d'Automne
Various venues. **Information** 156 rue de Rivoli, 1st (01.53.4517.00/www.festival-automne.com).
Admission €15.24-€38.11.
Keeping Paris at the cutting edge of all things intellectual and arty, the Festival d'Automne features challenging contemporary theatre, dance and modern opera, and is committed to bringing aspects of non-western culture into the French consciousness.

Sept: La Journée sans voitures
An attempt to save the environment by getting the French to leave their cars at home for the day.

28-9 Sept: Portes Ouvertes à la Garde Républicaine
18 bd Henri IV, 4th (01.49.96.13.26).
M° Sully Morland. **Admission** free.
The public is allowed a rare glimpse of the uniforms, arms and gleaming mounts of the Presidential Guard.

end of Sept: Salon Mix Move
Cité des Sciences et de l'Industrie, 30 av Corentin Cariou, 19th. M° Porte de la Villette. **Information** 01.40.05.70.00/www.mixmove.com. **Admission** €9.15-€15.24.
A techno salon spreading across the park, featuring concerts, conferences, DJ workshops and dance.

early Oct: Salon du Chocolat
Venue to be confirmed (01.45.03.21.26).
Admission €7.62.
Chocolatiers from around the world gather to show off their mastery of the art of chocolate-making.

Oct: Open Studios
Bastille, 11th, 12th (Artistes à la Bastille 01.53.36.06.73; Génie de la Bastille 01.40.09.84.03); Ménilmontant, 11th, 20th (01.40.03.01.61); 13ème Art, 13th (01.45.86.17.67). **Admission** free.

Painters, engravers, designers, sculptors and photographers open their studios to the public around the Bastille, Ménilmontant and the 13th.

5, 6, 7 Oct: Fête des Vendanges à Montmartre
rue des Saules, 18th. M° Lamarck-Caulaincourt. Mairie du XVIIIème, 1 pl Jules-Joffrin, 18th. M° Jules-Joffrin. **Information** 01.46.06.00.32/www.montmartrenet.com.
Music, speeches, locals in costume and a parade celebrate the Montmartre grape harvest.

5-6 Oct: Prix de l'Arc de Triomphe
Hippodrome de Longchamp, Bois de Boulogne, 16th (01.49.10.20.30/www.france-galop.com). M° Porte d'Auteuil plus free shuttle bus. **Admission** lawns free, enclosure €8.
France's richest flat race attracts the elite of horse racing amid much pomp and ceremony.

mid-Oct: Salon du Champignon
Jardin des Plantes, 36 rue Geoffroy-St-Hilaire, 5th (01.40.79.36.00/www.mnhn.fr). M° Gare d'Austerlitz. **Admission** free.
To coincide with mushroom season, the natural history museum exhibits fungi of all shapes, and gives lessons in distinguishing the deadly from the edible.

24-28 Oct: FIAC
Paris-Expo, Porte de Versailles. 15th. M° Porte de Versailles. **Information** OIP (01.41.90.47.80/www.fiac-paris.com). **Admission** €10.67.
The international contemporary art fair is hosted in the cavernous Paris-Expo convention centre.

1 Nov: All Saints' Day
Although commercially Halloween has suddenly become the big thing in France, 1 Nov remains the important date for traditionalists – a day for visiting cemeteries and remembering the dead.

early Nov: Festival Fnac-Inrockuptibles

La Cigale, Divan du Monde and other venues.
Information www.fnac.fr. **Admission** varies.
Originally indie-centred, Inrocks has lately admitted a more eclectic mix of genres, including trance, techno and trip hop. Still the place to discover the next big thing; in past years the festival has introduced Fiona Apple, Morcheeba and Travis to Paris.

8-17 Nov: Marjolaine

Parc Floral de Paris, Bois de Vincennes, 12th.
M° Château de Vincennes. **Information**
01.45.56.09.09/ www.spas-expo.com. **Admission**
€6.86.
The annual Marjolaine fair promotes organic food and wine, all-natural health and beauty products and alternative energy sources.

11 Nov: Armistice Day

Arc de Triomphe, 8th. M° Charles de Gaulle-Etoile.
At the remembrance ceremony for the dead of both World Wars, wreaths are laid by the President at the Tomb of the Unknown Soldier under the Arc de Triomphe. The remembrance flower is not the poppy but the *bleuet* (cornflower) after the colour of the *pantalons* worn by World War I infantry. *See also* **Compiègne** *in chapter* **Trips Out of Town**.

15 Nov: Fête du Beaujolais Nouveau

The arrival of Beaujolais Nouveau on the third Thursday in November is no longer the much-hyped event of a few years ago, but wine bars and cafés are still thronged (some from midnight on Wednesday, but especially Thursday evening) as customers gather to 'assess' the new vintage.

Winter

30 Nov-8 Dec Dec: Salon du Cheval, du Poney et de l'Ane

Paris Expo, pl de la Porte de Versailles, 15th.
M° Porte de Versailles. **Information** 01.49.09.64.27.
Admission €7.62-€9.91.
Inspect horses, ponies and donkeys at close quarters, or see them in action in the show jumping event.

5 Dec-1 Mar: Patinoire de l'Hôtel de Ville

pl de l'Hôtel de Ville, 4th (01.42.76.40.40). M° Hôtel de Ville. **Admission** free (skate hire €4.57).
Take to the ice on the fir tree-lined outdoor rink in front of the city hall, the perfect way to warm yourself up on a frosty evening.

6-16 Dec: Salon Nautique de Paris

Paris Expo, pl de la Porte de Versailles, 15th.
M° Porte de Versailles. **Information** 01.41.90.47.10/
www.salonnautiqueparis.com. **Admission** €4.57-€9.91.
Boat fans flock to see luxury yachts and leisure cruisers plus rowing boats, canoes and diving gear.

end of Dec: Africolor

Théâtre Gérard Philipe, 59 bd Jules-Guesde, 93200 St-Denis (01.48.13.70.00/www.africolor.com).
M° St-Denis Basilique. **Admission** €7.62.
The African music festival features traditional and new musical trends from the African continent, with a spirited end-of-festival party.

24, 25 Dec: Christmas

Christmas is a family affair in France, with a dinner on Christmas Eve, normally after mass, that traditionally involves foie gras or oysters, goose or turkey and a rich Yule log (*bûche de Noël*). Notre Dame cathedral is packed for the 11pm service. Children put out shoes for Father Christmas.

31 Dec: New Year's Eve

On the *Réveillon* or Fête de la St-Sylvestre, thousands crowd the Champs-Elysées and let off bangers. New Year is almost bigger than Christmas in France and nightclubs and restaurants put on expensive soirées. More foie gras and bubbly.

1 Jan: La Grande Parade de Paris

leaves 2pm bd Haussmann, 9th. M° Richelieu Drouot.
Information 03.44.27.45.67/www.parisparade.com.
Extravagant and colourful floats, giant balloons, bands and dancers parade along the Grands Boulevards via Opéra to the Madeleine.

6 Jan: Fête des Rois (Epiphany)

Pâtisseries sell *galettes des rois*, a flaky pastry cake with frangipane filling in which a *fève* or tiny charm is hidden. Whoever finds the charm dons a cardboard crown, becomes king or queen for a day, and chooses a consort.

Jan: Commemorative Mass for Louis XVI

Chapelle Expiatoire, 29 rue Pasquier, 8th (01.42.65.35.80). M° St-Augustin.
On the Sunday closest to 21 January, anniversary of the beheading of Louis XVI in 1793, members of France's aristocracy gather with die-hard royalists and assorted other far-right crackpots to mourn the end of the monarchy. Firm republicans are supposed to mark the day by eating *tête de veau*.

Jan/Feb: Nouvel An Chinois

Around av d'Ivry and av de Choisy, 13th. M° Porte de Choisy or Porte d'Ivry.
Head towards Chinatown, for lion and dragon dances and martial arts demonstrations in celebration of the Chinese New Year. Some restaurants offer special menus. Festivities take place on the nearest weekend(s) to the actual date.

early Feb: Festival Présences

Maison de Radio France, 116 av du Président-Kennedy, 16th (01.42.30.22.22). RER Kennedy-Radio France. **Admission** free.
Risk the contemporary at this free festival of new musical creation, by resident orchestras and guest performers, keeping tricky rhythms.

Arts & Entertainment

Circus, Cabaret & Comedy

No need to run away to join the circus – it's all here in Paris, from high kicks and high wires to *gitans* and jongleurs, and this is just the year to enjoy it.

Paris adores all things circus – it supports seven permanent circuses and welcomes others from as far afield as Mexico and Moscow. But *l'Année des arts du cirque* (summer 2001 until summer 2002) has led to an extra explosion of events centring around the home of avant-garde and experimental circus, La Villette. The programme for the year is constantly being enriched, so do check out the websites www. horslesmurs.asso.fr or www.la-villette.com.

In terms of cabaret and comedy, the boundaries between the genres are frequently blurred, with *café-théâtres* serving up a mix of dinner-theatre and stand-up. However, the **Moulin Rouge**, **Crazy Horse** and the like are still going strong with hardly a change to their programmes since last year. If it ain't broke... Probably a closer approximation to the *Moulin Rouge* as depicted by Baz Lurhman can be found at the **Cabaret Sauvage** and the new **Le Zèbre** where trapezists, lunatic clowns and jugglers mix freely with the party people.

No clowning around at **La Villette**: Cirque de la Licorne.

Circus

Traditional circuses

Cirque Alexandra Bouglione
Jardin d'Acclimatation, bois de Boulogne, 16th (01.45.00.87.00/www.bouglione.com). Mᵒ Porte Maillot. **Shows** vary. **Tickets** €12.20-€27.44 + garden entry €2.30. **Credit** AmEx, MC, V.
Alexandra, André Joseph and Sandrine Bouglione own this permanent circus venue which hosts visiting artists. Joseph has his own travelling circus.

Cirque Diana Moreno Bormann
1 bd du Bois Leprêtre, 17th (01.64.05.36.25). Mᵒ Porte de Clichy or Porte de Saint-Ouen. **Shows** 3pm Wed, Sat, Sun, school and public holidays. **Tickets** €9.15-€27.44. **Credit** V.
Claiming to have the most luxurious big top in town, this year-round traditional circus uses an array of exotic animals in the show. If your sympathies towards the animal kingdom run to any depth, you may want to give this one a miss.

Cirque d'Hiver Bouglione
110 rue Amelot, 11th (01.47.00.12.25). Mᵒ Filles du Calvaire. **Shows** vary. **Tickets** €9.15-€35.06. **Credit** V. **Map** p402 L5.
The beautiful winter circus was built in 1852 by Hittorff. Bouglione mounts his own extravaganza twice a year combining animals, tacky cabaret and some superb international performers.

Cirque de Paris
115 bd Charles de Gaulle, 92390 Villeneuve la Garenne (01.47.99.40.40/www.journeeocirque.com). Bus 137 Stade de France. **Open** Wed, Sun. Closed Jul-Sep. **Shows** 10am-5pm day of circus; 5pm circus performance. **Tickets** (day of circus) €24.50-€29 adults, €18.50-€24 children; (show only) €11-€24 adults, €7-€14.50 children. **Credit** AmEx, MC, V.
For the circus addict. Spend the day fulfilling your circus dreams, learn the tricks of the trade and even have lunch with the stars before watching the show.

Cirque Pinder
37 rue de Coulagnes, 94370 Sucy en Brie (01.45.90.21.25/www.cirquepinder.com) or Pelouse de Reuilly, emplacement Foire du Trône, 12th. **Open** all year; Pelouse de Reuilly Dec. **Shows** vary. **Tickets** €10-€30. **Credit** AmEx, MC, V.
A circus giant that's been around since 1855, Pinder is permanently stationed 40km south of Paris but moves into town for the Christmas season.

Romanès Cirque Tsiganes

*Cité Prost, 12 rue Paul Bert, 11th
(01.40.09.24.20/06.07.08.79.36). M° Faidherbe-
Chaligny.* **Open** call or check *Pariscope* for details.
Tickets €18.29, students €9.15, children €7.62.
No credit cards. Map p407 N7.

It's once seen forever smitten with the Romanès family circus. A gypsy band accompanies trapeze, juggling, contortionism and songs in the tiny *chapiteau*
that moves back here whenever they are in town.

Contemporary circus venues

Cabaret Sauvage

*parc de la Villette, 19th (01.40.03.75.15/www.
cabaretsauvage.com). M° Porte de la Villette.* **Shows**
Tue-Sun. **Tickets** €16.77-€22.87. **Credit** MC, V.
Map p403 inset.

Housed in an old circus venue, a mixture of tent,
Western saloon and hall of mirrors provides a stage
for jugglers, acrobats and other performers.

Espace Chapiteaux

*parc de la Villette, 19th (08.03.07.50.75/
www.la-villette.com). M° Porte de Pantin or Porte de
la Villette.* **Shows** Wed-Sat, Sun matinees. **Tickets**
€16.77-€22.87. **Credit** MC, V. **Map** p403 inset.

Celebrating the year of the circus, Parc de la Villette
is hosting a jam-packed calendar of superb events
at the Espace Chapiteaux. 2002's programme
includes a circus/opera hybrid by Carles Santos and
the acrobatic storytellers Cirque Desaccorde.

Olé Bodega

*square Victor, rue Lucien Bossourot, 15th
(01.53.02.90.85/www.olebodega.com). M° Balard.*
Open 8.30-2am Wed-Sat. **Shows** around 9.30pm.
Admission free, but shows for diners only. **Credit**
AmEx, MC, V. **Map** p404 D8.

A jamboree of astonishing acrobatic displays and
spirited partying. Catch the spinning, twisiting performers over dinner, before they make way for zeal-
ous gaggles of teenagers trampling the circular
wooden dancefloor to pop and French *chanson*.

Le Zèbre

*63 bd de Belleville, 20th (01.47.99.40.40). M° Père
Lachaise.* **Open** call for details. **Tickets** €20.

New for 2002, Francis Schoeller of the Cirque de
Paris has rescued the old Berry Zèbre cinema in
Belleville and plans to open it as a circus/cabaret
venue welcoming visiting artists and its own troupe,
the Cirque Cruel, while visitors eat and drink.

Cabaret & fringe

French comedy can range from stand-up to
satirical cabaret, often over dinner.

Caveau de la République

*1 bd St-Martin, 3rd (01.42.78.44.45/www.caveau.fr).
M° République.* **Show** Tue-Sat; Sun matinee. Closed
July, Aug. **Admission** €24 Tue-Thur; €30 Fri-Sun.
Credit MC, V. **Map** p402 L4.

Cabaret

Cheesy as an overripe camembert and
ripping good fun, the classic Parisian
cabarets are still great crowd-pullers.

Crazy Horse Saloon

*12 av George V, 8th (01.47.23.32.32).
M° Alma-Marceau or George V.* **Show**
8.30pm, 11pm Sun-Fri; 7.30pm, 9.45pm,
11.50pm Sat. **Admission** Champagne,
dinner and show €110; dinner €125-
€165. **Credit** DC, MC, V. **Map** p400 D4.

Enticingly named 'sculptural dancers' all
boast uniformly curvaceous bodies to
titillate a high-rolling clientele. The girls
are kept at a draconian distance from
audiences and weighed twice a month.

Le Lido

*116bis av des Champs-Elysées, 8th
(01.40.76.56.10/www.lido.fr). M° George V.*
Dinner 8pm. **Show** 10pm,12pm Sat.
Admission show €85.37 with drinks €58.69-
€70.13; dinner and show €124.25-
€157.74; matinees €70.13-€109. **Credit**
AmEx, DC, MC, V. **Map** p400 D4.

The 60 Bluebell Girls shake their stuff in
a classy show entitled *C'est Magique*.
Special effects include a fire-breathing
dragon and an ice rink. As popular as ever
with businessmen. *Wheelchair access.*

Moulin Rouge

*82 bd de Clichy, 18th (01.53.09.82.82).
M° Blanche.* **Dinner** 7pm. **Show** 9pm,
11pm daily. **Admission** €79-€89
champagne and show; €125-€155 dinner
and show. **Credit** AmEx, DC, MC, V.
Map p401 G2.

The Pigalle venue is the most trad of the
glitzy cabarets and still relies on feathers,
breasts and toothpaste smiles as the 60
Dorriss girls can-can across the stage.

La Nouvelle Eve

*25 rue Fontaine, 9th (01.48.78.37.96).
M° Blanche.* **Dinner & Show** 6.30pm,
9.45pm daily. Closed Dec-Mar. **Admission**
€73 show and half bottle of champagne,
€111 dinner and show. **Credit** AmEx, MC,
V. **Map** p401 H2.

Small-fry compared to the big-name
cabarets, La Nouvelle Eve offers a more
intimate peek, some would say flash, at
Pigalle traditions. Understandably, the
garish high-kicking show always leaves
its audiences bellowing for more.

Arts & Entertainment

The loneliest job in the world – stand up and be counted at **Hôtel du Nord**.

The *chansonnier* combines stand-up, verse-mono-logue and song, with a political-satirical bent. The older performers belong to that dinosaur-genre, the 'humourist'; younger acts are edgier and naughtier.

Chez Michou
80 rue des Martyrs, 18th (01.46.06.16.04/ www.michou.com). M° Pigalle. **Dinner** 8.30pm daily. **Show** 11pm (ring to check). **Admission** drink €30.49; dinner €89.94. **Credit** MC, V. **Map** p402 H2.
Blue-clad Michou guides proceedings from beside a stage inhabited by larger-than-life showbiz look-alikes. Book ahead if you want to dine.

Au Lapin Agile
22 rue des Saules, 18th (01.46.06.85.87/ www.au-lapin-agile.com). M° Lamarck-Caulaincourt. **Shows** 9pm Tue-Sun. **Admission** drink €19.82. **No credit cards. Map** p402 H1.
Accordionists and songsters perform traditional French songs largely for tourists' enjoyment.

Au Bec Fin
6 rue Thérèse, 1st (01 42 96 29 35). M° Palais Royal or Pyramides. **Shows** daily; matinee only on Sun. **Tickets** €7.62-€15.24; dinner & show €32.78. **Credit** MC, V. **Map** p401 H5.
The name implies good taste, and you get a chance to dine in the 300-year-old restaurant before head-ing for the intimate drama upstairs. Public auditions Monday nights are a guaranteed giggle.

Les Blancs Manteaux
15 rue des Blancs Manteaux, 4th (01.48.87.15.84/ www.blancsmanteaux.fr). M° Hôtel de Ville. **Shows** daily. **Tickets** €13.72; Mon €9.91; dinner and show €23.63. **No credit cards. Map** p402 L4.
Up to ten shows play at any one time: stand-up, text, children's shows, comedy, plays, young talent nights. *Wheelchair access.*

Café de la Gare
41 rue du Temple, 4th (01 42 78 52 51/ www.cafe-de-la-gare.fr.st). M° Hôtel de Ville or Rambuteau. **Shows** Tue-Sun. **Tickets** €18.29. **Credit** MC, V. **Map** p406 K6.
Since 1968 theatre lovers and stars of the fringe have flocked to Paris' most famous *café-théâtre* for an evening of farce or fancy.

Le Tartuffe
46 rue Notre-Dame-de-Lorette, 9th (01.45.26.21.37). M° St-Georges or Pigalle. **Shows** from 7:30pm daily. **Tickets** dinner, wine and three shows €25.92 Mon-Fri, €28.97 Sat. **Credit** MC, V. **Map** p402 H2.
True comic cabaret with great atmosphere. Three one-man-shows per night culminate in audience participation and certain embarrassment.

Le Grenier
3 rue Rennequin, 17th (01.43.80.68.01). M° Ternes. **Shows** Mon-Fri. **Tickets** €12.20; dinner and show €22.87. **Credit** MC, V. **Map** p400 D2.
If you're not fussed about history but you do like fresh decor, a sit-down meal and a stand-up routine *à la française*, then head for Le Grenier (the attic).

Comedy in English

Laughing Matters
Info (01.53.19.98.98/www.anythingmatters.com). Shows usually at Hôtel du Nord, 102 quai de Jemmapes, 10th. M° République or Jacques Bonsergent. **Tickets** €18.29. **No credit cards. Map** p402 L4.
An oasis for those gagging for some refreshing Anglophone laughs. Comic talents including Johnny Vegas and Eddie Izzard have played here, and it's a wonderful place for seeing up-and-comers just as they're up. And coming. As it were.

Children

Paris likes children, and so do Parisians. The city is full of delights for the young, and thus is full of excuses for the not-so-young to whoop it up simultaneously.

Despite the fact that French parents very often seem to be telling their offspring *not* to be doing something that looks remarkably like good fun, Paris is a most child-friendly city, and Parisians place children second only to toy dogs in their pantheon of cute. Many places have points of interest for kids; a lot of museums have play areas and exhibitions designed to set those inquisitive little brain cells into spasms of rapture (or at least keep them quiet for ten minutes).

As one might expect in a city with such intellectual cred, Parisians start buffing up their neurons at an early age: there are frequent adventurous theatrical productions, fledgling cinema seasons and any number of workshops. When it comes to soaking up the atmosphere, street markets offer plenty of entertainment, and buying a *baguette* in a bakery or sitting on a café terrace will always give the young a feel for the Paris lifestyle.

Seasonal events include fireworks in summer for the solstice and Bastille Day, animated department store windows at Christmas, the Hôtel de Ville ice rink and free merry-go-rounds (also at Christmas). Hallowe'en has taken off in a big way, too; reactionaries hate it, but children and retailers love it. The most colourful and joyous parade of the year is Gay Pride (late June), but, fun as it is, parents must prepare themselves for the possibility that it might provoke searching questions from inquisitive progeny.

The city gets more of a viable place in which to use bicycles and rollerblades each year, especially now that the distinctly Green and family-friendly Mr Delanoë is in charge of the town hall. Outings on both modes of transport are feasible along the newly created bike lanes and by the Seine and Canal St-Martin on Sundays. To find your feet, Roller Squad Institut (01.56.61.99.61/www.association.rsi. free.fr) organises roller tours and lessons for children seven and up. For swimmers, the

Piscine de la Butte-aux-Cailles has an outdoor pool, while Aquaboulevard offers fun with flumes and wave machines.

The city's hoteliers are very welcoming to children, and it's always a good idea when making your hotel reservation to ask for a baby's bed: given a week or two's notice, this can often be arranged. With cuisine a vital and proudly maintained aspect of French culture, *petits* Parisians are expected to start eating out at an early age. Even if the reverentially silent haute-cuisine temple or latest high-fashion restaurant is momentarily out of the question, it's perfectly possible to enjoy an authentic French restaurant experience with the kids in tow. Far from the frosty attitude often found in Britain, most places will happily accept children as long as they are kept under control.

Cafés are also a good bet with small children, offering an informal, fun atmosphere, speedy service, snacks and often simple hot dishes – not to mention the intrigue of espresso machines, beer pumps and lurid drinks.

Most kids' events take place on Wednesdays, weekends and holidays: see listings in *Pariscope*, *L'Officiel des Spectacles* and *Figaroscope*. The bi-monthly freebie *Paris-Mômes* is full of imaginative suggestions; it comes with *Libération* or can be picked up at the Office de Tourisme, Musée d'Orsay, MK2 cinemas and the Louvre's children's bookshop (for more outlets, call 01.49.29.01.21). The *Guide de la Rentrée*, free from the *mairie* (town hall) of each *arrondissement* or at the Kiosque Paris-Jeunes (25 bd Bourdon, 4th/01.42.76.22.60), has information about sports facilities and cultural activities for youngsters. The Comité Régional du Tourisme publishes the *Ile d'enfance*, which suggests sightseeing and activities for three-to-12s in Paris and the Ile de France, available at the Espace du Tourisme in the Carrousel du Louvre or on www.iledenfance.com.

Arts & Entertainment

Getting around

Public Transport

It is best to use public transport between 10am and 5pm to avoid the rush hour. Line 6 (Nation to Charles de Gaulle-Etoile) is mostly overground and crosses the Seine twice, once beside the Eiffel Tower. Scenic bus routes include the 24, 69 and 72, which follow the river and pass the Louvre and Musée d'Orsay. Buses 29 and 56 have an open deck at the back. Both the Montmartrobus minibus and the Montmartre funicular are part of the RATP public transport system, as is the Balabus (Apr-Sept, Sun and holidays), which takes in most of the sights. Under-fours travel free on public transport, four-ten year olds are eligible for a *carnet* (ten tickets) at half-price. The annual Carte Imagine-R (€230) gives ten-to-26s the freedom of the city – and Ile-de-France on weekends and holidays.

Taxis

Taxi drivers will generally take a family of four, as long as one of the travellers is under ten (under-tens count as half). Add €0.91 for the buggy.

Help & babysitting

The American Church

65 quai d'Orsay, 7th (01.40.62.05.00/www. americanchurchparis.org). M° Invalides. **Open** 9am-10pm Mon-Sat; 9am-7pm Sun. **Map** p402-3 D5/E5. The free noticeboard in the basement is a major source of information on recommended English-speaking baby-sitters and au pairs.

From cheeseboard to clapperboard

Mickey and his posse have done pretty well out of the movies, so it's appropriate that Disneyland Paris has celebrated its tenth anniversary by opening a second theme park, dedicated to the medium that has kept the high-pitched one in a job for years.

The new area, which is situated right next to Disneyland Paris, is called the Walt Disney Studios Park. Its aim is to bring the moving visual media to life for visitors of all ages.

The entrance is called the *Front Lot*. Visitors walk through a huge pair of studio gates to be confronted by a 33-metre-high water tower, just like the one at the entrance to the Disney Studios in California. The first complex you see is *Lights, Camera, Hollywood!*, a mock film set disguised as a street.

After the *Front Lot* comes the *Animation Courtyard*, a zone that is particularly fascinating for children as they can learn some of the methods behind the animation process before trying their hand at the art at interactive play stations. Slap bang in the midst of this paeon to all that is Hollywood

Ababa

(01.45.49.46.46). **Open** 8.30am-7.30pm Mon-Fri; 11am-7pm Sat. Childminding €5.64/hr plus €10.21 agency fee.

Ababa can provide experienced childminders or babysitters (mainly students) at the last minute.

Inter-Service Parents

(01.44.93.44.93). **Open** 9.30am-12.30pm, 1.30-5pm Mon, Tue, Fri; 9.30am-12.30pm Wed; 1.30-5pm Thur. Phone service lists babysitting agencies. Clients have to pay for the phone service only.

Message

(01.48.04.74.61/www.messageparis.org).
English-speaking support group for mothers and mothers-to-be of all nationalities living in Paris. This non-profit organisation gives advice and classes, as well as leisure activities for mothers.

comes *Animagique*, a show in which classic scenes from Disney cartoons are acted out in Czech 'black light' theatre mode. Things revert to loveable, downhome lunacy with *Flying Carpets Over Agrahbah*, where an actor playing the genie from *Aladdin* turns film director, using visiting children as his cast.

The next zone is *Production Courtyard*, which gives a real insight into the production process. The *Walt Disney Television Studios* are where theme park meets reality, as these are the actual production centre of the French Disney Channel. Visitors are able to view a functioning studio and can even have the chance to appear as extras in productions. *Cinemagique* celebrates the history of the moving image, with a combination of live performers and special effects where actors move in and out of screen scenes, giving a live quality to classic film moments.

The *Back Lot* has special effects and stunts, along with such treats as the *Rock 'n' Roller* rollercoaster, where rock band Aerosmith provide the soundtrack to a truly spectacular white-knuckle ride.

Marne-la-Vallée (01.60.30.60.30); from UK 0990 030 303. **Open** *Apr-June* 9am-8pm daily; *July, Aug* 9am-11pm daily, *Sept-Mar* 10am-6pm Mon-Fri; 9am-8pm Sat, Sun. **Admission** *high season* €34.30; €26.68 3-11s; free under-3s; *low season* €25.92; €21.34 3-11s; free under-3s. **Credit** AmEx, DC, MC, V. **Getting there**: RER A or TGV Marne-la-Vallée-Chessy. *By car* 32km by A4 Metz-Nancy exit 14.

Swings & roundabouts

Many public gardens offer mini playgrounds, sandpits and concrete ping-pong tables. Even the posh **place des Vosges** has small slides and rocking horses. The **Bois de Vincennes** and **Bois de Boulogne** provide picnic areas, boating lakes and cycle paths. For adventures there's the artificial cave and waterfall at the **Parc des Buttes-Chaumont**, the **Tuileries** has trampolines and pony rides, while the Jardin du Ranelagh has a vintage hand-cranked iron roundabout. As well as the natural history museum and Ménagerie zoo, the **Jardin des Plantes** offers an endangered species merry-go-round and spiralling yew maze. At postmodern **La Villette**, there are themed gardens, a dragon slide, prairies for picnicking and bright red *folies* housing everything from fast food to music workshops. Park-keepers seem to have got a little more lenient since the Berlin Wall came down, but the grass is still strictly out of bounds in the Luxembourg (except for one lawn), Tuileries, Monceau and Palais-Royal parks.

Any Parisian park worth its salt has its own théâtre de Guignol puppet theatre, named after its principal character, the French equivalent of Mr Punch. There is a lot of frantic audience participation, but the language can be hard to follow. Shows (around €3) are usually hourly on Wednesday afternoons, weekends and school holidays (not July and Aug).

Jardin d'Acclimatation

Bois de Boulogne, 16th (01.40.67.90.82/ www.jardin dacclimation.fr). M° *Les Sablons or Porte Maillot + Petit Train* (€1.10 every 15 mins from L'Orée du Bois restaurant). **Open** *winter* 10am-6pm daily; *summer* 10am-7pm daily. **Admission** €2.20; free under-3s. **Credit** MC, V.
Opened in 1860, this amusement park aims to cater for all the family, with zoo and farm animals, a hall of mirrors, puppets, mini-golf, table football, billiards, pony club, caterpillar and dragon rollercoasters, trampolines, mini racing circuit and new interactive Exploradome. Some attractions are free, others cost €2.13 each (book of 28 tickets €38.10).

Jardin des Enfants aux Halles

105 rue Rambuteau, 1st (01.45.08.07.18).
M° *Châtelet-Les Halles.* **Open** 9am-noon, 2-4pm Tue, Thur, Fri; 10am-4pm Wed, Sat; 1-4pm Sun (until 6pm Apr-June). July, Aug 10am-7pm Tue-Thur, Sat, Sun; 2-7pm Fri. **Admission** €0.50 one-hour session.
No credit cards. Map p406 J6.
This well-supervised garden with underground tunnels, rope swings, secret dens and pools of coloured ping-pong balls is great for seven-11s, and useful for parents visiting the adjoining Forum des Halles.

Arts & Entertainment

Running wild and floating easy at **Parc Floral.**

Jardins du Luxembourg

pl Edmond-Rostand, pl Auguste-Comte, rue de Vaugirard, 6th (01.42.34.20.00/ www.mairie-paris.fr). RER Luxembourg/ M° Odéon or St-Sulpice. **Open** *winter* 7.30am-7.45pm; summer 8am-8pm. **Map** p407 H7.

The quintessential urban park has very little wild nature, but plenty of amenities for flat-living children. The adventure playground boasts enough springy animals, slides and climbing frames to satisfy even the most frenzied toddler (entrance €1.37 children, €2.29 adults). There are swing boats, an adorable old-fashioned merry-go-round, toy sailing boats on the pond, marionnettes and pony rides.

Parc Floral de Paris

route de la Pyramide, Bois de Vincennes, 12th (01.55.94.20.20/www.parcfloraldeparis.com). M° Château de Vincennes. **Open** *summer* 9.30am-8pm; *winter* 9.30am-6pm. **Admission** €1.52 6-18s, over-60s; €2 adults. **No credit cards.**

A miniature train (€0.91) chugs between the majestic conifers of this attractive park. The adventure playground has a multitude of slides, swings, climbing frames and giant spider webs. This is also the home of the Maison Paris-Nature, a nature resource centre, and the Serre des Papillons, where children can wander among the butterflies. There are free concerts and children's shows at the Théâtre Astral.

Art & aircraft

Egyptian mummies at the **Louvre**, witty sculptures at **Musée Picasso**, Dali's surrealist sense of fun at the **Espace Dalí**, the intricate Lady and the Unicorn tapestries at the **Musée National du Moyen Age**, the costumes at the **Musée de la Mode et du Textile**, the Degas ballet dancers and the animal statues on the parvis at **Musée d'Orsay**, jets and space shuttles at the **Musée de l'Air et de** l'**Espace** all appeal to children, in limited doses. At many places under-18s get in free. *See chapter* **Museums**. Some museums (Louvre, Carnavalet, Fondation Cartier) offer guided visits by storytellers. Others (Orsay, Monnaie, Arts et Traditions Populaires, Gustave-Moreau, Halle St-Pierre) provide free activity sheets. Many organise Wednesday afternoon workshops (usually in French).

Centre Pompidou – Galerie des Enfants

4th (01.44.78.49.13). M° Hôtel de Ville/RER Châtelet-Les Halles. **Open** exhibition 1-7pm Mon, Wed-Sun; workshop Wed, Sat afternoon (and Mon, Thur, Fri during school holidays). **Workshop & exhibition** €7.62. **Map** p406 K6.

Beautifully thought-out exhibitions by top artists and designers introduce children to modern art, design and architecture, with hands-on workshops for six-to-12s. One Sunday a month (11.15am-12.30pm), *Dimanche en famille* explores painting and sculpture in a family visit to the museum.

Cité des Enfants/Techno Cité

Cité des Sciences et de l'Industrie, 30 av Corentin-Cariou, 19th (01.40.05.12.12/www.cite-sciences.fr). M° Porte de la Villette. **Open** 10am-6pm Tue-Sun. **Admission** €5.03 per session. **Credit** MC, V. **Map** p403 inset.

The whole of the futuristic Cité des Sciences et de l'Industrie at Parc de la Villette is a stimulating experience, with plenty of interactive exhibits. The Cité des Enfants (three-to-12s) and Techno Cité (11-up) are for children. Book ahead for sessions where three-fives can build a house using cranes and pulleys, and five-to-12s can learn about machines and the body. In Techno Cité, over-11s can get hands-on experience of design and technology.The Médiathèque library has a section for under-14s.

Musée de la Curiosité

11 rue St-Paul, 4th (01.42.72.13.26). M° St-Paul or Sully-Morland. **Open** 2-7pm Wed, Sat, Sun; daily during school holidays. **Admission** €6.86; €4.57 3-12s; free under-3s. **Map** p407 L7.

Come here for conjuring shows, optical illusions, psychic phenomena and an exhibition of magic props including boxes for sawing ladies in two. There are English-speaking guides and children's magic courses during the school holidays.

Musée en Herbe du Jardin d'Acclimatation

Jardin d'Acclimatation (see above). **Information** *(01.40.67.97.66).* **Open** 10am-6pm Mon-Fri, Sun; 2-6pm Sat. **Admission** €3; €2.50 3-18s, over-60s; free under-3s (plus €2.13 park entry). **No credit cards.**

Children aged four-to-12 are introduced to the history of European art from cave paintings to Picasso. There are also themed exhibitions and workshops (the circus workshop is especially good fun). *Wheelchair access.*

Musée National des Arts d'Afrique et d'Océanie

293 av Daumesnil, 12th (01.44.74.84.80/ www.musee-afriqueoceanie.fr). M° Porte Dorée. **Open** 10am-5.20pm Mon, Wed-Sun. **Admission** €4.57 (€5.79 with exhibition), €3.05 (€4.27 with exhibition) 18-25s; free under-18s. **No credit cards. Map** p407 M8.

There are ethnic artefacts from all over Africa and the Pacific, including some scary masks. The tropical aquarium downstairs is the real draw: a vast collection of colourful exotic fish placed at just the right height for children. Beware the crocodiles…

Muséum National d'Histoire Naturelle

36 rue Geoffrey-St-Hilaire, 5th (01.40.79.30.00). M° Gare d'Austerlitz or Jussieu. **Open** 10am-6pm Mon, Wed-Sun; 10am-10pm Thur. **Admission** €6.10; €4.57 students, 4-16s; free under-4s. **Credit** MC, V. **No credit cards. Map** p406 J9.

The Grande Galerie de l'Evolution borrows cinema techniques to recreate the atmosphere of the savannah, with a Noah's Ark of stuffed animals. Under-12s can play interactive games and use microscopes in the small Espace Découverte. The paleontology gallery has a renowned fossil collection, while the mineralogy museum displays giant crystals.

Palais de la Découverte

av Franklin D Roosevelt, 8th (01.56.43.20.21/www.palais-decouverte.fr). M° Franklin D Roosevelt. **Open** 9.30am-6pm Tue-Sat; 10am-7pm Sun. **Admission** €5.64; €3.05 5-18s, students; free under-5s; planetarium add €3.05 (no under-7s). **No credit cards. Map** p401 E5.

This vintage science museum manages to deliver the goods while retaining a historic, wood-panelled feel. Kids can see a colony of ants, learn about centrifugal force the hard way and play in an interactive section. Reserve ahead for the planetarium.

Animal magic

Ferme du Piqueur

Domaine National de St-Cloud, 92210 St-Cloud (01.46.02.24.53). M° Boulogne-Pont de St-Cloud/RER Garches-Marne la Coquette. **Open** 10am-12.30pm, 1.30-5.30pm Wed, Sat, Sun and school holidays. **Admission** €1.52. **No credit cards.**

Kids are introduced to farmyard fun at this small farm within the Parc de St-Cloud.

La Ménagerie

Jardin des Plantes, pl Valhubert, rue Buffon or rue Geoffroy-St-Hilaire, 5th (01.40.79.37.94). M° Gare d'Austerlitz or Jussieu. **Open** 9am-6pm daily. **Admission** €4.57; €3.05 4-16s, students, over-60s; free under-4s. **No credit cards. Map** p406 J8.

The Ménagerie, one of the oldest zoos in the world, is on a perfect scale for younger kids. It's a long way from the safari park ideal of modern zoos, but still offers plenty of vultures, monkeys, cats and reptiles.

Arts & Entertainment

Musée Vivant du Cheval

*60631 Chantilly (03.44.57.13.13/03.44.57.40.40).
SNCF Chantilly from Gare du Nord. By car 40km
from Paris by A1, exit 7.* **Open** Apr-Oct 10.30am-
5.30pm Mon, Wed-Sun (plus 2-5pm Tue July, Aug);
Nov-Mar 2-5pm Mon, Wed, Fri; 10.30am-5.30pm Sat,
Sun. **Admission** €7.62; €6.86 over-60s; €5.34 4-16s;
free under-4s. **Credit** MC, V.

Home to 40 breeds of horse and pony, the historic
stables of the Château de Chantilly are a dream for
the pony-mad. At 11.30am, 3.30pm, 5.15pm (winter
3.30pm), there are *haute-école* presentations.

Parc Zoölogique de Paris

*53 av de St-Maurice, 12th (01.44.75.20.10/00).
M° Porte Dorée.* **Open** Apr-Sept 9am-6pm daily;
Oct-Mar 9am-5pm daily. **Admission** €7.62; €4.57 4-
16s, students, over-60s; free under-4s. **Credit** MC, V.

Gibbons leaping around the trees and prowling big
cats looking for din-dins keep children and parents
amused for hours at the Paris zoo; most species wander in relative freedom. *Wheelchair access.*

Parc Zoölogique de Thoiry

*78770 Thoiry-en-Yvelines (01.34.87.52.25). By car
A13, A12 then N12 direction Dreux until Pont
Chartrain, then follow signs. 45km west of Paris.*
Open winter 11am-5pm daily; summer 10am-6pm
daily. **Admission** park €16.16; €13.72 over-60s;
€12.04 3-12s, students under 26; château €5.79;
€4.57 9-18s. **Credit** MC, V.

A hands-on approach at **Musée National
des Arts d'Afrique et d'Océanie**. See p289.

As you drive round the safari park (stay in car, keep
windows closed), zebras come up and nuzzle the
windscreen, lions laze under the trees and bears
amble past down a forest track. A second section
contains a zoo accessible on foot where rare species
include gigantic Komodo dragons, lions that can be
seen close up and beautiful snow leopards. Thoiry
is a clever mix of conservation and witty marketing,
all in the incongruous setting of château grounds.

Theme parks outside Paris

Disneyland Paris

*Marne-la-Vallée (01.60.30.60.30); from UK 0990
030 303.* **Open** *Apr-June* 9am-8pm daily; *July, Aug*
9am-11pm daily, *Sept-Mar* 10am-6pm Mon-Fri; 9am-
8pm Sat, Sun. **Admission** *high season* €34.30;
€26.68 3-11s; free under-3s; *low season* €25.92;
€21.34 3-11s; free under-3s. **Credit** AmEx, DC, MC,
V. **Getting there**: RER A or TGV Marne-la-Vallée-
Chessy. *By car* 32km by A4 Metz-Nancy exit 14.

Disney's French Empire now consists of two theme
parks, **Disneyland Paris** and **Walt Disney
Studios** (*see p286* **From Cheeseboard to
Clapperboard**). Since Mickey first invaded in 1992,
he's scuttled his way into French affections, and is
now something of a big cheese. Disneyland Paris'
pink portals are, cynicism aside, the entrance to a
great place to take kids. Fantasyland is good for
young children, and everybody with a pulse will
love the Giant Teacup ride.

France Miniature

*25 route du Mesnil, 78990 Elancourt
(01.30.16.16.30 or 01 30 16 16 40/
www.franceminiature.com). SNCF La Verrière from
Gare Montparnasse, then bus 411. By car A13, then
A12 direction St-Quentin-en-Yvelines/Dreux, then
Elancourt Centre.* **Open** Apr-mid-Nov 10am-7pm
daily (July, Aug 10am-11.30pm Sat). **Admission**
€12.50; €8.80 4-16s; free under-4s. **Credit** AmEx,
MC, V.

Over 200 models include Loire châteaux, the Mont
St-Michel, Eiffel Tower and Notre Dame. Mini interior sets have recently been added. *Wheelchair access.*

Entertainment

Fairytales, La Fontaine's fables, musical stories
and anything to do with witches and wizards
are all favourites in the numerous productions
for children staged at theatres and *café-théâtres*,
especially on Wednesdays and weekends (for
details look in French listings magazines).
Productions for very young children involving
music, clowning and dance are often accessible
for children with little or no French. Over-eights
with good French may enjoy Ecla Company's
performances of Molière and other classics
(01.40.27.82.05). A profusion of circuses pass
through Paris, especially at Christmas (*see
chapter* **Circus, Cabaret & Comedy**).

Marvelling at the sheer Gaul of it!

Even the closest student of history may not realise just how advanced a place Ancient Gaul was. Dodgems, kiddies' trains, the Three Musketeers and wicked rollercoasters were all to be found there. Sceptical? Visit Parc Astérix; the feisty little Roman-basher has his own theme park. Just as our hero could not rest while Caesar was on French territory, nor can he while the Emperor Disney is launching his own cultural invasion.

The park is split into historical zones that cover Ancient Greece, the Roman Empire, the Middle Ages and 19th-century Paris. A priority must be Astérix's own topsy-turvy village, where you'll meet actors dressed up as, among others, Getafix, Obélix and the lad himself. These characters are especially attentive and welcoming to small children.

Rides range from the fearful to the gently swinging. Daredevils should try *Goudurix*, a

terrifying loop-the-loop, or the water log frenzy that is *La Petite Tempête*. Children under one metre in height have to be accompanied by an adult, and for the more challenging rides there is a minimum size restriction of 1.2m. For those with motion sickness, there are gentler temptations, such as *La Descente Du Styx*, a water journey through hell, which is far less horrific than it sounds.

Open *Apr-mid-Oct* 10am-6pm daily; 10 *July-Aug* 9.30am-7pm daily. Closed mid Oct-Mar; ring to check extra closures. Admission 185F/E28.20; 135F/E20.58 3-11s; free under-3s. **Credit** AmEx, MC, V.
Getting there *60128 Plailly (03.44.62.34.34/www. parcasterix.fr).* RER B Roissy-Charles de Gaulle 1, then shuttle (9.30am-1.30pm, 4.30pm-closing time). By car A1 exit Parc Astérix.

High-flying basket cases at **Disneyland Sports**.

The Cité de la Musique at La Villette puts on Wednesday children's concerts and runs workshops in La Folie Musique. Selected classical concerts at the Maison de Radio France are free for under-12s accompanied by an adult (brochure 01.42.20.42.20), as are **Concerts du Dimanche Matin** (*see below*) workshops. Proto-clubbers can try the monthly Sunday afternoon 'Bal grenadine' at the Divan du Monde (*see chapter* **Clubs**).

ACT Theatre Company

(01.46.56.20.50). **Tickets** €7.62-€12.20.
This English-language company performs accessible adaptations of British works at the Théâtre de Ménilmontant and suburban MJC de Palaiseau.

The American Library

10 rue du Général-Camou, 7th (01.53.59.12.60/www. americanlibraryinparis.org). M° Ecole Militaire/RER Pont de l'Alma. **Open** 10am-7pm Tue-Sat (*Aug* noon-6pm Tue-Fri; 10am-2pm Sat). **Map** p400 D6.
The American Library offers storytelling sessions in English: for three-to-fives 10.15am and 2.30pm Wed; for one-to-threes, 10.30am first and last Thur of month; for six-to-eights monthly (day varies).

Concerts du Dimanche Matin

Châtelet, Théâtre Musical de Paris, 1 pl du Châtelet, 1st (01.40.28.28.40/children's programme 01.42.56.90.10). M° Châtelet. **Tickets** €18.29; under-26s; free 4-14s (reservation essential). **Map** p406 J6.
While parents attend the 11am classical concert on Sundays, four-to-nine-year-olds can explore instruments or composers. Budding warblers can join the choir, and well wikkid eight-to-12s can join DJ Mozart and manipulate sounds by computer.

La Croisière Enchantée

Bateaux Parisiens, Port de la Bourdonnais, 7th (01.44.11.33.44). M° Bir-Hakeim. **Trips** Oct-June 1.45pm, 3.45pm Sat, Sun, public holidays; daily school holidays. **Admission** €9.15.
Credit MC, V. **Map** p404 C6.
Two elves take three-to-ten-year-olds (and their parents) on a one-hour enchanted boat trip up the Seine, with songs and games laid on (in French).

Forum des Images

2 Grande Galerie, Porte St-Eustache, Nouveau Forum des Halles, 1st (01.44.76.63.44/47/ www. forumdesimages.net). **Après-midi des enfants** 3pm Wed, Sat. **Admission** €3.51 (€5.49 adults). **Credit** MC, V. **Map** p406 J6.
Movies go from previews to *Harry Potter*. Check to see if it is in VO (original language) or VF (French).

Théâtre Astral

Parc Floral de Paris (see above). **Information** *(01.43.71.31.10).* **Tickets** €5.50 (+€1.52 park entry). **No credit cards.**
The Astral offers three-to-eights attention-holding epics about ogres and princesses in a bucolic setting. The programme for 2002 includes an adaptation of *Grimm's Fairy Tales*. Reservation necessary. *Wheelchair access (call ahead).*

Théâtre Dunois

108 rue du Chevaleret, 13th (01.45.84.72.00). M° Chevaleret. **Tickets** €9.15; €6.10 3-15s. **No credit cards. Map** p407 M10.
Adventurous theatre, dance and musical creations will widen expectations of culture for kids. In 2002, plays include *Mange-Moi*, an intriguing offering about a bulimic girl and an anorexic ogre. *Wheelchair access (call ahead).*

Arts & Entertainment

Clubs

DJ bars are still an integral part of the scene, but the newest venues dare to be different with experimental programming and even drinks on the house. Chilled.

Clubbing in Paris veers between outstanding and immensely disappointing, depending on where you end up and on what night. There are hundreds of small clubs scattered around the city where the music policy doesn't go beyond 80s pop and *chanson française*. Thankfully, a handful of clubs maintain an up-to-date music policy with quality DJs, although genres rarely adventure further than house and techno. Fans of drum 'n' bass, ragga, trance and hip-hop have to wait for one-offs, usually organised by collectives such as Black Label or Under Pressure (drum 'n' bass), Gaia (trance) and MasIMas (hardcore). UK garage has so far failed to interest Paris clubbers.

DJ bars such as **OPA**, **Alcazar**, **Wax**, **Man Ray** and **La Fabrique** have become a regular part of the Paris clubbers' itinerary as they now compete with clubs, offering name DJs, late opening hours, a dance floor and often free entrance and cheapish drinks. However, huge club events with international headline

DJs such as Scream, Open House and Club Europa at **L'Elysée Montmartre**, BPM and House of Legend at **Enfer**, Trade and Respect is Burning at **Queen**, draw in the crowds at weekends. Big one-off nights are often linked to Fashion Week or other events such as Les Rendez-vous électroniques in September and the Mix Move salon in October, both of which create a massive buzz.

Another important aspect of Paris clubland is the after-hours party. These draw clubbers from all over the city into one venue to carry on clubbing until midday. **Folies Pigalle** and

Enfer's Diskotek hold 'afters' every Saturday and Sunday mornings. After Kwality has become *the* Sunday morning institution, and monthly Biyatch is the only 'after' that isn't tied down to a house/tec-house music policy

A respite from house, house and more house is found at the **Batofar**. The former lighthouse ship which is a favourite with the Anglophone crowd has now become a mini complex with restaurant, club and bar as well as outdoor events on the quayside in the summer such as Cake and Milk. The other alternative is the **Nouveau Casino**, the recently-opened annexe to the Café Charbon. Here concerts and club nights cover a wide range of musical genres including rock, electronica, drum 'n' bass, electro, dub and minimal techno.

World music nights offer another alternative, with Latino and African clubs and bars and distinctive one-off events. Latino and Antillais communities have their own bars and clubs and those who have a taste for close contact dancing are always welcome. There are one-off world festivals at the **Divan du Monde** and the **Cabaret Sauvage** (*see chapter* **Cabaret, Circus & Comedy**).

There is also a return to traditional *bals,* which have a high-school reunion atmosphere with live bands and quaintly retro DJs armed with microphones and prehistoric patter. Le Bal des Ringards at **Gla'zart** and Le Bal at **Elysée Montmartre** are two of the most successful.

The real alternative to the usual clubbing scene is free parties (better known as 'frees'), which are organised by sound systems throughout France. These nights, often held on the outskirts of Paris, are attracting more and more young Parisians as not only are they free or very cheap, but everyone is welcome. This is definitely not the case in more conventional clubs, which often have a very restrictive and often openly racist door policy.

USEFUL ADVICE
The coolest clubbers don't arrive until after 2am and often go to several clubs and DJ bars in one evening. This is not cheap at the weekends but many clubs hold free nights and invitations can often be found among normal flyers. Bouncers are often given free rein at the door, and have a particularly bad reputation for being rude and racist. The problem has been so bad that SOS Racism has enabled victims to prosecute.

GETTING IN: THE GOLDEN RULES
1) Be confident. Wimpish dithering at the door means instant refusal. Think: 'This is my club: I have the right to be here'.

2) For the more traditional clubs, wear black and avoid jeans and trainers. For the trendier clubs wear a total look or a trade-mark, for example a cowboy hat or purple fur coat.
3) Speak English loudly in the queue – tourists mean money, and clubs like to have an international clientele. That's you.
4) Don't arrive in a group unless you are girls dressed to kill (in which case you may even get in free). Boys, a model on your arm helps.
5) Once inside, order a bottle of champagne or Jack Daniels (*une bouteille).* This guarantees you a table and VIP treatment. And tipsiness.

ESSENTIAL VOCABULARY
Paris' club culture has, like that of most cities, developed its own language; it's useful to recognise a few words in order to know what to avoid as well as how to blend in with the crowd. **Bouncer** *physio;* **Hash** *shit;* **Ecstasy** *taz* or *X;* **Joint** *ouinj;* **Grass** *herbe;* **Great!** *mortel!;* **Guy** *mec;* **Girl** *nana, gonzesse* or *meuf;* **Police** *keufs;* **Money** *maille* or *ozaille.*

INFO AND GETTING HOME
Radio FG's Plans Capitaux (98.2 FM, throughout the day) and Radio Nova's Bons Plans (101.5 FM 6pm, 7pm, weekdays) and www.france-techno.fr and www.novaplanet.com provide up-to-date clubbing information. Shops such as Le Shop and Kiliwatch around rue

Etienne-Marcel (1st/2nd *arrondissements)* have flyers with club details; also try rue Keller (11th).

Getting home between the last (around 12.45am) and first Métro (5.45am) can be difficult, especially if you're feeling jaded after an evening on the dance floor. The best bet is a taxi but there are *bus de nuit* (night buses), which run between Châtelet and the suburbs; maps are available at Métro stations.

Gilded youth

Where teenybopping under-agers clink glasses with superannuated sugar daddies and their surgically-enhanced wives.

Club Castel

15 rue Princesse, 6th (01.40.51.52.80). M° Mabillon. **Open** 9pm-dawn Tue-Sat. **Admission** free (members and guests only). **Drinks** €15.25. **Credit** AmEx, DC, MC, V. **Map** p405 H7.
Paris as St-Tropez. The strict door policy – members and friends only – ensures an elite clientele. Pretend you've just minced in off your yacht.

Duplex

2bis av Foch, 16th (01.45.00.45.00). M° Charles de Gaulle-Etoile. **Open** 11pm-dawn Tue-Sun. **Admission** €15.25 Tue-Thur, Sun (girls free before midnight); €18.30 with drink Fri, Sat. **Drinks** €9.15. **Credit** AmEx, MC, V. **Map** p400 C3.

The Duplex caters for young wannabes and privileged youths. Regulars look as though they have raided a parent's wardrobe. A sultry restaurant upstairs is transformed into a chill-out room where champagne flows in rivers.

Le Monkey Club

67 rue Pierre-Charron, 8th (01.58.56.20.50). M° George V. **Open** 11pm-dawn Mon-Sat. **Admission** free. **Drinks** €12.20. **Credit** AmEx, DC, MC, V. **Map** p400 D4.
A newcomer in the 8th *arrondissement* where everybody goes bananas. After an attempt at laying on hip-hop and r'n'b for the wealthy, they've now settled for acid jazz and funk. The funky loos have pebbles in the sink and piped monkey noises (at least that's what we thought they were).

Cool clubs

Dress: on the cool side of trendy, but smart if it's your first time there. Avoid baseball caps and track suit bottoms. If in doubt wear shoes, although designer trainers are usually accepted. Flares would be a positive advantage. (That whirring sound you can hear is Fred Astaire spinning in his grave).

Les Bains

7 rue du Bourg-l'Abbé, 3rd (01.48.87.01.80). M° Etienne-Marcel. **Open** 11.30pm-5am daily. Restaurant 8.30pm-1am. **Admission** €15.25 Mon-Thur; €18.30 Fri-Sun. **Drinks** €10.70. **Credit** AmEx, MC, V. **Map** p402 K5.
The concentration of beautiful people at this club in a former public baths is impressive. Unfortunately, the music policy has become a little dated: house and garage. Look out for hip-hop stars at 'Be-Fly' (Wed). Booking a table at the restaurant will almost certainly ensure that you get in.

Batofar

11 quai François-Mauriac, 13th (01.56.29.10.00). M° Bibliothèque. **Open** 8pm-4am Tue-Sun. **Admission** €9.15. **Drinks** €2.30-€6.85. **Credit** AmEx, MC, V. **Map** p407 N10.
This waterborne club is a quayside complex with a restaurant bar on deck and the club on board with a chill-out room. Evenings start with live music, followed by DJs playing anything from electronica to drum'n'bass. Paris' fashion brigade turns up on Sunday mornings for the afters, and on summer Sunday afternoons for a musical tanning session.

La Coupole

102 bd du Montparnasse, 14th (01.43.20.14.20). M° Vavin. **Open** 11pm-5amThur- Sat; **Admission** €15.25. **Drinks** €8.40-€10.65. **Credit** AmEx, DC, MC, V. **Map** p405 G9.
This joint has true terpsichorean pedigree. It was one of the first venues in Paris to risk dancing the

tango in the 20s. After a ten-year stint as a salsa club it has now become home to house and garage nights such as *Cheers* on Fridays, which used to be a monthly night at Queen.

Le Divan du Monde

75 rue des Martyrs, 18th (01.44.92.77.66). M° Pigalle. **Open** 8.30pm/midnight-dawn daily. **Admission** free-€18.30. **Drinks** €3.80-€6.10. **Credit** MC, V. **Map** p402 H2.
Le Divan sees an eclectic mix of alternative club nights at weekends. There are regular jungle, raï, ragga, r'n'b, Brazilian and trance events. The drinks are cheap, the atmosphere is friendly and there is no strict dress code, so where better to chill?

Who's who in clubland

Movers and shakers

Their names are dropped in nocturnal conversation and everyone claims to know them. Famous for organising big events, DJing or just existing, meet the capital's brightest and most *branché*.

Cathy and David Guetta

Heavily influenced by the USA, UK and Ibiza club scenes, the couple's first events brought clubbing to the capital's youth. After a stint as the faces of the infamous Palace they are now the *Direction Artistique* (entertainment managers) for Les Bains. David Guetta also DJs and is part of 'Wake Up'. Their restaurant, Tanjia, attracts all the faces and the pair recently opened Paris' first upmarket lap dancing club, Platinum.

Sylvie Chateigner

This elegant lady of the night began her career as manageress of an exclusive second-hand clothes shop. From there she launched her Thanx God I'm a VIP nights, attracting clubbers and the fashion world.

Wake Up

The team that organises the biggest, flashiest events with international DJs Ludo and Jérome. The Scream nights – usually featuring David Guetta – are reputed to be the biggest gay events in town. Wake Up is also behind the hedonistic Diskotek after-parties (L'Enfer) as well as BPM and House of Legend.

Magic Garden

Siblings Béatrix and Brice Mourer have turned their one-off rave events into a huge money-spinning machine. As well as launching most of Paris' celebrity DJs and their own record label, they organise events around France and leave Paris for seasonal one-offs.

Fabrice Lamy

Responsible for the After Kwality parties and the lounge events held at the ultra-chic Mezzanine bar of the Alcazar, he is really making his mark on the scene.

Valéry B

The person to know for those who have made The Rex club their home. He started out as the 'Physio' at the Gibus and now plays a major role in the Rex's scene.

DJs

Most of Paris' star DJs stick to their own territory, and rarely reach international status. Maybe it's a language barrier thing; there's certainly no lack of talent. Once launched on the city, big-name DJs seem to appear on every flyer and at every event. Watch out for:

Breakfastisback

An Anglo-French DJ collective with FJlook, Dinahbird, Lea and X resident at Batofar and specialising in chill-out sessions, combining spoken word and beats. Style: anything from electronic to break-beat.

Dan Ghenacia

He is the man of the moment. Launched by Magic Garden, Ghenacia later became resident of After Kwality. Style: trippy Chicago-influenced house.

Jack de Marseille

Ignore the naffness of the moniker. This lively lad features in most big techno events around France. Style: banging Detroit-style techno.

Otis

An Englishman abroad, Otis launched himself in Paris as a Jungle MC. He is now one of the capital's leading drum & bass DJs. Style: UK-influenced drum 'n' bass, hard step.

Cut Killer

Most remember him as the DJ from Mathieu Kassovitz's film *La Haine*, but Cut Killer is, without a doubt, Paris' most wanted hip hop DJ. Style: French and US hip hop on the commercial side.

Dee Nasty

The veteran scratch DJ who makes appearances now and then at fashion events and house clubs. Style: Old school funk and hip hop.

Paco

He started as resident DJ for Open House and has joined the list of Paris' most wanted DJs. Style: Percussive House.

Sex Toy

Probably more famous for her tattoos than her mixing, but she remains the most media-friendly and high-profile female DJ in the city. Style: anything from commercial house to hardcore techno.

Elysée Montmartre

72 bd de Rochechouart, 18th (01.44.92.45.38).
Mº Anvers. **Open** varies. **Admission** €12.20-€38.
Drinks €3.80-€6.10. **Credit** AmEx, DC, MC, V.
Map p402 J2.
Originally a concert venue, at weekends l'Elysée is
home to regular monthly nights such as Scream
and Le Bal. Watch out for huge house events such
as Open House and Club Europa.

Folies Pigalle

11 pl Pigalle, 9th (01.48.78.25.26). Mº Pigalle.
Open midnight-dawn Tue-Sat; 6pm-midnight Sun.
Admission free Mon-Thur; €15.25 Fri-Sat; €6.10
Sun. **Drinks** €4.60-€7.60. **Credit** V. **Map** p401 G2.
This ex-strip joint attracts an assortment of weirdos
and transsexuals. Some have speculated that they
pump poppers through the air-conditioning: that
could explain a lot. Resident DJs spin house at weekends and after-parties are always packed.

Le Gibus

18 rue du Fbg-du-Temple, 11th (01.47.00.78.88).
Mº République. **Open** 9pm-dawn Tue; midnight-
dawn Wed-Sat. **Admission** €7.60 Tue; free Wed-
Thur; €15.25 Fri-Sun. **Drinks** €6-€7.60.
Credit AmEx, DC, MC, V. **Map** p402 L4.
The Wednesday free trance event is popular, but
most nights resident DJs simply rehash copies of
nights from the 1995 Paris club boom. Recent
attempts at r'n'b and world music are unlikely to
last. Big-name DJs crop up occasionally.

Glaz'art

7-15 ave de la Porte de La Villette, 19th
(01.40.36.55.65). Mº Porte de La Villette. **Open**
8.30pm-2am Thur (sometimes Weds); 10pm-5am Sat,
Sun. **Admission** €6.10-€10.70. **Drinks** €3-€4.60.
Credit MC, V. **Map** p403 inset.
From the outside this club looks like a scout hut on
the side of a motorway. Inside, the low ceilings make
the venue a little claustrophobic, but this must be
the only club with a garden, which makes summer
nights here very pleasant. Music varies from dub to
chanson and from disco to techno.

Le Queen

102 av des Champs-Elysées, 8th (01.53.89.08.90).
Mº George V. **Open** midnight-dawn daily.
Admission €7.60 Mon, Sun; free Tue, Thur;
€4.60 Wed; €15.25 Fri, Sat. **Drinks** from €7.60.
Credit AmEx, DC, MC, V. **Map** p400 D4.
This is the nearest Paris gets to London's super
clubs, with its own merchandising and magazine.
Wednesday night's Break is open to all, Saturday is
especially gay and Friday is the night to look out
for big names – London's Trade is invited once a
month. Mondays, Sundays and Thursdays rely on
kitsch disco to bring in the crowds. Brace yourself
for the bitchy drag queens on the door.

Nouveau Casino

109 rue Oberkampf, 11th (01.43.57.57.40).
Mº Parmentier or St-Maur. **Open** daily 9pm-2am,
sometimes till 5am. **Admission** free-€12.20.
Drinks €3-€4.50. **Credit** AmEx, MC, DC, V.
Map p403 M5.
This newcomer has started to make its mark.
Offering an alternative to the **Batofar**, it has an
eclectic music policy of live music and DJs. The
decor is a little cold and the early closing is maybe
a tad restricting, but this is a space to watch out for.

Pulp

25 bd Poissonniere, 9th (01.40.76.01.93). Mº Grands
Boulevards. **Open** Midnight-5am Wed-Sat.
Admission Free-€9.15. **Drinks** €4.57-7.62.
Credit MC,V **Map** p402 J4.
Officially a lesbian club on the weekends but
Wednesdays and Thursdays see top DJs and col-
lectives drawing in a mixed crowd. This has become
the (un)official music business hang-out.

Rex Club

5 bd Poissonnière, 2nd (01.42.36.28.83).
Mº Bonne Nouvelle. **Open** 11pm-dawn Wed, Thur,
Fri; 11.30pm-dawn Sat. **Admission** €9.15 Wed;
€10.70 Thur-Fri; €12.20 Sat. **Drinks** €4.60-€7.60.
Credit AmEx, MC, V. **Map** p402 J4.
The Rex prides itself on its quality DJs. Entry is
refused only when the club is too full, so arrive early
when big-name guests play. Friday's Automatik is
one of Paris' few authentic techno nights.

Mainstream

These clubs attract a mixed crowd. Dress: clean
and casual. Avoid trainers, baseball caps, etc.

La Loco

90 bd de Clichy, 18th (01.53.41.88.88). Mº Blanche.
Open 11pm-5am daily. **Admission** €10.70 with
drink Mon-Thur, Sun; €15.25 with drink Fri, Sat.
Drinks €7.60. **Credit** AmEx, MC, V. **Map** p401 G2.
The teen club of Paris, attracting kids from the outskirts as well as groups of exchange students who
don't know better. The three floors offer pop and
rock, Euro-dance and hip-hop played by radio DJs.
On Sundays, the doors open to the gay community
with an Ibizan tea-dance concept, 'Domingo Club'.

L'Atlantis

32 quai d'Austerlitz, 13th (01.44.23.24.00).
Mº Quai de la Gare. **Open** 11pm-dawn Fri-Sat,
public holidays. **Admission** €16.80.
Drinks €10.70 **Credit** MC, V. **Map** p407 M9.
One of the most popular French Caribbean clubs,
and you can feel why the minute you sample the
calm buzz that pervades the place. The dress code
fits all your cool dude stereotypes: women wear
painted-on dresses and men wear suits with barn-
door shoulders, but somehow all this seems to
enhance the mood. Those who like to erect barriers
around their personal body space, be warned; the
dancing is always close contact.

Latino, jazz & world

Parisians do Latino clubs well. Dress: it may be
a cliché, but red dresses and heels are the norm
(for the ladies); the men wear drainpipes, white
socks and loafers. Nice.

Le Balajo

9 rue de Lappe, 11th (01.47.00.07.87). Mº Bastille.
Open 9pm-2am Wed; 2.30-6.30pm, 10pm-5am Thur;
11.30pm-5.30am Fri, Sat; 2.30-6.30pm, 9pm-1am Sun.
Admission €12.20 Wed (€6.10 women); €15.25
Thur-Sat; €7.60 Thur afternoon, Sun. **Drinks** €7.60-
€9.15. **Credit** AmEx, DC, MC, V. **Map** p407 M7.
Bal-à-Jo (as it used to be called) has been going for
over 60 years. Wednesday's rock 'n' roll, boogie and
swing session attracts some colourful customers,
but these days it's starting to look a bit washed out.

Caveau de la Huchette

5 rue de la Huchette, 5th (01.43.26.65.05).
Mº St-Michel. **Open** 9.30pm-2.30am Mon-Thur, Sun;
9.30pm-3.30am Fri, Sat. **Admission** €9.15 Mon-
Thur, Sun; €8.40 students; €10.60 Fri, Sat. **Drinks**
from €4.60. **Credit** MC, V. **Map** p406 J7.
This is enduringly popular with ageing divorcées
and wannabe, pot-bellied Stones with dodgy feath-
er cuts during the week. Sublime. At weekends it

attracts a mixed bunch who boogie to soulful jazz or
enjoy live rock 'n' roll or jazz.

La Chapelle des Lombards

19 rue de Lappe, 11th (01.43.57.24.24). Mº Bastille.
Open 10.30pm-dawn Thur-Sat; concert Thur 8.30pm
(€9.15-€12.20). **Admission** €15.25 Thur (women
free before midnight); €18.30 Fri, Sat. **Drinks** €4.60-
€11.45. **Credit** AmEx, MC, V. **Map** p407 M7.
Tourists and Latino and African residents sweat it
out in this cramped venue. DJ Natalia La Tropikal
mixes salsa, merengue, zouk and tango at weekends.

Les Etoiles

61 rue du Château d'Eau, 10th (01.47.70.60.56).
Mº Château d'Eau. **Open** 9pm-3.30am Thur;
9pm-4.30am Fri-Sat; 6.30pm. **Admission** €18.30
with meal; €15.25-€9.15 with/without drink from
11pm. **Drinks** €3.05-€6.10. **No credit cards.**
Map p402 K3.
Top-notch musicians electrify a soulful crowd here.
There is not much space, but that doesn't stop the
night-owl crowd giving it some. Women are unlikely to be left standing still for more than a couple of
minutes, and veterans dish out footwork advice.

La Java

105 rue du Fbg-du-Temple, 10th (01.42.02.20.52).
Mº Belleville. **Open** 11pm-6am Thur Sat; Sun 2-7pm.
Admission €9.15-€12.20 Thur; €15.25 Fri, Sat;
€4.60 Sun. **Drinks** €5.35-€7.60. **Credit** AmEx, DC,
MC, V. **Map** p403 M4.
Hidden away in a disused Belleville market, La Java

is a Mecca for salsa lovers. DJs and live bands play
anything tropical and Latino to a fun-loving crowd.
Watch out: Thursday is trance night.

Bar clubs

These laid-back clubs are some of the better
places to watch live bands and hear the latest
music. Fashionable restaurants, such as Alcazar
and Man Ray, also increasingly hold DJ nights.

Cithéa

114 rue Oberkampf, 11th (01.40.21.70.95).
Mº Parmentier. **Open** 9.30pm-5am daily.
Admission free Mon, Tue, Sun; €4.60 Wed, Thur;
€9.15 Fri, Sat. **Drinks** €5.35-€9.15. **Credit** MC, V.
Map p403 M5.
The Cithéa has become a prime concert venue for

world music and jazz. At weekends, however, disco and funk nights pull everyone in at closing time – the result is a sweaty nightmare.

La Fabrique

53 rue du Fbg-St-Antoine, 11th (01.43.07.67.07).
M° Bastille. **Open** 11am-5am daily. **Admission** free
Mon-Thur; €7.60 Fri, Sat. **Drinks** €4.60-€6.10.
Credit AmEx, DC, MC, V. **Map** p407 M7.
A DJ bar which turns into a mini-club at weekends.
Top local DJs attract a trendy Bastille crowd,
although most are there for the club's kudos rather
than its music. The bouncers are especially rude.

Man Ray

34 rue Marbeuf, 8th (01.56.88.36.36). M° Franklin
D Roosevelt. **Open** 7pm-2am Mon-Thur.
Admission free. **Drinks** €6.10-€10.70. **Credit**
AmEx, MC, V. **Map** p400 D4.
With its mock-Chinese decor and be-seen restaurant,
Man Ray is at the heart of the Champs-Elysées
revival. From Mon to Thur relax to live jazz at the
mezzanine bar; from midnight onwards DJs spin
house, trip-hop and techno.

Mezzanine/Alcazar

62 rue Mazarine, 6th (01.53.10.19.99). M° Odéon.
Open 8pm-2am Wed-Sun. **Admission** free.
Drinks €3.80-€7.60. **Credit** AmEx, DC, MC, V.
Map p405 H7.
Terence Conran's Parisian brasserie has opened its
doors to house: the combination of the city's most
desirable DJs and the laid-back mezzanine bar works

its magic to draw in Parisian yuppies. 'Personalities'
and DJs are invited to play a down-tempo personal
selection on Friday's Lounge night.

Popin

105 rue Amelot, 11th (01.48.05.56.11).
M° Filles du Calvaire. **Open** 6.30pm-1.30am Tue-Sun.
Admission free. **Drinks** €2.15-€5.35. **Credit**
AmEx, MC, V. **Map** p402 L5.
Predominantly French, with more than a smattering
of students, Popin also attracts savvy young inter-
nationals looking for a pint or ten of the old falling
down lotion (€5.35 for Kilkenny or Guinness). On
weekends the tiny downstairs dancefloor heaves as
local DJs spin whatever they fancy, from big beat to
indie classics. Some even show a bit of imagination
in their choice of sounds.

Project 101

Project 101, 44 rue de La Rouchefoucault, 9th
(project101@ifrance.com). M° Pigalle or St-Georges.
Open 9pm-2am Wed, Fri, occasional Suns
Admission €10 non members, €8 members.
Drinks free. **No credit cards. Map** p402 H3.
Not strictly a bar or club but more of a living room
home-from-home. DJs and VJs perform to an arty
crowd who help themselves to the free bar and swap
ideas. The music is decidedly varied.

Wax

15 rue Daval, 11th (01.40.21.16.16).
M° Bastille. **Open** 8pm-2am Mon-Sat. **Admission**
free. **Drinks** €3.80-€9.15. **Credit** AmEx, DC, MC,
V. **Map** p407 M7.
Wax is worth going to just for the orange swirly
paintwork and plastic dinner tables. However, you
have to spend to be allowed near the comfy white
leather sofas. The music is essentially house.

Guinguettes

For a taste of authentic dance-floor style, head
to the *guinguette* dance halls along the Marne.

Chez Gégène

162bis quai de Polangis, 94340 Joinville-le-Pont
(01.48.83.29.43). RER Joinville-le-Pont. **Open** *Apr-*
Oct 9pm-2am Fri (live band); 7pm-midnight Sun
(recorded). **Admission** €32 (dinner); €13.70 (drink).
Credit AmEx, MC, V.
This is the classic *guinguette*, packed with elderly
French dance fiends, dapper *monsieurs*, multi-
generational families and young Parisians. Dine
near the dance floor and you can get up for a fox-
trot, tango or rock 'n' roll number between courses.

Guinguette du Martin-Pêcheur

41 quai Victor-Hugo, 94500 Champigny-sur-Marne
(01.49.83.03.02). RER Champigny-sur-Marne.
Open *1 Apr-15 Nov* 8pm-2am Tue-Sat; noon-8pm
Sun; *10 Nov-23 Dec* Fri-Sat 8pm-2am. **Admission**
free Tue-Sat; €6.10 Sun. **Drinks** €2.30-€3.05.
No credit cards.
The newest (built in the 1980s) and hippest of the
dance halls, on a tiny, tree-shaded island reached by
raft. There's a live orchestra Sat and Sun afternoon.

Dance

Whether you're looking to take in a classic ballet or learn some avant-garde tap, Paris can always offer you *quelque chose de* twinkle toes.

Paris has impeccable dance credentials, and in many ways, it's terpsichore city central. Toulouse-Lautrec immortalised its can-can girls; Gene Kelly set the *trottoirs* ablaze and paid an unforgettable tribute to French dance in '*An American in Paris*'; it was here that Nureyev made his pirouette to 'freedom', and the can-canning Moulin Rouge was the backdrop for Kidman and McGregor in 2001. That was then. Paris in 2002 is one of the leading cities in which to watch or perform dance. The scene is emerging from the relative slump that was caused by dance budgets being cut – as so often, tough times have brought benefits: the fittest have survived.

One event that the Paris dance world awaits with anticipation is the arrival this year of Brit Michael Clark and his iconoclastic style at the **Théâtre National de Chaillot**. It will be fascinating to observe both Clark's offering and the French reaction to it.

For those who harbour ambitions to be Chief Snowflake themselves, Paris has more dance studios than any other European city. Announcing that you have decided to learn how to rhumba is no admission of irredeemable posiness here (*see p302* **Stepping out**); you can find out what's on via www.ladanse.com, maintained by France's leading dance monthly, *Les Saisons de la Danse*.

Information

Centre National de la Danse (CND)
Administration *1 rue Victor Hugo, 93507 Pantin cedex (01.41.83.27.39/www.cnd.fr). M° Hoche.*
The headquarters of the state-funded national dance centre opened in Pantin in early 2000, and by the end of 2002, all its departments will be consolidated here. The CND also offers subscriptions to all the major venues, as well as careers advice to aspiring hoofers and exhibitions on the development of the art.

International Dance Council
1 rue Miollis, 15th (01.45.68.25.54). M° Ségur.
Open call for details. **Map** p404 D8.
The Council, housed in the UNESCO annex, has become ambitiously administrative: it is in the process of setting up the Global Dance Directory, a database of everything to do with dance.

Major dance venues

Ballet de l'Opéra National de Paris
Palais Garnier *pl de l'Opéra, 9th (08.36.69.78.68 /www.operadeparis.fr). M° Opéra.* **Box office** 11am-6.30pm Mon-Sat. Closed 15 July-Aug. **Tickets** €4.57-€60.22. **Credit** AmEx, MC, V. **Map** F4
Opéra de Paris Bastille *pl de la Bastille, 12th (08.36.69.78.68). M° Bastille.* **Box office** 11am-6.30pm Mon-Sat. Closed 15 July-Aug. **Tickets** €6.86-€60.22. **Credit** AmEx, MC, V. **Map** p406 L7.

Opéra de Paris: it's *allongé* to tip a fairy.

Highlights of the 2002 classical season are *Le Parc*, choreographed by Angelin Preljocaj, and *Don Quichotte*, choreographed by Nureyev. Modern treats include Kader Belarbi's *Hurlevent* and ballets set to the music of Stravinsky by Dunn, Bausch and Balanchine. *Wheelchair access (call ahead on 01.40.01.18.08).*

Théâtre des Champs-Elysées

15 av Montaigne, 8th (01.49.52.50.50/www.theatre-champselysees.fr). M° Alma-Marceau. **Box office** 1-7pm Mon-Sat; telephone bookings 10am-noon, 2-6pm Mon-Fri. Closed mid-July-Aug. **Tickets** €9.15-€59.46. **Credit** AmEx, MC, V. **Map** p400 C5.
This elegant hall was made famous by dance pioneer and scarf victim Isadora Duncan, and it's still viable and valid. 2002 sees a new production of Tango Pasion's *A los amigos* and the spectacular *Gala des Etoiles du XXIe siècle*. *Wheelchair access.*

Théâtre de la Ville

2 pl du Châtelet, 4th (01.42.74.22.77/www.theatre delaville-paris.com). M° Châtelet-Les Halles. **Box office** 11am-7pm Mon; 11am-8pm Tue-Sat; telephone bookings 11am-7pm Mon-Sat. Closed July-Aug. **Tickets** €14.48-€28.97; €7.62-€10.67 under 27s on day of performance, but phone ahead. **Credit** MC, V. **Map** p401 H6.
Paris' leading contemporary dance forum is still at the cutting edge. This season book well in advance for works by Régine Chopinot, Anne Teresa De Keersmaeker (celebrating 20 years of productivity) and Pina Bausch. Its sister Théâtre des Abbesses (31 rue des Abbesses, 18th) programmes ethnic dance. *Wheelchair access.*

Théâtre National de Chaillot

1 pl du Trocadéro, 16th (01.53.65.30.00/www. theatre-chaillot.fr). M° Trocadéro. **Box office** 11am-7pm Mon-Sat; 11am-5pm Sun; telephone bookings 9am-7pm Mon-Sat; 11am-5pm Sun. Closed July-Aug. **Tickets** 10.67-€28.97. **Credit** MC, V. **Map** p400B5.

With choreographer José Montalvo at the helm, world-class dance has now joined theatre at Chaillot. Highlights for 2002 include Jean-Claude Gallotta's *99 Duos*, the unveiling of Michael Clark's iconoclastic talent before a Paris audience via three special choreographies and a homage to Jacques Tati by Jérôme Deschamps and Macha Makeïeff. *Wheelchair access.*

Independent dance spaces

Centre Mandapa

6 rue Wurtz, 13th (01.45.89.01.60). M° Glacière. **Box office** 30min before performance or by phone. **Tickets** €12.20-€15.24; €9.15-€10.67 students; €6.10 under 16s. **No credit cards. Map** p401 H1.
This space is dedicated largely to traditional Indian dance and music. It stages works by companies from India, China, the Middle East, North Africa and Eastern Europe. It also organises some excellent classes. *Wheelchair access (call ahead).*

L'Etoile du Nord

16 rue Georgette-Agutte, 18th (01.42.26.47.47). M° Guy-Môquet. **Box office** 10am-6pm Mon-Fri. Closed July-Aug. **Tickets** €7.62-€18.29; €12.20 students, over 60s; €7.62 under-26s. **Credit** MC, V.
This theatre provides a much-needed platform for the contemporary multi-media dance scene. Les Jaloux in May promotes exciting short works by young dancemakers.

Le Regard du Cygne

210 rue de Belleville, 20th (01.43.58.55.93). M° Place des Fêtes or Télégraphe. Closed Aug. **Tickets** €4.57-€7.62. **No credit cards. Map** p403 N4/Q3.
Home to the Worksweek programmes designed to promote new choreographic talent, this dance space has also championed Spectacles Sauvages, during which (nearly) anybody can join in the dance – for a symbolic fee.

Stepping out

If Paris makes you feel like dancing you'll be spoiled for choice. Beyond the huge selection of ballet, jazz, modern and tap classes you might expect, Parisian dance classes also offer glimpses of other cultures. The Centre de Danse du Marais (41 rue du Temple, 4th, 01.42.52.07.29) offers an array of classes, from Afro-Cuban to yoga. Juju Alishina teaches two very different styles of Japanese dance: traditional 17th-century, involving kimonos and fans, and the beautiful buto form, which was developed in the 1950s.

A school of international reknown is **Studio Harmonic** (5 passage des Taillandiers, 11th, 01.49.23.40.43/ www.studioharmonic.fr), which holds summer workshops with world-famous teachers (generally not for beginners). If none of the 20 or so jazz and modern classes appeal, you can try Egyptian dance. The students, aged from early-20s to 70s, look the part in long, silky skirts and head scarves.

Flamenco en France (33 rue des Vignoles, 20th, 01.43.48.99.92) is one of the best places to develop Andalusian attitude – not only are teachers such as La Juana outstanding, but the setting feels like a genuine slice of Spain. La Juana's end-of-year show proves what dancers can accomplish after two to five years' study: this is no school recital but real flamenco.

Also in the 20th *arrondissement,* the **Centre Momboye** (25 rue Boyer, 20th, 01.43.58.85.01/www.parisdance.com) focuses solely on African dance. If you've ever wondered what distinguishes Togolese from Senegalese dance (and, let's face it: all of us have), this is the place to find out. You could start with Michel Gnivo-Correa's Afro-gym class, a get-fit introduction to African dance. Soon you might find yourself booking a flight to Senegal – once you're gripped by a dance form, the natural urge is to get to know its country of origin's culture better.

Raghunat Manet, a star Indian dancer based in Paris and Pondichery, warns against taking up a dance form without also taking its culture seriously. 'People take dance classes the way they would take aerobics, and I don't agree with that.' Bah! Humbug! Surely the love of a country can *begin* with a love of its artistry.

Théâtre de la Cité Internationale
21 bd Jourdan, 14th (01.43.13.50.50). RER Cité Universitaire. **Box office** 2-7pm Mon-Sat. Closed July-Aug. **Tickets** all seats €8.38 Mon. **Credit** MC, V.
The highlight of this year promises to be a visit by Emmanuelle Vo-dinh, performing to music by Björk collaborator, Zeena Parkins. *Wheelchair access.*

Dance classes

Salle Pleyel
252 rue du Fbg-St-Honoré, 8th (01.45.61.53.00) *M° Ternes.* **Open** 9am-6pm Mon-Fri. Closed Aug. **Map** p400 D3.
A number of ballet-oriented dance schools are housed in amazing spaces that seem to be straight out of a Degas painting.

Centre International Danse Jazz
54a rue de Clichy, 9th (01.53.32.75.00). M° Place de Clichy. **Open** 9am-10pm Mon-Fri; 11am-7.30pm Sat. **Classes** €11.89. **Credit** V. **Map** p401 G2/G3.
This epitome-of-cool school draws famous dancers, with an emphasis on ballet, jazz and hip hop.

International Isadora Duncan Center
175 av Ledru-Rollin, 11th (01.43.67.31.92). *M° Voltaire.* **Classes** €12.20. **Map** p403 N6.
Classes, workshops and videos promote contemporary, modern and early modern traditions.

Centre des Arts Vivants
4 rue Bréguet, 11th (01.55.28.84.00). M° Bastille. **Open** 10am-10pm Mon-Fri; 9.30am-7pm Sat. **Classes** €10.67. **Map** p407 M7.
This studio complex provides training for amateurs and pros alike in modern jazz, contemporary, flamenco, African dance and hip hop.

Espace Oxygène
168 rue St-Maur, 11th (01.49.29.06.77). M° Bastille. **Open** 11am-7pm Sat. **Classes** fees vary. **Map** p403 M3.
This studio in a converted loft offers classes including Afro-Brazilian, capoeira and tango, and holds exciting tango *bals.*

Ateliers de Paris-Carolyn Carlson
Cartoucherie de Vincennes, Bois de Vincennes, 12th (01.41.74.17.07). M° Château de Vincennes. **Open** 10am-6pm Mon-Sat. **Classes** fees vary.
The celebrated American dancer offers professional training in dance, improvisation, theatre and music via a series of one- to two-week master classes.

Académie des Arts Chorégraphiques
4bis Cité Véron, 18th (01.42.52.07.29). M° Blanche. **Open** 9am-10pm Mon-Sat; noon-9pm Sun. **Classes** average €11.
The clean and friendly Académie offers classes in ballet, modern jazz, hip hop and is also home to Paris' only school of Russian character dance. Russian characters should form a queue.

Film

The French cinema industry is big and booming, and skipping along in its vanguard is a doe-eyed sugar babe by the name of Amélie.

If the French film industry minted yearly commemorative medals, the issue for 2001 would have been a hefty golden disc emblazoned with the doe-eyed, butter-wouldn't-melt face of Amélie Poulain – possibly in a Delacroix-style 'Amélie leading the people' tableau. For the sweet heroine (played by Audrey Tautou, *see p305*) of Jean-Pierre Jeunet's smash hit movie, *Le Fabuleux Destin d'Amélie Poulain*, became the figurehead of an amazing reversal of fortunes in French film. After the doom and gloom of the previous year, 2001 dished up one Gallic success story after another: at the final tally, the top four box office winners were all French (Amélie scooping the first prize, natch – eight million viewers and rising), and French films accounted for a glowing 40 per cent of total takings. Everything was up: numbers of French or part-French productions (over 170, the highest number since the early-80s); numbers of tickets sold (a rise partly owing to the success of the 'cartes illimitées', or unlimited-view season tickets); and the public's level of satisfaction with home-grown product. It seemed like France's movie industry had finally cracked what film-goers wanted, and was giving it to them: big budget comedies like *Le Placard* and *La Vérité si je mens 2*, or SFX-heavy action-adventures like *Le Pacte des loups* and *Vidocq*. Hollywood was being pushed back by the doughty Gaul; and as a final morale booster, *Amélie* and *Le Pacte* set off for glittering international careers.

In artistic terms, too, 2001 was a solid year, notable for a number of return-to-form titles from established directors: films like André Téchiné's *Loin*, Eric Rohmer's *L'Anglaise et le duc*, Claude Miller's *Betty Fisher et autres histoires*, and Jacques Rivette's *Va savoir*. Other highlights included films from rising stars like Bertrand Bonello's *Le Pornographe* and Laurent Cantet's *L'Emploi du temps*.

So, champagne all round, then? Alas, not quite. Towards the end of the year, alarm bells rang out as newly-formed media monolith Vivendi-Universal lined up its torpedoes on the unique funding system which keeps the French industry so buoyant. Vivendi's boss, Frenchman Jean-Marie Messier (known by the molecular-sounding moniker J2M) has no sentimental feelings for the cinematic output of his home country: say the word 'culture', runs the rumour, and he reaches for his calculator. TV channel and Vivendi

subsidiary Canal+ backed up Messier's fighting talk by announcing its intention to slash investment in cinema – currently around a third of the cash pumped into new productions every year – come 2004. More cause for concern came from the growing obstacles to distribution facing foreign films from outside Hollywood: package deals and ever less adventurous distributors mean it's getting harder for unknown film-makers from abroad to get their films onto French screens and, once there, to make any kind of profit.

It would be a terrible shame if the amazing choice of films shown in France were strangled by purely financial considerations. France remains streaks ahead of anywhere else in its love of foreign film and willingness to programme the most obscure foreign director: the film-going public here has an enduring curiosity for foreign cinema, particularly films from the Far East and countries like Iran. Paris is truly a film lover's paradise. And if Amélie isn't just a flash in the pan, the future could be rosy.

For venues, times and prices, see the *Cinéscope* section of *Pariscope,* which lists all new titles ('*Films Nouveaux*'), films on general release ('*Exclusivités*'), re-releases ('*Reprises'*) and festivals. Foreign films are screened in 'VO' (original language with French subtitles) or 'VF' (dubbed into French).

Ciné showcases

Le Cinéma des Cinéastes

7 av de Clichy, 17th (01.53.42.40.20). Mº Place Clichy. **Tickets** €6.56; €5.34 Wed, students, under-12s, over-60s. **Map** p401 G2.
Once a famous cabaret, this three-screen showcase of world cinema (with France at the forefront, of course) was the brainchild of Jean-Jacques (*Betty Blue*) Beneix and Claude (*Garde à vue*) Miller. Decorated to evoke old-fashioned film studios, it holds regular meet-the-director sessions, and festivals of classic, foreign, gay and documentary films. It accepts *cartes illimitées* (season tickets). *Bar-restaurant. Wheelchair access.*

Gaumont Grand Ecran Italie

30 pl d'Italie, 13th (08.36.68.75.13). Mº Place d'Italie. **Tickets** €8.80; €7 students, over-60s; €5.50 under-12s. **Map** p406 J10.
The huge complex boasts the biggest screen (24m x 10m) in Paris: here blockbusters like *Titanic* and *Gladiator* really do bust blocks. *Wheelchair access.*

La Géode

26 av Corentin-Cariou, 19th (01.40.05.12.12). Mº Porte de la Villette. **Tickets** €8.75; €6.75 students. **Credit** MC, V. **Map inset** p403.
An OMNIMAX cinema housed in a glorious, shiny geodesic dome at La Villette. Most films feature 3D plunges through dramatic natural scenery. Booking is advisable. *Wheelchair access (reserve ahead).*

Le Grand Rex

1 bd Poissonnière, 2nd (08.36.68.05.96). Mº Bonne Nouvelle. **Tickets** €6.90; €5.35 students, over-60s, under-12s. **Map** p402 J4.
The blockbuster programming of this huge art deco cinema matches the vast screen. It also puts on Les Etoiles du Rex, an SFX-packed behind-the-scenes tour. *Wheelchair access.*

Max Linder Panorama

24 bd Poissonnière, 9th (01.48.24.88.88/ 08.36.68.00.31). Mº Grands Boulevards. **Tickets** €8; €6 students, under-20s Mon, Wed, Fri. **Map** p409 J9.

A state-of-the-art screening facility (THX sound) in a house founded in 1920 by silent French comic Linder. The walls and seating are all black, to prevent even the tiniest twinkle of reflected light distracting the audience from what's happening on the screen, so this is not the sort of place to start lobbing popcorn or rustling your crisp packet. Look out for all-nighters and one-offs such as rare vintage films. *Wheelchair access.*

MK2 sur Seine

14 quai de la Seine, 19th (01.53.26.41.77/ 08.36.68.47.07). Mº Stalingrad. **Tickets** €8.10; €6 Mon, Wed, students; €5.50 under-12s. **Map** p403 M2.
The stylish six-screen flagship of the MK2 group offers an all-in-one night out, complete with restaurant and exhibition space. The MK2 chain, which belongs to French producer Marin Karmitz, is a paradigm of imaginative programming, screening short films before each feature, just like the good old days. Voracious film buffs can buy the *Carte Le Pass*, which offers unlimited access for €18 per month. *Wheelchair access.*

UGC Ciné Cité Les Halles

7 pl de la Rotonde, Nouveau Forum des Halles, 1st (08.36.68.68.58). Mº Les Halles. **Tickets** €8.10; €5.95 students, over-60s; €5.50 under-12s. **Map** p402 J5.
This ambitious 16-screen development screens art movies as well as mainstream, and holds 'meet the director' screenings. UGC has gone two screens better at the Ciné Cité Bercy (2 cour St-Emilion, 12th/08.36.68.68.58/Mº Cour St-Emilion), and launched its *UGC Illimitée* card – unlimited access for €16.46 per month. *Internet café. Wheelchair access.*

Art cinemas

Action

Action Christine *4 rue Christine, 6th (01.43.29.11.30). Mº Odéon.* **Tickets** €6.50; €5 students, under-20s. **Map** p406 J7.
Action Ecoles *23 rue des Ecoles, 5th (01.43.29.79.89). Mº Maubert-Mutualité.* **Tickets** €6; €4.50 students, under-20s. **Map** p406 J8.
Grand Action *23 rue des Ecoles, 5th (01.43.29.79.89). Mº Cardinal-Lemoine.* **Tickets** €6.50; €5 students, under-20s. **Map** p406 K8.
A Left Bank feature since the early 80s, the Action group is renowned for screening new prints of old movies. Heaven for those nostalgic for 1940s and 50s Tinseltown classics and American independents, with anything from Cary Grant to Jim Jarmusch.

Accattone

20 rue Cujas, 5th (01.46.33.86.86). Mº Cluny La Sorbonne. **Tickets** €6; €5 Wed, students, under-20s. **Map** p406 J8.
Named after Pasolini's first film and housed in what was once the venue for France's first strip show, this temple to art house cinema screens films by Bresson, Oshima, Wenders and the like to an earnest crowd.

Cuteness and cutlery After Amélie Poulain, French cinema is over the spoon.

Le Balzac

1 rue Balzac, 8th (01.45.61.10.60/08.36.68.31.23).
M° George V. **Tickets** €7; €5.5 Mon, Wed,
students, under-18s, over-60s. **Map** p400 D4.
Built in 1935 with a mock ocean-liner foyer, Le
Balzac scores high for design and programming.

Le Champo

51 rue des Ecoles, 5th (01.43.54.51.60).
M° St-Michel. **Tickets** €7; €5.5 Wed, students,
under-20s. **Map** p406 J7.
Opened in 1939, this much-loved Latin Quarter art
house is now a listed historical monument. Its programming varies from Far Eastern cinema to retrospectives of French and US directors.

Le Cinéma du Panthéon

13 rue Victor-Cousin, 5th (01.40.46.01.21).
RER Luxembourg. **Tickets** €7; €5.5 Mon, Wed,
students, 13-18s; €4 under-13s. **Map** p406 J8.
Renamed in April 2001, Paris' oldest surviving
movie house (founded in 1907 in the Sorbonne gymnasium) is still a place to catch new, often obscure
international films.

Le Denfert

24 pl Denfert-Rochereau, 14th (01.43.21.41.01).
M° Denfert-Rochereau. **Tickets** €6.10; €4.60 stu-
dents, over-60s; €4.30 under-15s. **Map** p406 H10.
This valiant, friendly little spot was founded in 1933.
Its eclectic repertory selection ranges from François
Ozon and Kitano to short films and new animation,
as well as new foreign films you won't find any-
where else in Paris. *Wheelchair access.*

L'Entrepôt

7-9 rue Francis de Pressensé, 14th (08.36.68.05.87).
M° Pernéty. **Tickets** €6.41; €4.88 students, over-
60s. **Credit** MC, V. **Map** p405 F10.
The number of films screened each week is quite
modest, but the programme is wide-ranging: new
and Third World directors, shorts, gay cinema and
regular debate sessions. *Café. Restaurant.*

Le Latina

*20 rue du Temple, 4th (01.42.78.47.86). M° Hôtel de
Ville.* **Tickets** €7; €5 students, under-20s. **Map**
p406 K6.
Le Latina screens films from Italy, Spain, Portugal
and Latin America. There are also Latino dances, a
gallery and a restaurant.

La Pagode

*57bis rue de Babylone, 7th (01.45.55.48.48). M° St-
François-Xavier.* **Tickets** €7.30; €.5.80 Mon, Wed,
students, under-21s. **Map** p405 F7.
The seventh *arrondissement* only has this one cinema,
but what a cinema it is: two screens housed in a 19th-
century replica of a Far Eastern pagoda (not, as legend has it, a stone-by-stone import) that was given
Historic Monument status in 1986. Films shown here
tend to be of Far Eastern origin too.

Studio 28

10 rue Tholozé, 18th (01.46.06.36.07). M° Abbesses.
Tickets €6.80; €5.60 under-12s. **Map** p401 H1.
Montmartre's historic Studio 28 was the venue for
Cocteau's scandalous film L'Age d'Or in 1930.
Today it offers a decent repertory mix of classics
and recent movies.

La Pagode: Far Eastern on the outside, Far Eastern on the inside. *See p305.*

Studio Galande

42 rue Galande, 5th (01.43.26.94.08/ 08.36.68.06.24). M° St-Michel. **Tickets** €7; €5.35 Wed, students, under-18s. **Map** p406 J7.
This lovable hole in the wall holds high the tradition of the *Rocky Horror Picture Show* (10.30pm Fri, Sat) amid an extremely eclectic programme.

Public repertory institutions

Auditorium du Louvre

entrance through Pyramid, Cour Napoléon, 1st (01.40.20.51.86/www.louvre.fr). M° Palais Royal. **Tickets** €4.57; €3.35 under-18s. **Map** p402 H5.
This 420-seat auditorium was designed by IM Pei. Film screenings are sometimes related to the exhibitions; regulars are silent movies with live music, often specially composed, which benefit from the excellent acoustics. *Wheelchair access.*

Centre Pompidou

rue St-Martin, 4th (01.44.78.12.33/ www.centrepompidou.fr). M° Hôtel de Ville. **Tickets** €5; €3 students. **Map** p406 K6.
Themed series, along with experimental and artists' films and a weekly documentary session, give a flavour of what's on. There's also the Cinéma du Réel festival of rare and restored films. *Wheelchair access.*

La Cinémathèque Française

Palais de Chaillot, 7 av Albert-de-Mun, 16th (01.56.26.01.01/www.cinemathequefrancaise.com). M° Trocadéro. **Tickets** €4.73; €3 students. **Map** p400 C5.

Grands Boulevards, 42 bd Bonne-Nouvelle, 10th (01.56.26.01.01). M° Bonne Nouvelle. **Tickets** €4.73; €3 students, membership available. **Map** p400 J4.
The Cinémathèque played a key role in shaping the New Wave directors in the late 1950s. The fate of the still-shut film museum seems doubtful, as plans to develop a Maison du Cinéma at Bercy seem to be on indefinite hold. In the meantime, run by American Peter Scarlet, the Cinémathèque continues to hold seasons devoted to directors of all stripes and origins. The auditorium was recently renovated (though the grey colour scheme is slightly dull); as you buy your ticket, a modern LED screen tells you the quality of the print you are about to view – the sort of detail any film buff will appreciate.

Forum des Images

2 Grande Galerie, Porte St-Eustache, Forum des Halles, 1st (01.44.76.62.00/ www.forumdesimages.net). M° Les Halles. **Open** 1-9pm Tue, Wed, Fri-Sun; 1-10pm Thur. Closed 2 weeks in Aug. **Tickets** €5.50 per day; €4.50 students, under-30s, over-60s; membership available. **Map** p402 J5.
This is an addictive archive dedicated to Paris on celluloid from 1895 to the present. No matter how brief the clip – from the Eiffel Tower scene in *Superman II* to the opening of *Babette's Feast* – if Paris is on film, you'll find it here. A Star Trek-like consultation room has 40 video consoles. 2002 topics for the auditoria include 'Mum', 'Buenos Aires' and 'Intolerance'. The Forum also screens the Rencontres Internationales du Cinéma (*see below*), the trash treats of L'Etrange Festival and films from the critics' selection at Cannes. Something for every kind of film lover here. *Wheelchair access.*

Festivals & special events

Côté Court

Ciné 104, 104 av Jean Lolive, 93500 Pantin/ 01.48.46.95.08). M° Eglise de Pantin. **Dates** Mar-Apr.
A great selection of new and old short films from far and wide.

Festival International de Films de Femmes

Maison des Arts, pl Salvador-Allende, 94000 Créteil (01.49.80.38.98). M° Créteil-Préfecture. **Dates** Mar-Apr.
An impressive selection of retrospectives and new international films by female directors. *Wheelchair access (reserve ahead).*

Rencontres Internationales du Cinéma

Forum des Images (see above). **Dates** Oct-Nov.
A global choice of new independent features, documentary and short films, many screened in the presence of their directors. Audiences vote for the winner of the *Grand Prix du Public*; other attractions include a workshop series and debates galore.

City of lights, camera, action!

With a town as camera-friendly as Paris – both visually and bureaucratically – it's hardly surprising that it should be the set of some of the most memorable cinematic moments. The Eiffel Tower is often the star attraction, but it's worth looking out for the supporting cast, too.

Hôtel du Nord
(Marcel Carné, 1938)
Though most scenes for this hotel by the Canal St-Martin were actually shot in a studio, it's now a national monument – as was the leading lady Arletty. On the bridge (*pictured, below*), the film's shrill heroine uttered the immortal 'Atmosphere! Atmostphere!'

Funny Face
(Stanley Donen, 1956)
Audrey Hepburn was in her element filming in Paris. In this *très* fashion number with Fred Astaire, she sings '*Bonjour Paree*' to a range of sights, including the Eiffel Tower and Champs-Elysées. Most memorable is her existentialist shin-dig in a Montmartre bar.

A Bout de Souffle
(Breathless, Jean-Luc Godard, 1959)
A classic tale of girl meets vagabond, with Jean Seberg as the cutest *Trib* vendor on the Champs-Elysées. The offices where she picked up copies have sinced moved, but you can pitch up at the former building at 21 rue de Berri, in the 8th. Stand in the middle of

rue Campagne-Première in Montparnasse to relive a timeless Belmondo pose.

Zazie dans le Métro
(Louis Malle, 1960)
The ultimate New Wave Paris tour in the company of the impish Zazie. The whole city features, but the star is the Eiffel Tower, scene of some truly vertiginous images.

Last Tango in Paris
(Bertolucci, 1972)
Brando heads for a steamy rendezvous with Maria Schneider in an apartment overlooking the Passy Métro station. And don't forget the memorable crossing of the Pont Bir-Hakeim.

Subway
(Luc Besson, 1985)
Christophe Lambert and Isabelle Adjani (both suffering a bad hair day) run around the RER in La Défense and Les Halles, in Besson's subterranean *cinéma du look* tale of quirky hustlers and hassle.

La Haine
(Matthieu Kassovitz 1995)
This grainy black and white agitprop opus was mostly shot in the *banlieue* of Chanteloup-les-Vignes outside Paris but came downtown for the protagonists to meet the art bourgeoisie. The three likely lads outrage the art world at Galerie Gilbert Brownstone in the Marais.

Bridging the gap in Marcel Carné's classic film **Hôtel du Nord**.

Galleries

Contemporary art in Paris has become the scene of fertile exchanges between media, artists, disciplines, galleries and institutions.

Just as artists might well be producing paintings, sculptures, photos, installation, video or indeed all of these, many artists are also bridging disciplines as DJs, filmmakers, designers or writers. Networks of artists, curators and designers serve both as arenas for exchange and debate and sometimes even shared projects that challenge the idea of individual artistic authorship and identity, as in the manga cartoon heroine Anna Lee who has featured in films by Philippe Parreno, Pierre Huyghe and Dominique Gonzalez-Foerster. While some artists make works largely about art and art practice, others are more concerned with the outside world, creating works that comment on fashion, advertising and media, science and technology.

There's a symbiosis between Paris' commercial galleries and public institutions. Anyone interested in the gallery scene will also be watching what's going on at the **Centre Pompidou**, **Musée d'Art Moderne de la Ville de Paris**, **Site de Création Contemporaine**, **Centre National de la Photographie** and **Fondation Cartier** to name the most important. It is the gallery that will follow an artist over the long term and which is often also actively concerned with the production of works, not merely financially and technically, but in the organisation behind ambitious video and installation projects.

Paris gallery shows are wildly international: it's easy to get an idea of what's going on in Europe and even Asia, sometimes less so to get a fix on what's being produced locally. With neither the celebrity media hype of London nor the sheer scale and energy of New York, the Paris scene remains relatively low-key and elitist. But action there is. The city remains a draw for artists from all the world (Albanian Anri Sala, the Irish Malachi Farrell, Chinese Huang Yong Ping, Korean Koo Jeong-A, Swiss Thomas Hirschhorn for starters) and very much the centre of all activity in highly centralised France. Two recently established prizes, the Prix Ricard and Prix Marcel Duchamp, are bringing a higher profile to art made in France, and the 20- and 30-something generation are increasingly gaining attention alongside long-established names like Sophie Calle, Daniel Buren or Christian Boltanski.

THE ART CIRCUIT

Fortunately, like-minded galleries tend to cluster together, which makes tracking the art scene relatively simple. For new, innovative work and international names head for the northern Marais and the streets near the Centre Pompidou or to 'Louise', the growing nucleus of young galleries around rue Louise-Weiss in the 13th *arrondissement*. Galleries around the Bastille mainly present young artists, while those around St-Germain-des-Prés, home of the avant-garde in the 1950s and 60s, largely confine themselves to traditional sculpture and painting. Galleries near the Champs-Elysées present big modern and contemporary names, but are most unlikely to risk the untried. The International art fair **FIAC** in October gives a quick fix on the gallery scene. To be fair, the contemporary in the name is tempered by a hefty dose of establishment modern, although a new video section was added in 2001.

A growing circuit of alternative structures includes artist-run spaces, such as Glassbox and Public, and shows put on by curators in venues that vary from private apartments to churches or shopping centres. Look out also for art on the web, with the annual festival Art Outsiders (www.art-outsiders.com) run with the Maison Européenne de la Photographie and the Semaine électronique.

There are numerous chances to visit artists' studios. The Génie de la Bastille, Ménilmontant and 13ème Art are the best known, but there are also *'portes ouvertes'* (often in May or October) in Belleville, St-Germain, the 10th, 14th and 18th *arrondissements* and the suburbs.

INFORMATION & MAGAZINES

Local publications include monthlies *Beaux Arts*, *L'Oeil*, bilingual *Art Press* and the fortnightly news and market-oriented *Journal des Arts*, as well as hip quarterly fashion/art/sex volume *Purple*. For information on current shows, look for the *Galeries Mode d'Emploi* (Marais/Bastille/rue Louise-Weiss) and *Association des Galeries* foldouts (Left and Right Bank/suburban cultural centres), as well as more occasional artists' publications and flyers, which can be picked up inside galleries. Virtually all galleries close in August and often in late July and early September.

Arts & Entertainment

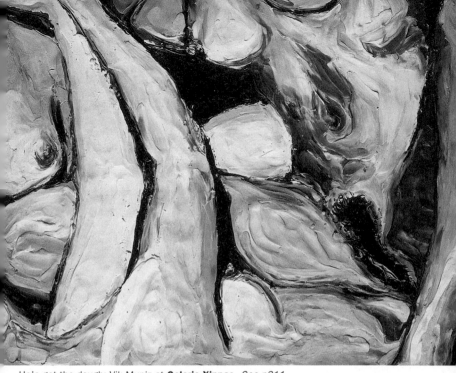

He's got the dough: Vik Muniz at **Galerie Xippas**. *See p311.*

Beaubourg & the Marais

Chez Valentin
9 rue St-Gilles, 3rd (01.48.87.42.55). M° Chemin Vert. **Open** 2.30-7pm Tue-Sat. **Map** p407 L6.
A sense of urban angst pervades the installations, photography and video art by the young French artists here. Look for the creeping detritus installations and videos of Véronique Boudier, photos by Nicolas Moulin and videos by François Nouguiès.

g-module
15 rue Debelleyme, 3rd (01.42.71.14.75/ www.g-module.com). M° Filles du Calvaire. **Open** 2-7pm Wed-Sat. **Map** p402 L5.
New Yorker Jeff Gleitch's recently opened gallery concentrates on introducing new New York artists, with a marked taste for fine draughtsmanship. Check out the comic strip-influenced paintings of Mark Dean Veca.

Galerie Chantal Crousel
40 rue Quincampoix, 4th (01.42.77.38.87/ www.crousel.com). M° Rambuteau/RER Châtelet-Les Halles. **Open** 11am-7pm Tue-Sat. **Map** p406 J6.
Crousel founded her Beaubourg gallery in 1980 and today focuses on the hottest of the new generation, including Abigail Lane, Rikrit Tiravanija, the politically inspired installations of Thomas Hirschhorn, the video works of Graham Gussin and Albanian-born Parisian Anri Sala. She also represents a few big names such as Tony Cragg. A maze of dark cellars makes for atmospheric video viewing.

Galerie Valérie Cuerto
10-12 rue des Coutures-St-Gervais, 3rd (01.42.71.91.89/www.valeriecueto.com). M° Rambuteau. **Open** 10am-1pm, 2.30-7pm Mon-Sat. **Map** p402 K5.
This new gallery alternates individual shows by young artists and imaginative themed gatherings.

Galerie de France
54 rue de la Verrerie, 4th (01.42.74.38.00). M° Hôtel de Ville. **Open** 11am-7pm Tue-Sat. **Map** p406 K6.
This is one of the rare galleries to span the entire 20th century. Shows have included Brancusi sculpture, Surrealist Meret Oppenheim and Raysse's Pop, as well as contemporary sculptor Alain Kirili and the mechanical devices of Rebecca Horn.

Galerie Marian Goodman
79 rue du Temple, 3rd (01.48.04.70.52). M° Rambuteau. **Open** 11am-7pm Tue-Sat. **Map** p406 K6.
The New York gallerist's Paris outpost is now in the beautiful 17th-century Hôtel de Montmor. Alongside established names, including Thomas Struth and Lothar Baumgarten, she has also snapped up brilliant young Brit videomaker Steve McQueen and fast-rising South African William Kentridge.

Galerie Karsten Greve

5 rue Debelleyme, 3rd (01.42.77.19.37/ www.artnet.com/kgreve). M° Filles du Calvaire or St-Paul. **Open** 11am-7pm Tue-Sat. **Map** p402 L5.
This historic Marais building is Cologne gallerist Karsten Greve's Parisian outpost and venue for retrospective-style displays of top-ranking artists, among them Jannis Kounellis, Louise Bourgeois, Cy Twombly and Tony Cragg.

Galerie du Jour Agnès b

44 rue Quincampoix, 4th (01.44.54.55.90/ www.agnesb.fr). M° Rambuteau/RER Châtelet-Les Halles. **Open** noon-7pm Tue-Sat. **Map** p402 J5.
Agnès b's gallery now occupies Fournier's old space. Many artists share the designer's interests in Third World and social observation: Brit photographer Martin Parr, Italian Massimo Vittali, Africa's Félix Brouly Bouabré and filmmaker Jonas Mekas.

Galerie Laage-Salomon

57 rue du Temple, 4th (01.42.78.11.71). M° Hôtel de Ville. **Open** 2-7pm Tue-Fri; Sat 11am-7pm. **Map** p406 K6.
Laage-Salomon alternates painters including Philippe Cognée and art photography from the likes of Hannah Collins and Axel Hütte.

Galerie Yvon Lambert

108 rue Vieille-du-Temple, 3rd (01.42.71.09.33). M° Filles du Calvaire. **Open** 10am-1pm, 2.30-7pm Tue-Sat. **Map** p402 L5.
Lambert, one of France's most important dealers, has redesigned his gallery with a skylit central space, a series of smaller rooms and a sociable browsing area, with a new video lounge at the front. European and US giants include Carl André, Julian Schnabel, Nan Golden, Andres Serrano, Anselm Kiefer, Christian Boltanski and Niels Toroni and younger-generation artists such as Douglas Gordon and Koo Jeong-A.

Galerie Moussion

121 rue Vieille-du-Temple, 3rd (01.48.87.75.91/ www.artnet.com). M° Filles du Calvaire. **Open** 10am-7pm Mon-Sat. **Map** p402 L5.
The undoubted star at Moussion is Pierrick Sorin, the funniest video artist around, but it also features Chrystel Egal, dealing with gender and sexuality, young US photographer Chris Verene, some older French artists, such as Degottex, and Korean artists concerned with environmental art.

Galerie Nathalie Obadia

5 rue du Grenier-St-Lazare, 3rd (01.42.74.67.68). M° Rambuteau. **Open** 11am-7pm Mon-Sat. **Map** p402 **K5.**
Obadia supports young talents, often women, from intellectual installations by Nathalie Elemento and Jessica Stockholder and feminist animals by Anne Ferrer to painters Fiona Rae and Carole Benzaken.

Delphine Kreuter's pertinent pucker at **Galerie Alain Gutharc.** *See p311.*

Galerie Nelson

40 rue Quincampoix, 4th (01.42.71.74.56/ www.galerie-nelson.com). M° Rambuteau/RER Châtelet-Les Halles. **Open** 2-7pm Tue-Sat. **Map** p406 J6.
Just upstairs from Chantal Crousel, this adventurous gallery features the work of Thomas Ruff, as well as that of the late Fluxus artist Filliou.

Gilles Peyroulet & Cie

80 rue Quincampoix, 3rd (01.42.78.85.11). M° Rambuteau or Etienne Marcel. **Open** 2-7pm Tue-Sat. **Map** p402 K5.
Peyroulet is at its strongest with photo-based artists including Marin Kasimir, Yves Trémorin and Nick Waplington. Across the street at No 75, Espace #2 features items commissioned from contemporary designers including Frédéric Ruyant and Matali Crasset, as well as archival-type shows of 20th-century pioneers such as Eileen Gray and Alvar Aalto.

Galerie Polaris

8 rue St-Claude, 3rd (01.42.72.21.27/www.galerie-polaris.com). M° St-Sébastien-Froissart. **Open** 11am-7pm Tue-Sat. **Map** p402 L5.
Bernard Utudjian makes the investment of working over the long term with a few artists. It pays off. Look out for photographers Stéphane Couturier and Anthony Hernandez and photo/performance artist Nigel Rolfe.

Galerie Rachlin Lemarié Beaubourg

23 rue du Renard, 4th (01.44.59.27.27). M° Hôtel de Ville. **Open** 10.30am-1pm, 2.30-7pm Tue-Sat. **Map** p406 **K6.**
When Galerie Beaubourg moved south to Vence, Rachlin and Lemarié kept on sculptors Arman and César and *nouvelle figuration* painter Combas, and added a few artists of their own, such as François Boisrand and Nichola Hicks.

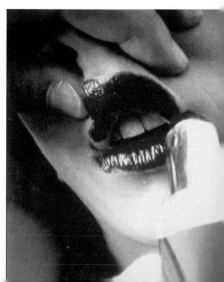

Galerie Michel Rein

42 rue de Turenne, 3rd (01.42.72.68.13/
www.michelrein.com). M° St-Paul or Chemin Vert.
Open 11am-1pm, 2-7pm Tue-Sat. **Map** p406 L6.
Rein moved his gallery from Tours in March 2000.
He works with contemporary artists in all media, but
check out in particular the photoworks of Ruyta
Amae and Guillaume Paris.

Galerie Thaddaeus Ropac

7 rue Debelleyme, 3rd (01.42.72.99.00/
www.ropac.net). M° St-Sébastien-Froissart or St-Paul.
Open 10am-7pm Tue-Sat. **Map** p402 L5.
The Austrian-owned gallery is particularly strong
on American Pop, neo-Pop and neo-Geo (Warhol,
Baechler, Fleury, Taaffe, Sachs), but also features
major artists Kabakov, Gilbert & George, Balkenhol,
Gormley, Sylvie Fleury and Bettina Rheims.

Daniel Templon

30 rue Beaubourg, 3rd (01.42.72.14.10).
M° Rambuteau. **Open** 10am-7pm Mon-Sat.
Map p402 K5.
Templon mainly shows well-known painters, which
is perhaps why his gallery is a favourite with the
French art establishment. David Salle, Jean-Marc
Alberola, Claude Viallat, Vincent Corpet are regu-
lars along with eternally youthful Raymond Hains
and he's recently added some young German artists.

Galerie Anne de Villepoix

43 rue de Montmorency, 3rd (01.42.78.32.24/
www.annedevillepoix.com). M° Rambuteau. **Open**
10am-7pm Tue-Sat. **Map** p402 K5.
In 2001 Anne de Villepoix opened her spacious new
quarters near the Centre Pompidou with a comeback
show by Fabrice Hybert. A mix of generations takes
in established older names John Coplans and
Suzanne Laffont as well as younger figures in all
media, including Franck Scurti, Gillian Wearing,
Jean-Luc Moulène and Valérie Jouve.

Galerie Anton Weller

57 rue de Bretagne, 3rd (01.42.72.05.62).
M° Temple or Arts et Métiers. **Open** 2-7pm Tue-Sat.
Map p403 M5.
Weller often takes an experimental approach, using
alternative venues, working with artists' groups or
new media. Recent finds include young artists
Isabelle Lévénez and Christelle Familiari, who use
video and installation to deal with sexuality.

Galerie Xippas

108 rue Vieille-du-Temple, 3rd (01.40.27.05.55/
www.xippas.com). M° Filles du Calvaire. **Open** 10am-
1pm, 2-7pm Tue-Fri; 10am-7pm Sat. **Map** p406 L6.
This gallery presents painters and photographers in a
stable including Vik Muniz, Joan Hernandez Pijuan,
Lucas Samaras, Ian Davenport and Valérie Belin.

Galerie Zurcher

*56 rue Chapon, 3rd (01.42.72.82.20). M° Arts et
Métiers.* **Open** 11am-7pm Tue-Sat; 2-6pm Sun.
Map p402 K5.

Young artists with a new take on painting include
Camille Vivier, Gwen Ravillous, Philippe Hurteau
and Dan Hays. *Wheelchair access.*

Bastille

Liliane et Michel Durand-Dessert

28 rue de Lappe, 11th (01.48.06.92.23/
www.lm.durand-dessert.com). M° Bastille.
Open 11am-7pm Tue-Sat. **Map** p407 M7.
Durand-Dessert has long been committed to artists
associated with *arte povera* (Pistoletto, Mario Merz),
major French names (Morellet, Garouste, Lavier)
and photographers (Wegman, Burgin, Rousse,
Burckhard) presented in an industrial space.

Galerie Alain Gutharc

47 rue de Lappe, 11th (01.47.00.32.10). M° Bastille.
Open 2-7pm Tue-Fri; 11am-1pm, 2-7pm Sat.
Map p407 M7.
Gutharc has an eye for picking young French artists.
Check out intimate photos by Agnès Propeck,
quirky text pieces by Antoinette Ohanassian, videos
by Joël Bartolomméo and FXC, and Delphine
Kreuter's disturbing slice-of-life images.

Espace d'Art Yvonamor Palix

*13 rue Keller, 11th (01.48.06.36.70). M° Bastille or
Ledru-Rollin.* **Open** 2-5pm Tue-Fri; 2-7pm Sat.
Map p407 N7.
Mexican Palix's small gallery includes artists Aziz
+ Cucher and Orlan, who use new technology to
manipulate images.

Galerie Patrick Seguin

34 rue de Charonne, 11th (01.47.00.32.35/
www.patrickseguin.com). M° Bastille or Ledru-Rollin.
Open 11am-1.30pm, 2.30-7pm Mon-Fri; 11am-7pm
Sat. **Map** p407 N7.
Patrick Seguin has remained in the gallery of former
Jousse Seguin, keeping some of the artists (Karin
Kneffel, Chuck Nanney). The design gallery in rue
des Taillandiers has been renovated by Jean Nouvel.

Champs-Elysées

Galerie Louis Carré et Cie

10 av de Messine, 8th (01.45.62.57.07).
M° Miromesnil. **Open** 10am-12.30pm, 1.30-6.30pm
Mon-Sat. **Map** p401 E3.
Founded in 1938, this gallery currently focuses on
nouvelle figuration painter Hervé di Rosa and
Haïtian-born sculptor Hervé Télémaque. You will
also find works by modern masters Calder, Dufy,
Delaunay and Léger in stock.

Galerie Lelong

13 rue de Téhéran, 8th (01.45.63.13.19).
M° Miromesnil. **Open** 10.30am-6pm Tue-Fri;
2-6.30pm Sat. **Map** p401 E3.
Lelong shows bankable, post-1945, international
names including Alechinsky, Bacon, Hockney,
Kounellis, Scully. Branches in New York and Zurich.

Arts & Entertainment

Nicole Tran Ba Vang at **Galerie Emmanuel Perrotin:** fur she's a hairy good fellow. *See p313.*

Galerie Jérôme de Noirmont

38 av Matignon, 8th (01.42.89.89.00/
www.denoirmont.com). M° Miromesnil. **Open**
10am-1pm, 2.30-7pm Mon-Sat. **Map** p401 E4.
The location could arouse suspicions that Noirmont
sells purely business art. Not a bit of it – eye-catching shows by A R Penck, Clemente, Jeff Koons,
Pierre et Gilles and Shirin Neshat make this gallery
worth the trip.

St-Germain-des-Prés

Galerie 1900-2000

8 rue Bonaparte, 6th (01.43.25.84.20/
www.galerie1900-2000.com). M° St-Germain-des-
Prés. **Open** 2-7pm Mon; 10am-12.30pm, 2-7pm
Tue-Sat. **Map** p406 H7.
Marcel and David Fleiss show a strong predilection
for Surrealism, Dada, Pop art and Fluxus. This is a
place strong on history; you can find works on paper
by anyone from Breton and De Chirico to
Lichtenstein and Rauschenberg.

Galerie Claude Bernard

7-9 rue des Beaux-Arts, 6th (01.43.26.97.07/
www.claude-bernard.com). M° Mabillon or
St-Germain-des-Prés. **Open** 9.30am-12.30pm,
2.30-6.30pm Tue-Sat. **Map** p406 H6.
This gallery shows mostly conservative, figurative
painting from the 1960s on.

Galerie Jeanne Bucher

53 rue de Seine, 6th (01.44.41.69.65).
M° Mabillon or Odéon. **Open** 9am-6.30pm Tue-Fri;
10am-12.30pm, 2.30-6pm Sat. **Map** p406 H7.
Based on the Left Bank since 1925, Bucher spe-
cialises in postwar abstract (De Staël, Da Silva,
Rebeyrolle) and Cobra painters..

Galerie Jean Fournier

22 rue du Bac, 7th (01.42.97.44.00). M° Rue du Bac.
Open 10am-12.30pm, 2.30-7pm Tue-Sat. **Map** p401 G6.
Fournier has changed *quartier* but still specialises
in the French 1970s Support-Surface painters and
US West Coast abstractionists.

Galerie Maeght

42 rue du Bac, 7th (01.45.48.45.15/
www.galeriemaeght.com). M° Rue du Bac. **Open**
10am-6pm Mon; 9.30am-7pm Tue-Sat. **Map** p405 G6.
The famous gallery founded by Aimé Maeght in
1946 is now run by his grandchildren, but today's
shows pale compared to a past that included Léger,
Chagall, Giacometti and Miró.

Galerie Denise René

196 bd St-Germain, 7th (01.42.22.77.57/
www.deniserene.com). M° St-Germain-des-Prés or
Rue du Bac. **Open** 10am-1pm, 2-7pm Tue-Fri;
11am-1pm, 2-7pm Sat. **Map** p406 H7.
Denise René is a Paris institution – as acknowledged
in a tribute show at the Centre Pompidou in 2001 –
and has remained committed to kinetic art, Op art
and geometrical abstraction ever since Tinguely
first presented his machines here in the 1950s.
Branch: 22 rue Charlot, 3rd (01.48.87.73.94).

Galerie Darthea Speyer

6 rue Jacques-Callot, 6th (01.43.54.78.41).
M° Mabillon or Odéon. **Open** 11am-12.45pm, 2-7pm
Tue-Fri; 11am-7pm Sat. **Map** p406 H6.
Colourful, representational painting and sculpture
and naïve artists are the speciality here. It can be
kitsch, but at best features the political expression-
ism of Golub or American dreams of Paschke.

Galerie Georges-Philippe et Nathalie Vallois

36 rue de Seine, 6th (01.46.34.61.07). M° Mabillon
or Odéon. **Open** 10.30am-1pm, 2-7pm Mon-Sat.
Map p406 H7.
The son of art deco specialist Vallois (at No 41) has
a contemporary bent, with hip young things Alain
Bublex, Gilles Barbier and Paul McCarthy, plus a few
older names such as *affichiste* Jacques Villeglé.

Galerie Lara Vincy

47 rue de Seine, 6th (01.43.26.72.51). M° Mabillon
or St-Germain-des-Prés. **Open** 2.30-7.30pm Mon;
11am-12.30pm, 2.30-7.30pm Tue-Sat. **Map** p406 H7.
Lara Vincy is one of the few characters to retain
something of the old St-Germain spirit and sense of
1970s Fluxus-style 'happenings'. Interesting theme
and solo shows include master of the epigram, Ben,
and artists' text, music, performance-related pieces.

Scène Est: rue Louise-Weiss

&:

10 rue Duchessedelaville, 13th (gb agency
01.53.79.07.13; in SITU 01.53.79.06.12;
Christophe Daviet-Thery 01.53.79.05.95).
M° Chevaleret. **Open** 11am-7pm Tue-Sat. **Map** p407
M10.
This gallery is shared in rotation between Fabienne
Leclerc's in SITU, whose artists include Mark Dion,
Patrick von Caeckenbergh, Gary Hill and Patrick
Corillon, gb agency, which works principally with
young artists, and artists' book publisher Christophe
Daviet-Thery.

Air de Paris

32 rue Louise-Weiss, 13th (01.44.23.02.77/
www.airdeparis.com). M° Chevaleret. **Open** 2-7pm
Tue-Fri; 11am-7pm Sat. **Map** p407 M10.
This gallery is named after Duchamp's bottle of air
and, true to its namesake, shows tend to be highly
experimental, if not chaotic. Neo-conceptual experiences mix video, performance, photo, objects and a
regularly changing artist's mural. A young international stable includes Philippe Parreno, Liam Gillick,
Pierre Joseph, Carsten Höller, Bruno Serralongue and
fashion photographer Inez van Lamsweede.

Art:Concept

16 rue Duchefdelaville, 13th (01.53.60.90.30/
www.galerieartconcept.com). M° Chevaleret.
Open 11am-7pm Tue-Sat. **Map** p407 M10.
Art:Concept has flown the Louise-Weiss nest to a
larger space around the corner, opening in March
with Martine Aballéa, Lothar Hempel and Jean-Luc
Blanc. Shows often have a psychedelic, clubby aura.

Galerie Almine Rech

24 rue Louise-Weiss, 13th (01.45.83.71.90/
galeriealminerech.com). M° Chevaleret. **Open** 11am-
7pm Tue-Sat. **Map** p407 M10.
Almine Rech often features photography/video or
works on paper. Artists have included Americans
James Turrell, Alex Bag, Italian Ugo Rondinone and
young French discovery Rebecca Bourgnigault.

Galerie Jennifer Flay

20 rue Louise-Weiss, 13th (01.44.06.73.60).
M° Chevaleret. **Open** 2-7pm Tue-Sat. **Map** p407 M10.
Flay picks up on interesting artists, ensuring this is
a place people watch. As well as installation, photo
and video from French thirtysomethings Xavier
Veilhan, Claude Closky and Dominique Gonzalez-
Foerster, and the slice-of-life photos of Richard
Billingham, a batch of interesting painters includes
John Currin, Chantal Joffe and Lisa Milroy.

Jousse Entreprise

34 rue Louise-Weiss, 13th (01.53.82.13.60/
www.jousse-entreprise.com). M° Chevaleret. **Open**
11am-1pm, 2-7pm Tue-Sat. **Map** p407 M10.
After breaking his partnership with Patrick Seguin,
Philippe Jousse moved to Art:Concept's old gallery
in January bringing Serge Comte, Matthieu Laurette
and Thomas Grünfeld with him. He keeps the 1950s
avant-garde furniture of Jean Prouvé as a sideline.

Galerie Emmanuel Perrotin

5 and 30 rue Louise-Weiss, 13th (01.42.16.79.79/
www.galerieperrotin.com). M° Chevaleret.
Open 11am-7pm Tue-Sat. **Map** p407 M10.
Perrotin is the best place to catch up on the provoca-
tive young Japanese generation including Noritoshi
Hirakawa, manga maniac Takashi Murakami
and glossy cyber-punkette Mariko Mori. Among
European artists look out for the fashion/body pho-
tos of Nicole Tran Ba Vang, multimedia collective
Kolkoz, and video/performance work of Jean-Pierre
Khazem as well as a recent project with Sophie Calle.

Artist-run spaces

Galerie Eof
15 rue St-Fiacre, 2nd (01.53.40.72.22). M° Bonne-Nouvelle. **Open** call for details. **Map** p402 J4.
This artist-run space puts on shows that vary from solo shows by individual painters to multi-media collaborations with other organisations.

Glassbox
113bis rue Oberkampf, 11th (01.43.38.02.82/www.icono.org/glassbox). M° Parmentier.
Open 2-7pm Fri, Sat. **Map** p403 N5.
Glassbox's politically oriented shows have included art, poetry, design and exchanges with other European collectives.

Livraisons
55 rue Bichat, 10th (06.60.97.18.71). M° République.
Open 2-7pm Thur-Sun. **Map** p402 L4.
Opened in November 2000 by five artists and an architect, this new space plans to deliver exhibitions, encounters and events.

Photography

The following galleries specialise in photography, but photoworks of all sorts have become an integral part of contemporary art and can also be found in many other galleries (see above), and at branches of Fnac. The biennial Mois de la Photo (the next one is in November 2002) covers both historic and contemporary photography, as does the annual Paris Photo salon in the Carrousel du Louvre (every Nov). In addition, the agencies Vu and Magnum have recently opened Paris galleries, indicative both of the growing market for photography and the interaction between photojournalism and photography as art, which is set to evolve in tandem with technology.

Galerie 213
213 bd Raspail, 14th (01.43.22.83.23). M° Raspail.
Open 11am-7pm Tue-Sat. **Map** p405 G9.
Photographers, often with a fashion world connection, are shown upstairs. Downstairs is a photography bookshop in a listed art nouveau dining room.

Galerie Anne Barrault
22 rue St-Claude, 3rd (01.44.78.91.67).
M° St-Sébastien-Froissart. **Open** 2-7pm Tue-Sat.
Map p406 L6.
In a small shop space, Barrault enthusiastically presents young French art photographers.

Michèle Chomette
24 rue Beaubourg, 3rd (01.42.78.05.62).
M° Rambuteau. **Open** 2-7pm Tue-Sat. **Map** p402 K5.
Classical and experimental photography. Alain Fleischer, Eric Rondepierre, Lewis Baltz, Felten & Massinger, Bernard Plossu, are regulars, shown alongside historic masters. Chomette has recently

made an effort to introduce recent graduates proposed by artist-teachers represented by the gallery.

Galerie Kamel Mennour
60 rue Mazarine, 6th (01.56.24.03.63/www.galeriemennour.com). M° Odéon.
Open 10.30am-7.30pm Mon-Sat. **Map** p405 H6/H7.
This recently established gallery is attracting buyers with an oh-so fashionable, often provocative, list that includes Nobuyoshi Araki, Peter Beard, Kriki, David LaChapelle, filmmaker Larry Clark and photographer Annie Leibovitz.

Galerie Françoise Paviot
57 rue Ste-Anne, 2nd (01.42.60.10.01). M° Quatre Septembre. **Open** Tue-Sat 2.30-7pm. **Map** p402 H4.
Paviot presents contemporary and historic photographers with an emphasis on the great Surrealists.

Design galleries

French design is currently flourishing as a whole new generation, often dubbed *les petits-enfants de Starck* (grandchildren of Starck), feature in galleries or are being commissioned to design shops and restaurants, continuing in the line of earlier Modern Movement designers and designer-architects. (*See also Gilles Peyroulet et Cie, p310*).

Galerie Downtown
33 rue de Seine, 6th (01.46.33.82.41/www.downtown.fr). M° Odéon. **Open** 10am-1pm, 2-7pm Tue-Sat. **Map** p406 H6.
François Laffanour is an expert on modernist architect-designers of the 1930s to 50s but also presents some contemporary artist-designers.

Galerie Kréo
22 rue Duchefdelaville, 13th (01.53.60.14.68).
M° Chevaleret. **Open** 11am-7pm Tue-Sat.
Map p407 M7.
Recently installed in the 'Louise' strip, Kréo combines retrospective style exhibitions and a design agency commissioning limited-edition pieces. Look for international names Ron Arad, Marc Newson and Jasper Conran as well as native Radi Designers and Martin Szekely and the up-and-coming hotshots of the moment, the Bourrellec brothers.

VIA
29-35 av Daumesnil, 12th/ 01.46.28.11.11/www.)
M° Ledru-Rollin or Gare de Lyon. **Open** 11am-7pm
Tue-Sat. **Map** p407 M8.
VIA, also known as Valorisation de l'Innovation dans l'Ameublement, is an industry-funded body whose function is to promote French design creation through providing finance for design prototypes and by establishing links between groups of designers and manufacturers. Group and solo ehxibitions held in three arches of the Viaduc des Arts can range from the subtlest evolutions in chair design to the wildly experimental.

Gay & Lesbian

If you fancy a fling with a phallic Gallic or a dalliance with a dykey 'demoiselle, here's how to find all the right openings for *la vie en rose*, Paris style.

With Bertie Delanoë as the fairy in the Mairie, Paris' gay community is easing up on the militancy and revving up the hedonism. The Marais is still the traditional major mincing manor, while Les Halles is turning pinker by the minute. The sapphic scene is very much improved, with places like **Les Scandaleuses** and **Pulp** showing that gay chicks are now way chic. **All listings are by order of** *arrondissement.*

Associations

CGPif (Fédération sportive gaie et lesbienne Paris Ile-de-France)
(01.48.05.55.17/www.cgpif.org).
This is the (virtual, hence the lack of a street address) umbrella organisation for Paris' 20 gay and lesbian sports associations. CGPif arranges events and meetings and is preparing the Paris entry for November 2002's Gay Games in Sydney.

SNEG (Syndicat National des Entreprises Gaies)
59 rue Beaubourg, 3rd (01.44.59.81.03).
M° Rambuteau. **Open** 2-6pm Mon-Fri. **Map** p402 K5.
The gay and lesbian business group unites more than 1000 companies across France. It organises HIV and safe sex awareness training and courses on drug abuse for staff, and hands out free condoms.

Act Up Paris
45 rue Sedaine, 11th (answerphone 01.48.06.13.89/ www.actupp.org). M° Bréguet-Sabin. **Map** p406 L6.
This worldwide anti-Aids group is now headed by an HIV-negative woman. Paris zaps have included a fluorescent pink condom over the obelisk on place de la Concorde. Meetings are held Tuesdays at 7pm in amphitheatre 1 of the Ecole des Beaux-Arts (*14 rue Bonaparte, 6th/M° St-Germain des Prés*).

Centre Gai et Lesbien
3 rue Keller, 11th (01.43.57.21.47/www.cglparis.org). M° Ledru-Rollin. **Open** 2-8pm Mon-Sat. **Map** p406 L7.
A valued community resource providing information and a meeting space, a library (2-6pm Fri, Sat), legal and other advice services. The *Association des Medecins Gais* (gay doctors) mans (or, rather, persons) a phone line (6-8pm Wed; 2-4pm Sat/ 01.48.05.81.71). The Centre also houses l'Association des parents et futurs parents gais et lesbiens, again contactable by phone (8-10pm Mon/06.16.66.56 .91/www.apgl.aso.fr). This association advises gay

They grow up in the most delightful way...

parents (as well as fighting for their rights), and, among its many worthy deeds, organises probably the cutest contribution to the annual Gay Pride march, the children's parade.

Bars & cafés

Banana Café
13 rue de la Ferronnerie, 1st (01.42.33.35.31).
M° Châtelet. **Open** 4pm-dawn daily. **Credit** AmEx, MC, V. **Map** p402 J5.
Throbbing nightly with hedonists of several proclivities, the theme nights here are legendary. Singers belt out showtunes in the cellar bar and upstairs you might find a beautiful buns contest (we're not talking cookery here). Très cruisey. *Wheelchair access.*

Le Tropic Café

66 rue des Lombards, 1st (01.40.13.92.62).
M° Châtelet. **Open** noon-dawn daily. **Credit** AmEx,
DC, MC, V. **Map** p405 G6.
This bright, upbeat bar is going through a renaissance with some groovy bashes that draw a loyal
band of party poppers. *Wheelchair access.*

Le Duplex

25 rue Michel-le-Comte, 3rd (01.42.72.80.86).
M° Rambuteau. **Open** 8pm-2am daily. **Credit**
AmEx, MC, V. **Map** p402 K5.
Monthly exhibitions and an eclectic music policy
attract all sorts to this smoky bar, but don't be fooled;
cruising here is an Olympic sport.

Onix

9 rue Nicolas-Flamel, 3rd (01.42.72.37.72).
M° Arts et Métiers. **Open** 3pm-2am daily.
Credit V. **Map** p402 K5.
This glossy, orange and terracotta bar with arty
fittings is often crowded with the smart set. It is also
a jumping-off point for clubbers.

Amnesia

42 rue Vieille-du-Temple, 4th (01.42.72.16.94).
M° Hôtel de Ville. **Open** 10am-2am daily.
Credit MC, V. **Map** p406 K6.
A warm meeting place with comfy sofas and easy-going clientele who decorate the facade with ferns
and hay bales. It's not all about pulling in here.
Intercourse of the social kind is high priority.

Le Bar du Palmier

16 rue des Lombards, 4th (01.42.78.53.53).
M° Hôtel de Ville. **Open** 5pm-5am daily.
Credit AmEx, MC, V. **Map** p406 J6.
The bar gets busy late, but is also good during
happy hour (6-8pm). It has a bizarre pseudo-tropical
decor and a nice terrace. This is one of the few
places (wise up, gay Paris, and get jiggy with the sisters) where women are welcome and numerous.

Le Central

33 rue Vieille-du-Temple, 4th (01.48.87.99.33).
M° Hôtel de Ville. **Open** 4pm-2am Mon-Fri; 2pm-2am
Sat, Sun. **Credit** MC, V. **Map** p406 K6.
One of the city's oldest gay hangouts, Le Central
still passes muster against its sprightly neighbours.

Coffee Shop

3 rue Ste-Croix-de-la-Bretonnerie, 4th
(01.42.74.24.21). *M° Hôtel de Ville.* **Open** 9am-2am
daily. **No credit cards. Map** p406 K6.
The laidback Coffee Shop is a popular rendezvous
and pick-up joint. MTV plays in a corner and decent
food is served until late. Great for gossip.

Le Cox

15 rue des Archives, 4th (01.42.72.08.00).
M° Hôtel de Ville. **Open** 1pm-2am daily. **No credit
cards. Map** p406 K6.
Charming name. One of the hottest Marais gay bars.
Afternoons are relatively calm, but evenings steam
up with loud music and dishy barmen.

Okawa

40 rue Vieille-du-Temple, 4th (01.48.04.30.69).
M° Hôtel de Ville. **Open** 11am-2am daily.
Credit AmEx, MC, V. **Map** p406 K6.
This French-Canadian bar/coffee shop is also
promisingly named: *Okawa* is native American for
peace pipe – and *pipe* is French slang for blow job.

Open Café

*17 rue des Archives, 4th (01.42.72.26.18). M° Hôtel de
Ville.* **Open** 10am-2am daily. **Credit** MC, V. **Map** p406 K6.
The Open Café has become a Mecca for gay boys
meeting up before heading off into the night. The
management also runs the Open Bar Coffee Shop
(see p318).

Quetzal

*10 rue de la Verrerie, 4th (01.48.87.99.07/www.
quetzalbar.com). M° Hôtel de Ville.* **Open** 5pm-5am
daily. **Credit** MC, V. **Map** p406 K6.
The cruisiest bar in the Marais (which is saying
something), with a history prancing all the way back
to the 1980s, Quetzal attracts a beefy crowd. The
venue is at the end of rue des Mauvais-Garçons (bad
boys' street) – you have been warned.

Sun Café

*35 rue Ste-Croix-de-la-Bretonnerie, 4th
(01.40.29.44.40). M° Hôtel de Ville.* **Open** 8am-2am
daily. **Credit** V. **Map** p406 K6.
Upstairs boasts cosy nests of low stools and a food
bar, while downstairs has sunbeds. Morning tanning is accompanied by a free breakfast.

Le Thermik

*7 rue de la Verriere, 4th (01.44.78.08.18). M° Hôtel
de Ville.* **Open** 4pm-2am daily. **Credit** AmEx, DC,
MC, V. **Map** p406 K6.
This is a friendly, intimate place for those who need
a break from crowded cruising bars and thumping
music. That said, screamingly camp karaokes are a
house speciality.

Gay restaurants

L'Amazonial

3 rue Ste-Opportune, 1st (01.42.33.53.13).
M° Châtelet. **Open** noon-3pm, 7pm-1am Mon-Fri;
noon-5pm, 7pm-1am Sat, Sun. **Prix fixe** €13.00,
€19.80 (dinner). **Lunch menu** €9.90; €13.00 (Mon-Fri). **Credit** AmEx, DC, MC, V. **Map** p402 J5.
Paris' largest gay restaurant has expanded its terrace with a lot of fake stone and tack. Decent French
cuisine and tightly T-shirted waiters.

Au Rendezvous des Camionneurs

72 quai des Orfèvres, 1st (01.43.54.88.74).
M° Pont-Neuf. **Open** noon-11pm Mon-Sat; noon- 5pm
Sun. **Average** €27.50. **Prix fixe** €21.50. **Lunch
menu** €13.50. **Credit** AmEx, MC, V. **Map** p406 J6.
Classic French favourites and a charming location
by Pont Neuf make this restaurant a consistent success for those with truck-driver fantasies. Careful
with the big end when you reverse.

Is it a bird? No, it's more likely to be a bloke at **Le Central**.

Aux Trois Petits Cochons

31 rue Tiquetonne, 2nd (01.42.33.39.69/www. auxtroispetitscochons.fr).M° Etienne-Marcel. **Open** 8.30pm-1am Tue-Sun. **Prix fixe** €22.11, €25.76. **Credit** AmEx, MC, V. **Map** p402 J5.

Three Little Pigs eschews the gimmickry of international boystown cuisine in favour of a daily-changing menu. The tarts are tasty.

Amadéo

19 rue Francois-Miron, 4th (01.48.87.01.02). M° St-Paul. **Open** 8-11pm Mon; noon-2pm, 8-11pm Tue-Thur; noon-2pm, 8-11.30pm Fri, Sat. **Average** €25.15. **Prix fixe** €16.77 Tue; €26.68. **Lunch menu** €11.43-95/€14.48. **Credit** MC, V. **Map** p406 K6.

The music is strictly tight-perm classical (well, it takes all sorts), and the ochre and petrol-blue colour scheme is *absolument* typical uptown Marais chic. Inventive *plats du jour* like goat's cheese ravioli.

The Open Bar Coffee Shop

23 rue du Temple, 4th (01.42.77.04.88). M° Hôtel de Ville. **Open** noon-midnight daily. **Average** €13. **Credit** MC, V. **Map** p406 K6.

The management of the Open Café has taken over the Rude and sensibly not departed much from its formula. It's a convivial spot with mostly gay diners and a reasonably priced, largely French menu.

Le Tibourg

29 rue du Bourg-Tibourg, 4th (01.42.74.45.25). M° Hôtel de Ville. **Open** 9am-1am daily. **Average** €19.90. **Prix fixe** €15.30 (dinner); **Lunch menu** €8.40. **Credit** AmEx, MC, V. **Map** p406 K6.

French cuisine in a warm atmosphere. Snails, duck and *cassoulet* are particularly dreamy.

Gay clubs & discos

Club 18

18 rue de Beaujolais, 1st (01.42.97.52.13). M° Palais Royal. **Open** 11pm-dawn Thur-Sat; 5pm-dawn Sun. **Admission** free Sun; €10.70 Fri, Sat. **Credit** AmEx, MC, V. **Map** p402 H5.

Time travel is made real in this soopa-doopa camp-as-a-billy-can club. Don't expect adventurous music.

L'Insolite

33 rue des Petits-Champs, 2nd (01.40.20.98.59). M° Pyramides. **Open** 11pm-5am daily. **Admission** free Mon-Thur, Sun; €7.70 Fri, Sat. **Credit** MC, V. **Map** p402 H4.

Bright and brassy with an 80s disco glitter ball, you can rely on this club pumping out dance classics.

Le Tango

13 rue au Maire, 3rd (01.42.72.17.78). M° Arts et Métiers. **Open** Thur 8pm-2am, Fri, Sat 10.30pm-5am; 6pm-2am Sun. **Admission** €9.00 Thur (with concert), €4.60 after 10.30pm; €6.10 Fri, Sat. **No credit cards**. **Map** p402 K5.

Le Tango has returned to its dancehall roots for dancing *à deux*, with a mixed clientele. There's a camp-to-the-nth accordion concert on Thursdays.

Le Dépôt

10 rue aux Ours, 3rd (01.44.54.96.96). M° Rambuteau. **Open** noon-7am daily. **Admission** €6.86 Mon-Thur; €8.38 Fri-Sun. **Credit** MC, V. **Map** p402 K5.

The decor in this colossal disco sin-bin is blockhouse chic with jungle netting and exposed air ducts. Ladies Night every Wednesday; those with refined sensibilities should note that the Gay Tea Dance on Sundays is not as restrained as its name suggests. (And one for the ladies here: Wednesday night is ladies' night).

Le Queen

102 av des Champs-Elysées, 8th (01.53.89.08.90). M° George V. **Open** 11.30pm-dawn daily. **Admission** €7.62 Mon; free Tue-Thur, Sun; €12.20 Fri, Sat. **Credit** AmEx, DC, MC, V. **Map** p400 D4.

Still the pick of the crop, even if going takes courage – the door staff are bitchily rude and ruthless, especially with women. Top DJs, flamboyant dress, drag queens and go-gos galore. Yer basic classic gay club.

Folies Pigalle

11 pl Pigalle, 9th (01.48.78.25.26). M° Pigalle. **Open** midnight-dawn Tue-Sat; 6pm-midnight Sun. **Admission** free Mon-Thur; €15.24 Fri-Sat; €6.10 Sun. **Drinks** €4.57-€7.62. **Credit** V. **Map** p401 G2.

Come here for Paris' most popular gay tea dance, the Black Blanc Beur (BBB) (6pm-midnight Sun; €6.10). You'll find an invigorating mix of world music dancing. Be warned: there is much close-contact dancing. *See also chapter* **Clubs**.

Slam that six-pack at **L'Insolite**. *See left.*

Scorp

25 bd Poissonnière, 9th (01.40.26.28.30).
M° Grands Boulevards. **Open** midnight-6.30am
daily. **Admission** free Mon-Thur, Sun; €10.67 Fri,
Sat. **Credit** AmEx, MC, V. **Map** p402 J4.
Shortened in name and sharpened in style (to the
point of snobbishness), the former Scorpion proves
that long relationships are possible in *gai Paris*.

Men-only clubs

Le Transfert

3 rue de la Sourdière, 1st (01.42.60.48.42).
M° Tuileries. **Open** midnight-dawn daily.
Credit MC, V. **Map** p401 G5.
Small but useful leather/SM bar.

Univers Gym

20 rue des Bons Enfants, 1st (01 42 61 24 83) M°
Palais Royal **Open** noon-1am daily. **Credit** V. **Map**
p401 H5.
Univers is the busiest Parisian sauna. Trailing
round in a tanga is entirely acceptable, though hot
action lies behind those loin cloths.

Bear's Den

6 rue des Lombards, 4th (01.42.71.08.20/www.
bearsden.fr). *M° Châtelet.* **Open** 4pm-2am daily.
Credit AmEx, MC, V. **Map** p406 K6.
Brimming with butch bearded blokes and strangers
bearing moustaches, the atmosphere is evocative of
more carefree, somehow more leatherette days.

QG

12 rue Simon-le-Franc, 4th (01.48.87.74.18/www.
qgbar.com). *M° Rambuteau.* **Open** 4pm-8am Mon-
Thur; 5pm-8am Fri, Sat; 2pm-6am Sun. **Credit**
AmEx, MC, V. **Map** p406 K6.
No entrance fee, cheap beer, late opening and a sense
of humour guarantee success. Things get rough
downstairs; don't even ask what the bath is for, especially if you like to go up the tap end.

Le Trap

10 rue Jacob, 6th (unlisted telephone).
M° St-Germain des Prés. **Open** 11pm-4am daily.
Admission free Mon-Thur, Sun; €7.62 Fri, Sat. **No
credit cards. Map** p406 H6.
Le Trap has been packing them in for nearly 20
years and has become hip with the fashion crowd.
Brace yourself for naked dancing (Mon, Wed).

Gay shops & services

Hôtel Saintonge

16 rue de Saintonge, 3rd (01.42.77.91.13/
fax 01.48.87.76.41). *M° Filles du Calvaire.*
Rates single €74.70-€79.27; double €85.37-€99.09;
suite €109.76-€120.43. **Credit** AmEx, DC, MC, V.
Map p402 L5.
Although this hotel is open to everyone, its owners
cultivate a gay clientele. All rooms have a shower.
Room services Hairdryer. Minibar. Safe. TV.

Lionel Joubin

10 rue des Filles-du-Calvaire, 3rd (01.42.74.37.51).
M° Filles du Calvaire. **Open** 11am-8pm Mon-Sat.
Closed Aug. **Credit** V. **Map** p402 L5.
Famous for its extravagant window displays, florist
Joubin decorates floats for Gay Pride. Just the place
to get a handful of pansies.

Space Hair

10 rue Rambuteau, 3rd (01.48.87.28.51).
M° Rambuteau. **Open** noon-10pm Mon; 9am-11pm
Tue-Fri; 9am-10pm Sat. **Credit** DC, MC, V.
Map p402 K5.
This Marais barber has become an institution on the
Paris gay scene. So successful on the coiffage that it
has expanded next door to Space Hair Classic.

Boy'z Bazaar

5, 38 rue Ste-Croix-de-la-Bretonnerie, 4th
(01.42.71.94.00). *M° Hôtel de Ville.* **Open** noon-
midnight Mon-Sat; 2-9pm Sun. **Credit** AmEx, DC,
MC, V. **Map** p406 K6.
No 5 caters for boyz' essential pectastically tight
T-shirts, sportswear and classics, while No 38 serves
up titillating videos.

Eurogays

23 rue du Bourg-Tibourg, 4th (01.48.87.37.77/
www.eurogays.com).M° Hôtel de Ville. **Open** *Oct-Mar*
10am-1.30pm, 2.30-7pm Mon-Fri. *Apr-Sept* 10am-
1.30pm, 2.30-7pm Mon-Fri; 11am-5pm Sat. **Credit**
MC, V. **Map** p406 K6.
This gay travel agent can book it all, and proposes
80 gay destinations around the globe.

Hôtel Central Marais

33 rue Vieille-du-Temple, 4th (01.48.87.56.08). *M°*
Hôtel de Ville. **Rates** single €68.60; double €81.60;
breakfast €5.40. **Credit** MC, V. **Map** p406 K6.
Paris' only strictly gay hotel (above Le Central) has
seven rooms (no private bathrooms spoiling the fun),
plus an apartment (€99.90-€121.20). Book in
advance. English spoken.
Room services Double glazing. Telephone.

Les Mots à la Bouche

6 rue Ste-Croix-de-la-Bretonnerie, 4th
(01.42.78.88.30). *M° Hôtel de Ville.*
Open 11am-11pm Mon-Sat; 2-8pm Sun.
Credit MC, V. **Map** p406 K6.
Stocks gay-interest literature from around the world,
including an English-language section.

Pause Lecture

61 rue Quincampoix, 4th (01.44.61.95.06/ www.
pauselecture.com). *M° Rambuteau.* **Open** 11am-
midnight Mon-Sat; 1pm-midnight Sun. **Credit**
AmEx, DC, MC, V. **Map** p406 J6.
A very cool environment in which to buy your tomes
(the selection is huge). You can pose your day away
in well-upholstered comfy chairs, have a vada at the
exhibitions and cultivate that intellectual look.

IEM

208 rue St-Maur, 10th (01.42.41.21.41/
www.dildos.co.uk). M° Goncourt. **Open** 10am-7.30pm
Mon-Sat. **Credit** AmEx, MC, V. **Map** p403 M4.
Scores of videos, clothes, books and condoms.
Upstairs houses all things leather and rubber.
Branches: 43 rue de l'Arbre-Sec, 1st (01.42.96.05.74);
33 rue de Liège, 9th (01.45.22.69.01).

Lesbian Paris

Lesbians share the **Centre Gai & Lesbien**
with the men (*see above*), holding lectures,
debates and drinks (Fri, 8-10pm); several
militant groups are based at the **Maison
des Femmes** (*see chapter* **Directory**).
Look out for club nights run by Ladies Room
at **Le Dépôt**.

La Champmesle

4 rue Chabanais, 2nd (01.42.96.85.20).
M° Pyramides. **Open** 5pm-dawn Mon-Sat.
Credit AmEx, MC, V. **Map** p402 H4.
This bar is a pillar of the Paris lesbian community.
It is a classy, comfortable place with a very relaxed
vibe. It is busiest at weekends and on Thursdays,
when there's cabaret. There are changing art shows,
too. *Wheelchair access.*

Pulp

25 bd Poissonniere, 2nd (01.40.26.01.93).
M° Grands Boulevards. **Open** midnight-dawn
Wed-Sat. **Admission** €7.62 Fri, Sat.
Credit AmEx, MC, V. **Map** p402 J4.
Pulp has become the happening club: small and
intimate, with friendly staff. The musical mix takes
in a broad range including soul, funk, reggae, house,
techno and Latin; regulars include DJ Sex Toy. It
publishes the witty fanzine *Housewife*. Men admitted if accompanied.

Unity Bar

176-178 rue St-Martin, 3rd (01.42.72.70.59).
M° Rambuteau. **Open** daily 4pm-2am. Closed one
week in Dec. **No credit cards**. Map p402 K5.
A studenty clientele wears denim, plays pool and
sings along to a range of music as diverse as Queen
and Suzanne Vega at this refreshingly visible *bar
féminin* by the Centre Pompidou. Cards and board
games are available at the bar. Accompanied men
are welcome.

Utopia

15 rue Michel-le-Comte, 3rd (01.42.71.63.43)
M° Rambuteau. **Open** 5pm-2am Mon-Sat.
No credit cards. Map p402 K5.
Opened by Antoinette and Anne in June 1998, the
Utopia has quickly gained a reputation with house
beat, billiards tournaments, pinball, Internet, music
and *café-theatre* showcases and not forgetting the
fancy dress parties and exhibitions of the work of
lesbian artists. *Wheelchair access.*

It's cool to take care in Paris.

L'Alcântara

*30 rue de Roi-de-Sicile, 4th (01.42.74.45.00). M° St-
Paul.* **Open** daily 6pm-2am. **Credit** MC, V.
Map p406 K6.
The newest women's bar in the Marais. From the out-
side, it doesn't look like much, but inside, the lounge is
stylish. Basement dance floor. *Wheelchair access.*

Les Scandaleuses

8 rue des Ecouffes, 4th (01.48.87.39.26). M° St-Paul.
Open 6pm-2am daily. **Credit** MC, V. **Map** p406 K6.
Chrome bar stools and high tables maximise the
space, and the cellar rooms extend mixing potential.
Video monitors and changing exhibits by female
artists adorn the walls. Accompanied men welcome.

Les Archives, Recherches, Cultures Lesbiennes (ARCL)

*Maison des Femmes, 163 rue de Charenton, 12th
(01.43.43.41.13/01.43.43.42.13). M° Reuilly-Diderot.*
Open 7-9.30pm Tue. Closed Aug. **Map** p407 N8.
ARCL produces audiovisual documentation and
bulletins on lesbian and women's activities, and runs
an archive of lesbian and feminist documents.

Quand les Lesbiennes se font du cinéma

Information Cineffable 01.48.70.77.11. **Dates** late
Oct-early Nov.
Women-only film festival screens world premiers,
from documentaries and experimental videos to
lesbian features; also debates, exhibitions and bar.

Music: Classical & Opera

The Paris classical scene is infused with new blood, and its vital signs are a-glow. So whip out your opera glasses and let those crotchets go all quavery.

In the Parisian musical world, where politics play a more important part than the first violins, it is encouraging that the new Socialist mayor of Paris has left the running of **Châtelet** untouched for the time being. Previously a change of administration would have brought about wholesale changes in this, the flagship of municipal culture. 'If it works, don't fix it!' will hopefully be remembered this years. The **Opéra National** has enjoyed a stable period under the direction of Hugues Gall and James Conlon, and any potential successors should build on their achievement rather than systematically opt for radical change. Myung-Whun Chung and Christoph Eschenbach are both establishing fine reputations at the **Orchestre Philharmonique de Radio France** and **Orchestre de Paris** respectively, while several of the smaller orchestras are heading for major changes, with the newly restored **Salle Gaveau** at least partly solving the increasing problem of affordable city centre venues. The only major disappointment this season has been the new regime at the **Opéra Comique**, for despite Jérôme Savary's exciting plans, the institution has been starved of cash.

The Early Music scene has begun the century as a stable, ongoing passion. The year began with a revival of the splendid new production of Offenbach's *La Belle Hélène* at the Châtelet, conducted by Marc Minkowski, who was in danger of becoming pigeon-holed as an Early Music specialist. Otherwise Christie, Rousset, Eliot Gardiner et al continue to dust down pre-Baroque scores and come up with shining new purified versions. The new recording of Verdi's *Aida* by Harnoncourt and Eliot Gardiner's *Falstaff* proves that this approach could be spiralling out of control when applied to the 19th century, but the thirst for musical scholarship seems unquenchable.

The tradition of contemporary creation has been well served in the past year, with exciting premieres at Châtelet and the Opera National. The **Ensemble Intercontemporain** remains one of the great sources of European creation, and this year's group is programmed at the **Cité de la Musique**, as well as the **Centre Pompidou**, **IRCAM** and, even, Peter Brooks' **Bouffes du Nord**.

INFORMATION AND RESOURCES

For listings, see *Pariscope* and *L'Officiel des Spectacles*. The monthly *Le Monde de la Musique* and *Diapason* also list classical concerts, while *Opéra International* provides the best coverage of all things vocal. *Cadences* and *La Terrasse*, two free monthlies, are distributed outside concerts. Many venues offer cut-rate tickets to students (under-26) an hour before curtain.

Orchestras & ensembles

Les Arts Florissants

(01.43.87.98.98/www.arts-florissants.com).
William Christie's 'Arts Flo' remains France's most highly regarded Early Music group. In 2002 the group is focusing on openings for young singers from all over Europe in an exciting project called Le Jardin des Voix.

Concerts Pasdeloup

Based at the Salle Pleyel and the Opéra Comique.
Modestly effective orchestra under the direction of Jean-Pierre Wallez, with popular programming, enlivened by the occasional gifted soloist such as French pianist Anne Queffelec.

Ensemble InterContemporain

(www.ensembleinter.com). Based at the Cité de la Musique.
The world-famous contemporary music ensemble is now performing under Jonathan Nott and gives around 70 concerts a year. The standard is consistently high, while the repertoire ranges from early 20th-century classical pieces to the avant garde.

Ensemble Orchestral de Paris

(www.ensemble-orchestral-paris.com). Based at Salle Pleyel.
John Nelson presides over this Mozartzean/Haydnesque chamber orchestra, whose fortunes seem to be on an upward spiral, and deservedly so for an outfit with such a wide-ranging repertoire.

Orchestre Colonne

(01.42.33.72.89/www.orchestrecolonne.fr). Based at Salle Pleyel, Théâtre des Folies Bergère.
This orchestra often fails to live up to its past and its Paris appearances in 2002 are thin on the ground. The excellent educational Concerts Eveil (aimed at young listeners) has now moved to the Salle Gaveau, which should bring an improvement.

Orchestre d'Ile de France

Based at Salle Pleyel and the Cirque d'Hiver.
This orchestra continues its solid work under its longstanding musical director Jacques Mercier. The programming remains imaginative, and this season will be dominated by organ pieces.

Orchestre Lamoureux

(01.58.39.30.30/orchestrelamoureux.com). Based at the Théâtre des Champs-Elysées.
Rising from near extinction two seasons ago, the Lamoureux has found a new home in the prestigious Théâtre des Champs-Elysées and looks set for happier times playing experimental pieces under principal conductor Yutaka Sado.

Orchestre National de France

(01.40.28.28.40). Based at the Maison de Radio France and Théâtre des Champs-Elysées.
Director Kurt Masur should make this season a touch more adventurous than of late. There is even hope of the performance of a work by the Soviet composer, Alfred Schnittke.

Orchestre de Paris

(01.45.61.65.60/www.orchestredeparis.com). Based at Salle Pleyel and Châtelet.
Christoph Eschenbach takes over the reins of this leading orchestra in a blaze of positive publicity. His first season looks promising with a good mix of contemporary creation and orchestral standards. Eschenbach will not be pandering to popular taste, but is a rigorous musician. Programming centres on the build-up to the Berlioz 2003 bicentennial, with a series entitled *Berlioz, Lord Byron et l'Italie.*

Orchestre Philharmonique de Radio France

(www.radio-france.fr). Based at the Maison de Radio France and Salle Pleyel.
Myung-Whun Chung has now put his stamp on things, and he has promised to continue the adventurous contemporary programming of the orchestra, as well as performing the French classics 'to a standard never before attained in this country'. This season will also include works by Bellini, Bach and Stravinsky.

Les Talens Lyriques

(www.lestalenslyriques.com).
Christophe Rousset's Early Music spin-off from Les Arts Florissants has established its own personality and a soaring reputation. Its aim of 'restoring to life the whole of French musical and theatrical heritage' is unquestionably worthy.

Concert halls

Théâtre des Bouffes du Nord

37bis bd de la Chapelle, 10th (01.46.07.34.50). M° La Chapelle. **Box office** 11am-6pm Mon-Sat. **Tickets** €13.72-€24.39. **Credit** AmEx, MC, V. **Map** p403 L2.

Peter Brook and Stéphane Lissner continue to give an important place to chamber music in their programming. This season will feature the Beethoven string quartets by the Quatuor Prazak.

Châtelet - Théâtre Musical de Paris

1 pl du Châtelet, 1st (01.40.28.28.40/www.chatelet-theatre.com). M° Châtelet. **Box office** 11am-7pm daily; telephone 10am-7pm Mon-Sat. Closed July-Aug. **Tickets** phone for details. **Credit** AmEx, MC, V. **Map** p406 J6.
Jean-Pierre Brossmann's inspirational reign continues at municipal-run Châtelet with imaginative programming of concerts, ballet and opera. He certainly isn't frightened of getting talent in from abroad. This season, the theatre is playing host to orchestras from Toulouse, Amsterdam, London and Cleveland. *Wheelchair access*

Cité de la Musique

221 av Jean-Jaurès, 19th (recorded information 01.44.84.45.45/reservations 01.44.84.44.84/www. cite-musique-fr). M° Porte de Pantin. **Box office** noon-6pm Tue-Sun/telephone 11am-7pm Mon-Sat, 10am-6pm Sun. **Tickets** phone for details. **Credit** MC, V. **Map insert**
Exciting, energetic programming focuses on contemporary creation, but takes in a vast repertoire. The museum has a smaller concert space (*see chapter* **Museums**). The Conservatoire (01.40.40.45.45) is host to world-class performers and professors, with free concerts. *Wheelchair access.*

IRCAM

1 pl Igor-Stravinsky, 4th (01.44.78.48.16/www. ircam.fr). M° Hôtel de Ville. **Open** phone for details. **Tickets** €13.72; €9.15 students. **Credit** AmEx, MC, V. **Map** p406 K6.
The underground bunker, designed to create a new music for a new century, as part of the Centre Pompidou, now plays a full part in the musical mainstream, and the reactionary old farts have taken it to their hearts. This season's highlights will be a series of electronic pieces, some music for young people and a focus on contemporary choral song.

Maison de Radio France

116 av du Président-Kennedy, 16th (concert information 01.56.40.22.22/www.radiofrance.fr). M° Passy/RER Kennedy Radio France. **Box office** 11am-6pm Mon-Sat. **Tickets** free-€18.29. **Credit** MC, V. **Map** p404 A7.
Radio station France Musique programmes an impressive range of classical concerts, operas and ethnic music here. The main venue is the rather charmless Salle Olivier Messiaen, but the quality of music compensates. Under-26s can buy a *Passe Musique*, €18.29, for admission to four concerts. Watch out for free events. *Wheelchair access.*

Getting down for the low notes at **Opéra National de Paris Bastille** (*see p323*).

Opéra National de Paris Bastille

pl de la Bastille, 12th (08.36.69.78.68/www.opera-de-paris.fr). M° Bastille. **Box office** 130 rue de Lyon 9am-9pm Mon-Sat; 11am-11pm Sun. **Tickets** €10-€105. **Credit** AmEx, MC, V. **Map** p407 M7.

There now seems to be a consensus that the Opéra Bastille is a poorly designed building. However Hughes Gall's tenure, with solid musical direction from James Conlon, has been notable for stability and competitive standards of performance. Gall has not ignored contemporary creation, with commissions from composers Philippe Manoury, Pascal Dusapin and Matthias Pintscher in the pipeline. This season's highlights include productions of *Billy Budd, Wozzeck, Macbeth* and *Rusalka.*
Guided visits (01.40.01.19.70). Wheelchair access (01.40.01.18.08, two weeks in advance).

Opéra National de Paris Garnier

pl de l'Opéra, 9th (08.36.69.78.68/www.opera-de-paris.fr). M° Opéra. **Box office** 11am-6.30pm Mon-Sat/telephone 9am-7pm. **Tickets** €10-€105. **Credit** AmEx, MC, V. **Map** p401 G4.

The restored Palais Garnier is again functioning as an opera house, though the Bastille still gets the lion's share of performances. An evening here is a privilege, even if the building's tiara shape means that some seats have poor visibility. Productions to get excited about in 2002 are *La Petite Fille aux allumettes* and *Platée. See chapters* **Right Bank, Museums** and **Dance.**
Visits 10am-4.30pm daily; guided visits (01.40.01.22.63). Wheelchair access (01.40.01.18.08, two weeks in advance).

Péniche Opéra

Facing 42, quai de la Loire, 19th (01.53.35.07.76/www.penicheopera.com). M° Jaurès. **Box office** 10.30am-6.30pm Mon-Fri/telephone 01.53.35.07.77. **Tickets** €23.00. **Credit** MC, V. **Map** p403 M1/M2.

A boat-based opera company producing a programme of chamber-scale rarities, often comic. In previous seasons, productions came ashore to the Opéra Comique, but from now on it's all aboard for some educational works for children.

Salle Cortot

78 rue Cardinet, 17th (01.47.63.85.72). M° Malesherbes. **No box office. Tickets** are sold 30 minutes before concerts begin; prices vary. **Map** p400 D2.

This intimate concert hall in the Ecole Normale Supérieure de Musique has excellent acoustics for chamber music.

Salle Gaveau

45 rue La Boétie, 8th (01.49.53.05.07). M° Miromesnil. **Box office** 11.30am-6.30pm Mon-Fri. **Tickets** €25. **Credit** MC, V. **Map** p401 E3.

The charmingly antiquated Salle Gaveau has finally begun its long-promised facelift. The plan was to improve the acoustics to allow larger Baroque performances, but it remains to be seen quite how far the restoration will go.

Salle Pleyel

252 rue du Fbg-St-Honoré, 8th (01.45.61.53.01/www.salle-pleyel.fr). M° Ternes. **Box office** 11am-6pm Mon-Sat; telephone (08.25.00.02.52) 9am-9pm Mon-Fri. **Tickets** phone for details. **Credit** MC, V. **Map** p400 D3.

The Salle Pleyel is vast and unatmospheric, but functions as the home to many orchestras. The sale by the government to an individual buyer has produced soaring rehearsal fees, but also an undertaking that Pleyel will remain the city's main concert hall. Plans are afoot for restoration. *Wheelchair access.*

Théâtre des Champs-Elysées

15 av Montaigne, 8th (01.49.52.50.50/www.theatrechampselysees.fr). M° Alma-Marceau. **Box office** 1pm-7pm Mon-Sat; telephone 10am-noon, 2-6pm Mon-Fri. **Tickets** phone for details. **Credit** AmEx, MC, V. **Map** p400 D5.

This beautiful theatre, with bas-reliefs by Bourdelle, witnessed the première of Stravinsky's *Le Sacre du Printemps* in 1913. Director, Dominique Meyer, is rightly proud of the theatre's unsubsidised status and has continued the tradition of high-quality programming. As well as big-name orchestral visitors, vocal treats for 2002 include *Le Nozze di Figaro, Il Matrimonio Segreto, La Serva Padrona* and *Falstaff.*

Théâtre du Tambour-Royal

94 rue du Fbg-du-Temple, 11th (01.48.06.72.34). M° Belleville or Goncourt. **Box office** 6.30-8pm Tue-Sat; telephone 10am-8pm Mon-Sat. **Tickets** €12.20-€19.82. **Credit** MC, V. **Map** p403 M4.

This venue continues to do a worthy job promoting the careers of young singers and instrumentalists. Works presented in 2002 include Offenbach's *La Grande Duchesse de Gérolstein* and Rossini's *Le Barbier de Séville.*

Théâtre de la Ville

2 pl du Châtelet, 4th (01.42.74.22.77/www.theatredelaville-paris.com). M° Châtelet. **Box office** 11am-7pm Mon; 11am-8pm Tue-Sat; telephone 11am-7pm Mon-Sat. **Tickets** phone for details. **Credit** MC, V. **Map** p406 J6.

The occasional concerts in this vertiginously raked concrete amphitheatre feature hip classical outfits like the avant-garde Kronos Quartet, Fabio Biondi, as well as top pianist Piotr Anderszewski. (*See chapters* **Dance, Music: Rock, Roots & Jazz** and **Theatre.**) *Wheelchair access.*

Music in museums

Auditorium du Louvre

Entrance through Pyramid, Cour Napoléon, 1st (01.40.20.51.86/reservations 01.40.20.84.00/www.louvre.fr). M° Palais Royal. **Box office** 9am-7.30pm Mon, Wed-Fri. Closed July Aug. **Tickets** phone for details. **Credit** MC, V. **Map** p406 H5.

The Louvre provides a regular programme of concerts (generally chamber music), both in the evening and at lunch time (*Les Midis du Louvre*), as well as seasons devoted to music on film.

Liberty, equality and do-re-mi

You don't have to be sitting atop a euro mountain to hear classical music in Paris – there are ample opportunities to enjoy performances that are free or, at least, substantially reduced in price.

For the best way of finding out what's on free, log on to www.journal-laterasse.com and then search under *entrée libre*. You'll find yourself spoilt for choice. **La Fête de la Musique**, on 21 June, and the seasonal events in the Parc Floral (see chapter **Paris By Season**) stage the most popular free concerts in Paris, and these really are just the tip of the Brandenburg.

Fête de la Musique

The **Maison de Radio France** (01.56.40.15.16) lays on as many as ten free shows each week, including the annual **Présences** festival in early February, devoted to new musicial creation. Do phone up first in order to reserve your freebie.

Châtelet offers the readily affordable **Midis Musicaux** (€9), weekday lunchtime chamber music in the Foyer, and the excellent Sunday **Concerts du Dimanche Matin** (€10-€20). If you're under 26, the following offer reductions:

Ensemble Orchestral de Paris (08.00.42.67.57); **Opéra Comique** (08.25.00.00.58); **Opéra National de Paris; Orchestre des Concerts Lamoureux** (01.44.84.77.00).

To combine listening with sightseeing, many churches provide a beautiful environment in which to enjoy pieces. **The Festival d'Art Sacré** (01.44.70.64.10) highlights religious music in the weeks before Christmas. **Les Grands Concerts Sacrés** (01.48.24.16.97) and **Musique et Patrimoine** (01.42.50.96.18) offer concerts at churches including Eglise St-Roch, Eglise des Billettes, Eglise St-Julien-le-Pauvre, Eglise St-Séverin, the Madeleine and the Val-de-Grâce. The emphasis is on Baroque and choral, and although ensembles are often semi-amateur, standards have risen greatly in recent years with visits by Early Music specialists such as Sigiswald Kuijken and Philippe Herreweghe. Music in Notre-Dame is handled by **Musique Sacrée à Notre Dame** (01.44.41.49.99/01.42.34.56.10).

Bibliothèque Nationale de France

quai François-Mauriac, 13th (01.53.79.40.45/ reservations 01.53.79.49.49/www.bnk.fr). M° Bibliothèque or Quai de la Gare. **Box office** 10am-7pm Tue-Sat; noon-7pm Sun. **Tickets** €15.24; €7.60 students. **Credit** MC, V. **Map** p407 M10.
The new library is building a loyal customer base for its song recitals by the cream of international artists, with programming exploring the rose-water, nay, perfumed, nay, delicately fragranced world of the French *mélodie*. *Wheelchair access.*

Musée National du Moyen Age (Cluny)

6 pl Paul-Painlevé, 5th (01.53.73.78.00). M° Cluny-La Sorbonne. **Tickets** €3.05-€15.24 (some include museum entry). **No credit cards. Map** p407 J7.
The museum presents medieval concerts that are in keeping with the collection in the atmospheric setting of the Roman baths. Pieces are played, as far as is possible, on original instruments, to create deeply atmospheric performances. Fans of the lute and lyre will be in heaven here.

Music: Rock, Roots & Jazz

French music knows no half measures: the bad stuff's in a universe beyond redemption; the good stuff's innovative, influential and the peak of cool.

Paris' music scene benefits from France's cultural diversity. Algerian *raï* has been mainstreamed (think Cheb Mami in Sting's '*Desert Rose*'), and rap and ragga continue to evolve. France's leading rapper, MC Solaar, is back on form with a sound evoking R'n'B and Latino. K2R Riddim and Massilia Sound System lead the roots and reggae pack, and the emergence of rap/ragga crossover act Saïan Supa Crew shows the influence of rap on more established genres. More cause for joy is that music from the suburbs is thriving, as La Brigade, Oxmo Puccino, Faf Larage and Lady Laistee prove.

Rock's condition is harder to diagnose, though Mirwais is flying the flag with a hybrid of rock, indie and electro, as are fusion-funksters FFF. In fact, 'fusion' typifies all that is French in the music world, be it the techno-jazz of St Germain, the shift of former hardcore rapper Doc Gynéco towards a more *chanson française*-inspired sound or the revival of disco via the French Touch phenomenon (but namechecking Air and Daft Punk no longer does justice to the breadth of the genre; Cassius, Superfunk and Kojak are equally crucial).

As one would expect in a city where an ensemble of bifocal Miklis, goatee, the black polo neck, loafers and white socks can be worn without attracting guffaws, Paris' love affair with jazz continues, with a blend of hard bop, fusion and world music currently being served up in the capital.

Chanson française lives on in the form of Johnny Hallyday (*see p331* **Heeeeere's Johnny!**), the voluptuously-nosed dauphin of grizzled French *rockeurs*, Eddy Mitchell, or the incessantly revamped Florent Pagny, but artists of today tend to refer to a generation further back (Piaf, Brassens and Aznavour) when searching for inspiration. That's a tasty (and tasteful) manoeuvre.

French music 2002-style is in good shape: freer from the influence of American rock and moving on from the decade in which only rap seemed to be happening. Air started recording a new album in January 2002, and the finished product should be a reliable yardstick of the mainstream's direction. Electro's in, hand in hand with a return to the songwriting tradition (*see p238* **Chansons for a New Generation**). All that French rock needs to do now is to put its past behind it and start strutting its funky stuff. For ticket agencies, *see chapter* **Directory**.

Stadium venues

Palais Omnisports de Paris-Bercy
8 bd de Bercy, 12th (08.03.03.00.31/www.bercy.fr).
M° Bercy. **Box office** 9am-8pm Mon-Sat.
Admission €22.87-€89.94. **Credit** MC, V.
Wheelchair access. Map p407 N9.
A veritable kaleidoscope of talent performs here, but you have to get in quick for the better acoustics and superior comfort of the upper tiers.

Zénith
211 av Jean-Jaurès, 19th (01.42.08.60.00/ www.zenith.com). M° Porte de Pantin. **No box office. Admission** from €15.24. **Credit** MC, V. **Map** p403 inset.
This large amphitheatre has built its reputation on rap and rock gigs (in that order). Dinkier than Bercy, though you wouldn't think it from the sound the system (whose knobs all go up to eleven) generates.

Rock venues

Le Bataclan
50 bd Voltaire, 11th (01.43.14.35.35/www.bataclan.fr).
M° Oberkampf. **Box office** 10.30am-7pm Mon-Fri.
Concerts 8pm. Closed 2 wks in Aug. **Admission** from €15.24-€27.44. **Credit** MC, V. **Map** p403 M5.
This charming old theatre hosts a varied bill of French and foreign acts for seated or standing/ dancing concerts. *Wheelchair access.*

Café de la Danse
5 passage Louis-Phillipe, 11th (01.47.00.57.59/ www.cafedeladanse.com). M° Bastille. **Box office** 12-6pm Mon-Sat. **Concerts** from 7.30pm.
Admission €9-€23. **No credit cards.**
Map p407 M7.
Overseas pop/rock acts dominate the bill at this medium-sized former dance hall. Half the seating is removed on boogie nights for that rarest of sights: a French crowd grooving. *Wheelchair access.*

La Cigale/La Boule Noire
120 bd de Rochechouart, 18th (01.49.25.89.99).
M° Pigalle. **Box office** noon-7pm Mon-Sat. Closed 15 July-15 Aug. **Admission** prices vary. **Credit** MC, V. **Map** p402 H2.
One of the most reliably groovy venues in Paris. The old horseshoe-shaped vaudeville house holds up to 1,900 punters for local and international acts. Seats are removed for dancier occasions. Downstairs, La Boule Noire hosts up-and-coming bands.

To the left, to the right – Stereo MC's at the **Elysée Montmartre.**

Le Divan du Monde
75 rue des Martyrs, 18th (01.44.92.77.66).
Mº Pigalle. **Concerts** 7.30pm Mon-Sat; 2pm Sun.
Admission €9.15-€18.29. **Credit** MC, V.
Map p402 H2.
A healthy dose of world music, a twist of electro-dance, a dollop of hip-hop and a sprinkle of indie rock/pop keeps this venue at the cutting edge.

Elysée Montmartre
72 bd de Rochechouart, 18th (01.55.07.06.00/
www.elyseemontmartre.com). Mº Anvers. **Concerts**
7.30pm most nights. Closed Aug. **Admission**
€15.24-€22.87. **No credit cards**. **Map** p402 J2.
This spacious venue offers tango to techno and vintage reggae, and often attracts overseas artists. Plenty of atmosphere, even if acoustics are not great.

L'Olympia
28 bd des Capucines, 9th (01.55.27.10.00/
reservations 01.47.41.25.49/www.olympiahall.com).
Mº Opéra. **Box office** 9am-7pm Mon-Sat. **Concerts**
8.30pm. **Admission** €24.39-€60.98. **Credit** MC, V.
Map p401 G4.
None have refused this *grande dame's* seductive invitation, from Sinatra to Piaf. But not even *grandes dames* are immune to the charms of big business; in 2001, the Olympia was acquired by Vivendi.

Le Trabendo
211 av Jean-Jaurès, 19th (01.49.25.89.99).
Mº Porte de Pantin. **Concerts** from 8pm, days vary.
Admission €12.20-€24.39. **No credit cards**.
Map p403 inset.
Formerly the Hot Brass jazz club, Le Trabendo has been redone in a more futuristic manner. Holds largely underground rock, world, and electro-jazz concerts. Frequent overseas acts. *Wheelchair access.*

Rock in bars

Le Cavern
21 rue Dauphine, 6th (01.43.54.53.82). Mº Odéon or
Pont Neuf. **Bar** 7pm-3am Tue-Thur; 7pm-5am Fri,
Sat. **Concerts** 10.30pm-2am. Closed Aug.
Admission free. **Credit** MC, V. **Map** p406 H6.
A godsend for young groups seeking an audience, and therefore a good place to spot up-coming stars.

Chesterfield Café
124 rue La Boétie, 8th (01.42.25.18.06). Mº Franklin
D Roosevelt. **Bar/restaurant** 9am-5am daily.
Concerts 11pm Tue-Sat; gospel concerts 2pm Sun.
Admission free. **Credit** AmEx, V. **Map** p401 E4.
Music can seem secondary to bizarre mating rituals, but it does run from quiffed-up rock and posey pop to Sunday blues and soulful gospel.

Le Réservoir
16 rue de la Forge-Royal, 11th (01.43.56.39.60/
www.reservoir-dogs.com). Mº Ledru-Rollin. **Bar** 8pm-
2am Mon-Thur; 8pm-dawn Fri-Sat; noon-6pm Sun
(jazz brunch). **Admission** free. **Credit** AmEx, MC,
V, **Map** p407 N7.
Live acts range from soul, funk, groove to world, reggae, trip hop and house. This venue boasts celebrity visits and a juicy Sunday jazz brunch.

La Scène
2bis rue des Taillandiers, 11th (01.48.06.50.70/
reservations 01.48.06.12.13). Mº Ledru-Rollin.
Bar/restaurant 8pm-2am. **Concerts** 9.30pm Mon-
Thur; 11pm Fri, Sat. Closed Sun. **Admission** free.
Credit AmEx, MC, V, **Map** p407 M7.
This superbly designed bar and split-level restaurant has a relaxed, earthy feel thanks to its cool, stone interior and low lights.

Arts & Entertainment

Chansons for a new generation

Until recently, French rock and pop had been suffering from a rather staid (spot the euphemism) reputation, with the traditional *chanson* style of artists like Cabrel, Obispo (the writer of musicals such as *Romeo and Juliet*) and Johnny Hallyday (*see p331* **Heeeeere's Johnny!**) dominating the charts. Rock singers with the ambition to corner the youth or export market had been forced to sing in English. Happily for the music scene, a new generation of singers is today elbowing its way to the forefront with a crossover style of chanson/rock and electronic music, and stars from the 1980s are re-vamping their sound with help from younger producers. Singer-songwriter Etienne Daho has experimented with drum'n'bass (akin to Phil Collins doing gangsta rap), Les Rita Mitsouko have added house tempos to recent tracks and Les Negresses Vertes' last album *Trabendo* was produced by English knob twiddler Howie B.

The international interest in the French house scene has not only produced a post-Daft Punk phenomenon of house artists such as Modjo, Alex Kid and Dax Riders but has opened doors for new rock talent. Turns such as shrinking violet and well-oiled gyrator Sinclair, Louise Attaque and Katrine have all proved that the rock scene is alive and thrashing. Young singers such as M (Mathieu Chedid, who looks like a cartoon character with his hair coiffed neatly into demonic horns) and Bosco have used the kind of visual backdrops usually associated with infamous dance acts such as Prodigy or Chemical Brothers as well as hip-hop, house and rock influences in their music.

Another successful crossover is the electronic be-bop/jazz of groups such as Paris Combo and newcomer Kelly Joyce, who combines French *chanson* with a 40's sound, breakbeat and soul.

Tracklisting:
Les Negresses Vertes *Trabendo* Virgin 1999
Les Rita Mitsouko *Cool* Frenesie Delabel 2000
M *Le Tour de M* Delabel 2001
Kelly Joyce *KJ* Polydor 2001

Le Bee Bop
64 rue de Charenton, 12th (01.43.42.56.26/ www.bee-bop.cityvox.com). M° Ledru Rollin. **Bar** 6pm-2am daily. **Concerts** 9-11.30pm. **Admission** free. **Credit** AmEx, DC, MC, V. **Map** p407 M7.
A French-run, English-style pub that serves up a banquet of local bands. Rock, blues, funk, world, *chanson* – the programme is wide open and predominantly electric. Cheap pints. *Wheelchair access.*

La Flèche d'Or
102bis rue de Bagnolet, 20th (01.43.72.42.44/ www.flechedor.com). M° Gambetta. **Bar/restaurant** 6pm-2am Tue; 10am-2am Wed-Sun. **Concerts** 9pm Tue-Sat; 5pm Sun. **Admission** free-€4.57. **No credit cards**. **Map** p407 Q6.
This ex-train station is home to old hippies and new alternatives. Music is an eclectic feast of world, ska, reggae and rock. *Wheelchair access.*

Le Gambetta
104 rue de Bagnolet, 20th (01.43.70.52.01). M° Gambetta. **Bar** 9.30am-2am daily. **Concerts** 9pm. **Admission** €3.05-€4.57 **Credit** MC, V. **Map** p407 Q6.
This unpretentious rock and rumble haunt has an edgy student-union feel and bands that thump and rattle. Punk, rock, alternative electric guitar, plus regular world music nights. *Wheelchair access.*

Chanson

Not all *chanson* involves impassioned, aged crooners singing covers from 30 years ago. The following venues offer an eclectic mix of new singer-songwriters, jazz, gypsy music and poetry, but the spiritual home of the form will always be **L'Olympia**, *p327.*

Sentier des Halles
50 rue d'Aboukir, 2nd (01.42.61.89.96). M° Sentier. **Concerts** 8pm, 10pm Mon-Sat. Closed Aug. **Admission** €7.62-€6.77. **No credit cards**. **Map** p402 J4.
This celebrated cellar seats 120 people for a wide variety of acts (many of them big cheeses), from *chanson* to camembert reggae and roquefort rap.

L'Attirail
9 rue au Maire, 3rd (01.42.72.44.42). M° Arts et Métiers. **Bar/restaurant** 10am-2am daily. **Concerts** 9pm. **Admission** free. **Credit** AmEx, DC, MC, V. **Map** p402 K5.
This low-key Algerian bar offers *chanson*, plus ocasional world music and theatre. Sitting in the back section with the musicians, you will be encouraged not to smoke too much.

Le Limonaire
18 cité Bergère, 9th (01.45.23.33.33/ http://limonaire.free.fr). M° Grands Boulevards. **Bar** 6pm-1am Tue-Sun. **Concerts** 10pm Tue-Sat; 6pm Sun. **Admission** free. **Credit** MC, V. **Map** p402 J4.
Down an atmospheric passageway a *bistro à vins*

that takes its *chanson* seriously – don't come here for a drink and a chat as the room becomes wrapped in reverent silence while the artistes perform. And don't come here to do your Inspector Clouseau impressions, either. The venue does wonderful accordion *bals* and silent movies with piano accompaniment.

Chez Adel

10 rue de la Grange-aux-Belles, 10th (01.42.08.24.61). M° Jacques Bonsergent. **Bar** 11.30am-2am Mon-Thur; 6.30pm-2a, Fri, Sat; noon-2am Sun. **Concerts** 9pm Mon-Fri; from 3pm Sun. **Admission** free. **Credit** MC, V. **Map** p402 L3.
What a place to whoop it up. Great sangria, frescoed walls, good-value meals (homemade Syrian at weekends) and a cosy audience. French, folk and gypsy tunes add to the warm and welcoming little village vibe. *Wheelchair access.*

Le Panier

32 rue Ste-Marthe, 10th (01.42.01.38.18). M° Belleville. **Bar** 11am-2am daily. **Concerts** 8pm Weds, Fri, Sat (call to check). **Admission** free. **No credit cards. Map** p403 M3.
Nestled in a quietly hip Belleville square, Le Panier oozes incense smoke and kitsch cool. Splay out on the terrace and listen to the echo of *chanson* and jazz, or huddle inside with the musicians in shades.

Nice 'n' queasy at the **Batofar**.

Le Magique

42 rue de Gergovie, 14th (01.45.42.26.10). M° Pernéty. **Bar/restaurant** 8pm-2am Wed-Sun. **Concerts** 9.30pm Wed-Thur; 10.30pm Fri-Sun. **Admission** free. **No credit cards. Map** p405 F10
Enjoy politically incorrect *chanson*, gypsy swing or hypnotico-futurist song before or after a palatable, discount meal. Donations €4.50 minimum.

Le Pataquès

8 rue Jouye-Rouve, 20th. No telephone number listed. M° Pyrénées. **Bar** 10am-midnight Tue-Fri and every second Mon; 10pm-1am Sat, Sun. **Concerts** 7.30-10.30pm **Admission** free. **No credit cards.**
Enter the retro timewarp and savour the alternative ambience or dance the java with strange and/or friendly locals. Le Pataquès has built up a reputation for slam poetry nights but occasionally has music and off-beat theatre too.

Barges

La Balle au Bond

(01.40.51.87.06/www.laballeaubond.fr). (Oct-Mar) 55 quai de la Tournelle, 5th, M° Maubert-Mutualité; (Apr-Sept) quai Malaquais, 6th. M° Pont Neuf. **Bar** 11am-2am Mon-Sun. **Concerts** 9pm Mon-Sat. **Admission** €6.10. **Credit** AmEx, MC, V. **Map** p406 K7.
Mainstream commotion on mid-river. Come over all 'hello, sailor' as you swing and sway to the party-honk of rock, pop, jazz and *chanson*.

Péniche Déclic

7 quai St-Bernard, 5th (01.45.79.08.42). M° Jussieu/Gare d'Austerlitz. **Bar** 9pm-midnight Thur-Sun. **Concerts** 9pm. Closed Aug. **Admission** €6.10. **No credit cards. Map** p406 L8.
This modest little packet, no larger than a dingo's donger, is home to an unpretentious crowd of hipsters for didgeridoo and rootsy rhythm nights.

Batofar

quai François-Mauriac, 13th (01.56.29.10.00/www.batofar.org). M° Quai de la Gare/Bibliothèque. **Bar** 5pm-2am Tue-Sat. **Concerts** 8pm Tue-Sat. **Admission** free-€9.15. **Credit** MC, V. **Map** p407 N10.
An unsinkable pleasure fest for those who can stomach writhing to electro-modern music such as techno, house and dub with a fair bit of wave motion underfoot. *See also chapter* **Clubs***.*

Péniche Blues Café

quai de la Gare, 13th (01.45.84.24.88). M° Quai de la Gare/Bibliothèque. **Concerts** advertised ten days in advance in *Lilo* magazine. **Admission** €7.62. **No credit cards. Map** p407 M9.
A jazz barge that's gone increasingly indie of late, if such a concept is possible. Just near the Bibliothèque Nationale if you fancy a read instead (the Blues Café is notoriously restrained, so don't come if you're in the mood for head-banging).

Péniche El Alamein

quai François-Mauriac, 13th (01.45.86.41.60).
M° Quai de la Gare/Bibliothèque. **Bar** 7pm-2am
daily. **Concerts** 9pm. **Admission** €4.57-€7.62.
No credit cards. Map p407 N10.
For all you sea-legged lovebirds. Serenades are predominantly *chanson*, with the odd pop-rock or
ragga-reggae mutiny. Things tend towards the
chicken-in-a-basket; if they happened anywhere else,
the perpetrators would have to walk the gangplank.
Wheelchair access.

Péniche Makara

quai François-Mauriac, 13th (01.44.24.09.00).
M° Quai de la Gare/Bibliothèque. **Bar** 7pm-2am Tue-
Sun. **Concerts** 9.30pm. **Admission** €4.57-€7.62.
Credit MC, V. **Map** p407 N10.
A relaxed crowd sways in a decidedly herbal man-
ner to world, reggae and roots vibes. Definitely the
place to go to check out local talent before they
become stars. *Wheelchair access.*

Blues bars

See also **Lionel Hampton Jazz Club** *and*
New Morning, *both on p333.*

Utopia

79 rue de l'Ouest, 14th (01.43.22.79.66). M° Pernéty.
Concerts usually 10pm daily. **Admission** €7.62-
€10.67. **Credit** MC ,V. **Map** p405 F10.
Bluesmen from home and away dig deep into the
soulful territory of their predecessors. Country blues,
delta blues, swing and blues rock are laid down with
gusto as any considerations of Gallic cool are swept
aside by the power of the real thing.

Quai du Blues

17 bd Vital-Bouhot (Ile de la Jatte), Neuilly sur Seine,
(01.46.24.22.00). M° Pont de Levallois. **Bar/**
restaurant 8.30pm-2am. **Concerts** 10.30pm Thur-
Sat. Closed July-Aug. **Admission** €15.24; €12.20
under 25s (Thur); €38.11 (dinner & show). **Credit**
AmEx, V.

The best Venues

French chanson

You'll regret rien at **Le Limonaire** (*see p329*).

Rock

L'Olympia world-famous, world class (*see*
p326).

Jazz

OK, cats, let's play spot-the-melody at
Duc des Lombards (*see p332*).

Indian

Head-bangras convene at **Centre Mandapa**
(*see p331*).

This atmospheric refurbished garage invites only
genuine Afro-American artists to grace its stage.
The positively discriminatory policy is clearly a
quality control measure, and it usually pays off.

World & traditional music

Théâtre de La Ville

(01.42.74.22.77/ www.theatredelaville-paris.com).
2 pl du Châtelet, 4th. M° Châtelet. 31 rue des
Abbesses, 18th. M° Abbesses. **Box office** 11am-7pm
Mon; 11am-8pm Tue-Sat; 11am-7pm Mon-Sat
(telephone). **Concerts** 8.30pm Mon-Fri; 5pm, 8.30pm Sat.
Closed July-Aug. **Admission** €15-€22; €11 under 27s
on day. **Credit** MC, V. **Map** p406 J6.
Wheelchair access.
At the Châtelet theatre and its Abbesses offshoot the
musical programme presents and celebrates rare
and exotic forms – rare and exotic to we blinkered
westerners, that is.

Au Train de Vie

85 rue de la Verrerie, 4th (01.42.77.33.80). M° Hôtel
de Ville. **Restaurant** noon-1am daily. **Concerts** 9.30pm
Mon-Sat; 5.30pm, 9.30pm Sun. **Admission** €13.72.
Credit AmEx, MC, V. **Map** p406 K6.
Brainbox Claude Berger invites the best Eastern
European and Yiddish musicians to his downstairs
den for wild and vibey sessions in a little tea-
room/restaurant.

Institut du Monde Arabe

1 rue des Fossés-St-Bernard, 5th (01.40.51.38.38/
www.imarabe.org). M° Jussieu. **Box office** 10am-
5pm Tue-Sun; 7.30-9pm show nights. **Concerts**
8.30pm Fri, Sat. **Admission** €12.20-€15.24. **Credit**
V. **Map** p406 K7.
A quality auditorium with wonderful, lounge-like
leather seats. The institute is lucky enough to be able
to attract a great number of top-class performers
from the Arab world.

La Vieille Grille

1 rue du Puits-de-l'Hermite, 5th (01.47.07.22.11/
http://vielle.grille.free.fr). M° Place Monge.
Restaurant 7 30pm-12.30am Tue-Sat. **Bar** 6pm-
1am Tue-Sun. **Concerts** 6.30pm, 9pm Tue-Sun.
Admission €10 (6.30pm concert); €16 (9pm
concert); €10 students; €5 children. **No credit**
cards. Map p406 K8.
A cute, café-théâtre style niche. Regular Latin and
Klezmer nights alternate with traditional jazz, world
music and text readings (yes, that's right: text readings, metal fans) at weekends.

Kibélé

12 rue de L'Echiquier, 10th (01.48.24.57.74).
M° Strasbourg St Denis. **Restaurant** noon-3pm,
7pm-2am Mon-Sat. **Concerts** 9.30pm Wed-Sat.
Admission free. **Credit** AmEx, MC, V.
Map p402 K4.
Dine in the friendly Turkish restaurant and then
drop down to the snug cellar and drift to the sound
of Eastern Europe and North Africa.

Heeeeere's Johnny!

500,000 people are swaying in misty-eyed unison on the Champs-de-Mars. On a Harley, on a stage, is a chubby dude in a skin-tight leather jumpsuit. His capped teeth and genetically-modified hair seem to emit light as he opens the motorcycle's throttle; the roar of the engine rises to meet that of the crowd. Just then, the giant letters fixed to the Eiffel Tower burst into flame and broadcast their desperate message: **100% Johnny**. Oh, it's just another Johnny Hallyday gig.

Johnny remains a hazy character to the Anglophone world. The name tends to evoke a pathetic Gallic Elvis, Beatles' covers in French, and a tenuous link with Hendrix (with whom Johnny did have social relations. He considered Hendrix his soul brother, which must have flattered the Jimi no end). But there is more. There must be. A 40-year career?

Behind the sequins is the raunchily named Jean-Philippe Smet, son of Léon, born in the 9th *arrondissement* in 1943. By 1958 he has developed a passion for cowboys and rock (or was that cowboys *called* Rock?). He changes his name to sound American and gets a band together. They release their first album in 1960 but don't have any success until 1962 when *Johnny Sings America's Rockin' Hits* slays the country's youth. The cut *C'est le Mashed Potatoes* (sic), is a hit; fans scarcely have time to take it all in before *Mashed Potato Time* does it to them one more time.

Never the first man to leave a party, Johnny records no fewer than five songs exploring Twist possibilities. In fact, Hallyday's career has been sustained by his ability to spot a trend and milk it. In 1967, just months after the release of *Sergeant Pepper*, Johnny released *Johnny 67*, the cover of which shows our man smoking an elaborate pipe and wearing military dress uniform with bath-brush epaulettes. No pudding is left under-egged.

This multi-genre straddler never shied away from a concept project (among them a double-album interpretation of *Hamlet*) but it's his all-American rock ballads that have kept his fans coming back for more. And more. Hallyday is fertile, and he inspires fecundity in others: he is the subject of 56 books, has appeared in over 20 films and released ten albums in 2000 alone. 2001 was a quiet year for Johnny, but teasing rumours of a novel abound.

Why do the French love Johnny like they do? His fans know that he doesn't write his songs (not even *Laura*, the song dedicated to his daughter). But his concerts are long, he sweats a lot, he's got all his rockstar stripes and has even been reported dead by AFP.

In the era of the super-slick, market-dictated popstar, Johhny romps home on innocent charm. The thing is, the French just can't do rock'n'roll; Johnny can't either, but he doesn't let a little thing like that stop him, and that's proof that he is 100% rock'n'roll in outlook.

Cava Cava
9 rue Moret, 11th (01.43.55.18.84).
M° Ménilmontant. **Bar/restaurant** 7.30pm-2am
Mon- Sun. **Concerts** 11pm Fri-Sat; 7 30pm Sun.
Admission €6.10 Fri-Sat; €7.62 Sun. **Credit.**
Map p403 N4.
A buoyant spot for lithe, Latin groovers in search of a sinful turn on the dancefloor. Daily dance lessons and a Cuban buffet on Sunday.

Sattelit' Café
44 rue de la Folie-Méricourt, 11th (01.47.00.48.87).
M° Oberkampf. **Bar** 8pm-4am Tue-Thur; 10pm-6am
Fri-Sat. **Concerts** 8.30pm Mon-Thur. **Admission**

€7.62. **Credit** AmEx, MC, V. **Map** p403 M5.
Sizzling, blues-tinged delights provide the soul food to send you into a nocturnal orbit to remember.

Centre Mandapa
6 rue Wurtz, 13th (01.45.89.01.60). M° Glacière.
Box office *(telephone)* 11am-7pm Mon-Sat.
Concerts 8.30pm. Closed July-mid-September.
Admission €12.20-€15.24; students €9.15-€10.67.
No credit cards. Map p406 J10.
If you have never been lucky enough to experience the hypnotic beauty of the live *sitar* or *tabla* in full flight, this is where you get your ticket. *Wheelchair access (call ahead).*

Stop press

If you're looking for a wider perspective on the music scene and you can read a bit of French, there's no shortage of magazines that are as informative as they are diverse. (Don't let the occasional cringe-worthy anglicised title put you off, and try to ignore the regular, seemingly mandatory, articles on the Princess Margaret of French pop, Serge Gainsbourg).

Les Inrockuptibles
www.lesinrocks.com.
A weekly, pseudo-intellectual look at music, literature and most anything cultural. It's become an opinion-former, and has a refreshing penchant for the off-beat. No self-respecting Anglophone poser would be caught dead calling it anything other than 'les inrocks'.

Rock 'n' Folk
Does what it says on the tin. Pretty mainstream, but leans towards the harder end of rock. Also solid on funk, soul and reggae. Especially good news section.

Rock Sound
(www.wattmusic.com).
A rocky read indeed, far more Slipknot than Sting. Frequent freebie CDs come along as part of the package.

L'Affiche
Definitely one for the homies, dedicated as it is to rap, R'n'B and ragga. One of the cornerstones of the rise and rise of French rap a decade ago, this is still relevant, and, for many, essential.

Jazz Magazine
(www.jazzmagazine.com).
The most forward-looking and designerish of the nation's jazz publications, but not at the expense of neglecting the history behind the music. Tussles it out with *JazzHot* (which has been around for 60 years) for first place.

Vibrations
(www.lesite.fr/vibrations/).
Actually Swiss-based, this favourite among hip Parisians is very good for world music, reggae and modern jazz. Particularly pleasing on the eye, and not in the usual cliché rap-mag style.

Cité de La Musique
221 av Jean-Jaurès, 19th (01.44.84.44.84/ www.cite-musique.fr). Mᵒ Porte de Pantin. **Concerts** 8pm Tue-Sat; 4.30pm Sat; 3pm, 4.30pm Sun. **Admission** €6-€33. **Credit** MC, V. **Map** p403 inset.
Spacious, comfortable and acoustically superb, the auditorium at La Villette's music complex attracts first-class world, jazz and classical musicians.

La Maroquinerie
23 rue Boyer, 20th (01.40.33.30.60). Mᵒ Gambetta. **Restaurant** 11am-1am Mon-Sat. **Bar** 11am-1am. **Concerts** 8.30pm. **Admission** €4.57-€16.77. **Map** p407 Q5.
This old leather factory has become a happening locale for world, rock, jazz and country, poetry and debate. That's right: debate. None of that sitting around just enjoying the sounds. *Wheelchair access.*

Jazz

Le Baiser Salé
58 rue des Lombards, 1st (01.42.33.37.71). Mᵒ Châtelet. **Bar** 7pm-6am Mon-Sat. **Concerts** 7pm, 8pm. **Admission** €6.10-€15.24. **Credit** AmEx, DC, MC, V. **Map** p406 J6.
This little Châtelet club offers 'happy concerts' of pop, soul-funk or *chanson*, followed by Afro-jazz.

Duc des Lombards
42 rue des Lombards, 1st (01.42.33.22.88). Mᵒ Châtelet. **Bar** 8pm-2am Mon-Sat. **Concerts** 9pm-1.30am. **Closed** weekdays in Aug. **Admission** €12.20-€18.29. **Credit** MC, V. **Map** p406 J6.
No frills but plenty of atmosphere. You're practically on top of the many jazz acts (mainly French, though the odd biggish US outfit passes through), so you get a great vibe and you almost feel like having a good time in public, bro.

Le Petit Opportun
15 rue des Lavandières-Ste-Opportune, 1st (01.42.36.01.36). Mᵒ Châtelet. **Bar** 9pm-5am Tue-Sat. **Concerts** 6pm, 10.30pm-2.30am Tue-Sat. **Admission** €12.20. **No credit cards**. **Map** p406 J6.
Top French jazzers go for the high notes in this tiny medieval cellar, although if it's packed you may not actually be able to see them.

Le Slow Club
130 rue de Rivoli, 1st (01.42.33.84.30). Mᵒ Châtelet. **Bar** 10pm-3am Tue, Thur; 10pm-4am Fri, Sat. **Concerts** 10pm. **Admission** €9.15-€11.43; €8.38 students Tue, Thur. **Credit** MC,V. **Map** p406 J6.
A little cellar with big beat boogie-woogie orchestras, R&B, washboard jazz and swing bands.

Le Sunset/Le Sunside
60 rue des Lombards, 1st (01.40.26.46.60 Sunset/ 01.40.26.21.25 Sunside). Mᵒ Châtelet. **Bar** 9.30pm-2am Mon-Sat. **Concerts** 10pm (Sunset). **Admission** €12.20-€18.29. **Credit** MC, V. **Map** p406 J6.

The sun doesn't look anywhere near setting on the centre of Paris' jazz solar system. Le Sunset concentrates on electric jazz and world music, Le Sunside focuses on acoustic.

Les 7 Lézards
10 rue des Rosiers, 4th (01.48.87.08.97). M° St-Paul. **Bar** noon-2am daily. **Concerts** 9.30pm. **Admission** €9.15-€10.67; €7.62 Wed. **No cards. Map** p406 L6.
A jazz hubbub of locals, ex-pats and visiting US maestros. Prepare yourself for the bippidy-boppidy fury of free-bopping improvisation.

Café Universel
267 rue St-Jacques, 5th (01.43.25.74.20). RER Luxembourg. **Bar** 9am-2am Mon-Sat. **Concerts** 9.30pm. Closed Aug. **Admission** free. **Credit** MC, V. **Map** p406 J8.
Friendly bar showcases local bebop, modern, Afro and Latin acts to a student and ex-pat crowd.

Caveau de la Huchette
5 rue de la Huchette, 5th (01.43.26.65.05). M° St-Michel. **Concerts** 9.30pm daily. **Admission** €9.15 Mon-Thur, Sun; €11.43 Fri-Sat; €8.38 students Mon-Thur. **Credit** MC, V. **Map** p406 J7.
Set in the tourist trap part of the Latin Quarter but worth every last euro. The intimate venue is a hit in itself, even if you're not really a jazz cat.

Le Bilboquet
13 rue St-Benoît, 6th (01.45.48.81.84). M° St-Germain-des-Prés. **Concerts** 10.30pm-2.30am Mon-Sun. **Admission** €20.58 (incl one drink). **Credit** AmEx, MC, V. **Map** p406 H6.
Its 50s heyday (Miles Davis played here) may be over but traditional jazz standards remain.

New Morning
7-9 rue des Pétites-Ecuries, 10th (01.45.23.51.41/ www.newmorning.com). M° Château d'Eau. **Box office** 4.30-7.30pm Mon-Fri. **Concerts** 9pm daily. **Admission** €16-€20. **Credit** V. **Map** p402 K3.
This prestigious venue attracts a rapt audience with top-end jazz, blues and world music artists.

Le Cithéa
114 rue Oberkampf, 11th (01.40.21.70.95/ www.cithea.com). M° Parmentier/Ménilmontant. **Bar** 10pm-5.30am. **Concerts** 11.30pm. **Admission** free Mon, Tue, Sun; €4.57 Wed, Thur; €9.15 Fri, Sat. **Credit** MC, V. **Map** p407 N5.
Amateur jazz(y) musicians fuse Afro, Latin, soul-funk, hip hop and dance styles. After the show, the DJ creeps slowly towards a techno meltdown.

Parc Floral de Paris
Bois de Vincennes, 12th (01.55.94.20.20/ www.parcfloraldeparis.com). M° Château de Vincennes. **Concerts** May-July 4.30pm Sat, Sun. **Admission** €1.50. **No credit cards.**
The cream of the international jazz world congregates every summer at this little gazebo in the park.

Petit Journal Montparnasse
13 rue du Commandant-Mouchotte, 14th

Heavy fretting at **Studio des Islettes**.

(01.43.21.56.70). M° Gaité. **Bar/restaurant** noon-3.30pm, 8pm-2am Mon-Sat. **Concerts** 10pm. Closed 15 July-15Aug. **Admission** €15.24-€27.44; €30.49-€60.98 (dinner & show). **Credit** MC, V. **Map** p405 F9.
This jazz brasserie offers R&B, soul-gospel, Latin and Afro-fusion in an evolutionary atmosphere of harmony and experimentation that many other Parisian venues would do well to emulate.

Lionel Hampton Jazz Club
81 bd Gouvion-St-Cyr, 17th (01.40.68.30.42). M° Porte Maillot. **Bar** 7am-2am daily. **Concerts** 10.30pm, 2am daily. **Admission** €21.50 (incl one drink). **Credit** AmEx, DC, MC, V. **Map** p400 B2.
This upmarket hotel bar offers R&B, soul and gospel. 75% of acts are from America, but local talent gets the opportunity to swing here, too.

Studio des Islettes
10 rue des Islettes, 18th (01.42.58.63.33). M° Barbès-Rochechouart. **Bar** 8pm-1am Mon-Sat. **Jam sessions/concerts** 9pm. Closed Aug. **Admission** €7.62 Fri, Sat; €3.81 Mon-Thur. **No credit cards. Map** p402 J2.
Jazz chart wallpaper and a loose, blues-used feel help pro or amateur musicians get in the groove and home in on the source.*Wheelchair access.*

Les Instants Chavirés
7 rue Richard Lenoir, 93100 Montreuil (01.42.87.25.91/www.instantschavires.fr.st). M° Robespierre. **Concerts** 8.30pm-11.30pm Tue-Sat. Closed Aug. **Admission** €6.10-€12.20, free under 12s. **No credit cards.**
Contemporary, improvised music of all genres (frequently jazz and electronic) attracts a plethora of international musicians. *Wheelchair access.*

Sport & Fitness

To Parisians, urban sport no longer means the free-style doggie-do slide
or miniature poodle carrying: it's decidely chic to have a sleek physique.

Something astonishing happened on 12 July
1998: France won the soccer World Cup; as a
consequence, the nation realised that you can be
French and still be a winner. Since then, city
authorities have invested in the city's sports
infrastructure, primarily in an effort to be
selected to host the 2008 Olympics. In the
summer of 2001, it was announced that China
had won that particular race, but, of course, that
hasn't changed the fact that visitors now have a
range of good, cheap municipal sporting
facilities at their disposal. (2001 was not a year
of total disappointment for the French: they
clinched the World Handball Championships in
Paris.) In many ways, the biggest event of
Paris' sporting 2002 takes place in South Korea
and Japan, where all eyes are looking to see if
France can retain that soccer World Cup. The
best source of information for sport in Paris is
the comprehensive *Guide du Sport à Paris*,
published annually by the Mairie de Paris and
available from the *mairie* (town hall) of each
arrondissement. To use certain sports centres,
you will need a *carte* for which you must show
an identity card or passport (take an extra
photo too) and, for sports perceived as risky,
such as inline skating or rock climbing, you will
usually need proof of insurance, which you can
buy in specialist shops. Alternatively, insurance
may be included when you join a club.

Spectator sports

A number of first-class international sporting
events are held in the city throughout the year
(*see p338*, **The sporting year 2002**). For
international events, the usual venue is the
Stade de France (rue Francis de Pressensé,
93210 St-Denis/01.55.93.00.00/reservations
01.44.68.44.44/www.stadedefrance.fr).
Alternatively, the Palais Omnisports de Paris-
Bercy (8 bd de Bercy, 12th, M° Bercy/
01.40.02.60.60/reservations 01.44.68.44.68/
www.popb.fr) hosts everything from martial
arts to indoor jet skiing. Tickets can be obtained
from branches of Fnac and Virgin Megastores.

Head in contact
with ball equals
'une tête'.

Basketball

Paris Basket Racing
*Stade Pierre de Coubertin, 82 ave Georges Lafont,
16th (01.45.27.79.12). M° Porte de St-Cloud.*
Basketball is very popular in France, and the French
first division, the Pro A, is of a good level by
European standards. Paris Basket Racing is a consistent mid-table performer.

Football

Paris Saint-Germain
*Parc des Princes, 24 rue du Commandant-Guilbaud,
16th (01.42.30.03.60/www.psg.fr). M° Porte d'Auteuil.*
Tickets *by Internet or phone 08 25 07 50 78.
Prices range from €9-€83.*
Paris' only top-division football team Paris Saint-
Germain has had difficulty in consistently living up
to its fans' high expectations (*see p337* **PSG: Please
score goals**). Having failed to become French cham-
pions for several years now, a recent spending spree
will, it is hoped, produce a reversal of fortunes.
Matches at the 48,000-seat Parc des Princes.

Friday night fever

Cruising along pavements, roads and quaysides, weaving through people and traffic alike, Parisian skaters have been braving both the potential disgrace of a spectacular fall and the wrath of infringed pedestrians for a couple of years now. Everybody's at it.

If, on a Friday evening stroll, you notice traffic at a standstill and rabid drivers honking their horns, you'll be witnessing the effects of 40,000 roller maniacs on their Friday Night Fever run. This free weekly roll averages 25km and the route changes each week, passing along the Champs-Elysées once every two months. The run is not for delicate blossoms, and as Paris isn't flat knowing how to stop on a steep slope is imperative. The head of the skate can reach speeds of 60km per hour on downhill slopes, so you need to be able to control your direction and speed. You should also know how to brake, avoid obstacles, navigate rough pavements and, of course, how to fall with the finesse of a prima ballerina.

Having said that, don't let the prospect of a few nose-dives deter you. The buzz is worth rolling for and ambulances and the Pari Roller team staff in their bright yellow T-shirts are on hand at all times to deal with mishaps. There is a stop towards the end of the run and iced tea is distributed amongst the crowd (with bin bags to clean up the litter; that's how organised it is). Do take water as the run is energetic. It's always a good idea to make sure that you are insured. If you're not a regular, head for the large yellow Pari Roller

truck parked at the start of each race (the starting point is at 40 av d'Italie, 13th, M° Place d'Italie, at 7.45pm and the run finishes here three hours later); here you can equip yourself with a special visitor privilege package for €15.24. This covers you for insurance all-year-round and gives you full membership of the Roller Association. It is possible join the run at any point and the route is announced on Thursday on the **Pari Roller** website: www.pari-roller.com (01.43.36.89.81). The Friday night run is not just for participants; it is hugely enjoyable just to watch 40,000 people whizzing along the roads, creating an impressive spectacle and a carnival atmosphere.

For those who want the sensation without the fear there is a far more sedate beginner's skate every Sunday at 2.30pm, organised by **Rollers Nomades** and meeting at their shop just off place de la Bastille (37 bd Bourdon, 4th. M° Bastille. 01.44.54.07.44/www.rollernet.com/nomads).

One of the best aspects of Paris skating is that it attracts no snobbery. The nervous neophyte, crawling along with all the grace of a new-born foal and emitting banshee wails every time things almost go out of control, is accorded as much respect as some Astaire-on-wheels. And if you are thinking of mowing down a roller-less pedestrian who's been getting in your way and cramping your style for almost an entire *arrondissement*, don't let it be a blue-rinsed old lady. Those chicks are like rottweilers.

Horse racing

There are seven racecourses in the Paris area. *France Galop* publishes a full racing list (01.49.10.20.30/www.france-galop.com) in its *Calendrier des Courses*. **Auteuil**, Bois de Boulogne, 16th (01.40.71.47.47/M° Porte d'Auteuil). Steeple- chasing. **Chantilly** (41km from Paris/03.44.62.41.00/train from Gare du Nord). Flat racing. **Enghien** (18km from Paris/ 01.34. 17.87.00/train from Gare du Nord). Steeplechasing and trotting. **Longchamp**, Bois de Boulogne (16th/01.44.30.75.00/M° Porte d'Auteuil, then free bus). Flat racing. **Maisons-Laffitte** (1 av de La Pelouse, 78600 Maisons-Laffitte/01.39.62.90.95/RER A Maisons-Laffitte and then bus). Flat racing. **St-Cloud** (1 rue du Camp Canadien, 92210 St-Cloud/01.47.71.69.26/RER A Rueil-Malmaison). Flat racing. **Paris-Vincennes** Bois de Vincennes, 12th (01.49.77.17.17/ M° Vincennes/RER Joinville le Pont).

Rugby

Stade Français CASG
Stade Jean-Bouin, 26 av du Général-Sarrail, 16th (01.46.51.00.75/www.stade.fr). M° Porte d'Auteuil. **Tickets** €6.10-€38.11.
Le **Stade Français** has put Paris on the national rugby map. The arrival of coach Bernard Laporte was a turning point for the club. Under his guidance the team earned promotion to the first division and went on to become champions in 1998. Since 1999 the side has been managed by Georges Coste. In 2001 the team lost in the European Cup final to Britain's Leicester.

Gyms & fitness

The city has a relatively small number of *clubs de forme*. Nonetheless, they are well equipped, with a broad range of activities available and helpful staff.

Club Quartier Latin
19 rue de Pontoise, 5th (01.55.42.77.88/ www.clubquartierlatin.com). M° Maubert-Mutualité. **Open** 9am-midnight Mon-Fri; 10am-7pm Sat, Sun. **Membership** Fitness section annual €533.57. **Credit** MC, V. **Map** p406 K7
The gym has plenty of well-maintained machines, together with a range of stretch, cardio and other classes. There's also a squash membership which grants you access to the centre's four squash courts (in varying states of repair). The club does, however, get crowded at peak times. Both memberships include access to the Piscine Pontoise (*see p340* **Making a splash**).

Espace Vit'Halles
48 rue Rambuteau, 3rd (01.42.77.21.71). M° Rambuteau. **Open** 8am-10.30pm Mon-Fri; 10am-7pm Sat; 10am-6pm Sun. **Membership** annual €678.40, student €609.80; one month €137.20, student €123.48; one visit €15.24. **Credit** AmEx, MC, V. **Map** p402 K5
The gym here is good, the changing rooms are clean and the crowd is non-posey. A range of classes from Tai Chi to Pump is run by tolerant instructors.

Gymnase Club
20 locations in and around Paris, contact 01.44.37.24.24/www.gymnaseclub.fr for full list. **Membership** annual €795.78. **Credit** AmEx, MC, V.
The clubs are large, clean, well-equipped and instruction standards are generally good. They offer the usual classes, plus martial arts and weight loss.

Gymnasium
25 locations in and around Paris; visit www. gymnasium.tm.fr for the full list. Branches include: 62 bd Sébastopol, 3rd (01.42.74.14.56). M° Etienne-Marcel; 129 bd Haussmann, 8th (01.42.89.89.14). M° Miromesnil; 60 rue Ordener, 18th (01.42.51.15.15). M° Jules-Joffrin. **Membership** approximagely €76.22 per month. **Credit** MC, V.
The Gymnasium franchise offers rowing and cycling machines and cardio-training equipment, and some branches have pools. Courses include aerobics, step, stretching and water-based workouts.

Vitatop
Vitatop Plein Ciel Hôtel Sofitel, 8 rue Louis-Armand, 15th (01.45.54.79.00). M° Balard. **Open** 8am-10pm Mon, Wed-Fri; 8am-midnight Tue; 8am-7pm Sat; 9am-5pm Sun. **Vitatop Porte Maillot** *Hôtel Concorde Lafayette, 1 pl du Général-Koenig, 17th (01.40.68.00.21). M° Porte-Maillot.* **Open** 8am-10pm Mon-Fri; 9am-5pm Sat, Sun. **Membership** one year €1,135.75. **Credit** AmEx, MC, V.
These posh, executive gyms are located in two modern, functional hotels. The Porte Maillot branch also has a swimming pool and golf-driving range.

Activities & team sports

All-round sports clubs
The **Standard Athletic Club** (Route Forestière du Pavé de Meudon, 92360 Meudon-la-Forêt/01.46.26.16.09) is a private, non-profit-making club aimed at English speakers living in Paris. Full membership is €625 per year, plus an initial joining fee. It fields a cricket side (May-Sept), hockey and football teams. There are eight tennis courts, two squash courts, a heated outdoor pool and billiards table. Some top-level French clubs also run teams in various sports, such as **Racing Club de France** (01.45.67.55.86/www.racingclubdefrance.org), **Paris Université Club** (01.44.16.62.62/ www.puc.asso.fr) and **Le Stade Français** (01.40.71.33.33).

PSG: Please Score Goals

France has a love affair with football; Paris does not. The heart of French soccer beats elsewhere, probably down in Marseille; in Paris, it needs a pacemaker. Paris St-Germain is the only Parisian club in the French Premier League, and it's not a high achiever. Its followers have an attitude towards their team that borders on full-blown nihilism. Anglophone as many of them are, it is claimed that the club's initials stand for 'Please Score Goals'. So why is the capital city's team so dismally average when the national side is sublime? One of the answers lies in the way it was brought up.

PSG, founded in 1974, is the youngest club in French soccer. It seems to have grown up dysfunctionally. Its development policy has been short-termist, aimed at creating a good team rather than a good club. It buys in rather than grows talent, and has a history of being beaten to the punch by clubs from Italy, Spain and the UK when it comes to bagging promising French players. And wisdom has not always been the hallmark of the purchasing policy: the club frequently buys players who turn out to be clapped-out divas.

Although the last two seasons have been catastrophic, the club hasn't always managed to avoid success: it won the European Cup in 1996, and the National League in 1986 and

1994. That's not so bad, but it's not enough.

The reason why Parisians have not taken the team to their hearts is that it plays without the panache, the 'football champagne' they crave: merely winning isn't enough when there are so many more attractive things to do in Paris on a Saturday night than catch pneumonia on the half-empty terraces of the Parc des Princes. And it's not only the terrace chill factor that keeps people away in droves – until 1998, the club had problems with racist supporters, which dissuaded people from the suburbs or from the working-class north-eastern part of the city from lending their support. The problems have been dealt with, but the stigma prevails.

PSG also lives under the burden of being owned by the TV channel Canal Plus, whose philosophy seems to be soccer as showbiz; the pressure of being expected to sparkle at showtime every two weeks has seen three managers and four coaches come and go in the last four years. Added to that is the fact that the city council grants the club 30 million francs of taxpayers' money each year: taxpayers' expectations are justifiably high, but they just add a heavier burden onto the players' delicate constitutions.

Paris St-Germain stands at a point where politics, money and civic image meet; the pressure tells. PSG should be one of the eight best clubs in Europe; as it is, it struggles to be one of the eight best clubs in France.

American football

Though there are no teams in Paris itself, there are 15 teams in the area. Many teams have some Americans in them, whether players or coaches,. Contact the **Fédération Française de Football Américain** (01.43.11.14.70/ www.ffa.org or www.efafofficiating.org for those interested in learning how to referee) to find the club nearest you.

Athletics & running

Paris has many municipal tracks (including eight indoor ones) which are generally of a good standard. To find the track nearest you, consult the *Guide du Sport* or call Paris Infos Mairie. For an open-air run, the **Bois de Boulogne** and the **Bois de Vincennes** are the only large green expanses in Paris. Runners using the former should be aware that it is a cruising spot.

The sporting year 2002

Paris hosts enough top-notch events to satisfy even the most discerning sports enthusiast. This is the line-up for 2002.

January

Horse racing Prix d'Amérique, Hippodrome de Paris-Vincennes. France's glitzy trotting race.

February

Rugby France's finest take on their five rivals in the Six Nations Cup. Matches are held at the Stade de France in February, March and April. www.stadefrance.com

Tennis Open Gaz de France at the Stade Pierre de Coubertin (82 av Georges-Lafont, 16th/ 01.44.31.44.31/Mº Porte de St-Cloud). Stars of the women's circuit compete at this WTA indoor event. Information and tickets 0803.804.000/ www.gazdefrance.fr/open

March

Gymnastics Internationaux de France at the Palais Omnisports de Paris-Bercy.

Showjumping Jumping International de Paris, at Bercy. Tickets and details for both events via www.ticketnet.fr/bercy/

April

Athletics Paris Marathon starts at 9am on the Champs-Elysées, 7 April, finishing av Foch. Information or entry forms on 01.41.33.15.68/ www.parismarathon.com

Fencing World Grand Prix at Coubertin (a chance to see Laura 'The Wasp'Flessel in action).

Horse racing Prix du Président de la République, a top steeplechase race, at Auteuil, third Sun of April.

May

Fencing World Cup for individual and teams.at Coubertin.

Football French clubs compete for glory and a ticket to the UEFA Cup in the Coupe de France and Coupe de la Ligue finals, both at the Stade de France.

Tennis France's Grand Slam event, the French Open, is held at the Stade Roland-Garros (01.47.43.48.00) at the end of May/early June. www.frenchopen.org

June

Rugby The domestic season reaches its climax with the final of the Championnat de France at the Stade de France.

Horse racing The Prix de Diane Hermès, French equivalent of the Derby, at Chantilly.

July

Athletics IAAF Gaz de France meeting at the Stade de France, a Golden League event.

Cycling The Tour de France arrives in Paris for a grand finale on the Champs-Elysées at the end of July/early Aug (information 01.41.33.15.00/www.letour.fr)

Golf The French Women's Open at the Paris International Golf Club, 18 route du Golf, 95160 Baillet-en-France (01.34.69.90.00) in mid-July.

September

Golf The Trophée Lancôme, at Golf de St-Nom-la-Brétèche, 78860 St-Nom-la-Brétèche. Information and ticket reservations 0803.804.000. www.trophee-lancome.com

October

Horse-racing Flat race and society event Prix de l'Arc de Triomphe at Longchamp.

November

Tennis The Paris Open, a top-ranking international men's indoor tournament, at Bercy.

Skating Lalique Skating Trophy at Bercy. International ice champions and contenders.

Supercross Mud, high jumps, wheel flangers, superskids and all those other things you're not allowed to do with your bike on the roads: do all of this vicariously at Bercy.

December

Go-karting This is no longer a hobby for geeky wannabees in skid-lids. Karting is now officially cool. Formula One drivers get into smaller-than-usual vehicles and race each other round an indoor track at Bercy in the Elf Masters.

Showjumping Concours Hippique International at Paris-Expo, Porte de Versailles, 15th, in association with the annual Salon du Cheval, du Poney et de l'Ane.

Arts & Entertainment

Cutting and faking on the weakside.

Baseball

Baseball clubs are predictably Americanised and many of the players are English speakers. The best way to find a team near you is to contact the **Fédération Française de Baseball, Softball et Cricket** (01.44.68.89.30/www.ffbsc.org).

Basketball

Basketball is very popular in Paris, and virtually every municipal sports centre has a court and club. The **Comité Parisien de Basketball** (01.53.94.27.90/www.basketfrance. com) lists clubs, public and private, including **Racing Club de France and Paris Université Club**. There are also a number of public courts in the city where anyone can play. Popular spots include two courts under the Métro tracks near the Glacière stop in the 13th *arrondissement* and at M° Stalingrad in the 19th.

Bowling & boules

The Paris region has more than 25 tenpin bowling centres. The two we list below are among the most pleasant; both rent out shoes and have restaurants, games rooms and late hours. There are eight lanes at the centrally located and lively **Bowling-Mouffetard** (73 rue Mouffetard, 5th/01.43.31.09.35/ M° Place Monge/open 3pm-2am Mon-Fri, 10am-2am Sat, Sun). The **Bowling de Paris** (Jardin d'Acclimatation, Bois de Boulogne, 16th/01.53.64.93.00/M° Les Sablons/open

9am-3am Mon-Fri; 9am-5am Sat, Sun) has 24 lanes, pool, billiards and video games. Bear in mind that you have to pay €2.13 to get into the Jardin d'Acclimatation before you get to the centre. You can play *boules* or *pétanque* in most squares. There are also some *boulodromes* at **Jardins du Luxembourg**.

Climbing

The wall at the **Centre Sportif Poissonnier** (2 rue Jean-Cocteau, 18th/01.42.51.24.68/ M° Porte de Clignancourt) is the largest municipal facility and has a little 'real rock' section, as well as a 21m-high unlit outside wall. For more of a workout and an even closer acquaintance with fear, there is the privately run **Mur Mur** (55 rue Cartier Bresson, 93500 Pantin/01.48.46.11.00/M° Aubervilliers-Pantin Quatre Chemins), said to be the best climbing wall in Europe, with 1,500 m² of wall, 10,000 holds and an even greater number of ways of falling off. It costs €9.15-€12.20 for adults, €5.34-€6.10 for under-12s per session, though there is a joining fee of €22.87 for adults and €11.43 for under-12s. There is kit for hire and tuition on offer. Newly added is a section to practise ice-climbing (or 'dry-tooling', as they so picturesquely call it).

If you prefer real rock, you can train on the huge, slightly surreal boulders strewn around the forêt de Fontainebleau. Contact **l'Association des amis de la forêt de Fontainebleau** (01.64.23.46.45/www.aaff.org) .

Arts & Entertainment

Cycling

Bike lanes have been expanded by Mr Delanoë, and increasing numbers of cyclists are taking to the streets. The Bois de Boulogne and the Bois de Vincennes offer good cycling. The quais de Seine and the Canal St-Martin are the nicest.

Paris has many cycling clubs, both in the competition-based and more leisurely categories. You can find your nearest club by phoning the **Fédération Française de Cyclotourisme** (01.44.16.88.88/www.ffc.fr). The **Stade Vélodrome Jacques-Anquetil** (Bois de Vincennes, 12th/01.43.68.01.27) is a functional racing track open to cyclists on a regular basis. The **Maison du Vélo** (11 rue Fénélon, 10th/01.42.81.24.72) sells and repairs all types of bikes. There are also companies offering bike tours in and around Paris.

Diving

If you are in Paris for some time it's worth joining a club as it works out cheaper. If time is limited, a pricier, commercial outfit will get you your certificate. For a diving shop, try **Plongespace** (80 rue Balard, 15th/ 01.45.57.01.01/www.plongespace.fr). **The Club de Plongée du 5ème Arrondissement** (01.43.36.07.67) is a friendly club where you can train for the French licence. It organises trips to the Med and meets at the **Piscine Jean-Taris** (*see below*). There are well-qualified, friendly and experienced instructors at **Surplouf** (06.14.10.26.11/ 01.42.21.18.14), which offers courses in English. Courses for beginners, including textbooks, insurance and gear rental, cost €256.11 for the French licence or €282.03 for the PADI.

Making a splash

The fashion-conscious and finely honed should beware: most swimming pools in Paris insist that men wear trunks rather than shorts, and that women don swimsuits instead of bikinis. Swimming caps must often also be worn. Quite right, too.

Public pools

Paris's state-run pools are generally of a good standard, clean and cheap. They cost €2.44 for adults and €1.37 for children. With varying opening hours due to school use, it's best to check availability in advance.

Piscine Saint-Merri

16 rue du Renard, 4th (01.42.72.29.45). Mº Hôtel de Ville or Rambuteau. 25m pool with greenery.

Piscine Jean-Taris

16 rue Thouin, 5th (01.43.25.54.03). Mº Cardinal Lemoine. Look out on to the Panthéon from this lovely 25m pool.

Piscine du Marché St-Germain

12 rue Lobineau, 6th (01.43.29.08.15). Mº Mabillon. Underground 25m pool in St-Germain.

Piscine Cour-des-Lions

11 rue Alphonse-Baudin, 11th (01.43.55.09.23). Mº Richard-Lenoir. A 25m pool near the Marais.

Piscine Butte-aux-Cailles

5 pl Paul-Verlaine, 13th (01.45.89.60.05). Mº Place d'Italie. One main pool (33m) and two outdoor pools built in the 1920s.

Piscine Didot

22 av Georges-Lafenestre, 14th (01.42.76.78.14). Mº Porte de Vanves. This 25m pool welcomes diving clubs and practitioners of aquagym as well as individual swimmers.

Piscine Armand-Massard

66 bd du Montparnasse, 15th (01.45.38.65.19). Mº Montparnasse-Bienvenüe. An underground sports centre with three pools.

Football

Those expecting to find a grass pitch for a kickabout will be disappointed. The city's 80 public pitches tend to be either dirt, artificial turf, or a place where grass once grew. To find a pitch near you, consult the *Guide du Sport* or call Paris Infos Mairie. To find an amateur team to play for, call the **Ligue Ile de France de Football** (01.42.44.12.12/www.ffr.fr) and ask for a contact number in your *arrondissement*.

Golf

There are no courses in central Paris, but scores in the Paris region. For a full list, contact the **French Golf Federation** (68 rue Anatole France, 92309 Levallois Perret/01.41.49.77.00/ www.ffg.org). The **Golf Clément Ader** (Domaine du Château Péreire, 77220 Gretz Armainvilliers/ 01.64.07.34.10/SNCF Gretz Armainvilliers) is challenging. The **Golf Disneyland Paris Marne-la-Vallée** (77777 Marne-la-Vallée/ 01.60.45.68.90/RER Marne-la-Vallée-Chessy then taxi) has everything. Closer to central Paris is the **Académie de Golf de Paris** at the Paris Country Club, Hippodrome de Saint-Cloud (1 rue du Camp Canadien, 92210 St-Cloud/ 01.47.71.39.22/ SNCF Suresnes Longchamp), which has a nine-hole course within its horse-racing track.

Horse riding

Both the Bois de Boulogne and the Bois de Vincennes are beautiful riding areas. You can join one of theses clubs: **La Société d'Equitation de Paris** (01.45.01.20.06), the

Piscine Emile-Anthoine
9 rue Jean-Rey, 15th (01.53.69.61.59/ 01.42.76.78.18). Mº Bir-Hakeim. Modern 25m pool with a view of the Eiffel Tower.

Piscine Henry-de-Montherlant
32 bd Lannes, 16th (01.40.72.28.30). Mº Porte-Dauphine. Popular, modern 25m pool (plus beginners' pool) with chic clientele.

Piscine Hébert
2 rue des Fillettes, 18th (01.46.07.60.01). Mº Marx-Dormoy. Crowded 25m pool with retractable roof.

Private Pools

Private pools often offer extra attractions and services, and have longer opening hours.

Piscine Suzanne-Berlioux
Forum des Halles, 10 pl de la Rotonde, 1st (01.42.36.98.44). Mº Les Halles. **Admission** €3.81, €3.05 children. This 50m pool with tropical greenhouse attracts a young clientele.

Piscine Pontoise Quartier Latin
19 rue de Pontoise, 5th (01.55.42.77.88). Mº Maubert-Mutualité. **Admission** €4.27, €2.90 under-16s, €3.35 students; €6.71 at night (9pm-midnight) incl gym access. Art deco 33m pool has music.

Aquaboulevard
4 rue Louis-Armand, 15th (01.40.60.15.15). Mº Balard. **Admission** six hours in peak periods €18.29, under-11s €9.15.

This extravagant indoor-outdoor complex is great fun for kids. Its tropical lagoon makes you feel as if you're in a Wham! video.

Piscine Georges-Hermant
4-6 rue David d'Angers, 19th (01.42.02.45.10). Mº Danube. **Admission** €3.35, €2.90 under-16s. This is Paris' biggest pool, measuring 50m x 20m. When it's full, there's a great atmosphere of bonhomie.

Centre Hippique du Touring (01.45.01.20.
88) or the Cercle Hippique du Bois de
Vincennes (01.48.73.01.28). Beginners can
learn in the unpretentious Club Bayard
Equitation (Bois de Vincennes, Centre Bayard/
UCPA de Vincennes, av de Polygone, 12th/ 01.
43.65.46.87). Membership runs for three months
(€209.92) or you can do a five-day course in
July or August (€205.96). The Haras de
Jardy (bd de Jardy, 92430 Marnes-la-Coquette
/01.47.01.35.30) is a lovely equestrian centre
near Versailles, which organises group rides.

Ice skating

In winter the place de l'Hôtel de Ville is
transformed into an open-air ice rink. If
temperatures drop extremely low, there is
skating on Lac Supérieur in the Bois de
Boulogne. Indoor all-year round rinks include
the Patinoire de Boulogne (1 rue Victor
Griffuelhes, Boulogne Billancourt/
01.46.94.99.74/M° Marcel Sembat) and the
Patinoire d'Asnières-sur-Seine (bd Pierre
de Coubertin, 92600 Asnières/ 01.47.99.96.06/
M° Gabriel Péri/Asnières-Gennevilliers).

Rowing & watersports

You can row, canoe and kayak (Wed, Sat;
equipment is provided) in the 600m x 65m basin
at the Base Nautique de la Villette (15-17
quai de la Loire, 19th/ 01.42.40.29.90/M° Jaurès).
La Défense-based Société Nautique de la
Basse Seine (26 quai du Président Paul
Doumer, 92400 Courbevoie/01.43.33.03.47) has
both competitive and recreational sections; or
you can hire boats on Lac Daumesnil and Lac
des Minimes in the Bois de Vincennes or on
Lac Supérieur in the Bois de Boulogne.

Rugby

Top-level rugby goes on at Racing Club de
France. For a good club standard try the
Athletic Club de Boulogne (Saut du Loup,
route des Tribunes, 16th), which fields two
teams. The British Rugby Club of Paris
(01.40.55.15.15/ 01.39.16.33.56) fields two teams
in the corporate league.

Snooker/billiards

For snooker try the Bowling de Paris (see
above Bowling) or the Académie de Billard
Clichy-Montmartre (84 rue de Clichy, 9th/
01.48.78.32.85/M° Place de Clichy). For French
and American tables: Blue-Billard (111-113
rue St-Maur, 11th/01.43.55.87.21/M° Parmentier);
ditto at the popular bar Indiana Club (77 av

du Maine, 14th/ 01.43.22.50.46/M° Gaîté); and
the elegant Hôtel Concorde St-Lazare (108
rue St-Lazare, 8th/01.40.08.44.44/M° St-Lazare)
for French billiards only.

Squash

You can play at Club Quartier Latin or the
Standard Athletic Club (see above), or try
Squash Montmartre (14 rue Achille-
Martinet, 18th/ 01.42.55.38.30/M° Lamarck-
Caulaincourt). Membership is 3,400F/€518.33
per year or 900F/€137.20 for three months, or
you can pay each visit (80F/€12.20 per hour).

Tennis

The Jardins du Luxembourg (6th/ 01.43.25.
79.18/ M° Notre-Dame-des-Champs/ RER
Luxembourg) is great. The Centre Sportif La
Falguère (route de la Pyramide, Bois de
Vincennes, 12th/ 01.43.74. 40.93/M° Château de
Vincennes) has 21 acrylic courts. Centre
Sportif Henry-de-Montherlant (30-32 bd
Lannes, 16th/ 01.40.72.28.33/M° Porte-
Dauphine) has seven hard courts.

Private clubs. The Tennis de Longchamp
(19 bd Anatole-France, 92100 Boulogne/
01.46.03.84.49/M° Boulogne-Jean Jaurès) has
20 hard courts. Club Forest Hill (4 rue
Louis-Armand, 15th/01.40.60.10.00/M° Balard/
RER Boulevard Victor) has 14 branches in the
Paris region.

Académie de Billard, breeding
ground of fast Edouards.

Theatre

It's not all cute mime and avant garde experimentation: the broad church of
Paris theatreland gives you Shakespeare and show tunes, too.

These days, you'll find Shakespeare performed
in Paris more frequently than you'll find Racine
or Corneille; it'll be in French, *mais vas-y*,
Macduff. In fact, language need not be a barrier
to your enjoyment of a lot of the capital's
theatrical offerings (*see below*). Quite often, just
the merest smattering of French will be enough
to enable you to enjoy performances. Reading a
bit of French is helpful as, at the moment,
Parisian producers are big on presenting plays
in their original language, with French subtitles
(or should that be 'epititles'?) running above the
actors. You'll easily get the idea, and if you do
find yourself struggling to understand, the
person sitting next to you will almost certainly
be Anglophone and able to help.

With the current craze for musicals at its
peak (*see p344*, **Holy Moses, it's all gone
Showbiz!**), all you really need for a rollicking
night out is an ear for a catchy tune and a
distinct lack of artistic snobbery.

You'll find much stimulating work staged
beyond the Périphérique. Audiences are
attracted by large-budget productions of
ambitious new takes on the classic/modern
repertoire, as well as experimental work under
the management and artistic direction of many
of France's leading young directors. Of course,
such theatre always has to strike a balance
between artistic experimentation and financial
viability, and 2001 saw some out-of-town
theatres in difficulty, but good management
will help these theatres survive. Stanislas
Nordey has massively increased audiences at
the Théâtre Gérard Philipe, and new director
Alain Olivier looks set to continue the good
work. At Nanterre's Théâtre des Amandiers,
Jean-Louis Martinelli of the Théâtre National de
Strasbourg (TNS) is taking over from Jean-
Pierre Vincent, who is tired of dealing with the
administrative nightmare, and hopes are high
for this renowned theatre. It's always worth
wandering into the suburbs for a different kind
of experience; don't, for example, be surprised
to find yourself sitting on a cushion in a disused
factory, with the play going on around you.

PLAYING IN ENGLISH

English-language theatre is booming. Besides
the prestigious visiting companies occasionally
hosted by the Odéon, MC93 Bobigny and

Bouffes du Nord, an ever-growing number of
resident theatre companies are performing an
increasingly adventurous repertoire alongside
staples Wilde, Pinter and Mamet. Dear
Conjunction, On Stage Theatre Co, Walk &
Talk Productions and Glasshouse Theatre Co
perform new and established plays, as does
Bravo Productions which also gives free play
readings every Monday at the **Café de Flore**.
Regular venues are the **Petit Hébertot**, Théâtre
de Nesle (8 rue de Nesle, 6th/01.46.34.61.04) and
Théâtre des Déchargeurs (3 rue des Déchargeurs,
1st/01.42.36.00.02). For less highbrow
entertainment, the amateur International
Players (01.34.62.02.19) stages a musical or
comedy every spring in St-Germain-en-Laye.

National theatres

Comédie Française

Salle Richelieu *2 rue de Richelieu, 1st
(01.44.58.15.15/www.comedie-francaise.fr). M°
Palais-Royal.* **Box office** 11am-6pm daily. **Tickets**
€4.57-€28.97; €9.91 under-27s (1hr before play).
Credit AmEx, MC, V. **Map** p403 H5. **Théâtre du
Vieux-Colombier** *21 rue du Vieux-Colombier, 6th
(01.44.39.87.00). M° St-Sulpice.* **Box office** 1-6pm
Mon, Sun; 11am-7pm Tue-Sat. **Tickets** €24.39;
€16.77 over-60s; €12.96 under-27s. **Credit** MC, V.
Map p405 G7. **Studio Théâtre** *pl de la Pyramide
inversée, Galerie du Carrousel (99 rue de Rivoli), 1st
(01.44.58.98.58). M° Palais Royal.* **Box office**
5.30pm on day (Mon, Wed-Sun). **Tickets** €12.20;
€6.86 under-27s. **Credit** MC, V. **Map** p401 H5.
Founded in 1680 by Louis XIV, France's oldest
company moved to its building adjoining the Palais-
Royal just after the French Revolution. This is the
only national theatre to have its own permanent
troupe, the *pensionnaires*, whose repertoire ranges
from Molière and Racine to modern classics
(Genet, Anouilh, Stoppard). The Théâtre du Vieux-
Colombier offers a range of classic and contemporary plays and readings, while the Studio Théâtre
in the Carrousel du Louvre hosts early evening short
plays (6.30pm) and salons.
Wheelchair access (call ahead).

Odéon, Théâtre de L'Europe

*1 pl de l'Odéon, 6th (01.44.41.36.36/www.theatre-
odeon.fr). M° Odéon/RER Luxembourg.* **Box office**
11am-6.30pm Mon-Sat; *telephone* 11am-7pm Mon-Sat
(Sun if play on). **Tickets** €4.57-€27.44; €7.62
student on day. **Credit** MC, V. **Map** p406 H7.

Holy Moses, it's all gone showbiz!

In a city where serious theatre is sacred, it must be galling to the Molière devotee that the most popular soirée in Paris nowadays is a trip to a glitzy musical. The Parisians have voted with their feet, and the era of the mega-musical is upon us; your average French audience would rather be entertained with cheesy ballads and up-tempo dance than endure two hours of Sartrean malaise.

It all started in 1979, when Michel Berger's rock opera, *Starmania*, debuted at the Palais des Congrès. Since then, the tale of love among the skyscrapers has been endlessly revived, revamped and restyled and has paved the way for other musicals. The lyricist of *Starmania*, one Luc Plamondon, continued in fine show-stopping style with the record-breaking phenomenon: *Notre-Dame-de-Paris*.

Could Victor Hugo ever have envisaged French popstrel Hélène Ségara dressed in bosom-hugging frocks and pouting out melodies inspired by his novel? Dubbed by many British cynics as nothing more than a 'romantic Euro-pop sideshow' (and so what if it is?), *Notre-Dame* is not your average musical: there is no orchestra to complement the singers, just a backing track and microphones, and the whole production is carried off with a lot of whirlygig lighting and melodrama. That's entertainment, and the show has won the heart of many a hardened luvvie, so if you can suspend your disbelief for a few hours you may leave the theatre in rapture. And it's hats off to Plamondon for knowing what the people want: the show sold over 600,000 tickets in the first six months after its opening night in Paris in September 1998, 3.5 million copies of the original cast studio album have been sold in Europe and Canada — the album stayed at the number one spot in the French charts for 17 weeks.

When this tale of doomed love and injustice raked in the euros, everyone wanted a piece of the action; exhibit A, French pop crooner Pascal Obispo, with his musical version of the life of Moses, *Les Dix Commandements*.

And it's not just the Bible that has been pounced upon for song and dance; politics and history aren't safe, either. Musical versions of the life of Charles de Gaulle, Napoléon and the Dreyfus affair have also been crafted for the stage (this is getting perilously close to *The Producers* territory, but it's a fact). A gaggle of famous literary lovers – Tristan and Iseult, Romeo and Juliet and Beauty and the Beast, are all doing the hearts and flowers routine in Paris theatres, and an adaptation of *Les Liaisons Dangereuses* will hit the boards at any minute.

Popular entertainment on stages more used to seeing wan thesps droning on about philosophical concepts? That's showbiz!

Notre-Dame-de-Paris — very à la quasimode.

Comédie Française, aka *la maison de Molière*. See p343.

One of the more adventurous venues in terms of repertoire, the main Odéon (directed by Georges Lavaudant) is based in a beautiful neo-classical theatre. *Wheelchair access (call ahead)*.

Théâtre National de Chaillot
Palais de Chaillot, 1 pl du Trocadéro, 16th (01.53.65.30.00/www.theatre-chaillot.fr).Mº Trocadéro. **Box office** 11am-7pm Mon-Fri; 11am-5pm Sun; *telephone* 9am-7pm Mon-Sat; 11am-7pm Sun. **Tickets** €24.39; €18.29 over-60s; €12.20 under-25s; €7.62 Thur on day. **Credit** MC, V. **Map** p400 B5.

Popular, accessible plays (classic and modern) and musical theatre are programmed for Chaillot's mammoth 2,800-seat, 1930s theatre, while more experimental fare can be found in its smaller theatre space. The highlights of 2002 promise to be Dan Jemmett's *Presque Hamlet* and Irina Brook's *Juliette et Roméo*. *Wheelchair access (call ahead)*.

Théâtre National de la Colline
15 rue Malte-Brun, 20th (01.44.62.52.52/www.colline.fr). Mº Gambetta. **Box office** 11am-6pm Mon-Fri; 1pm-7pm Sat; 2-5pm Sun if play on; *telephone* Mon-Sat only. **Tickets** €24.39; €19.82 over-60s; €12.20 under-30s; €16.77 Tue; €7.62 Thur on day. **Credit** MC, V. **Map** p407 Q5.

This is France's national theatre for contemporary drama. Productions to look forward to in 2002 include *Histoires de Famille*, *Les Voisins* and *Les Paravents*. The works of lesser-known playwrights tend to be scheduled for the Petit Théâtre upstairs. *Wheelchair access (call ahead)*.

Right Bank

Théâtre de la Ville/Les Abbesses
2 pl du Châtelet, 4th (01.42.74.22.77/ www.theatredelaville-paris.com). Mº Châtelet. **Box office** 11am-7pm Mon; 11am-8pm Tue-Sat; *telephone* 11am-7pm Mon-Sat. **Tickets** €14.48-€21.34; half-price on day under-27s. **Credit** MC, V. **Map** p406 J6.

This venue mixes dance productions with some important contemporary theatre, varying from first-rate to controversial. Top banana show for 2002 will be Koltès's *'Quai Ouest'* directed by Jean-Christophe Saïs. Les Abbesses (31 rue des Abbesses, 18th/01.42.74.22.77) is its second, Montmartre-based space. *(See also chapters Dance, Music: Classical & Opera and Music: Rock, Roots & Jazz).*

Bouffes du Nord
37bis bd de la Chapelle, 10th (01.46.07.34.50/ bouffesdunord.com). Mº La Chapelle. **Box office** 11am-6pm Mon-Sat. **Tickets** €12.20-€21.34. **Credit** MC, V. **Map** p402 L2.

This famously unrenovated theatre is home to Peter Brook's experimental company the CICT; Stéphane Lissner's co-direction has added classical and opera. The venue sometimes hosts productions in English.

Théâtre de la Bastille
76 rue de la Roquette, 11th (01.43.57.42.14/theatre-bastille.com). Mº Bastille/Voltaire. **Box office** 10am-6pm Mon-Fri; 2-6pm Sat, Sun. **Tickets** €18.29; €12.20 under-26s, over-60s. **Credit** AmEx, MC, V. **Map** p407 M6/P6.

Experimental theatre, music and dance score full marks for daring, though quality can be hit or miss. *Wheelchair access (lower theatre only).*

Cartoucherie de Vincennes

Route du Champ de Manoeuvre, bois de Vincennes, 12th. Mº Château de Vincennes, then shuttle bus or bus 112. Each theatre operates independently. An old cartridge factory houses a complex that includes Mnouchkine's Théâtre du Soleil (01.43.74.24.08), Théâtre de l'Epée de Bois (01.48.08.39.74), Théâtre de la Tempête (01.43.28.36.36), Théâtre de l'Aquarium (01.43.74.99.61), Théâtre du Chaudron (01.43.28.97.04).

The Tempête's programme in particular is worth a look, with a top-class mix of modern classics and new contemporary writing from authors including Catherine Anne and Eugène Durif.

Théâtre de l'Athénée-Louis Jouvet

7 rue Boudreau, sq de l'Opéra-Louis-Jouvet, 9th (01.53.05.19.19/www.athenee-theatre.com). Mº Opéra. **Box office** 1-7pm Mon-Sat. **Tickets** €5.34-€24.39. **Credit** MC, V. **Map** p401 G4.

Beautiful old theatre famed for its illustrious past does French and foreign classics in a beautiful Italianate main theatre, with studio theatre upstairs for the smaller contemporary world. *Wheelchair access (call ahead).*

La Bruyère

5 rue La Bruyère, 9th (01.48.74.76.99). Mº St-Georges. **Box office** 11am-7pm Mon-Sat. **Tickets** €18.29-€32.01; €10.67 under-26s (Mon-Thur); €22.87 over-60s (Mon-Thur). **Credit** MC, V. **Map** p402 H2.

This archetypal boulevard theatre is the place to go if you want to take in big box-office smasheroos from home and abroad.

Théâtre Hébertot/Le Petit Hébertot

78bis bd des Batignolles, 17th (01.43.87.23.23/Petit Hébertot 01.44.70.06.69). Mº Villiers or Rome. **Box office** 11am-5.30pm Mon; 11am-7pm Tue-Sat; 11am-2pm Sun. **Tickets** €16.01-€40.40; Petit Hébertot Mon-Wed, Sun €7.62; Thur-Sat €15.24. **Credit** MC, V. **Map** p401 F2.

Home to popular (rather than controversial) contemporary writers and 20th-century classics, with regular English productions.

Left Bank

Théâtre Lucernaire

53 rue Notre-Dame-des-Champs, 6th (01.45.44.57.34). Mº Notre-Dame-des-Champs. **Box office** 2-9pm Mon-Sat. **Tickets** €11.43-€21.34. **Credit** AmEx, MC, V. **Map** p405 G9.

Two 130-seat theatres, a cinema, a café and exhibitions co-exist in this bustling arts centre: the repertoire occasionally features new work from contemporary authors, but usually reverts to guaranteed box-office hits.

Théâtre de la Huchette

23 rue de la Huchette, 5th (01.43.26.38.99). Mº St-Michel. **Box office** 5-9pm Mon-Sat. **Tickets** €15.24; €12.20 students under 25; €10.67 Tue, Wed, Thur. **No credit cards. Map** p406 J7.

Home to Nicolas Bataille's original production of Ionesco's *'The Bald Primadonna'* since 1950, in double bill with more works by Ionesco and others in a tiny venue often crowded out with students there to see their set texts in the flesh. *Wheelchair access.*

Théâtre de la Cité Internationale

21 bd Jourdan, 14th (01.43.13.50.50/www.theatredelacite.ciup.fr). RER Cité Universitaire. **Box office** 2-7pm Mon-Sat. **Tickets** €16.77; €12.20 over-60s; €8.38 students, under-26s, Mon. **No credit cards.**

A well-equipped modern theatre based on the university campus in the south of Paris, offering a mixture of experimental rather than traditional theatre and dance from around the world.

Guichet-Montparnasse

15 rue du Maine, 14th (01.43.27.88.61). Mº Montparnasse-Bienvenüe. **Box office** *telephone* 2-7pm Mon-Sat. **Tickets** €15.24; €12.20 students, over-60s, Mon. **No credit cards. Map** p405 F9.

In a tiny 50-seat auditorium, this lively fringe venue features everything from classics to new writing, by small companies and new directing and acting talent. Several short productions are shown each night, offering the perfect taster of French theatre.

Booking and tipping

For details of programmes see the *Time Out Paris* section of *Pariscope*. Tickets can be bought direct from theatres, or at agencies (*see chapter* **Directory**). Specialists include Agence Chèque Théâtre (33 rue Le Peletier, 9th/01.42.46.72.40; open 10am-7pm Mon-Sat) and Kiosque Théâtre (opposite 15 pl de la Madeleine, 9th, and in front of Gare Montparnasse, 15th; open noon-8pm Tue-Sun) which sells same-day tickets at half-price, plus €2.44 commission per seat. Tickets are also sold via the Minitel, on 3615 THEA. Many private theatres offer 50% reductions on previews and students can also get same-day deals. A discount for under-26s gives access to the best seats in 46 theatres (€10.62 (0800 800 750). As for tipping, it is customary to tip the person who shows you to your seat in a *private* theatre. Tips are not given in public theatres.

Trips Out
of Town

Trips Out of Town

Paris is surrounded by locations that are accessible and fascinating in their own right, so why not make the city your base camp for some intriguing trips out?

Stately Châteaux

Versailles

Until 1661 Versailles was a simple hunting lodge and boyhood refuge of Louis XIV. In a fit of envy after seeing Vaux-le-Vicomte (*see p353*), he decided on a building to match his ego and his ambitious dream of absolute power over the aristocracy. Painter Charles Le Brun began transforming the château, while André Le Nôtre set about the gardens, turning marshland into terraces, pools and paths.

In 1678 Jules Hardouin-Mansart took over as principal architect and dedicated the last 30 years of his life to adding the two main wings, the Cour des Ministres and Chapelle Royale. In 1682 Louis moved in and thereafter rarely set foot in Paris. The palace could house the entire court and its entourage – some 20,000 people in all. With the King holding all the strings of power, nobles had no choice but to leave their provincial châteaux or Paris mansions and spend years in service at court, at great personal expense. In the 1770s, Louis XV chose his favourite architect Jacques Ange Gabriel to add the sumptuous Opéra Royal, sometimes used for concerts by the Centre de Musique Baroque (01.39.20.78.10). With the fall of the monarchy in 1792, most of the furniture was dispersed and after the 1830 Revolution Louis-Philippe saved the château from demolition.

Versailles was the Graceland to the Louis' Elvis. Voltaire described Versailles as 'a masterpiece of bad taste and magnificence', yet you can't help but be impressed at the architectural purity of the vast classical facades, before being bowled over by the 73m-long Hall of Mirrors, where 17 windows echo the 17 mirrors in a brilliant play of light; the King's Bedroom, where Louis held his celebrated *levées* in the presence of the court; the Apollo Salon, the Sun King's appropriately named throne room; and the Queen's Bedroom, where queens gave birth in full view of courtiers, there to confirm the sex of the child and to ensure no substitutes were slipped in in cases when the royal child wasn't sufficiently coochie coochie coo or easy on the eye.

Outside, the **gardens** stretch over 815 hectares comprising formal *parterres*, ponds, wooded parkland and sheep-filled pastures, dominated by the grand perspectives laid out by Le Nôtre. Statues of the seasons, elements and continents, many commissioned by Colbert in 1674, are scattered throughout the gardens, and the spectacular series of fountains is served by an ingenious hydraulic system. One cannot but be amazed by their grandeur, though one understands why those who didn't enjoy quite such sumptuous living conditions eventually revolted. Nearby is Hardouin-Mansart's Orangerie, whose vaulted gallery could house over 2,000 orange trees. The Potager du Roi, the King's vegetable garden, has been restored. Uncannily enough, Le Nôtre's original plans for the gardens appear to present the form of a certain big-eared, high-pitched American mouse, whose own fairytale kingdom was established not so far away, not so long ago…

The main palace being a little unhomely, in 1687 Louis XIV had Hardouin-Mansart build the **Grand Trianon**, in the north of the park, a pretty, but still hardly cosy palace of stone and pink marble, where Louis stayed with Mme de Maintenon. Napoléon Bonaparte also stayed there with his second Empress, Marie-Louise, and had it redecorated in Empire style.

The **Petit Trianon** is a perfect example of Neo-Classicism, and was built for Louis XV's mistress Mme de Pompadour, although she died before its completion. Marie-Antoinette, however, managed to take advantage of the nearby **Hameau de la Reine**, the mock farm arranged around a lake where she could play at being a lowly milkmaid and give vent to her let-them-eat-cake routine.

Each Sunday afternoon from April to October (plus Sat July, Aug, Sept) the great fountains in the gardens are set in action, to music, in the Grandes Eaux Musicales, while seven times a year the extravagant Grandes Fêtes de Nuit capture something of the splendour of the celebrations of the Sun King.

Château de Versailles

(01.30.83.76.20; reservations 01.30.83.77.43; guided tours 01.30.83.77.88/www.chateauversailles.com). **Open** *May-Sept* 9am-6pm Tue-Sun; *Oct-Apr* 9am-5pm Tue-Sun. **Admission** €7.60; free under-18s and history/architecture students; €5.30 for after 3.30pm.

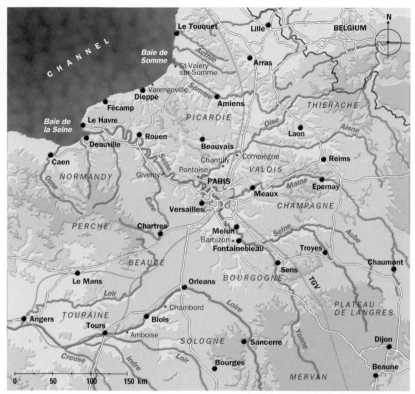

Grand Trianon/Petit Trianon

Open *May-Oct* noon-6pm daily; *Nov-Apr* noon-5pm daily. **Admission** €4.57; free under-18s.

Gardens

Open dawn-dusk daily. **Admission** free (Grandes Eaux €4.57; free under 10s). Note that most statues are protected by a tarpaulin in winters. **Guided Tours** *Potager du Roi* (01.39.24.62.62). **From** Apr-Oct, Sat, Sun, times vary. **Tickets** €6.10

Where to eat

Le Chapeau Gris (5 rue Hoche/ 01.39.50.10.81) has a good-value €25 *menu*.

Getting there

By car

20km from Paris by A13 or D10.

By RER

RER C Versailles-Rive Gauche.

Chantilly

In the middle of a lake, cream-coloured Chantilly with its domes and turrets looks like the archetypal French Renaissance château. In fact, the over-the-top main wing is a largely 19th-century reconstruction, as much of the original was destroyed during the Revolution. Restored by the eccentric Duc de Condé, Chantilly is notable for the Duc's remarkable art collection, among which are three paintings by Raphael; Filippino Lippi's *Esther and Assuarus*; a cabinet of portraits by Clouet; several mythological scenes by Poussin; and the medieval miniatures from the *Très Riches Heures du Duc de Berry* (facsimiles only are usually on show). In fact the Musée Condé has one of France's richest collections.

Today, Le Nôtre's park is rather dilapidated, but still contains an extensive canal system, an artificial 'hamlet' predating that of Versailles and a 19th-century 'English garden'. In summer, a ten-minute ride in a hot-air

Trips Out of Town

Montgolfière balloon gives an aerial view of château, park and forest. 2002 sees the spectacular bi-annual Nuits de Feux (firework competition) in the park, during the third weekend of June (03.44.45.92.12).

Chantilly is also an important equestrian centre: this is where the most important trainers have their stables, and the town has a major racetrack. The 18th-century Great Stables once housed 240 horses, 500 dogs and almost 100 palfreys and hunting birds, and today contain the Musée Vivant du Cheval et du Poney (*see chapter* **Children**).

South of the château spreads the **Forêt de Chantilly**, which has numerous footpaths and is these days besieged by picnickers in summer. A pleasant walk (approx 7km) circles the four Etangs de Commelles (small lakes) and passes the 'Château de la Reine Blanche', a mill converted in the 1820s into a pseudo-medieval hunting lodge.

Senlis, 9km east of Chantilly, has been bypassed since its glory days as the royal town where Hugh Capet was elected king in 987. Its historical centre contains several quaint, half-timbered streets, some ruggedly handsome mansions, a fine, predominantly Gothic cathedral, some chunks of Gallo-Roman city ramparts and the remains of a Roman amphitheatre. It is worth a visit.

Château de Chantilly

Musée Condé (03.44.62.62.62/03.44.62.62.60 /www.chantilly.com). **Open** *Mar-Oct* 10am-6pm Mon, Wed-Sun; *Nov-Feb* 10.30am-12.45pm, 2-5pm Mon, Wed-Sun. **Admission** €6.40; €5.64 12-18s; €2.29 3-11s; free under 3s; *park only* €2.59; €1.52 3-11s. **Credit** MC, V.

Montgolfière balloon

(03.44.57.29.14). **Open** *Mar-Nov* 10am-7pm daily (weather permitting). **Balloon** €7.47; €6.56 12-17s; €1.52 3-11s (plus park entrance).

Where to eat & stay

La Carrousel du musée vivant du cheval (entry via the château/03.44.57.19.77) has an excellent €10 menu. **Les Relais d'Aumale** (Montgrésin, 60560 Orry-la-Ville/ 03.44.54.61.31) is a welcoming hotel where a double room will set you back €106.71 per night.

Getting there

By car

41km from Paris by A1, exit Chantilly or N16 direct.

By train

SNCF Chantilly from Gare du Nord, then 30 min walk or short taxi ride.

Compiègne & Pierrefonds

North of Paris on either side of the substantial hunting forest of Compiègne stand two very different châteaux, each with an imperial stamp.

On the edge of the old town of Compiègne, the **Château de Compiègne** looks out over a huge park and surrounding dense forest, and is a monument to the French royal family's obsession with hunting. Although there had been a royal residence at Compiègne since the Capetians, the château was remodelled in its present form by Louis XV. In 1751 Louis entrusted its reconstruction to architect Jacques Ange Gabriel, who created something of a classical pleasure palace.

Although some of the decoration dates from the 18th century (in particular an elegant, circular bathroom), most of the interior was ruthlessly remodelled by Napoléon for his second wife Marie-Louise and is stuffed with imperial eagles, bees, palms and busts of the great self-publicist. The Empress' state apartments include fully furnished boudoirs, the ballroom (used as a military hospital in World War I) and her bedroom with its wonderfully over-the-top gilded bed and crimson damask furnishings. The only 18th-century piece is a commode, which belonged to Marie-Antoinette, put there as Marie-Louise wanted a souvenir of her unfortunate aunt.

Napoléon III also left his mark at Compiègne, where he and Empress Eugénie hosted lavish house parties every autumn. His most popular legacy was the highly efficient heating system he installed which still works today and makes a visit to the château bearable even in the depths of winter.

In one wing, the **Musée de la Voiture** is devoted to early transport. On view are Napoléon I's state coach, Napoléon III's railway carriage and early motorcars, including an 1899 Renault and the 1899 Jamais Contente electric car.

In a clearing in the forest 4km from Compiègne is the **Clairière de l'Armistice**, a memorial to the site where the Germans surrendered to Maréchal Foch, ending World War I, on 11 November 1918 (it is also where in 1940 the French surrendered to the Germans). There is the mark where the two railway lines met, a statue of Foch and a reconstruction of his railway-carriage office.

At the other edge of the forest, a sudden dip in the land gives a view of strange turrets. At first sight, the neo-medieval **Château de Pierrefonds** is so clearly a fake it's almost

The arrogant grandeur of **Versailles**.

Villandry: just a load of vegetables. *See p354.*

grotesque. Yet it deserves a detour. Napoléon bought the ruins of a 14th-century castle for 2,950F. In 1857, Napoléon III, staying nearby at Compiègne, asked Viollet-le-Duc to restore one of the towers as a romantic hunting lodge. But the project grew and the fervent medievalist ended up recontructing the whole edifice, in part using the remaining foundations, in part borrowing elements from other castles, or simply creating medieval as he felt it should be. Admire the crocodile waterspouts in the courtyard; the grand baronial halls harbour elaborate Gothic chimneypieces carved with beasts, dragons and figures. The magnificent Salle des Preuses was designed as a ballroom, with a minstrels' gallery; the fireplace is sculpted with figures of nine ladies (one a likeness of Empress Eugénie). One wing has a display about Viollet-le-Duc. Another fantasist, Michael Jackson, once expressed interest in buying the château, but it was not for sale.

Château de Compiègne

5 pl du Général-de-Gaulle, 60200 Compiègne (03.44.38.47.00). **Open** 10am-6pm Mon, Wed-Sun. **Admission** €5.48; €3.51 18-25s; free under 18s. **No credit cards.**

Château de Pierrefonds

60350 Pierrefonds (03.44.42.72.72). **Open** *Nov-Apr* 10am-12.30pm, 2-5pm Mon-Sat; 10am-5.30pm Sun; *May-Oct* 10am-6pm daily. **Admission** €4.88; €3.20 students, 12-25s; free under 12s. **No credit cards.**

Clairière de l'Armistice

route de Soissons (03.44.85.14.18). **Open** (museum) *Apr-15 Oct* 9am-12.15pm, 2-6pm; *16 Oct-Mar* 9-11.45am, 2-5pm Mon, Wed-Sun. **Admission** €1.52; €0.91 7-14s; free under 7s. **No credit cards.**

Where to eat & stay

Rive Gauche (13 cours Guynemer/ 03.44.40.29.99) does inventive cuisine (*menu* €40). The **Hôtel Les Beaux-Arts** (33 cour Guynemer/03.44.92.26.26, double €60) is a cosy place to lay your head.

Getting there

By car

Compiègne is 80km from Paris by A1. The Clairière de l'Armistice is 4km east of Compiègne by D973. To reach Pierrefonds from Compiègne take the N31 towards Soissons, then follow signs.

By train

From Gare du Nord.

Fontainebleau

Fontainebleau would be just another sleepy provincial French town were it not for the sumptuous palace which dominates it. In 1528 François Ier brought in Italian artists and craftsmen – including Rosso and Primaticcio – to help architect Gilles le Breton transform what was a neglected royal lodge into the finest Italian Mannerist palace in France. This style is noted for its grotesqueries, contorted figures and crazy fireplaces, which gave sculptors an ideal chance to show off their virtuosity, still visible in the Ballroom and Long Gallery.

Other monarchs brought their own touches, so that much of the palace's charm comes from its very disunity. Henri IV added a royal tennis court, Louis XIII built the celebrated double-horseshoe staircase that dominates the principal courtyard, Louis XIV and XV added further classical trimmings, while Napoléon redecorated in Empire style before taking leave of his troops and leaving France for exile from the front courtyard, known ever since as the Cour des Adieux.

With its ravines, rocky outcrops and mix of forest and sandy heath, the Fontainebleau Forest, where François Ier liked to hunt, is the wildest slice of nature near to Paris and now popular with Parisian weekenders for walking, cycling, riding and rock climbing. The GR1 is a popular hiking trail signposted straight from the station at Bois-le-Roi, 30 minutes from Gare de Lyon. Don't miss the fabulously Atmospheric Café de la Gare close by, stuffed with the owner's wacky collection of lunacy.

Château de Fontainebleau
77300 Fontainebleau (01.60.71.50.70).
Open *Nov-Apr* 9.30am-12.30pm, 2-5pm Mon, Wed-Sun; *May, June, Sept, Oct* 9.30am-5pm Mon, Wed-Sun; *July, Aug* 9.30am-6pm Mon, Wed-Sun. **Admission** €5.34; €3.51 18-25s, all on Sun; free under-18s. **Credit** V.

Where to eat & stay

Le Caveau des Ducs (24 rue Ferrare/ 01.64.22.05.55, menus €18-€33) does good, simple food. The **Hôtel Victoria** (112 rue de France/01.60.74.90.00/www.hotel.victoria.com, double €55) is a groovy hotel.

Getting there

By car
60km from Paris by A6, then N7.

By train
Gare de Lyon to Fontainebleau-Avon (50 mins), then bus marked Château.

Vaux-Le-Vicomte

This is a monument to the fear and mistrust generated by men of intellect, taste and influence in the hearts of pompous egotists like Louis XIV. Nicolas Fouquet (1615-1680), protégé of the ultra-powerful Cardinal Mazarin and a

friend of many of the luminaries of his day, including the poet Jean de La Fontaine, bought the site in 1641. In 1653 he was named *Surintendant des Finances*, and set about building himself an abode to match his position. He assembled three of France's most talented men for the job: painter Charles Lebrun, architect Louis Le Vau and landscape gardener André Le Nôtre.

In 1661 Fouquet held a huge soirée to inaugurate his château and made the fatal mistake of inviting the Sun King. They were entertained by jewel-encrusted elephants and spectacular, imported Chinese fireworks. Lully wrote music for the occasion, and Molière a comedy. The King, who was 23 and ruling de facto for the first time, was outraged by the way in which Fouquet's grandeur seemed to overshadow his own. Shortly afterwards Fouquet was arrested, and his embezzlement of state funds exposed in a show trial. His personal effects were taken by the crown and the court sentenced him to exile; Louis XIV commuted the sentence to solitary confinement. Fouquet is sometimes mooted as the infamous 'Man in the Iron Mask', privy to damaging state secrets and locked away for life.

As you round the moat, the square, sober frontage doesn't prepare you for the Baroque rear aspect. The most telling symbol of the fallen magnate is the unfinished, domed ceiling in the elliptical Grand Salon, where Lebrun only had time to paint the cloudy sky and one solitary eagle. Fouquet's *grand projet* did live on in one way, however, as it inspired Louis XIV to build Versailles – using Fouquet's architect and workmen to do it.

Watch out for the spectacular fountains, which spout from 3-6pm on the second and last Saturday of the month, Apr-Oct. The biggest draw, though, are the candlelit evenings, which transform the château into a palatial jack-o-lantern.

Vaux-Le-Vicomte
7950 Maincy (01.64.14.41.90). **Open** 11 Mar-12 Nov 10am-1pm, 2-6pm Mon-Fri; 10am-6pm Sat, Sun. **Admission** €9.60; €7.47 6-16s, students, over-60s; free under-6s. **Candlelit visits** 7 May-mid Oct 8pm-midnight Thur, Sat. **Price** €12.50; €10.67 6-16s; students, over-60s. **Credit** MC V.

Getting there

By car
60km from Paris by A6 to Fontainebleau exit; follow signs to Melun, then N36 and D215.

By coach
Paris-Vision run half-day and day trips from Paris.

Châteaux of the Loire

Seat of power of the Valois kings, who preferred to rule from Amboise and Blois rather than Paris, the Loire valley became the wellspring of the French Renaissance, when aristocratic residences became pleasure palaces rather than fortresses. François Ier was the main instigator, bringing architects, artists and craftsmen from Italy to build his palaces, and musicians and poets to keep him amused. Royal courtiers followed suit with their own elaborate residences. The valley is now an easy weekend trip from Paris.

The enormous **Château de Chambord** (02.54.50.40.00/02.54.50.40.28) is François Ier's masterpiece, and was probably designed in part by Leonardo da Vinci. It's a magnificent but also rather playful place, from the ingenious double staircase in the centre – it was possible to go up or down without crossing someone coming the other way – to the wealth of decoration and the 400 draughty rooms. Built in the local white stone, with decorative diamonds applied in black slate, it is an extraordinary forest of turrets, domes and crazy chimneys. Chambord's huge, forested park is popular during late September/early October, when people come from all over to hear the annual stag rut at night. Nice.

In total contrast of scale is the charming **Château de Beauregard** (02.54.70.40.05) nearby at Cellettes. Its main treasure is the unusual panelled portrait gallery, depicting in naïve style 327 famous men and women. The precious character of the room is accentuated by its fragile, blue and white Dutch Delft tiled floor. The château also boasts the tiny Cabinet des Grelots. The park contains a modern colour-themed garden designed by Gilles Clément.

From here the road to Amboise follows an attractive stretch of the Loire valley, under the looming turrets of the **Château de Chaumont** (02.54.51.26.26) and past roadside wine cellars dug into the tufa cliffs (with numerous opportunities to indulge). Chaumont is worth visiting for its innovative garden festival (02.54.20.99.22; mid-June-mid-Oct) when international garden designers, artists and architects create gardens on a set theme.

The lively town of Amboise, not far from Tours, grew up at a strategic crossing point on the Loire. The **Château Royal d'Amboise** (02.47.57.00.98) was built within the walls of a medieval stronghold, although today only a (still considerable) fraction of Louis XI's and Charles VIII's complex remains. The château's interiors span several styles from vaulted Gothic to Empire. The exquisite Gothic chapel has a richly carved portal, vaulted interior and,

supposedly, the tomb of Leonardo da Vinci.

It's a short walk up the hill, past several cave dwellings, to reach the fascinating **Clos Lucé** (02.47.57.62.88), the Renaissance manor house where Leonardo lived at the invitation of François Ier for the three years before his death in 1519. There's an enduring myth of a – so far undiscovered – tunnel linking it to the château. The museum concentrates on Leonardo as Renaissance Man: artist, engineer and inventor. It is part furnished as a period manor, part filled with models derived from Leonardo's drawings of inventions. An oddity just outside town is the pagoda of Chanteloup, built in the 18th century when *chinoiserie* was the rage.

South of Amboise, the **Château de Chenonceau** (02.47.23.90.07) occupies a unique site spanning the river Cher. Henri II gave the château to his beautiful mistress Diane de Poitiers, until she was forced to give it up to a jealous Catherine de Médicis, who commissioned Philibert Delorme to add the three-storey gallery that extends across the river. Chenonceau is packed with tourists in summer, but its watery views, original ceilings, fireplaces, tapestries and paintings (including *Diane de Poitiers* by Primaticcio) are well worth seeing.

Seeming to rise out of the water, **Azay-le-Rideau** (02.47.45.42.04), built on an island in the river Indre west of Tours, must be everyone's idea of a fairytale castle. Built 1518-27 by Gilles Berthelot, the king's treasurer, it combines the turrets of a medieval fortress with the new Italian Renaissance style.

At **Villandry** (02.47.50.02.09), it's the Renaissance gardens that are of interest. One part is a typical formal garden of neatly cut geometrical hedges; more unusual is the *jardin potager*, where the patterns done with artichokes, cabbages and other vegetables compose the ultimate kitchen garden.

Where to stay

Amboise is a pleasant, centrally placed stopping-off point. Within town, try the **Lion d'Or** (17 quai Charles Guinot/ 02.47.57.00.23/ double €46.50-€49.55) or the grander **Le Choiseul** (36 quai Charles Guinot/ 02.47.30.45.45/double €144-€221.05), both of which have restaurants. For a taste of château life, try the **Château de Pray** (02.47.57.23.67) at Chargé, 3km outside town (€83.85-€109.76). There are more hotels and restaurants in Tours.

Getting there

By car

By far the best way to explore the region. Take the A10 to Blois (182km), or leave at Mer for Chambord.

Discreet charm at **Beauregard**. *See left*.

An attractive route follows the Loire from Blois to Amboise and Tours, along the D761.

By train

Local trains from Gare d'Austerlitz run to Amboise (2hrs) and Tours (2 1/2 hours); the TGV from Gare Montparnasse to Tours takes 70 mins.

Artists' Haunts

Japanese bridges, peasants, cornfields and absinthe: visit the places where some of the world's greatest artists found inspiration.

Van Gogh at Auvers-sur-Oise

Auvers-sur-Oise has become synonymous with Van Gogh, who rented a room at the **Auberge Ravoux** on 20 May 1890 to escape the noise of Paris. During his stay, he executed over 60 paintings and sketches. On 27 July, he fired a bullet into his chest, and died two days later. He is buried in the cemetery, alongside his brother, Theo. The tiny attic room where he stayed for 3.50F a day gives an evocative sense of the artist's stay; there is also a well-prepared video.

Van Gogh was not the only painter to be attracted by Auvers. The **Atelier de Daubigny** was built by the successful

Barbizon school artist in 1861 and decorated with murals by Daubigny, his son and daughter and his friends Corot and Daumier. There is also a **museum** dedicated to the artist.

Auvers retains a surprising degree of rustic charm. Illustrated panels around town let you compare paintings to their locations today. The cornfields, where Van Gogh executed his last painting *Crows*, the town hall and the medieval church, famous worldwide because of the painting of it which is now in the Musée d'Orsay, have barely changed. Cézanne also stayed here for 18 months in 1872-74, not far from the house of Doctor Gachet, doctor, art collector and amateur painter, who was the subject of portraits by both him and Van Gogh.

The 17th-century **Château d'Auvers** offers an audiovisual display about the Impressionists, while the **Musée de l'Absinthe** is devoted to their favourite (long-banned) drink, whose psychedelic possibilities are sometimes thought to have contributed to the vivid colours and hazy visual effects of their work, as well as to the tempestuous episodes of their private lives (the loss of Van Gogh's ear, for example).

Atelier de Daubigny
61 rue Daubigny (01.34.48.03.03). **Open** *Easter-1 Nov* 2-6.30pm Thur-Sun. **Admission** €4.27; free under-12s.

Auberge Ravoux
pl de la Mairie (01.30.36.60.60). **Open** 10am-6pm daily. Closed 25 Dec-7 Jan. **Admission** €4.57; free under-18s.

Château d'Auvers
rue de Léry (01.34.48.48.50). **Open** 10.30am-6.30pm Tue-Sun (closes 4.30pm Nov-Apr). **Admission** €8.38-€9.15; €6.86-€7.62 over-60s; €6.10 6-25s; free under-6s. **Credit** AmEx, MC, V.

Musée de l'Absinthe
44 rue Callé (01.30.36.83.26). **Open** *June-Sept* 11am-6pm Wed-Sun; *Oct-May* 11am-6pm Sat, Sun. **Admission** €3.81; €3.05 students; €1.52 7-15s; free under-7s.

Musée Daubigny
Manoir des Colombières, rue de la Sansonne (01.30.36.80.20). **Open** 2-6pm Wed-Sun. **Admission** €3.05; free under-12s.

Where to eat

Auberge Ravoux (pl de la Mairie/ 01.30.36.60.60, menu €40) does good, simple food.

Getting there

By car
35km north of Paris by A15 exit 7, then N184 exit Méry-sur-Oise for Auvers.

By train

Gare du Nord or Gare St-Lazare direction Pontoise, change at Persan-Beaumont or Creil, or RER A Cergy-Préfecture, then bus (marked for Butry).

By coach

Paris-Vision runs tours from Paris.

Monet at Giverny

In 1883, Claude Monet moved his large personal entourage (one mistress, eight children – how did he find the time and energy to get all those paintings done?) to Giverny, a rural retreat west of Paris. He died in 1926, having immortalised both his flower garden and the water lilies beneath his Japanese bridge. Don't be put off by the tour buses or the enormous gift shop and naff presents – the natural charm of the pink-brick house, with its blue and yellow kitchen, and the rare glory of the gardens survive intact. A little tunnel leads (under the road) between the flower-filled Clos Normand garden to the Japanese water garden, with all the pools, canals, little green bridges, the punt, willows and water lilies familiar from the paintings. Up the road, the modern **Musée Américain Giverny** is devoted to American artists who came to France, inspired by the Impressionists.

Fondation Claude Monet

27620 Giverny (02.32.51.28.21). **Open** *Apr-Oct* 10am-6pm Tue-Sun. **Admission** €5.34; €3.81 students; €3.05 7-12s; free under-7s. **Credit** (shop) AmEx, MC, V. *Wheelchair access.*

Musée Américain Giverny

99 rue Claude Monet (02.32.51.94.65). **Open** *Apr-Oct* 10am-6pm Tue-Sun. **Admission** €5.34; €3.05 students, over 60s; €2.29 7-12s; free under-7s. **Credit** AmEx, MC, V. *Wheelchair access.*

Where to stay

Chambre d'hôte Le Bon Maréchal (1 rue du Colombier/02.32.51.39.70, double €40) is a comfy bed and breakfast.

Getting there

By car

80km west of Paris by A13 to Bonnières and D201.

By train

Gare St-Lazare to Vernon (45 mins); then taxi or bus.

Millet at Barbizon

A rural hamlet straggling along a lane into the forest of Fontainebleau, Barbizon was an ideal sanctuary for the pioneer outdoor landscape painters Corot, Théodore Rousseau, Daubigny and Millet. From the 1830s onwards, these artists (the Barbizon School) showed a new concern with peasant life and landscape, paving the way for Impressionism. The main sights are all on the Grande rue and, although very touristy, some of the atmosphere remains. Plaques point out who lived where.

Other artists soon followed them to Barbizon.

The inspirational colours of **Giverny**.

Many stayed at the **Auberge du Père Ganne**, painting on the walls and furniture of the long-suffering (or perhaps far-sighted) Ganne, in lieu of rent. After years of dilapidation, the inn is now a smartly restored museum, where the artists' charming sketches and paintings can still be seen in situ. The **Office du Tourisme** is in the former house of Théodore Rousseau. Prints and drawings by Millet and others can be seen in the **Maison-atelier Jean-François Millet**, where Millet moved in 1849 to escape cholera in Paris. Millet and Rousseau are both buried at nearby Chailly.

In the woods not far from Barbizon, but coming from a quite different art perspective, is an extraordinary 20th-century monster. The **Cyclope** (open Fri-Sun, May-Oct reserve on 01.64.98.83.17), a clanking confection of mirrors and iron cogs, was the work of Swiss artist Jean Tinguely, who began it in 1969, in a rare collaboration with Nikki de Saint Phalle and other artists, although it was only finished after his death and opened to the public in 1994.

Musée de l'Auberge du Père Ganne
92 Grande rue, 77630 Barbizon (01.60.66.22.27). **Open** 10am-12.30pm, 2-6pm Mon, Wed-Sun (closes 5pm Nov-Mar). **Admission** €3.81, €1.98 12-25s, students; free under 12s. **Credit** MC, V.

Maison-atelier Jean-François Millet
27 Grande rue (01.60.66.21.55). **Open** 9.30am-12.30pm, 2-5.30pm Mon, Wed-Sun. **Admission** free.

Office du Tourisme
55 Grande rue (01.60.66.41.87). **Open** 1-5pm Wed-Fri; 11am-12.30pm, 2-5pm Sat, Sun.

Where to eat & stay
La Bohème (35 Grande rue/01.60.66.48.65) has a good-value €24 *menu*.

Getting there

By car
57km from Paris by A6, then N7 and D64.

Heading for the Coast

The Baie de Somme offers bird reserves and quiet villages, while Dieppe provides seaside bustle.

Dieppe & Varengeville

An important port since the Middle Ages, Dieppe is also the nearest seaside town to Paris, ideal for a dip and a fish meal. The charming area around the harbour along quai Henri IV is prettier than ever now that ferries from Britain go to a new container port and the old railway terminal has been demolished. At one end the Tour des Crabes is the last remnant of fortified wall. The interesting maze of old streets between the harbour and the newer quarters fronting the promenade contains numerous sailors' houses built in brick with wrought-iron balconies, many being renovated, and the fine Gothic churches of St-Jacques, once a starting point for pilgrimage to Compostella (note the pilgrims' shell motifs), and St-Rémi.

The beach is shingle except at low tide, but the seafront offers plenty of interesting activities for kids, with mini-golf, pony rides, a children's beach and lawns filled with kite flyers (look out for the international kite festival in September). The beach is overlooked from the clifftop by the gloomy **Château de Dieppe** (02.35.84.19.76), now the municipal museum, known for its collection of alabasters and paintings by Pissarro and Braque.

Leave town by the coast road for a twisting, breathtakingly scenic drive along the cliff. Just along the coast to the west is chic Varengeville-sur-Mer, celebrated for its clifftop churchyard where Cubist painter Georges Braque (who also designed one of the stained-glass windows in the church) and composer Albert Roussel are buried, for the **Parc du Bois des Moustiers** (02.35.85.10.02), planted by Lutyens and Gertrude Jekyll, famed for its rhododendrons and views, as well as for the unusual 16th-century Renaissance **Manoir d'Ango** (02.35.85.14.80) which has a fascinating galleried courtyard and unusual dovecote. A steep, narrow lane leads down to a beautiful little sandy cove.

Also just outside Dieppe (8km south) is the decorative early 17th-century **Château de Miromesnil** (02.35.85.02.80) where the writer Guy de Maupassant was born in 1850. The building has a fascinating historic kitchen garden. Nearby, dominating a little hill at Arques la Bataille, are the ruins of a tenth-century castle.

Where to eat & stay
Head towards the harbour, along quai Henri IV. Here you'll find countless little fish restaurants offering endless variations on mussels, skate and sole, plus the delicious local cider.

Getting there

By car
Dieppe is 170km north-west from Paris. Take the A13 to Rouen and then the A151.

By train
From Gare St-Lazare (2 1/2 hours).

Tourist information

Office du Tourisme de Dieppe
Pont Jehan Ango, 76204 Dieppe (02.32.14.40.60).
Open *Apr-Sept* 9am-1pm, 2-8pm daily; *Oct-Mar*
9am-noon, 2-6pm Mon-Sat.

Baie de Somme

Although the Somme remains forever
synonymous with the horror and carnage of
World War I battlefields (the Battle of the
Somme in 1916 cost an incredible 800,000 lives),
the area is, by nature, quite beautiful: its coastal
area boasts a rich variety of wildlife and has a
gentle, ever-changing light that has attracted
artists and writers alike. There are many
picturesque villages and a wild, beautiful
coastline that varies from long beaches and
rolling dunes to pebbles and cliffs. A very
popular tourist steam train, the **Chemin de
Fer de la Baie de Somme,** tours the bay in
summer along 27km of tracks between Le
Crotoy, Noyelles, St-Valery and Cayeux.

The panorama around the bay at the small
fishing port of **Le Crotoy** inspired Jules Verne
to write *20,000 Leagues Under the Sea* and
drew Colette, Toulouse-Lautrec and Arthur
Rimbaud. It boasts the only sandy beach in
northern France that is south-facing and as
such is a busy resort, with numerous
restaurants and brasseries serving excellent
fresh fish, as well as hotels, guest houses and
camp sites, and opportunities for watersports
(03.22.27.04.39), hunting, fishing and tennis.

Across the bay, **St-Valery-sur-Somme**
still retains its historic character, with a well-
preserved medieval upper town and a
domineering position over the bay. The area is
full of historic import. It was from here that
William the Conqueror set sail in 1066 to
conquer England, and Joan of Arc passed
through as a prisoner in 1430. The upper town
contains a Gothic church, while a second
gateway leads to a château that was once part
of an abbey. Beyond here a small chapel,
overlooking the bay, houses the tomb of St-
Valery. In the lower town, the **Ecomusée
Picarvie** recreates aspects of traditional village
life. Strolling from the port to the bay, you can
see some impressive villas from the turn of the
century. Consult tide times: at low tide the sea
goes out nearly 14km; it comes back again in
less than five hours.

At the tip of the bay, **Le Hourdel** consists of
a few fishermen's houses and a dock where the
fishing boats sell their catch of the day. Here
you have your best chance to see seals from the
largest colony in France. Lying below sea-level,
Cayeux, three miles south, was a chic resort in
the early 1900s. It has beautiful sand beaches at
low tide, and they are often almost completely
deserted. During the summer, the seafront is
captivatingly dressed with wooden cabins and
planks in a 2km promenade. Continue
southwest along the coast to explore Ault
Onival, Le Bois de Cise, Eu and Le Tréport.

The bay has an astounding 2,000 hectares of
nature reserves and France's first maritime
reserve was created here in 1968, with some 200
bird species, notably winter migrants, recorded
at the **Parc Naturel du Marquenterre**.

Chemin de Fer de la Baie de Somme
Information 03.22.26.96.96. **Open** *Apr-June* Wed,
Sat, Sun in Sept. **Tickets** €6.56-€12.35; under-18s
€5.34-€9.91.

Ecomusée Picarvie
*5 quai du Romeral, St-Valery-sur-Somme
(03.22.26.94.90).* **Open** Mar-Sept.

Parc Naturel du Marquenterre
Information: 03.22.25.03.26. **Open** *15 Mar-11 Nov*
9.30am-7pm daily; *12 Nov-10 Mar* guided tours only
4pm Sat; 10am, 4pm Sun. **Admission** €9.15; €6.86
students.

Where to eat & stay

In St-Valery-sur-Somme, **Le Nicol's** (15 rue de
la Ferté/03.22.26.82.96, *menu* €20) does
excellent fare. The **Relais Guillaume de
Normandie** (46 quai Romerel/03.22.60.82.36,
double €50) is a welcoming hotel.

Getting there

By car
Le Crotoy is 190km from Paris by N1 or A15 and
N184, then A16 motorway (exit Abbeville Nord).

By train
The closest train station is Noyelles-sur-Mer, just
after Abbeville, about 2 hours from Gare du Nord.

Getting around

Limited local buses serve villages on the bay. Bikes
can be hired at St-Valéry-sur-Somme (03.22.26.96.80).

Tourist information

Office de Tourisme: Le Crotoy
1 rue Carnot, Le Crotoy (03.22.27.05.25). **Open**
Sept-June 10am-noon, 3-6pm Mon, Wed-Sat; 10am-
noon Sun; *July, Aug* 10am-7pm daily.

Office de Tourisme: St-Valery-
sur-Somme

A typically beautiful **Rouen facade.** *See page 362.*

2 pl Guillaume le Conquérant (03.22.60.93.50).
Open *Sept-June* 10am-noon, 2.30-5pm Tue-Sun. *July, Aug* 10am-noon, 2.30-7pm Tue-Sun.

Cathedral Cities

Stubby spires, Gothic vaults, flying buttresses and even some Champagne: France's beautiful cathedral cities show the results of divine inspiration at its best.

Beauvais

Beauvais is both one of the strangest and most impressive of French cathedrals. It has the tallest Gothic vault in the world and a spectacular crown of flying buttresses. The cathedral had a very challenging nativity. The task of building it entailed numerous construction problems, as first the choir had to be rebuilt – you can still see where an extra column was added between the arches – and then the spire collapsed. The nave was never built at all; the church suddenly stops in a wall at the transept, which only accentuates the impression of verticality.

Left of the choir is a curious astrological clock, made in the 1860s by local watchmaker Lucien-Auguste Vérité, and a typically 19th-century extravagance of turned wood, gilt, dials and automata; around the corner is a clock dating from the 14th century.

Next to the cathedral, a medieval gateway leads into the 16th-century bishop's palace, now the **Musée Départemental de l'Oise** (03.44.11.43.83), tracing the region's illustrious heritage in wood and stone sculptures from destroyed houses and churches, Nabis paintings and art nouveau furniture and the tapestries for which Beauvais was famed. The tapestry industry reached its peak in the 18th century and then stopped when the factory was evacuated to Aubusson in 1939, but it has recently been revived at the **Manufacture Nationale de la Tapisserie** where you can watch weavers making astonishing tapestries under natural light.

Most of Beauvais was well and truly flattened by bombing during World War II, but the centre was rebuilt not unpleasantly in the 1950s in a series of low-rise squares and shopping streets. One other impressive medieval survivor remains, the Eglise St-Etienne, a curious mix of Romanesque and Gothic styles, with elaborate gargoyles sticking out in the centre of a traffic island.

Manufacture Nationale de la Tapisserie
24 rue Henri Brispot, 60000 Beauvais (03.44.05.14.28). **Demonstrations** 2-4pm Tue-Thur.

Where to eat

Two reliable addresses are restaurant-bar **Le Marignan** (1 rue Malherbe/03.44.48.15.15), and Alsatian brasserie **Taverne du Maître Kanter** (16 rue Pierre Jacoby/ 03.44.06.32.72).

Trips Out of Town

Getting there

By car
75km from Paris by A16 or N1.

By train
From Gare du Nord.

Tourist information

Office du Tourisme
1 rue Beauregard (03.44.15.30.30). **Open** *Apr-Oct*
10am-1pm, 2-6pm Mon, Sun; 9.30am-7pm. Tue-Sat.
Nov-Mar 10am-1pm, 2-6pm Mon, 9.30am-6.30pm
Tue-Sat; 10am-1.20pm Sun.

Chartres

Chartres cathedral was described by Rodin as
the 'French Acropolis'. Certainly, with its two
uneven spires – the stubbier from the 12th
century, the taller one completed only in the
16th century – and doorways bristling with
sculpture, the cathedral has an enormous
amount of slightly wonky charm.

Chartres was a pilgrimage site long before
the cathedral was built, ever since the Sacra
Camisia (said to be the Virgin Mary's lying-in
garment) was donated to the city in 876 by the
Carolingian King Charles I. When the church
caught fire in 1194, locals clubbed together to
reconstruct it, taking St-Denis as the model for
the new west front, 'the royal portal' with its
three richly sculpted doorways. The stylised,
elongated figure columns above geometric
patterns still form part of the door structure.

Inside yet another era of sculpture is
represented in the lively, 16th-century scenes of
the life of Christ that surround the choir. Note
also the circular labyrinth of black and white
stones in the floor; such mazes used to exist in
most cathedrals but most have been destroyed.

Chartres is above all famed for its stained-
glass windows depicting Biblical scenes, saints
and medieval trades in brilliant 'Chartres blue',
punctuated by rich reds. To learn all about
them, take one of the erudite and entertaining
tours given in English by Malcolm Miller (*see
below* **Tourist information**), who specialises
in deciphering the medieval picture codes.

The cathedral may dominate the town from a
distance, but once in the town centre's narrow
medieval streets, with their overhanging gables,
glimpses of it are only occasional. Wander past
the iron-framed market hall, down to the river
Eure, crossed by a string of attractive old
bridges, past the partly Romanesque Eglise St-
André and down the rue des Tanneries, which
runs along the banks. There's more fine stained
glass in the 13th-century Eglise St-Pierre.

There's a good view from the Jardin de
l'Evêché, located at the back of the cathedral
and adjoining the **Musée des Beaux-Arts**
(02.37.36.41.39/29 Cloître Notre-Dame). Housed
in the former Bishop's palace, the collection
includes some fine 18th-century French
paintings by Boucher and Watteau, as well as a
large array of medieval sculpture, some of
which is distinctly creepy.

The other main tourist attraction is very
much of our times and a reminder that Chartres
towers over the Beauce region, known as the
'bread basket of France' for its prairie-like
expanses of wheat. The **COMPA** agricultural
museum (pont de Mainvilliers/ 02.37.36.11.30) in
a converted engine shed near the station has a
small but lively presentation of the history of
agriculture and food (and consequently, of
course, society) from 50,000BC to today, with
the emphasis very much on the machinery,
from vintage tractors and threshing machines
to old fridges.

Where to eat & stay

La Vieille Maison (5 rue au Lait/
02.37.34.10.67) has good classical cooking in an
ancient building, and a good-value €25.61
menu. Simpler, but with an attractive setting
facing the cathedral, the **Café Serpente**
(2 Cloître Notre Dame/02.37.21.68.81) triples as
a café, a tearoom and a restaurant.

Getting there

By car
88km from Paris by A11.

By train
From Gare Montparnasse.

Tourist information

Guided cathedral tours
Contact Malcolm Miller (02.37.28.15.58).
Tours noon, 2.45pm Mon-Sat, Easter-mid-Nov.
Price €6.10 adults; €3.05 students.

Office du Tourisme
pl de la Cathédrale,(02.37.18.26.26). **Open** *Apr-Sept*
9am-7pm Mon-Sat; 9.30am-5.30pm Sun; *Oct-Mar*
10am-6pm Mon-Sat; 10am-1pm, 2.30-4.30pm Sun.

Reims

Begun in the 13th century, the Cathédrale
Notre-Dame is of dual importance to the French,
as the coronation church of most monarchs
since Clovis in 496 and for the richness of its
Gothic decoration. Thousands of figures on the
portals and the Kings of Judea high above the

It's the Lille thing

Selected as European City of Culture for 2004, Lille is buzzing: a lively mix of popular and high culture, from crowded karaoke bars to opera, and home to futuristic Eurolille, the showcase business city. One of the great wool towns of medieval Flanders, it became part of France in 1667. *La Braderie* or 'great clear-out' on the first weekend in September attracts two million visitors annually from the Netherlands, France, Belgium, Germany and Britain. Streets are lined with jumble and antiques stalls, while mussel shells mount up outside cafés. The fair has existed since the Middle Ages and is still wonderfully anarchic.

In Vieux Lille, Renaissance buildings have been renovated, including the 1652-53 *Vieille Bourse* on the Grand' Place at the heart of the city. Adjoining place du Théâtre has the 19th-century Nouvelle Bourse, a pretty opera house and the rang de Beauregard, a row of late 17th-century houses. The tourist office is in the Palais Rihour started in 1454 by Philippe Le Bel, Duc de Bourgogne. Nearby is the Gothic Eglise St-Maurice.

The **Musée de l'Hospice Comtesse** (32 rue de la Monnaie/03.20.49.50.90) contains Flemish art, furniture and ceramics. Nearby on place de la Treille is Lille's cathedral, begun 150 years ago after a public subscription but only completed in 1999. Visit the modest brick house where **de Gaulle** was born (9 rue Princesse/03.28.38.12.05).

The palatial **Musée des Beaux-Arts** (pl de la

République/03.20.06.78.00) includes paintings by Rubens, El Greco, Goya, David, Delacroix and Courbet. Further out, the **Musée d'Art Moderne** (1 allée du Musée, Villeneuve-d'Ascq/03.20.19.68.68) houses works by Picasso, Braque, Derain and Modigliani. The stunning new **Musée d'Art et d'Histoire** (Hôtel de Ville, Roubaix/ 03.20.66.47.41) showcases 19th- and early 20th-century paintings, ceramics and textiles in an art deco former swimming pool.

Where to eat & stay

Bistros line Rue de Gand. Try chic **L'Huîtrière** (3 rue des Chats-Bossus/03.20.55.43.41), or brasserie **Alcide** (5 rue des Debris-St-Etienne/03.20.12.06.95). Stop for tea at pâtisserie **Méert** (27 rue Esquermoise/ 03.20.57.07.44). **Hôtel de la Treille** (7-9 pl Louise de Bettignies/ 03.20.55.45.46) is a pleasant modern hotel (double €62.50-€68.60); otherwise try the simple **Hôtel de la Paix** (46bis rue de Paris/03.20.54.63.93/ double €62.50-€68.60).

Getting there

By car
220km from Paris by A1; 104km from Calais.

By train
TGV from Gare du Nord; Eurostar from London.

Tourist information

Office du Tourisme
Palais Rihour, pl Rihour, 59002 Lille (03.20.21.94.21). **Open** 9.30am-6.30pm Mon-Sat; 10am-noon, 2-5pm Sun.

Pool your thoughts at Roubaix's **Musée d'Art et d'Industrie.**

rose window show how sculptural style developed over the century. Heavy shelling in World War I, together with erosion, means that many of the carvings have been replaced by copies; the originals are on show next door in the Palais de Tau, the Bishop's palace. It is possible that some of the masons from Chartres also worked on Reims, but the figures generally show more classical influence in their drapery and increasing expressivity. Look out for the winsome 'smiling angel' sculpture and St Joseph on the facade. Inside take a look at the capitals decorated with elaborate, naturalistic foliage with birds hiding among the leaves.

A few streets south of the cathedral, the **Musée des Beaux-Arts** (8 rue Chanzy/ 03.26.47.28.44) has some wonderful portraits of German princes by Cranach, 26 canvases by Corot and the famous *Death of Marat* by Jean-Louis David. From the museum, head down rue Gambetta to the Basilique de St-Rémi, which honours the saint who baptised Clovis. Built 1007-49, it is a fascinating complement to the cathedral. Subsequent alterations allow you to see just how the Romanesque style evolved into the Gothic. Don't miss the ten remarkable 16th-century tapestries depicting the life of St-Rémi in the **Musée St-Remi** (53 rue Simon/ 03.26.85.23.36) in the restored monastic buildings next door.

Reims is also, of course, at the heart of the Champagne region. Many leading producers of the famous bubbly are based in the town and offer visits of their cellars, an informative insight into the laborious and skilful Champagne-making process. The **Champagne Pommery** cellars (03.26.61.62.56) occupy Gallo-Roman chalk mines 30m below ground and are decorated with art nouveau bas-reliefs by Emile Gallé. **Taittinger** (03.26.85.84.33) doesn't look like much until you descend into the *cave*: on the first level are the vaulted Gothic cellars of a former monastery; below are the strangely beautiful, Gallo-Roman chalk quarries.

Where to eat

Haute-cuisine mecca is Gérard Boyer's **Château des Crayères** (64 bd Henri-Vanier/ 03.26.82.80.80) in a Second Empire château to the southeast of town. Boyer no longer owns the lively bistro **Au Petit Comptoir** (17 rue de Mars/03.26.40.58.58), but the chef has stayed on. Run by another Boyer-trained chef, **La Vigneraie** (14 rue de Thillois/03.26.88.67.27) has good-value *menus*. Also within town, there are numerous brasseries, restaurants and cafés around place Drouet d'Erlon.

The Gothicism of **Troyes**. *See right.*

Getting there

By car
150km by A4.

By train
From Gare de l'Est about 1/2 hour.

Tourist information

Office du Tourisme
2 rue Guillaume-de-Machault (03.26.77.45.25). **Open** *mid-Apr-mid-Oct* 9am-7pm Mon-Sat; 10am-6pm Sun; *mid-Oct-mid-Apr* 9am-6pm Mon-Sat; 10am-5pm Sun.

Rouen

The capital of Normandy is a cathedral town, featuring a historic centre with lots of drunken half-timbered buildings and narrow streets, while the port areas by the Seine were almost totally destroyed by bombing during World War II. Begun at the start of the 13th century, the **Cathédrale Notre-Dame**, depicted at all times of the day by Monet in a famous series of paintings, spans the Gothic periods. The north tower dates from the early period while the Flamboyant Tour de Beurre is from the late 15th century. Nearby, the famous **Gros**

Horloge gateway, with its ornamental clock over busy medieval rue du Gros-Horloge, leads to picturesque streets of half-timbered houses.

Two more Gothic churches are worth a visit, the **Abbatiale St-Ouen** and the **Eglise St-Maclou**, as well as an enormously fanciful Flamboyant Gothic Palais de Justice. Just near the Abbatiale St-Ouen, the newly reopened **Musée de l'Education** (185 rue Eau-de-Robec/02.32.82.95.95) presents a lively view of French education since the 15th century over two floors of a half-timbered house. The striking, contemporary **Eglise Ste-Jeanne d'Arc**, adjoining a funky modern market hall on place du Vieux-Marché, is a boat-shaped structure with a swooping wooden roof and stained glass windows that were recuperated from a bombed city church. The **Musée des Beaux Arts** (1 pl Restout/02.35.71.28.40) numbers masterpieces by Gérard David, Velázquez, Perugino and Caravaggio, some wonderful oil studies by Géricault (a native of Rouen) and several Impressionist paintings by Monet and Sisley.

Where to eat

Best-known gourmet stop is **Restaurant Gill** (9 quai de la Bourse/ 02.35.71.16.14), home to fish specialist Gilles Tournadre (menus €27.44-€91.47). There are several cheaper bistros, especially on pl du Vieux-Marché, or the quietly formal **L'Orangerie** (2 rue Thomas-Corneille/ 02.35.88.43.97).

Getting there

By car
137km west of Paris by A13.

By train
From Gare St-Lazare.

Tourist information

Office du Tourisme
25 pl de la Cathédrale (02.32.08.32.40).
Open *May-Sept* 9am-7pm Mon-Sat; 9.30am-12.30pm, 2.30-6.30pm Sun; *Oct-Apr* 9am-6.30pm Mon-Sat; 10am-1pm Sun.

Troyes

Troyes, with its remarkably preserved half-timbered houses and Gothic churches, is still a delightful city. Stroll along rue Champeaux at the heart of the old city, and don't miss the ruelle des Chats, a narrow lane full of medieval atmosphere which leads up to the **Eglise Ste-Madeleine**, the city's oldest church. Nearby,

the **Basilique St-Urbain** was built in 1262-86 on the orders of Pope Urbain IV, a native of Troyes. This church represents an early apogee of Gothic architecture and its ambitions of replacing the heavy masonry of the Romanesque period with lacy stone work and glass.

Heading down rue Champeaux, pass through café-lined place du Maréchal-Foch, with the handsome 17th-century Hôtel de Ville, and cross a canal into the oldest part of the city around the **Cathédrale St-Pierre St-Paul**. Part of the impressive facade is by Martin Chambiges, who also worked on the cathedrals at Sens and Beauvais. The triforium of the choir was one of the first in France to be built with windows instead of blind arcading.

Next door to the cathedral, in what used to be the bishop's palace, the **Musée d'Art Moderne** (pl St-Pierre/03.25.76.26.80) is an absolute must for art-lovers, and for André Derain fans in particular. It contains numerous canvases by Derain, in both his Fauvist and later styles, in addition to several works by Braque, Courbet, Degas, Seurat and Vuillard, and modern sculpture and drawings. The **Maison de l'Outil** (7 rue de la Trinité/ 03.25.73.28.26) has a fascinating array of craftsmen's tools on display. The **Musée des Beaux-Arts et d'Archéologie** in the Abbaye St-Loup (4 rue Chrétien de Troyes/ 03.25.76.21.68) next to the cathedral, has some fine Gallo-Roman bronzes and a fantastic treasure of arms and jewellery that was discovered in a fifth-century Merovingian tomb.

Where to eat

Many consider **Le Clos Juillet** (22 bd du 14-Juillet/03.25.73.31.32) to be the best table in town; its young chef Philippe Colin specialises in modernised regional dishes.

Getting there

By car
150km southeast of Paris by A6 and A5.

By train
From Gare de l'Est (75 mins).

Tourist information

Office du Tourisme
*16 bd Carnot (03.25.82.62.70).***Open** 9am-12.30pm; 2-6.30pm Mon-Sat.
Branch: rue Mignard (03.25.73.36.88).
Open 9am-12.30pm, 2-6.30pm Mon-Sat; 10am-12.30pm, 2-5pm Sun.

Trips Out of Town

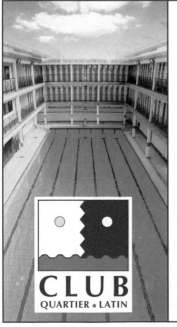

Directory

Directory

Getting Around

By air

Roissy-Charles-de-Gaulle airport

Most international flights arrive at Roissy-Charles-de-Gaulle airport, 30km north-east of Paris. Its two main terminals are some way apart, so it's important to check which is the right one for your flight if you are flying out. 24-hr information service in English: 01.48.62.22.80.

The **RER B** is the quickest and most reliable way to central Paris (about 35 minutes to Gare du Nord; 45 minutes to Châtelet-Les Halles, €7.62 single). A new station gives direct access from Terminal 2 (Air France flights); from Terminal 1 you take the free shuttle bus. RER trains run every 15 minutes, 5.24am-11.58pm daily. SNCF information: 01.53.90.20.20.

Air France buses (€9.91) leave every 12-20 minutes, 5.45am-11pm daily, from both terminals, and stop at Porte Maillot and pl Charles-de-Gaulle (35-50 min trip). Air France buses also run to Gare Montparnasse and Gare de Lyon (€11.43) every 30 minutes (45-60 minute trip), 7am-9.30pm daily. There is also a bus between Roissy and Orly (€12.20) every 20-30 minutes, 6am-11pm daily. Information: 01.41.56.89.00. The RATP **Roissybus** (€8.08) runs every 15 minutes, 5.45am-11pm daily, between the airport and the corner of rue Scribe/rue Auber, near pl de l'Opéra (at least 45 minutes); tickets are sold on the bus. Information: 08.36.68.77.14. The **Airport Shuttle** is a door-to-door minibus service between the airports and hotels, running 4.30am-7.30pm daily. It works on a 'the passengers the less you pay' system. Roissy prices from €23 for one person to €11.25 each for eight people sharing; Orly €19-€61. (reserve ahead on

08.21.80.08.01). **Airport Connection** (01.44.18.36.02, reservations 7am-8pm) runs a similar service, 4am-8pm, at €23 per person, €14 each for two or more. **Taxis** are the least reliable and most expensive means of transport. A taxi to central Paris can take 30-60 mins depending on traffic and your point of arrival. Expect to pay €26-€45, plus €0.90 per piece of luggage. **Km2** (01.45.16.27.27) run **motorbike taxis** aimed largely at executives. Roissy-Charles de Gaulle to Versailles €73; Orly to La Défense €51.

Orly airport

French domestic and several international flights use Orly airport, 18km south of the city. It also has two terminals: Orly-Sud (mainly international flights) and Orly-Ouest (mainly domestic flights). English-speaking information service on 01.49.75.15.15, 6am-11.30pm daily. **Air France buses** (01.41.56.89.00; €7.62) leave both terminals every 6 minutes, 6am-11pm daily, and stop at Invalides and Montparnasse (30-45 minutes). The RATP **Orlybus** at Denfert-Rochereau leaves every 15 minutes, 6am-11pm daily (30-minute trip); tickets (€5.64) are available on the bus. Information: 08.36.68.77.14. The high-speed **Orlyval** shuttle train runs every 7 minutes (6am-8.30pm Mon-Sat; 7am-11pm Sun) to RER B station Antony (Orlyval and RER together cost €8.69); getting to central Paris takes about 40 minutes. Alternatively, catch the courtesy bus to RER C station Pont de Rungis, where you can get the **Orlyrail** to central Paris (€5.18). Trains run every 12 minutes, 5.45am-11.10pm daily; 50-minute trip. A **taxi** into town takes 20-40 minutes and costs €16-€26, plus €0.90 per piece of luggage. The minibus and Km2 services listed above also run to and from Orly.

Beauvais Tillé airport

Ryan Air (03.44.11.41.41) flies from Dublin and Glasgow to Beauvais, 70km from Paris, with a 90-120 minute bus link to Porte Maillot (€9.15, tickets can be bought at the airport or from the James Joyce pub, 71 bd Gouvion-St-Cyr, 17th, across from the Concorde La Fayette hotel).

Major airlines

Aer Lingus 01.55.38.38.55.
Air France 08.02.80.28.02.
American Airlines 08.10.87.28.78.
British Airways 08.25.82.54.00.
British Midland 01.48.62.55.65.
Continental 01.42.99.09.09.
KLM & NorthWest 08.10.55.65.56.
USAir 01.49.10.29.00.

By car

For travelling between France and the UK by car, options include tunnel **Le Shuttle** (Folkstone-Calais 35mins) (01.43.18.62.22/08.01.63.03.04/ www.eurotunnel.com); **Hoverspeed** (Dover-Calais, Newhaven-Dieppe) (08.20.00.35.55/03.21.46.14.00); ferry **Brittany Ferries** (08.03.82.88.28), **P&O Stena Line** (01.53.43.40.00) and **SeaFrance** (08.03.04.40.45).

Shared journeys

Allô-Stop *8 rue Rochambeau, 9th (01.53.20.42.42).* **Open** 9am-1pm, 2-6.30pm Mon-Fri; 10am-1pm, 2-5pm Sat. **Credit** MC, V.
Call several days ahead to be put in touch with drivers. There's a fee (€4.57 under 200km; up to €10.67 over 500km), plus €0.03 per km to the driver. Routes most travelled: Lyon, Toulouse, Rennes, Nantes, Cologne.

By coach

International coach services arrive at the Gare Routière Internationale

Paris-Galliéni at Porte de
Bagnolet, 20th (M° Galliéni).
For reservations (in English) call
Eurolines on 08.36.69.52.52
(€0.34 min), or in the UK 01582-
404511/www.eurolines.fr.

By rail

The **Eurostar** train between
London and Paris takes three
hours. You must check in at least
20 minutes in advance. Passports
must be carried on the Eurostar.
Eurostar trains from London
Waterloo (01233-617575/www.
eurostar.com) arrive at Gare du
Nord (08.36.35.35.39, €0.34/min;
Minitel 3615 SNCF, www.sncf.fr),
with easy access to public
transport. **Bicycles** can be
transported as hand luggage
provided they are dismantled and
carried in a bike bag. You can also
check them in at the Eurodispatch
depot at Waterloo or the Sernam
depot at Gare du Nord up to 24
hours in advance. A Eurostar
ticket must be shown and the
service costs £20/€32.20.

Travel agencies

Havas Voyages
*26 av de l'Opéra, 1st (01.53.29.
40.00). M° Opéra.* **Open** 10am-
7.30pm Mon-Sat. **Credit** AmEx, V.
General travel agent with more
than 15 branches in Paris.

Maison de la Grande Bretagne
*19 rue des Mathurins, 9th
(01.44.51.56.20/www.grandebretag
ne.net). M° Havre-Caumartin/RER
Auber.* **Open** 9.30am-6pm Mon-Fri;
10am-5pm Sat. **Credit** MC, V.
All under one roof, the British
Tourist Office and other services
for travelling to or in the UK
including ferry companies, Le
Shuttle, British Rail (01.44.51.06.00)
and Global Tickets (01.45.96.35.00),
a theatre ticket agency for the UK.

Nouvelles Frontières
*13 av de l'Opéra, 1st
(08.03.33.33.33/08.25.00.08.25).
M° Pyramides.* **Open** 9am-7pm
Mon-Sat. **Credit** DC, MC, V. Agent
with 18 branches in Paris.

USIT *6 rue de Vaugirard, 6th
(01.42.34.56.90/telephone bookings
01.42.44.14.00). M° Odéon.*
Open 10am-7pm Mon-Fri; 9.30am-
6.30pm Sat. **Credit** MC, V. Coach,
air and train tickets for under-26s
and others.

Maps

Free maps of the Métro, bus and
RER systems are available at
airports and Métro stations.
Other brochures from Métro
stations are *Paris Visite – Le
Guide*, with details of transport
tickets and a small map, and the
Grand Plan de Paris, a fold-out
map that also indicates
Noctambus night bus lines.

Public transport

The public transport system
(**RATP**) consists of bus routes,
the Métro (underground), the **RER**
suburban express railway which
interconnects with the Métro
inside Paris and two suburban
tramways. Pick up a free map at
any Métro station. Paris and its
suburbs are divided into five
travel zones; zones 1 and 2 cover
the city centre. Information 6am-
9pm daily, 08.36.68.77.14/in
English 08.36.68.41.14 (€0.34/
min); www.ratp.fr. **SNCF**, the
state railway system, serves the
French regions and international
(*Grandes Lignes*) and the suburbs
(*Banlieue*). Information:
08.36.35.35.35/ www.sncf.fr/
Minitel 3615 SNCF.

Fares & tickets

RATP **tickets** and passes are
valid on the Métro, bus and
RER. Tickets and *carnets* can be
bought at Métro stations, tourist
offices and *tabacs* (tobacconists).
Keep your ticket in case of spot
checks and to exit from RER
stations. Individual tickets cost
€1.30; it's more economical to buy
a *carnet* of ten tickets for €9.30.
Carte Orange travel passes
(passport photo needed) offer
unlimited travel in the relevant
zones for a week or month. A
Coupon Mensuel (valid from the
first day of the month) zones 1-2
costs €44.36. A weekly *Coupon
Hebdomadaire* (valid Mon-Sun
inclusive) zones 1-2 costs €13.26
and is better value than *Paris
Visite* passes – a three-day pass
for zones 1-3 is €18.29; a five-day
pass is €26.68, with discounts on
some tourist attractions. A one-
day Mobilis pass goes from €5.03
for zones 1-2 to €17.99 for zones 1-
8 (not including airports).

Métro & RER

The Paris **Métro** is at most times
the quickest and cheapest means
of travelling around the city.
Trains run daily 5.30am-12.40am.
Individual lines are numbered,
with each direction named after
the last stop. So Line 4
northbound is indicated Porte de
Clignancourt, while southbound
is designated Porte d'Orléans.
Follow the orange *correspondance*
signs to change lines. Some
interchanges, notably Châtelet-Les
Halles, Montparnasse-Bienvenüe
and République, involve a long
walk. The exit (*sortie*) is indicated
in blue. The high-speed Line 14,
Météor, opened in 1998, links the
new Bibliothèque Nationale to
Madeleine. It is impossible to
travel on the Métro without being
confronted with buskers and
beggars. The sound of accordion
playing may well ring in your ears
long after your return home.
Determined buskers work their
way through carriages, no matter
how packed. These are most likely
the unauthorised musicians who
have not made it through the
selective RATP casting process
and paid €152.50 to sport an
official photo ID badge. If spotted
by the RATP staff (who survey
the Métro with a beady eye and
seem keener on stamping out the
buskers than catching the fare
dodgers) they have to pay a fine
of €60.98. Those with an official
badge tend to set up position in
corridors at major stations and
liven up the seemingly
interminable journeys between
Métro line connections. The
consensus regarding giving
money to them is: if they have
some talent, drop a few cents into
their coffers. Beggars often
frequent the Paris Métro stations
in the hope of earning the
sympathy of a pitying tourist.
Obviously payment is down to
your own discretion.
The five **RER** lines (A, B, C, D
and the new Eole) run 5.30am-1am
daily across Paris and into the Ile-
de-France commuter land. Within
Paris, the RER is useful for
making faster journeys – for
example, Châtelet-Les Halles to
Charles de Gaulle-Etoile is only
two stops on the RER compared
with eight on Métro Line 1.

Buses

Buses run from 6.30am until
8.30pm, with some routes
continuing until 12.30am, Mon-
Sat, with a more limited service
on selected lines on Sundays and
public holidays. You can use a
Métro ticket, a ticket bought from
the driver (€1.30) or a travel pass.
Tickets should be punched in the
machine next to the driver; passes
should be shown to the driver.
When you want to get off, press
the red request button, and the
arrêt demandé (stop requested)
sign above the driver will light up.

Night buses

After the Métro and normal
buses stop, the only public
transport – apart from taxis –
is the 18 **Noctambus** lines,
between place du Châtelet and
the suburbs (hourly 1.30am-
5.30am Mon-Thur; half-hourly
1am-5.30am Fri, Sat). Routes A
to H, P, T and V serve the Right
Bank and northern suburbs; I to
M, R and S serve the Left Bank
and southern suburbs. Look out
for the owl logo on bus stops.
A ticket costs €2.44 and allows
one change; travel passes are valid.

Trams

Two modern tramlines operate in
the suburbs, running from La
Défense to Issy-Val de Seine and
from Bobigny Pablo Picasso to
St-Denis. They connect with the
Métro and RER and fares are the
same as for buses.

Rail services

Several attractions in the suburbs,
notably Versailles and Disneyland
Paris, are served by the RER. Most
locations farther from the city are
served by the SNCF state railway;
there are few long-distance bus
services. The TGV high-speed
train has revolutionised journey
times and is gradually being
extended to all the main regions.

SNCF Reservations/Tickets
SNCF national reservations
and information: 08.36.35.35.35
(€0.34 per min) www/sncf.com.
Open 7am-10pm daily.

**SNCF information (no
reservations)** in the Ile de
France: 01.53.90.20.20.

You can buy tickets at counters
and machines in any SNCF station
and at travel agents. If you reserve
on Minitel 3615 SNCF or by phone,
you must pick up and pay for the
ticket within 48 hours. Regular
trains have both full-rate White
and cheaper Blue periods. You can
save on TGV fares by purchasing
special cards. Carte 12/25 gives
under-26s a 50% reduction;
without it, under-26s are entitled
to 25% off. Pensioners over 60
benefit from similar terms with a
Carte Vermeil. Before you board
any train, validate your ticket in
the orange composteur machines
located by the platforms, or you
might have to pay a hefty fine.

Paris mainline stations

Gare d'Austerlitz: Central and
SW France and western Spain.
Gare de l'Est: Alsace,
Champagne and southern
Germany.
Gare de Lyon: Burgundy, the
Alps, Provence, Italy.
Gare Montparnasse: West
France, Brittany, Bordeaux, the
Southwest.
Gare du Nord: Northeast France,
Channel ports, Eurostar, Belgium
and the Netherlands.
Gare St-Lazare: Normandy.

Taxis

Paris taxi drivers are not known
for their charm, nor for infallible
knowledge of the Paris street plan
– if there's a route you would
prefer, say so. Taxis can also be
few and far between, especially at
rush hour. Your best bet is to find
a taxi rank (*station de taxis*) – on
major roads, crossroads and at
stations – marked with a blue
sign. The white light on a taxi's
roof indicates the car is free. A
glowing orange light means the
cab is busy. Taxi charges are
based on area and time: A (7am-
7pm Mon-Sat, €0.60 per km); B
(7pm-7am Mon-Sat, all day Sun;
7am-7pm Mon-Sat suburbs and
airports, €1.00 per km); C (7pm-
7am daily suburbs and airports,
€1.20 per km). Most journeys in
central Paris average €6-€12;
there's a minimum charge of
€2.00, plus €0.90 for each piece of
luggage over 5kg or bulky objects,
and a €0.70 surcharge from
mainline stations and a minimum

journey charge of €4.57. Most
drivers will not take more than
three people, although they should
take a couple and two children.
Don't feel obliged to tip, although
rounding up by €0.30-€0.70 is
polite. Taxis are not allowed to
refuse rides because they are too
short and can only refuse to take
you in a particular direction
during their last half-hour of
service – however, in practice
these rules are blatantly ignored.
If you want a receipt, ask for *un
reçu* or *une fiche* (compulsory for
journeys of €15.25 or more).
Complaints should be made in
writing to the **Bureau de la
réglementation publique de
Paris**, 36 rue des Morillons, 75732
Paris Cedex 15.

Phone cabs

The following accept telephone
bookings 24-hr. However, you also
pay for the radioed taxi to get to
where you are and there is no
guarantee they will actually turn
up. If you wish to pay by credit
card, mention this when you order.

**Accept credit cards over
€7.62**: **Alpha** 01.45.85.85.85.
**Accept credit cards over
€15.24**: **Artaxi** 01.42.03.50.50;
G7 01.47.39.47.39/ 01.41.27.66.99
(in English); **Km2** (motorbikes
01.45.16.28.56/www.k-m-2.com
(Mon-Fri 7.30am-7pm);
Taxis Bleus (01.49.36.10.10/
www.taxis-bleus.com).

Driving

If you bring your car to France,
you will need to bring the
registration and insurance
documents – an insurance green
card, available from insurance
companies and the AA and RAC
in the UK, is not compulsory but
is advisable. As you come into
Paris you will inevitably meet the
Périphérique, the giant ring road
that carries traffic in, out and
around the city. Intersections,
which lead onto other main roads,
are called *portes* (gates). Driving
on the Périphérique is not as hair-
raising as it might look, even
though it's often congested,
especially during rush hour and at
peak holiday times. The key word
is confidence.

If you've come to Paris by car, it can be a good idea to park at the edge of the city and use public transport. A few hotels have parking spaces which can be paid by the hour, day or by various types of season tickets. In peak holiday periods, the organisation Bison Futé hands out brochures at the motorway *péages* (toll stations), suggesting less-crowded routes. French roads are divided into *Autoroutes* (motorways, with an 'A' in front of the number), *Routes Nationales* (national 'N' roads), *Routes Départementales* (local, 'D' roads) and tiny, rural *Routes Communales* ('C' roads). *Autoroutes* are toll roads (*péages*), although some sections, including most of the area immediately around Paris, are free. Motorways have a speed limit of 130km/h (80mph), though this is not adhered to with any degree of zeal by many French motorists. The limit on most *Routes Nationales* is 90km/h (56mph); within urban areas the limit is 50km/h (30mph), 30km/h (20mph) in selected residential zones.

Traffic information for the Ile-de-France: 01.48.99.33.33.

Breakdown services

The AA or RAC do not have reciprocal arrangements with an equivalent organisation in France, so it is advisable to take out additional breakdown insurance cover, for example with *Europ Assistance* (01.44 44.22.11/ www.europ-assistance.co.uk). If you don't have insurance, you can use its service (01.41.85.85.85) but it will charge you the full cost. Other 24-hour breakdown services in Paris include **SOS Dépannage** (01.47.07.99.99); **Action Auto Assistance** (01.45.58.49.58); **Adan Dépann Auto** (01.42.66.67.58).

Driving tips

• At intersections where no signposts indicate the right of way, the car coming from the right has priority. Many roundabouts now give priority to those on the roundabout. If this is not indicated (by road markings or a sign with the message *Vous n'avez pas la*

priorité), priority is for those coming from the right.
• Drivers and all passengers must wear seat belts.
• Children under ten are not allowed to travel in the front of a car, except in special babyseats facing backwards.
• You should not stop on an open road; pull off to the side.
• When drivers flash their lights at you, this means that they will not slow down and are warning you to keep out of the way.
• Friendly drivers also flash their lights to warn you when there are *gendarmes* lurking in the vicinity.
• Try to carry plenty of change, as it's quicker – and less stressful – to make for the exact-money line on *péages*; but, if you are caught short, cashiers do give change and *péages* accept credit cards.

Parking

There are still a few free on-street parking areas left in Paris, but they are often full. If you park illegally, you risk having your car clamped or towed away (*see below*). It is forbidden to park in zones marked for *livraisons* (deliveries) or taxis. Parking meters have now been replaced by *horodateurs*, pay-and-display machines, which either take coins or cards (€15.24 or €30.49 available from *tabacs*). Parking is often free at weekends and after 7pm, and in August. There are numerous underground car parks in central Paris. Most cost €1,83-€2.29 per hour; €12.20-€19.82 for 24 hours; some offer lower rates after 6pm and many offer various types of season ticket.

Clamps & car pounds

If you've had your car clamped, contact the local police station. There are eight car pounds (*préfourrières*) in Paris. You'll have to pay a €91.47 removal fee plus €4.57 storage charge per day, and a parking fine of €35.06 for parking in a no-parking zone. Bring your driving licence and insurance papers. If your car is confiscated at night, it goes first to *préfourrière* Bercy for southern Paris or Europe for the north; and will be sent to the car pound for the relevant *arrondissement* after

48 hours. For details call 08.36.67.22.22 (€0.34 per min). **Les Halles** 1st, 2nd, 3rd, 4th (01.40.39.12.20). **Bercy** 5th, 6th, 7th, 12th, 13th, 14th (01.53.46.69.20). **Pantin** 10th, 11th, 19th, 20th (01.44.52.52.10). **Balard** 15th, 16th (01.45.58.70.30). **Foch** 8th, 16th, 17th (01.53.64.11.80). **Pouchet** 8th, 9th, 17th, 18th (01.53.06.67.68).

Car hire

To hire a car you must normally be 25 or over and have held a licence for at least a year. Some agencies accept drivers aged 21-24, but a supplement of €7.62-€5.24 per day is usual. Take your licence and passport with you.

Hire companies

Ada 01.45.54.63.63/08.36.68.40.02. **Avis** 08.02.05.05.05. **Budget** 08.25.00.35.64. **Calandres** 04.93.76.03.50. **EasyRentacar** www.easyRentacar.com. **Europcar** 01.30.43.82.82. **Hertz** 01.39.38.38.38. **Rent-a-Car** 01.45.22.28.28/ 08.36.69.46.95. **Valem** 01.43.14.79.79. There are often good weekend offers (Fri evening to Mon morning). Week-long deals are better at the bigger hire companies – with Avis or Budget, for example, it's around €18.16 a week for a small car with insurance and 1,700km included. The more expensive hire companies allow the return of a car in other French cities and abroad. Supposedly bargain companies may have an extremely high charge for damage. Budget has joined with Calandres to present a new *flotte prestige* which boasts luxury cars and motorbikes from cabriolets to Ferraris. You must be 30 or over with at least three year's driving licence.

Chauffeur-driven cars

Les Berlines de Paris
(01.41.40.84.84). **Open** 24 hours daily. **Prices** from €135 sedan airport transfer; €62 for four hours. **Credit** AmEx, DC, MC, V.

International Limousines
(01.41.66.32.00). **Open** 24-hr. **Prices** from €132.78 chauffeur-driven car service and multi-lingual guided tours, airport transfer; from €213.43 four-hour hire. **Credit** AmEx, DC, MC, V.

Directory

Cycling

Since 1996, the Mairie de Paris has been energetically introducing cycle lanes and, with the election of Mayor Delanoë, this looks set to continue. If Mr Delanoë has his way, things will only get greener. The quais along the Seine and the Canal St-Martin are usually closed to cars on Sundays (9am-4pm Seine, 2pm-6pm Canal) and summer 2002 may again see the *Rive Droite* reserved for cyclists and rollerbladers daily from mid-July to mid-Aug. The bike path by the Canal de l'Ourcq is another good open stretch. The Bois de Boulogne and Bois de Vincennes offer paths away from traffic although they are still criss-crossed by roads. Cycle lanes (*pistes cyclables*) run mostly N-S and E-W; you could be fined (€35.06) if you don't use them. N-S routes include rue de Rennes, bd St-Germain, bd de Sébastopol and av Marceau. E-W routes take in the Champs-Elysées, bd St-Germain, the rue de Rivoli, bd St-Jacques, bd Vincent-Auriol and av Daumesnil. Lanes are at the edge of the road or down *contre-allées*. Only a small percentage are separated from motorised traffic, so you may encounter delivery vans, scooters and pedestrians blocking your way; the €137.20 fine for obstructing a cycle lane is barely enforced. There are now approximately 165km of bike lanes and there are even plans for a bicycle 'Périphérique' circling Paris. You can get a free map of Paris' cycle routes (*Paris à Vélo*), with advice and addresses, at any Mairie or from bike shops.

The RATP is working on a project called *Roue Libre* in conjunction with Maison Roue Libre bike hire shop to promote cycle use in the city. It offers two guided bike rides per day in a choice of five languages, (90mins €12.96 adults, €8.38 children; 3hrs €20.58 adults, €14.48 children) from March-November, weekends only in winter. Price includes bike hire, insurance, guide and '*Accueil du Boulanger*' (hot drinks and pastries) on Sunday mornings.

Maison Roue Libre
95bis rue Rambuteau, 1st (01.46.28.29.68). M° Rambuteau. **Open** 9am-7pm daily. **Credit** MC, V.

Cycles, scooters & motorbikes

Note that bike insurance may not cover theft: be sure to check before you sign on the dotted line.

Atelier de la Compagnie *57 bd de Grenelle, 15th (01.45.79.77.24).* **Open** 10am-7pm Mon-Sat. **Credit** MC, V. A scooter for €30.00 per day or €150 per week; motorbike from €55 per day or €250 per week. Deposits of €1,300 for a scooter or €2,300 for a motorbike, plus passport, are required.

Maison du Vélo *11 rue Fénelon, 10th (01.42.81.24.72). M° Gare du Nord or Poissonnière.* **Open** 10am-7pm Tue-Sat. **Credit** MC, V. Bikes for hire, new and used cycles on sale, repairs.

Paris-Vélo *2 rue du Fer-à-Moulin, 5th (01.43.37.59.22). M° Censier-Daubenton.* **Open** 10am-12.30pm, 2-6pm daily. **Credit** MC, V. Mountain bikes and 21-speed models for hire. Bicycles can also be hired 15 Apr-15 Oct in the Bois de Boulogne (rond-point du Jardin d'Acclimatation) and the Bois de Vincennes (av Daumesmil, beside lac Daumesnil).

Property & personal safety

In 2001, more than 30,000 people reported having their pockets picked in Paris. Theft in public areas jumped by 41% in the first half of that year, and crimes on the Métro rose by 25%. Violent crime increased by 50%. Many thieves operate in the big tourist and shopping areas such as Boulevard Haussmann, Rue de Rivoli, Les Halles, the Arc de Triomphe and Montmartre, but almost half the incidents occur on the Métro. The pickpockets' favourite strategy is to hold a light jacket over one forearm and to reach under the victim's jacket with the other arm; sometimes the thief slips a plastic bag over his hand so that it can slide into bags and pockets with minimum friction. Another favourite method is for one person to bump into you and, while he is apologising and checking that you're OK, he and/ or an accomplice will take your wallet. All this can be done in a crowded Métro carriage but pickpockets are more likely to strike during the bustle that ensues when the carriage empties and refills, grabbing a wallet from a boarding passenger just as the doors are closing, and hopping off as the unsuspecting victim rides away. If you discover that you have been pick-pocketed it is worth going back to the street or the Métro station where you think it happened: thieves are normally just after cash and ditch wallets in the nearest rubbish bin (*for information on reporting lost property see p380*). When carrying a passport and credit cards, try to conceal them in several places rather than putting them all in a wallet or pouch. Keep an eye on your mobiles, too – 2,000 cell phones are now being snatched per month. If you realise that you are being robbed, it's often the safest course of action not to resist in too frenzied a manner, as thieves are increasingly carrying knives and gas canisters: it may be safer to let them take what they want. Do heed the above warnings to be on the safe side – but keep in mind that most cautious travellers are able to navigate Paris unscathed.

Walking

Exploring by foot is the very best way to discover Paris; just remember that to anything on wheels (and this includes cyclists and in-line roller skaters), pedestrians are the lowest form of life. Crossing Paris' multi-lane boulevards can be lethal to the uninitiated, and Brits, of course, must realise that traffic will be coming in an opposite direction from the one to which they are used. By law, drivers are only fully obliged to stop when there is a red light. Even then, a lot of drivers will take a calculated risk (your personal safety is not likely to be a high factor in that calculation) and simply not bother to stop. Where there is a crossing, whether or not it has a flashing amber light or a sign saying *Priorité aux Piétons*, most drivers will ignore pedestrians and keep going. It often seems that the green man crossing signal represents nothing more to a Parisian driver than a distinct challenge.

Resources A-Z

Addresses

Paris *arrondissements* are reflected in the postal code, eg. the 5th *arrondissement* 75005, the 12th 75012. The 16th *arrondissement* is subdivided into two sectors, 75016 and 75116. Some business addresses have a more detailed postcode, followed by a Cedex number which indicates the *arrondissement. Bis* or *ter* is the equivalent of 'b' or 'c' after a building number.

Age restrictions

You must be 18 or over to drive, and 18 in order to consume alcohol in a public place. There is no age limit for buying cigarettes. The age of consent for heterosexuals and homosexuals is 15.

Attitude and etiquette

Parisians take manners seriously and are generally more courteous than their reputation may lead you to believe. If someone brushes you accidentally on the Métro they will more often than not say '*pardon*'; you can do likewise, or reply '*C'est pas grave*' (don't worry). If you don't feel sufficiently bilingual to utter those phrases, a humble yet forgiving smile will do the trick. When entering a shop you should say '*Bonjour madame*' or '*Bonjour monsieur*' and when leaving '*au revoir madame*' or '*monsieur*'. Although a great proportion of people who work in shops speak at least some English, Parisians do appreciate it if you try a few words of French in the spirit of friendship, be they only '*Parlez-vous anglais?*'. Everybody who isn't a close friend or relative should be addressed in the polite '*vous*' form: to a French person, addressing a stranger in the familiar '*tu*' form is as shocking as calling one's boss 'sugar'. If you are invited to a *soirée*, arrive with flowers or wine. Try to arrive in a state of reasonable sobriety: the French are often tickled by Brits' alleged propensity for turning up to social engagements drunk.

Business

The best first stop in Paris for anyone initiating business is the Bourse du Commerce or CCIP (*see* **Useful Organisations**, *below*). Banks can refer you to lawyers, accountants and tax consultants. Several US and British banks provide expatriate services.

Conventions & conferences

The leading centre for international trade fairs, Paris hosts over 500 exhibitions a year.

CNIT *2 pl de la Défense, BP 321, 92053 Paris La Défense (01.46.92.28.66/fax 01.46.92.15.78). M° Grande Arche de La Défense.* Mainly computer fairs.

Palais des Congrès *2 pl de la Porte-Maillot, 17th (01.40.68.22.22). M° Porte-Maillot.*

Paris-Expo Porte de Versailles, *15th (01.43.95.37.00/fax 01.53.68.71.71). M° Porte de Versailles.* Paris' biggest exhibition centre, from agriculture to pharmaceuticals.

Parc des Expositions de Paris-Nord Villepinte *SEPNV 60004, 95970 Roissy-Charles de Gaulle. (01.48.63.30.30/ fax 01.48.63.33.70). RER B Parc des Expositions.* Trade fair centre near Roissy airport.

Courier services

Chronopost (*Customer service: 08.03.801.801).* **Branch:** *34 rue Croix des Petits Champs, 1st (01.49.27.90.74). M° Palais Royal.* Open 9am-8pm Mon-Fri; 9am-1pm Sat. **Credit** AmEx, MC, V. This overnight delivery offshoot of the state-run post office is the most widely used service for parcels of up to 30kg.

DHL *59 av d'Iéna, 16th (08.00.20.25.25). M° Iéna.* Open 9am-8pm Mon-Fri; 9am-5pm Sat. **Credit** AmEx, MC, V. Big name in international courier services. **Branch:** *6 rue des Colonnes, 2nd.*

Europstar *(01.41.31.40.30/fax 01.41.31.40.56).* **Open** 8.30am-7.30pm Mon-Fri, deliveries until 9pm. **No credit cards**. A local bike messenger company with later operating hours than most.

Secretarial services

ADECCO International *4 pl de la Défense, 92974 Paris La Défense (01.49.01.94.94/ fax 01.49.01.45.09). M° Grande Arche de La Défense.* **Open** 8.30am-12.30pm,2-6.30pm Mon-Fri. This branch of the large international employment agency specialises in bilingual secretaries and office staff – permanent or temporary.

Translators & interpreters

Certain documents, from birth certificates to loan applications, must be translated by certified legal translators, listed at the CCIP (*see below*) or embassies. For business translations there are dozens of reliable independents.

Association des Anciens Elèves de L'Esit *(01.44.05.41.46).* **Open** by phone only 9am-6pm Mon-Fri. A translation and interpreting cooperative whose 1,000 members are graduates of L'Ecole Supérieure d'Interprètes et de Traducteurs.

International Corporate Communication *3 rue des Batignolles, 17th (01.43.87.29.29/ fax 01.45.22.49.13). M° Place de Clichy.* **Open** 9am-1pm, 2-6pm Mon-Fri. Translators of financial and corporate documents plus simultaneous translation services.

Useful organisations

American Chamber of Commerce *104 rue Miromesnil, 8th (01.53.89.11.00/ www.faccparisfrance.com). M° Villiers.*

British Embassy Commercial Library *35 rue du Fbg-St-Honoré, 8th (01.44.51.34.56/ fax 01.44.51.34.01, www.ambgrandebretagne.fr). M° Concorde.* **Open** 10am-1pm, 2.30-5pm Mon-Fri, by appointment.

Climate

Month	Average monthly Temperature:		Average monthly Rainfall:	
	Centigrade	Fahrenheit	mm	inches
January	7.5º	45.5º	56	2.0
February	7.1º	44.8º	42	1.7
March	10.2º	50.4º	36	1.4
April	15.7º	60.3º	40	1.6
May	16.6º	61.9º	56	2.2
June	23.4º	74.1º	52	2.0
July	25.1º	77.2º	58	2.3
August	25.6º	78.1º	60	2.4
September	20.9º	69.6º	53	2.1
October	16.5º	61.7º	48	1.8
November	11.7º	53.1º	48	1.8
December	7.8º	46.0º	48	1.8

Stocks trade directories, and assists British companies that wish to develop or set up in France.

Bourse du Commerce
2 rue de Viarmes, 1st (01.55.65.39.27). Mº Louvre-Rivoli or RER Châtelet-Les Halles. **Open** 9am-5pm Mon-Fri.
Business information clearing house, including a *Centre de Formalités* to facilitate filings.

Chambre de Commerce et d'Industrie Franco-Britannique *31, rue Boissy d'Anglas, 8th (01.53.30.81.30/ fax 01.53.30.81.35/ www.francobritishchamber.com). Mº Madeleine.* **Open** 2-5pm Mon-Fri. This organisation promotes contacts through conferences and luncheons. Annual membership is a cool €221.05. Enquiries library provides information including British Interests in Ile de France.

Centre de Formation
8 rue de la Michodière, 2nd (01.42.68.79.95). Mº Opéra. **Open** 9am-7pm Mon-Thur; 9am-5pm Fri; 9am-1pm Sat.
Run by the CCIFB. This institution runs French and English courses in business communication.

CCIP (Chambre de Commerce et d'Industrie de Paris) *27 av de Friedland, 8th (01.55.65.55.65/ fax 01.42.89.78.68/ www.ccip.fr). Mº George V.* **Open** 9am-6pm Mon-Fri. A huge organisation providing services for businesses. In the same building is an information centre,

and the best business library in the city (open 1-6pm; €7.62 per day; €45.73 per year). Its very useful publication *Business and Commerce Undertaken by Non-French Nationals* (for small businesses) in English, costs €7.32. Trade and export information is available on Minitel 3615 CCIP.

US Embassy Commercial Section *4 av Gabriel, 8th (library 01.43.12.25.32/fax 01.43.12.21.72). Mº Concorde.* **Open** 9am-6pm Mon-Fri, by appointment. Business library provides advice on US companies in France, as well as contacts and information. Minitel 3617 USATRADE will respond to all enquiries within 24 hours (Mon-Fri).

Customs

There are no limits on the quantity of goods you can take from one EU country to another for personal use, provided tax has been paid in the country of origin.

Quantities accepted as being for personal use are:
• 800 cigarettes, 400 small cigars, 200 cigars or 1kg loose tobacco.
• 10 litres of spirits (over 22% alcohol), 90 litres of wine (under 22% alcohol) or 110 litres of beer.

For goods from outside the EU:
• 200 cigarettes, 100 small cigars, 50 cigars or 250g loose tobacco.

• 1 litre of spirits (over 22% alcohol) or 2 litres of wine and beer (under 22% alcohol)
• 50g perfume
Visitors can carry up to €7,600 in currency.

Tax refunds

Non-EU residents can claim a refund (average 13%) on VAT if they spend over €182.94 in any one shop, and if they've been in the country less than three months. At the shop ask for a *détaxe* form, and when you leave France have it stamped by customs. Then send the stamped form back to the shop, who will refund the tax, either by bank transfer or by crediting your credit card. *Détaxe* does not cover food, drink, antiques or works of art.

Disabled travellers

An excellent English-language guide, *Access in Paris*, by Gordon Couch and Ben Roberts (Quiller Press), is available for £6.95 (including UK postage) from RADAR, Unit 12, City Forum, 250 City Road, London EC1V 8AS (+44 (0)207 250 3222).

The Comité national de liaison pour la réadaptation des handicapés
(CNRH) 236bis rue de Tolbiac, 13th (01.53.80.66.63) publishes a free guide to Paris for the disabled in English or French, called Paris et Ile-de-France Pour Tous; to order from abroad send a Eurocheque for €3.06 to cover P&P.

Association des paralysés de France *22 rue du Père-Guérain, 13th (01.44.16.83.83). Mº Place d'Italie.* **Open** 9am-12.30pm, 1.30-6pm Mon-Fri. Publishes *Guide 98 Musées, Cinémas* (€3.81) listing cinemas and museums accessible to those with limited mobility.

Platforme d'accueil et d'information des personnes handicapées de la Marie de Paris has a Freephone 08.00.03.37.48 which gives advice (in French) to disabled persons living in or visiting Paris. The Office de Tourisme's website **www.paristourismoffice.com** gives information for disabled visitors. We've put wheelchair access in the listings where applicable, but it's always wise to check beforehand. Other places are accessible to wheelchair users but do not have accessible or specialised toilets.

Getting around

Neither the Métro nor buses are wheelchair-accessible, except Métro line 14 (Méteor), bus lines 20, PC (Petite Ceinture) and some No 91s. Forward seats on buses are intended for people with poor mobility. RER lines A and B and some SNCF trains are wheelchair-accessible in parts. All Paris taxis are obliged by law to take passengers in wheelchairs. The following offer adapted transport for the disabled. You should book 48 hours in advance.

Aihrop *(01.41.29.01.29)*. **Open** 8am-noon, 1.30-6pm Mon-Fri. Transport to and from the airports.

GiHP *24 av Henri Barbusse, 93000 Bobigny (01.41.83.15.15)*. **Open** 7am-8pm Mon-Fri.

Drugs

French police have the power to stop and search anyone; it's always wise to keep any prescription drugs in their original containers, and, if possible, to carry copies of the original prescriptions. If you're caught in possession of illegal drugs you can expect a prison sentence and/or a fine. If you experience any kind of drug-consumption-related emergency, contact or visit: Centre Hospitalier Ste-Anne, *1 rue Cabanis, 14th (01.45.65.80.64). Mº Glacière.* Hôpital Marmottan, *17-19 rue d'Armaillé, 17th (01.45.74.00.04). Mº Argentine.* The best phone service for help with drug problems is **SOS Drogue International** *(01.43.13.14.35* or *01.43.13.14.35)*. **Centre DIDRO** (01.45.42.75.00) is an excellent source of advice for young people with drug problems.

Electricity & gas

Electricity in France runs on 220V. Visitors with British 240V appliances can change the plug or use an adapter (*adaptateur*), available at better hardware

shops. For US 110V appliances, you will need to use a transformer (*transformateur*) available at the Fnac and Darty chains or in the basement of BHV. Gas and electricity are supplied by the state-owned Electricité de France-Gaz de France. Contact EDF-GDF (01.45.44.64.64/www.edf.fr/ www.gazdefrance.com) about supply, bills, or in case of power failures or gas leaks.

Education

Language
Alliance Française *101 bd Raspail, 6th (01.42.84.90.00). Mº St-Placide or Notre Dame des Champs.* **Fees** enrolment €38.11; €248.49-€496.98 per month. A highly regarded, non-profit French-language school, with beginners and specialist courses starting every month, plus a *médiathèque*, film club and lectures. A very good means of making new friends from around the world and developing one's social life.

Berlitz France *38 av de l'Opéra, 2nd (01.44.94.50.00). Mº Opéra.* **Fees** €579.31-€3,811.23. Well known and effective classes; mainly used by businesses.

British Institute *11 rue Constantine, 7th (01.44.11.73.73/70). Mº Invalides.* **Fees** €259.16-€1,036.65 per term. Linked to London University, the 4,000-student Institute offers both English courses for Parisians, and French courses (not beginner) in translation, commercial French, film and literature. It is possible to study for a three-year French degree from the University of London (details from Senate House, Malet Street, London WC1/0207-636 8000, 9am-1pm).

Ecole Eiffel *3 rue Crocé-Spinelli, 14th. (01.43.20.37.41/ fax 01.43.20.49.13). Mº Pernety.* **Fees** €160.07-€442.10 per month. Intensive classes, business French, and phonetics.

Eurocentres *13 passage Dauphine, 6th (01.40.46.72.00). Mº Odéon.* **Fees** four weeks €1,240.94. This international group offers intensive classes for up to 13 students. Courses emphasise communication and include a *médiathèque*.

Institut Catholique de Paris *12 rue Cassette, 6th (01.44.39.52.68). Mº St-Sulpice.* **Fees** enrolment €76.22 (dossier test); registration €571.68; 15-week course (6 hrs per week) €617.42. Reputable school offers traditional courses in French language and culture. The equivalent of a *bac* is required, plus proof of residence. Students must be 18 or above, but don't have to be Catholic.

Institut Parisien *87 bd de Grenelle, 15th (01.40.56.09.53). Mº La Motte Picquet-Grenelle.* **Fees** enrolment €38.11; 15 hours per week €164.64 per term; 25 hours per week €274.41 per term. This dynamic private school offers courses in language and French civilisation, business French, plus evening courses if there's enough demand. Except for beginners, you can enrol all year.

La Sorbonne – Cours de Langue et Civilisation *47 rue des Ecoles, 5th (01.40.46.22.11 ext 2664/75). Mº Cluny-La Sorbonne/RER Luxembourg.* **Fees** €564.06-€1,981.84 per term. Classes for foreigners at the Sorbonne ride on the name of this eminent institution. Teaching is grammar-based. The main course includes lectures on French art, history and literature. Courses are open to anyone over 18, and fill up very quickly.

Specialised
American University of Paris *31 av Bosquet, 7th (01.40.62.07.20). RER Pont de l'Alma.* **Fees** €15,854.70 per year. Established in 1962, the AUP is an international college awarding four-year American liberal arts degrees (BA/BSc). It has exchange agreements with colleges in the US, Poland and Japan. A Summer Session and Division of Continuing Education (102 rue St-Dominique, 7th/ 01.40.62.05.76) are also offered.

Christie's Education Paris *Hôtel Salomon de Rothschild, 8 rue Berryer, 8th (01.42.25.10.90). Mº George V.* The international auction house offers a one-year diploma in French fine and decorative art (*Sept-June*; €8,357.26), shorter courses on Modern Art (*Apr-June*; €2,548.95) and an evening photography course (*Feb-Apr*; €381.12), based on a combination of lectures and visits (in French). New in 2002 is a four-day course in English on the art of living at the court of Louis XIV.

Cours d'Adultes *Information: Hôtel de Ville, pl de l'Hôtel de Ville, 4th (01.44.61.16.16). Mº Hôtel de Ville.* **Fees** €60.98 per term. A huge range of inexpensive adult-education classes are run by the City of Paris.

CIDD Découverte du Vin *30 rue de la Sablière, 14th (01.45.45.44.20). Mº Pernéty.* Fees from €66.32 (for 3 hrs). Wine tasting and appreciation courses (some in English) from beginner to advanced.

Cordon Bleu *8 rue Léon-Delhomme, 15th (01.53.68.22.50). Mº Vaugirard.* **Fees** €36.59-€6,387.61. Three-hour sessions on classical and regional cuisine, one-week workshops and ten-week courses aimed at those refining skills or embarking on a culinary career.

Ritz-Escoffier Ecole de Gastronomie Française *38 rue Cambon, 1st (01.43.16.31.43/ www.ritzparis.com). Mº Madeleine.* **Fees** €44.21-€10,823.88. From afternoon demonstrations in the Ritz kitchens to 12-week diplomas. Courses are in French with English translation. Attendance is a very good way to impress the ladies, fellas.

Ecole du Louvre *Porte Jaugard, Aile de Flore, Palais du Louvre, quai du Louvre, 1st (01.55.35.19.35).* **Fees** €216.48-€266.79. This prestigious school runs art history and archaeology courses. Foreign students not wanting to take a degree (*Licence*) can enrol (May-Sept) to attend lectures.

INSEAD *bd de Constance, 77305 Fontainebleau (01.60.72.40.00).* Fees €27,898.17. Highly regarded international business school, with 520 students from across theworld, offers a ten-month MBA in English. Not a bad place to name-drop on your CV (but only if you've actually been here).

Parsons School of Design *14 rue Letellier, 15th (01.45.77.39.66). Mº La Motte-Picquet-Grenelle.* **Fees** €45.73

registration; 8 sessions €304.90-€381.12. Subsidiary of New York art college offers courses in fine art, fashion, photography, computer, interior and communication design.

Spéos – Paris Photographic Institute *7 rue Jules-Vallès, 11th (01.40.09.18.58). Mº Charonne.* **Fees** €68.60-5,640.61. Bilingual photo school affiliated with the Rhode Island School of Design.

Students & unions

Cartes de séjour and housing benefit

Take a deep breath before you read this lot: it may be worth your while, though. Foreign students wishing to qualify for housing benefit or to work legally during their course in Paris must get a *Carte de Séjour*. You need to present your passport or national identity card; proof of residence; an electricity bill; student card; student social security card; visa (if applicable); a bank statement, accompanied by a parental letter (in French) proving that you receive at least €381.12 per month. Add to this three black-and-white passport photos. Expect the *Carte de Séjour* to take around two months.You may then (note the 'may' – French bureaucracy works in mysterious ways) be eligible for the ALS (*Allocation Logement à Caractère Social*), which is handled by three CAFs, by *arrondissement*. Depending on their living situation, students may receive an ALS benefit of €91.47-€152.45 a month.

Centre de Réception des Etudiants Etrangers (non-EU students) *13 rue Miollis, 15th (01.53.71.51.68). Mº Cambronne.* **Open** 9am-4pm Mon-Fri.

Préfecture de Police de Paris (EU Students) *7 bd du Palais, 4th (01.53.71.51.68). Mº Cité.* **Open** 8.30am-4pm Mon-Fri.

CAF (Centre de Gestion des Allocations Familiales) *101 rue Nationale, 13th (01.40.77.58.00). Mº Natuionale; 18 rue Viala, 15th (01.45.75.62.47). Mº Dupleix; 67 av Jean-Jaurès, 19th (01.44.84.74.98). Mº Laumière.* **Open** 8.30am-4pm/5.30pm Mon-Fri.

Student accommodation

The simplest budget accommodation for medium-to-long stays are the Cité Universitaire or *foyers* (student hostels). Another option, which is more common for women than men, is a *chambre contre travail* – free board in exchange for childcare, housework or English lessons. Look out for ads at language schools and the American Church. For cheap hotels and youth hostels, *see chapter* **Accommodation**. As students often cannot provide proof of income, a *porte-garant* (guarantor) is required who must write a letter (in French) declaring that he/she guarantees payment of rent and bills.

Cité Universitaire *19 bd Jourdan, 14th (01.42.53.51.44). RER Cité Universitaire.* **Open** offices 9am-3pm Mon-Fri. Foreign students enrolled on a university course, or current *stagiaires* who have done two years of career work, can apply for a place at this campus of halls of residence in the south of Paris. Excellent facilities, funky themed architecture and a friendly atmosphere compensate for basic rooms. Rooms must be booked for the entire academic year. Rents are around €259.16-€335.39 per month for a single room, €182.94-1,€247.73 per person for a double. Prices vary according to which *maison* you live in. UK citizens must apply to the Collège Franco-Britannique, and Americans to the Fondation des Etats-Unis.

UCRIF (Union des centres de rencontres internationales de France) office: *27 rue de Turbigo, 2nd (01.40.26.57.64/ www.ucrif.asso.fr). Mº Les Halles.* **Open** 9am-6pm Mon-Fri.Operates cheap, short-stay hostels. It has three help centres: 5th (01 43.29.34.80); 13th (01.43.36.00.63); 14th (01.43.13.17.00).

Student employment

EU students can legally work up to 30hrs per week. Non-EU members studying in Paris may apply for an *autorisation provisoire de travail* after one year to work a 20hr week.

CIDJ (Centre d'information et de documentation jeunesse)

101 quai Branly, 15th (01.44.49.12.00). M° Bir-Hakeim/ RER Champ de Mars. **Open** 9.30am-6pm Mon-Fri; 9.30am-1pm Sat.

The CIDJ is not a form of mad cow disease but is, in fact, mainly a library giving students advice on courses and careers. It also houses the youth bureau of ANPE (Agence Nationale Pour l'Emploi), the state employment service, which provides assistance with job applications. Many ANPE job offers are part-time or on the menial side, but divisions do exist for professional jobs.

Student & youth discounts

Despite Paris' expensive reputation, a wide range of student discounts makes budget living possible. To claim the *tarif étudiant* (around €1.52 off some cinema seats, up to 50% off museums and standby theatre tickets), you must have a French student card or an International Student Identity Card (ISIC), available from CROUS, student travel agents and the Cité Universitaire. ISIC cards are only valid in France if you are under 26. Under-26s can get up to 50% off rail travel on certain trains with the SNCF's Carte 12/25.

Universities

Registration in Paris universities takes about three weeks; each course has to be signed up for separately, and involves queueing at a different office to obtain a reading list.

CROUS (Centre régional des oeuvres universitaires et scolaires) *39 av Georges-Bernanos, 5th (01.40.51.36.00/ Service du Logement 01.40.51.37.17/21, fax 01.40.51.37.19). RER Port-Royal.* **Open** 9am-5pm Mon-Fri.

Manages all University of Paris student residences. Most rooms are single-occupancy (around €114.34 month). Requests for rooms must be made by 1 April for the next academic year. CROUS posts ads for rooms and has a list of hostels, some of which

overlap with UCRIF. In summer, university residences are open to under-26s (around €15.24 per night).

CROUS also issues the ISIC card, organises excursions, sports and cultural events, provides information on jobs, and offers discount theatre, cinema and concert tickets. It is the clearing house for all *bourses* (grants) issued to foreign students. Call the Service des Bourses on 01.40.51.35.50.

Useful organisations

Exchange schemes

Socrates-Erasmus Programme

Britain: *UK Socrates-Erasmus Council, RND Building, The University, Canterbury, Kent CT2 7PD (0122-7762712).* **France:** *Agence Erasmus, 10 pl de la Bourse, 33080 Bordeaux Cedex (05.56.79.44.00).*

The Socrates-Erasmus scheme enables EU students with reasonable written and spoken French to spend a year of their degree following appropriate courses in the French university system. The UK office publishes a brochure and helps with general enquiries, but applications must be made through the Erasmus Co-ordinator at your home university. Non-EU students should find out from their university whether it has an agreement with the French university system such as the US 'Junior Year Abroad' scheme via **MICEFA** (26 rue du Fbg-St-Jacques, 14th/01.40.51.76.96).

Resto-U

3 rue Mabillon, 6th (01.43.25.66.23). M° Mabillon. **Open** 11.30am-2pm, 6-8pm Mon-Fri. **No credit cards.**

A chain of cheap university canteens run by CROUS. If you have a student card from a Paris university you can buy a carnet of 10 tickets for €23.32.

Embassies & consulates

There's a full list of embassies and consulates in the *Pages Jaunes* (or www.pagesjaunes.fr) under '*Ambassades et Consulats*'.

Consular services are for citizens of that country (passport matters, etc) while a separate visa service operates for foreign nationals applying for visas. Since the 11 September 2001 terrorist attacks, the US and UK embassies are under particularly strict security. Horseplay in the vicinity of either is not recommended.

Australian Embassy *4 rue Jean-Rey, 15th (01.40.59.33.00/ www.austgov.fr). M° Bir-Hakeim.* **Consular services** 9.15am-noon, 2-4.30pm Mon-Fri; **Visas** 10am-12am Mon-Fri.

British Embassy *35 rue du Fbg-St-Honoré, 8th (01.44.51.31.00/www.amb-grandebretagne.fr). M° Concorde.* **Consular services** *18bis rue d'Anjou, 8th.* **Open** 9.30am-12.30pm, 2.30-5pm Mon, Wed-Fri; 9.30am-4.30pm Tue. **Visas** *16 rue d'Anjou, 8th (01.44.51.33.01/ 01.44.51.33.03).* **Open** 9.30am-noon Mon-Fri.

Canadian Embassy *35 av Montaigne, 8th (01.44.43.29.00/ www.amb-canada.fr). M° Franklin D. Roosevelt.* **Consular services** appointments 2.30-4.30pm Mon-Fri. **Visas** *37 av Montaigne (01.44.43.29.16).* **Open** 8.30-11am Mon-Fri.

Irish Embassy *12 av Foch, 16th.* **Consulate** *4 rue Rude, 16th (01.44.17.67.00). M° Charles de Gaulle-Etoile.* **Open** for visits 9.30am-noon Mon-Fri; by phone 9.30am-1pm, 2.30-5.30pm Mon-Fri.

New Zealand Embassy *7ter rue Léonard de Vinci, 16th (01.45.01.43.43/ www.nzembassy.com/france). M° Victor-Hugo.* **Open** 9am-1pm, 2pm-5.30pm Mon-Fri. July/Aug 8.30am-1pm, 2-5.30pm Mon-Thur; 8.30am-2pm Fri. **Visas** 9am-12.30pm Mon-Fri (*www.nzis.org).*

South African Embassy *59 quai d'Orsay, 7th (01.53.59.23.23/ www.afriquesud.net). M° Invalides.* **Open** 8.30am-5.15pm Mon-Fri, by appointment. **Consulate and visas** 8.30am-noon.

US Embassy *2 av Gabriel, 8th (01.43.12.22.22.www.amb-usa.fr). M° Concorde.* **Consulate/Visas** *2 rue St-Florentin, 1st (01.43.12.22.22). M° Concorde.* **Passport service** 9am-12.30pm, 1-3pm Mon-Fri. **Visas** phone between 2-5pm for an appointment.

Emergencies

Most of the following services operate 24 hours a day. In a real medical emergency such as a road accident, call the Sapeurs-Pompiers, who have trained paramedics.

Police	**17**
Fire (Sapeurs-Pompiers)	**18**
Ambulance (SAMU)	**15**
Emergency	
(from a mobile phone)	**112**
GDF (gas leaks)	0 810.433.275
EDF (electricity)	0 811.126.126
Centre	
anti-poison	01.40.05.48.48

See also **Health: Accident & Emergency, Doctors; Helplines**.

Health

All EU nationals staying in France are entitled to use of the French Social Security system, which refunds up to 70% of medical expenses (but sometimes much less, eg. for dental treatment). To get a refund, British nationals should obtain form E111 before leaving the UK (or E112 for those already in treatment). Nationals of non-EU countries should take out insurance before leaving home. Consultations and prescriptions have to be paid for in full, and are reimbursed, in part, on receipt of a completed *fiche*. If you undergo treatment the doctor will give you a prescription and a *feuille de soins* (statement of treatment). The medication will carry little stickers which you must stick onto your *feuille de soins*. Send this, the prescription and form E111, to the local **Caisse Primaire d'Assurance Maladie**. Refunds can take over a month to come through.

Accident and emergency

Following are listed most of the Paris hospitals that have 24-hour accident and emergency departments:

Hôpital d'Instruction des Armées du Val de Grâce, 5th *(01.40.51.45.08)*; Hôpital Lariboisière, 10th *(01.49.95.64.43)*; Hôpital St-Louis, 10th *(01.42.49.91.17)*; Hôpital d'Enfants Armand Trousseau, 12th *(01.44.73.60.10)*; Centre Hospitalier Ste-Anne, 14th, *(01.44.12.37.86)*; Hôpital St-Vincent de Paul, 14th *(01.40.48.81.33)*; Hôpital Robert Debré, 19th, *(01.40.03.22.73)*. For a complete list of Parisian hospitals consult the *Pages Blanches* under *Hôpital Assistance Publique*, or ring 01.40.27.30.00/ 01.40.27.30.52.

Specialisations

Burns: Hôpital Cochin, *27 rue du Fbg-St-Jacques, 14th (01.58.41.41.41)*. Mº St-Jacques/RER Port-Royal. Hôpital St-Antoine, *184 rue du Fbg-St-Antoine, 12th (01.49.28.26.09)*. Mº Faidherbe-Chaligny or Reuilly-Diderot. **Open** 24-hr.

Children: Hôpital St Vincent de Paul, *74 av Denfert Rochereau (01.40.48.81.11)*. Mº Denfert-Rochereau. Hôpital Necker, *149 rue de Sèvres, 15th (01.44.49.40.00)*. Mº Duroc. **Open** 24-hr.

Children's Burns: Hôpital Armand-Trousseau, *26 av du Dr-Arnold-Netter, 12th (01.44.73.74.75)*. Mº Bel-Air.

Poisons: Hôpital Fernand Widal, *200 rue du Fbg-St-Denis, 10th (01.40.05.48.48)*. Mº Gare du Nord. **Open** 24-hr.

American Hospital in Paris

63 bd Victor-Hugo, 92202 Neuilly (01.46.41.25.25). Mº Porte Maillot, then bus 82. **Open** 24-hr. A private hospital. Please note that French Social Security will refund only a small percentage of treatment costs. All medical staff speak English.

Hertford British Hospital

(Hôpital Franco-Britannique) *3 rue Barbès, 92300 Levallois-Perret (01.46.39.22.22)*. Mº Anatole-France. **Open** 24-hr. Most of the medical staff speak English.

Complementary medicine

Académie d'homéopathie et des médecines douces

2 rue d'Isly, 8th (01.43.87.60.33). Mº St-Lazare. **Open** 10am-6pm Mon-Fri. Health services include acupuncture, aromatherapy and homeopathy.

Association française d'acuponcture *3 rue de l'Arrivée, 15th (01.43.20.26.26)*. Mº Montparnasse-Bienvenüe. **Open** 8.30am-12.30pm, 1.30-5.30pm Mon-Thur; 8.30am-4.30pm Fri. Lists professional acupuncturists.

Contraception

To obtain the pill (*la pilule*) or the coil (*stérilet*), you need a prescription, available on appointment from the first two places below or from a *médecin généraliste* (GP) or gynaecologist. Note that the morning-after pill (*la pilule du lendemain*) is available from pharmacies without prescription and is not reimbursed. Spermicides and condoms (*préservatifs*) are sold in pharmacies, and there are condom machines in Métros, club lavatories and on street corners.

Centre de planification et d'éducation familiales *27 rue Curnonsky, 17th (01.48.88.07.28)*. Mº Porte de Champerret. **Open** 9am-5pm Mon-Fri. Free consultations on family planning and abortion. Abortion counselling on demand; otherwise phone for an appointment. For tests you will be sent to a laboratory.

MFPF (Mouvement français pour le planning familial) *10 rue Vivienne, 2nd (01.42.60.93. 20)*. Mº Bourse. **Open** 9.30am-5pm Mon-Fri. Phone for an appointment for contraception advice and prescriptions. For abortion advice, just turn up at the centre. **Branch:** 94 bd Masséna, 13th (01.45.84.28.25/ open 10.30am-3.30pm Fri only).

Dentists

Dentists are found in the *Pages Jaunes* under *Dentistes*. For emergencies contact:

Urgences Dentaires de Paris

(01.42.61.12.00). **Open** 8am-10pm Sun, holidays. For emergency dental appointments.

SOS Dentaire *87 bd Port-Royal, 13th (01.43.37.51.00)*. Mº Gobelins, RER Port-Royal. **Open** 9.45am-midnight daily. Telephone service for emergency dental care.

Directory

**Hôpital de la Pitié-
Salpêtrière** *47 bd de l'Hôpital,
13th (01.42.16.00.00). M° St-
Marcel.* **Open** 24-h. For
emergency dental care when the
above services are closed.

Doctors

A complete list of general
practitioners is in the *Pages
Jaunes* under *Médecins: Médecine
générale.* To get a Social Security
refund, choose a doctor or dentist
registered with the state system;
look for *Médecin Conventionné*
after the name. Consultations cost
€17.53 upwards, of which a
proportion can be reimbursed.
Seeing a specialist rather than a
generalist costs more.

Centre Médical Europe
*44 rue d'Amsterdam, 9th
(01.42.81.93.33/* dentists
01.42.81.80.00). M° St-Lazare.
Open 8am-7pm Mon-Fri; 8am-
6pm Sat.
Practitioners in all fields under
one roof, charging minimal
consultation fees (€17.53
for foreigners).

House calls

SOS Infirmiers (Nurses)
*(01.43.57.01.26/06.08.34.08.92/
01.40.24.22.23).* House calls 8pm-
midnight; daytime Sat-Sun; the
cost is generally €22.87.

SOS Médecins *(01.47.07.77.77/
01.43.37.77.77).* A home visit is
€42.69 if you don't have French
Social Security; €22.87 if you do,
before 7pm; from €47.26 after.

Urgences Médicales de Paris
(01.53.94.94.94). Doctors make
house calls around the clock. Some
speak English, but don't assume
that they are all fluent, so prepare
to explain your problem simply.

Opticians

Branches of Alain Afflelou and
Lissac are abundant. They stock
hundreds of frames and can make
prescription glasses within the
hour. For an eye test you will
need to go to an *ophtalmologiste*
– ask the optician for a list of
those in the area.

SOS Optique (01.48.07.22.00/
www.sos-optique.com). 24-hr
repair service. Glasses repaired at
your home by a certified optician.

Pharmacies

Pharmacies sport a green neon
cross. They have a monopoly on
issuing medication, and also sell
sanitary products. Most open
9am/10am-7pm/8pm. Staff can
provide basic medical services
like disinfecting and bandaging
wounds (for a small fee) and will
indicate the nearest doctor on
duty. French pharmacists are
highly trained; you can often
avoid visiting a doctor by
describing your symptoms and
seeing what they suggest. Paris
has a rota system of *pharmacies
de garde* at night and on Sunday.
A closed pharmacy will have a
sign indicating the nearest open
pharmacy. Toiletries and
cosmetics are often cheaper
in supermarkets

Night pharmacies

Pharma Presto
(01.42.42.42.50). **Open** 24-hr.
Delivery charge €38.11 from
8am-6pm; €53.36 6pm-8am.
Delivers prescription medication
(non-prescription exceptions can
be made), in association with
Dérhy.

Pharmacie des Halles
*10 bd de Sébastopol, 4th
(01.42.72.03.23). M° Châtelet.*
Open 9am-midnight Mon-Sat;
9am-10pm Sun.

**Dérhy/Pharmacie des
Champs** *84 av des Champs-
Elysées, 8th (01.45.62.02.41).
M° George V.* **Open** 24-hr.

Matignon *2 rue Jean-Mermoz,
8th (01.43.59.86.55).* M° Franklin
D. Roosevelt. **Open** 8.30am-2am
daily.

**Pharmacie Européenne de la
Place de Clichy** *6 pl de Clichy,
9th (01.48.74.65.18). M° Place de
Clichy.* **Open** 24-hr.

**Pharmacie de la Place de la
Nation** *13 pl de la Nation, 11th
(01.43.73.24.03). M° Nation.*
Open 8am-midnight daily.

Pharmacie d'Italie *61 av
d'Italie, 13th (01.44.24.19.72).
M° Tolbiac.* **Open** 8am-midnight
Mon-Sat; 9am-midnight Sun.

STDs, HIV & AIDS

AIDES *52 rue du Fbg-Poissonière,
10th (01.53.24.12.00). M° Bonne.
Nouvelle.* **Open** 2-6pm Mon-Fri.

Volunteers provide support for
AIDS patients.

Le Kiosque Info Sida
*36 rue Geoffroy l'Asnier, 4th
(01.44.78.00.00). M° St-Paul.*
Open Mon-Fri 10am-7pm; 2pm-
7pm Sat. Youth association offering
info on AIDS, youth and health.

**Dispensaire de la Croix
Rouge** *43 rue de Valois, 1st
(01.42.61.30.04). M° Palais-Royal.*
Centre specialising in sexually
transmitted diseases offers safe,
anonymous HIV tests (*dépistages*),
free consultation. Make an
appointment on 01.42.97.48.29.

FACTS *(01.44.93.16.69).* Open 6-
10pm Mon, Wed, Fri. English-
speaking crisis line gives info and
support for those touched by
HIV/AIDS and runs groups for
friends and relatives.

SIDA Info Service
(08.00.84.08.00). **Open** 24-hr.
Confidential AIDS-information in
French (some bilingual
counsellors).

Helplines

SOS Dépression
(01.45.22.44.44). People listen
and/or give advice, and can send
a counsellor or psychiatrist to
your home in case of a crisis.

SOS Help *(01.47.23.80.80).*
English-language helpline
3-11pm daily.

**Alcoholics Anonymous in
English** *(01.46.34.59.65/
www.aaparis.org).* 24-hour
recorded message gives details
of AA meetings at the American
Church or Cathedral (*see p384,*
Religion*)* and members' phone
numbers for more information.

Narcotics Anonymous
(01.48.58.38.46/ 01.48.58.50.61).
Meetings in English three times
a week.

The Counseling Center
(01.47.23.61.13) English-
language counselling service,
based at the American Cathedral.

SOS Avocats *(08.03.39.33.00).*
Open 7-11.30pm Mon-Fri. Free
legal advice by phone.

SOS Racisme *28 rue des Petites
Ecuries, 10th (01.53.24.67.67).
M° Château d'Eau.* **Open**
9.30am-1pm, 2-6pm Mon-Fri.
A non-profit association defending
the rights of ethnic minorities.

Directory

ID

French law demands that some form of identification is carried at all times. Be ready to produce a passport or *Carte de Séjour* in response to that old police refrain *'Papiers, s'il vous plaît'.*

Insurance

See p377, **Health.**

Internet

After a slow start, use has skyrocketed. It is now possible get cable access in most of Paris.

ISPs

Noosnet (08.25.34.54.74/ 08.00.114.114/www.noos.com).

America Online (freephone 01.71.71.71.71/ www.aol.fr)

Club-Internet (01.55.45.46.47/ www.club-internet.fr)

CompuServe (08.03.00.60.00/ www.compuserve.fr)

Imaginet (01.43.38.10.24/ www.imaginet.fr)

Microsoft Network (08.01.63.34.34/www.fr.msn.com)

Wanadoo (France Télécom) (08.01.63.34.34/www.wanadoo.fr)

Internet access

Café Orbital *13 rue de Médicis, 6th (01.43.25.76.77). RER Luxembourg.* **Open** 10am-9pm Mon-Sat; noon-8pm Sun.

Clickside *14 rue Domat, 5th (01.56.81.03.00). Mº Maubert-Mutualité.* **Open** 10am-midnight Mon-Fri; 1pm-11pm Sat-Sun.

Cyber Café Latino *13 rue de l'Ecole-Polytechnique, 5th (01.40.51.86.94). Mº Maubert-Mutualité.* **Open** 11.30am-2am Mon-Sat; 4-9pm Sun.

Cyber Cube *12 rue Daval, 11th (01.49.29.67.67). Mº Bastille.* **Open** 10am-10pm Mon-Sat.

easyEverything *31-37 bd de Sébastopol, 1st (01.40.41.09.10) Mº/RER Châtelet-Les Halles.* **Open** 24-hrs.

Most hotels offer Internet access, some from your own room. *See p42,* **Accommodation.**

Language

See p388, **Essential Vocabulary,** and *p184,* **Menu Lexicon,** for food terms.

Legal advice

Mairies can answer some legal enquiries. Phone for times of free *consultations juridiques.*

Direction départementale de la concurrence, de la consommation, et de la répression des fraudes

8 rue Froissart, 3rd (01.40.27.16.00). Mº St-Sébastien-Froissart. **Open** 9-11.30am, 2-5.30pm Mon-Fri. This subdivision of the Ministry of Finance deals with consumer complaints.

Palais de Justice Galerie de Harlay

Escalier S, 4 bd du Palais, 4th (01.44.32.48.48). Mº Cité. **Open** 9.30am-noon Mon-Fri. Free legal consultation. Arrive early.

Libraries

All *arrondissements* have free public libraries. For a library card, you need ID and two documents proving residency.

American Library

10 rue du Général-Camou, 7th (01.53.59.12.60). Mº Ecole-Militaire/RER Pont de l'Alma. **Open** 10am-7pm Tue-Sat (shorter hours in Aug). **Admission** day pass €10.67; annual €86.90. Claims to be the largest English-language lending library in mainland Europe, and also organises talks and readings. Receives 350 periodicals, plus popular magazines and newspapers (mainly American).

Bibliothèque Historique de la Ville de Paris Hôtel Lamoignon,

24 rue Pavée, 4th (01.44.59.29.40). Mº St-Paul. **Open** 9.30am-6pm Mon-Sat. **Admission** free (bring ID and a passport photo). Reference books and documents on Paris history in a Marais mansion.

Bibliothèque Marguerite Durand

79 rue Nationale, 13th (01.45.70.80.30). Mº Tolbiac or Place d'Italie. **Open** 2-6pm Tue-Sat. **Admission** free. 25,000 books and 120 periodicals on women's history and feminism,

many of which were assembled by feminist pioneer Durand. The collection includes letters of Colette and Louise Michel.

Bibliothèque Nationale de France François Mitterrand

quai François-Mauriac, 13th (01.53.79.55.01). Mº Bibliothèque. **Open** 10am-7pm Tue-Sat; noon-8pm Sun. **Admission** day pass €3.05; annual €30.49. Books, papers and periodicals, plus titles in English, for anyone over 18. An audio-visual room lets you browse photo, film and sound archives.

Bibliothèque Publique d'Information (BPI)

Centre Pompidou, 4th (01.44.78.12.33). Mº Hôtel de Ville/RER Châtelet-Les Halles. **Open** 12am-10pm Mon, Wed-Fri; 11am-10pm Sat, Sun. **Admission** free. Now on three levels, the Centre Pompidou's vast reference library has a huge international press section, reference books and language-learning facilities.

Bibliothèque Ste-Geneviève

10 pl du Panthéon, 5th (01.44.41.97.97). RER Luxembourg. **Open** 10am-10pm Mon-Sat. This reference library, with a spectacular, iron-framed reading room, is open to students over 18. Bring ID and a photo to register (by 6pm).

BIFI (Bibliothèque du Film)

100 rue du Fbg-St-Antoine, 12th (01.53.02.22.30). Mº Ledru-Rollin. **Open** 10am-7pm Mon-Fri. Film buffs' library offers books, magazines film stills and posters, as well as films on video and DVD.

BILIPO (Bibliothèque des Littératures Policières)

48-50 rue du Cardinal-Lemoine, 5th (01.42.34.93.00). Mº Cardinal-Lemoine. **Open** 2-6pm Tue-Fri; 10am-5pm Sat. Non-lending library of crime, spy and detective fiction.

British Council Library

9-11 rue Constantine, 7th (01.49.55.73.23/library@ britishcouncil.fr). Mº Invalides. **Open** 11am-6pm Mon-Fri (until 7pm Wed). **Admission** day pass €6.10; annual €53.36; €44.21 students. Reference and lending library stocks British press and offers an Internet and CD-rom service.

Documentation Française
29 quai Voltaire, 7th (01.40.15.70.00). Mº Rue du Bac. Open 10am-6pm Mon-Wed, Fri; 10am-1pm Thur. The official government archive and central reference library has information on contemporary French politics and economy since 1945.

Locksmiths

Numerous 24-hr emergency repair services deal with plumbing, locks, car repairs and more. Most charge a minimum of €22.87 call-out (déplacement) and €30.49 per hour, plus parts; more on Sunday and at night.

Allô Assistance Dépannage
(08.00.00.00.18). No car repairs.

Numéro Un Dépannage
(01.40.71.55.55). No car repairs.

SOS Dépannage
(01.47.07.99.99). double the price, but claims to be twice as reliable. €48.78 call-out, then €48.78 an hour. 8am-7pm Mon-Sat; nights and Sun €60.98 call out, €60.98 an hour.

Lost property

General

Bureau des Objets Trouvés
36 rue des Morillons, 15th (01.55.76.20.20). Mº Convention. Open 8.30am-5pm Mon, Wed, Fri; 8.30am-8pm Tue, Thur (except July, Aug). Visit in person to fill in a form specifying details of the loss. This may have been the first lost property office in the world, but it is far from the most efficient. Horrendous delays in processing claims mean that if your trip to Paris is short you may need to nominate a proxy to collect found objects after your return, although small items can be posted. If your passport was among the lost items you will need to get a single-entry temporary passport in order to leave the country.

Media

Magazines

Arts & listings

Three pocket-sized publications compete for basic Wed-to-Tue listings information: **Pariscope**

(€0.40), the Parisian cinema-goer's bible, which includes **Time Out Paris** in English; the thinner **Officiel des Spectacles** (€0.35); and new trendy **Zurban** (€0.80). Linked to Radio Nova, monthly **Nova** gives rigorously multi-ethnic information on where to drink, dance or hang out. **Technikart** tries to mix clubbing with the arts. Highbrow TV guide **Télérama** has good arts and entertainment features and a Paris listings insert. *See also below* **Le Monde** *and* **Le Figaro**. There are specialist arts magazines to meet every interest. Film titles include intellectual **Les Cahiers du Cinéma**, glossy **Studio** and younger, celebrity-geared **Première**.

Business

Capital, its sister magazine **Management** and the weightier **L'Expansion** are worthwhile monthlies. **Défis** has tips for the entrepreneur, **Initiatives** is for the self-employed.

English

On the local front, **Time Out Paris** is a six-page supplement inside weekly listings magazine **Pariscope**, available at all news stands, covering selected Paris events, exhibitions, films, concerts and restaurants. The quarterly **Time Out Paris Free Guide** is distributed in bars, hotels and tourist centres and **Time Out Paris Eating & Drinking Guide** is available in newsagents across the city. **FUSAC** (France-USA Contacts) is a small-ads free-sheet with flat rentals, job ads and appliances for sale.

Gossip

Despite strict privacy laws, the French appear to have an almost insatiable appetite for gossip. 1998 saw the arrival of **Oh La!** from Spain's *Hola!* (and UK's *Hello!*) group. **Voici** is France's juiciest scandal sheet whilst **Gala** tells the same stories without the sleaze. **Paris Match** is a French institution founded in 1948, packed with society gossip and celebrity interviews, but still regularly scoops the rest with photo shoots of international affairs. **Point de Vue** specialises in royalty and disdains showbiz fluff. Monthly **Entrevue** tends

toward features on bizarre sexual practices, so is very useful as reference, but still somehow clinches regular exclusives. **Perso** presents the stars as they would like to be seen.

News

Weekly news magazines are an important sector in France, taking the place of weighty Sunday tomes and offering news, cultural sections as well as in-depth reports. Titles range from solidly serious **L'Express** and **Le Point** to the traditionally left-wing **Le Nouvel Observateur** and sardonic, chaotically arranged **Marianne**. Weekly **Courrier International** publishes a fascinating selection of articles from newspapers all over the world, translated into French.

Women, men & fashion

Elle was a pioneer among women's mags and has editions across the globe. In France it is weekly and spot-on for interviews and fashion. Monthly **Marie-Claire** takes a more feminist, campaigning line. Both have design spin-offs (**Elle Décoration**, **Marie-Claire Maison**) and Elle has spawned foodie **Elle à Table**. **DS** aims at the intellectual reader, with lots to read and coverage of social issues. **Vogue**, read both for its fashion coverage and big-name guests, is rivalled when it comes to fashion week by **L'Officiel de la Mode**. The underground go for more radical publications **Purple** (six-monthly art, literature and fashion tome), **Crash**, and the new wave of fashion/lifestyle mags: **WAD** (We Are Different), **Citizen K**, **Jalouse** and **Numéro**. Men's mags include French versions of lad bibles **FHM**, **Maximal**, **Men's Health**, and the naughty **Echo des Savanes**.

Newspapers

The national dailies are characterised by high prices and relatively low circulation. Only 20% of the population reads a national paper; regional dailies hold sway outside Paris. Serious, centre-left daily **Le Monde** is essential reading for business people, politicians and intellectuals, who often also publish articles in it. Despite its highbrow reputation, subject matter is surprisingly eclectic, although international coverage is selective. It also publishes *Aden*, a Wednesday Paris-listings supplement. Founded post-68 by a group that included Sartre and de Beauvoir, trendy **Libération** is now centre-left, but still the read of the *gauche caviar*, worth reading for wide-ranging news and arts coverage and guest columnists. The conservative middle classes go for **Le Figaro**, a daily broadsheet with a devotion to politics, shopping, food and sport. Sales are boosted by lots of property and job ads and the Wednesday *Figaroscope* Paris listings. Saturday's edition contains three magazines which rockets the price from €1 to €4. For business and financial news, the French dailies **La Tribune**, **Les Echos** and the weekly **Investir** are the tried and trusted sources. Tabloid in format, the easy-read **Le Parisien** is strong on consumer affairs, social issues, local news and events and vox pops, and has a Sunday edition. Downmarket **France Soir** has gone tabloid. **La Croix** is a Catholic, right-wing daily. The Communist Party **L'Humanité** has kept going despite the collapse of the Party's colleagues outside France. Sunday broadsheet **Le Journal du Dimanche** comes with *Fémina* mag and a Paris section. **L'Equipe** is a big-selling sports daily with a bias towards football; **Paris-Turf** caters for horse-racing fans.

English papers

The Paris-based **International Herald Tribune** is on sale throughout the city; British dailies, Sundays and **USA Today** are widely available on the day of issue at larger kiosks in the centre.

Satirical papers

Wednesday-published institution **Le Canard Enchaîné** is the Gallic *Private Eye* – in fact it was the inspiration for the *Eye*. It's a broadly left-wing satirical weekly broadsheet that's full of in-jokes and breaks political scandals, but in recent years it has lost some of its bite. **Charlie Hebdo** is mainly bought for its cartoons.

Radio

A quota requiring a minimum of 40% French music has led to overplay of Gallic pop oldies and to the creation of dubious hybrids by local groups that mix some words in French with a refrain in English. Trash-talking phone-in shows also proliferate. Wavelengths are in MHz.

87.8 France Inter State- run, MOR music, international news and Pollen – concerts by rock newcomers.

90.4 Nostalgie As it sounds.

90.9 Chante France 100% French *chanson*.

91.3 Chérie FM Lots of oldies.

91.7/92.1 MHz France Musiques State classical music channel has added an 's' and brought in more *variété* and slush to its highbrow mix of concerts, contemporary bleeps and top jazz. *See also p321* **Maison de Radio France** *in* **Music: Classical & Opera.**

93.1 Aligre From local Paris news to literary chat.

93.5/93.9 France Culture Verbose state culture station: literature, history, cinema and music.

94.8 RCJ/Radio J/Judaïque FM/ Radio Shalom Shared wavelength for Paris' Jewish stations.

95.2 Paris FM Municipal radio: music, traffic and what's on.

96 Skyrock Pop station with loudmouth presenters. Lots of rap.

96.4 BFM Business and economics. Wall Street in English every evening.

96.9 Voltage FM Dance music.

97.4 Rire et Chansons A non-stop diet of jokes – racist, sexist or just plain lousy – and pop oldies.

97.8 Ado Local music station for adolescents.

98.2 Radio FG Gay station. Techno music, rave announcements and very explicit man-to-man lonely hearts.

99 Radio Latina Great Latin and salsa music, increasingly adding *raï,* Spanish and Italian pop.

100.3 NRJ Energy: national leader with the under-30s.

101.1 Radio Classique More classical pops than France Musique, but also less pedagogical.

101.5 Radio Nova Hip hop, trip hop, world, jazz and whatever is hip.

101.9 Fun Radio Now embracing techno alongside Anglo pop hits.

102.3 Ouï FM Ouï rock you.

103.9 RFM Easy listening.

104.3 RTL The most popular French station nationwide mixes music and talk programmes. *Grand Jury* on Sunday is a debate between journalists and a top politician.

104.7 Europe 1 News, press reviews, sports, business, gardening, entertainment, music. Much the best weekday breakfast news broadcast, with politicians interviewed live.

105.1 FIP Traffic bulletins, what's on in Paris and a brilliant mix of jazz, classical, world and pop, known for the seductive-voiced *Fipettes*, its female programme announcers.

105.5 France Info 24-hr news, economic updates and sports bulletins. As everything gets repeated every 15 minutes, it's guaranteed to drive you mad – good though if you're learning French.

106.7 Beur FM Aimed at Paris' North African community

English

You can receive the **BBC World Service** (648 KHz AM) for its English-language international news, current events, pop and drama. Also on 198KHz LW, from midnight to 5.30am daily. At other times this frequency carries **BBC Radio 4** (198 KHz LW), for British news, talk and *The Archers* directed at the home audience. **RFI** (738 KHz AM) has an English-language programme of news and music from 3-4pm daily.

Television

TF1 The country's biggest channel, and first to be privatised in 1987. Game shows, dubbed soaps, gossip and audience debates and football are staples. The latest big draw as been *Star Academy*, in which wannabe stars are shut up in a château. Detective series *Julie Lescaut* is a perennial favourite. The 8pm news has star anchors Patrick Poivre d'Arvor ('PPDA'), and Claire Chazal.

Directory

France 2 State-owned station mixes game shows, chat, documentaries, and the usual of cop series and films.

FR3 The more heavyweight of the two state channels offers lots of regional, wildlife and sports coverage, on-screen debating about social issues, and *Cinéma de Minuit*, late-night Sunday classic films in the original language.

Canal+ Subscription channel draws viewers with recent films (sometimes in the original language), exclusive sport and late-night porn. *The Simpsons* and satirical puppets *Les Guignols* are available unscrambled.

Arte/La Cinquième Franco-German hybrid Arte specialises in intellectual programming. Arte shares its wavelength with educational channel *La Cinquième* (5.45am-7pm).

M6 M6 is winning the 20s and 30s audience, with imports like *Ally McBeal* and the *X-Files* and some excellent homegrown programmes, such as *Culture Pub* (about advertising) and finance mag *Capital*. It broadcast the phenomenally successful reality show *Loft Story*.

Cable TV & satellite

France offers a decent range of cable and satellite channels but content in English remains limited. CNN and BBC World offer round-the-clock news coverage. BBC Prime keeps you up to date on *Eastenders* (omnibus Sun 2pm), while Teva features original-language comedy *Sex and the City*. **Noostv** (08.25.34.54.74/ 08.00.114.114/www.noos.com) offers packages from €9.91 per month. There are more than 135 channels which the customer is free to change each month. Noos is the first cable provider to offer an interactive video service.

Money

The euro

On 1 January 2002 euro currency became the official currency in France. French francs can be exchanged free of charge at most banks and post offices until 30 June 2002, after which only Banque de France will offer free

exchanges (coins until 2005, notes until 2012). The crossover period does not extend to paying in francs on debit and credit cards, or writing cheques: debit and credit card transactions and cheques must be in euros. But you have until the beginning of 2003 to cash cheques written in francs. Foreign debit and credit cards can automatically be used to withdraw and pay in euros. Travellers cheques are also available in euros. To convert roughly from euros to francs:

Take two thirds of the figure in euros and multiply by 10 (eg. Two thirds of €6 is 4; x 10 = 40F)

To convert roughly from francs into euros:

Take the price in francs, add half again and divide by 10 (eg. 40F + 20 = 60; divided by 10 = €6)

Useful euro addresses: Freephone official helpline 08.00.01.20.02 (in service until November 2002). www.euro.gouv.fr. Official website: information, updates and online converter.

ATMs

Withdrawals in euros can be made from bank and post office automatic cash machines. The specific cards accepted are marked on each machine, and most give instructions in English. Credit card companies charge a fee for cash advances, but rates are often better than bank rates.

Banks

French banks usually open 9am-5pm Mon-Fri (some close at lunch 12.30-2.30pm); some banks also open on Sat. All are closed on public holidays, and from noon on the previous day. Note that not all banks have foreign exchange counters. Commission rates vary between banks. The state Banque de France usually offers good rates. Most banks accept travellers cheques, but may be reluctant to accept personal cheques even with the Eurocheque guarantee card, which is not widely used in France.

Bank accounts

To open an account (*ouvrir un compte*), French banks require proof of identity, address and your

Quick Conversion

euro	pound*	dollar*
€0.10	6p	$0.08
€0.50	31p	$0.45
€1	62p	$0.89
€2	£1.24	$1.78
€3	£1.86	$2.67
€4	£2.48	$3.56
€5	£3.09	$4.45
€6	£3.71	$5.33
€7	£4.33	$6.22
€8	£4.95	$7.11
€9	£5.57	$8.00
€10	£6.19	$8.89
€20	£12.38	$17.78
€30	£18.57	$26.67
€40	£24.76	$35.56
€50	£30.95	$44.45
€60	£37.15	$53.34
€70	£43.35	$62.23
€80	£49.54	$71.12
€90	£55.73	$80.00
€100	£61.93	$88.90
€500	£309.63	$444.47

Based on rates at time of going to press.

income (if any). You'll probably be required to show your passport, *Carte de Séjour*, an electricity/gas or phone bill in your name and a payslip/letter from your employer. Students need a student card and may need a letter from their parents. Of the major banks (BNP, Crédit Lyonnais, Société Générale, Banque Populaire, Crédit Agricole), Société Générale tends to be most foreigner-friendly. Most banks don't hand out a *Carte Bleue/Visa* until several weeks after you've opened an account. A chequebook (*chéquier*) is usually issued in about a week. *Carte Bleue* is debited directly from your current account, but you can choose for purchases to be debited at the end of every month. French banks are tough on overdrafts, so try to anticipate any cash crisis in advance and work out a deal for an authorised overdraft (*découvert autorisé*) or you risk being blacklisted as '*interdit bancaire*' –

forbidden from having a current account – for up to ten years. Depositing foreign-currency cheques is slow, so use wire transfer or a bank draft in francs to receive funds from abroad.

Bureaux de change

If you arrive in Paris early or late, you can change money at the **Travelex** bureaux de change in the terminals at Roissy (01.48.64.37.26) and at Orly (01.49.75.89.25) airports, which are open 6.30am to 10.30pm or 11pm daily. **Thomas Cook** has bureaux de change at the main train stations. Hours can vary.

Gare d'Austerlitz
01.53.60.12.97. **Open** 7.15am-9pm Mon-Sun.

Gare Montparnasse
01.42.79.03.88. **Open** 8am-7pm daily (until 8pm in summer).

Gare St-Lazare 01.43.87.72.51. **Open** 8am-7pm Mon-Sat; 9am-5pm Sun.

Gare du Nord 01.42.80.11.50. **Open** 6.15am-11.30pm daily.

Gare de l'Est 01.42.09.51.97. **Open** Mon-Sat 6.45am-9.50pm, 6.45am-7pm Sun.

Credit cards

Major international credit cards are widely used in France; Visa (in French *Carte Bleue*) is the most readily accepted. French-issued credit cards have a special security microchip (*puce*) in each card. The card is slotted into a card reader, and the holder keys in a PIN number to authorise the transaction. Non-French cards also work, but generate a credit slip to sign. In case of credit card loss or theft, call the following 24-hr services which have English-speaking staff: **American Express** 01.47.77.72.00; **Diners Club** 01.49.06.17.17; **MasterCard** 01.45.67.84.84; **Visa** 08.36.69.08.80.

Foreign affairs

American Express *11 rue Scribe, 9th (01.47.14.50.00). M° Opéra.* **Open** 9am-4.30pm Mon-Fri. *Bureau de change* (01.47.77.79.50). **Open** 9am-6.30pm Mon-Fri; 9am-5pm Sat;

10am-4pm Sun. Bureau de change, *poste restante*, card replacement, travellers cheque refund service, international money transfers and a cash machine for AmEx cardholders.

Barclays *6 rond point des Champs-Elysées, 8th (01.44.95.13.80). M° Franklin D. Roosevelt.* **Open** 9.15am-4.30pm Mon-Fri. Barclays' international Expat Service handles direct debits, international transfer of funds, etc.

Chequepoint *150 av des Champs-Elysées, 8th (01.42.56.48.63). M° Charles de Gaulle-Etoile.* **Open** 24-hr. Other branches have variable hours; some are closed on Sun. No commission.

Thomas Cook *52 av des Champs-Elysées, 8th (01.42.89.80.32). M° Franklin D. Roosevelt.* **Open** 8.30am-10.30pm daily. Hours of other branches (over 20 in Paris) vary. They issue travellers cheques and deal with bank drafts and bank transfers.

Western Union Money Transfer *CCF Change, 4 rue du Cloître-Notre-Dame, 4th (01.43.54.46.12). M° Cité.* **Open** 9am-5.15pm daily. CCF is an agent for Western Union in Paris, with several branches in the city. 48 post offices now provide Western Union services as well (call 08.25.00.98.98 for details). Money transfers from abroad should arrive within 10-15 minutes. Charges paid by the sender.

Citibank *125 av des Champs-Elysées, 8th (01.53.23.33.60). M° Charles de Gaulle-Etoile.* **Open** 10am-6pm Mon-Fri. Existing clients get good rates for transferring money from country to country, preferential exchange rates and no commision on travellers cheques. European clients can make immediate on-line transfers from account to account on ATM with a Cirrus cashcard.

Opening hours

Standard opening hours for shops are 9am/10am-7pm/8pm Mon-Sat. Some shops close on Mon. Shops and businesses often close at lunch, usually 12.30-2pm. Many

shops close in August. While Paris doesn't have the 24-hr consumer culture beloved of some capitals, most areas have a local grocer that stays open until around 9.30 or 10pm, as do larger branches of Monoprix.

24-hour newsagents include: *33 av des Champs-Elysées, 8th. M° Franklin D. Roosevelt; 2 bd Montmartre, 9th. M° Grands Boulevards.*

Select Shell *6 bd Raspail, 7th (01.45.48.43.12). M° Rue du Bac.* **Open** *24-hr.* **Credit** *AmEx, MC, V.* This round-the-clock garage has a large if pricey array of supermaket standards from the Casino chain. No alcohol sold 10pm-6am.

Photo labs

Photo developing is often more expensive than in the UK or USA. **Photo Station** and **Fnac Service** have numerous branches.

Police stations

If you are robbed or attacked, you should report the incident as soon as possible. You will need to make a statement (*procès verbal*) at the commissariat in the *arrondissement* in which the crime was committed. To find the appropriate commissariat, phone the Préfecture Centrale (01.53.71.53.71) day or night, or look in the phone book. Stolen goods are unlikely to be recovered, but you will need the police statement for insurance purposes.

Postal services

It is quicker to buy stamps at a tobacconist (*tabac*) than at a post office. Post offices (*bureaux de poste*) are open 8am-7pm Mon-Fri; 9am-noon Sat. All are listed in the phone book: under Administration des PTT in the *Pages Jaunes*; under Poste in the *Pages Blanches*. Most post offices have automatic machines (in French and English) that weigh your letter, print out a stamp and give change.

Main Post Office *52 rue du Louvre, 1st (01.40.28.20.00). M° Les Halles or Louvre-Rivoli.* **Open** 24-hr for Poste Restante, telephones, telegrams, stamps and fax. This is the best place to get your mail sent if you haven't got a fixed address in Paris. Mail should be addressed to you in block capitals, followed by Poste Restante, then the post office's address. There is a charge of €0.46 for each letter received.

Recycling & rubbish

Green hive-shaped bottle banks can be found on street corners, although many have been removed for security reasons. Building recycling bins fall into two categories: blue lids for newspapers and magazines, white for glass. Green bins are for general household refuse. For getting rid of furniture and non-dangerous rubbish, look for green skips on street corners.

Allô Propreté (08.01.17.50.00). **Open** 9-12am, 2-5pm Mon-Fri. Recycling information and collection of cumbersome objects.

Religion

Churches and religious centres are listed in the phone book (*Pages Jaunes*) under *Eglises* and *Culte*. Paris has several English-speaking churches. The *International Herald Tribune*'s Saturday edition lists Sunday church services in English.

American Cathedral *23 av George V, 8th (01.53.23.84.00). M° George V.*

American Church in Paris *65 quai d'Orsay, 7th (01.40.62.05.00). M° Invalides.*

St George's Anglican Church *7 rue Auguste-Vacquerie, 16th (01.47.20.22.51). M° Charles de Gaulle-Etoile.* The YWCA-Cardew club for under-28s meets here.

St Joseph's Roman Catholic Church *50 av Hoche, 8th (01.42.27.28.56). M° Charles de Gaulle-Etoile.*

St Michael's Church of England *5 rue d'Aguesseau, 8th (01.47.42.70.88). M° Madeleine.*

Kehilat Geisher *10 rue de Pologne, 78100 St Germain-en-Laye (01.39.21.97.19).* The Liberal English-speaking Jewish community has rotating services in Paris and the western suburbs.

La Mosquée de Paris *2 pl du Puits de l'Ermite, 5th (01.45.35.97.33).*

Renting a flat

The best flats often go by word of mouth. Northern, eastern and southeastern Paris is generally cheapest. Expect to pay roughly €15 per month/m^2 (€525 per month for a 35m^2 flat, and so on). Studios and one-bedroom flats fetch the highest prices proportionally; lifts and central heating will also boost the rent.

Rental laws

The legal minimum rental lease (*bail de location*) on an unfurnished apartment is three years; one year for a furnished flat. During this period the landlord can only raise the rent by the official construction inflation index. At the end of the lease, the rent can be adjusted, but tenants can object before a rent board if it seems exorbitant. Tenants can be evicted for non-payment, or if the landlord wishes to sell the property or use it as his own residence. It is illegal to throw people out in winter. Before accepting you as a tenant, landlords will probably require you to present a dossier with pay slips (*fiches de paie/bulletins de salaire*) showing three to four times the amount of the monthly rent, and for foreigners, in particular, to furnish a financial guarantee. When taking out a lease, payments usually include the first month's rent, a deposit (*une caution*) equal to two month's rent, and an agency fee, if applicable. It is customary for an inspection of the premises (*état des lieux*) at the start and end of the rental, the cost of which (around €150) is shared by landlord and tenant. Landlords may try to rent their flats *non-déclaré* – without a written lease and get rent in cash. This can make it difficult for tenants to establish their rights – which is one reason landlords do it.

Flat hunting

The largest lists of furnished (*meublé*) and unfurnished (*vide*) flats for rent are in Tuesday's *Le Figaro*. There are also assorted free ad brochures that can be

picked up from agencies. Flats offered to foreigners are advertised in the *International Herald Tribune* and English-language fortnightly *FUSAC*; rents tend to be higher than in the French press. Short-term flat agencies can simplify things, but are not cheap either. Local bakeries often post notices of flats for rent direct from the owner. Non-agency listings are also available in the Thursday weekly *Particulier à Particulier* and via Minitel 3615 PAP. Fortnightly *Se Loger* is mostly agencies but has good online listings at www.seloger.com. There's a minitel flat rental service on 3615 LOCAT. Landlords often list a visiting time; prepare to meet hordes of other flat-seekers and take documents and cheque book.

Bureau de l'information juridique des propriétaires et des occupants (BIPO) *6 rue Agrippa-d'Aubigné, 4th (01.42.76.31.31). M° Sully-Morland.* **Open** 9am-5pm Mon-Thur; 9am-4.30pm Fri. Municipal service provides free advice (in French) about renting or buying a flat, housing benefit, rent legislation and tenants' rights.

Centre d'information et de défense des locataires *115 rue de l'Abbé-Groult, 15th (01.48.42.10.22). M° Convention.* **Open** 9.30am-1pm, 5-7pm Mon-Fri. For problems with landlords, rent increases, etc.

Shipping services

Hedley's Humpers *6 bd de la Libération, 93284 St-Denis (01.48.13.01.02). M° Carrefour-Pleyel.* **Open** 9am-6pm Mon-Fri. *102 rue des Rosiers, 93400 St-Ouen (01.40.10.94.00). M° Porte de Clignancourt.* **Open** 9am-1pm Mon; 9am-6pm Sat, Sun. Specialised in transporting furniture and antiques. In UK: *3 St Leonards Rd, London NW10 6SX, UK (0208 965 8733).* In USA: *21-41 45th Road, Long Island City, New York NY 11101, USA (1.718.433.4005).*

Smoking

Despite recent initiatives, France remains a country of smokers. Restaurants are obliged to provide a non-smoking area (*espace non-fumeurs*), however, you'll often end up with the worst table in the house, and there's no guarantee other people seated in the section won't light up anyway. Smoking is banned in most theatres, cinemas and on public transport.

Telephones

Dialing & codes
All French phone numbers have ten digits. Paris and Ile de France numbers begin with 01; the rest of France is divided into four zones (02-05). Portable phones start with 06. 08 indicates a special rate (*see below*). If you are calling France from abroad leave off the 0 at the start of the ten-digit number. Country code: 33. To call abroad from France dial 00, then country code. Since 1998 other phone companies have been allowed to enter the market, with new prefixes (eg. Cégétel numbers starting with a 7).

France Telecom English-Speaking Customer Service *08.00.36.47.75*. **Open** 9.30am-5.30pm Mon-Fri. Freephone information line in English on phone services, bills, payment, Internet.

Public phones
Most public phones in Paris use phonecards (*télécartes*). Sold at post offices, tobacconists, airports and train and Métro stations, cards cost €7.47 for 50 units and €14.86 for 120 units. Thomas Cook have introduced their own International Telephone Card which costs €7.62 or €15.24 and has a PIN code, usable on any type of phone in France and more than 80 countries. Available from Thomas Cook agencies (01.47.58.21.00 gives a list of salespoints). Cafés have coin phones, while post offices usually have card phones. In a phone box, the digital display screen should read *Décrochez*. Pick up the phone. When *Introduisez votre carte* appears, insert your card into the slot. The screen should then read *Patientez SVP. Numérotez* is your signal to dial. *Crédit épuisé* means that you have no more units left. Finally, hang up (*Raccrochez*), and don't forget your card. Some public phones take credit cards.

If you are using a credit card, insert the card, key in your PIN number and *Patientez SVP* should appear.

Operator services
Operator assistance, French directory enquiries (*renseignements*), dial 12. To make a reverse-charge call within France, ask to make a call *en PCV*.

International directory enquiries 32.12, then country code (eg. 44 for UK, 1 for US).

Telephone engineer dial 10.13.

International news (French recorded message, France Inter), dial 08.36.68.10.33 (€0.34 per min).

Telegram all languages, international 08.00.33.44.11; within France 36.55.

Time dial 36.99.

Traffic news dial 01.48.99.33.33.

Weather dial 08.36.70.12.34 (€0.34 per min) for enquiries on weather in France and abroad, in French or English; dial 08.36.68.02.75 (€0.34 per min) for a recorded weather announcement for Paris and region.

Airparif (01.44.59.47.64). Mon-Fri 9am-5.30pm. Information about pollution levels and air quality in Paris: invaluable for asthmatics.

Telephone directories
Phone books are found in all post offices and most cafés. The *Pages Blanches* (White Pages) lists people and businesses alphabetically; *Pages Jaunes* (Yellow Pages) lists businesses and services by category.

Telephone charges
Local calls in Paris and Ile-de-France beginning with 01 cost €0.11 for three minutes, standard rate, €0.04 per minute thereafter. Calls beyond a 100km radius (province) are charged at €0.11 for the first 39 seconds, then €0.24 per minute. International destinations are divided into 16 zones. Reduced-rate periods for calls within France and Europe: 7pm-8am during the week; all day Sat, Sun. Reduced-rate periods for the US and Canada: 7pm through to 1pm Mon-Fri; all day Sat, Sun. France Telecom's **Primaliste** offers 25% off on calls to six chosen numbers.

Cheap rate providers
The following providers offer competitive rates from France: **Fast Telecom** (01.46.98.20.00); **Teleconnect** (08.05.10.25.05). The local access number for **AT&T Direct** is 0800-99-00-11.

Special rate numbers
08.00 Numéro Vert Freephone.

08.01 Numéro Azur €0.11 under 3 min, then €0.04 per min.

08.02 Numéro Indigo I €0.15 per min.

08.03 Numéro Indigo II €0.23 per min.

08.36 €0.34 per min. This rate applies not just to chat lines but increasingly to cinema and transport infolines.

08.67 €0.23 per min

08.68 €0.34 per min

08.69 €0.34 per min

Special rate information: **10.14**

Minitel
France Telecom's Minitel is a videotext service available to any telephone subscriber, although it is rapidly being superceded by the Internet. Hotels are often Minitel-equipped and most post offices offer use of the terminals for directory enquiries on 3611. Hundreds of services on the pricier 3614, 3615, 3616 and 3617 numbers give access to hotel and ticket reservations, airline and train information, and scores of recreational lines that include 'dating' hook-ups. For French telephone directory information, dial 3611 on the keyboard, wait for the beep and press *Connexion*, then type in the name and the city   of the person or business whose number and/or address you're looking for, and press *Envoi*. You can also search for name and/or phone number by typing a street address. Minitel directory use is free for the first three minutes, €0.06 per minute thereafter. For Minitel directory in English dial 3611, wait for the beep, press *Connexion*, type MGS, then *Envoi*. Then type *Minitel en anglais*.

Ticket agencies

Fnac Forum des Halles, *1st (01.40.41.40.00/www.fnac.com). M° Les Halles/RER Châtelet-Les Halles.* **Open** 10am-7.30pm Mon-Sat. **Credit** AmEx, MC, V. Bookings in person, or via 3615 FNAC or on www.fnac.fr.

Fnac France Billet *(08.92.68.36.22).* **Open** 9am-9pm Mon-Sat. **Credit** MC, V. Telephone bookings linked to Fnac.

Virgin Megastore *52 av des Champs-Elysées, 8th (01.49.53.50.00). M° Franklin D. Roosevelt.* **Open** 10am-midnight Mon-Sat (ticket sales by phone on 08.25.02.30.24); 9am-8pm Mon-Sat. **Credit** AmEx, DC, MC, V.

Time & seasons

France is one hour ahead of Greenwich Mean Time (GMT). In France time is based on the 24-hr system.

Tipping

Service is legally included in your bill at all restaurants, cafés and bars. However, it is polite to either round up the final amount for drinks, and to leave a cash tip of €1-€2 or more for a meal, depending on the restaurant and, of course, on the quality of service you receive.

Toilets

Automatic street toilets are not as terrifying as they look. And it's just as well when you think about it. You place your coin in the slot, and – open sesame – you're in a disinfected wonderland (each loo is completely disinfected after use, so don't try to sneak in as someone is leaving: you'll end up covered in bleach). Once in, you'll have fifteen minutes in which to do the bizzo. If a space-age-style parking of the breakfast doesn't appeal, you can always nip into the loos of a fast-food chain. Café toilets are theoretically reserved for customers' use: the only café owners that seem to turn a blind eye when interlopers sneak down the stairs are the ones who've installed coin-op stalls.

Tourist information

Office de Tourisme de Paris *127 av des Champs-Elysées, 8th (08.36.68.31.12/ recorded information in English and French, www.paris-touristoffice.com). M° Charles de Gaulle-Etoile.* **Open** *summer* 9am-8pm daily; *winter* 9am-8pm Mon-Sat; 11am-6pm Sun. Closed 1 May. Information on Paris and the suburbs. It has a souvenir shop, bureau de change, hotel reservation service, and sells phonecards, museum cards, travel passes and tickets for museums, theatres, tours and other attractions. Multilingual staff.

Espace du Tourisme d'Ile de France *Carrousel du Louvre, 99 rue de Rivoli, 1st (08.03.80.80.00/ from abroad 33-1.56.89.38.00).* **Open** 10am-7pm Mon, Wed-Sun. Information showcase for Paris and the Ile de France.

Visas

European Union nationals do not need a visa to enter France, nor do US, Canadian, Australian or New Zealand citizens for stays of up to three months. Nationals of other countries should enquire at the nearest French Consulate before leaving home. If they are travelling to France from one of the countries included in the Schengen agreement (most of the EU, but not Britain, Ireland, Italy or Greece), the visa from that country should be sufficient. For stays of over three months, *see below, Cartes de Séjour*.

Weights & measures

France uses only the metric system; remember that all speed limits are in kilometres. One kilometre is equivqlent to 0.62 mile (1 mile = 1.6km). Petrol, like other liquids, is measured in litres; one UK gallon = 4.54 litres; 1 US gallon = 3.79 litres).

Size Charts

Women's Clothes

British	French	US
4	32	2
6	34	4
8	36	6
10	38	8
12	40	10
14	42	12
16	44	14
18	46	16
20	48	18

Women's Shoes

British	French	US
3	36	5
4	37	6
5	38	7
6	39	8
7	40	9
8	41	10
9	42	11

Men's Suits

British	French	US
34	44	34
36	46	36
38	48	38
40	50	40
42	52	42
44	54	44
46	56	46
48	58	48

Men's Shoes

British	French	US
6	39	7
7 1/2	40	7 1/2
8	41	8
8	42	8 1/2
9	43	9 1/2
10	44	10 1/2
11	45	11
12	46	11 1/2

Women's Paris

Paris is not especially threatening for women, although the precautions you would take in any major city apply: be careful at night in areas like Pigalle, the rue St-Denis, Stalingrad, La Chapelle, Château Rouge, Gare du Nord, the Bois de Boulogne and Bois de Vincennes. British and American women can expect to be on the receiving end of more attention from strangers than they get at home. You will possibly receive compliments in the street – this is a cultural difference rather than sexual harrassment. *Dragueurs* (men on the pull) can be persistent; usually a few choice words of invective in any language is enough to shoo them away, as they are generally all mouth and trousers (without much in those trousers). A polite *'N'insistez pas!'* (don't push it) should do. If things get too heavy, go into the nearest shop or bar and wait or ask for help.

CNIDFF *7 rue du Jura, 13th (01.42.17.12.34). Mᵒ Gobelins.* **Open** 1.30-5.30pm Tue-Thur (phone 9am-12.30pm).The Centre National d'Information et de Documentation des Femmes et des Familles offers legal, professional and health advice for women.

Violence conjugale: Femmes Info Service/SOS Femmes Battues *(01.40.33.80.60).* **Open** 7.30am-11.30pm Mon-Fri; 10am-8pm Sat.Telephone hotline for battered women, directing them towards medical aid or shelters.

Viols Femmes Informations *(08.00.05.95.95).* **Open** 10am-6pm Mon-Fri. This is a freephone in French for giving help, support and advice to rape victims.

Working in Paris

Anyone from abroad coming to live in Paris should be prepared for the sheer weight of bureaucracy to which French officialdom is devoted, whether it's for acquiring a *Carte de Séjour* (resident's permit), opening a bank account,

reclaiming medical expenses or getting married. Among documents regularly required are a *Fiche d'Etat Civil* (essential details translated from your passport by the embassy/consulate) and a legally approved translation of your full birth certificate (embassies will provide lists of approved legal translators; for general translators, *see p372,* **Business***)*. All EU nationals can work legally in France, but must apply for a French social security number and *Carte de Séjour*. Some job ads can be found at branches of the **Agence nationale pour l'emploi (ANPE)**, the French national employment bureau. This is also the place to go to sign up as a *demandeur d'emploi,* to be placed on file as available for work and possibly to qualify for French unemployment benefits. Britons can only claim French unemployment benefit if they were already signed on before leaving the UK. Non-EU nationals need a work permit and are not entitled to use the ANPE network without valid work papers.

CIEE *1 pl de l'Odéon, 6th (01.44.41.74.74). Mᵒ Odéon.* **Open** 9am-6pm Mon-Fri. The Council on International Educational Exchange provides three-month work permits for US citizens at or recently graduated from university, has a job centre, mostly for sales and catering, and provides a three-month permit to those with a pre-arranged job.

Espace emploi international (OMI et ANPE) *48 bd de la Bastille, 12th (01.53.02.25.50). Mᵒ Bastille.* **Open** 9am-5pm Mon, Wed-Fri; Tue 9-12am. The OMI provides work permits of up to 18 months for Americans aged 18-35 and has a job placement service. *Stagiaires* should pick up a permit, which takes eight-ten weeks, in their home country.

Job ads

Help-wanted ads sometimes appear in the *International Herald Tribune*, in *FUSAC* and on noticeboards at language schools

and Anglo establishments, such as the American Church. Most are for baby-sitters, dog-walkers and English-language teaching. Positions as waiters and bar staff are often available at international-style watering holes. Sometimes a strong sense of self-worth is needed in such positions. Bilingual secretarial/PA work is available for those with good written French. If you are looking for professional work, have your CV translated, including French equivalents for any qualifications. Most job applications require a photo and a handwritten letter; strange as it may seem, employers often use graphological analysis, so try to ensure that your upward strokes aren't too redolent of 'slacker' or 'dangerous pervert'.

Cartes de Séjour

Officially, all foreigners, both EU citizens and non-Europeans, who are in France for more than three months must apply for a *Carte de Séjour*, valid for one year. Those who have had a *Carte de Séjour* for at least three years, have been paying French income tax, can show proof of income and/or are married to a French national can apply for a *Carte de Résident*, valid for ten years.

CIRA (Centre interministeriel de renseignements administratifs). *(01.40.01.11.01)* **Open** 9am-12.30pm, 2-5.30pm Mon-Fri. Advice on French administrative procedures.

Préfecture de Police de Paris Service Étrangers *7 bd du Palais, 4th (01.53.71.51.68/ www.prefecture-police-paris.interieur.gouv.fr). Mᵒ Cité.* **Open** 8.30am-4pm Mon-Fri. Information on residency and work permits.

Cosmopolitan Services Unlimited *113 bd Pereire, 17th (01.55.65.11.65/ fax 01.55.65.11.69). Mᵒ or RER Pereire.* **Office** hours 9am-6pm Mon-Thur; 9am-5pm Fri. A good but pricey relocation company. Services include getting work permits and *Cartes de Séjour* approved.

Essential Vocabulary

In French the second person singular (you) has two forms. Phrases here are given in the more polite *vous* form. The *tu* form is used with family, friends, young children and pets; you should be careful not to use it with people you do not know sufficiently well. You will also find that courtesies such as *monsieur, madame* and *mademoiselle* are used much more than their English equivalents.

General expressions

good morning/afternoon, hello *bonjour;* good evening *bonsoir;* goodbye *au revoir;* hi (familiar) *salut;* OK *d'accord;* yes *oui;* no *non;* How are you? *Comment allez vous?/vous allez bien?;* How's it going? *Comment ça va?/ça va?* (familiar); Sir/Mr *monsieur (M);* Madam/Mrs *madame (Mme);* Miss *mademoiselle (Mlle);* please *s'il vous plaît;* thank you *merci;* thank you very much *merci beaucoup;* sorry *pardon;* excuse me *excusez-moi;* Do you speak English? *Parlez-vous anglais?;* I don't speak French *Je ne parle pas français;* I don't understand *Je ne comprends pas;* Speak more slowly, please *Parlez plus lentement, s'il vous plaît ;* Leave me alone *Laissez-moi tranquille;* How much?/how many? *combien?;* Have you got change? *Avez-vous de la monnaie?* I would like... *Je voudrais...* I am going *Je vais;* I am going to pay *Je vais payer;* it is *c'est;* it isn't *ce n'est pas;* good *bon/bonne;* bad *mauvais/ mauvaise* small *petit/petite;* big *grand/grande;* beautiful *beau/belle;* well *bien;* badly *mal;* expensive *cher;* cheap *pas cher;* a bit *un peu;* a lot *beaucoup;* very *très;* with *avec;* without *sans;* and *et;* or *ou;* because *parce que* who? *qui?;* when? *quand?;* what? *quoi?;* which? *quel?;* where? *où?;* why? *pourquoi?;* how? *comment?;* at what time/when? *à quelle heure?;* forbidden *interdit/défendu;* out of order *hors service (hs)/en panne;* daily *tous les jours (tlj);*

On the phone

hello (telephone) *allô;* Who's calling? *C'est de la part de qui?/Qui est à l'appareil?;* Hold the line *Ne quittez pas*

Getting around

Where is the (nearest) Métro? *Où est le Métro (le plus proche)?;* When is the next train for... ? *C'est quand le prochain train pour... ?;* ticket *un billet;* station *la gare;* platform *le quai;* entrance *entrée;* exit *sortie;* left *gauche;* right *droite;* straight on *tout droit;* far *loin;* near *pas loin/près d'ici;* street *la rue;* street map *le plan;* road map *la carte;* bank *la banque;* is there a bank near here? *est-ce qu'il y a une banque près d'ici?;* Post Office *La Poste;* a stamp *un timbre*

Sightseeing

museum *un musée;* church *une église;* exhibition *une exposition;* ticket (for museum) *un billet;* (for theatre, concert) *une place;* open *ouvert;* closed *fermé;* free *gratuit;* reduced price *un tarif réduit*

Accommodation

Do you have a room (for this evening/for two people)? *Avez-vous une chambre (pour ce soir/pour deux personnes)?;* full *complet;* room *une chambre;* bed *un lit;* double bed *un grand lit;* (a room with) twin beds *une chambre à deux lits;* with bath(room)/shower *avec (salle de) bain/douche;* breakfast *le petit déjeuner;* included *compris;* lift *un ascenseur*

At the café or restaurant

I'd like to book a table (for three/at 8pm) *Je voudrais réserver une table (pour trois personnes/à vingt heures);* lunch *le déjeuner;* dinner *le dîner;* coffee (espresso) *un café;* white coffee *un café au lait/café crème;* tea *le thé;* wine *le vin;* beer *la bière;* mineral water *eau minérale;* fizzy *gazeuse;* still *plate;* tap water *eau du robinet/une carafe d'eau;* the bill, please *l'addition, s'il vous plaît*

Behind the wheel

give way *céder le passage;* no parking *stationnement interdit/ gênant;* toll *péage;* speed limit 40 *rappel 40;* petrol *essence;* traffic jam *embouteillage/ bouchon;* speed *vitesse;* traffic moving freely *traffic fluide;* dangerous bends *attention virages*

Shopping

may I try this on? *est-ce que je pourrais essayer cet article?;* do you have a smaller/ larger size? *auriez-vous la taille au-dessous/en dessus?;* I'm a size 38 *je fait un 38;* I'll take it *je le prends;* does my bum look big in this? *cela me fait-il des grosses fesses?*

The come on

do you have a light? *vous avez du feu?;* what's your name? *comment tu t'appelles?;* would you like a drink? *tu veux boire une verre?;* your place or mine? *chez toi ou chez moi?*

The brush-off

fuck off *va te faire foutre;* leave me alone *laissez-moi tranquille*

Staying alive

be cool *restez calme;* I don't want any trouble *je ne veux pas d'ennuis*

Numbers

0 *zéro;* 1 *un, une;* 2 *deux;* 3 *trois;* 4 *quatre;* 5 *cinq;* 6 *six;* 7 *sept;* 8 *huit;* 9 *neuf;* 10 *dix;* 11 *onze;* 12 *douze;* 13 *treize;* 14 *quatorze;* 15 *quinze;* 16 *seize;* 17 *dix-sept;* 18 *dix-huit;* 19 *dix-neuf;* 20 *vingt;* 21 *vingt-et-un;* 22 *vingt-deux;* 30 *trente;* 40 *quarante;* 50 *cinquante;* 60 *soixante;* 70 *soixante-dix;* 80 *quatre-vingts;* 90 *quatre-vingt-dix;* 100 *cent*

Days & months

Mon *lundi;* Tues *mardi;* Wed *mercredi;* Thur *jeudi;* Fri *vendredi;* Sat *samedi;* Sun *dimanche;* Jan *janvier;* Feb *février;* Mar *mars;* Apr *avril;* May *mai;* June *juin;* July *juillet;* Aug *août;* Sept *septembre;* Oct *octobre;* Nov *novembre;* Dec *décembre*

Further Reference

Books

Non-fiction

Antony Beevor & Artemis Cooper *Paris after the Liberation* Rationing, liberation and existentialism.

Rupert Christiansen *Tales of the New Babylon* Napoléon III's Paris; blood, sleaze and bulldozers.

Vincent Cronin *Napoleon* A fine biography of the great megalomaniac.

Noel Riley Fitch *Literary Cafés of Paris* Who drank where.

Alastair Horne *The Fall of Paris* Detailed chronicle of the Siège and Commune 1870-71.

Ian Littlewood *Paris: Architecture, History, Art* Paris' history and its treasures.

Patrick Marnham *Crime & the Académie Française* Quirks and scandals of Mitterrand-era Paris.

Nancy Mitford *The Sun King; Madame de Pompadour* Great gossipy accounts of the courts of the *ancien régime*.

Douglas Johnson & Madeleine Johnson *Age of Illusion: Art & Politics in France 1918-1940* French culture in a Paris at the forefront of modernity.

Renzo Salvadori *Architect's Guide to Paris* Plans, illustrations and a guide to Paris' growth.

Simon Schama *Citizens* Giant but wonderfully readable account of the Revolution.

Alice B Toklas *The Alice B Toklas Cookbook* How to cook fish for Picasso, by the companion (and cook) of Gertrude Stein.

Theodore Zeldin *The French* Idiosyncratic and entertaining survey of modern France.

Fiction

Petrus Abaelardus & Heloïse *Letters* The full details of Paris' first great romantic drama.

Louis Aragon *Paris Peasant* A great Surrealist view of the city.

Honoré de Balzac *Illusions perdues; La Peau de chagrin; Le Père Goriot; Splendeurs et misères de courtisanes* Some of the most evocative in the 'Human Comedy' cycle.

Baudelaire *LeSpleen de Paris* Baudelaire's prose poems with Paris settings.

Louis-Ferdinand Céline *Mort à crédit* Vivid account of an impoverished Paris childhood.

Simone De Beauvoir *The Mandarins* Paris intellectuals and idealists just after the Liberation.

Michel Houellebecq *Plateforme* Naughty boy of French literature tackles sexual tourism.

Victor Hugo *Notre Dame de Paris* Quasimodo and the romantic vision of medieval Paris.

Guy de Maupassant *Bel-Ami* Gambling and dissipation.

Catherine Millet *La vie sexuelle de Catherine M* Bonkographie par excellence.

Patrick Modiano *Honeymoon* Evocative story of two lives that cross in Paris.

Georges Perec *Life, A User's Manual* Intellectual puzzle in a Haussmannian apartment building.

Nicolas Restif de la Bretonne *Les Nuits de Paris* The sexual underworld of Louis XV's Paris, by one of France's most famous defrocked priests.

Raymond Queneau *Zazie in the Metro* Paris in the 1950s: bright and very *nouvelle vague*.

Jean-Paul Sartre *Roads to Freedom* Existential angst as the German army takes over Paris.

Georges Simenon The *Maigret* series All of Simenon's books featuring his laconic detective provide a great picture of Paris and its underworld.

Emile Zola *Nana, L'Assommoir, Le Ventre de Paris* Vivid accounts of the underside of the Second Empire.

The ex-pat angle

Ernest Hemingway *A Moveable Feast* Big Ern drinks his way around 1920s writers' Paris.

Henry Miller *Tropic of Cancer; Tropic of Capricorn* Low-life and lust in Montparnasse.

Anaïs Nin *Henry & June* More lust in Montparnasse with Henry Miller and his wife.

George Orwell *Down & Out in Paris & London* Orwell's stint as a lowly Paris washer-up.

Gertrude Stein *The Autobiography of Alice B Toklas* Ex-pat Paris, from start to finish.

Film

A Bout de Souffle (1959) Jean-Luc Godard's still fresh and stunning convention breaker.

Carry On Don't Lose Your Head (1966) Brit-pack *Carry On* team's take on the ins and outs of the revolution.

Le Dernier Métro (1980) François Truffaut pairs Deneuve and Depardieu in Nazi-occupied Paris.

The Rebel (1960) Tony Hancock satire on ex-pat artistes who come to Paris for the sake of their art. Our hero founds the *Infantile* school of painting.

Sounds

Couleur Café, *Serge Gainsbourg* A sixties platter cut before the booze, drugs and women got hold of the poor lamb.

Discovery, *Daft Punk* A blast of innovative acid disco via the drum machine and vocoder French dudes.

Frank Sinatra and Sextet live in Paris 1962 He came, he swung, he conquered.

Moon Safari, *Air* Relaxing, ambient beeps and sonics from that *rara avis,* a credible French pop group.

Parisian Walkways, *Phil Lynott and Gary Moore* Two wild rockers go mainly instrumental and terribly atmospheric.

Song for Europe, *Roxy Music* Bryan Ferry croons like a *chansonnier* in immaculate heart-broken Geordie style.

Websites

www.fnac.com
Great for booking tickets to all sorts of events.
www.liberation.com
Trendy *Libé's* site provides current affairs and cultural coverage.
www.leparisien.com
The capital's daily newspaper.
www.timeout.com
A list of the month's current events, and an extensive guide to hotels, restaurants and the arts. Simply the best.

Teamsys.

A WORLD OF SERVICES

 Teamsys is always with you, ready to assure you all the tranquillity and serenity that you desire for your journeys, 365 days a year.

Roadside assistance always and everywhere, infomobility so not to have surprises, insurance... and lots more.

To get to know us better contact us at the toll-free number **00-800-55555555**.

...and to discover Connect's exclusive and innovative integrated infotelematic services onboard system visit us at:

www.targaconnect.com

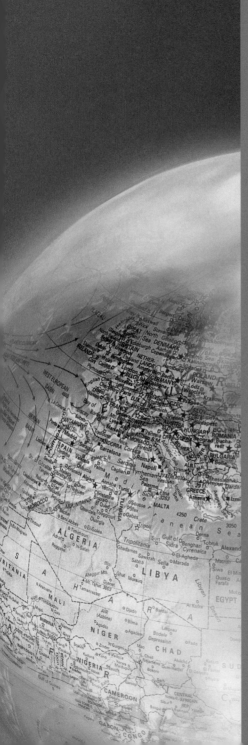

Central Paris Maps Key

Place of Interest and/or Entertainment . . .

Hospital or College . . . .

Pedestrians only . . . .

Arrondissement Boundary & Number . . . ─ 16

Railway Line & Station . . . .

Paris Métro & RER Station . . . . (M) (RER)

Maps

Paris Arrondissements

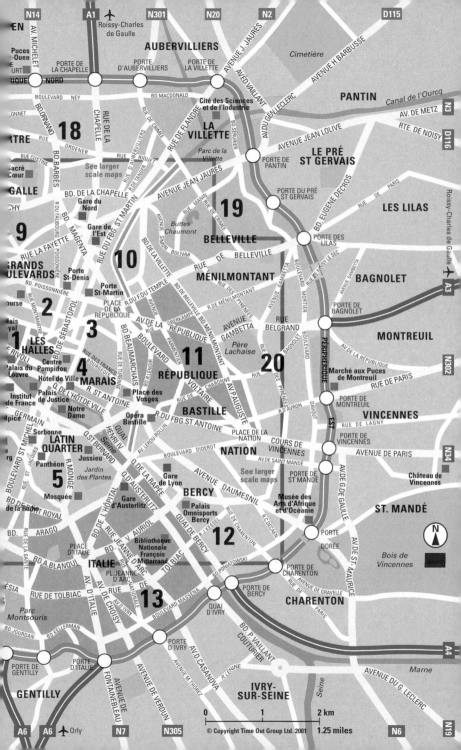

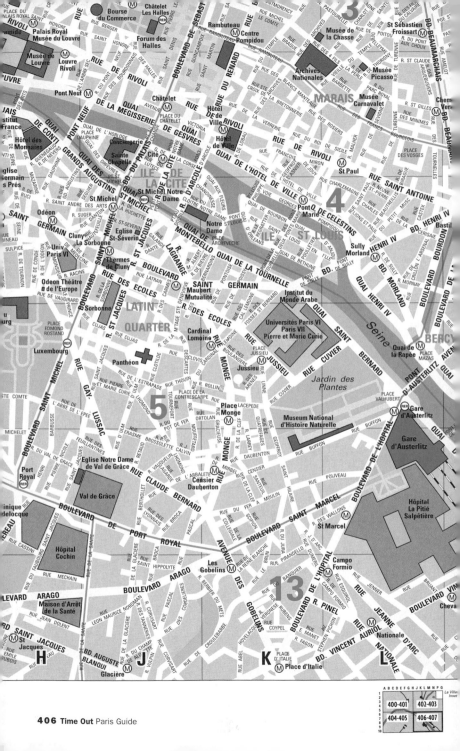

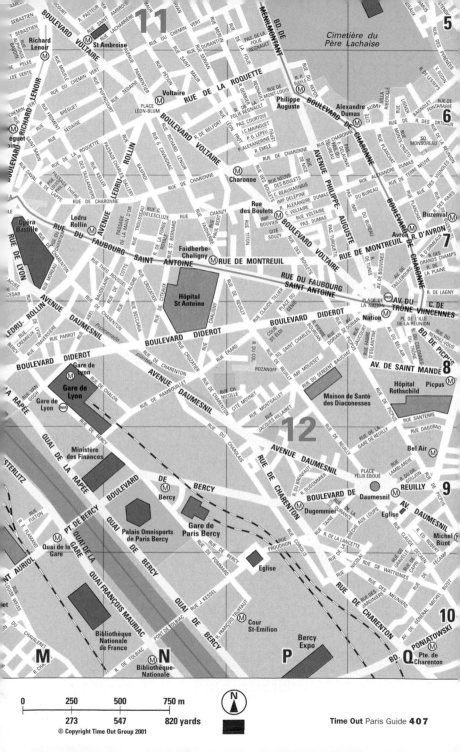

Street Index

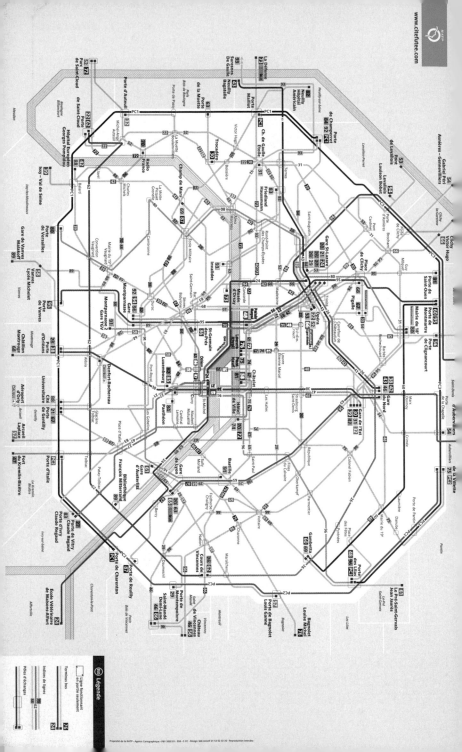

Paris Please let us know what you think

About this guide...

1. How useful did you find the following sections?

	Very	Fairly	Not very
In Context	☐	☐	☐
Accommodation	☐	☐	☐
Sightseeing	☐	☐	☐
Eat, Drink, Shop	☐	☐	☐
Arts & Entertainment	☐	☐	☐
Trips Out of Town	☐	☐	☐
Directory	☐	☐	☐
Maps	☐	☐	☐

2. Did you travel to Paris...?

Alone ☐	With children ☐
As part of a group ☐	On vacation ☐
On business ☐	To study ☐
With a partner ☐	I live here ☐

3. How long was your trip to Paris? (write in)

_____ days

4. Where did you book your trip?

Time Out Classifieds ☐
On the Internet ☐
With a travel agent ☐
Other (write in) ☐

_____

5. Where did you first hear about this guide?

Advertising in Time Out magazine ☐
On the Internet ☐
From a travel agent ☐
Other (write in) ☐

_____

6. Is there anything you'd like us to cover in greater depth?

_____

7. Are there any places that should/ should not* be included in the guide?
(*delete as necessary)

_____

8. How many other people have used this guide?

none ☐ 1 ☐ 2 ☐ 3 ☐ 4 ☐ 5+ ☐

9. What city or country would you like to visit next? (write in)

_____

About other Time Out publications...

10. Have you ever bought/used Time Out magazine?

Yes ☐   No ☐

11. Have you ever bought/used any other Time Out City Guides?

Yes ☐   No ☐

If yes, which ones?

_____

12. Have you ever bought/used other Time Out publications?

Yes ☐   No ☐

If yes, which ones?

_____

About you...

13. Title (Mr, Ms etc):

First name:

Surname:

Address:

_____   P/code:

Email:

Nationality:

14. Date of birth: ☐☐/☐☐/☐☐

15. Sex: male ☐   female ☐

16. Are you...?

Single ☐
Married/Living with partner ☐

17. What is your occupation?

_____

18. At the moment do you earn....?

under £15,000 ☐
over £15,000 and up to £19,999 ☐
over £20,000 and up to £24,999 ☐
over £25,000 and up to £39,999 ☐
over £40,000 and up to £49,999 ☐
over £50,000 ☐

☐ Please tick here if you do not wish to receive information about other Time Out products.
☐ Please tick here if you do not wish to receive mailings from third parties.

Time Out Guides

FREEPOST 20 (WC3187)
LONDON
W1E 0DQ

2 1

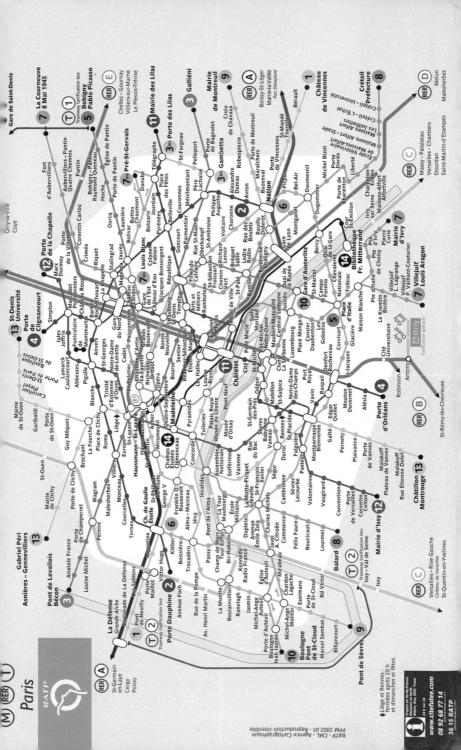

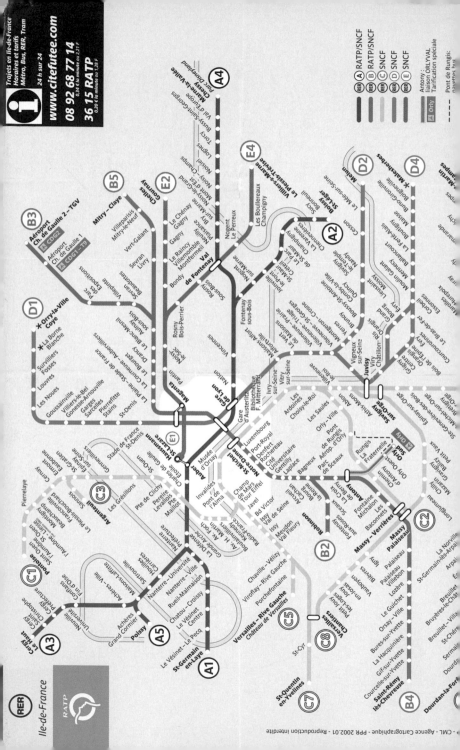